Opera

A LISTENER'S GUIDE

Opera

A LISTENER'S GUIDE

JACK SACHER

Schirmer Books
AN IMPRINT OF SIMON & SCHUSTER MACMILLAN
New York

PRENTICE HALL INTERNATIONAL
London • Mexico City • New Delhi • Singapore • Sydney • Toronto

Schirmer Books
An Imprint of Simon & Schuster Macmillan
1633 Broadway
New York, NY 10019

Library of Congress Catalog Number: 97-11271

Printed in the United States of America

Printing number:

1 2 3 4 5 6 7 8 9 10

Library of Congress Cataloging-in-Publication Data

Sacher, Jack
    Opera : a listener's guide / Jack Sacher.
        p.   cm.
    Includes bibliographical references (p.   ) and index.
    ISBN 0-02-872272-8
    1. Opera.   I. Title.
    ML1700.S13 1997   97-11271
    782.1—dc21   CIP
                                                                       MN

This paper meets the requirements of ANSI/NISO Z39.48-1992 (Permanence of Paper).

Contents

Preface   **xi**

Acknowledgments   **xv**

PART I: OPERA AND ITS TOOLS

Chapter 1   The Nature of the Beast   **3**

Is Opera "About" Anything?   3
Opera's Focus: Drama Through Music   5
Different Strokes: Opera and the Musical   6
Humanity Through Symbol   8
Word and Music, Music and Word   9
Good or Bad?   10

Chapter 2   The Filter of History   **11**

Opera is What We Make of It   11
Music as Symbol   12
Orfeo ed Euridice and *Giulio Cesare*:
    The Same Century but Different Worlds   13
Voice as Symbol   19
Opera's History—an Overview   20

**Chapter 3   How Opera's Music Works:
                Sound as Symbol and Metaphor**   **23**

Symbolism in Music: Some General Comments   23
Knowing It When You Hear It   23
Context   27
Archetypes   33
  Song and Singing   33
  The Structure of Music   35
  Instrumental Genres   36
  Melody, Rhythm, and Harmony   41
  Chromaticism   56

PART II: OPERA AND THE HUMAN CONDITION

Opera and Us   61

Chapter 4   The Search Within   **62**

Introspection   62
Conscience and the Sense of Good and Evil   71

Chapter 5   The Search Beyond   **80**

Spirituality and Wonderment   80
Atonement and Redemption   87

Chapter 6   Extremes: The Absurd and the Beautiful   **94**

A Sense of the Ridiculous   94
Aesthetics   104

PART III: SOME DRAMAS AND THEIR MUSIC

Introduction   116
Why These?   116
On Pronunciations   116
Scenes and "Numbers"   117

Chapter 7   *Giulio Cesare in Egitto*   **118**

Giulio Cesare and Opera Seria   118
Music and Drama   118
Handel's Vocal Idioms   118
Pictorialization   120
Bel Canto: The Ideal of Singing   121
Handel and the Conventions of Opera Seria   123
The Historical Background of the Plot   125
The Plot and Its Music   129
ACT I   129
ACT II   136
ACT III   141
The Characters   145
Bibliography   153

Chapter 8   *Iphigénie en Tauride*   **156**

The Myth   158
The Plot and Its Music   158
ACT I   159
ACT II   160
ACT III   162
ACT IV   164
The Characters   167
Bibliography   173

Chapter 9   *Don Giovanni*   **174**

   Sui Generis: The Opera as Synthesis   174
   Ambiguity and "Là ci darem la mano"   175
   Energy and Unity   177
   The Plot and Its Music   182
      ACT I   189
      ACT II   199
   The Characters   209
   Bibliography   220

Chapter 10   *Fidelio*   **222**

   The Plot and Its Music   225
      PRE–ACT I ACTION   225
      ACT I   225
      ACT II   229
   The Characters   233
   Bibliography   240

Chapter 11   *Il barbiere di Siviglia*   **242**

   The Plot and Its Music   245
      PRE-ACT I ACTION   245
      ACT I   245
      ACT II   250
   The Characters   256
   Bibliography   264

Chapter 12   *Rigoletto*   **265**

   The Plot and Its Music   267
      PRE-ACT I ACTION   267
      ACT I   268
      ACT II   274
      ACT III   276
   The Characters   279
   Bibliography   288

Chapter 13   *Die Walküre*   **290**

   Wagner's Principles of Music and Drama   290
   Der Ring des Nibelungen—An Overview   295
   The Motives of *Die Walküre*   296
   The Plot and Its Music   307
      ACT I   307
      ACT II   313
      ACT III   322
   The Characters   327
   Bibliography   340

Chapter 14 *Carmen* 342

Carmen as Heroine: "Reading" the Opera 343
Realism and Romanticism 345
Convention and Controversy 351
The Fate Motive 352
The Plot and Its Music 354
ACT I   354
ACT II   358
ACT III   362
ACT IV   365
The Characters 368
Bibliography 378

Chapter 15 *Salome* 380

Salome and the Dawn of Modernism 380
Music: Imagery and Obsession 381
The Historical Background 387
The Plot and Its Music 389
The Characters 401
Bibliography 411

Chapter 16 *Porgy and Bess*® 414

Idiom and Motive 414
The Plot and Its Music 420
ACT I   420
ACT II   423
ACT III   428
The Characters 431
Bibliography 436

Chapter 17 *Peter Grimes* 437

The Opera as Symbol 437
The Opera as a Point of View 438
The Threads of the Music 440
The Pervasiveness of the Sea 443
The Plot and Its Music 447
PRE-CURTAIN ACTION   447
PROLOGUE   447
ACT I   448
ACT II   451
ACT III   456
The Characters 458
Bibliography 467

A Glossary of Operatic Terms **469**

Works Consulted, Recommended **487**
   Key to the Bibliography 487
   Bibliography 488

Index **495**

Preface

This book evolved from two sources, the lectures that I have given since 1964 for the Metropolitan Opera Guild, focusing on operatic music and how it illuminates character and plot, and explorations with the students of my General Humanities classes at Montclair State University of what it is to be a human being. Part I of this book deals with the former, Part II the latter. Part III then applies these discussions to detailed studies of eleven operas, varied in style and content but all reflective, in one way or another, of the materials of Parts I and II.

I have long felt that the opera lover tends to hear the surface and not the depth, to know the general nature of a plot and its characters but not the details, and to think of opera only in terms of singers and melodies. There is, however, great joy and philosophical and esthetic enrichment in the details. I offer what follows as invitations to explore some of the ways in which opera composers have used these details to show us opera's many "faces." The possible readings and interpretations of the symbols of text and sound are infinite, of course, as is the depth of perception that comes with repeated hearing, so the chapters within are but starters and primers. If my studies shed some light on the unseen, my intention is fulfilled; if my discussions generate outrage and thinking anew, I will have served some purpose, even if it is not the one I set out to achieve.

I have written for those who have come to love the opera as well as those who are just starting. For each, the vocabulary of musical description may be forbidding at first but is most useful in dealing with the nonverbal aspects of opera. I define every term that I use when it comes along; those terms and a number of others used in the vocabulary of opera are also defined in the Glossary.

For the reader who cannot make heads or tails of notation, have no fear—the examples are illustrative, not essential, although often the visual appearance of notes on a page gives a genuine sense of the sound (and dramatic meanings) that they represent. In most cases, a minimal keyboard ability is all that is needed to play them.

The Bibliography is in part a recommended reading list for opera in general and in part a summary of works I have consulted. Sources that are primarily relevant to one of the operas in Part III are listed at the end of the appropriate essay.

I am grateful to the many who read, carped, suggested, and supported. Frederic Mayer, James Wilson, David Reeves, and Bob Glick went through the manuscript with eagle eyes and a depth of personal knowledge that brought to the fore many a slip and many a useful thought. Sandra Darling, especially, reviewed the text with a care and eye for detail that were tremendously helpful. I am indebted to all of them for the work of virtually every page. Fred's assistance in obtaining production photos from European companies took far more effort and time than friendship should have asked of anyone. Andreas Wendholz, Geschäftsführender Dramaturg of the Stadttheater und Philharmonie Essen, was also helpful in this regard.

Sylvia Eversole and Wallace Sokolsky came into the picture early in my work and helped me refine my approach with encouragement and critique; so did Sally Chichester. Don and Merrilea Trawin and John and Doris Langsdorf, inveterate operagoers all, gave the manuscript the once over when the book was in its early stages and helped as much by what they tactfully did not say as by what they voiced specifically. Silences can, after all, be truly informative. Gladys Torres-Baumgarten caught many slips and helped me edit through the eyes of a genuine music lover eager to learn more.

I am grateful to Marie Brdik for help with the translations from the Czech and Caroline Scielzo for her assistance with Russian. Evan Baker and Eric Diamond offered helpful advice in the areas of production and casting; Robert Laudon and Theresa Muir gave instructive comments on Wagner; I found Ralph Locke's internet comments on *Carmen* and Richard Mix's on the instrumentation of Bizet and Gluck very helpful. Michael G. Werner's assistance with Handel and his proofreading the texts of the examples from *Salome* and *Die Walküre* caught many a lapse.

A particular word of thanks to my son, Bobby, for rejecting the serpent's tooth while being a most sharp-eyed critic of my writing and pointedly quizzing my attempts to solve the perplexities of opera appreciation.

I am very appreciative of the effort spent by Jane Poole and Aris Morelli of *Opera News* for the hours they contributed in my behalf in poring through an enormous collection of photographs and expediting my gaining permission to use them. The several photographers were wonderfully helpful as deadline approached; while they receive appropriate credit in the captions to their work, the captions do not tell of their willingness to put in extra hours on my behalf. I am also very grateful to Rebecca Sherman of the Dallas Opera, Elena Park of the San Francisco Opera, Lucy Bourke of the Santa Fe Opera, Tina Ryker and Monte Jacobson of the Seattle Opera, and Lee Pecht and Ava-Jean Mears of the Houston Grand Opera for their efforts in identifying photographic sources, cast lists, and the like.

Sage advice on singing came most generously from Gordon and Harriet Myers, Sandra Darling, James Wilson, Frederic Mayer, and Eric Diamond. All are seasoned professionals in opera and/or musical theater and I thank them for sharing their wisdom and experience with me.

The work conducted with the Gershwin estate on my behalf by David Olsen and Rosemarie Gawelko, of Warner Brothers Publications, and Wade DeCroce, of the Sukin Law Group, also helped with some of the difficulties of writing and publishing.

I owe special appreciation to Richard Carlin and Jonathan Wiener, my editors at Schirmer Books, not only for their editorial acumen but also for their encouragement, and, not least, their patience. James Hatch caught many a glitch, and I am much in his debt.

To all of them, my thanks.

My start as a lover of opera I owe to my father, who bought the Philco radio (to which I became a Saturday addict) that stood in the corner of our living room; my first visit to a live performance was a gift from my Aunt Esther. They both have a special place in my heart whenever I turn to this musical art form that I love so much. I shall also always be indebted to my mother for her unfailing support morally, financially, and spiritually.

Most of all, I extend my embrace to my wife Jo. For encouragement, critique, caring, detailing, endless hours, checking, editing—and understanding. She's been everything; to her this book is dedicated with my love.

J. S.
June 23, 1997

Acknowledgments

Quotation from *The Musical Quarterly* 78, no. 1 (Spring 1994), "The Opera Revival" by Leon Botstein, pp. 1–8, by permission of Oxford University Press.

For all musical selections from *Porgy and Bess®:*
Music and Lyrics by George Gershwin, Du Bose and Dorothy Heyward and Ira Gershwin; © 1935 (Renewed 1962) George Gershwin Music, Ira Gershwin Music and DuBose and Dorothy Heyward Memorial Fund. All rights administered by WB Music Corp. All Rights Reserved. Reprinted by Permission of Warner Bros. Publications, Miami, Fl. *Porgy and Bess®* is a registered trademark of Porgy and Bess Enterprises; Gershwin® and George Gershwin® are registered trademarks of Gershwin Enterprises. All rights reserved.

Excerpts from Poulenc's *Dialogues des Carmélites*
©1959 Casa Ricordi—B.M.G./Ricordi, Copyright owner. Henden Music, inc., Agent. Used by permission.

Excerpts from *Peter Grimes*
©1945 by Boosey and Hawkes Ltd.; Copyright Renewed. Used by permission of Boosey and Hawkes, Inc.

Excerpt from *West Side Story*:
©1956, 1957 (Renewed) by Leonard Bernstein and Stephen Sondheim. The Leonard Bernstein Music Publishing Company, LLC, U.S. and Canadian Publisher. G. Schirmer, Inc., Worldwide print rights and publisher for the rest of the World. International Copyright Secured. All Rights Reserved. Reprinted by Permission.

PART I

Opera and Its Tools

Chapter 1

THE NATURE OF THE BEAST

Is Opera "About" Anything?

*I*n the mid-1970s, in a major effort to get school children enthusiastic about opera, the Metropolitan Opera and the Met Opera Guild sponsored performances of a special program called a "Look-In." It showed the workings of the stage, presented some arias and ensembles, and staged a scene, all with great vivacity, charm, and theatricality. No less a star than Danny Kaye was the host for some of the presentations. In his movies, musicals, and television appearances, Kaye was a marvel of spontaneity, wit, creative intelligence, good nature, and general attractiveness. His manner at the Look-In was no less. But he began his introductory comments to these children with the remark, "If you didn't know better, you'd think opera was about something."

I begged to differ then, and I do now.

People have often avoided opera like the plague because they think about it just as Danny Kaye did. They have held to the ideas that opera is loud singing by overweight, excessively temperamental people, that their elaborate phrases and high notes—presumably the essence of opera—are a rather bizarre music-making utterly irrelevant to the real world, and that the whole business is interesting only to moneyed snobs who attend performances because that's what high-society folk do.

Kaye gave modern voice to Samuel Johnson's eighteenth-century view that opera is an "exotick and irrational entertainment"[1] and added one more item to a long list of pejorative comments about opera. Here are some of them:

---

[1] Although Johnson (1709–1784) was referring specifically to Italian opera, the sense of his remark has remained and has been applied to opera in general. Johnson went on to observe with irritation that opera survived in spite of criticism: ". . . [it] has been always combated [sic], and has always prevailed." See "[John] Hughes," in *Lives of the English Poets*, Oxford English Classics, *Dr. Johnson's Works*, vol. 7, p. 475, (New York: AMS Press, 1970 [1825]).

3

Anything not worth saying, they sing nowadays. (Beaumarchais 1732–1799, *Le barbier de Séville*, Act I; 1775)

Opera is when a guy gets stabbed in the back and, instead of bleeding, he sings. (Ed Gardner, on "Duffy's Tavern," a radio program of the 1940s.)

No good opera plot can be sensible, for people do not sing when they are sensible. (W. H. Auden, 1907–1973)

People are wrong when they say the opera isn't what it used to be. It is what it used to be. That's what's wrong with it. (Noël Coward, 1899–1973)

[Opera] is a bizarre mixture of poetry and music where the writer and the composer, equally embarrassed by each other, go to a lot of trouble to create an execrable work. . . . Nonsense filled with music, dancing, stage machines and decorations may be magnificent nonsense; but it is nonsense all the same. (Charles de Saint-Évremond, 1677)[2]

With all the complaining about opera's potential for disaster and what is perceived as a lack of intellectual substance, one would think that opera would have faded long ago and that Kaye's wisecrack would be generally accepted. The opposite seems to be the case, however. I am very fond of a suggestion by Leon Botstein, who notes that modern media (television and cinema) are "notoriously stained with inaccuracy, unfairness, hidden agendas, and out-and-out falsification," while opera, because it recognizes its inherent artificiality and because it does not even pretend to be real, is actually

more real to us because it never attempts to deceive. . . . It has become the most trustworthy, honest, effective and magical of any of the art forms with a potential for a mass audience. It possesses an unimpeachable integrity and real connection to life.[3]

Kaye, Beaumarchais, Saint-Évremond, and their friends to the contrary, opera *is* about something. Of course it's an entertainment—all the theatrical and musical arts are—and it's beautiful singing and vocal display.[4] And a story. But as theater it is therefore also about human deeds and feelings. Even as it entertains, it reveals and reflects who we are and what we think, and, at times, how we would like things to be. What, then, is opera about? It's about us. "The She-Ancient," of George Bernard Shaw's *Back to Methuselah: A Metabiological Pentateuch* (1922), referring to the arts in general—and therefore also to opera—says it this way:

. . . art is the magic mirror you make to reflect your invisible dreams in visible pictures. You use a glass mirror to see your face: you use works of art to see your soul.[5]

---

[2] Littlejohn, p.2

[3] Leon Botstein. "The Opera Revival," in *The Musical Quarterly* 78, no. 1 (Spring 1994): 5.

[4] A diva to a conductor questioning her wild improvisation: "Well, since I could, I thought I would. . . . "

The mirror may show our darker side, too; when it does, the meaning of "entertainment" deepens. Presumably, we attend the opera to feed our souls by diverting our minds from the rigors of everyday life, but feeding and diversion don't have to be lighthearted and frivolous. *Wozzeck* (1925) and *Peter Grimes* (1945), for example, are unrelievedly serious. Yet they are wonderfully restorative works, not only because of their musical beauties but also because both Berg and Britten—in very different operas—demand that our collective conscience renew itself in order to make us think in fresh ways about the nature of humanity and about our social responsibilities. "Entertainment" may thus be much more than diversion, and it is in this larger sense that we should understand just what opera is and how it goes about its task.

Opera's Focus: Drama Through Music

Opera presents its people and their worlds primarily through vocal and instrumental sound; words, acting, visual effect, and, at times, dance, are contributory but secondary. Although the progress of time in some sections of an opera approximates reality, its key moments are those when time stands still and physical action slows or halts to allow the musical expression of inner thoughts and emotions.[6]

From its beginning around 1600, opera's focus has been on these "frozen moments." The elements of plot—who does what to whom, when and where it is done, and how—are the framework for this focus, but only a framework. The facts of history, the presentation of a logical series of events, or the fidelity to a story source are all encumbrances that are not central to the heart of what opera tries to do. Composers and librettists have long shown sympathy with Busenello's comment in 1641 that "poets are privileged to alter not only fiction, but even history."[7]

Although there have been adjustments this way or that in terms of the importance of plot and the way music has related to it, the focus on music as the means of knowing the feelings and desires of its characters has remained

---

[5] John Freeman, a former editor of *Opera News*, noted that "Because he supposedly tells the truth and holds the mirror up to society, every artist is a potential revolutionary." ("Viewpoint," in *Opera News* 53, no. 10 [Feb. 4, 1989]): 4. In fairness to Shaw and his sometimes dyspeptic avoidance of the pretentious, I should point out that this "She-Ancient" is speaking to a young woman who has said, "There is a magic and mystery in art that you know nothing of." This naiveté and self-righteousness has elicited both the arts-as-mirror thought quoted in the text as well as the following put-down of the young by one older and, presumably, wiser: "But we who are older use neither glass mirrors nor works of art. We have a direct sense of life. When you gain that you will put aside your mirrors and statues, your toys and your dolls." The passage is in Part V, p. 250, of the 1921 Brentano edition.

[6] See Luca Zoppelli, "'Stage Music' in Early Nineteenth-Century Italian Opera," in *Cambridge Opera Journal* 2, no. 1 (March 1990):36ff, for a discussion of a specific usage of this element of time. The nature of time is a vital aspect of the Marschallin's musing about life in Richard Strauss's *Der Rosenkavalier* (The Knight of the Rose, 1911).

[7] Gian Francesco Busenello, "Preface" to Cavalli's *Didone*.

and distinguishes opera from all other types of musical theater. Some operas, such as those by Handel, Mozart, and Rossini, alternate melodic peaks (arias, ensembles) with narrative or conversational valleys (sung recitative or, in some cases, spoken dialogue[8]); some, such as the later works of Verdi and all of Wagner's important operas, offer a more sustained stylistic approach in which the contrasts between the peaks and valleys are less noticeable. Whatever the genre or the style, if it's an opera, the music is the primary means by which we know about the drama and its characters.

Different Strokes: Opera and the Musical

Chief among the differences between opera and other forms of music theater is the nature of the singing itself. The musical has generally shied away from anything resembling the vibrant timbre of the operatic voice as too artificial and aristocratic. The typical hero and heroine of the musical is rarely from the upper classes, so the resonance of their voices must be close to the everyday person's concept of simple songfulness. Thus composers of musicals tend to write melodies that lie fairly low in the vocal range, and the singers of musicals tend to develop the lower parts of their voices; except for basses (whose fortunes lie in sonorous low pitches), opera singers develop their upper voices and make careers out of high notes. The leading singers of musicals are often said to have nice voices or exciting personalities and deliveries, rarely are they described as singing beautifully.

Operatic diction relies on stylized vowel production, whereas the singers of musicals relate their diction to the speaking habits of their characters. Operatic singing demands a seamless transition from one vocal register to another. In the musical, singers often extend the lower register (the "chest voice") into their high notes, a technique called "belting"; when the singer suddenly goes to "head voice," there is an abrupt register switch. While this is a common and expected phenomenon in the musical, it would bring critical anathema on the head of a performer who would dare to sing this way in an opera.

Operatic singing is expected to show nuance, flexibility, and, whatever the orchestration, enough power to be heard comfortably without electronic amplification; nuance and flexibility is indeed treasured among those performers of the musical who are capable of them, but amplification is virtually a given in the musical today, possibly because of such factors as a long tradition of brassy orchestration (that makes amplification necessary if a singer is to show any nuance at all) and a tendency to prefer looks and acting to vocal technique and non-belting power.

A simple set of distinctions like this has exceptions, of course. The musical has drawn on "crossovers" from the operatic world for such baritone

---

[8] Mozart's *Die Entführung aus dem Serail* (1782) (The Abduction from the Seraglio) and *Die Zauberflöte* (1791) (The Magic Flute), Beethoven's *Fidelio* (1814), Bizet's *Carmen* (1875), and Weill's *Down in the Valley* (1948) are examples of operas using speech instead of sung recitative. *Singspiel* (*Entführung, Zauberflöte, Fidelio*) and *opéra comique* (*Carmen*) are operatic genres that, by definition, include both spoken and sung portions.

roles as Tony Esposito in *The Most Happy Fella* (1956) and Billy Bigelow in *Carousel* (1945), the bass-baritone role of Emile in *South Pacific* (1949), or the dramatic soprano parts of Hattie in *Carousel*, and the Mother Superior in *Sound of Music* (1960).[9] For that matter, some entire musicals are almost entirely crossovers, including Sondheim's *A Little Night Music* (1973) and Weill's *Lady in the Dark* (1941).

Musicals (and operettas, for that matter) depend on a close connection between casting and believability of appearance. In opera, characterization all too often relies exclusively on voice and instrument (and some acting, if you're lucky), rather than on looks. It is not at all uncommon to have a twenty-something Rodolfo (in Puccini's *La bohème*, 1896) sung by a fifty-something tenor, with his beloved Mimi to match, because the music demands vocal technique that comes only with years of experience and physical maturity. So when the Mimi (who is dying of consumption) is amply dimensioned, an audience's regretful sighs are soon forgotten if the voice works for the part. Operatic performers must sound wonderful, while the actor-singers of the musical must look good and sound attractive: try watching *Oklahoma!* (1943) with a fifty-year-old Curly or *Guys and Dolls* (1950) with a middle-aged Sarah.

To be fair, this distinction is not always true, especially in regional theaters and televised or filmed presentations of opera. As a rule, however, if there's a choice between a singer who looks good but sounds bad and one who looks bad but sounds good, the smart opera impresario will always choose the latter over the former.

It will seem strange (if not contradictory to what I have just written) to suggest that acting is at least as important in opera as in the musical, yet I think this is the case. The musical's songs, ensembles, and choruses are choreographed rather than acted, whereas virtually *all* operatic numbers are acted through mime and gesture. If there is to be dancing in the opera, it is because the plot calls for it; in the musical, dance is a fundamental mode of staging for everything that is sung; the "stand-up-and-sing" solo in a musical is often a key point in the show simply because of its unexpectedly simple, nonchoreographic staging.

For characters in an opera, music is the *normal* mode of communication; in the musical, it is the *special* mode of communication, because the actions and feelings are set out more in spoken dialogue than in song. In the musical, music is *incidental* to our learning about characters and events, even though it's the primary reason for attending the show in the first place; in opera, music is the *primary* means of expression.

What happens in the orchestra pit is also a matter of major difference. In the musical, orchestration is the work of an arranger whose job is to provide color along with rhythmic, harmonic, and melodic support; if the musical's words or dramatic situation are illuminated by the instruments, it's a happy event but one not central to the thinking of the arranger (more often

---

[9] Each of these roles, interestingly enough, is for an older person for whom the operatic timbre, or sound quality, of a "big" voice has come to seem appropriate. Younger roles, of course, have also been "legit": Cunegonde, in Leonard Bernstein's *Candide* (1956) and Christine in Andrew Lloyd Webber's *Phantom of the Opera* (1986) are just two examples.

than not, someone other than the composer). Operatic music, on the other hand, uses instruments as important tools of mood, plot development, and characterization.

In principle, all the music of an opera—and therefore the heart of the drama—comes from a single musical imagination focused on the emotional meaning of text through instruments, harmony, rhythm, form, and melody, even though the history of opera is rife with departures from this fundamental concept. These factors combine into something unique. Opera has its own way of doing things that requires its audience to deal with it on its own terms. The concluding line of Richard Strauss's *Arabella* (1933), said by Arabella to Mandryka, her true love, is good advice to the opera-goer: "Ich kann nicht anders werden, nimm mich, wie ich bin!"—"I can't become anything else, take me as I am!"

Humanity Through Symbol

Perhaps the most distinctive aspect of human thought is our use of abstractions and symbols. Music itself is a special form of symbolism—its notation is a graphic suggestion of ups and downs, longs and shorts, louds and softs; its sounds have been used to represent events, moods, places, times, and even specific objects. These representations are, of course, highly abstract. Their use is a uniquely human achievement, wonderfully flexible, creatively diverse, and, by virtue of their being, allusive, capable of great powers of meaning even though inherently subtle and imprecise.[10]

Music and theater are continually evolving. What was shocking thirty years ago has become quite acceptable in the 1990s, and what was symbolically unmistakable to a Mantuan audience of 1607 (the year of the first important opera, Monteverdi's *L'Orfeo, Favola in musica*—"The Orpheus Legend in Music") can be utterly opaque in our time.

Although opera is a remarkably complex array of symbols and metaphors and thus one of the most problematic forms of human expression, the allusive power of its music is one of its greatest strengths. It allows us to conjure up images free of the limiting and defining powers of words and thus invites us into the workings of the mind and heart.

The way humans think is, of course, crucial to our understanding of ourselves, but no less important are the purposes to which our thinking

---

[10] The interpretation of notation itself is often vague: the number of vibrations per second of "concert A" (a[1]) is generally described as 440Hz, but the tuning fork of that pitch in Dresden from about 1754–1824 was 415 vibrations per second (identified as *hertz*; abbreviated as "Hz"); in Paris, during the time of Lully (c. 1675), a[1] was even lower, about 410Hz. The difference may seem inconsequential, but it is significant for performers who have to tune instruments that have only a narrow range of adjustability or whose singing comfort can be affected drastically by even a small move up or down. Pitch has varied among contemporaries, too: in 1723, for example, the pitch in Milan and other Lombardian cities was more than a half-step higher than in Rome. Even today, performers speak of the "Paris A" and the "Boston A." The conflict between the higher A of 442 or 443Hz preferred by modern wind players and the lower tuning that contributes to the comfort of singers often rubs raw.

process is applied. Opera's special interest is the awareness of self—the center part of virtually every scene is the cessation of time for the purpose of personal expression and response to a situation—and so it provides us with a special lens to see ourselves as we really are: content with simple virtues,[11] frustrated and tormented,[12] steadfast and loving,[13] or ridiculous and pompous.[14] We find operatic characters mirroring ourselves as we ponder our relation to those around us and to the abstract forces that we feel compelled to try to understand,[15] as we struggle with the concepts of good and evil[16] and examine figures who represent our nether side.[17]

Whatever the process, we find that when our frailties and inadequacies do us in, we have within us the power to grow and change,[18] atone,[19] forgive,[20] and to extend compassion.[21] We poor fools may dig holes for ourselves, but we find in our hearts and souls the capacity to climb out of them and soar. And we find it in opera.

Word and Music, Music and Word

Opera is not a very practical medium for discussing anything, although that hasn't stopped librettists and composers from trying. Rational discourse and clinical study are the functions of words, not melodies. Groups of notes (melismas)[22] stretch syllables beyond recognition, and so do notes that are long and/or high, where all we perceive is vowel rather than consonant. Opera's syntax is that of the lyrical phrase and the patterns and symmetries of harmony and form, not that of written or spoken grammar; words are obliterated by overlapping vocal entries and different texts sung at the same time. Moreover, the way we hear music always gives pride of place to melody rather than poetry: a laundry list set to beautiful music "works"; *Hamlet* set to trivial music flops.

In fact, the apparent conflict between the mutually contradictory demands of text and music lay at the core of the invention of opera in the

---

[11] Beethoven's Marzelline and Rocco (*Fidelio,* 1805; rev. 1806, 1814).

[12] Verdi's Rigoletto (1851), Gluck's Oreste, in *Iphigénie en Tauride* (1779).

[13] Gilda (*Rigoletto*), the Gershwins' Porgy (*Porgy and Bess®*, 1935).

[14] Mozart's Osmin (*Die Entführung aus dem Serail*), Rossini's Bartolo (*Il barbiere di Siviglia*—The Barber of Seville, 1816), Handel's Tolomeo (*Giulio Cesare*—Julius Caesar, 1724).

[15] Richard Strauss's Marschallin (*Der Rosenkavalier*—The Knight of the Rose, 1911), Wagner's Brünnhilde (*Die Walküre*—The Valkyrie, 1870), and Britten's Peter Grimes (1945).

[16] The Gershwins' Bess and Musorgsky's Boris (comp. 1868–69, rev. 1871)

[17] Mozart's Don Giovanni (1787), Verdi's Iago (*Otello,* 1887), Beethoven's Pizarro (*Fidelio*).

[18] Handel's Cleopatra (*Giulio Cesare*), Wagner's Wotan (*Die Walküre*).

[19] Dvořák's Prince (*Rusalka,* 1901), Musorgsky's Boris.

[20] Dvořák's Rusalka, Mozart's Elvira (*Don Giovanni*), the Gershwins' Porgy.

[21] Britten's Ellen (*Peter Grimes*), Wagner's Sieglinde (*Die Walküre*).

[22] See Lindenberger, p. 130, for a pointed discussion of this particular problem.

first place. The intricate part writing of the Italian madrigal in the late six-teenth century was one of the glories of Western art, but it was useless for delineating character or plot and resulted in "il lacerato delle parole" ("the dismembering of the words"). It is a delightful irony that opera should have been invented so that music would be simply a supportive platform for the purpose of clear text declamation[23] and that, within just a few decades of its inception, it should have almost completely lost that purpose.

People of music and letters have forever argued about text and music as if they were warring factors, but words and music are not enemies. They are partners. The text of an opera almost always gives birth to the music: words inspire, music fulfills. Words create and define meaning, music expresses and enriches it. At times *what* the character says is paramount; at other times, *how* it is said tells all.

Good or Bad?

Opera lovers are often bedeviled by what experts praise and what they themselves find wonderful. How does one evaluate the worth of a work of art? What makes an opera "good," and by what criteria is one work dubbed a masterpiece and another one not?

I propose some criteria that work for me, beginning with one of my memories: I once thought that Gounod's *Faust* (1859) was the most enrich-ing musical experience of my life and now—some forty or fifty years later—I find it still a delight but supplanted in my personal pantheon by *Peter Grimes*, *Die Walküre* (The Valkyrie, 1870), and some others. I was right then and I'm right now, for the acceptance or rejection of a work is personal, not absolute. What rewards me has changed, just as I have changed. That the perception of value depends extensively on knowledge and understanding is an old saw, but a good one. I find an opera beautiful if its music speaks to me of who people are and how they feel, and of their time, place, and atmos-phere, and I find it interesting if harmonies, colors, melodies, forms, and textures seem fresh and inventive no matter how many times I hear them. I also impose one other criterion—I must be moved.

A weak work can be turned into a marvelous experience by a fine perfor-mance; a great work can be made excruciating by a bad one. Is there a perfect opera? Only when there's a perfect performance perfectly understood.

---

[23] The earliest operas (i.e., those in the nine years before Monteverdi's *Orfeo* of 1607) were true to their aesthetics: no musical values could interfere with the clarity of declamation, and any musical values were governed by the flow of word accents, vowel forms, etc. Little wonder, then, that the complaint against the madrigal's sundering of text was replaced by Domenico Mazzocchi's irritation with "il tedio della recitativo"—"the boredom of the recitative."

Chapter 2

THE FILTER OF HISTORY

*P*ut a colored gel on a camera lens, a fiberglass screen in an air condi-
tioner, or a metal mesh in a coffee maker: what passes through is altered
from its original state by the color of the gel, the density of the screen, and
the fineness of the mesh, as well as its own density and general nature. The
passage of time works the same way—we understand the events of our past
only in terms of the ways we are introduced to them and the various "filters"
that have come between them and us.

Opera Is What We Make of It

Everything we hear or see on the stage is conditioned by who we are and
what has happened to us. Consider, for example, the new power of the
Gershwins' *Porgy and Bess®* (1935). In the first few decades of its life, its mostly black casting, its references to "happy dust," and its sense of Gullah[1] music
and dialect were exotic and entertaining for Broadway audiences who were
predominantly whites from the middle and upper classes. *Porgy and Bess®*
was considered a musical, not an opera, and it was an entertainment rather
than a "mirror of our soul." At the end of the twentieth century, however,
cocaine is not restricted to "others," African-Americans have entered the
mainstream of modern American life, the spiritual is universally acknowledged as one of the glories of American music, and *Porgy and Bess®* has not
only found its way to the world's opera houses but has also become the subject of dissertations and scholarly analysis. Its music and characters have
empowered audiences to look into and beyond themselves.

Wagner's *Die Meistersinger von Nürnberg* (The Mastersingers of Nuremberg, 1868) is another opera that today is heard very differently from the
way it was during its first years. Its nationalist fervor, with a closing admoni-
tion by Hans Sachs for Germans to revere their "holy German art" and to
beware of foreign leaders, communicated potently to German audiences

---

[1] The Gullah are the black Americans inhabiting the Sea Islands and the coastal regions of
South Carolina, Georgia, and northeastern Florida. *Porgy and Bess®* is set specifically on the
mainland near Charleston, SC, the second scene of Act II taking place on a nearby island.

11

aching for national unity; it offers very different faces to Germans today, for modern Germany embraces diverse generations who have shared shockingly different national experiences.

Berlioz's *Les Troyens* (The Trojans, 1856–58) is also heard in an ambience wholly different from its first performances. Aeneas's escape from Troy, the promises and compulsions of divine forces, and Aeneas's journey toward eternal glory and the founding of Rome comprise a story that bears a message of unremitting pursuit of military prowess and national destiny. It is also a message of misfortune for those who get in the way. *Les Troyens* speaks clearly of a Western outlook that once acclaimed its own progress as inexorable and right, even if it meant trampling the less powerful into the dust. But militarism is no longer universally held to be glorious, and the sacrifice of innocents for a higher cause is no longer acceptable. When we remember the words of Gray's *Elegy Written in a Country Churchyard* (1750): ". . .the paths of glory lead but to the grave"—we "read" Berlioz's setting of Aeneas's departure and the founding of the Roman Empire with grim recognition of unpalatable costs.[2]

Music as Symbol

The story of Orpheus and Euridice is one of the most ancient and often told. There are descents to the world of the dead in many cultures, but the connection of the descent to the power of music is particularly Western and exclusive to this legend. The earliest opera still performed, Monteverdi's *Orfeo*, is based on this story, as is Gluck's reworking of it as *Orfeo ed Euridice* (1762; rev. Paris, 1774). The legend and the librettos of the operas based on it[3] vary in details and denouements, but the basic elements are these: Euridice, beloved of the singer-poet, Orpheus, has died; his song of lament has so moved the gods that they relent, permitting him to enter the world of the dead and lead Euridice back to life, provided he not look back until they have returned to the light.

At the gates of the Underworld, Orpheus begs admission from the Furies (or the boatman, Charon, who ferries souls across the River Styx), his song charming and soothing them so that he is granted passage into Elysium, the abode of happy shades. There he finds Euridice and, without looking at her or speaking to her, begins to lead her back to the land of the living. The narrations vary at this moment: some say that Euridice's complaints of his seeming coldness cause Orpheus to forget the conditions of his journey and turn to explain; others suggest that he loses faith in himself and the promise of the gods, turning to be sure she is there. In either case, she is reclaimed by Death.

Orpheus sings once more of his unrelenting grief, and once more the gods respond, legend and opera diverging again. In the legend, Orpheus is inconsolable to the point of rejecting the love of any woman; as a result of

[2] A study of this opera as "a musical embodiment of the Hegelian idea of history," is found in Robinson, pp. 109f. Berlioz's masterpiece is in two parts, *La prise de Troie* (The Capture of Troy) and *Les Troyens à Carthage* (The Trojans in Carthage).

[3] See Barsham, pp. 1–9.

what is perceived as unnatural behavior, he is torn apart by female adherents of Bacchus/Dionysus, who hurl his corporeal remnants into the river Hebrus. Eventually, the Muses gather the fragments of his body and bury them at the foot of Mount Olympus, where, it is said, the nightingales sing more sweetly than anywhere else in the world. Orpheus's lyre is taken by Jupiter to the realm of the stars.

In Monteverdi's setting, Apollo raises the grieving Orfeo[4] into the heavens. The premiere of Gluck's work, however, coincided with the name day of Emperor Francis I, and any ending other than a happy one simply would not do; the gods therefore relent and the opera ends with reunion and rejoicing.

Orfeo ed Euridice and Giulio Cesare: The Same Century, but Different Worlds

Gluck's setting of the entry of Orfeo into the Underworld, in the second act of *Orfeo ed Euridice*, has some fairly obvious pictorializations. Fast tempos and driving scales are common symbols for turmoil in the operas of all eras, so the connection of them with the terrifying, raging Furies who guard the Underworld is simple and direct (Example 2.1a). So is the use of a harp playing gentle arpeggios (notes of a chord played successively instead of all at once) as an allusion to Orfeo's accompanying his song of pleading on his lyre (Example 2.1b).

Other elements of the scene, however, are somewhat arcane to modern listeners. Although the text's mention of Hercules and of Pirithous the Lapith will not mean much to those who have not kept up with the details of the Greek and Roman myths,[5] it is a passing one and not essential to grasping the dramatic and musical nature of the scene. Gluck's orchestral reference to the barking of Cerberus,[6] however, is another matter, because it is very prominent in the music without being described by the words. Not only must you know that Cerberus is a three-headed, dragon-tailed dog guarding the gate to Tartarus, permitting spirits to enter but not to return, but you must also be attuned to Gluck's stylized representation of the dog's barking through the use of low instrumentation and a threefold scalar motive (Example 2.1c).

Aside from such particularized musical references as the depiction of a three-headed dog and a musician's lyre, symbolic considerations exist on a broader plane and boil down to two essential problems.

The first requires us to think about the psychological and philosophical meanings of words and actions. Since it is the power of art to mean many

---

[4] Henceforth I will use the anglicized name of a character when dealing with it generically; when dealing with a specific opera, I will refer to the characters as they are named in the opera's original language.

[5] Pirithous the Lapith was enamored of Persephone, spouse of Pluto. Pirithous, accompanied by his friend Theseus, entered the underworld to carry her off; only Theseus made it back. Hercules went there to bring Alcestis back to Admetus (in one version of that myth).

[6] The creature is also musically represented in Lully's *Alceste* (1674).

Gluck, *Orfeo ed Euridice* (1762; rev. Paris 1774), Act II, scene i: in a performance of the Paris version, Orphée (Vinson Cole) struggles with the Furies
(The Mark Morris Dance Group). Seattle Opera, 1988: sets by Thomas Lynch,
costumes by Martin Pakledinaz. Photo Mary McInniss.

things, with what is "right" as a matter of individual reception, interpretations vary: Winton Dean sees the opera as a "fertile symbol of the artist's
predicament,"[7] John Drummond as "a simple tale of love,"[8] and Edward
Rothstein as a tale of "the ordinary man, the bourgeois placed in an unten-
able position by the whims of the gods" and thus powerful in "impact in pre-
Revolutionary Paris [where] there were many Orphées in attendance."[9]
Orfeo's foray into the land of the dead may be seen as a challenge to the
order of the universe, or as a victory of imagination over convention (and
thus of Romanticism over Classicism), wisdom over superstition, or the
Enlightenment over the Age of Despotism. It may be viewed as the creative
spirit lonely in a world of philistinism, as the resurrection of the soul, as a
metaphor of human courage and loyalty to principle, or as a study of the
price for any kind of human achievement. Perhaps it is simply a hymn of
thanks to the Muse or a paean to the power of music.[10]

The second problem, however, is more obscure, for it is the coming to
terms with the musical vocabulary of two centuries ago, when aesthetics were
changing from the prevalence of extravagant ornamentation to a preference
for tasteful elegance and restraint. Consider the stark contrast between Orfeo's
music and the music of the Furies: the Furies are given rushing scales punc-

[7] *Essays on Opera*, p. 92.

[8] *Opera in Perspective*, p. 167.

[9] Edward Rothstein, "Gluck's Doomed Lovers of 1774," in *New York Times*, (January 14,
1995), p. 13. Rothstein's review is of a performance of the Paris version of the opera.

[10] Shakespeare, *Henry VIII*, Act III, sc. i: "Orpheus with his lute made trees, / And the
mountain tops that freeze, / Bow themselves when he did sing."

EXAMPLE 2.1 GLUCK, *Orfeo ed Euridice*, ACT II

a) Dance of the Furies.

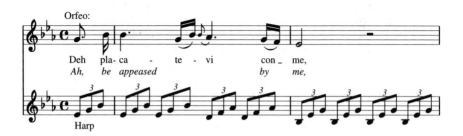

b) Orfeo's plea to the Furies.

c) Cerberus motive.

tuated by snapping chords; Orfeo is provided with an uncluttered melody[11] and a placid accompaniment of arpeggios. The Furies, consequently, seem wild and barbaric, while Orfeo's music implies self-control and courage of conviction. The Furies's dance and song of challenge are mostly an "empty" unison, but the limpid arpeggios provided by Orfeo as accompaniment to his simple melody are full chords: flowing gently and changing slowly from one harmony to another, they evoke serenity and steadfast purpose.

On the simplest level, this great scene gives us obvious musical pictorializations: Cerberus's barking, the Furies's primitive dancing, and the steadying influence of Orfeo's quiet and dignified music making. In terms of the immediate confines of the story, we are given song as metaphor for Orfeo's sincerity, for his station as poet and musician, and for his defiance of death as ultimate heroism.

On the other hand, if we compare the melodic nature of Handel's *Giulio Cesare* (Julius Caesar, 1724, thirty-eight years earlier than *Orfeo*) with that of Gluck's opera, we gain insight into changing aesthetics and ideals of behavior. This is very different from simple pictorialization. Gluck's "gestures" of melody mark a change from the grandiloquence of the Baroque to the new aesthetics of the Enlightenment. All of Handel's characters are given ornate melodic expression (with a few exceptions striking not only for their beauty but also because they sound so different from the rest of the opera). In *Giulio Cesare*, wholly contrasting thoughts and moods find voice in melodic ornament: when Cleopatra vows that, even in death, her ghost will torment Tolomeo, who has humiliated her and put her in chains, her melody explodes in melismas (Example 2.2a), and when Cesare compares the sweet music of the gorgeous vision staged by Cleopatra to the singing of a hidden bird, his melody is no less elaborate, even though the runs are garlands, not explosions (Example 2.2b).

This elaborate model of vocal writing and its highly abstract and artificial expression of feeling represented a heritage of art and manners against which Gluck was striking out. It is not just that Orfeo represents the power

EXAMPLE 2.2 HANDEL: *Giulio Cesare*

a) Act III, scene iii: Cleopatra vows to haunt Tolomeo after her death.

---

[11] The custom of singers providing ornamentations was prevalent in Gluck's time in accordance with a long-standing tradition of Italian opera, but the monumental simplicity of the music as Gluck notated it (drawing on a French tradition of restraint in ornamentation) is clearly an aesthetic statement by the composer, whether or not singers and audiences were sympathetic to it.

EXAMPLE 2.2 *(Continued)*

b) Act II, scene ii: Cesare, having seen a staged spectacle with Cleopatra at its center, compares its music to the beautiful singing of an unseen bird.

of music by singing beautifully and that he demonstrates courage by daring to enter the Underworld. His venture into the new and the perilous, his strength of heart, his sense of purpose, and all the metaphorical meanings lie in the fact that he sings simply.

Gluck's use of instruments also marked a major shift from the musical thinking of Handel's day. While the sense of melody is largely consistent in *Giulio Cesare*, the sense of orchestration is not, even though the string instruments are used throughout: at one time we hear strings in harmony, but at another only in unison; in one aria, the violas play, but in another they do not; we hear bassoons in one aria, but not in others; oboes are here, but not there; and so on.

One of the reasons for the tremendous impact of the Parnassus Scene, when Cleopatra suddenly appears before Cesare costumed as "Virtue Surrounded by the Muses," is that Handel presents a small combination of instruments not encountered anywhere else in the opera: oboe, harp, viola da gamba, and the lute-like theorbo are an "exotic" group, immediately suggesting to Handel's audience the Egyptian setting of the story, even though none of these instruments is Egyptian or—for Handel's audience—ancient.

Each expression of sentiment—the aria—is accompanied by some sort of orchestral group, but the exposition of plot through dialogue is strikingly different. The setting of the words leading to almost every aria is in the style of the *recitativo secco*.[12]

In other words, Handel's orchestra is an *ensemble d'occasion*—a group of players that varies from one aria to another, albeit with a basic set of strings and *basso continuo*.[13] Thus each new instrumental sound presented in an aria gains special emphasis and symbolic weight because it is unique to that moment.

Gluck's orchestra is also richly varied: the solo oboe accompanying Orfeo's entry into Elysium, accompanied by murmuring strings and flute ornaments, is the epitome of pastoral beauty, evoking images of shepherds piping, purling brooks, and birdcalls; and the blaring trombones of the chorus of Furies make a sound not found elsewhere in quite the same way. But there is no recitativo secco in *Orfeo*: the orchestra plays throughout, with a fairly consistent complement of instruments: strings, woodwinds (flutes, oboes, bassoons), and French horns. The result is a certain uniformity of sound that lends a tone of majesty and dignity to the whole opera even though the music is as varied in tempo and mood as *Giulio Cesare*.

The relative "steady state" of Gluck's orchestra is as symbolic as anything in the opera. It is an easily heard illustration of a basic principle set out by Gluck and his librettist, Ranieri di Calzabigi, in one of music's most famous manifestos, the Preface to Gluck's later opera *Alceste* (1767): the quixotic and the bizarre were to be set aside in favor of "simplicity, truth, and naturalness."

---

[12] A non-melodious/limited range/one-note-per-syllable singing of text accompanied only by harpsichord and a cello, without orchestra (hence *secco*—"dry").

[13] An accompanying pair of players: a bass instrument and a harpsichord improvising chords and figurations over the written-out bass line.

Voice as Symbol

What are modern audiences to make of the fact that, in performances today the roles of Cesare—hero, general, lover—and Orfeo are often sung by female voices (or by countertenors, who sound like female voices)? A very special abstraction is at work in both of these operas, the association of heroic achievement, grandeur, aristocratic bearing, and, not least, the words and sentiments of wooing, with a high voice capable of sweetness of tone, power, and skill in vocal display and agility. The practice in the seventeenth century and most of the eighteenth century was to assign the roles of heroes/lovers to the unique sound of the castrato, a male soprano or alto whose voice resulted from his castration when he was a promising boy singer and the subsequent marriage of his preserved treble register with years of intense training in singing (and musicianship), adult male lung capacity, and physical and vocal maturation.[14]

A successful castrato could rival the clarin trumpet in brilliance and pitch, and its player in strength, articulation, ornamental skill, and endurance.[15] In eighteenth-century serious opera, the castrati were the idols of their time; people flocked to their appearances and heaped adulation and applause on their performances, on occasion substituting "Evviva il coltello"—"Long live the little knife"—for "bravo." There are none around these days, so their roles must either be given to women or be transposed down, slightly for countertenors and greatly for tenors or basses. When basses or tenors are used, we have a genuine violation of the sound ideal of the original composition: in Monteverdi's *L'incoronazione di Poppea* (The Coronation of Poppea, 1643) for example, Nerone's voice is meant to be higher than anyone else's, including Poppea's. When women take the roles, we are offered a sound and a stage picture that are galaxies away from the present standards of theatrical reality, in spite of costuming and appropriate reining in of the female figure. In either case, our perceptions are twisted away from the composer's intent, and the ambience of the original performance is experienced through a very dense filter indeed.

---

[14] "Marriage" is a strange word choice under the circumstances, but it will do. Gluck rewrote the role of Orfeo for tenor (thus "Orphée") for the Paris revision, since the French could not countenance operatic castrati. It is said that Frenchmen hated them because the very idea was a threat to their masculinity, whereas the Italians cherished castrati because they were so relieved that the mutilation had not happened to themselves (Rogers, p. 359). Although the last professional castrato, Alessandro Moreschi (1858–1922), was active at the turn of the twentieth century, the last important castrato role was in Giacomo Meyerbeer's *Il crociato in Egitto* (The Crusader in Egypt, 1824). Heriot's monograph is the standard in-depth study. The details of the various surgical procedures are described by Burney in his *Music, Men, and Manners*, p. 163n. For other discussions, see Celletti (p. 8ff), *Oxford Dictionary of Opera* (p. 122), Rosselli (p. 32ff), and Bergeron. See also my discussion of *bel canto* in Chapter 7.

[15] "Clarin" or "clarino" refers to the upper registers of the modern trumpet and clarinet. In the Baroque trumpet, the clarin register was the only pitch area in which melodic playing was possible, and the brilliance of the sound of such high-note playing became a hallmark of passages dealing with heroism, grandeur of achievement, the glory of God, etc. Burney offers an account of a musical contest between the famous castrato Farinelli (né Carlo Broschi, 1769–1836) and a trumpeter (Antonio Crespi?): Farinelli won hands down. (See *Musical Tours*, p. 153; reprinted in Weiss and Taruskin, p. 227.)

The very sound of a soprano or mezzo-soprano as hero becomes highly problematic for a large number of listeners and viewers who demand that, at least on stage, men be men (which is to say tenors, baritones, and basses) and sound like them. Even in the late twentieth century, supposedly an era of gender liberation, the idea of lover and beloved being acted by singers of the same sex causes unease and restlessness among many in the often conservative opera audience.

In *Orfeo ed Euridice* and *Giulio Cesare*, then, both hero and heroine are trebles in the female range, providing a subtle and sensuous mix of similar voice types. It is vital to the blend of voice in the final duets of both operas and is central to the sensuous impact of the Parnassus Scene.

Both *Giulio Cesare* and *Orfeo ed Euridice* draw on classical subject matter and share the role of treble voices as heroes. But they represent enormous changes in taste and operatic expression, even though they are less than four decades apart. Some of the differences between them are right on the surface; others require an understanding of points of view that are long gone. If we are to get anywhere beyond the simple gratification of pretty tunes and sounds in opera, we will need to examine its changing faces and the metaphorical symbols they offer to us.

Opera's History—An Overview

The complexity of the history of opera is such that any attempt to distill it borders on the simplistic. For the reader who prefers a précis, I offer the following glib summary, with the admission that such an attempt to cover four centuries of opera history in two or three pages deserves a Surgeon General's warning.

The invention of opera around 1600 is a benchmark for the Baroque era, a period whose stylization of dramatic conflict and abstract expression of feeling found the opera to be its most cogent and popular form of musical expression. The musical symbols of Baroque opera are embedded partly in the general musical traits of a century-and-a-half of evolution—rhythmic drive, harmonic energy, and instrumental brilliance—but especially in solo song, in which the singing of long-phrased melodic line was characterized by tones made sweet or powerful at will, by varieties of expression, and ornamentation shaped by taste and highly refined technical skill.

Opera seria ("serious opera") plots were a freely mixed brew of characters, locales, and incidents drawn from all sorts of historical events, liberally spiced with the exotic and the imagined. Love was more the focus than heroism, intrigue more fascinating than the events of which they were a part, and the need for entrancing locales and emotion-laden situations precluded any concerns for historical or legendary accuracy.[16] Comic opera did not emerge as an independent genre until the mid-eighteenth century; before then it was a scene (or group of scenes) performed between the acts of an opera seria. Major composers of the Baroque era were Monteverdi (1567–1643) at

---

[16] See Jellinek for a lively comparison of historical goings-on with opera's treatment of them.

the start of it, Alessandro Scarlatti (1660–1725) and Jean-Baptiste Lully (1632–1687) in the middle of it, and George Frideric Handel (1685–1759) at the end.[17]

The Classical era (1770–1820) began with a devotion to principles of simplicity, naturalness, and dignified restraint, but these ideals represented only one side of the operatic coin: while melodies of elegant simplicity or comic tunefulness were deemed the paragons of good music, elaborate melody remained as an important tool of the trade for such theatrical goals as setting off the nobility from the simpler tunes given to common folk, characterizing flights of feeling, or satirizing excessive emotion. Moreover, the composers of the Classical era developed a fabric of voices and instruments that, in the ensemble, offered a continually interchanging array of melodies or motives that gave each of the simultaneously singing characters highly individualized music. For all its loyalty to simplicity, the Classical sound in opera was characterized primarily by constant variety, interchange of motives among vocal and instrumental parts, and mercurial plot development.

Classic elegance and restraint were given to serious opera by Gluck; the combination of wit and naturalness in comic opera is represented by the sprightly *La serva padrona* (The Maid-Mistress, 1733) of Giovanni Battista Pergolesi (1710–1736). The synthesis of these dissimilar elements was the particular gift of Wolfgang Amadeus Mozart (1756–1791), who commingled the comic and the serious in a unique way and meshed them with the realities of life. While the Classical era is usually dated from mid-eighteenth century through the career of Beethoven (who died in 1827), it is Mozart to whom we must turn for any understanding of its greatest days: he gave expression not only to its ideals but also to the passions and turmoil that affected the decades of the 1770s, '80s, and '90s.

If line was the distinguishing element of Baroque music and fabric that of Classic music, Romantic music made its impact through tone. During the whole of the nineteenth century and much of the twentieth, the hallmark of serious opera was the urgent, dramatic singing of the now-familiar soprano, mezzo-soprano, tenor, baritone, and bass voices. An orchestral accompaniment of richly varied colors supported flowing melody, and both instrumental and vocal sounds were at the service of passionate emotionalism. Such music purveyed the stories of heroes and heroines who suffered mightily, nobly, and tragically. The archetypical vehicle of these troubled characters was grand opera, a genre that used legends and historical events as frames for their complicated lives and provided a special theatrical mix of solos, ensembles, choruses, and ballets set against elaborate scenery and stage effects.

A list of the Romantic era's major composers would represent today's standard repertory. The first four decades of the 1800s are the years of Gioacchino Rossini (1792–1868), Carl Maria von Weber (1786–1826), Vincenzo Bellini

---

[17] Henry Purcell (1659–1695), composer of *Dido and Aeneas* (1689) was certainly one of the master composers, but his work was restricted to an English public soon to be overwhelmed by Italian opera seria, and the brevity of his life prevented him from exerting more than a minimal influence on the expansion of native English opera.

(1801–1835), and Gaetano Donizetti (1797–1848); the next four, while dominated by Giuseppe Verdi (1815–1901) and Richard Wagner (1815–1883), are also the years of the central Europeans Modeste Musorgsky (1839–1881), Pyotr Ilich Tchaikovsky (1840–1893), and Antonín Dvořák (1841–1904), and the Parisian triumphs of Giacomo Meyerbeer (1791–1864), Charles Gounod (1818–1893), Georges Bizet (1838–1875), and Jacques Offenbach (1819–1880). The final decades of the era, which carried over into the twentieth century, are primarily the years of the very different Giacomo Puccini (1858–1924), Claude Debussy (1862–1918), and Richard Strauss (1864–1949).

A special development in Italy during these latter years was the interest in an unsentimentalized treatment of characters and events (often violent) from everyday life. This so-called "verismo" movement has continued to exert an important influence on opera through the present.

The modern era defies stylistic generalization, because there is no single or predominant style of composition that identifies it. Its most startling feature seems to be the fundamental change in the relationship between audience and composer: after three centuries or so of audiences not only being congenial to new works but demanding them, we find in our own time a distinct coolness between composers (who naturally work at or near the cutting edge of contemporary styles) and audiences who find much more pleasure in the conventions, sounds, and symbols of the past than they seem to do in works of their own time.[18]

It is clear that some names have become firmly established in opera's pantheon, Leoš Janáček (1854–1928), Richard Strauss, Alban Berg (1885–1935), and Benjamin Britten (1913–1976) among them, but the vote is not yet in as to which of the many other figures will endure: Gian Carlo Menotti (b. 1911) gets more performance than critical prestige, and Sergei Prokofiev (1891–1953), Francis Poulenc (1899–1963), Dmitri Shostakovich (1906–1975), Samuel Barber (1910–1981), Hans Werner Henze (b. 1926), and Carlisle Floyd (b. 1926) more prestige than performance, although all are well represented in recordings. Only the attendance and performance statistics of 2050 will sort out the household names from those relegated to references in history books.

There is, to be sure, a constant supply of new operas performed in important theaters around the world; whether they will become consistent elements of the repertory remains to be seen. Given that performance in the 1990s may include both old works in new ways (or in "authentic performance practice") as well as brand new works that either offer obeisance to the old or reject it entirely, it may be that our era will have to survive under a moniker such as "The Age of Eclecticism" until our great-grandchildren make better sense of it.

---

[18] The problem is discussed by Sutcliffe, pp. 53–78.

Chapter 3

HOW OPERA'S MUSIC WORKS: SOUND AS SYMBOL AND METAPHOR

Symbolism in Music: Some General Comments

Symbolism is enormously complex and varied, and any attempt to deal with it as an introduction to listening to opera is bound to be perfunctory at times. There are, of course, levels of symbolism, some symbols dealing with a momentary emotion, object, or action, while others may represent all-embracing philosophical concepts. A melody or melodic fragment in a Wagner opera, for example, may refer to an object that is associated with a character; the character may in turn stand for an aspect of the human psyche that tells us something about humanity; and the aspect of the psyche may reflect on civilization as a whole. I will offer some approaches to the understanding of differing levels of meaning, but the discussions that follow are only preliminary thoughts on the actual sounds of music and their more obvious symbolisms.

Music's special power, notes Suzanne Langer, derives from its being free of fixed association. While severely limited in its capacity to be precise, it is especially powerful symbolically and "by virtue of its dynamic structure . . . can express the forms of vital experience which language is peculiarly unfit to convey. Feeling, life, motion and emotion constitute its import."[1]

The interrelationship of the expressive powers of music and poetry has knit the brows of many. It is not my purpose here to take up the cudgels of one side or another, but rather to point out some of the ways in which composers of opera have used the abstract art of music and the intellectual/emotional aspects of words to illuminate human behavior, emotion, and thought.

Knowing It When You Hear It

The effect of symbolism depends on recognition: if the perceiver is isolated from the intent of the symbol, its meaning is lost, no matter how deftly and creatively it has been used. Symbols are directly related to time, place, and

---

[1] Langer, p. 32.

person, so what made sense to the audience of one era may be quite lost to the audience of another. Citizens of the present century do not normally "ride a-hunting" to the tune of French horns, nor are they apt to associate the simple intervals of the unison and the octave with the perfection of God, yet the former was a common experience for aristocratic audiences throughout the seventeenth and eighteenth centuries, and the latter was a basic element of musical thinking for much of the Middle Ages. The audiences who attended the operas of Handel and the congregations who heard the chant settings of Leoninus (ca. 1163–1201) did not need to be clued in when they heard these things, but we who are near the dawn of a new millennium certainly do.

Except for words like "boom" and "crackle," music and speech are artificial sounds with no direct connection to their meaning.[2] Meanings are learned.

Opera is not just luxuriant in its use of musical symbols, it depends on them and on audience perception of them. Much of the language of music is immediate in its impact; we don't need a Music Appreciation course to appreciate the effects of pitch, loudness, instrumentation, bold dissonance, urgent melody, and so on. The "syntax" of this language, however, is made up of complex textures, harmonic sequences, or musical structures; their meanings are no less potent than other musical devices, but they are much more subtle and require astute listening if they are to be perceived fully and appreciated. At times, even the most refined listening skills are stretched to the limit, because composers will use symbolisms that require hearing perceptions that are gifts rather than learned skills.

Example: in Britten's *Peter Grimes*, we are given the townspeople and fisherfolk who are hardhearted, sanctimonious, set in their ways, and eager to place blame on someone who is different from them. Mending their nets and setting about their business, they appear in Act I singing consistently in the key of A major. In Act II, they attend church on Sunday morning, piously singing the *Benedicite* and intoning other liturgies in the key of E-flat. Much music (and an intermission) has come between the two keys, hence all but the most sophisticated listeners will probably have forgotten the sound of their key of Act I. Yet the relationship between the two keys is dramatically important and musically potent: E-flat and A are the gratingly dissonant pitches of the augmented fourth, the tritone;[3] keys based on them are distant, harmonically conflicting, and harsh when played at the same time or heard in close succession.

So here we have these people in church singing in a key that is dissonant with the key of their singing in everyday life—in musical terms, then, they say what pious folk are supposed to say in church, but it has no relation to their real world. Sounds familiar, doesn't it? And when the people return to

[2] Steven Pinker: "[Words] are arbitrary. The word "duck" does not look, walk or quack like a duck, but we all know it means duck because we have memorized an arbitrary association between a sound and a meaning." *The New York Times* OpEd. (April 5, 1994): A5.

[3] The interval is familiar from Sportin' Life's song, "It ain't necessarily so," from *Porgy and Bess*® (see Example PB–3b). The dissonance was so coarse to theorists of the Middle Ages that it was known as *diabolus in musica*—"the devil in music." "Tritone" is a term derived

Britten, *Peter Grimes* (1945), Act 1, scene i: The people of the Borough at their daily work. The tableau of the first scene will be the same at the end of the opera. Metropolitan Opera, 1966–67: Design by Tanya Moiseiwitsch. Courtesy *Opera News*, Metropolitan Opera Guild. Photo Louis Mélançon.

their A-major tonality in the final scene of the opera, giving only passing attention to the possibility of a tragedy at sea (Peter has ended his life by sailing his boat far from shore and by sinking it), we are given a harmonic insight into their unvarying mindset that is compositionally and theatrically quite wonderful, even if the cause of this effect is undetected by most in the audience. We may not know why we are so affected, but we are. And if we know why, we are affected intellectually as well as emotionally. It is a good combination.

Sadly, even in works where listening skills are less sorely tested, musical symbolisms are often so barely understood that audiences lose the essence of the action—the musical intensification of character and plot— and are aware of little else beyond the outlines of the story. The mirror that opera holds to the soul becomes fogged.

from the fact that this interval comprises three whole steps: E-flat to F is the first, F to G the second, and G to A the third. E-flat and A-flat occur early in the acoustic overtone series and sound so pure and somehow "right" that the interval of the fourth formed by them is called a "perfect" interval. A-natural, however, comes very late in the series; the ratio of the frequency of A-natural to the frequency of E-flat is hopelessly complex, 739:512 (!), a far cry from the perfect fourth's simple ratio of 4:3. The more complex the relationship, the more dissonant the interval is perceived.

The singing of opera in a language other than that of its audience has long been a problem,[4] and it is not solved by projecting or singing translations. Assume that the translation is superb and that the dramatic juxtaposition of a key word and its music—such as an expressive chord or a high note—is eminently appropriate; words still get drowned in ensembles and mangled by melismas (many notes per syllable), entire poems get washed away by the sweep of the music, and projected subtitles are pithy at best. Moreover, even when the listeners get every word, musical abstractions can be wholly foreign.

Mozart's *Le nozze di Figaro* (The Marriage of Figaro, 1784) and Rossini's *Il barbiere di Siviglia* (The Barber of Seville, 1816), for example, have some of the funniest moments in the world of theater, yet performances of them are often not unlike the respectful ambience of a *Tenebrae* service on Good Friday: amidst the most delightful and pointed *musical* jokes—told through purely musical devices—silence prevails.

On the other hand, when a listener is "in tune" with the vocabulary of the music, symbols can be readily grasped, whatever the language. Suppose an Italian tenor performs Pinkerton in Puccini's *Madama Butterfly* (1904) and overvowelizes the words "America forever" to a point of utter gibberish. The meaning can still be unmistakable because the fragment of *The Star Spangled Banner* to which these words are appended makes strikingly clear the several meanings of Puccini's music to anyone who recognizes the national anthem of the United States: the tenor is portraying an American. Moreover, given the quasi-oriental music and the dramatic contexts preceding this passage, Pinkerton emerges as an American quite out of touch with the delicacy and customs of Japanese culture and quite unaware that a culture other than his own might be worth something.

No less effective in its communication of meaning is "America," from Bernstein's opera-musical, *West Side Story* (1957). This song-dance, inflected by the alternation of a rhythmic group of 2 beats with one of 3 beats, is immediately recognizable as Caribbean to those familiar with Latin-American

EXAMPLE 3.1 BERNSTEIN, *West Side Story* ACT I: "AMERICA"

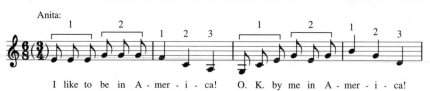

[4] Joseph Addison, in *The Spectator* of March 21, 1711, noted sarcastically that "our great Grand-children will be very curious to know the Reason why their Forefathers used to sit together like an Audience of Foreigners in their own Country, and to hear whole plays acted before them in a Tongue which they did not understand." Addison went on to ridicule performances in which each cast member sang in his own language and foolish translations ("soft Notes that were adapted to Pity in the Italian, fell upon the Word Rage in the English. . . . It oftentimes happen'd likewise, that the finest Notes in the Air fell upon the most insignificant Words in the Sentence. I have known the word *And* pursu'd through the whole Gamut, have been entertain'd with many a melodious *The,* and have heard the most beautiful Graces, Quavers and Divisions bestow'd upon *Then, For,* and *From;* to the eternal Honour of our English Particles"). Quoted in Grout/Williams, p. 167f.

rhythms. No American audience mistakes the ethnic identity of this 2 + 3 pulse; in theaters from San Francisco to Montauk, the mood of sarcasm and irony is explicit because of the music.

Context

Symbolism changes with context and depends on it, for no musical sound is absolute in its meanings. The sense of the text, the interplay of the characters, the substance of the story, the way it is performed, the choice of instruments, the nature of the harmony—all affect the perception of any musical sound; moreover, a sound's repetition or return can be laden with suggestions far removed from its original appearance.

Consider a simple dance tune in *Peter Grimes*, for example. In Act II, Ned Keene brushes off Mrs. Sedley's suspicion that Peter's apprentice has been murdered; Keene's dismissal of her suggestion is accompanied by the bright woodwind scoring of a fragment (marked "x" in Example 3.2a) of the

EXAMPLE 3.2 BRITTEN, *Peter Grimes*:
DANCE FRAGMENT AND ITS RETURN

a) Act III, scene i: Keene's response to Mrs. Sedley, accompanied by dance tune heard coming from the Moot Hall.

b) Act III, scene i: The people of the Borough intent on killing Peter.

Ländler[5] to which the townsfolk are dancing in the Moot Hall, and thus his remark seems to give the quietus to Mrs. Sedley's dark thoughts. This fragment, however, becomes something else on its return, for Britten turns it into a wordless howl of mob frenzy when the villagers stream out into the fog to find Peter and inflict on him their own brand of justice.

Context will lend subtle differences to a musical device. The cruel torment of conscience afflicting Oreste, the murderer of his mother (Gluck's *Iphigénie en Tauride,* 1779; Example 3.3a), is quite different from the guilt felt by Berlioz's Dido (*Les Troyens,* Example 3.3b), who pines for love even as she feels she should continue mourning for her dead husband; yet syncopation, a displacement of a rhythmic accent and thus an archetype for unrest and anguish, is used for both.

To complicate the matter a bit, syncopation can also be used for the exactly opposite sentiments of buoyancy of spirit and companionship. The peasants of Mascagni's *Cavalleria rusticana* (Rustic Chivalry, 1890; Example 3.3c)

EXAMPLE 3.3 SYNCOPATIONS IN DIFFERING CONTEXTS

a) Gluck, *Iphigénie en Tauride* Act II, scene iii: the troubled sleep of Oreste, who is besieged with guilt for having murdered his mother.

---

[5] A *Ländler* is a slow folk dance in triple time, originating mostly in Austria and southern Germany; it was a harbinger of the waltz.

are happily heading home to their wives; Constance, the young novitiate of Poulenc's *Dialogues des Carmélites* (Dialogues of the Carmelites, 1957; see below, Example 5.1), chatters in a charming and childlike way about death being as amusing as life. In each case, the displacement of the beat has the effect of insouciance and good feeling because of the impact of dramatic con-

EXAMPLE 3.3 (*Continued*)

b) Berlioz, *Les Troyens*, Part II (*Les Troyens à Carthage*), Act I, scene iv: Dido, in mourning for her husband, feeling guilt for wanting to be relieved of the "strange sadness" of life without love.

c) Mascagni, *Cavalleria rusticana*: villagers heading home after the Easter service.

text and the shaping forces of other musical factors such as melody, tempo, and harmony.

Then there is *Porgy and Bess®*, in which the emulation of Gullah music and dialect makes syncopation fundamental to its idiom, whether the situation is happy (Example 3.3d) or sad (Example 3.3e).

Timbre[6] also assumes a symbolism in accordance with its context. The French horn, for example, signifies hunting in both Handel's *Giulio Cesare* and Weber's *Der Freischütz* (The Free Marksman; also The Charmed Bullet, 1821), but the layers of meaning are vastly different because of such factors

EXAMPLE 3.3 (*Continued*)

d) The Gershwins, *Porgy and Bess®*, Act I, scene i: Clara daydreams a happy song of summer while some of the men shoot craps.   ©WB MUSIC CORP. (Adm.)

e) The Gershwins, *Porgy and Bess®*, Act I, scene ii: At the funeral of Jake Robbins, a collection is taken for his proper burial.   ©WB MUSIC CORP. (Adm.)

---

[6] The sound quality of an instrument or voice.

as when the works were composed, audience expectations and perceptions of musical symbolism, and the nature of the plot and characters.

In *Giulio Cesare* we have a simple "metaphor aria,"[7] "Va tacito e nascos-to" ("Go silently and stealthily"): Cesare has just engaged in a not-too-subtle duel of words and innuendos with Tolomeo; left alone, he compares the conniving Tolomeo to a cunning hunter stalking his prey in secret, just as one disposed to evil wishes his nefarious designs to go unsuspected.

The most immediate symbol in Handel's music for this aria is its scoring: the aria is accompanied by the French horn, whose distinctive tone was immediately symbolic of hunting to the landed aristocracy of the eighteenth century and thus clearly evocative of the hunter/prey-deceiver/victim metaphor of the text. Its legato is at once elegant, quite in keeping with its audience and the high station of the character singing it, and restrained, appropriate to the idea of hunting as stealthy pursuit.

Der Freischütz is also about hunting and hunters, but it came to the stage with heavy baggage: surging German nationalism that had made Berliners resentful of foreign influence and privilege, and the association of Weber's patriotic music[8] with the German cause. That he was to compose music for a plot set in and dealing with the superstitions of the forests of Bohemia and its Teutonic devil Samiel, rather than the gods and goddesses in some Greco-Roman Arcadia, got German nostrils flaring. Weber responded with music that was acutely descriptive and atmospheric, with French horns being especially important.

In scene after scene, four French horns lend their timbre so tellingly that they have become famous as "the Freischütz horns." Although they inform the overture and two choruses of huntsmen with bold and characteristic fanfares, it is in the famed "Wolf Glen Scene" of Act II that they are used most innovatively. There they howl in acerbic dissonance, accompanying the casting of a magic bullet and a supernatural vision of huntsmen, stags, and hounds, and the evil Caspar crying "Wehe! das Wilde Heer" ("Woe! The wild chase"). Handel never imagined hunting music like this.

But the French horn is not only associated with hunting. It has been a prominent harmony instrument in orchestration ever since the latter third of the eighteenth century and thus a part of our musical environment, not just in opera (no matter what the story is about) but in symphonies and concertos as well. Sometimes it takes on a dramatic significance worlds apart from what I have just described.

The French horn often assumes a bluntly comic—not to say salacious—function when reference is made to a husband's being "given the horns" of cuckoldry. This image is employed with special deliciousness in Verdi's *Falstaff* (1893), when Ford learns that Falstaff has just arranged a tryst with Ford's wife and that Ford is very likely to be "wearing the horns" within the hour. Ford conjures up a grotesque picture of the horns erupting from his

---

[7] In the operas of the Baroque era, this was a common genre of song in which both text and music represented a situation and an emotion in allegorical terms.

[8] Among his nationalistic works before *Der Freischütz* are the song cycle *Leyer und Schwert* ("Lyre and Sword," 1814) and the cantata *Kampf und Sieg* ("Battle and Victory," 1815).

forehead as he imagines his neighbors gossiping about him and his wife degrading his honor. The orchestra's French horns suit the sound to the thought, their raucous call blazoning at every opportunity to take advantage of a musical pun: "corno" is Italian for both the name of the musical instrument and the humiliating protuberance itself.

Two other particularly well-known examples of the French horn sounding the excitement of sexual activity are the opening of Strauss's *Der Rosenkavalier* (The Knight of the Rose, 1911), in which the instrument's wild braying has been assigned by some writers to the depiction of the premature climaxing of the adolescent Octavian in his lovemaking with the Marschallin, and the second duet of *Le nozze di Figaro,* where Susanna suggests to Figaro, her fiancé, that not only might the Countess's bell be ringing for her—"din, din," sung with pointed notes from flute and oboe—but the Count's too, "don don." The French horns snort from the orchestra, with a vengeance.

Here's a final illustration of the importance of context. Chromaticism[9] is an oft-encountered symbol, but it too will vary in its meaning with where and how we hear it.

It is difficult to imagine two characters more disparate than Mrs. Sedley, of *Peter Grimes,* and Zdenka, of Richard Strauss's *Arabella.* Mrs. Sedley is an expert in character assassination and gossip, malevolently suspecting evil and taking vicious delight in finding it. Zdenka is a vivacious seventeen-year-old girl, in love madly and for the first time. For both we have chromatic ups and downs, but they are remarkably different because of the contextual subtleties of voicing (Zdenka's motive high, Mrs. Sedley's low), dynamics and tempo (the swell and ebb of Mrs. Sedley's motive is consistent and always at

EXAMPLE 3.4 CHROMATIC RISE AND FALL

a) Britten, *Peter Grimes,* Act III, scene i: Mrs. Sedley's creed.

b) R. Strauss, *Arabella*: Zdenka's motive.

---

[9] The use of notes not found in the scale or key on which a passage is based; these "added" or "altered" notes will be indicated in the notation by the symbols for flat, sharp, and natural (the so-called "accidentals"). A series of half-steps in either direction (A, A-sharp, B, C, C-sharp, etc.; or A, A-flat, G, G-flat, etc.) is called a "chromatic scale."

a slow tempo), and rhythmic stress (Zdenka's motive is at times waltz-like, at other times flighty; Mrs. Sedley's music has none of these qualities). Therefore, *when* and *how* we hear is as symbolic as *what* we hear.

Archetypes

Some symbols speak to us in spite of the barriers of time and style. Lest I overstate the universality of some of these musical signs, let us remember that most of our listening repertory comes from the nineteenth and the first third of the twentieth centuries, with some extension back through Mozart to Gluck and forward to twenty operas or so composed between 1930 and 1980. That's a fairly narrow window into opera's history, so when I suggest that archetypes transcend the barriers of time, note that my generalization has its limits. Some of the following examples are indeed transgenerational; but the bulk of them permeate only the operas written between 1800 and 1930, give or take a few decades either way.

Song and Singing

Song, of course, is the central element of opera and is its "natural" mode of communication, whether through dialogue, soliloquy, or choral expression. In *Porgy and Bess®* the element of song is a crucial metaphor for the "real" people of the opera. Song is given only to the blacks in this opera; they are the focal characters, and therefore Gershwin has them "speak" and reveal their actions through the "real" idiom of opera, vocal music. The few whites of the cast—outsiders to the life of Catfish Row—are speakers only.

Porgy and Bess® is not unique in separating out a character by denying him or her song: Samiel, in *Freischütz* and Pasha Selim, in Mozart's *Die Entführung aus dem Serail* (The Abduction from the Seraglio, 1782), are speaking parts only. Tadzio, in Britten's *Death in Venice* (1973), is danced, not voiced; Dvořák's Rusalka is consigned to muteness in the presence of mortals, but can "speak" to other supernatural creatures.

Beyond the realm of melody as the essence of operatic communication, however, is the archetype of song itself—not sung recitative or aria but ballad, drinking song, and entertainment for others presented as musical moments as part of the carrying out of the plot.[10] They are musical props or tuneful scenery, in other words—songs characters "do" as opposed to songs that show us what they are thinking. I suppose psychiatrists might have a field day when considering opera's fascination with itself, for opera is thickly populated with musicians, both amateur and professional; for them, singing is not just the way they speak to those around them but the essence of their being.

---

[10] Such a song *qua* song is usually listed in the score as a *canzone* ("La donna è mobile," No. 15 in *Rigoletto,* and "Se il mio nome," No. 3 in *Il barbiere di Siviglia*) or a *canzonetta* ("Deh vieni alla finestra," No. 16 in *Don Giovanni,* and "Halte-là," No. 16 in *Carmen*).

The singing of Monteverdi's Orfeo to Caronte, the gatekeeper and ferryman of the Underworld, is opera's first great testament to the wonder of song. Orfeo's "Possente spirto" ("Potent spirit") charms the ferryman to the world of death by bringing to bear a metaphorical diversity of music's riches: simple and complex melody and changing combinations of string, woodwind, and brass instruments.

Orpheus, the protagonist of hundreds of operas over the years, is a member of a large fraternity of amateur and professional singers that includes Manrico in Verdi's *Il trovatore* (The Troubadour, 1853) and Antonia in Offenbach's *Les contes d'Hoffmann* (The Tales of Hoffmann, 1881),[11] the title roles of Wagner's *Tannhäuser* (1845; rev. Paris, 1861), Ponchielli's *La Gioconda* (1876), and Puccini's *Tosca* (1900), and all the important male characters of Wagner's *Die Meistersinger*.

Serenades abound, especially from the amateurs: Mozart's Don Giovanni (1787) and Gounod's Mephistopheles (*Faust*) sing outside the windows of fair ladies, both strumming very nicely as they do; Ernesto (Donizetti's *Don Pasquale*, 1843) also gets to sing a serenade, with a whole chorus imitating a guitar as his accompaniment; and Almaviva (in Rossini's *Barber*) gets to sing two in a row, the first with a ragged assemblage of musical oafs, the second with Figaro on guitar.

Some of opera's singers appear in public: Lakmé's "Bell Song" (Delibes' *Lakmé*, 1883); Iago's drinking song (Verdi's *Otello*, 1887); Barnaba's "Fisherman's Song" (*La Gioconda*); and Porgy's "I got plenty o' nuttin'" are sung for the edification of throngs. Some sing for themselves, although Debussy's Mélisande (*Pelléas et Mélisande*, 1902), Mozart's Osmin (*Entführung*), Verdi's Duke of Mantua (*Rigoletto*, 1851), and Berlioz's Hylas (*Les Troyens*) are overheard. Some of opera's singers aim their music at intimate audiences: Cherubino sings his "Voi che sapete" for the Countess and Susanna in *Le nozze di Figaro,* and Carmen performs very privately for Don José in both the "Seguidilla" of Act I (No. 10) and her "tra-la-la" bit with the castanets in Act II (No. 17). *Die Meistersinger*'s Walther sings for Hans Sachs alone, then performs the finished version of the song before all of Nuremberg.

The point of this catalogue is not only to illustrate the frequency of song *qua* song in opera but also to suggest that this isolation of singing as apart from the dialogue- and soliloquy-singing of opera is a metaphor for the power of music. Each one of these "songs" reveals something about the character of the person singing: both Mephistopheles and Iago are given chromatic runs that belie an apparent simplicity and goodheartedness and thus emerge as evil in spite of the seeming conviviality of their singing; Walther's earnestness, creativity, and poetry of soul is no less apparent in his "studio work" with Sachs than in the public competition at the end of the opera; Rossini's Almaviva is a fancy dan whose elaborate melody speaks directly of his aristocratic heritage, dress, and station in life.[12]

---

[11] Olympia, in the same opera, is also devoted to song as basic to her expression, but she doesn't really count—she's a mechanical doll. 1881 is the date of this opera's first production, but with recitatives, revisions, and some orchestrations completed by Ernest Guiraud (1837–1892), Offenbach having died in 1880 without completing the music. Guiraud provided the same service for the Vienna premiere of Bizet's *Carmen*.

[12] Mozart's Almaviva is cut from more serious cloth—no serenades for *him*.

Songs that are the natural expression of their singers are as revealing and symbolic as the rest of the music of opera, for hypocrisy and deception will out no less clearly than goodness and virtue, as witness the obvious insincerity of the music of Don Giovanni and Mephistopheles. Characters may lie; their "songs" do not.

The Structure of Music

Because the way we set out our thoughts may be as illuminative as the thoughts themselves, it is not suprising that the patterns of melodic repetition and contrast—the forms of music—are themselves metaphorical. The strophic principle—the repetition of a melody with changing words, harmonizations, or accompaniments (or all, or at least some of them)—is one of the oldest ways of organizing music and one of the most widespread among the world's cultures. It has served as a symbol for many of opera's characters.

In Monteverdi's *Orfeo*, for example, Orfeo's appeal to Caronte is a series of repetitions of a melody in the bass[13] with ever more elaborate figurations

Bizet, *Carmen* (1875), Act I: Carmen (Grace Bumbry) tells of her philosophy of love in the "Habanera." Metropolitan Opera, 1967–68: sets by Jacques Dupont. Courtesy *Opera News*, Metropolitan Opera Guild. Photo Louis Mélançon.

---

[13] See Example 6.7. The same approach was later applied by Purcell to Dido's lament, "When I am laid in earth," in his *Dido and Aeneas* (1689; see Example 3.16b). A repeated bass figure with a sense of melodic coherence is called a "ground" or "ground bass."

above it until the final verse, which is poignantly simple. Carmen's strophic music is no less appropriate, even though her character is about as far removed from Orfeo as one can get. She has "been around," as they say, so this most basic approach to musical form becomes a metaphor for her earthiness and her frank approach to life's primal urge, both represented in her familiar "Habanera"[14] (a testament to the uncontrollable—not to say dangerous—nature of love) and her "Seguidilla" (in which she offers seductive suggestions to José of the delights in store for him should he free her).

The ABA pattern[15] is also archetypical, its musical symmetry serving as a fundamental pattern for arias of every period of opera. It may represent tradition, formalism, or the like: in Gounod's *Faust*, for example, Valentin's prayer, an ABA, is in marked contrast with the strophic street song and serenade of Mephistopheles; in *Carmen*, Micaëla's ABA prayer (No. 22, "Je dis que rien ne m'épouvante"—"I say that nothing frightens me") represents convention and prayerful sincerity quite unknown to Carmen; and in *Don Giovanni*, both of Don Ottavio's arias (Nos. 10a and 21) are in this "ternary" form, in keeping with a character who represents traditional values in an opera dominated by a Don Giovanni, who has no values at all other than self-interest and personal gratification.

Some of the forms used in opera derive from the forms of instrumental music, especially those developed during the Classical era. The rondo, the sonata form, and the theme and variations (a kind of strophic pattern) are among the basic organizing principles of all music for the past 250 years, although they have not acquired particularly symbolic functions.

Instrumental Genres

The first sound of the first enduring opera, Monteverdi's *Orfeo* (Example 3.5a), is a set of fanfares, each a flourish of repeated notes or of pitches derived from the overtone series.[16] Fanfares have been used in hundreds of operas since, as heralds of grand events, at the arrival of dramatic moments, or at the imposition of curses and other pronouncements of great import.

Marches and processionals abound, sometimes militant and bright, others dark and funereal; some of them are rung in for the sake of display, some as clear metaphors for the inner meanings of the stories. *Les Troyens* is the most "public" of operas, because so much of it is enacted in full view of its

---

[14] This is not only a Spanish dance type but the name given to the song sung by Carmen at her first appearance.

[15] In describing musical forms, a different letter is used for each recognizable section of a composition. "ABA" thus describes a pattern in which an opening section (A) returns after a contrasting middle one (B).

[16] The first notes of the overtone series used in fanfare writing consist of a fundamental pitch, then the octave above it, the fifth above that, the next octave above the fundamental, then the third above the fundamental; in C major, the notes would be c, c^1, g^1, c^2, e^2, and g^2. Bugle calls draw on the last four of these. A simple but thorough explanation of the overtone series may be found in Levenson, p. 26f. A discussion related to vocal registers and singing techique is offered by Giles, pp. 159ff.

EXAMPLE 3.5 INSTRUMENTAL AND VOCAL FANFARES

Recorders, Violins,
Oboe, Trumpet (Cornetto)

a) Monteverdi, *Orfeo:* Toccata before the Prologue.

Trumpet

b) Beethoven, *Fidelio*, Act II, scene i: fanfare announcing the sudden arrival of the Consul at the climax of the Dungeon Scene.

Shuisky:

Da zdravst - vu - et car' Bo - ris Fe - o - do - ro - vič!
Long live Tsar Boris Feodorich!

c) Musorgsky: *Boris Godunov* (comp. 1868–69; rev. 1871–72), Act I, scene ii: Shuisky proclaims Boris as Tsar.

many participants; processional music is therefore its *sine qua non* in terms of its theatrical personality and, more important, in terms of what the drama and music say to us symbolically. Its martial passages include an arrogant, cock-of-the-walk march for the triumphant Trojans in Act I, a trumpet-bedecked ballet to entertain Dido, and a brooding Dead March for Dido's preparation for suicide.[17]

In one of opera's most familiar moments, Figaro's "Non più andrai, far-fallone amoroso" ("No more will you gad about, you amorous butterfly"; end of Act I, of *Le nozze di Figaro*), the march is used to humorous effect: Figaro twits the soon-to-be-commissioned adolescent, Cherubino, whose dandy clothes and fandango-dancing will soon give way to a soldier's uniform and slogging in the mud. Mozart's flourishes of trumpets, horns, and drums are the sound-equivalent of Figaro's elbows digging into Cherubino's discomfited ribs.

The first part of the same act of *Le nozze* includes yet another orchestral genre as archetype: the dance. Having just learned that the Count has sexual designs on his fiancée, Susanna, Figaro sings of an ironic invitation to the

---

[17] The use of a throbbing ostinato (itself an archetype) in this Dead March has an echo in the procession to the scaffold that brings Poulenc's *Dialogues des Carmélites* (1957) to its close. See Example 5.2 below.

Count[18] to join Figaro's "dancing school," in which the servant, not the master, will call the tune. Figaro's soliloquy "Se vuol ballare" ("If you wish to dance") uses the triple meter and symmetrical form of the minuet (a dance type appropriate for a Count but not for a Count's valet), but he makes the music his own and turns its elegant bearing inside out. Phrases that ought to end on the first beat of a measure are misplaced to high-note accents ("x" in Example 3.6a) on the second beat, twisting the minuet's grace and rhythmic predictability quite out of shape. The device thus becomes symbolic of both anger and determination on Figaro's part, while an occasionally scurrying accompaniment ("y" in the example) provides the overtones of plotting that give the genre of this courtly dance very special significance.

Mozart also uses a minuet to mock the aristocracy when he provides a mincing 3/8 rhythm for Susanna's exiting the closet in *Le nozze's* Act II, the music twitting the discomfited Count in one of opera's funniest and most telling moments (Example 3.6b).

In both epic theater (Wagner's *Die Walküre,*) and comedy (Rossini's *Il barbiere di Siviglia*), the instrumental representation of tempest serves a variety of functions, ranging from an intermezzo to show the passage of time (*Il barbiere*) to the representation of psychological stress (Vanderdecken's torment and eternal punishment in Wagner's *Der fliegende Holländer* [The Flying Dutchman], 1843), societal hatreds and fears (*Peter Grimes*), and the tumult of action and passion (*Die Walküre*).

The orchestral tempest as metaphor is very frequent in Baroque serious opera, but there it is most often an accompaniment to an aria rather than a separate instrumental movement. Rapid string passages or angular figures suggesting, for example, lightning, are typically background accompaniments or reinforcements and echoes of figures set out more prominently in the voice part. Cleopatra's "Da tempeste il legno infranto" ("When from the tempest his vessel is safe . . .") is an example (see Example 3.7).

Examples from the Classical era include the overture and first scene of *Iphigénie en Tauride*, in which storm music implies the fury of pre-curtain action and then continues into the first scene to serve as a metaphorical counterpoint to the anguished opening cries of Iphigénie and her companions, and Mozart's *Idomeneo* (1781), where the tempest music of the overture underlies the awful vow of Idomeneo to sacrifice the first person he sees and symbolizes the ravages of a sea serpent sent by the angry Neptune when Idomeneo fails to keep his word.

In the nineteenth century, composers often used the "storm in heaven to reflect a crime on earth."[19] Given the propensity of operatic plots for nefarious scheming and dramatic contretemps, the weather in the 1800s got pretty riled up when there was dirty work afoot (*Rigoletto*, 1851), a major confrontation in the works (Donizetti's *Lucia di Lammermoor,* 1835), or supernatural forces on the loose (*Der Freischütz*).

Perhaps the most celebrated use of storm as metaphor is the stunning opening of *Otello,* where Verdi simultaneously depicts two aspects of Otello's

---

[18] The Count is, of course, not around to hear it; given that Beaumarchais's story is set in aristocratic times, Figaro needs discretion, not effrontery.

[19] Frank Martin, *Aspects of Verdi*, pp. 175–177. The passage provides a discussion of the symbolism of the storm in *Rigoletto*.

EXAMPLE 3.6 MINUET-AS-SYMBOL IN MOZART'S *Le nozze di Figaro*

a) Act I: Figaro's "Se vuol ballare."

b) Act II: Susanna exits the closet.

character. The rampaging turbulence of wind and wave is clearly metaphorical for a man whose psyche is subject to the impulse of the moment and whose passions are extreme. At the same time, Otello is shown as a conqueror of Nature itself. The dramatic exposition that took Shakespeare almost an entire act to depict is compressed into ten minutes of orchestral and choral sound: rolling timpani, rushing strings, and ripping brass fanfares are the most forward elements of Verdi's fulminating orchestra, with the chorus providing such specific verbal images as "lampi" ("lightning")

EXAMPLE 3.7 HANDEL, *Giulio Cesare* ACT III, SCENE VII:
NO. 37, CLEOPATRA'S TEMPEST ARIA

and "tuoni" ("thunder"). Even the most advanced staging and lighting can't come close to Verdi's incarnation of shrieking wind and piling waves; given Verdi's music, we don't really need the stage picture at all.

The vessels survive; when Otello strides into view with his glorious arioso,[20] "Esultate! L'orgoglio musulmano sepulto in mar"("Exult! The glory of the Turks has been drowned in the sea"), the orchestra suddenly turns from violent motion and its role as the most dominant music to the

---

[20] Literally, "in the manner of an aria"; i.e., songful without being in the formal shape of a self-sufficient song. Arioso is a pliant style of sung declamation that has the through-composed structure of recitative but is not bound to its one-note-per-syllable tradition. There may be some text repetition and some small ornamentation of a single syllable but far less than in an aria.

stasis of sustained chords in the lower brass and a role as subordinate accompaniment. The effect is a pictorialization of the triumph of vocal song over instrumentation, of control over turmoil, and thus of human being over Nature. Through musical means, then, Verdi is able to establish Otello as a man whose grandeur and nobility transcend the turmoil of the world around him; his fall from this high state and the calamitous effect of surrendering to his more primitive instincts is thus made all the more wrenching and tragic.

Melody, Rhythm, and Harmony

The fundamental building blocks of music are interconnected. It is not possible to have melody without rhythm—although the reverse is true—and our listening habits have been so conditioned by the music of the past three centuries that we tend to sense a harmonic underpinning to music even when none is provided or intended. I will separate these elements artificially for the sake of discussion.

Melodic types are too diverse to list here, but the use of elaborate melody as opposed to simplicity provides a useful starting point. Olympia's coloratura[21] in the Coppelius scene of *Les contes d'Hoffmann* is the epitome of artificiality and thus is closely related to the archetype of ornate melody as symbolic of madness (Lucia di Lammermoor's is the most famous derangement, but she has many cousins), excess (the Queen of the Night in *Die Zauberflöte*—The Magic Flute, 1791), and romantic fantasizing (Gilda, in *Rigoletto*). Coloratura has also symbolized sprightly raillery (Zerbinetta, in Richard Strauss's *Ariadne auf Naxos*—"Ariadne on Naxos," 1912), and a resigned awareness of the complexities and disappointments of life (Ellen's "Embroidery of childhood," in *Peter Grimes*).

An archetype for innocent figures is a song of simple melody[22]— Marguerite's "Il était un roi de Thulé," ("There once was a King of Thule," in *Faust*), Mélisande's tower song (in Debussy's *Pelléas et Mélisande*), Clara's "Summertime" (*Porgy and Bess*®). Other kinds of people also get to sing that way, however. Don Giovanni's serenade, for example, "Deh vieni alla finestra," ("Ah, come to your window") is a purposefully simple song used with dramatic irony by a very complex person to seduce a serving girl (Donna Elvira's maid). The famed Barcarolle of *Les contes d'Hoffman* is another instance of simplicity used ironically: an elegantly harmonized, simple tune over a generic background accompaniment, it is a duet sung by the courtesan Giulietta, who represents Hoffmann's destructive sexual appetite, and Nicklausse, Hoffmann's muse who has forsaken him at this moment—to them is given music that is ravishingly beautiful, while Hoffmann, the poet, meets only with frustration and despair.

From its beginning days, the primary subjects of opera have been love and hate, life and death. Flowing melody and rising lines have a long-standing association with life and love; hesitant rhythms and descending lines are

---

[21] That is, bravura singing that uses such vocal flourishes as fast runs, trills, and high notes.

[22] The simplicity of notation is deceiving; an unadorned tune may be supremely difficult to sing in tune, or to perform stylishly.

correspondingly associated with death. Loyalty has frequently found its voice in solidity of rhythm; hatred has been given dissonant harmonies or aggressiveness of dynamics and rhythmic drive.

That the musical imagery of love has been fairly constant through the several generations of opera, from its birth to the present, is quite remarkable when one considers the enormous diversity of operatic genres, historical styles, and the individual traits of composers. Ever since the invention of opera, the indication between lovers that their hearts beat together has been for them to sing the same tune (or phrases clearly related melodically), either in alternation or in the parallel harmony of thirds and sixths.

EXAMPLE 3.8 LOVERS SINGING THE SAME OR SIMILAR MELODY, EITHER IN ALTERNATION OR IN HARMONY

a) Monteverdi–Sacrati,[23] *L'incoronazione di Poppea* Act III, scene viii: Nerone–Poppea duet.

---

[23] It is probable that Monteverdi did not complete the opera and that the finale is the work of Francesco Sacrati (1605–1660). The question is discussed in detail by Alan Curtis in the preface to the Novello score of the opera (1989); the technical aspects leading to this ascription are set out by Curtis in his *"La Poppea Impasticciata,* or Who Wrote the Music to 'L'incoronazione' 1643)?," in *Journal of the American Musicological Society* 42, no. 1 (Spring 1989): 23–54.

EXAMPLE 3.8 (*Continued*)

b) Berlioz, *Les Troyens*, Part II (*Les Troyens à Carthage*), Act II, scene vii:
Aeneas–Dido duet.

c) R. Strauss, *Der Rosenkavalier*, Act III: Sophie and Octavian in wonderment
and joy at the prospect of their marriage.

EXAMPLE 3.9 MUSORGSKY, *Boris Godunov,* ACT III, SCENE II:
CONCLUDING TRIO PASSAGE

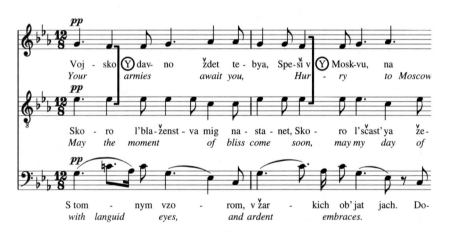

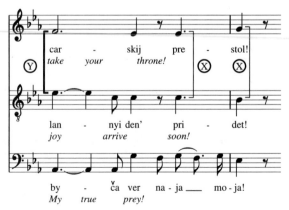

Lest this association of parallel thirds and sixths with love be carried too far, I should point out that any situation involving two characters singing at once will probably be harmonized in this way, because the interval of a third (and its inversion, the sixth) has been a standard harmonic building block for almost four centuries of tonal music. The result is some strange harmonic bedfellows: in *Faust*'s Act IV trio we have the joining of a very pious Valentine and a very impious Mephistopheles (with the morally addled Faust melodically out on his own) and Verdi's *La forza del destino* (The Force of Destiny, 1862, rev. 1869) parallels two men who are ready to cut each other to pieces at the end of the Act IV duet, "Invano Alvaro te celasti al mondo" (Don Carlo: "In vain, Alvaro, have you hidden yourself from the world"). On the other hand, the Act I duet between Otello and Desdemona (Verdi's *Otello*) has none of this until the last two measures, and then there is simply—and exquisitely—a pair of sustained notes, her F and his A-flat.

Musorgsky offers an effective parody of this archetype in the Marina-Dmitri scene of *Boris* (Example 3.9). Here, Marina's goal in sharing sentiments of love is motivated not by affection but by lust for power. The flowing effect of amorous thirds and sixths (marked in the example with "x") is occasionally jolted by dissonant intervals (marked "y"); the passage of parallel singing is much too brief for anyone but the hapless Dmitri to be convinced that love has anything to do with Marina's thoughts; and the sneering comments by the conniving Jesuit Rangoni add more discordance to a scene of superficial crooning and swooning.

While we are on the subject of intervals, let us return to the augmented fourth, the infamous tritone that has historically been so dissonant and sonically grating. It has inevitably been associated with betrayal, evil intent, tragic foreboding, dishonesty, and the like, and, these being not infrequent aspects of operatic villainy and misfortune, it lurks under many an operatic rock.

EXAMPLE 3.10 THE TRITONE

a) Monteverdi, *Orfeo*, Act IV: On the way out of the Underworld, Euridice dies when Orfeo turns to look at her.

EXAMPLE 3.10 (*Continued*)

b) Dvořák, *Rusalka*, 1901, Act III: The Prince, in spiritual torment, seeks Rusalka, even if finding her means his death; reference to gods and devils uses the tritone D → G-sharp [A-flat], call to the beloved uses perfect fifth.

c) Leoncavallo, *Pagliacci* (Clowns, 1892). Act I: Tonio promises to help Canio learn the identity of Nedda's secret lover.

Quite the opposite are the so-called "perfect" intervals, the unison, octave, fifth, and fourth. These are the first notes of the overtone series and so are the simplest relationships in music. By extension they have become associated with the most basic forces of our universe and thus the most true: nature, innocence, love, the ancient, the fundamental qualities of a nation's folk, and so on.

In *Peter Grimes*, a remarkable unaccompanied duet between Peter and Ellen begins with each singing in separate keys (Example 3.11a), as Peter is obsessed with the injustice of an inquest accusing him of negligence in the death of his apprentice, while Ellen tries to reach him with words of gentleness and understanding. At the end of the duet (Example 3.11b), Ellen's gentleness has finally done its soothing work, and the two, planning to marry, sing in a tender and very beautiful unison.

Given the vagaries of context, perfect intervals have been applicable to very different moods, situations, and characters, yet there is a certain consistency and logic to their use. In Wagner's *Der fliegende Holländer*, for example, we have a sea captain, Vanderdecken, whose blasphemy against God has brought upon him a sentence to sail raging seas to eternity until he finds a woman true to him until death. The perfect intervals of the motive associated with him (Example 3.12a) derive from the fundamental sin of his defiance of God and also from the oneness of his sentence with the eternal element of the sea.

The street urchins of Catfish Row (*Porgy and Bess*®), on the other hand, are as innocent as Vanderdecken is sinful. Like him, however, they inhabit a world of their own—the "real" world of ordinary folk is not theirs—so, as pure children of nature, they sing their song with many perfect fourths as well as the minor thirds drawn from the blues (Example 3.12b).

The people of *Boris Godunov* are, in effect, like the *Porgy and Bess*® children. They are representative of Mother Russia, hence they are symbols of the natural goodness of their nation. Their singing (Example 3.12c) transcends the frailty of individuals and draws on Russian folk music, itself a

EXAMPLE 3.11 BRITTEN, *Peter Grimes*: END OF PROLOGUE

a) Peter and Ellen in different keys, different psychological worlds.

EXAMPLE 3.11 (*CONTINUED*)

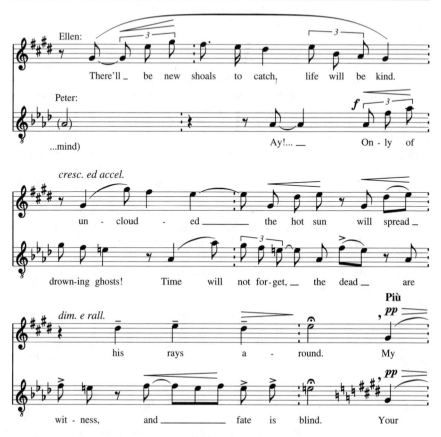

b) Ellen and Peter move off, sharing the assuaging influence of love and compassion.

melodic storehouse of perfect fourths and fifths and thus a national musical symbol of virtue and strength.

Verdi used this kind of sound for a very different purpose, building up an orchestral picture of an ancient Egyptian night's serenity in the Prelude to Act III of *Aida* (1871). A series of violin octaves and tremolos on an open fourth introduce, then accompany, a melody using fifths and fourths in its opening phrases; the result is a fusion of timbre and interval that evokes the ancient and the exotic in a way that is utterly magical.

The open fifth has also symbolically embraced the Far East. Its "gapped" sound characterizes many oriental folk melodies, and thus has come to represent China and Japan whenever opera has presented characters or stories drawing on those countries. Puccini, among others, capitalized effectively on this linkage by his dramatic quotation of Chinese melodies in *Turandot* (1924), Japanese melodies in *Madama Butterfly*, or by inventing melodies or

EXAMPLE 3.11 (*CONTINUED*)

motives that evoked these folk sources.[24] Example 3.14 offers a Japanese folksong and adaptations of it by Puccini for *Butterfly* and Arthur Sullivan for *The Mikado* (1885). In both cases, there is an element of comedy, for Puccini used the tune for Yamadori, the wealthy suitor for whom Butterfly has no use and whom she finds ridiculous, and Sullivan used it for the pompous greeting of the Emperor's arrival in the ridiculous town of Titipu.

Music associated with death has assumed two particularly archetypical forms. One is a sullen and hesitantly rhythmic fanfare (Example 3.15a–c, the last of these being a spoof in Mozart's comic *Così fan tutte* [Thus Do All

---

[24] Puccini also used the pentatonic scale (a five-note pattern represented by the pitches of the black keys of the piano) as an orientalism. But then, he used it also in his *La fanciulla del West*—"The Girl of the [Golden] West," 1910), which is about as Western as you can get, given its Italian-American patrimony and its California scenery.

EXAMPLE 3.12 USE OF PERFECT INTERVALS

a) Wagner, *Der fliegende Holländer*: "Dutchman" motive.

b) The Gershwins, *Porgy and Bess*®, Act III, scene iii: Children's song.
©WB MUSIC CORP. (Adm.)

c) Musorgsky, *Boris Godunov*, Act I, scene i: The people, under the whips of Shuisky's policemen, follow orders to beg Boris to become Tsar.

EXAMPLE 3.13 VERDI, *Aida* ACT III: PRELUDE

EXAMPLE 3.14 A JAPANESE FOLKSONG WITH THE SPAN OF A PERFECT FIFTH AND DERIVATIONS FROM IT

a) Folksong, "The Prince."

b) Puccini: *Madama Butterfly,* Act II: Entrance of Yamadori.

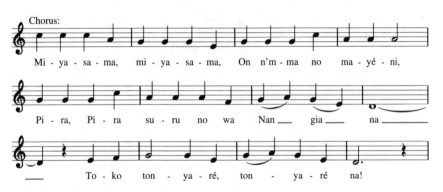

c) Sullivan: *The Mikado,* Act II: Entrance of the Mikado.

EXAMPLE 3.15 RHYTHMIC MOTIVES OF DEATH

a) Berlioz, *Les Troyens*, Part II (*Les Troyens à Carthage*), Act IV, scene iii: Dido resolves to die (descending scale, then death fanfare).

Mozart, *Così fan tutte* (1790), Act I, scene xv: Unaware that the lovesick Albanians are actually their boyfriends, Ferrando (Dénes Gulyás) and Guglielmo (Stephen Dickson), and are feigning death from poison, Fiordiligi (Etelka Csavlek) and Dorabella (Diana Montague) express great dismay. San Francisco Opera, 1988: production by Jean-Pierre Ponnelle. Photo Larry Merkle.

EXAMPLE 3.15 (*Continued*)

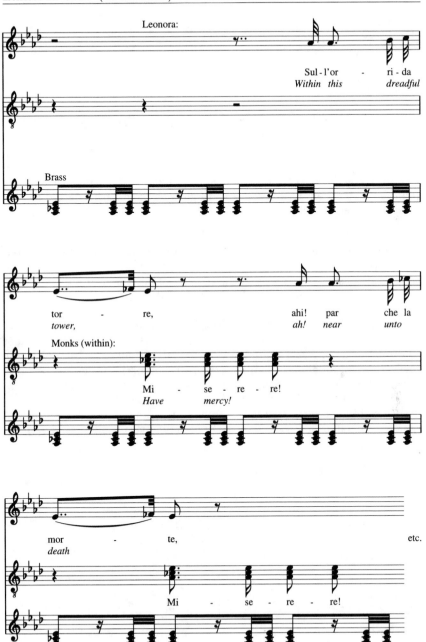

b) Verdi, *Il trovatore*, Act IV, scene i: Death motive in orchestra accompanying monks' intoning the *Miserere* while Leonore anguishes over the forthcoming execution of Manrico.

EXAMPLE 3.15 (*Continued*)

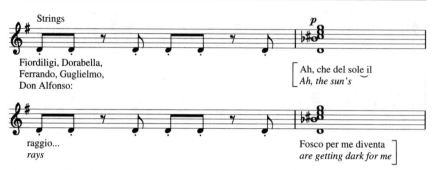

Fiordiligi, Dorabella,
Ferrando, Guglielmo,
Don Alfonso:

Ah, che del sole il
Ah, the sun's

raggio...
rays

Fosco per me diventa
are getting dark for me

c) Mozart, *Così fan tutte,* Act I, scene; xiv: Ferrando and Guglielmo, having returned as Albanians to woo each other's girlfriend and having been duly rejected, pretend to die of poison.

Women], 1790) and/or a descending scale (Example 3.16), which is often chromatic.

An anapestic rhythm—as in the pattern of accents in the name "Peter Grimes"—is also a common archetype for death. The rhythm ⏑ ⏑ — is used with chilling effect toward the end of Britten's opera, when the mob of townsfolk, believing Peter to be guilty of murder, sets out in the fog to find him and bring him to justice; their rhythmic calling of his name echoes through the action like a death knell. In Richard Strauss's *Salome* (1905), the final notes are an anapest hammered out by full orchestra as a brutal and shattering metaphor for Salome's death and the manner of her execution: she is crushed to death under the shields of Herodes's soldiers.

One of the most frequently encountered rhythmic archetypes is a pattern of notes separated by rests, the resultant halting quality suggestive of gasping,

EXAMPLE 3.16 DEATH AS SCALAR DESCENT

When I am laid, ___ am laid _____ in earth,   etc.

a) Purcell, *Dido and Aeneas* (1689), Act III: Ground bass accompanying Dido's determination to die.

EXAMPLE 3.16 (*Continued*)

b) Dvořák, *Rusalka,* Act III, final scene: Water Goblin (Rusalka's father) laments the sad fate of Rusalka (chromatic descent followed by Death rhythm).

anxiety, and choking sobs. Examples are legion; *Fidelio* makes special use of it to the point that it is a distinctive characteristic (see Example FI-2). A variant of this is the two-note rhythmic unit separated by rests. Called the *sospiro* ("sigh"), it is associated with sighs or sobs. The dramatic orchestral cries accompanying Donna Anna's discovery of her father's corpse (in *Don Giovanni*, see Example DG-3a), Gilda's weeping in the *Rigoletto* quartet (see also the *Rigoletto* Prelude, Example RI-5b), and the grieving of Sesto and Cornelia in the duet that closes Act I of *Giulio Cesare* (Example GC-6c) are examples.

Chromaticism

The ancient tradition of Western music has built its tunes on a simple array of pitches: the eight notes of any of several scale patterns, with the eighth note a repetition of the first at the octave. Chromaticism, however, deals with the division of the octave into twelve pitches, and the whole business of melodic and harmonic writing gets much more complex. The direction of the music gets slippery, for the movement of a series of pitches by half-steps or the skip to a note that is foreign to the key tends to weaken our ability to sense a single pitch as the tonic.[25] It becomes easy to lose our aural pathway.

Thus deceit, death, loss of self-control, drunkenness, and, certainly not least, the moods and conditions of love—ecstasy, swooning, infatuation—have found their métier in half-step melodic patterns, skips to unexpected notes not found in the key, and/or chords derived from left field. The most famous example is the opening of the Prelude to Wagner's *Tristan und Isolde* (1865; Example 3.17); not only is it the embodiment of the anguish of frustrated passion and longing—and thus in an exquisite fraction of time represents the essence of the opera—but also it represents a major change in Western music toward chromaticism as one of the central ways composers could think about music in general.

The examples illustrating the descent into death provide other instances of chromatic scales, and so does the comparison of the evil Mrs. Sedley (*Peter Grimes*) with the adolescent Zdenka (Richard Strauss's *Arabella*) in Example 3.4 (see above). Zdenka's music is about love, the love of an adolescent whose

EXAMPLE 3.17 WAGNER, *Tristan und Isolde:* PRELUDE

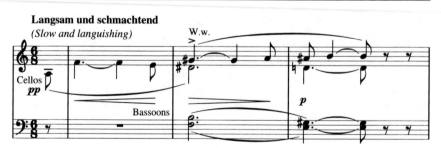

---

[25] I.e., the "arrival point" or main note of a scale by which a key—or tonality—gets its name.

giddy infatuation with Matteo finds its expression in chromatic snippets that are by turns in languorous waltz time or quick blips of half-steps, this way and that.

You can look at almost any opera score to find examples of chromaticism associated with the more sensual aspects of the human condition. One of the most familiar melodies in all opera is the "Habanera" sung by the ultimate femme fatale of the lyric stage, Bizet's Carmen: over an irresistible, hip-switching dance rhythm, her melody is a very simple white-key-black-key descent that is a benchmark for the connotations of chromatic side-slipping.

The love of Berlioz's Dido and Aeneas in *Les Troyens* is more elevated in its poetic diction, to be sure (it draws on the text of Shakespeare's *The Merchant of Venice*), but its chromatic ardor is as unmistakable as Carmen's (see the third measure of Example 3.8b, above, which shows a fragment of their duet). Berlioz pulls out a number of stops here—orchestration, parallel voicing, descending half-steps, ebb and flow of loud and soft—all working together to create an inimitable and unforgettable image of sensuality and epic love.

⚜

I have focused on details—short fragments of music—in this overview of the way music may work symbolically. Certainly the discussion need not stop here, for we may examine the music and texts of entire works as allegories and metaphors.[26] The visual element of stage design may also add to the performance as symbol, offering scenery, costuming, and staging as interpretations of the symbols heard in the music. (Or not heard, for that matter: the imaginations and reinterpretive ambitions of modern directors and designers know no limits.)

In the following chapters and in the detailed discussions of individual operas in Part III, I offer some perceptions and interpretations of musical symbolisms that reflect some aspects of the human spirit. Searching for these symbols and recognizing them are equally rewarding. And unending.

---

[26] Iain Fenlon and Peter Miller offer a particularly engrossing study of this sort of symbolism in their study of *L'incoronazione di Poppea*, in *The Operas of Monteverdi*, ed. Nicholas John, pp. 129ff. See also Nattiez's study of Wagner's *Ring* cycle as a metaphor for Wagner's conception of the history of music in terms of the union of poetry (Brünnhilde) and music (Siegfried) in *Wagner Androgyne*, chap. 3. Chailley's study of *Die Zauberflöte* is another example of an examination of an entire opera as symbolic.

PART II

Opera and the Human Condition

Opera and Us

While opera deals importantly with aspects of humanity, it does not deal with all of them equally well. The realities of poverty, for example, while a major element of the harshness of the music of Berg's *Wozzeck* and an important sub-text for the love story of *La bohème* (1896), is rather ignored by opera as a whole. Poverty is usually presented as an idealized condition of happy shepherds, peasants, or gypsies, as if there were no starvation or back-breaking labor at all: the arcadian peasants of Monteverdi's *Orfeo* and Donizetti's *L'elisir d'amore* (The Elixir of Love, 1832) are laborers sans sweat, and Nemorino's pennilessness in *L'elisir* is only a comic premise of the piece. Slavery gets some emphasis and compassion (Verdi's *Nabucco*—Nebuchadnezzar, 1842, and *Aida,* and Saint-Saëns's *Samson et Dalila*, 1877), but not as much as one might expect.

Man-the-toolmaker is also only a peripheral operatic concern. Verdi's gypsies make a real racket with their anvils in *Il trovatore* and the Nibelung miners of Wagner's *Das Rheingold* (1869) are similarly noisy, but the former give no sense of real manufacture, and the latter are squealing, sub-human slaves serving only as a foil to Alberich's greed and the power[1] he holds as possessor of the magic Ring and Tarnhelm.[2]

While every reader will have his or her own list of human qualities that are fascinating and seem worthy of theatrical treatment, I have drawn the following three chapters from some of those characteristics that I think warrant some special attention and that have not only been found to be congenial to lyric expression but seem to me to be wholly unique to the human animal.

The ability to examine oneself, the interest in the spiritual, the awareness of moral choice, and the capacities of the human mind to be ridiculous and to search for the sublime—these are quintessentially human. All have found expression in the music of opera; thus they are the substance of what follows and essential aspects of the eleven operas examined in detail in Part III.

---

[1] Not to mention that Alberich may be heard as a vicious anti-Semitic metaphor. Wagner's stage directions instruct the performers of Alberich and his brother Mime to use "the Jewish manner of speech—shrill hissing, buzzing, a wholly foreign and arbitrary distortion of our national idiom."

[2] The Tarnhelm is a helmet that allows its owner to be invisible or to assume any shape.

Chapter 4

THE SEARCH WITHIN

Introspection

*T*he willingness and ability to turn inward lead to the work of conscience and guilt and our sense of good and evil. From our ability to examine ourselves comes our sense of our relation to others, our shaping of our future, our respect (or embarassment) for our past, and the knowledge that we are responsible for who we are and what we do.

The ability to probe is a remarkable attribute of music, for the workings of the mind go beyond words into feelings that are no less strong, even though they may be indefinable. The whole of an opera can be an exercise in introspection, for it may hold out for our examination our glories and humiliations, our ambitions and our shortsightedness, and all the polarities that make us human. Wagner's *Tannhäuser*,[1] for example, may be read as the conflict in the mind of an artist between the contrary worlds of innovation/tradition and freedom/conformity. In such a reading, the grotto of Venus represents freedom of expression and emotional richness, while the Wartburg and its customs represent arid formalism and meaningless abstractions. *Die Meistersinger*, too, may be read this way, with Walter symbolizing untrammeled poetic expression and Beckmesser representing the sterility of rigid conventions and rules.

Thus the plots of these operas are metaphors for the self-study of their protagonists, each case coming to a fuller realization or synthesis of mental conflicts through the intercession of a third person: Elizabeth, in *Tannhäuser*, Hans Sachs in *Die Meistersinger*. To carry the reading a step further, one might see these operas as introspections of Wagner himself, exploring his own life as a creator and seeking the proper balance between the old and the new even as he recognized his revolutionary position in the world of Romanticism.

Yet, despite music's symbolic powers, it is surprising that so few operatic characters examine themselves with the frankness that true introspection demands. Although they vent their feelings, wonder about their world and their problems, and even use musical and textual metaphors to describe the

---

[1] The full title is *Tannhäuser und der Sängerkrieg auf Wartburg* ("Tannhäuser and the Singers' Contest on the Wartburg").

contrary moods that assail them, rarely do they seek causes, motivations, or explanations about themselves. This failure is given special bite in the Olympia scene of Offenbach's *Les contes d'Hoffmann*, when Hoffmann accepts the delusion provided by magic eyeglasses and falls in love with a spring-wound doll. The disintegration of her machinery and Hoffmann's resultant public humiliation drive home the point that the failure to be honest with oneself may result in the disintegration of the spirit. There are nonetheless a number of operatic figures who do turn inward, even though they rarely like what they see in themselves.

Just such a moment occurs near the start of the second scene of Verdi's *Rigoletto*, when the humpbacked dwarf's indictments of himself (and those who have tormented him) are expressed not only through uncompromising words but through music that is precisely descriptive. Rigoletto has just been accosted by a professional assassin, Sparafucile, who has suggested that there is a rival for the affections of Rigoletto's "mistress" and that, for an appropriate financial consideration, the rival[2] could easily be dispatched. Rigoletto's monologue, "Pari siamo" ("We are equals") follows. A vividly expressive arioso, it is in the vein of a metaphor: both are assassins, notes Rigoletto, he stabbing with his acid words and caustic affronts, Sparafucile with a murderer's dagger. A lurching scale figure (Example 4.1a) not only provides an image of the night, through scoring for low strings, but also suggests the hobbled walk caused by Rigoletto's deformity, and, by extension, his mental torments. We are given at once the gloom of the scene, the visual aspect of the character, and the twists of the character's thoughts.

Each of Rigoletto's mental turns is reflected in powerfully descriptive music: the repeated notes of Monterone's curse (Ex. RI-1a, p. 267) are recalled twice with hushed terror; Rigoletto's resentment over his life of mistreatment because of his deformity boils with tremolos and motivic bursts (Example 4.1c); his bitterness over having to obey every whim of the amoral Duke is reflected in pizzicatos and short woodwind pitches that remind him of the Duke's life of revelry and pleasure (Example 4.1b); and his thoughts of Gilda's innocence and of his love for her are lyrical and represented by the symbolically pure sound of a solo flute (Example 4.1d).

Would that Rigoletto continued to look at things with a firm eye through the rest of the opera: his sensitivity to Gilda's sad tale after the seduction of Act II is only momentary, and the blindness of his lust for revenge leads to the tragedy of her death and the emotional devastation of his life.

Another Verdi character, Iago of *Otello*, is crassly frank in his "Credo,"[3] a self-examination that is a stunning expression of nihilism and cynicism. Because it is sung in the opera after a few measures of grace and seeming

---

[2] Sparafucile is unaware that the lovely young woman living in Rigoletto's house is Rigoletto's sixteen-year-old daughter Gilda. Rigoletto is unaware that the Duke of Mantua, disguised as a poor student, has been making good eye contact with Gilda during her visits to church (the only times she is allowed out of the house and its walled garden).

[3] The "Credo" is a musical and textual expansion of but a snippet of Shakespeare's *Othello*, Act II, sc. 3, lines 344–347, where Iago, after giving his advice to Cassio, mutters "Divinity of hell! / When devils will the blackest sins put on, / They do suggest at first with heavenly shows, / As I do now."

EXAMPLE 4.1 VERDI, *Rigoletto* ACT I, SCENE II:
MOTIVES FROM RIGOLETTO'S "PARI SIAMO"

a) Motive suggesting Rigoletto's awkward gait and, by extension, the bitterness in his mind.

b) Piquant suggestion of Duke's pleasure-loving.

c) Tremolos and triadic motive of anger.

Verdi, *Rigoletto* (1851), Act I, scene ii: In the deserted street outside his house, Rigoletto (Matteo Manuguerra) learns of the murderous skills of Sparafucile (Dimitri Kavrakos), to whom he then compares himself in the arioso "Pari siamo" ("We are equals"). Houston Grand Opera, 1983: production by Jean-Pierre Ponnelle, costumes by Martin Schlumpf. Photo James Caldwell.

EXAMPLE 4.1 (*Continued*)

d) Tender thoughts of the innocent, young Gilda.

friendship, its arrogance and hatefulness make it quite possibly the most chilling passage in opera in spite of its musical grandeur and power.

Cassio has been demoted for being drunk while on duty; at the opening of Act II, Iago, in soothing and supportive language, urges him to stop torturing himself and to ask Desdemona to intercede with Otello on his behalf. The trusting Cassio leaves to put Iago's advice into action, not suspecting that Iago will persuade Otello that Desdemona's intercession speaks of adultery with Cassio and not simply goodwill on her part.

Iago's seeming helpfulness to Cassio is suggested by the gentle triplets and simple harmonies of the accompaniment to their conversation (Example 4.2a), but, when Iago is alone, the triplets become harsh and crude, and they roll through the soliloquy as a venomous mockery of all that Iago has

EXAMPLE 4.2 VERDI, *Otello* ACT II, SCENE II: MOTIVES FROM
IAGO'S "CREDO"

a) False friendliness toward Cassio.

b) Fanfare announcing Iago's creed.

seemed to be. Brass fanfares (Example 4.2b) are a blatant and base mockery
of the panoply of church music, testifying caustically to Iago's crass view of
the universe. Iago's creed of nothingness, lack of purpose, and derision of
the human search for meaning is fully realized in the orchestra's final measures, at first virtually empty, then noisy and contemptuous (Example 4.2c).

Rosina, in Rossini's *Il barbiere di Siviglia* (1816), also offers a soliloquy
about herself, the "Una voce poco fa qui nel cor mi risuono" ("There is a little voice echoing in my heart," No. 5), but what a difference from Iago's
sense of himself as "viltà d'un germe o d'un atomo" ("born from some vile

germ or atom")! Rosina's look at herself is delightful and comic, and if she has more than a little of the vixen in her, it is a most attractive fault. She tells us in a flowing and moderately decorative melody (Example 4.3a) that she's very docile, respectful, and obedient unless she is crossed (repeated notes, staccato; start of Example 4.3b); that she then becomes a viper "sarò una

EXAMPLE 4.2 (*Continued*)

c) Suggestion of emptiness, then blatant scorn.

EXAMPLE 4.3 ROSSINI, *Il barbiere di Siviglia* ACT I, SCENE II:
NO. 5, ROSINA'S "UNA VOCE POCO FA"

a) Rosina professes that she is docile, sweet, and obedient.

b) But admits to being quite something else if she does not get her way.

vipera" snaps at us with a coloratura downward swoop that shows she means business (end of Example 4.3b), after which the aria frolics to its crowd-pleasing end.

Two of opera's most introspective and fascinating figures are Wagner's Wotan (*Die Walküre*) and Musorgsky's Boris Godunov. They have a good deal in common, for both made an unprincipled grab for power earlier in their lives, have sought to nobly and sincerely better their realms, and are tortured with guilt and the realization that all their good wishes have been compromised fatally since the start.

Wotan's introspection would seem to be a confession rather than a self-study, for he blames Loge (the god of fire) for his foolishness, and his thoughts are spoken to his daughter Brünnhilde. Loge, however, may be read as a symbol of Wotan's own guile, rather than an autonomous person; Brünnhilde, born of his affair with Erda, the earth goddess, and not of the traditional rites of matrimony by Wotan's wife, Fricka (the goddess of wedlock), exists at the beginning of Act II only as the symbol of Wotan's desires and innnermost thoughts: "mit mir nur rath' ich, red' ich zu dir" ("I am only talking with myself when I talk to you").[4] His turn inward is established by

---

[4] Her emergence as a person of self-will and independence is a major element of the plot.

the music: admitting that he has set out on a path of self-destruction by faithless acts and deceitful behavior, Wotan's acknowledgement of his downward path is marked by the scalar descent of the motive associated with his despondent recognition of a grim future.

For long stretches we hear only the gloom of softly played low instruments: the dotted rhythm of the motive labeled "Dejection" (Example 4.4a) plods in the cellos over sustained low strings; trombones and tubas intone fragments of the motive associated with Valhalla, a hall of the gods (Example 4.4b) paid for with stolen goods; bass clarinets and bassoons mutter fanfare fragments associated with death; French horns softly give out the motive of the Valkyries (the warrior maidens sired by Wotan to carry out his wishes;

EXAMPLE 4.4 WAGNER, *Die Walküre* ACT II, SCENE II: MOTIVES ASSOCIATED WITH WOTAN'S BROODING OVER HIS PAST ACTIONS

a) He acknowledges his acting faithlessly.

EXAMPLE 4.4 (*Continued*)

b) Fragment of motive of Valhalla ("x"), a castle representing lofty ambitions but purchased with the ring (and the gold from which the ring was made) stolen from Alberich.

Example 4.4c); and a duet of tubas whispers the motive of the Ring that gives its possessor dominion over the world (Example 4.4d).

When the violins finally get to play, their part is as a restless, syncopated accompaniment, either to Wotan's statement of frustration at being enslaved by his own actions and treaties, or to the guttural thrust of a motive (Example 4.4e) associated with the debased Nibelung dwarfs and their leader, Alberich, who has placed power and wealth above love.

Dishonest introspection, of course, is an oxymoron, and genuine introspection is much more than feeling good or bad about one's actions. Wallowing in self-justification or self-pity is as profitless in opera as in real life, no matter how moving the sentiment or beautiful the music. In Leoncavallo's *Pagliacci* (Clowns, 1892), for example, Canio, convinced that his wife Nedda should be grateful that he rescued her from poverty and orphanhood, fails to recognize that being married to him is anything but a source of happiness for her, he thinks only of the insult and grief brought to

EXAMPLE 4.4 (*Continued*)

c) Motives of Death ("a") and the Valkyrie Maidens ("b").

him by her infidelity. His "Vesti la giubba" ("Put on your costume") laments his sad lot—he must entertain and be a clown while his real life is a shambles—but he goes no further.

His only answer—murdering Nedda and Silvio—is brutal and vengeful, leaving him with an existence that is bleak and, as Iago tells us in *Otello*, without meaning. Like Rigoletto, Canio will find that revenge is a bitter and empty reward; like Verdi's jester, Leoncavallo's clown is cursed by self-obsession without the grace of full self-examination.

Conscience and the Sense of Good and Evil

The awareness of ourselves is one thing; concern for the implications of who we are is something else. Certainly there is a profusion of operatic characters who seem not to think about morality (if they think at all). There are good and bad folk whose minds are never touched by conscience or the debate between good and evil: Papageno, in *Die Zauberflöte*, is a prime example; so

Wagner, *Die Walküre* (1870), Act II, scene i: Wotan (Jerome Hines), having yielded to the demands of Fricka (r, Irene Dalis) and agreed not to assist Siegmund in his battle with Hunding, awaits the grim duty of telling his story of frustration and gloom to Brünnhilde (l, Birgit Nilsson). Metropolitan Opera, 1965: production by Lee Simonson. Courtesy *Opera News*, Metropolitan Opera Guild. Photo Louis Mélançon.

EXAMPLE 4.4. (*Continued*)

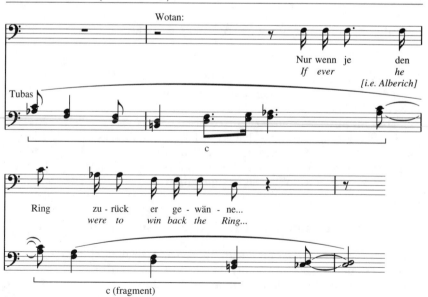

d) Motive of the Ring ("c").

EXAMPLE 4.4. (*Continued*)

e) Wotan's brooding and troubled spirit, suggested by syncopated accompanying music associated with Alberich and the Nibelungs.

is Oscar, the page in Verdi's *Un ballo in maschera*, (A Masked Ball, 1859). Both are given music that bounces along, almost totally without a serious thought in the world.[5] And, of course, there are characters who do think about such matters but whose music is so bland as to render their thoughts hopelessly inconsequential (Siebel, in *Faust*, for example).

When true introspection occurs, it can result in atonement or a determination to change that becomes redemptive, although Iago's frankness is of a kind that makes redemption utterly unthinkable. The stature of Boris Godunov (Musorgsky, 1874) as one of opera's greatest figures is the result of a mixture of musical ingredients that show him racked by guilt over his past vicious unscrupulousness, even as he has become completely devoted to others. Musorgsky provides the troubled Tsar with a simple style—at times declamatory, at times lyrical—and orchestral accompaniments that reveal the soul within: the recognition of the fatuousness of flatterers and connivers (Example 4.5a) is given a clarinet theme of dignity and eloquence; as Boris empathizes with the grief of his daughter, whose fiancé has suddenly died,

---

[5] Papageno, nonetheless, has a profound and beautiful duet with Pamina about the richness of the love between man and wife.

the strings play a tender song that is at once simple and loving (Example 4.5b); cellos and basses double a more purposeful melody that bears his words about the wrath of God on high (Example 4.5c); and, as Boris's thoughts become more agitated with his spiritual sickness, triplet rhythms in flutes and oboes (Example 4.5d) suggest the restlessness that eventually becomes hysteria through the use of chromatic descent, string tremolos, and lower instrumentation. His spiritual exhaustion is expressed in a tremolo for violas—all other instruments are silent.

Gluck's *Iphigénie en Tauride* also gives us a musical study of the workings of conscience in a scene celebrated in writings about opera but, sad to say, scarce-

EXAMPLE 4.5 MUSORGSKY, *Boris Godunov* ACT II:
BORIS LOOKS WITHIN

[Boris: Naprasno mne kudesniki suljat, Dni dolgie, dni vlasti bezmjatežnoj.]
[*In vain my prophets have assured me of many days of life and an untroubled reign.*]

a) Melody associated with Boris's majesty, authority, and recognition of truth.

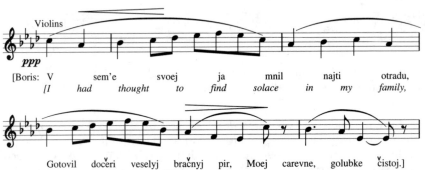

[Boris: V sem'e svoej ja mnil najti otradu,
[*I had thought to find solace in my family,*

Gotovil dočeri veselyj bračnyj pir, Moej carevne, golubke čistoj.]
I was readying a wedding feast for my princess, my pure darling.]

b) Boris thinks of his daughter's bereavement.

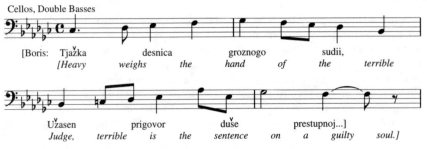

[Boris: Tjažka desnica groznogo sudii,
[*Heavy weighs the hand of the terrible*

Užasen prigovor duše prestupnoj...]
Judge, terrible is the sentence on a guilty soul.]

c) Motive associated with Boris's sense of guilt.

EXAMPLE 4.5. *(Continued)*

d) The music of Boris's torment.

ly ever performed. Oreste, slayer of his mother, Clytemnestra, in revenge for her murder of his father, Agamemnon, collapses into exhausted and presumably peace-granting slumber. But the Furies, a mythical metaphor for the anguish of conscience (here a musical one as well), enter his dreams, first via the restless orchestral syncopation (see Example 3.3a) that belies his self-delusion, then, with both text and music savaging his conscience.

In *Aida*'s Act III, Aida is reviled by her father for hesitating to betray her beloved Radames for the military benefit of her country. Amonasro calls her a vile slave of the Pharaohs and throws her to the ground; the following violin syncopations lend her sense of deep guilt and the devastation of her spirit to the sad unison of bassoons, cellos, and violas.

Mozart's Count Almaviva (*Le nozze di Figaro*) has some of the most melting conscience music in opera, but it's arguable that he is more sorry that he has been caught than that he is genuinely remorseful. At the end of Act IV he begs forgiveness and is given it, but his only punishment is a momentary embarrassment. While that may be severe for a person of his pride and station, one suspects that he will soon enough be pursuing every skirt in sight, even though there is genuineness in the elegant simplicity of his appeal to his wife for pardon.

Lest those utterly without remorse be forgotten, attention should focus for a moment on some of opera's devils. Samiel (*Der Freischütz*), Mephistopheles (in both Gounod's *Faust*, 1859, and Boito's *Mefistofele*, 1868), and Stravinsky's Nick Shadow (*The Rake's Progress*, 1951) would be poor Satans indeed if they were afflicted by even a passing hint of regret. As demons go, however, they are uniformly qualified and can vent utter ferocity when they need to: Gounod's devil sets the villagers spinning with the swirling of his Calf of Gold aria; and Nick Shadow's "I burn I freeze," sung when Tom barely saves his soul by beating Nick at cards, is venom personified. Both use obsessive repetitions of short rhythmic patterns or melodic fragments to suggest that these devils have only one thing in mind: the destruction of those around them. Until their ultimate frustration, however—the devil always loses in opera—they cajole, entertain, and serve their targets with apparently unrestrained good will. All but Samiel have a good deal of charm, wit, and elegance, both musically and textually.

Devils in everyday life lurk everywhere, their temptations, jolliness, and honeyed words working their wiles. They are no less cajoling and frequent in opera, where evil often masquerades as sincerity, and the course of negativism and destruction is often marked by the signposts of self-indulgence, easy answers, glib solutions, and superficial attractiveness.

EXAMPLE 4.6 VERDI, *Aida* ACT III: AIDA IN GUILTY DESPAIR

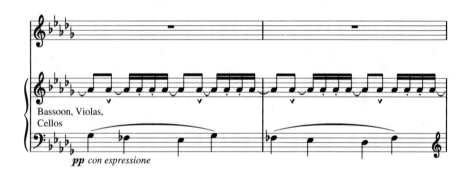

Boito's Mefistofele, who has these attributes in abundance, also works on a different plane, for the opera overtly engages a major theological question: will Faust select good or evil? The Prologue's debate-wager between Mefistofele and the Supreme Ruler is one of the few intellectual discussions in opera. There is no pretense of action whatever—the five-sectioned scene is devoted only to the interplay of satanic mind and eternal good—but it has some of opera's most impassioned choral and orchestral colorations, ranging from the whistles and piccolo shrieks of Mefistofele's scherzando sarcasm to thunderous brass fanfares and a battery of vocal and orchestral effects.

Among the most magical elements of Boito's cosmic confrontation is the mystic choral work given to boys' voices as the cherubim et al., who serve as the voice of God.

Although these supernatural forces of evil stand boldly before us as metaphors of the struggle of morality and immorality in our conscience, there are plenty of human miscreants, many with no remorse at all.

After banishing his wife and ordering the suicide of his mentor and critic Seneca, Monteverdi's Nerone (*L'incoronazione di Poppea*) is given a wholly conscience-free bachelor party (and one of opera's first and best drinking songs: "Cantiam, Lucano"—"Let's sing, Lucano"; see Example 6.2c); Beethoven's Pizarro (*Fidelio*) and Puccini's Scarpia (*Tosca*) are vicious and unrepentant to the end, as are Verdi's Paolo (*Simon Boccanegra*, 1857; rev. 1881), and Wagner's Alberich (in the first and last of the four operas of *Der Ring des Nibelungen* [The Ring of the Nibelung], 1876[6]). Britten's Claggart (*Billy Budd*, 1951) is the incarnation of evil, and there are any number of cold-hearted dastards in Handel (Garibaldo in *Rodelinda*,1725, Tolomeo in *Giulio Cesare*, and Polinesso, who confesses guilt unrepentantly in *Ariodante*, 1735).[7]

The face of evil is multifaceted, of course, and operatic depictions of evil have followed suit: Crown and Sportin' Life offer two strikingly different and brilliantly drawn pictures of evil in *Porgy and Bess*®, Crown a brutal savage, Sportin' Life cynical and ingratiating; in Offenbach's *Les contes d'Hoffmann*, the different aspects of Hoffmann's penchant for self-destruction and evil are given form in the characters of Lindorf (cynicism), Coppelius (chicanery), Dr. Miracle (destructiveness), and Dapertutto (carnality and materialism).[8]

Perhaps the quintessential unrepentantly evil characters of opera are Verdi's Iago and the title figure of Mozart's *Don Giovanni* (1787). Both are men of grace and elegance: the former applies his attractiveness to hedonism and self-gratification, the latter to evil for its own sake. Given the central position each holds in his plot, it is remarkable that each has but one soliloquizing aria; the bulk of their musical time is spent working their wiles on someone by sharing that person's musical personality and turning it to evil purpose in ensemble. When they are alone, however, their real natures emerge. In both cases, we have true scoundrels who wear different colors but serve the same cause of self-interest: Iago's evil is based on savage hatreds and the worship of an infernal deity in whose image he has been cast; Giovanni adores no God, good or evil, hates nothing except, perhaps, boredom derived from abstinence, and is most truly himself when he mocks the accepted decorum of his world.

---

[6] *Das Rheingold* was premiered in 1869; *Götterdämmerung* in 1876.

[7] There's also a foul villain in Berlioz's *Les Troyens*, in which we hear about one Iarbus who invades Dido's land with lecherous and rapacious intent. He never appears on stage, however, and has not a note to sing. It's not exactly a good debut part.

[8] A somewhat related approach is used with striking effectiveness by Liszt in *A Faust Symphony* (1854), in which the entire "Mephisto" movement (the third) is a sardonic variation of the "Faust" motives of the first movement. See Derek Watson, *Liszt* (New York: Schirmer Books, 1989), pp. 275f.

In his Act I "Fin ch'an dal vino calda la testa" (No. 11, "While their heads are still hot from the wine"), a solo of blistering speed, Giovanni orders his servant Leporello to scout up wine and other delectables, including young, pretty females, in heady anticipation of an evening's debauchery. The opening orchestral phrase is the distillation of all that the aria represents because of its rushing quality. Hedonism, loss of self-control, and spiritual dissoluteness are all implied by it, and Giovanni's "Senza alcun ordine / la danza sia" ("Without regard to any [customary] order, let there be dancing") gives the aria special point: the order of dance types in the ballroom is to be cast aside and, by analogy, so are the strictures of any moral code. Phrase follows phrase in the vocal line with no notated rests and thus no clear place where a comfortable breath may be taken by the singer. At the one spot where there is a break in the vocal line, the orchestra takes up the rhythmic germ of the music and pushes on with it, so that the music moves forward pell mell and reels with excitement and the anticipation of self-pleasure.

The sense of giddiness is intensified by tiny, slithering, chromatic descents given to the voice part when Giovanni urges Leporello to try to bring him damsels from the town ("Se trovi in piazza / qualche ragazza / teco ancor / quella cerca menar"—"If in the square you find some young girls, try to bring them with you"). When he lists the dances to be played (minuet, folia, alemanna), he virtually assaults the fabric of society, for each dance is associated with a certain segment of society—respectively aristocracy, peasantry, middle class—and commingling them in an age when classes were kept distinct and apart is an invitation to social chaos and upheaval.[9]

Headliners and superstars are not the only ones that merit attention. We need to look at ordinary folk whose sense of moral purpose—or lack of it—is just as much the stuff of life. Opera's magic lends insight into their souls, too.

Leporello, Don Giovanni's valet and sometime procurer, goes just so far and no farther in the Cemetery Scene, where he will not blaspheme against the voice of the Commendatore's statue; Ping, Pang, and Pong, the three ministers in Puccini's *Turandot*, regret deeply their roles in furthering the Princess Turandot's awful decree of death to any self-proffered lover who cannot solve three riddles; Dansker, Billy's friend (in *Billy Budd*), defies orders forbidding contact with condemned prisoners to bring some solace and some grog to Billy, chained in the bowels of the HMS *Indomitable*; and Narraboth, the young army captain in *Salome*, torn between his passion for Salome and revulsion over the lasciviousness of her obsession with Jokanaan, falls on his own sword.

There is the darker side of ordinary people, too, for the choices between good and evil do not always produce the right decision. Rocco, Pizarro's jailer in *Fidelio*, hates the murderous plan of his master, yet he obeys orders to dig the grave for Florestan and to be present when the deed is done. Wagner's Gutrune (*Götterdämmerung* [The Twilight of the Gods], 1876) furthers Hagen's nefarious plot by knowingly giving Siegfried a potion that will cause him to forget his vows to Brünnhilde; Gutrune is late to admit the moral implications of what she has done, but she gains a measure of redemption by confessing the evil of which she was a part.

---

[9] See Till, *Mozart and the Enlightenment,* pp. 200–214, for a penetrating study of Don Giovanni's character as a violation of the spirit of the Enlightenment.

Mozart, *Don Giovanni* (1787), Act I, scene v: Contemplating the addition of another conquest to Don Giovanni's list (which Giovanni will later comment on ecstatically in his "Fin ch' han dal vino / calda la testa"—"While their heads are still hot from the wine"), Leporello (Ezio Flagello, left) and Giovanni (Cesare Siepi) observe the anguish of Donna Elvira (Gabriella Tucci), whom they do not yet recognize. Metropolitan Opera, 1957: production by Eugene Berman. Courtesy *Opera News*, Metropolitan Opera Guild. Photo Louis Mélançon.

The whole crowd of townsfolk in *Peter Grimes* are a mean-spirited lot, excessively comfortable in their ways with not one whit of compassion or understanding. Britten's use of the same music (see Example 3.2) for both the lighthearted dance tune near the start of Act III, scene i, and the howl of the people-as-mob at the end of the scene, as they set out to get Peter, is one of opera's most telling metaphors for the ease with which a rigidly conventional and insensitive society can turn to mob violence, insensate persecution, and evil incarnate.

The world is made of such little people. We may be proud on occasion, ashamed on others. However we feel, these characters on the operatic stage are reflections of ourselves, for better or worse.

Chapter 5

THE SEARCH BEYOND

Spirituality and Wonderment

We don't know everything, and that bothers us. We reach continually for the unattainable, we ponder the inscrutable, and we seek to understand what we cannot even define. We do pretty well in some respects, for our inquisitive nature results in scientific achievement, artistic expression, the expansion of knowledge, and deeper understanding of ourselves and our world.

When we sense the boundary between what we can know and what we can only believe in, we move from the confines of the mind to the spirit beyond it. Opera's capacity to explore the metaphysical is limitless and has produced some of its most exquisite moments. I propose to ignore opera's frequent allusions to angels watching from on high and the seemingly ubiquitous prayer scenes that divas have come to regard as a muse-given right. There is a huge difference between spirituality and religiosity, the latter an oft-grabbed opportunity in nineteenth-century operas[1] for such audience-pleasing devices as delicate strings, flute arpeggios, choirs of nuns or monks, hymn-like chord progressions, or strumming of harps.[2]

While there is a host of musical sounds associated with religious observance, there is nothing sacred or secular in sound itself; a good tune is a good tune, and any associations it may conjure up are added, not inherent.[3] Bach's most sacred music is rife with dance rhythms (see the *Christe eleison* of the Mass in b minor, for example), and the settings of the *Gloria* by such dis-

---

[1] When the doyens of the French Revolution sought to de-Christianize their world and to establish a new religious order replacing the God of the Old and New Testaments with a more "rational" Supreme Being, the operatic stage became a permissible platform for theatrical spectacle and quasi-ritual in Christian dress. Since the bulk of the standard operatic repertory comes from the nineteenth century, pseudo-religiosity is a too-frequent blight.

[2] It happens in the final moments of *Faust*. Inasmuch as Gounod was a marvelous organist, I will perhaps be forgiven for suggesting that, in this finale, he pulled out all the stops.

[3] See, for example, the variety of sources for the chorale (hymn) melodies of the early Protestant churches discussed in Gustave Reese, *Music in the Renaissance Era* (New York: W. W. Norton, 1954), pp. 356f and 674f.

parate composers as Vivaldi and Poulenc are deliciously enriched by musical styles usually associated with the nonliturgical: in the case of Vivaldi, the *Domine Deus* is a *siciliano* (a graceful, slow dance in 6/8); in Poulenc the *Laudamus te* bounces with the spice of café songs.[4]

Poulenc's *The Dialogues of the Carmélites* illustrates how music can become powerfully spiritual even when using qualities not generally associated with spirituality.[5] A young novice, Sister Constance, engages in a dialogue with the troubled heroine of the opera, Blanche, who, more from an escapist urge than a religious one, has entered the Carmelite order amid the social travails of the exploding French Revolution. Constance's good-hearted, joyous, buoyant, and unquestioning acceptance of the possibility of an early death and her total acceptance of a life in the service of God are expressed sometimes with a repeated-note quality that derives from the familiar pattersong style of comic opera and operetta, and at other times in a gentle songfulness that one would normally associate more with the café than the convent. Her lighthearted and simple melodic style is at once reminiscent of the high spirits of Poulenc's early adulthood[6] and richly expressive of Constance's ebullient and unrestrained devotion to the joy of the spiritual life.

The chattering of Constance is illustrated by the repeated notes, quick triplets and one-note-per-syllable setting of the first eleven measures of Example 5.1; her innocent willingness to yield her own life to God yields to a more songful style where her philosophical naiveté ("But then, fifty-nine years old—isn't that high time to die?") is mirrored in a lighthearted melody sung over the "vamping" style of popular-song accompaniment.

This irrepressibly good-humored element is but one aspect of an opera that offers a powerfully dramatic juxtaposition of mystical faith and the temporal world. Courageous loyalty to high ideals and the struggle to overcome the infirmities of mind, soul, and body are the ennobling and spiritual processes that are the main themes of the opera.

At the brutal finale of *Dialogues*, when the nuns take their places in line to accept the guillotine rather than deny their faith, they sing the words of the medieval plainchant "Salve Regina, Mater misericordiae" ("Hail, Queen, Mother of Mercy"). Poulenc sets them (Example 5.2) in the flowing melody and steady rhythms appropriate to their unshakable faith, but he also provides music for the stark cruelty of the event: a throbbing ostinato (marked "x" in the example) in low strings symbolizes death and its inexorability for the condemned during the Reign of Terror; the crowd is given only vowels

---

[4] Poulenc's joie de vivre in sacred settings is not to everyone's taste. Roger Nichols describes the *Gloria*'s choral writing as "unsanctimonious to the point of wilfulness" (p. 208). Poulenc himself noted that "When I wrote this piece, I had in mind those frescoes by Gozzoli where the angels stick out their tongues. And also some serious Benedictine monks I had once seen revelling in a game of football." Mellers, p. 147.

[5] See Ellison, "Cafés and Catechisms," for study of the mix of musical opposites in Poulenc and a brief study of the Constance/Blanche scene.

[6] This period of Poulenc's life was shaped by the iconoclasm of both Dadism and the musical thinking of Eric Satie. Even while he was a serious student of music, Poulenc became something of a boulevardier, or man-about-town.

EXAMPLE 5.1 POULENC, *Les Dialogues des Carmélites*, ACT I,
SCENE III: CONSTANCE'S INNOCENT ACCEPTANCE OF DEATH

and chords, not words and melodies, so they appear musically as a faceless grim presence; through it all, at unpredictable moments, thuds the vicious sound (marked ↓ in the example) of the guillotine, heard as "a muffled and heavy noise."

As each Sister is killed by the fall of the blade, the number of voices is reduced, the last, Sister Constance's, broken in mid-phrase. At that point Blanche steps from the crowd to join in her Sisters' martyrdom. She mounts the scaffold while singing the closing quatrain ("Deo Patri sit gloria"—"To

EXAMPLE 5.2 POULENC, *Les Dialogues des Carmélites*
ACT III, SCENE IV: THE MARCH TO THE SCAFFOLD

God the Father be the glory") of the ancient chant text *Veni Creator,* her affirmation of faith and recommitment to her holy orders violated by the final
swoosh of the guillotine. There is a hushed "Ah" from the crowd, five measures of attenuated sound, then a soft pizzicato—and the opera ends.

This finale is as theatrical as any scene in theater. Yet, for all its extract-
ing the most from every device of sound and sight, it rings true and gives
any audience a deep concern for the meaning of the human spirit and the
consequences of defiling it.

Spirituality of a different stamp, although no less impassioned or fulfilling, may be illustrated by two works of a profoundly different character, both
from the twentieth century. The first is from the second act of *Peter Grimes*
when, amid the fury of a terrible storm, people have come to the town's tavern for companionship and carousing. Peter's sudden arrival ("looking
wild," says the stage direction) brings the action to a halt. Distrusted and dis-
liked, he sits alone, musing in words that are a model of the poetry of human
wonderment, although they are inexplicable to those around him. Every
detail of his thoughts is mirrored in Britten's music.

Peter's first words float on a single pitch above a canon in the strings
(Example 5.3a), just as the starry sky that he describes hovers above the
incomprehensible movements of life and nature on earth; ". . . breathing
solemnity in the deep night" is given a musical darkness by quadruple softness (*pppp*), and an enormous spread of octaves between high violins and
the lowest pitch of the double basses (Example 5.3b) becomes a picture of the
vastness of space.

A change of key and mode (e minor to C major; Example 5.3c) is the
musical symbol for "As the sky turns the world for us to change," and a flurry of disjointed scale fragments in quick and angular triplets (Example 5.3d)
depicts the "flashing turmoil of a shoal of herring" to which life's confusion
is compared. Syncopations lend the rhythmic uncertainty appropriate to
"who can turn skies back. . ."; a quiet return to the key of the opening of the
monologue provides the musical metaphor for ". . . and begin again."

At the end of each of the three verses there is a gentle descent of a major
scale, each with an accompaniment subtly different from the others, related
to Peter's sense of a universe that has meaning for the soul of man, even if
he does not understand it fully.

Richard Strauss's *Der Rosenkavalier* also has its hurly-burly: there is a
crowded Act I levee scene when it seems that all Vienna has come to get
something from the Marschallin, vigorously boorish lechery and some
swordplay in Act II, and an uproariously comical Act III that is jam-packed
with noise and activity. But the opera is also endowed with moments when
the participants turn inward, marveling at the beauty and mystery of life, the
meaning of love, and the passage of time.[7]

One of these moments, near the start of Act II, is the Marchallin's presentation to Sophie von Faninal of a silver rose on behalf of her fiancé,

---

[7] "Time is a strange thing" ("Die Zeit, die ist ein sonderbar Ding") says the mature
Marschallin (she is thirty-two) to her adolescent lover, Octavian, in Act I, realizing that he
will soon leave her for the embraces of another younger woman. See Kennicott, "Poised in
Time," for an insightful examination of the perception of time in this opera.

Octavian's lecherous, boorish, and forty-something cousin Baron Ochs. Octavian is seventeen (and two months), handsome, and charming; Sophie is fifteen and lovely. When Octavian suddenly appears, we are transported to fairyland: traditionally, the costumes of the protagonists are silver, the servants are liveried in bold colors, and the setting is a room of cream colored and silver-gilt walls with glassed doors. Everything—sound as well as sight— glitters; the two youngsters are transfixed by the sight of each other and with

EXAMPLE 5.3 BRITTEN, *Peter Grimes* ACT I, SCENE II: PETER PONDERS THE MEANING OF LIFE

a) Peter's vision of the arching sky above a world of sorrows.

EXAMPLE 5.3. (*CONTINUED*)

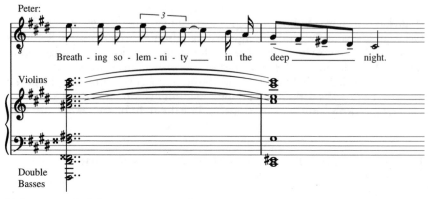

b) Imagery of night.

c) Change of mode (minor to major) and key as musical imagery of "sky turns the world for us to change."

d) Life's bewilderments

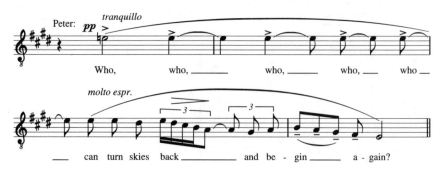

e) Return to the key of the opening of the monologue.

instant love beyond what either of them had ever dreamed. For Sophie and Octavian, suggested librettist Hugo von Hoffmannsthal, it is the exquisite "moment of meeting [which is] the most sensual and spiritual of any in human life, when the attractions of body and intellect are at their maximum because no faults have been discovered."[8]

The music is transformed breathtakingly from an enormous Straussian climax, reached by fanfares and boiling scale patterns, to a moment when time stands still: under a delicate string tremolo, an oboe melody's tenderness, innocence, and loveliness are the musical embodiment of Sophie; the motive of the Rose seems otherworldly and magical, because it is orchestrated for the exotic combination of celesta,[9] three flutes, harp, and three muted violins, and it is harmonized with chords that seem to float rather than to progress.

These elements accompany Octavian's formal presentation and Sophie's equally polite response. Heaven knows it is all beautiful beyond words, but when Sophie speaks as if to herself of the Rose's heavenly perfume ("Wie himmlische, nicht irdische, wie Rosen vom hochheiligen Paradies"—"How heavenly, not earthly, like the roses of most blessed Paradise"), her floating melody, accompanied by high violins, moves the music from the simply wonderful to the spirituality of wonderment (Example 5.4).

The mood of rapture is continued in a duet that is a celestial blend of treble voices in parallel thirds, with fluidly interacting orchestral motives. It is a duet only in the technical sense that both are singing at the same time; actually, each is speaking inwardly. Sophie's thoughts, to the music of Example 5.4, are of the unforgettable beauty of a passage in her life that "ist Zeit und Ewigkeit in einem sel'gen Augenblick" ("is time and eternity in one blessed moment"); Octavian's are questions that mingle awe with youthful puzzlement and incomparable joy. Their vow never to forget this sublime rite of passage tapers to a pianissimo that ends with the silvery motive of the Rose.

Like us, they will never fully understand or find words for the world they have entered and will leave too soon for the fits and starts of everyday life. Also like us, Octavian and Sophie will find that this precious if transient voyage into the world of the spirit will give a special and glorious dimension to their being.

Atonement and Redemption

Some operatic finales offer nothing but grief and disaster. The passing of Mimi in *La bohème,* while quite possibly the most moving denouement of the standard repertory, is without grandeur or heroism; the deaths of Leonora and Don Carlo, in Verdi's *La forza del destino,* leave no feelings of fulfillment or of a better world to come; Macbeth and Lady Macbeth perish, deservedly unloved; Carmen's murder is a tawdry affair, her bravery muddied by her callousness and amorality; and the killing of a lover by a jealous husband at the end of *Cavalleria rusticana* is without honor or point.

---

[8] Mann, *Strauss*, p. 125.

[9] An instrument with metal bars that are struck by hammers activated by a piano-like keyboard. The sound is delicate, bell-like, and, well, silvery.

EXAMPLE 5.4 RICHARD STRAUSS, *Der Rosenkavalier*, ACT II:
SOPHIE'S WONDERMENT AT THE BEAUTY OF THE MOMENT WHEN
OCTAVIAN PRESENTS THE SILVER ROSE AS SYMBOLIC OF HER
ENGAGEMENT TO BARON OCHS

For most of its history, however, opera has assured us that, no matter how tribulation has infected the plot, some ultimate destiny will soften the blows. Indeed, the *lieto fine* ("happy ending") was a virtually inescapable feature of opera from its earliest days until the second decade of the nineteenth century. Monteverdi's Orfeo loses Euridice for eternity, but at least he gets to the celestial realms to provide the music of the spheres. Other than the seamy and torrid affair of Nero and Poppea in *L'incoronazione*—both of whom triumph over the good people—opera saw its most dastardly deeds undone and couples happily joined correctly for its first two centuries.[10] Even in those nineteenth-century operas where death befalls the hero and/or heroine, the Romantic idea of death as a release or as an ennoblement was standard, albeit with some exceptions.

Redemption, however, is of another dimension, well beyond angelic strings or the blessing by the decedent of those left behind. Redemption is the forgiveness earned from atonement for sins such as hubris and betrayal. Some of opera's most powerful and convincing climaxes are evocations of this distinctively human goal.

In *Der fliegende Holländer*, the Act III redemption of Vanderdecken, the legendary Dutchman who defied God, is precisely etched by music specifically identified earlier in the opera with his salvation. In Act II, Senta sings for her friends the ballad of the man who wanders the sea under an eternal curse; at the end of the second verse, the girls wonder who will be the one to redeem him (Example 5.5a) and then are startled when Senta exclaims that she wants to be that person (Example 5.5b). The final phrases of the

---

[10] The *lieto fine* ("happy ending") often resulted from a miraculous appearance of a deity who would set things right. This *deus ex machina* (lit., "a god from the machine,") descended from the "heavens" above the stage by virtue of various mechanical contrivances. The term dates from Greek and Roman theater and is applied to unexplained solutions and last-minute rescues of all types, whether from human, natural, or supernatural causes.

EXAMPLE 5.5 WAGNER, THEMES FROM *Der fliegende Holländer*

a) Act II: Maidens wonder who will redeem the legendary Dutchman.

b) Act II: Senta's urgent wish to fulfill the legend.

c) Act III: reworking of music of (a) and (b) as accompaniment to the opera's final tableau.

opera, when Senta plunges into the sea to prove her continued love and faithfulness to Vanderdecken, accompany a vision of the two ("in the red glow of the rising sun . . . in a close embrace,. . . soaring upwards") by following a trombone-powered statement of the Dutchman theme with a transfiguring, exalting reworking (Example 5.5c) of Senta's theme of redemption.

Tannhäuser is another example of Wagner's interest in the topic of redemption. Tannhäuser, a minstrel who has committed the sins of abandonment to carnal love and praise of Venus, seeks absolution from the Pope after enduring a painful journey of penitence but is denied forgiveness by the Pope's harsh judgment that redemption may come to him only when the Papal staff bursts into greenery. Tannhäuser is bitterly ready to take up a life with Venus once again, but the prayers of the devoted Elizabeth have redeemed him: pilgrims return from Rome bearing the crozier itself, now bursting with leaves and proclaim the miracle of redemption, their exuberant message told over rippling woodwind triplets and crowned by a thrilling return of the famed Pilgrims' Chorus.

Der Ring des Nibelungen (1876) is yet another exploration of this subject. While some people regard the destruction of Valhalla by fire and the flooding of the earth by the overflowing Rhine at the end of *Götterdämmerung* as a nihilistic return to nothingness, others see it as a musically luxuriant metaphor for some form of redemption. For Brünnhilde and Siegfried, it is the culmination and symbol of their mutual return to truth, understanding, and undiluted love for each other; for the world at large, it is a ridding of the earth of the forces of spiritual corruption and a cleansing of it as a new opportunity for the powers of love and compassion.

Wagner's *Parsifal* (1882) avoids any veiling of its story as a metaphor and deals directly with the themes of repentance, mercy, and redemption, although the theology behind these themes is a typically Wagnerian mix of Christianity, paganism, nihilism, and Buddhism.[11] It is a story of the perfect naif who, by suffering, maturing, and searching, gains a wisdom tempered by compassion that makes him a knight of surpassing virtue.

Two of the characters have long suffered for their sins: Kundry for laughing at Christ as He bore the cross; Amfortas, King of the Knights of the Grail, for allowing himself to be so distracted by the pleasures of the flesh that he lost possession of the Sacred Spear to the evil magician, Klingsor. That both Kundry and Amfortas are sincerely and agonizingly remorseful is shown in their music.

The metaphor of Amfortas's heaviness of soul is represented dramatically by frequent reference to the eternal pain of a wound in his side (parallel to that of Christ); musically his remorse is given expression in a descending line accompanied by syncopations (both are archetypes for unease, sorrow, and suffering) that seem to throb with heartache (Example 5.6a).

Kundry, one of opera's most complex women,[12] is less easily represented by a single melody, for she presents varying personas of wildness, bitterness, and seductiveness that eventually give way to penitence and compassion: in all of Act III, she says only the word "dienen" ("to serve"). Her motive of devotion (Example 5.6b), heard in Act III as accompaniment to her offering of a drink of spring water to the exhausted Parsifal, is short and gentle. The supple harmonies and woodwind colorations suggest her move toward her own redemption because they are so different from the bestial cries, angular melodies, and harsh harmonies associated with her earlier.

The healing acts of Parsifal and the groping toward forgiveness of Kundry and Amfortas reach their climax in concluding passages that present an ecstatic summation of motives associated with the Grail, Communion, and Faith. Wagner's harp arpeggios and angelic women's voices singing from on high are perhaps opera's most celebrated metaphor for the redemption of humanity.

Another of opera's most redemptive moments is the death of Verdi's Otello, when, realizing how tragically he has been led astray and how cruelly he has mistreated his beloved Desdemona, he takes his own life. To the yearning strings' recall of the climax of the Act I Otello/Desdemona duet,

---

[11] See Millington, *Wagner,* p. 270f, for a summary of possible interpretations of this opera.

[12] See Leonie Rysanek, "Total Woman," in *Opera News* 49, no. 15 (April 13, 1985): 30f.

EXAMPLE 5.6 WAGNER, MOTIVES FROM *Parsifal*

a) Amfortas's motive of suffering.

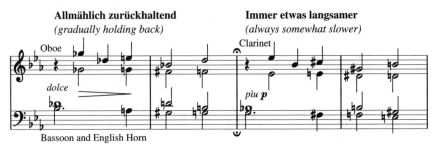

b) Kundry's motive of devotion.

Otello sings its text[13] as his dying words ("Un bacio. . .un bacio ancora . . . ah! un altro bacio"—"A kiss, a kiss again . . . ah! another kiss"). This tender affirmation of his true love is then followed by solemn, organ-like chords of a hushed tutti, the horns and trombones filling in the texture with timbres of solemn dignity.

Dvořák's *Rusalka* offers a particularly appealing approach to this element of the human condition, for the release from the opera's curse comes not only from the Prince's atonement but from the gentleness and uncompromising love of a nonhuman, the nymph Rusalka. Even though this heroine is not of this world, it is her desire to attain the fulfillment of human love that sets the plot in motion, and it is her human warmth of soul (although her embraces have had the coolness of her watery natural existence) and steadfast love that shape the emotional thrust of the opera's final moments.

Rusalka has accepted the curse of eternal banishment to the depths of the lakes as a man-destroying water nymph should the Prince she loves be faithless. The condition of her metamorphosis to the world of mortals, however, is voicelessness. Unable to understand her silence and falling prey to the ridicule and physical allure of a mortal woman, the Prince rejects Rusalka,

---

[13] But not precisely: in Act I, Otello sings "Un bacio, un bacio, ancora un bacio."

thus unknowingly forcing her to submit to the rigors of the curse. In the closing pages of the opera, he repents his cruelty and betrayal and returns to the
shore of the lake where he had first felt Rusalka's allure. There Rusalka lovingly and sadly warns him of the death her embrace must bring; it is his
knowledge of this fate and his willing surrender to it that serve as the symbol
of his atonement and as the agent of his spiritual redemption.

The opera's transcendent moment comes with two themes, one the lyric
and triadic melody of the Prince's acceptance of his fate (Example 5.7a), the
other a transformation of the curse motive (Example 5.7b) into a theme of
release (Example 5.7c) that is melodically soaring and orchestrally fullbodied,
even though trumpets punctuate it with fanfares derived from one of the
archetypical rhythms associated with death. Both are rich and warm in orchestration and both are pointed toward a climactic reaching that, through operatic means, expresses one of humanity's tenderest and most fulfilling concepts,
forgiveness.

There are any number of operatic villains for whom redemption is out of
the question. Pizarro in *Fidelio* is led off to prison, unrepentant; Salome gets

EXAMPLE 5.7 DVOŘÁK, THEMES FROM *Rusalka*

a) Act III: The Prince, knowing that it means his death, begs for Rusalka's kiss.

b) Act I: Curse motive, original form.

c) Act III: Curse motive transformed into theme of redemption.

crushed beneath soldiers' shields without the slightest admission of having done anything wrong; and Giovanni is dragged down to Hell, defiant to the end. Although Crown (*Porgy and Bess®*) is a rapist and murderer, he gains some measure of redemption by his efforts in Act II to rescue Clara's husband from a rampaging hurricane; his redemptive act is for naught, however, for in Act III he seeks to kill Porgy and reclaim Bess as his sexual property.[14]

Some of opera's scoundrels express remorse, but *caveat auditor*. In the previous chapter I noted that the contrition of Count Almaviva (Mozart's *Le nozze di Figaro*) is probably only momentary; in this respect he has lots of company. Count Di Luna (Verdi's *Il trovatore*, "The Troubadour," 1853) is abashed at committing his own brother to the flames, but one suspects that a redemptively guilty conscience is out of the question. Enrico di Lammermoor (brother of Donizetti's Lucia) feels the pangs when his sister appears in her famous state of derangement, but returns to form in the next scene to beard Edgardo of Ravenswood in the ruins of Wolf's Crag castle. Enrico's regrets are as transient as Di Luna's.

Then there are the evil wretches who may be defeated but survive, presumably to wreak their nefarious work in a more auspicious future. Alberich (*Götterdämmerung*) survives to plot another day; Nerone may look forward (in Monteverdi's *L'incoronazione*, if not in history) to a lifetime of lechery; the Captain, Doctor, and Drum Major are cruelly indifferent to the misery of Berg's humble soldier, Wozzeck; and the fisherfolk of *Peter Grimes* are utterly unmindful of the suicide of the opera's protagonist and quite untroubled by any remorse over their vengeful persecution of him.

---

[14] Porgy takes care of Crown once and for all by stabbing and strangling him.

Chapter 6

EXTREMES: THE ABSURD
AND THE BEAUTIFUL

A Sense of the Ridiculous

We hear so much from page, stage, and pulpit calling attention to our less-than-perfect characteristics that it seems to be in our genes to sermonize on the weakness of our flesh and the waywardness of our spirit. Certainly, some of our sermonizing has been very important and serious. Orations on human frailty, however, are but a hairsbreadth away from tiresome hectoring, and they can become self-important, overblown, and themselves worthy of orations on human frailty. If we have an inherent bent for self-criticism, it seems we also have an inherent inclination to be excessive about it. We can be absurdly overbearing and wearying, although, as Dr. Johnson pointed out, seldom to ourselves.

Rossini's Dr. Bartolo (*Il barbiere di Siviglia*) never gets that message. He has listened to his teenage ward Rosina duck and dodge his suspicions about a letter he is sure she has sent to a suitor: the ink on her finger was simply a balm for when she burned herself, she says, the sheet of paper missing from the desk was used to wrap candy for Figaro's sick daughter, and the quill pen was sharpened so she could make a design for her embroidery.

Bartolo can't stand her defiance a second longer and explodes into one of opera's great comic moments, a pompous blast about the knowledge, wisdom, and experience of "Un dottor della mia sorte" ("A doctor of my station") and the deference due to him. The aria is filled with dotted rhythms that speak of the musical panoply presumably appropriate to great men, obsessive repetitions of individual words and phrases, fanfare accompaniments, and a mincing chromatic violin melody that suggests at one point his awareness of every jot and tittle of her little lies and, on its repeat, his momentary turn to cajolery. When he turns to his ultimate threat of locking her in her room, the aria turns to a breakneck *allegro vivace* that is melodically simple because it is almost all scalar, but is also a real test of a singer's virtuosity in declaiming words and a masterpiece of bluster.

Effectively pointed satire is at once the self-criticism unique to human intelligence and our immunization against pompousness. We are often inclined to conform to a point of view even when it is proved wrong or inef-

94

fective—principle, and all that—but we cannot stand to be proved ridiculous. When we recognize that we are absurd, our motivation to change is more powerful than all the threats of hellfire and brimstone.

Neither wearying oration nor effective satire is wanting in the realm of opera. The serenade given to Beckmesser in Act II of *Die Meistersinger* takes the dagger of scorn and rams it right into the guts of pretentiousness, mediocrity, obsessive reliance on rule and tradition (instead of inspiration and imagination), and, not least (given opera's narcissistic interest in matters of song), bad singing. The lute introduction (Example 6.1a) is hopelessly arid in its decoration, word accents are misplaced ("GEfall'n" instead of "geFALL'N," "guTEN" instead of "GUten"; see also Example 6.1b), and he spurts out melismas that are grotesquely awkward and unlovely (also in Example 6.1b) even as they are technically appropriate because they draw on the serenade's introduction. Beckmesser's wretched ornamentation has a good deal in common with the music given Mozart's Osmin (the lecherous and self-important overseer of Mozart's *Entführung*) whose melisma on "singen" we will encounter shortly.

Beckmesser's song is a pretty gruesome affair. Besides the wrong accents and sterile ornaments, there are nonsequiturs in his text, phrases end on unimportant words, melody is forced into symmetries that make no sense, and nothing approaches good taste, beauty, or imagination.

The delivery of his serenade is complicated by Hans Sachs, who is working outside his house on a pair of shoes he has promised Beckmesser for the next day. Sachs's hammering is most disconcerting, so Beckmesser decides to make the best of it by inviting Sachs to correct any errors in his song with

EXAMPLE 6.1 WAGNER, *Die Meistersinger* ACT II, SCENE VI: BECKMESSER'S SERENADE

a) Lute introduction.

b) Melisma (with musical accents coming incorrectly on the second syllables of "Werben" and "Mägdelein").

the stroke of his hammer on the last. Sachs complies with energy unbound-
ed, the pounding clearly reminding us of Beckmesser's own noisy tallying of
Walther's errors in the Act I trial song.

The noise of hammering and Beckmesser's ever more strident singing
catches the attention of Sachs's apprentice, David, who thinks Beckmesser is
serenading Magdalene, David's girlfriend. David's assault on Beckmesser is
like a spark in a tinderbox: first a few, then many of the townsfolk, motivated
by years of personal rivalries and resentments, and aware of the advantages of
the cloak of darkness, seize the moment to get even with one and all. Even the
Mastersingers themselves join the fray. Ridiculousness, it seems, is catching.

In the final act, Beckmesser's mangling of words is one of the wonders of
poetic misanthropy. Having stolen the words written by Walther for the song
competition, Beckmesser stands before the judges and the crowd and tries to
graft Walther's text onto the melodic shapes of his lumpen serenade. Not only
is the effort musically preposterous, but Beckmesser also forgets Walther's
words. Instead of Walther's "Morgenlich leuchtend im rosigen Schein / von
Blüth' und Duft / geschwellt die Luft" ("Warm in the sunlight of dawning day,
the air swelled with blossoms and perfume"), out comes "Morgen ich leuchte
in rosigem Schein / voll Blut und Duft / geht schnell die Luft" ("In the morning I shine in a rosy light, the air was quick with blood and scent"). Little wonder that the onlookers and judges are at first puzzled, then derisive.[1]

Contemporary composers have certainly not shied away from the
bizarre, either. Shostakovich drew on an 1835 story by Gogol for *The Nose*
(*Nos*, 1930), a biting satire on bureaucratese, academicism, official poppy-
cock, and self-importance: a minor civic official's nose disappears, then is
seen at church dressed as a privy councillor; after an extensive police drag-
net, the nose is arrested and, with additional brouhaha, eventually returned
to the man's face. Elaborate percussion, a trombone evoking the breaking of
wind, vulgarly bright timbres, and a madcap array of styles and sounds
punctuate an opera at once zany and brilliantly penetrating.

Hans Werner Henze's *Der junge Lord* (The Young Lord, 1965) also takes
society on a bumpy ride. It portrays the people of a small town willing to
accept outrageous behavior from a young man whom they believe to be rich
and therefore worthy of respect; the revelation that the object of their sycophantic approval is a circus ape dressed in a man's clothing is a very creamy
pie in the face of pretension and false values.

The earliest, fully worked out example of operatic human foolishness is
the character of Nerone in *L'incoronazione di Poppea*. All powerful in rank and
privilege, Nerone is shown to be hopelessly weak of spirit in every situation.
That he is putty in the hands of the courtesan Poppea, with whom he is infat-

---

[1] An additional dimension to the Beckmesser disaster is Wagner's antipathy for Eduard
Hanslick, a respected and widely read critic. Wagner's audiences knew that Beckmesser
(whose original name in the libretto was to be "Hans Lick") was a barely disguised parody
of a writer about music, who held to traditional views of the nature of the art. Hanslick
deserved better; Beckmesser does not. There is a serious nether side here that is treated
by Barry Millington in "Nuremberg Trial: Is there anti-semitism in *Die Meistersinger?*," in
Cambridge Opera Journal 3, no. 3 (November 1991): 247–260. Pages 251ff deal especially
with the nature of Beckmesser's serenade as a parody of the Jewish cantorial style and may
serve as an introduction to Wagner's vicious anti-Semitism.

uated beyond control, is clearly indicated in their scene in Act I, where Nerone's music is limited to short responses, while she is given pliant, richly melodious music at every turn (Example 6.2a). Only at the end of the scene (following a night of extensive love-making, we are given to understand) does Nerone's music gain rhythmic solidity and musical expansion.

His dealings with his tutor and chief senator, Seneca, are dominated by outbursts of petulance and impatience, for Seneca will neither tolerate nor forgive Nerone's cruelties and immoral lusts. The musical result in an angry confrontation with Seneca is that Nerone's music is denied any arched melodic flow or stately rhythm associated with power and majesty; instead, it is spasmodic and irregular (Example 6.2b).

The emperor's spiritual nakedness is revealed even more glaringly during Act II's bachelor party. Having banished his wife, Ottavia, and ordered Seneca to commit suicide, Nerone celebrates his forthcoming bedding of Poppea in a vividly drunken duet with his courtier Lucano. Nerone's music

EXAMPLE 6.2 MONTEVERDI, *L'incoronazione di Poppea*: NERONE'S UNMELODIOUSNESS AS SYMBOL OF HIS BARRENNESS OF SPIRIT

a) Act I, scene iii: Poppea's cajoling, Nerone's response.

EXAMPLE 6.2. (*CONTINUED*)

b) Act II, scene ix: Nerone's contemptuous outburst against Seneca (the example shows separate segments).

is lilting and buoyant at the start of things, but melismas on individual words ("cantiam"—"let's sing," "glorie"—"glories," and, not unexpectedly, "bocca"—[Poppea's] "mouth") become more extended and seem to wobble all over the staff[2] (Example 6.2c) as the characters stagger about Nerone's apartment in the palace. As the duet progresses, the melismas become more and more frequent; eventually, Nerone is so completely addled with liquor and with his anticipation of sexual delights that he loses any sense of phrase or structured musical expression and gives himself over to meaningless cries ("Ahi!") and thoughts of his own glory ("Destin!"—"Destiny!").

The Beggar's Opera, in 1728, took a swipe at what was perceived by literati as the absurdity of opera itself and landed a haymaker on opera seria's chin by reversing everything typical of it: the protagonist is a bass, not a castrato; he and the other characters are lowlifes in station and behavior, not paragons of virtue; the stage pictures London's tawdry streets and hovels, not Arcadia or the marbled palaces of history and myth; and the words (by John Gay, 1685–1732) are sharply satirical, bawdy English rather than elaborately metaphorical Italian. Nor are the garlanded melodies of opera seria

---

[2] Beethoven used a similar quality in the "Ode to Joy" movement of his Ninth Symphony (1824), where humanity's ecstasy at drinking from the breast of nature evoked from the composer a mood of emotional inebriation via trills, rhythms, and melismas. Verdi did the same thing for Cassio's drunkenness in the first act of *Otello.* The context in Beethoven's work makes these devices gorgeous and spiritually uplifting; in Verdi they are theatrically vivid and exciting.

EXAMPLE 6.2 (*CONTINUED*)

c) Act III, scene v: The drunken singing of Nerone and Lucano.

exploited here—the musical idiom is a pastiche of simple songs and melodies cobbled by John Christopher Pepusch (1667–1752) from a variety of sources (including Italian opera). The emphasis is on natural action with the plot line developed through spoken dialogue rather than recitative.[3] *The Beggar's Opera* is a touchstone for the emergence in the eighteenth century

[3] These are the characteristics of the so-called "ballad opera," a comic genre popular in England, Ireland, and America in the mid- and late eighteenth-century. The evolution of the Singspiel can be traced to the exporting of ballad operas to Germany, in translation and with new music.

of distinct and self-sufficient comic genres: opera buffa, ballad opera, Singspiel, and opéra comique. It therefore marks a major directional change of thinking in the eighteenth century toward a more natural presentation of human character and situation and toward the use of satiric wit to underscore the frequent foolishness of human behavior.

Die Entführung aus dem Serail also hurls the lance of ridicule at over-confident, fatuous, and self-important people who don't see the pothole waiting to swallow them cap-à-pie. Set in a nameless near-Eastern land ruled by the enlightened despot Pasha Selim, Mozart's Singspiel offers a wonderfully funny aria by Osmin, the Pasha's overseer and chief steward. Osmin has thwarted an attempted elopement by two Western couples from the court; as reward, he expects to gain one of the girls as his bride and the joy of seeing the torture of the two men.

The singer who created the role had a wondrously deep bass; Mozart capitalized on that by giving the part low Ds galore. With the first notes of Osmin's aria, however, we are given the sound of a piccolo. For Mozart's audience that sound was an immediate association with the Janissary bands of the once-feared Turkish armies,[4] thus associating Osmin with the Near East while at the same time mocking Osmin's bass timbre by its shrill tone and skittering high pitches. The sound of the orchestra is the complete opposite of the timbre of the singer and thus turns the aria from a vehicle of menace into one of buffoonery. Osmin means business, but the reality is his gross foolishness.

The grotesquerie of the graceless melisma on "singen" (Example 6.3b) is clear: in an opera, how better could one be reminded of self-indulgent excess than to have an excessive display of the singer's art? The staccato rising scale at the end of that melisma, the extreme low notes, the wider-than-octave skips (Example 6.3a), the obsessive repetition of text, and the rondo-reiteration of his salivating glee are uproariously comical and potent in their ridicule.

The use of repeated notes as symbols of obsession is common to both Osmin and Rigoletto (see Examples RI-1a and RI-3c), but the dramatic and musical contexts make the device brooding and laden with fear in *Rigoletto*, hyperactive and preposterous in *Entführung*.

The operatic recognition of human absurdity took a rollicking and farcical direction in the operettas of Gilbert and Sullivan. Sullivan's ability to treat human inanity through musical means reveals itself in the grand huffing and puffing of Pooh-Bah's music in the "To sit in solemn silence" trio of *The Mikado* and the recitatives of Katisha's dire pronouncements in the same work.

Gilbert and Sullivan give opera a going-over, too: the chorus of policemen and young ladies in *The Pirates of Penzance* (1879) gets right to the musical heart of bloated operatic finales; Mabel's "Poor Wandering One" (also from *Pirates*) clearly has soprano coloratura on a spit; and "With cat-like tread" of

---

[4] Fifes and double-reed instruments, often accompanied by jangling instruments such as triangles and cymbals and the rolling of drums, were the basic devices of the Janissary bands and became part and parcel of western music's embrace of the sound. Mozart's *Rondo alla turca*, K. 331 (1781–83), is a keyboard evocation of it, and the orchestrations of Beethoven's Ninth Symphony finale and *Die Ruinen von Athen* (The Ruins of Athens, 1811) and Haydn's Symphony No. 100, ("Military," 1793–94) also took advantage of it. The sound is, in addition, a feature of the Scythian choruses of Gluck's *Iphigénie en Tauride*.

EXAMPLE 6.3 MOZART, *Die Entführung aus dem Serail*
ACT II, SCENE V: OSMIN'S "HA! WIE WILL ICH TRIUMPHIEREN"
("AH, HOW I SHALL TRIUMPH!")

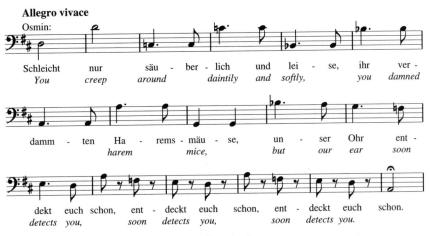

a) Wide skips, humorous repetitions, detached notes.

b) Comic melisma.

HMS Pinafore (1878) gives the elbow-in-the-ribs to stereotyped conspirators'
ensembles. The satiric delights of Gilbert and Sullivan's works are also carried
along via the patter delivery of delicious verbal rhymes, puns, and jokes.

Offenbach was another composer who ridiculed both opera and societal
self-importance. My particular favorite is the Act I finale of his *La grande-
duchesse de Gérolstein* (1867), when the Grand Duchess, infatuated with a young
private whom she has elevated to general, presents him with her father's
sacred sabre to wear into battle (to be waged against a nearby chateau in a
"war" invented by the Grand Duchess's advisor to keep her entertained). After
the obligatory variations on the main tune of "Voici le sabre de mon papa"

("Here is my daddy's sword"), all rush off to combat only to be stopped in their tracks by the Grand Duchess's "Arrêtez! Vous oubliez le sabre!" ("Stop! You've forgotten the sword!"), whereupon all must ring the changes on the same tune with the new words, "Nous oublions le sabre," and so on and so on.

The awareness of human idiocy has its serious side, too. In Act I of Handel's *Giulio Cesare* (1724), Cesare delivers one of the more probing indictments of the human penchant for pomp and empty display in his musing on an urn containing the ashes of the great Pompey. There Handel composed an arioso, departing from the bare-bones accompaniment and relatively rapid delivery of recitativo secco and setting aside the formal melodiousness of the *aria da capo*[5] in favor of a hushed, through-composed declamation accompanied by strings. There is a brooding, pensive quality achieved through the somber dotted motion of the introduction (Example 6.4a) and the moves between major ("x" in Example 6.4b) and minor harmonies ("y"). Strong dissonances ("z") also give emphasis and depth to Cesare's recognition of the fatuousness of human glory.

EXAMPLE 6.4 HANDEL, *Giulio Cesare* ACT I, SCENE VII: CESARE'S "ALMA DEL GRAN POMPEO" ("SOUL OF GREAT POMPEY")

a) Introduction.

---

[5] "Da capo" = "from the beginning." This indication was written at the end of a B section of an ABA aria instead of having to write the repeat of the notes of the A section. The *aria da capo* is the quintessential aria type of the Baroque era.

EXAMPLE 6.4. (*CONTINUED*)

b) The emptiness of human grandeur, set to expressive harmonies.

Cesare's monologue would seem to have common cause with Iago's "Credo," but the two are far apart. Iago is contemptuous of everything, Cesare is respectful of fundamental values; Iago's music is harsh and blatant, Cesare's is pensive and melancholy.

❧

What of our indifference to the needs of others or our capacity to inflict cruelty? We would like to refer to such behaviors as "inhuman," but of course they are very much a part of our being. They are absurd in that they are beyond understanding and far removed from what we would like to think is "normal" human behavior.

There is no more vivid indictment of human indifference than Berg's *Wozzeck*, in which a maniacal doctor and a perverted army captain prey on Wozzeck, a lowly and impoverished army private, the doctor through idiotic research, the captain through ridicule. Their insensitivity is a rebuke to society as a whole.

The final scene of the opera is shattering: Wozzeck has committed suicide after murdering his mistress Marie, and their child is now totally alone in an uncaring society. Not understanding the comments of the children who are excited over the discovery of Marie's body, the three-year-old toddler continues to play innocently on his hobby horse until one of the others calls bluntly before running off to see Marie's body, "Du, dein Mutter is tod!" ("You, your mother's dead!"). The last words of the opera are the toddler's "hop, hop . . . hop, hop" as he moves after the others; there are some quiet string chords, and the curtain falls. The atonal music, of course, has no harmonic resolution, in effect posing the question and musically demanding that society find answers. *Wozzeck* causes us to leave the theater aware that when we deny our humanity by acting against the welfare of the human condition—or by our failure to act for it—we commit the ultimate absurdity.

Aesthetics

Beauty as separate from content or function is primarily a Western idea— some non-Western cultures have no word for "art" and would be quite puzzled by a discussion of aesthetics.[6] Nonetheless, all cultures are interested in manner as well as substance, even if the beauty of an object is inseparable from its function.

The world of opera has been concerned with itself ever since its invention at the dawn of the seventeenth century. That it is a union of the beautiful and the meaningful has been agreed on by everyone, but how this union is to be achieved has been a rub and an irritant through the ages. Writers, performers, composers, and listeners have continuously hissed and snarled about words versus music, Italian versus French versus German styles, orchestra versus voice, and drama versus entertainment.

---

[6] The Western idea of the aesthetic as opposed to other cultures is discussed in Merriam, Chapter 6.

The issue of how music best serves the needs of poetry and drama has been raised in every generation. Although it has usually taken words to argue the thing out, the very earliest opera that still holds the boards in our time, Monteverdi's *Orfeo*, provided an answer through the language—and symbolism—of music.

Guided by the Goddess of Hope, Orfeo has resolved to enter the underworld to rescue Euridice from Death. At the banks of the River Styx, he confronts Caronte (Charon) with his plea. "Possente spirto e formidabil nume" ("Puissant spirit and dreadful god") is a plaint in the form of six verses, five of which are sung over a ground (a repeated melody heard in the bass line), with each of the first four verses progressively more elaborate in both melody and instrumentation. In the first verse (Example 6.5a), Monteverdi offers a highly ornamented vocal part, its intricacy and accompaniment of two violins playing fast scales suggesting urgency and breathless desperation.

The second verse is also ornamented, but the phrases are shorter and more impassioned; in the third verse (Example 6.5b), the ornamentation

EXAMPLE 6.5 MONTEVERDI, *Orfeo* ACT III:
ORFEO'S APPEAL TO CARONTE

a) start of first verse.

EXAMPLE 6.5 (*CONTINUED*)

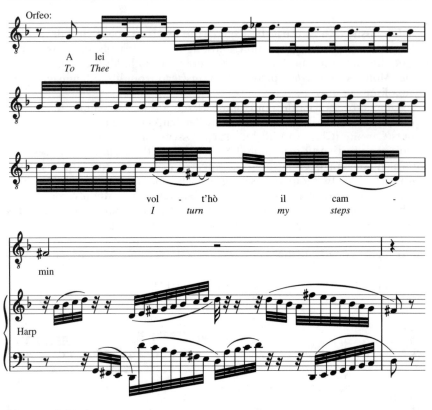

A   lei
To   Thee

vol - t'hò   il   cam -
I   turn   my   steps

min

Harp

b) start of third verse.

O ____   de le lu - ci mie,   lu - ci se -
Oh,   to my eyes,   the serene

re - ne,   S'un vo - stro sguar - do   può tor - nar - mi in
eyes   of   one   look   from you   can   return me

vi - ta,   ahi   chi   nie - ga il con - for - to à le ____
to   life,   ah,   who   would deny   solace

____ mie pe - ne, _____
for   my   torments?

c) start of fifth verse.

becomes frenzied, and the accompaniment is given to a harp as emblematic of Orfeo's desperate playing of his lute. The idea of impassioned complexity continues unabated in verse 4, but verse 5 (Example 6.5c) suddenly presents plainness; Orfeo's emotional bursts have been exhausted and are now replaced by resolve and dignified reserve expressed through recitative.

EXAMPLE 6.5 (CONTINUED)

d) sixth verse, in toto.

Orfeo's ultimate appeal—the most moving of them all—is an arioso (Example 6.5d), the merging of melodic warmth with the language-shaped accents of recitative.

Although he is charmed and lulled to sleep by Orfeo's song, Caronte's obedience to the laws of nature is inflexible. Orfeo, in despair, utters one more plea, this time in the style of a recitative that in effect has abandoned song and therefore hope. But Proserpina, Queen of the Underworld, has heard Orfeo's song and is deeply moved; it is her appeal to Pluto that results in permission for Orfeo to reclaim Euridice, albeit with the conditions Pluto imposes.

Orfeo's song poses some problems of interpretation. Are we to understand that ornate music is less effective than plain declamation because the simplest music "has the last word?" Or is the impact on Caronte and Proserpina the result of the whole of the song and not just part of it? Or should we consider that gods speak elaborately and mortals simply,[7] and therefore it is Orfeo's human qualities of fidelity, courage, and expressiveness that win the day? Perhaps Monteverdi is suggesting that words and music share the glory, that they ebb and flow in their relation to each other, and that the artist who recognizes the inherent worth of each is ultimately the most persuasive.

Richard Strauss's *Ariadne auf Naxos* takes up the issue of beauty in quite a different way. Its plot begins with an artistic crisis: a young composer learns that his opera seria (a genre of "high art") is not just to share an evening with a farcical entertainment (very *low* art) but is actually to be fused with it. The plots, texts, and music are to be intertwined and the dramatis personae are to be conjoined so that the whole theatrical business will be completed in time for the fireworks scheduled for later that night, dramatic and musical logic and the purity of art being of no importance. The Composer's protests are to no avail.

Amid the frantic final moments before the bizarre mix of comedy and tragedy is to be rushed onto the stage, the Composer bursts into a gorgeously lyrical tribute to music as a holy art that unites courageous souls of every sort like cherubim around a gleaming throne. Its majestic message is not just the result of Strauss's inspired melody but also its contrast with the busyness of the music that has preceded it. The arguing and bustle of the backstage scene has been characterized by short phrases, extremely complex motivic work in the orchestra, and lots of words with many consonants and fast rhythms derived from normal conversation; suddenly there is a burst of true song, with words and melody that could be on the coat of arms of every opera house and concert hall (Example 6.6).

The Prologue of *Ariadne* is a lesson in the harsh business of compromise, the naive Composer having to face up to the mingling of diverse genres— comedy and tragedy—if his work is to be performed at all. He must learn from the comedienne Zerbinetta that common sense is a necessary leavening

---

[7] Celletti, in *Bel canto*, p. 7, attributes to Monteverdi a suggestion that mortals should sing simply while divinities should be given the musical language of trills, runs, and other ornaments.

EX. 6.6 RICHARD STRAUSS, *Ariadne auf Naxos* ACT I: THE
COMPOSER'S TRIBUTE TO THE POWER OF MUSIC

of high ideals: when the ordinary folk represented by the clowns and servants enter the realm of serious opera, she says "Jetzt kommt Vernunft in die Verstiegenheit" ("Reasonableness now enters amidst extravagance").

The plot of Richard Strauss's *Capriccio* (1942) is about the struggle between words and music, allegorized by the passion of Olivier, a poet, and Flamand, a composer, for a beautiful Countess. Strauss's preface to the score proposes that words and music are brother and sister, and the message of the opera's text is that each nourishes the other. But whatever the opera says in its words,[8] the music of the opera says something else.

In *Capriccio*'s closing scene, the Countess gazes into a mirror, lamenting that she is torn between two loves and asking her reflection, "O Madeleine, willst du zwischen zwei Feuren verbrennen?" ("Oh Madeleine, do you want to be consumed by two fires?"). The Countess is unable to choose between them, and the opera ends with her simply going in to sup-

---

[8] The scenario and text are the result of a clutch of contributors, including Clemens Krauss (usually identified as the principal librettist), Stefan Zweig, Hans Swarowsky, Rudolf Hartmann, Joseph Gregor, and Strauss himself. Hugo von Hoffmannsthal, librettist for the bulk of Strauss's great works, had died in 1929.

per. Her inclinations, however (and Strauss's), are suggested by the orchestra: it quotes the music of Flamand, recalling the music to which the Countess had sung these words and providing Strauss's answer to opera's most pervasive mystery:

Die Worte der Dichter	The poet's words
schätze ich hoch,	I treasure highly,
doch sagen sie nicht alles,	but they don't say everything
was tief verborgen!	that is deeply hidden.

The nature of drama and its relation to music was taken up more extensively by Wagner than by anyone else. *The Artwork of the Future* (1849), *Opera and Drama* (1851), and *A Communication to My Friends* (1851) are among the most important and extensive documents on the nature of music and drama and remain fascinating and influential (if difficult) reading.[9]

Wagner's music dealt only once with the nature of beauty, albeit in a most potent and enduring way. The lyric grace and suppleness of verse in Walther's prize song, in *Die Meistersinger von Nürnberg*,[10] makes an obvious case for the importance of imagination and innovation, but the shaping of its music and words by the traditional Bar form (two verses and a refrain) is no less powerful a tribute to inherited practices and respect for the achievments and principles of past masters.

There are other statements about aesthetics in this opera and they are just as important. One of them is that the leadership of a community cannot be concerned only with pragmatics; the leaders of *Die Meistersinger's* Nuremberg are not only the most respected businessmen of the city but also some of its finest craftsmen (in cobbling, tinsmithing, gold working, et al.). Their concern for excellence goes still further, for they are all Mastersingers, men who are as concerned for the dignity and beauty of song as they are for the everyday demands of commerce.[11]

The phrases of Beckmesser's poetically and musically corrupt serenade become the building blocks of the choral fugue that provides the music for the second act's remarkable finale (it features as many as sixteen vocal parts at once!). While a fugue is one of the most tightly structured procedures of musical composition, its constant imitation of one part by another and its tossing around of snippets of melody and rhythm invite feelings of tumult and disorder, with motives coming seemingly from all directions. Wagner's elaborately contrapuntal texture is a musical melee, a metaphor for the social chaos sundering the strands that have bound the members of the Nuremberg com-

---

[9] The contents of these complex essays are summarized, described, and quoted from extensively in Newman's *Wagner As Man and Artist*. A précis of Wagner's principles is offered in the discussion of *Die Walküre* in the next part of this book.

[10] *Tannhäuser's* dramatis personae is strong in singer-poets: Wolfram von Eschenbach (fl.1170–1220), Walther von der Vogelweide (ca.1170–ca.1230), and Tannhäuser (ca.1205–ca.1270) were minstrels ("Minnesingers"), whose melodies were vehicles for elevated poetry about both the spiritual and the sensual aspects of love. The plot of the opera includes a Song Contest that occasions tremendous controversy among the characters, although their argument is over the nature of love and the poetic expression appropriate to it rather than the nature of beauty.

[11] Our modern society would profit much from such a business community.

munity in civilized acceptance of each other. That Beckmesser's wretched cat-erwauling not only precipitated this to-do but also is the substance of its music seems to be a clear statement by Wagner and a clarion message to all who would profit from a profound truth: bad art and philistinism sap the moral fiber of society.[12]

The Prologue to Leoncavallo's *Pagliacci* provides a special pointing of the issue of the beautiful in drama. As with the various settings of the legend of Orpheus, the opera tells a story in which plot, poetry, and music need no justification other than themselves. That they are moving and beautiful in their own right is enough.

Tonio, a member of a travelling commedia dell'arte[13] group, tells us, however, that there is more to the play than that, for the story we are about to be told is drawn from reality and the performers speak from their hearts. Attired in a clown's costume and make-up, he pokes his head through the curtain to announce that he is the Prologue. Some introductory musical business in the form of a fanfare and a fast, chirping scalar figure appropri-ate to the comic work of a clown is dispensed with quickly so that Tonio can get to the point.

The author's purpose is serious, he tells us, and the actors are real peo-ple whose messages are worthy of respect. The author's "voice" is in the sound of a solo cello (Example 6.7a) accompanying Tonio's mention of the

EXAMPLE 6.7 LEONCAVALLO, *Pagliacci*: TONIO'S PROLOGUE

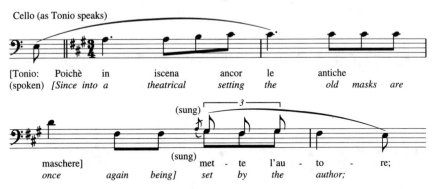

a) Cello as the author's voice (note: most performers sing the cello's melody, instead of following the score's direction to speak the words while the cello plays).

---

[12] Robinson, in *Opera and Ideas* (pp. 226ff), points out the importance of artists as the lead-ers of Nuremberg. I have drawn the mention of the relation of Beckmesser's serenade to the music of the riot scene from Robinson's persuasive analysis, pp. 226ff.

[13] The *commedie* were touring companies improvising farcical routines (*lazzi*) and dialogue around stock characters (*zanni*; among them were Arlecchino [Harlequin], Colombina, Scaramuccio, and Pantalone) and situations, often with interspersed songs, acrobatics, and other techniques of entertainment. They flourished in Italy from the time of the Renaissance, exerting a strong influence on both spoken drama and comic opera.

EXAMPLE 6.7. (*CONTINUED*)

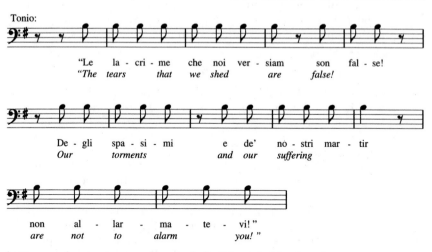

Tonio:

"Le la - cri - me che noi ver - siam son fal - se!
"The tears that we shed are false!

De - gli spa - si - mi e de' no - stri mar - tir
Our torments and our suffering

non al - lar - ma - te - vi! "
are not to alarm you! "

b) Repeated notes as a tuneless symbol of theatrical hackwork.

(♩. = 40)
Tonio:

Un ni - do di me - mo - rie in fon - do a
A nest of memories in the depth

l'a - ni - ma can - ta-va un gior - no, ed e - i con ve - re
of his soul sang one day, and he, with real

con dolore
alt.

la - cri - me scris-se, e i sin - ghioz - zi il
tears wrote, and his sobs

tem - po gli bat - te - va - no!
beat the time!

c) The inspiration from the depth of the author's soul.

masks the actors will wear as symbols of ancient theater; his rapid recitation of a single pitch suggests the arid conventions of meaningless playacting (Example 6.7b); the inspiration that has deeply moved the author is given expression by a flowing line above syncopations (Example 6.7c); the violent passions of the story and its characters come through in phrases that are shorter, more chromatic, and more angular (6.7d), with roiling and syncopated accompaniment; and the humanity of actors under those masks is given dignity and sincerity in an elegant, long-breathed, and passionate lyricism (Ex. 6.7e).

This music is free of preconceived musical patterns; instead, one textual/musical idea leads naturally to the next. Like Verdi's Rigoletto, Bizet's Don José, and Handel's Cesare, the character speaks from the heart, not from custom. Tonio's words and music form a powerful statement on the aesthetics of drama in general that is one of opera's great assertions of its self-worth. It reminds us forcefully—Danny Kaye to the contrary—that opera is indeed about something.

EXAMPLE 6.7. (*CONTINUED*)

d) The strong emotions enacted and felt by the performers.

EXAMPLE 6.7. (*CONTINUED*)

e) The humanity of the actors.

Although the librettos of opera have been silent on the nature of beauty itself, the whole of opera is a testament to the human penchant for achievement beyond the tools of survival.

Opera serves the cause of the beautiful simply by being.

Operas

SOME DRAMAS AND THEIR MUSIC

INTRODUCTION

Why These?

Any small selection of operas to illustrate the ways composers work is bound to be arbitrary, but I think there will be little quarrel with any of those I have chosen. Each is an acknowledged masterpiece, each represents a genre, a historical style, and a national spirit, and each deals tellingly with one or more of the aspects of the human condition dealt with so briefly in Part II. These eleven operas "worked" in terms of my goal: to show how operas "are about something" and how composers reveal some of the dimensions of their subjects. In some cases I chose them because I felt they haven't been given the attention they deserved; for others I have the temerity to think I have something to say about them that I have not read from the pens of opera's many superb analysts and friends.

The characters of the operas are listed in order of their vocal appearance.

On Pronunciations

I have indicated vowel sounds without recourse to the specialized symbols of the International Phonetic Alphabet, since I believe that many of my readers will not be familiar with them.

I have used an "h" to warn against the English diphthong in dealing with Italian's "pure" vowels. Thus "toh loh MEH oh" advises the reader to avoid "toe-oo" or "may-ee." "Ah" and "oo" present no problems, but the Italian "eh" should be like the first vowel of "chaotic."

German's umlauted "a" as the vowel sound in "bet" and the umlauted "o" as the "u" in "hurt" are straightforward, but the "u"-umlaut requires an "ee" sound in an "oo" shape of the mouth that is more difficult to describe than to do. The German "ch" is also difficult to pictorialize other than to suggest that it is some sort of low-throat pre-gargle/expectoration that is akin to the "h" in "human" and not like the "ch" in "itch." I'll leave it at that.

French vowels are less broad than German or Italian ones and in some cases impossible to represent by transliteration. To suggest that the French "u" is like the German "u"-umlaut is in the right direction but misses the nuance of language significantly.

The same problem of nuance applies to all the sounds of vowels and consonants: my guide is preliminary.

Scenes and "Numbers"

In the operas of the Baroque era and in most operas of later periods, a roman numeral identified a new scene in both score and libretto in accordance with the arrival or departure of a principal role; an arabic number was used for set vocal pieces such as arias and ensembles (but not for orchestral movements or recitativo secco). In the discussions that follow, scenes and set pieces are numbered as they are found in the score; in cases where they are not indicated in the score I have provided them for ease of reference.

Breaks in the poetic line are marked by a solidus (/).

Chapter 7

GIULIO CESARE IN EGITTO

MUSIC: George Frideric Handel (1685–1759)
LIBRETTO: Nicola Haym (1678–1729), after a libretto by Giacomo
  Francesco Bussani (fl. 1673–1680) for an opera of the same title (1676) by
  Antonio Sartorio (1630–1680)
PREMIERE: London (King's Theatre), February 20, 1724
TIME AND PLACE OF THE STORY: The period of the Roman Civil War,
  between September 48 B.C.E. and March 47 B.C.E.; Egypt

Giulio Cesare and Opera Seria

Music and Drama

Opera seria is the quintessential theatrical genre of the Baroque era; *Giulio
Cesare in Egitto* (Julius Caesar in Egypt) is one of its greatest exemplars. It is
like a brilliantly jeweled dramatic necklace: its links are the dialogues
through which the action takes place; its sapphires and rubies are the songs
that represent emotional responses and states of mind.

There is a special relationship between music and drama in opera seria
that has long been a sticking point: that which should presumably be the
most exciting—the music for the action of the story and the dialogue among
characters—is given the least interesting music, while the greatest musical
attention is given to the least galvanic action—the expression of feeling.

Handel's Vocal Idioms

The action of opera seria is vested in *recitativo secco* (i.e., "dry recitative"), a
bare-bones declamation of dialogue or narration in which note values and
pitch changes are governed by word accents and vowel colors; the music is
restricted to one note per syllable and a limited range of pitch and rhythm
that is stylized speech rather than song; and its accompaniment is limited to
harmonic bass notes and chord patterns provided by the two-instrument
basso continuo.

118

Audiences of Handel's day found the musical interest of the secco to be so low[1] that during it they turned to card playing, amorous activities, and other diversions—their attention turned to the stage only for the songs sung by the principal singers or for exciting visual delights.[2]

The dominating element of an opera seria is the "da capo" aria, an elaborate song in which a character sings about how he or she feels, offers a contrasting emotional state, and then—instead of doing something about it—repeats the first part, adding ornament limited only by the singer's taste and skill. Of *Giulio Cesare*'s twenty-nine arias, fourteen return to their beginning (thus "da capo"—"from the head" or "top"); twelve return to a spot marked by a symbol near the beginning ("dal segno"—"from the sign"). Each aria is a point of dramatic arrival rather than a springboard for future action—it is the summation of events and dialogue leading up to it and usually ends with the character's exit. Each mood represented in an aria—there are never more than two—is an undiluted "affection," an abstraction of an idea that is represented through symbols of rhythm, melody, instrumentation, and harmony.

Much of the poetry set to the music of arias is metaphorical: a villain given over to crafty deceit is like a huntsman stalking his prey (Cesare's description of the plotting Tolomeo, in "Va tacito e nascosto,"—[The knowing hunter] "moves quietly and stealthily," No. 14); a boy's defiance of a tyrant and villain is like a snake that writhes angrily if stepped on (Sesto determining to avenge the death of his father in "L'angue offeso mai riposa"—"The offended serpent will not rest," No. 23); and a heroine whose heart has found comfort after near disaster is like a sailor whose ship has survived a storm and reached the safety of harbor (Cleopatra's "Da tempeste il legno infranto"—"When a storm-tossed vessel [finds safety in port]," No. 37).

The secco and the aria are the polarities of *Giulio Cesare* but not its only elements. Handel's use of orchestrally accompanied recitative—the *recitativo accompagnato*—is among the wonders of opera in its affective harmony, dramatic highlighting of words, orchestral color, and pliant melody, and so is his *arioso*, a particular hybrid of song and declamation. Both of these genres allow for through-composition (the music changing as the text changes) and free movement between songfulness and declamation; they also allow for effective changes in rhythmic pulse and for sudden turns of harmony that would perhaps seem out of place in the more consistent flow of aria writing. (See Example 6.4.)

Arioso is turned to ironic effect in the seraglio scene, where Tolomeo greets his assembled beauties with ogling eyes and lustful heart in dotted rhythms and empty octaves appropriate to his adolescent sexual posturing.

---

[1] Secco can indeed be formulaic, but enterprising performers and composers can make it spirited and effective. The recording conducted by René Jacobs (Harmonia Mundi 901385.87) is especially felicitous in this regard; see, for example, the wonderful exposition of the secco in Act II (between Nos. 24 and 25), the scene where Cleopatra casts away her disguise as a serving maid and reveals that she is the Queen of Egypt to a Cesare suddenly and desperately in need of troops.

[2] The Baroque's opera seria was a sociological phenomenon as well as a musical one; people went there to be seen and to conduct business of varying sorts as well as to hear a favorite singer, hiss a singer under the protection of a rival, and so forth. They also went to hear gorgeous music, of course.

His opening phrases are melodic enough, but, at just the point where he ought to go into a contrasting B section, they disintegrate into recitativo secco, a style associated with musical emptiness just as his mouthing of flattery about the beauties around him is vapid and insincere.

Pictorialization

The signal moments of arias, ariosos, and accompanied recitatives are the musical representations of the imagery of significant words and/or the basic thoughts of the poetry. These pictorializations are most familiarly undertaken through ornamental extensions (see Examples 2.2a and b), but *Giulio Cesare* abounds in examples of other illuminations of text that are just as potent, if at times more subtle.

Changes of key and rhythm, for example, have a striking effect when, immediately after Cleopatra sings her aria of despair (No. 32, "Piangerò la sorte mia"—"I shall weep for my fate"), Cesare emerges from his desperate swim across Alexandria harbor to sing his orchestrally accompanied recitative "Dall' ondoso periglio" (No. 33, "From the perilous waters") in a key a half-step higher. The listener may not recognize the technical specifics of this move[3] but will feel the revivified life force represented by it. Also effective here is the move from the steady rhythmic pulses of Cleopatra's formal aria to the mix of halting phrases and lyric extensions illustrative of Cesare's conflicting emotions of relief at surviving, spiritual exhaustion at the defeat of his forces, and concern for his beloved (see below, Example GC-2).

Instrumentation is itself a potent factor in the illumination of text: the solo French horn of Cesare's "Va tacito e nascosto" immediately calls on the imagery of hunting; in Handel's day, the plaintive sound of the flute in Cornelia's "Priva son d'ogni conforto" (No. 4, "I am deprived of every solace") was a standard symbol for a woman who is wretched beyond comfort; the recorders in the slow section of "Svegliatevi nel core" (No. 5, "Rise up in my heart") lend a related timbre for a slightly different kind of mournfulness when Cornelia's son Sesto imagines the voice of his beloved father calling to him from across the chasm of death.

The orchestration of the second scene of Act II is justly celebrated not only for the exotic beauty of its sound but also for its atmospheric aptness: from behind the stage picture are heard the exquisite sounds of oboe, viola da gamba, harp, and theorbo.[4] This unusual array produces a magical sound that stops Cesare in his tracks and focuses his attention on the stage set (arranged by Cleopatra) of Parnassus (the mythological mount sacred to Apollo, Dionysus, and the Muses) that opens to reveal Cleopatra depicted as "Virtue Attended by the Nine Muses." That Cleopatra, supreme schemer and mistress of sex for the attainment of power, should assume an allegorical role of Virtue is deliciously ironic, but Cesare is quite unaware of her

---

[3] Especially if the role of Cesare is sung by a bass instead of the more appropriate treble voice.

[4] "Gamba" = leg, thus a relatively large member of the viol family held between the legs rather than by the arm against the shoulder. The viols were fretted instruments played with bows and produced a somewhat less vibratoed, more intimate sound than members of the violin family. The theorbo is a large lute.

propensities and ambitions. Moreover, the scene is musically so rapturous in both timbre and melody that only the most cynical cad in an audience would allow the truth to obscure the pleasure of the moment.

The several elements of music as pictorialization come together in "Se pietà di me non senti" (No. 27, "If you feel no pity for me"),[5] when Cleopatra believes that all is lost and avers her readiness to die if the gods have forsaken her. Example GC-1 shows the sweetly drooping violin figure ("a") that communicates sadness and the nearness of death, the change from short note values to syncopated long values that highlight "io morirò" ("I shall die;" "b" in the example), and the dramatic dissonance ("c") between the high note of the soprano and the bass note of the harmony that points the final syllable of "morirò" so poignantly. There is another instrumental force that is richly emotional by its *not* being present: the bassoons have darkly colored the first part of the aria but are absent from the passage shown; when they return after the singer falls silent, they deepen the gloom of the moment most effectively.

An interesting aspect of Handel's use of color for atmosphere and characterization in this opera is his assignment of female singers to female roles, quite in contrast to the then-frequent practice of giving these parts to castrati. In this most artificial of dramatic genres, the natural sound of women singing as women is a subtle but influential device.

Bel Canto: The Ideal of Singing

Bel canto ("beautiful singing") has of course been at the center of operatic performance from its earliest days. What beautiful singing should sound like, however, has changed drastically over the centuries of opera's history. Although the term was not coined until the nineteenth century, the principles of bel canto as understood from about 1660 to 1800 are clearly set out in any number of treatises[6] as a means of declaiming poetry through melody and a technique of articulation that allowed for clarity of diction, preciseness of pitch, and the ability to move smoothly from phrase to phrase, note to note, and from loud to soft and back again. That the most common epithets applied to the sound quality of "beautiful singing" were sweetness and purity suggests that lovers were to be mellifluous rather than overtly passionate.

Taste was vital, and the ability to apply it to expression and ornament was fundamental: the singer who, "in repeating the air . . . [did] not vary it for the better [was] no great master," wrote Tosi,[7] and "the higher the notes, the more it is necessary to touch them with softness, to avoid screaming."[8]

The images of hero and lover were vested in the treble ranges of soprano and alto, where voices could provide the sweetness of swains and the car-

---

[5] Lang (*Handel*, p. 181) appropriately describes this aria as "one of the great moments in opera."

[6] Perhaps the one most often cited is Piero Francesco Tosi's *Opinioni de' cantori antichi e moderni* (1723), available in English as *Observations on the Florid Song*, trans. J. E. Galliard (1723) and *Opinions of Singers Ancient and Modern . . .*, trans. Edward Foreman.

[7] Tosi, p. 94. An especially helpful review of vocal technique as applied to ornamentation in the Baroque is provided by Rogers, p. 354f.

[8] Tosi, p. 19.

rying strength of heroes.[9] In spite of the fame and respect accorded to women as they gained in importance as singers, by the dawn of the eighteenth century the castrato voice dominated casting for both male and female roles[10] everywhere but in France.[11]

We can only guess at the sounds of the voices of such remarkable performers as Farinelli, Senesino (creator of the role of Giulio Cesare), Caffarelli, and others who sent audiences into frenzies and faintings, although a recording[12] that exists of the last castrato, Alessandro Moreschi (1858–1922), gives a hint of what can be described as pure, stratospheric, and sopranoish. The descriptions of two French visitors to Italian opera houses give us some idea of the special qualities of the castrato sound:

> One must grow accustomed to these castrato voices to enjoy them. Their timbre is as clear and piercing as that of choir boys, and much stronger. . . . they sing an octave above the natural women's voice . . . [with] a dry and thin quality, far distant from the young and velvety quality of women's voices; but they are brilliant, light, full of *éclat*, very strong, and with a wide range.[13]

> No man or woman in the world can boast of a voice like theirs; they are clear, they are moving, and affect the soul itself. . . . a voice . . . clear and at the same time equally soft. . . They'll execute passages of I know not how many bars together, they'll have echoes on the same passages and swellings of a prodigious length . . . these charming voices acquire new charms by being in the mouth of a lover; . . . in this the Italian lovers have a very great advantage over ours, whose hoarse masculine voices ill agree with the fine soft things they are to say to their mistresses. Besides, the Italian voices being equally strong as they are soft, we hear all they sing very distinctly.[14]

Handel and the Conventions of Opera Seria

As in the thousands of operas that fall under the rubric of opera seria, the leading personages are trebles (in *Giulio Cesare*, Achilla is the only aria-singing bass, and there are no arias for tenor) whose characters are revealed

---

[9] Although tenors enjoyed major roles early in the history of opera (Monteverdi's *Orfeo*, for example) and at the end of the reign of opera seria (Mozart's *Idomeneo* and *La clemenza di Tito*), during the intervening period they were mostly relegated to the minor roles of wicked rivals, wise counselors, fathers, and comic servants. They also played comic female parts (so-called *travesti* roles), such as old nurses of loose morals or lecherous intent toward young men. The basso profondo voice was given to priests, sages, military leaders, and aged tutors; bass voices, somewhat lighter in timbre, played comic servants (especially stupid ones) and various travesti or clownish parts.

[10] Handel, however, assigned almost all of his women's roles to female singers.

[11] See Chapter 2, note 14.

[12] Opal CD 9823, *The Complete Recordings of Alessandro Moreschi, 1902–04.*

[13] Charles de Brosses, *Lettres familières en Italie en 1739 et 1740*, in MacClintock, p. 275. This paragraph is also quoted by Heriot, p. 14.

[14] François Raguenet, *Parallèle des Italiens et des Français* [1702], in Strunk, p. 483f.

in full dimension through a sequence of mono-emotional responses to events. The action is set out in recitativo secco. Also typical of the opera seria is its use of the soloists for the choral episodes (there being no mass of choristers available or sought),[15] the obligatory *lieto fine* ("happy ending"), the relegation of much of the physical action to offstage, and the distribution of the number and elaborateness of arias in accordance with the prestige of the singers and the prominence of their parts.

That Achilla and Tolomeo die violently on stage is a jolting of convention, however (as ordinary as it may seem to modern audiences), and so is the omission of a third section of the overture in order to go directly into the opera's opening chorus of triumph. They are relatively minor aberrations, however.

A departure from convention that is far more important is Handel's extension of a scene—normally simply some recitative and the exit aria occasioned by it—to include a complex of feelings and musical styles. The Parnassus Scene, for example, threads recitativo secco into separate movements of orchestral music and a da capo aria, extending the scene across independent sections that are themselves interconnected with related rhythmic units and orchestral timbres.

Cesare's survival of his desperate swim across the harbor (No. 33, "Dall' ondoso periglio" ["From the perilous waters"]) is wonderful by any standard; within the practice of opera seria musical form and dramatic construction, it is astonishing. Upper strings are answered smoothly by the lower strings, the smooth parallel thirds of both suggesting the quiet flow of both wave and breeze (Example GC-2a). After Cesare comments with relief on his escape, string fanfares suddenly punctuate his sense of personal loss at the death of his loyal soldiers, then meld into a dissonant chord that underscores his sense of isolation in the desert (measures 1–5 of Example GC-2b). Then comes another nonconventional stroke: Cesare calls to the breezes with but two notes, slow and unaccompanied,[16] at which point the string figure of the scene's first measure returns as accompaniment to a gracious aria (at the *andante* of Example GC-2b) in which he asks the Nile breezes to bring him solace. Aria and recitative have become one.

Even having reached the aria, however, Handel stretches the convention still further: melodic and rhythmic flow decay as a sign of Cesare's despair for Cleopatra's welfare (first part of Example GC-2c), and,when his mind turns once again to his lost companions and military defeat, the traditional return to the opening is delayed by the intrusion of recitative and a recall of the string fanfares.

That Handel was able to create highly individual characters instead of the opera seria's abstract idealizations is yet another departure from the tra-

---

[15] This would usually result in some awkward staging problems if one of the characters needed to round off a mixed voice ensemble should have the misfortune of having been killed off prior to a choral episode. In such a case, the singer would presumably sing his or her part from behind the scenery. In *Giulio Cesare* the problem is not as pressing, since Curio survives to cover the bass part and the loss of Tolomeo's alto voice is more than covered by the survival of Nireno, Cornelia, and Cesare, all altos. The score indicates, however, that the final chorus was sung by every singer of the cast, dead or alive.

[16] Perhaps Handel expected that a cadenza would be interpolated at this point. To my modern ears, the two unadorned pitches are sublime; but then, tasteful ornamentation is no less so.

EXAMPLE GC-2 ACT III, SCENE IV: NO. 33, "DALL' ONDOSO
PERIGLIO" ("FROM THE PERILOUS WATERS")—CESARE, HAVING
SURVIVED THE SURPRISE ATTACK OF TOLOMEO'S RUFFIANS AND
HAVING ESCAPED BY SWIMMING ALEXANDRIA'S HARBOR, NOTES
THE APPARENT HOPELESSNESS OF HIS SITUATION; HE IMPLORES
THE WINDS TO BECOME FAVORABLE AND TO TELL HIM OF THE
FATE OF HIS BELOVED

a) String introduction suggesting the ebb and flow of wave and breeze.

ditions of the genre, as is the freedom of the action from a complexity of sub-
plots, sudden disclosures of long-ago events, and hidden identities (although
Cleopatra's disguise as Lidia is certainly within that mold).

Of course, as with any great opera, the gorgeousness of *Giulio Cesare*'s
music is itself perhaps the most significant departure from the conventional.

The Historical Background of the Plot

Julius Caesar (100–44 B.C.E.), conqueror of Gaul and Britain, was ordered
by the Senate to leave his armies and return to Rome to face various
charges, most of them drummed up by fear and jealousy among a Roman
aristocracy riddled with corruption and misconduct. When Caesar instead
crossed the magic boundary of the Rubicon River with his army, the Senate
called upon Gnaeus Pompey (106–48 B.C.E.) to lead armies against him.
Pompey's forces were in the East; Caesar pursued him there, crushing him
in defeat at the Battle of Pharsala, Greece, in 48 B.C.E. Caesar pursued
Pompey to Egypt, where Pompey was murdered by Cleopatra's father,
Ptolemy XII. Caesar's subsequent affair with Cleopatra needs no detailing
here, given the fact that writers from Shakespeare to Shaw, not to mention
some of our most celebrated cinematic and stage performers, have dealt
handsomely with the topic.

b) Transition to the aria, with the strings' introduction (see Example GC-4a) becoming its ritornello.

EXAMPLE GC-2. (*Continued*)

c) Decay of melody and rhythm and passage of recitative before the return of
the aria's first section.

Haym's libretto plays freely with history. Tolomeo, Cleopatra's younger
brother, is the treacherous slayer of Pompeo. All the characters are youthful,
a feature purveyed by Handel's music as much as anything the words say,
even though the real Caesar was in his fifties during his sojourn by the Nile;
Cleopatra (69–30 B.C.E.) was but twenty-one, and her brother Ptolemy XIII
(63–47 B.C.E.) fifteen—his behavior in the opera gives all teenagers a bad
name.

Cornelia is apparently a delight to behold, for Cesare's aide-de-camp
Curio has loved her for a long time (in Act I he proposes to take Pompey's

EXAMPLE GC-2 *(Continued)*

c) *(Continued)*

place as her husband) and both Tolomeo (fifteen years old!) and Achilla are eager to bed her. The historical Cornelia had been married to Pompey for only four years and, in keeping with the practices of the time, may have been only sixteen when she was wed. That, however, would make it awkward for her to be the mother of Sesto, who must be at least twelve but no more than in his early teens (Cornelia expresses pride that her son even thinks of bearing arms). The historical Sextus, aged twenty-seven in 48 B.C.E., was actually Cornelia's stepson, his mother having been Pompey's third wife. It is better just to go along with Haym and not quibble on this.

The events of the opera are relatively close to the known events of Caesar's Egyptian adventure, save for Cesare's first recitative, where he says "Curio, Cesare venne, e vide e vinse" ("Curius, Caesar came, and saw, and conquered"). History has it that Caesar sent his message "veni, vidi, vici" ("I came, I saw, I conquered") in a letter to the Roman Senate a year later, after winning the battle of Zela.

THE PLOT AND ITS MUSIC

NOTE: In the account below, all recitatives are secco unless identified otherwise. Any performance and recording of this opera will include extensive ornamentations provided (appropriately and necessarily) by the singers and players, especially in sections that are repetitions. The comments that follow refer only to the music as notated. Basso continuo is present in all orchestrally accompanied passages as well as in the recitativo secco. "Bass" refers to a bass line given to cellos, with a double bass or two doubling at the octave. "DC" refers to an aria that returns to its beginning (da capo) after a contrasting middle section; "DS" to a return that skips the repeat of an orchestral introduction and begins anew at an identified place (thus dal segno).

OVERTURE *The first section is in a relatively slow tempo, its chordal texture and dotted rhythm providing a sense of grandeur; a blistering fugue is the substance of the second section. The repeated notes of the fugue subject will inform Cesare's call to arms (No. 25, Al lampo dell' armi) in Act II; the rapidly descending scales and dotted rhythms are also military in character.*[17]

Act I

SCENE I

An Egyptian landscape, with Cesare, Curio, and soldiers crossing an ancient bridge over a branch of the Nile River.

1 CHORUS (Egyptian people) *Viva, viva il nostro Alcide* ("Hail, our Alcides")[18] Cesare has conquered the forces of Pompeo, and the Egyptian populace greet him enthusiastically.

---

[17] This overture is in the pattern standardized by Lully and identified ever since as the French overture. Most of Handel's oratorio and opera overtures are constructed this way, regardless of their subject matter, so the piece may seem to be generic rather than descriptive. On the other hand, a repeated-note fugue subject is found in the overtures of such works as *Judas Maccabaeus* (1747) and *Jephtha* (1752), both of which have combat as the background to their opening scenes. It is tempting, therefore, to describe this overture as an orchestral description of the battle that has taken place before the rise of the curtain for Act I.

[18] In his search for the apples of the Hesperides, Alcides (aka Herakles) came to Egypt, where the cruel king Busiris annually sacrificed a stranger to Zeus. Alcides slew Busiris and freed the Egyptians from his yoke, hence the allusion to Cesare as Alcides and as a liberator rather than conqueror.

Handel, *Giulio Cesare* (1724), Act I, scene 1: Cesare's (Huguette Tourangeau) triumphant arrival in Egypt. Hamburg State Opera, 1969: production by Ming Cho Lee. Courtesy *Opera News,* Metropolitan Opera Guild. Photo Elisabeth Speidel.

The reedy sound of oboes, graceful triple time, and a dance-like dotted rhythm capture the swaying of the Nile's reeds and the waving of palm leaves, all evocative of a European composer's musical concept of the Egyptian. The addition of four French horns adds mellowness and festivity. Handel worked creatively within the conventions of the opera seria overture by substituting this choral minuet for the expected instrumental one.

2 ARIOSO (Cesare) *Presti omai l'Egizia terra / le sue palme al vincitor* ("Let the Egyptian nation now present its palms to the victor") Cesare delights in his triumph, expecting and enjoying the plaudits of the crowd.[19]

Cesare's firm rising triad and vigorous 4/4 time are in marked contrast to the preceding chorus. His greeting and self-pride are angular and, compared with the grace of the Egyptians' music, rather coarse.[20] His melismas on palme *("palms") are rhythmically driving, as befits a man of action who has little patience with the fussy etiquette of the Egyptian court.*

RECITATIVE (Cesare, Curio) *Curio, Cesare venne e vide e vinse* ("Curio, Caesar came, and saw, and conquered). Cesare and Curio comment briefly on the completeness of their triumph, noting that Pompeo apparently is seeking aid from the Egyptian king.

---

[19] Although there was probably a goodly array of extras on Handel's stage for this opening scene, it should be remembered that Handel's operatic choruses were "crowds" in imagination only, the parts being sung by the soloists of the cast; those recently deceased in the story sang from offstage or from a spot hidden by scenery.

[20] Strauss's Salome describes the Romans attending Herodes's fete as "brutal, ungeschlacht" (brutal, coarse) and their speech as "plumpe Sprache" ("uncouth jargon").

Handel, *Giulio Cesare,* Act I, scene ii: Cesare (Axel Köhler) is horrified when Achillas (Michael Nelle, kneeling) shows him the head of Pompey. Cornelia (Claudia Rüggeber) and Sesto (Susanne Blattert) are distraught, as Curio (Joachim Maass-Geiger) observes. Aalto Musiktheater Essen, 1996: set design by Nicholas Broadhurst, costumes by Simon Higlett. Photo Majer-Finkes, Dortmund.

SCENE II

RECITATIVE (Cesare, Curio, Cornelia, Sesto) *Questa è Cornelia* ("This is Cornelia") Seeing Cornelia and Sesto approaching, Curio remembers his former love for her. In response to Cornelia's plea for peace, Cesare offers Pompeo forgiveness and brotherhood.

SCENE III

RECITATIVE (Achilla and the above) *La reggia Tolomeo t'offre in albergo* ("Tolomeo offers you his palace as residence") Arriving with a retinue bearing gifts of gold, Achilla brings a message of hospitality and submission from Tolomeo. One of the Egyptians uncovers a charger, revealing on it the head of Pompeo. As Cornelia faints in shock, Curio goes to her with words and thoughts of affection for her, and Achilla is struck with her beauty. Outraged and in tears, Cesare orders Pompeo's head to be given appropriate internment in an urn, then, vowing to enter the palace that very day, sends Achilla back to Tolomeo with a message of contempt and anger.

3 ARIA DC (Cesare) *Empio, dirò tu sei* ("I say you are a villain") Cesare's message is that Tolomeo should not dare to show his face and that one with the heart of a king does not behave with such cruelty. Cesare and Achilla leave separately with their attendants.

Boiling rage is the spirit of plummeting scales, fast tempo, minor mode, open orchestration (violins and bass), repeated notes (empio, dirò, tu sei—"I say you are a miscreant"); the melismas on crudeltà *("cruelty") are compressed in range and thus indicate tight-lipped fury.*

SCENE IV

RECITATIVE (Curio, Sesto, Cornelia) *Già torna in sè* ("She is recovering now") Cornelia, reviving from her collapse, snatches Sesto's sword from his side to commit suicide, but Curio prevents her and offers himself as a successor husband who will avenge her wrong. At her angry rejection Curio exits, promising not to harm her. Sesto despairs at their loss.

4 ARIA DC (Cornelia) *Priva son d'ogni conforto* ("I am deprived of every solace") Bereft of all comfort, Cornelia wishes to die, exiting the scene mournfully.

The usual formal introduction of the aria is omitted, as Cornelia's grief cannot be held back. The aria's rhythms and melodic contours are simple and dignified. The flute, which at times doubles the violins and at others offers its own voice, is a symbol of melancholy. The vocal line's frequent rests on the first beat of a measure and an instrumental trill on the weak beat at the end of the first section are subtle but effective weakenings of the rhythmic movement of the piece and thus contribute to the mood of deep sadness.

RECITATIVE (Sesto) *Vanni sono i lamenti* ("Lamentations are useless") Sesto determines to avenge the death of his father.

5 ARIA DC (Sesto) *Svegliatevi nel core / furie d'un alma offesa* ("Rise up in my heart the furies of an offended soul") Sesto calls on the Furies of his dead father's soul to come to his defense and inspire him to merciless revenge. He exits quickly.

Sesto's naive courage is set out in the fast tempo and orchestration of bustling unison violins over a somewhat echoing bass line. The middle section, however, suggests a depth of character that is endearing musically as well as textually, for the tempo is an unexpected largo, *and it is given the sound of harmonizing recorders that suggest youth and innocence.*

SCENE V

A room in the palace. Cleopatra with attendants, then Tolemeo with guards.

RECITATIVE (Cleopatra, Nireno, Tolemeo) *Regni Cleopatra ed al mio seggio intorno / popolo adorator arabo e siro / sù questo crin la sacra benda adori* ("Let Cleopatra rule and around my throne let all the peoples of Arabia and Syria adore me and bow before my sacred crown") Nireno interrupts Cleopatra's preening before her attendants to tell her of the beheading of Pompeo and of the sending of Pompeo's head to Cesare. Cleopatra, horrified, dismisses all but Nireno, resolving to go to Cesare and persuade him to suport her cause against Tolemeo.

Accompanied by a retinue of guards, Tolemeo enters and challenges Cleopatra's daring to claim the throne, sneering that she should do a woman's work instead of seeking to reign. Cleopatra meets sneer with sneer, suggesting that Tolemeo would do better in his harem than in the throne room.

6 ARIA DC (Cleopatra) *Non disperar; chi sa? / se al regno non l'avrai, / avrai sorte in amor* ("Despair not, for who knows? If you cannot rule, you will have good fortune in love") Cleopatra disdains Tolemeo's power to reign and urges him to capitalize on his good looks by pleasuring himself with sexual entertainment. She exits, followed by Nireno.

A quicksilver but driving and ornamented violin passage establishes a mood of chin-up defiance and sarcasm (Ex. GC-5a), as do her brittle melismas on amor *and* consolar *("to console" [your heart]).*

SCENE VI

RECITATIVE (Tolomeo, Achilla) *Sire, Signor!* ("Sire, Lord!") Achilla enters to narrate the story of Cesare's reception of the gift of Pompeo's head and that Cesare has accused Tolomeo of incompetence and rashness.[21] Achilla advises Tolomeo to deal with Cesare as he had dealt with Pompeo and promises to do the dirty deed himself if Tolomeo will give him Cornelia as reward. Tolomeo agrees; dismissing Achilla to make the necessary plans, Tolomeo relishes the thought of securing his kingdom by killing Cesare.

7 ARIA DC (Tolomeo) *L'empio, sleale, indegno,/ vorria rapirmi il regno* ("Infidel, traitor, miscreant, who would steal my kingdom from me") Fearing Cesare's ambition, Tolomeo vows to destroy him.

Pompous indignation comes through the jagged intervals of the voice line and interrupted rhythmic groups of the orchestra; even the melisma on disturbar *("to disturb") is awkwardly disjunct as if to suggest Tolomeo's perturbation. Repeated notes and scales tumble about in the bass line. A slower passage briefly underscores Tolomeo's reference to his peace of mind (*la pace mia). *In the B section, the orchestra accompanies Tolomeo's eagerness to have Cesare die, using the music of the A section, while Tolomeo moves into a more chromatic melisma for* cor *([Cesare's avaricious] "heart") to suggest his own growing irritation and petulance.*

SCENE VII

Cesare's military encampment in a grove of trees; in the center, atop a mound of trophies of war, is an urn holding Pompeo's ashes.

8 ACCOMPANIED RECITATIVE (Cesare) *Alma del gran Pompeo / che al cener suo d'intorno / invisibil t'aggiri* ("Soul of great Pompey, hovering invisibly above your ashes") Cesare muses on the transitory nature of glory, noting that a man's beginning is but earth (*il principio è di terra*), his ending is a stone (*il fine è un sasso*), he is formed with a sigh (*un soffio*), and is destroyed by a breath (*un fiato*).

(See Exs. 6.4a and b) Beginning in a minor harmony jarringly at odds with the major tonality of Tolomeo's outburst, the dotted-rhythm strings provide a dirge-like introduction and a mood of brooding and introspection. The continually unexpected chords of the recitative suggest the transitory and unpredictable nature of life, and each set of words is given an interval or a melodic inflection that responds to its meaning: grandezza *("grandeur"), for example, is given a rising sixth;* un mondo in guerra *("a world at war") is given a sudden turn to the minor, as is the feebleness of life (*quanto è fral tuo stato); *and a rising chromatic phrase illustrates the final words,* ti distrugge un fiato *("a breath destroys you").*

RECITATIVE (Curio, Cesare, Cleopatra) *Qui nobile donzella / chiede chinarsi al Cesare di Roma* ("A noble lady seeks to kneel to the Roman Caesar") Curio announces the arrival of a lovely lady who seeks to pay homage. She is Cleopatra disguised as Lidia, a noble woman whose fortune has been stolen by Tolomeo. She kneels before Cesare and weeps. Both Cesare and Curio are utterly taken with her beauty. Cesare raises her to her feet and promises to assist her.

9 ARIA DS (Cesare) *Non è si vago e bello / il fior nel prato, / quant' è vago e gentile / il tuo bel volto* ("The flower in the meadow is not as charming and beautiful as the loveliness and sweetness of your face") Cesare is hooked, sighing that "all of a fair April is gathered in you" (*tutto un vago Aprile / è in te raccolto*) Cesare leaves with Curio.

---

[21] In the Age of Reason, rashness was one of the least desirable attributes for a ruler.

Cesare as lover sings this pretty song that is all melody (violins doubling the voice) over a lightly stepping bass line. Ornamentations are brief, with only vago ("pretty") given any real extension. The middle section is accompanied by continuo only, suggesting the delicacy of April's flowers.

RECITATIVE (Nireno, Cleopatra) *Cleopatra, vincesti* ("Cleopatra, you've won") Adding to Nireno's assurance that Cesare has been beguiled totally, Cleopatra is confident that she will conquer Tolomeo because the god of love has given her the power she needs.

10 ARIA DC (Cleopatra) *Tutto può donna vezzosa* ("A pretty woman can do every-thing") Cleopatra rejoices in the power given her by her beauty and sexual attractiveness.

This is another pretty song that serves as a companion to Cesare's Non è si vago, but Cleopatra's delight in the power of her beauty is musically more subtle than Cesare's expression of rapture, just as her motivations and plans are. The longer phrases that describe how a woman will amorously part her lips (s'amorosa scioglie il labbro) and gaze provocatively (gira il guardo, lit. "turn her look") are supple in their rhythmic twists and syncopations and quite different from her coy repetitions of tutto ("everything"). A sprightly oboe pipes along with equally sprightly violins, in keeping with her kittenish mood.

RECITATIVE (Nireno, Cleopatra) *Ferma, Cleopatra, osserva* ("Wait, Cleopatra, observe") Cleopatra is about to retire from the scene when Nireno observes the arrival of a weeping woman. Noting that the woman seems to be of lofty station, Cleopatra remains aside, to watch without being seen.

SCENE VIII

11 ARIOSO (Cornelia) *Nel tuo seno amico sasso, / stà sepolto il mio tesoro* ("Within thy bosom, friendly urn, is interred my treasure") Cornelia expresses her sense of loss.

A descending dotted scale in empty octaves makes the somber introduction throb with the anguish of Cornelia's heart; her first words are unaccompanied, the sound thus resonating with the introduction to suggest the hollowness of her life. As her thoughts progress, the first violin line plies its song mournfully and dissonantly against the other strings, just as Cornelia must make her way unhappily through the world.

RECITATIVE (Cornelia, Cleopatra, Sesto) *Ma che! Vile e negletta / sempre starai, Cornelia?* ("But what then! Will you remain always lowly and despised, Cornelia?") As Cleopatra muses that this may be Pompeo's wife, Cornelia grasps a sword from the pile of war trophies and vows to wreak vengeance on Tolomeo. Sesto enters quickly and takes the sword from her, claiming that he is the prop-er agent of retribution and vowing to bring it about. Cornelia expresses pride at her young son's strength of purpose and courage. When Sesto wonders how to find his way to the palace, Cleopatra steps forward impetuously; heeding Nireno's caution, she retains her identity as Lidia, promising that Cleopatra will comfort and reward them when she gains the throne. Cleopatra identifies Nireno as their guide. Sesto's heart is filled with the hope and satisfaction of humbling the tyrant Tolomeo.

12 ARIA DS (Sesto) *Cara speme questo core / tu cominci a lusingar* ("Dear hope, you begin to entice my heart") Sesto feels growing confidence that their fortunes will turn and that heaven will look well on his quest for revenge. All exit save Cleopatra.

Accompanied only by basso continuo, Sesto's aria seems as empty in its own way as his moth-er's. The bass line is hesitant and rhythmically complex, appropriate to a sense of hope that is tenuous at best. Lusingar ("to entice" or "flatter") is the only word treated melismatically, and it is significant that it has the same uncertainty as the bass line.

RECITATIVE (Cleopatra) *Vegli pure il germano / alla propria salvezza* ("Look well, my brother, to your own protection") Cleopatra is pleased that the forces of Cesare have now been joined by Pompeo's widow and son.

13 ARIA DS (Cleopatra) *Tu la mia stella sei, / amabile speranza* ("You are my star, kind hope") Cleopatra feels renewed confidence that all her hopes will be ful-filled and that the power of love will triumph. She exits.

This is another buoyant tune for Cleopatra, luxuriant in melodic turns (Ex. GC-5b) and melismas (on grato—*"pleasant"), all swaying in a confident siciliano²² style (in 6/8) appro-priate to a person who is certain that her future is golden.*

SCENE IX

A formal audience chamber in the palace of Tolomeo. Tolomeo enters with his attendants led by Achilla; entering from another side is Cesare, with Roman attendants.

RECITATIVE (Tolomeo, Cesare, Achilla) *Cesare, alla tua destra / stende fasci di scettri / generosa la sorte* ("Caesar, in your right hand destiny has generously placed a clus-ter of sceptres") The two rulers exchange formal greetings of elaborate praise, but their mutual distaste for each other is muttered in venomous asides. Tolomeo offers Cesare lavish apartments as his residence.

14 ARIA DC (Cesare) *Va tacito e nascosto, / quand' avido è di preda, / l'astuto cacciator* ("The knowing hunter moves quietly and stealthily when he is avid for his prey") Suspicious of Tolomeo's penchant for deviousness, Cesare notes to himself that, like a hunter stalking his prey, an evil man does not want his treachery to be evi-dent. Cesare leaves the hall with his adherents.

The only moment in all of Handel's operas that employs a solo French horn obbligato, this "metaphor aria"²³ moves quietly along but in a very steady flow. The melisma on cacciator *("huntsman") evokes the sound of horn calls because of its partly triadic character and one moment of a dotted rhythm (both invite the archetype of fanfare), but the melodic line as a whole is scalar and thus allows for a smoothness suggestive of stealth.*

SCENE X

RECITATIVE (Achilla, Tolomeo, Cornelia, Sesto) *Sire, con Sesto il figlio / questa è Cornelia* ("Sire, this is Cornelia with Sesto her son") Cornelia and Sesto are led in and promptly indict Tolomeo for his crime. Tolomeo orders both to be imprisoned but, at Achilla's remonstrance, sends only Sesto to the dungeon and orders Cornelia to be put to labor in the garden of his harem. Tolomeo promises

---

²² A graceful, slow dance in 6/8 or 12/8 time, with simple harmonies, flowing melody, and lilting rhythm. Its tenderness made it especially favored in seventeenth- and eighteenth-century opera as symbolic of pastoral situations or poignant moods.

²³ A term applied to an aria (also called a "simile aria") in which a character uses text and appropriately descriptive music to compare his/her mood and situation to an aspect of nature. Other examples in this opera are Nos. 18 ("Se in fiorito"), 23 ("L'angue offeso"), 34 ("Quel torrente"), and 37 ("Da tempeste").

Achilla that Cornelia shall be his; but he sneers in an aside that Achilla is deluding himself.

SCENE XI

RECITATIVE (Achilla, Cornelia, Sesto) *Cornelia, in quei tuoi lumi / stà legato il mio cor* ("Cornelia, in your eyes my heart stands enchained") When Achilla proposes to help them escape if Cornelia marries him, Cornelia angrily rejects him as a barbarian who could not dare to marry a Roman. Achilla orders Sesto to be taken away to prison but insists that Cornelia remain, warning her that her prayers for deliverance will be unanswered unless she submits to his ardor.

15 ARIA DC (Achilla) *Tu sei il cor di questo core* ("You are the heart of my heart") Achilla protests his love for Cornelia, then leaves her alone with her son.

Abrupt and sharply accented two-note groups at the end of each phrase of the orchestral introduction and throughout the aria give the lie to this vile person's expression of affection. The use of bassoons to double the voice part reinforces the bass timbre of Achilla's role and thus helps separate him musically from the other characters. We have seen emptiness of spirit earlier in the work; here the openness between violins and bass line indicate emptiness of soul as well.

RECITATIVE (Sesto, Cornelia) *Madre! Mia vita!* ("Mother! My life!") Cornelia runs to embrace her son, but the guards separate them. Their words of farewell are brief.

16 DUET DS (Cornelia, Sesto) *Son nata a lagrimar* ("I was born to weep") Mother and son lament their tragic destiny, expecting never again to enjoy happiness.

This tender siciliano movement ends Act I in a most touching way. The descending two-note groups and the gently arching flow of the melodic phrases (Ex. GC-4c) inflect both instruments and voices with poignancy and despondency; the exchange of single-note sobs on "ah" point up the wrenching heartbreak of the separation and imprisonment; the long-short rhythmic pattern of the bass is sorrowful and unrelenting. The desolation that faces them is given a subtle stress when the chord-providing harpsichord is silenced at the entry of the voices. The da capo is also subtly expressive, for the instrumental passage (the ritornello) that begins it is shortened, thus compressing its emotional impact.

Act II
SCENE I

A lovely grove of cedars, amidst which is a construction representing Mount Parnassus, the Palace of Virtue on its slopes.

RECITATIVE (Cleopatra, Nireno) *Eseguisti, o Niren, quanto t'imposi?* ("Have you completed all that I ordered you to do, Nireno?") To Cleopatra's questions, Nireno answers that all has been arranged and that Cesare is even now approaching. Cleopatra tells him that she plans to make him a prisoner of love (*prigionier d'amor*); Nireno is to lead Cesare into the grove to observe the spectacle she has planned, then he is to take him to her chambers, telling him that "Lidia" will meet him there before sunset in order to reveal Tolomeo's plots against him. She departs.

SCENE II

RECITATIVE (Nireno alone, then with Cesare) *Da Cleopatra apprenda / chi è seguace d'amor l'astuzie e frodi* ("From Cleopatra the follower of love will learn about artifice and deceit") Nireno plans to carry out Cleopatra's orders. Cesare arrives eagerly, Nireno promising that Lidia will appear in a moment.

SINFONIA[24] and RECITATIVE (Cesare, Nireno) *Cieli! e qual delle sfere / scende armonico suon, che mi rapisce?* ("Heavens, from which of the spheres descends this harmony that enraptures me so?") Sweet music is heard offstage. Cesare is struck with its beauty. A second SINFONIA accompanies the opening of the Parnassus construction to reveal Virtue (Cleopatra in costume) on her throne, surrounded by the nine Muses. Cesare is stunned.

Oboe, viola da gamba, harp, theorbo, and basses offer a sweet and gentle dotted-rhythm melody, punctuated by secco gasps from Cesare and Nireno. As the stage flats open to reveal the tableau of Virtue and the Nine Muses, the rhythmic flow intensifies; when the pit orchestra joins in, the richness of sound is sublime. Considering the contrast of this music with the secco response of Cesare, it is clear that he has been confronted with a wondrous magic indeed.

17 ARIA DC (Cleopatra) WITH BRIEF PASSAGE OF RECITATIVE (Cesare) *V'adoro, pupille, / saette d'amore* ("I adore you, eyes, darts of love") Cleopatra sings of love directly to Cesare; he sighs that not even heaven can sing so sweetly.

A quite simple melody with delicate coloration of the full ensemble, the violins now muted. The phrases at first are short, as if hesitant and shy; Cleopatra knows how to work her wiles indeed. The middle section is yet another part of Cleopatra's plan, for "Lidia's" grief is given special effectiveness: its rhythmic motion is gracious and flowing, orchestration is reduced (presumably this is more sincere), the minor mode colors the harmonies and melodies, and choking sobs are suggested by separated note groups. The interpolation of recitativo secco by Cesare before the da capo is unexpected and again points up how he is at the mercy of this staged enchantment.

RECITATIVE (Cesare) *Vola, vola mio cor* ("Fly, fly my heart") Cesare runs toward Cleopatra, but the set closes and the grove appears as before. He admits to Nireno that he is completely enchanted with Lidia. Nireno informs him that Lidia awaits him and will take him to Cleopatra. Cesare demands to be led there at once.

18 ARIA DC (Cesare) *Se in fiorito ameno prato / l'augellin tra fiori e fronde / si nasconde* ("If in the lovely flowered meadow, a little bird hides itself among blossoms and leaves") Cesare compares the unseen instruments and the disappearance of Lidia to the sound of a bird who is all the more entrancing when it is heard but not seen. Nireno leads him off to Cleopatra's quarters.

A violin solo (without continuo) provides the necessary bird calls; bass pedal points suggest the drone of bagpipes and thus a rural setting. There is some back-and-forth between voice and violin, as if the speaker were engaging in a duo with the unseen singer. The melisma on grato *serves the same purpose as it had in Cleopatra's No. 13, but here it has the added pleasure of bird-evoking trills and carols (Ex. 2.2b). Passages in parallel thirds and the mellowness of divided bassoons contribute further to the metaphorical allusions of Cesare's thoughts.*

SCENE III

The garden in the harem of Tolomeo's palace, where Cornelia is working with a small hoe. On the other side of the wall is the palace zoo, where wild animals roam.

---

[24] A generic term for an orchestral composition (of any length) without voices. The present case is exceptional, because snippets of astonishment from both Cesare and Nireno are declaimed during it.

19 ARIOSO (Cornelia) *Deh, piangete, o mesti lumi* ("Alas, weep, oh my sad eyes") Cornelia, now a slave condemned to hard toil in the garden of the seraglio, sees no hope, only sadness.

The use of basso continuo as the only accompanying element contributes to yet another of Cornelia's moments of spiritual dejection. The minor mode, spare instrumentation, halting descent of each phrase of the bass line, and one-note-per-syllable setting of Cornelia's text seem especially strong in emotional weight because they come immediately after the mellow instrumentation and pastoral pleasures of Cesare's lavish major-mode song of the little bird.

RECITATIVE (Achilla, Cornelia) *Bella, non lacrimare!* ("Beautiful woman, weep not!") Achilla presses his suit; despising him, Cornelia turns to leave.

SCENE IV

RECITATIVE (Tolomeo, Cornelia, Achilla) *Bella, placa lo sdegno!* ("Fair one, calm your anger!") Cornelia's departure is halted by the arrival of Tolomeo, who takes her hand. He pretends to further Achilla's cause; drawing Achilla aside, he learns that Achilla plans to slay Cesare this very day. Tolomeo hypocritically sends Achilla on his murderous path, promising him his reward but noting aside that Achilla is mad if he believes Tolomeo will keep his word.

20 ARIA DS (Achilla) *Se a me non sei crudele, / ogni sarà fidele / a te questo mio cor* ("If you were not so cruel to me, this heart would be forever faithful to you") Achilla again pleads his suit.

Achilla's clumsy villainy is at work again: angular dotted rhythms, a broken melisma on cor *("heart") and an ungainly one on* fidel *("faithful"), and the large gap between unison violins and lumpy bass line suggest that Achilla is not the most gracious of wooers.*

RECITATIVE (Tolomeo, Cornelia) *Bella, cotanto aborri / chi ti prega d'amar?* ("Beautiful one, do you abhor so much one who proffers love to you?") At first seeming to further Achilla's cause, Tolomeo places his hand on her breast and presses his own lust upon Cornelia, who violently rejects him and exits in high dudgeon. Tolomeo vows to use force to take her virtue from her.

21 ARIA DS (Tolomeo) *Sì, spietata, il tuo rigore / sveglia l'odio in questo sen* ("Aye, merciless one, your unbending rouses hatred in my breast") He leaves determinedly.

Out of context, this aria might seem to be one of boisterous gaiety. Snapping two-note groups offer some of the same grossness of spirit found in Achilla's No. 15, but Tolomeo has a veneer of aristocratic bearing implied by the flowing triplets of his aria, even though he is patently insincere and superficial. Expressing blatant resentment of Cornelia's hatred (with its expected melisma on odio—*"hatred"), Tolomeo comes across as distinctly unpleasant and not to be trusted.*

SCENE V

RECITATIVE (Cornelia, Sesto) *Sù, che si tarda?* ("Now then, why delay?") Cornelia returns. She is convinced that suicide is her only recourse but is prevented from jumping into the adjoining lair of wild beasts by the sudden arrival of Sesto, freed secretly from his cell by Nireno. He shrugs aside her concern for his life; he must live for as long as it takes to kill Tolomeo.

SCENE VI

RECITATIVE (Nireno, Sesto, Cornelia) *Cornelia, infauste nove* ("Cornelia, ill-starred news") Telling them that Tolomeo has ordered Cornelia to become one of his concubines, Nireno suggests that he help Sesto to hide in the seraglio, where Sesto will find the opportunity to kill an unsuspecting and defenseless Tolomeo. Mother and son agree gratefully.

22 ARIA DS (Cornelia) *Cessa omai di sospirare!* ("Cease now your sighing!") Cornelia feels hope returning, for heaven is not always angry. She compares herself to the steersman of a vessel, who never abandons hope even amid the tempest at sea. She departs with Nireno.

> *Finally, Cornelia is given music with emotional life: the 3/8 meter and alternating snippets of violin and recorder coloration (Ex. GC-4a) suggest a breath of hope, but the changing dynamics and timbres also suggest some uncertainty as to whether or not triumph will eventually be hers. Vendetta gets its due in trilled runs that are more tuneful than violent; it is a subtle characterization that separates her from the angry outbursts of her son. The simile of the middle section is in the same vein—the raging sea is not found in her music, only the lightness of spirit offered by hope.*

RECITATIVE (Sesto) *Figlio non è, chi vendicar non cura / del genitor lo scempio* ("There is not a son who is not devoted to avenging the murder of his father") Sesto summons his courage for the task before him.

23 ARIA DS (Sesto) *L'angue offeso mai riposa / se il veleno pria non spande / dentro il sangue all' offensor* ("The offended serpent will not rest until its venom is spread through the blood of the offender") Sesto likens himself to a serpent that has been stepped on and writhes with anger while it seeks to punish the transgressor. He heads off toward the harem quarters of the palace.

> *A moderate tempo controls a spirited bass line that steps vigorously under a full complement of strings. The result of the rhythmic vigor and melodic independence of the vocal line is that Sesto seems more mature here and less impetuous, even though the sentiments are not unlike those given him earlier. The spread of the snake venom at the heart of his simile finds voice in the long run of notes for* spande *("spreads"). The middle section begins with reduced instrumentation, as suggested by the text's reference to the need for cunning; it ends on a dramatically dissonant chord when he pauses at the thought of Tolomeo's* empio cor *("impious heart") before returning to the first section of the aria.*

SCENE VII

A garden.

RECITATIVE (Cleopatra) *Esser qui deve in breve / l'idolo del mio sen* ("Surely the idol of my breast will be here soon") Now in love with Cesare, Cleopatra eagerly awaits his coming. She determines to test his devotion.

24 ARIA DC (Cleopatra) *Venere bella, / per un istante, / deh, mi concedi / le grazie tutte / del dio d'amor!* ("Fair Venus, for just a moment grant me all the graces of the God of Love!") She prays to Venus that the god of love will aid her and that her beauty will inspire passion in Cesare's heart. She feigns sleep.

> *Cleopatra is in a semi-confident mood, trusting that Venus will eventually come to her aid but not yet certain that Cesare is hooked. A lively 3/8 meter with playful violin echoes and punctuations reflect her optimism; the theme of the aria is, of course,* amor, *hence the extended attention given to that word and its relative* amante *("loving" [to be inspired in Cesare's royal heart]).*

RECITATIVE (Cesare, Cleopatra) *Che veggio, oh numi?* ("What do I see, oh gods?") Cesare, as usual, is smitten with her beauty and speaks aloud his wish that she might feel the same toward him as he does toward her and might wish to become his wife. Cleopatra takes the cue and quickly rises, confessing her love for him. Cesare, still believing her to be "Lidia," draws back, warning her that a person of her station could not aspire to a marriage with a person of his stature. Cleopatra responds with injured dignity, vowing to return to her sleep, since that apparently is the only way Cesare is inspired to love her.

SCENE VIII

RECITATIVE (Curio, Cesare, Cleopatra) *Cesare, sei tradito* ("Caesar, you are betrayed") Sword in hand, Curio rushes in to warn Cesare that he has heard murderers storming their quarters. Cesare draws his sword, preparing to stand and fight, whereupon Cleopatra, fearing for his life, begs him to stay. Vowing that *in tua difesa / sino agli stessi abissi / scenderia Cleopatra* ("in your defense even into that very abyss Cleopatra will descend"), she inadvertently reveals her true identity. Cesare is, of course, astonished. Cleopatra hastens off to defy the intruders herself but returns in panic because her royal presence has not stemmed the tide. She begs Cesare to flee.

25 ARIA DS (Cesare) *Al lampo dell' armi / quest' alma guerriera / vendetta farà* ("In the gleam of arms this warrior's soul will take revenge") Before charging into battle with Curio at his side, Cesare exults in the coming of battle and the conquering of his enemies. The cries of the approaching horde of Tolomeo's assassins are heard.

An aria di bravura, this bristles at a furious tempo, with violins depicting the frenzy of battle by repeated notes and activity across the entire staff (Ex. GC-3a); the vocal line is similarly active, its wildfire delivery of syllables and brilliantly fast melismas (armi—"arms" and farà— "will wreak" [vengeance]) appropriate to the wild stabbing and struggling of the warrior surrounded by foes. The continuance of the strings' music under the unexpected and potently brief murderers' chorus extends the aria form, heightens the drama, and stretches the conventions of opera seria.

26 ACCOMPANIED RECITATIVE (Cleopatra) *Che sento! O Dio!* ("What do I hear? Oh God!") Cleopatra at first begs for death but then vows to be warlike herself and prays that the gods protect her beloved.

There is no recitativo secco between the chorus just heard and the dissonant harmony (a diminished seventh) that sharpens the focus on Cleopatra's shock and fear. Repeated dissonances in the strings announce the clamor of battle. As the chords change mercurially, with a melodic tritone marking her move from despair to determination at the word vendicarmi *("to avenge me"), Cleopatra becomes more and more fully limned as a woman in love and willing to fight to the death for her beloved.*

27 ARIA DS (Cleopatra) *Se pietà di me non senti, / giusto ciel, io morirò* ("If you feel no pity for me, just heaven, I shall die") Cleopatra prays to the gods for mercy and relief.

Factors that make this aria a supreme moment in theatrical music: dark coloration of an independent line for bassoons (effectively laid aside while the singer's line is presented); division of the strings into three parts so that both first and second violins can give proper strength to the drooping figures of a poignant obbligato; a throbbing bass line; dissonances at io morirò ("I shall die"); a syncopation at an extended return of these words; and a beauty of melody as it is interwoven with its accompaniment that can be heard but not described adequately. (See Ex. GC-1.)

SCENE IX

A room in the harem. Tolomeo is surrounded by his favorites and other beauties of the seraglio. Cornelia is among them.

28 ARIOSO and RECITATIVE (Tolomeo, Cornelia, Sesto) *Belle dee di questo core, /
voi portate il ciel nel volto* ("Lovely goddesses of my heart, you bear heaven in your
faces") Delighting in the beauties about him, Tolomeo takes his ease. He lays his
sword aside and turns his attention to Cornelia, to whom he gives a white ker-
chief as sign that she is to come to his bed that evening. She contemptuously
throws it down.

Sesto enters suddenly; seizing Tolomeo's sword, he prepares to stab the
Egyptian king but is prevented by the timely arrival of Achilla.

*Hollow octaves in a dotted rhythm are an aggressive and pointedly crude introduction.
Tolomeo begins with genuine lyricism, but his music dissolves into recitativo secco, and thus
his flattery becomes sterile.*

Scene X

RECITATIVE (Achilla, Tolomeo, Sesto, Cornelia) *Sire, prendi!* ("My Lord, take
it!") Snatching the sword from Sesto and returning it to Tolomeo, Achilla informs
all that Cesare, seeking to flee Achilla's troops, had plunged into the waters of
the bay; both Curio and Cesare, he reports, have perished. Cleopatra, he continues, has fled to the Roman camp and is leading Cesare's soldiers toward the
palace. When Achilla demands his prize—Cornelia—Tolomeo brushes him off
and orders him out. Achilla bitterly notes that one owes no faith to the faithless.

Tolomeo leaves with his attendants to engage in battle, vowing to return victorious over Cleopatra.

Scene XI

RECITATIVE (Sesto, Cornelia) *Ecco in tutto perduta / la speme di vendetta* ("Behold,
all hope of revenge is lost") Drawing a sword, Sesto prepares his own death.[25]
Cornelia prevents this, reminding him that they have an ally in Nireno; she
urges him to go to the Roman camp by himself and challenge Tolomeo fearlessly, even though he may face death.[26] Left alone, Sesto once again vows revenge.

29 ARIA DC (Sesto) *L'aure che spira, / tiranno e fiero, / egli non mertà di respirar*
("Tyrannical and cruel, he does not deserve to breathe the air that flows") Sesto
avers that he can find rest only in Tolomeo's richly merited death.

*Oboes serve for trumpets in Sesto's call to bring the tyrant to heel; his militant attitude is given
punches of rising and falling scales. Both voice and instruments drive excitedly.*

Act III

Scene I

A wooded spot near the shore of Alexandria's harbor. Achilla is there with his troops.

RECITATIVE (Achilla) *In tal modi si premia / il mio lungo servir, la fede mia?* ("Is this
the way you reward my long service and loyalty?") Bitterly, Achilla reviles

---

[25] It is not clear where this weapon comes from, Tolomeo's sword having been taken from
him by Achilla. Perhaps one of the ladies left hers behind.

[26] This is a somewhat different Cornelia in terms of mother/son relationships. Earlier she
was somewhat pridefully tolerant of his even deigning to pick up a weapon. Now she tells
him to be ready to die. Children mature rather quickly in opera.

Tolomeo for his perfidy and calls his soldiers to join him in allegiance to Cleopatra.

30 ARIA DC (Achilla) *Dal fulgor di questa spada / vo' che cada / umiliato un empio cor* ("By this flashing blade I wish to see a contemptible soul fall in humiliation") Achilla lusts for revenge, justifying his own behavior as a defense of his country. He leads his troops toward the battle.

Unison violins bustle along and the bass line is busy in keeping with Achilla's bellicose intentions. That his most important melisma is a rising figure instead of a descending one for cada *([I wish that my enemy should] "fall") is perhaps an indication of ornament made meaningless just as Achilla's raging is futile; perhaps it is but a warlike figure meant to illustrate the text generally.*

SCENE II

SINFONIA A battle takes place between the forces of Cleopatra and Tolomeo. Tolomeo enters in triumph, Cleopatra now his prisoner.

Oboes again serve instead of trumpets; the musical expression of the passions of battle is boilerplate material for an opera of the Baroque era: bold accents in the bass and scurrying by the violins.

RECITATIVE (Tolomeo, Cleopatra) *Vinta cadesti* ("Vanquished you have fallen") Tolomeo gloats, but Cleopatra is defiant. Tolomeo angrily orders her put in chains and directs that she be taken to the palace, where she will be forced to bow in homage before his throne.

31 ARIA DS (Tolomeo) *Domerò la tua fierezza / ch'il mio trono aborre e sprezza* ("I shall humble your pride that my royalty hates and despises") Nose in the air, Tolomeo heads off to his palace, exulting in his victory and in the coming humiliation of his sister.

Elaborate posturing and strutting by Tolomeo comes from the fast tempo, staccato delivery, and wide intervals in all parts: unison violins, striding bass, and elaborate voice line. Tolomeo gives special emphasis to umiliato *("humbled") by blunt descending settings or by long-breathed melismas, as if he were rubbing Cleopatra's face in the mire.*

SCENE III

RECITATIVE (Cleopatra) *E pur così in un giorno / perdo fasti e grandezze?* ("And thus do I lose my ceremonies and greatness in a single day?") Left under guard, Cleopatra contemplates the loss of love, liberty, and hope for life.

32 ARIA DC (Cleopatra) *Piangerò la sorte mia* ("I shall weep for my fate") Expressing grief at her tragic future, she vows that her ghost will return to assail her tormentor.

As poignant and melodically beautiful as Tolomeo's previous aria is blatant and pompous, this aria gains in dimension by the plaintive sound of an accompanying flute and a syllabic and exquisitely simple first part. The angry B section is as descriptive a melisma for agiterò *("I shall torment"; Ex. 2.2a) as one could ask, its aggressive repetitions of a short motive relentless in both music and symbolism.*

SCENE IV

The shore by the harbor. Cesare enters from one side; Achilla is seen lying mortally wounded on the other side of the scene.

33 ACCOMPANIED RECITATIVE and ARIA (Cesare) *Dall' ondoso periglio / salvo mi porta al lido / il mio propizio fato . . . Aure, deh, per pietà / spirate al petto mio, / per dar conforto, o Dio! / al mio dolor* ("From the perilous waters my happy fortune has carried me to shore. . . . Breezes, ah, for mercy's sake, breathe into my breast to give comfort to my sorrow") Cesare emerges from his perilous swim across the harbor. While grateful for remaining alive, he mourns the loss of his companions and feels desperate and isolated. He calls to the winds to send fair fortune and bring him word of the fate of his beloved. Looking about him at the desert sands strewn with corpses and weapons, he senses disaster, yet again prays for a happier turn of events and for news of Cleopatra.

The music begins after Cleopatra's resignation to death without intervening recitative and at a key a half-step higher, thus abruptly moving music and mood into a plane of optimism. Upper strings alternate with lower strings in an ebb-and-flow figure that simulates both waves and zephyrs (Ex. GC-2a). Brief hints of a fanfare rhythm suggest the echoes of the combat that Cesare has barely survived. An unaccompanied measure highlights his call to the winds (aure), then the figure of Ex. GC-2a returns as accompaniment to the aria (Ex. GC-2b). With a sudden jolt into the minor mode as Cesare is reminded of the death of his soldiers and his personal defeat, accompanied recitative intrudes before the return of the aria's opening music as Cesare's thoughts dwell desperately on Cleopatra (Ex. GC-2c).

RECITATIVE (Sesto, Achilla, Cesare, Nireno) *Cerco invan Tolomeo per vendicarmi* ("Vainly do I seek Ptolemy to take my revenge") Sesto comes upon the scene, still seeking Tolomeo; Nireno recognizes the dying Achilla. Cesare overhears Achilla confess to plotting the death of Pompeo in order that he might wed Cornelia.

Revealing that he has suffered his mortal wound in the fight against Tolomeo and hoping to be avenged even in death, Achilla gives Sesto a seal that assures its holder the loyalty of a body of troops and admission to the palace by an underground passage. Sesto orders the body of Achilla to be dumped into the sea.

Cesare steps forward and takes the seal from Sesto's hand, explaining how he survived and that he will lead them all to triumph or die in the attempt.

34 ARIA DC (Cesare) *Quel torrente che cade dal monte / tutto atterra che incontro gli stà.* ("This torrent that falls from mountains sweeps down to earth everything that stands around it.") Cesare compares himself to the raging mountain torrent that sweeps away all before its path. He leaves to marshall his forces.

Another simile aria, replete with the plummeting scales and vigorous rhythms appropriate to the text. A bit of canon at the outset and frequent overlapping of vocal line and violin part are stylizations of the crashing of water against rock; the bravura run on atterra *("brings to earth") is amply descriptive of Cesare's intent to ravage his foes.*

Scene V

RECITATIVE (Sesto, Nireno) *Tutto lice sperar, Cesare vive.* ("All is hopeful, Caesar lives") Sesto girds himself joyfully for the final struggle.

35 ARIA DS (Sesto) *La giustizia ha già sull'arco / pronto strale alla vendetta, / per punire un traditor* ("Justice has now placed the arrow of revenge upon its bow to punish the traitor") Sesto rejoices in the prospects of ultimate victory and revenge. He goes off with Nireno to join Cesare's final venture.

A rather formulaic aria, with the predictable treatment of vendetta.

Scene VI

Cleopatra's apartments in the palace.

36 ACCOMPANIED RECITATIVE (Cleopatra) *Voi, che mie fide ancelle un tempo foste* ("You who were my faithful handmaidens") Cleopatra, believing herself about to be slain, bids farewell to her ladies in waiting. Hearing the clash of arms, she feels that the final moment has come.

The oboe begins with a recall of the rhythm and mood of the first motive of the Parnassus music and thus lends a special poignancy to her words of farewell. Her music moves mournfully to minor harmonies until fanfare repetitions are heard in the strings as emblematic of the battle nearing her quarters. The repetitions slow down as she prepares to meet death with dignity and courage, but they are brusquely interrupted by Cesare's charging in with a no-nonsense secco.

RECITATIVE (Cesare, Cleopatra) *Forzai l'ingresso a tua salvezza, o cara* ("My dear one, I have forced my way in to save you") With sword drawn, Cesare and his troops charge in. Cleopatra is freed, and her guards are ordered to obey or die. Cleopatra rushes into his arms. After a passionate embrace, Cesare tells her to hasten to the port and reassemble their troops; he will rejoin her there. He runs off to continue the fighting.

37 ARIA DC (Cleopatra) *Da tempeste il legno infranto, / se poi salvo giunge in porto, / non sa più che desiar* ("When a storm-tossed vessel finds safety in port, it no longer knows what it desires") Cleopatra, ecstatic over the turn of fortune's wheel, likens herself to a vessel that has survived a tempest at sea.

Ebullient triads, ornamented melismas, jagged intervals, and scale runs sparkle through an aria that is brilliant in its display and a sparkling embodiment of renewed vitality and excitement (Ex. 3.7).

SCENE VII

The royal apartments.

RECITATIVE (Tolomeo, Cornelia) *Cornelia, è tempo omai / che tu doni pietàde a un re che langue* ("Cornelia, it is now time for you to give solace to a king who languishes for you") Gilding his sexual desire with fancy words, Tolomeo demands satisfaction from Cornelia. Twice she eludes his embraces; as he moves toward her again, she draws a dagger.

SCENE VIII

RECITATIVE (Sesto, Tolomeo, Cornelia) *T'arresta, o genitrice* ("Stop, mother!") Sesto arrives with sword in hand and kills Tolomeo. Gazing briefly at his victim, Sesto exits (presumably to rejoin Cesare).

38 ARIA DS (Cornelia) *Non ha più che temere / quest' alma vendicata* ("This avenged soul has nothing more to fear") Cornelia has finally found joy and release from torment. She leaves.

Quick-moving and bouncy, this is not as vindictive an aria as one might read into the text and its happy-sounding music.[27] Its trills and melismas are short, save for a pair of runs on respirar *("breathe"); sighing figures in the accompanying violins remind one of Cornelia's earlier trials and sorrows.*

---

[27] Described by Humphrey Procter-Gregg in his notes to the International piano-vocal score (p. 257) as "a merry dance over the corpse" of Tolomeo. On the other hand, the subtlety ascribed to it by Dean-Knapp (p. 498) seems to me to go too far the other way.

FINAL SCENE

The harbor of Alexandria.

SINFONIA Cesare, Cleopatra and Egyptian attendants, then Curio, Nireno, Sesto, and Cornelia enter in procession, led by trumpets and drums, with a Page bearing the crown and sceptre of the Ptolemaic dynasty.

Four French horns used in antiphonal pairs contribute to the brilliance and excitement of this orchestral piece. (The pairs contrast in timbre because they are pitched differently from each other.) The orchestra also enjoys a full complement of winds (i.e., oboes and bassoons) and strings. The rhythm is festive, the form is that of a full ABA, the middle section given over to a brief and slow interplay of the horns—unaccompanied—before the excitement of the A section returns.

RECITATIVE (Nireno, Cesare, Sesto, Cornelia, Cleopatra) *Qui Curio vincitor, qui tuo l'Egitto* ("Here Curio is victor, Egypt is yours") Nireno proclaims Cesare as master of the world and emperor of Rome; Cesare praises Curio for his exploits.

Sesto, kneeling before Cesare, reports the death of Tolomeo; Cornelia reports her son's valor in defense of her honor.

Cesare welcomes them both as friends.

Cornelia presents him with the symbols of Tolomeo's power, which Cesare then bestows on Cleopatra. She in turn offers herself and her kingdom as vassals to him.

39 DUET (Cesare, Cleopatra) *Caro! / Bella! / Più amabile beltà / mai non si troverà / del tuo bel volto* ("Dear one! Beautiful one! A more amiable beauty than your visage cannot be found") The two lovers rejoice in each other's arms.

Parallel thirds in violins and oboes make this lovely piece flow pastorally, as well it might. The idea of the lover's "fair face" (bel volto) is not so much described as it is given pride of place.

RECITATIVE (Cesare) *Goda pur or l'Egitto / in più tranquilllo stato* ("Now let Egypt rejoice in more peaceful state") Cesare proclaims an era of peace for Egypt.

40 CHORUS and DUET (Romans and Egyptians, Cesare and Cleopatra) *Ritorni omai nel nostro core / la bella gioia ed il piacer . . . Un bel contento il sen già si prepara* ("Fair joy and delight now return to our hearts . . . A great joy now swells within my breast") All celebrate the happy ending.

A bourrée rhythm sparks this wonderfully buoyant finale, with horns and oboes again lending the vitality of their sounds. The insertion of another love duet passage in a sharply contrasting key with strings only is another of Handel's theatrical strokes, for it places the lovers into a world of their own, where lovers ought to be. The music of the joyous chorus returns to end the opera with joy and triumph.

The Characters

Giulio Cesare (alto castrato) *[JOOL-ee-oh CHEH-zah-reh]*

Cesare is warrior, lover, thinker. The first music we hear from him is a bold rising triad that suggests at once the fanfares of military music; although the instrumentation is for strings alone, the key of D major implies a trumpet-like association, since the clarin trumpet was pitched in D. The unison violins introducing "Al lampo dell' armi" (No. 25, "In the gleam of arms," Example GC-3a), his excited (and exciting) response to the surprise attack by Tolomeo's henchmen in Act II is bellicose and suggestive of the clash of arms and the frenzy of battle; the canonic beginning and the succeeding plummeting scales of "Quel torrente" (No. 34, "This torrent," Example GC-3b) are not only warlike but are specifically related to a textual metaphor that likens his charging against the enemy to a flood that sweeps all before it.

Cesare is reduced to a few gasps of recitativo secco when he sees Cleopatra enthroned as Virtue but is much more articulate in his arias related to love. The earliest of these, "Non è si vago" (No. 9, ["The flower in the meadow] is not as charming"), is lighthearted and pleasant; its instrumentation is very open, with the bass line stepping lightly along while violins play merrily above it, doubling the vocal line at the upper octave. While it is an aria of delight rather than deep affection (Cesare has just met Cleopatra in her disguise as a servant), the addition of violas at the end of the A section is

EXAMPLE GC-3 CESARE IN MUSIC

a) Act II, scene viii: No. 25, "Al lampo dell' armi" ("In the gleam of arms")
Battle music in the violins introduces Cesare's excited preparation to fight against the surprise attack of Tolomeo's murderers.

EXAMPLE GC-3. (*Continued*)

b) Act III, scene v: No. 34, "Quel torrente che cada dal monte" ("This torrent that falls from mountains")—He compares his determination to destroy his enemies to a torrent that sweeps all before it.

quite unexpected and may be read as a deepening of Cesare's interest in this pretty young girl standing before him in apparent innocence and grief. "Se in fiorito ameno prato" (No. 18, "If in the lovely flowered meadow") is somewhat more involving, for now, having witnessed the Parnassus spectacle and Cleopatra's sudden disappearance from his sight, Cesare is infatuated. He compares her to the bird that seems more beautiful when its song is heard but its body not seen, a poetic and dramatic situation that summoned pastoral images from Handel: a pedal point suggests the drone of rustic bagpipes; violins in thirds purl graciously, their pitches mellowed by the atmospheric sound of divided bassoons; and the echo effect of a solo violin and flowing melismas (some with triplets; see Example 2.2b) evoke the avian singing that is the basic metaphor of the poetry.

The pensive Cesare is found most expressively in his accompanied recitatives, but the quiet and smooth "Va tacito e nascosto," (No. 14) with its superbly metaphorical French horn obbligato and steady rhythmic progress evocative of stealth, also represents this facet of his character.

Curio (bass) [KOO-rree-oh]

Cesare's aide-de-camp, based on the historical personage of Caius Scribonius Curio. At one time in love with Cornelia, he still has the momentary effrontery to offer himself as her new husband. That she rejects him out of hand does not distill his loyalty to Cesare nor his admiration for her. Curio has no arias.

Cornelia (alto) [kawr-NEHL-yah)

Pompeo's widow, mother of Sesto. Cornelia's music presents her consistently as a figure of dignified sadness. Even when she is given a ray of hope near the end of the opera, her aria there (No. 22, "Cessa omai di sospirare!"— "Cease now your sighing!") is an *andante* not an *allegro*, and, in spite of the brightness of recorders in the orchestra, the music's hesitant rhythm (see Example GC-4a) suggests that she dare not trust fortune too much.

From her first appearance, Cornelia is a figure of melancholy. Her first aria (No. 4, "Priva son d'ogni conforto"), marked *largo* ("slow"), begins without the usual formality of an orchestral introduction and thus suggests an immediacy of deep feeling. The accompaniment by a flute lends it a plaintive quality, as does the absence of any extended melismas; Cornelia's music here is direct and simple. The two-note groups (*sospiri*) are musical sighs; the approach to the final note of the vocal line seems to be a gasp of one choked with sorrow (Example GC-4b). A particularly interesting effect is the pathos that comes from the extension of "misera" ("unhappy") across several measures.

Simplicity is also a feature of her lament for Pompeo (No. 11, "Nel tuo seno"—"Within thy bosom") and of her despair in her ultimate degradation, when she is consigned to slavery in Tolomeo's garden (No. 19, "Deh, piangete, o mesti lumi"—"Alas, weep, oh my sad eyes"). Each is a pliant arioso without melismas or extended melodic repeats. The accompaniment of the "Deh, piangete" is the barest possible: basso continuo without any orchestral work at all as a musical metaphor for a prisoner deprived of everything.

The duet with Sesto (No. 16, "Son nata a lagrimar"—"I was born to weep") is one of the great moments in the opera. Sung at the point where she and her son are being led off into separate captivity, it is a gentle *siciliano*, a graceful dance type often associated with tenderness and sadness. Its steady long-short rhythmic accompaniment is like the throbbing of aching hearts, and its sweetly falling motives ("x" in Example GC-4c) epitomize dignity and pathos.

Sesto (soprano) [SEHSS-toh]

Son of Cornelia and Pompeo. Sesto is barely into his teens, if that. Sesto's music is heavy on defiance, with frequent melismas that bespeak courage if not wisdom. Save for a brief aria of optimism (No. 12, "Cara speme"—"Dear hope"), he is given over to thoughts of revenge, always in minor keys.

EXAMPLE GC-4: CORNELIA IN MUSIC

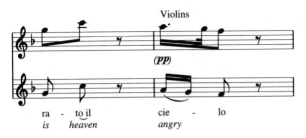

a) Act II, scene vi: No. 22, "Cessa omai di sospirare" ("Cease now your sighing")—Offered support by Nireno, Cornelia feels a touch of hope.

b) Act I, scene iv: No. 4, "Priva son d'ogni conforto" ("I am deprived of every solace")—In deep sadness, she sees no comfort in her life to come.

EXAMPLE GC-4 (*Continued*)

c) Act II, scene xi: No. 16, "Son nata a lagrimar" ("I was born to weep")—She bids farewell to her son as they are taken into captivity ("x" = sospiro, the "sigh effect).

Nonetheless, Handel gives his character some depth in his first aria (No. 5, "Svegliatevi nel core"), where the vigor of the A section is abruptly set aside when the B section offers a slow tempo, recorders that lend poignance to his thoughts, and repeated notes in the bass line that suggest the heartbeats of a grieving son.

Achilla (bass) *[ah-KEEL-lah]*

Achilla's villainous stature is a basic feature of the serious operas of the Baroque era, and there is little in his music that distinguishes him from other characters of his stripe. He suggested the murder of Pompeo, lusts after Cornelia, and leads a treacherous attack against Cesare. Achilla has no redeeming values in life but, like Edmund in *King Lear*, seeks to gain them in death: mortally wounded in battle against Cesare's forces, he gets his revenge against an even more villainous Tolomeo by surrendering a seal that will guarantee the obedience of a special troop of soldiers and grant entrance to Tolomeo's palace via a secret passage. In terms of the dignity of Achilla's soul, it is too-little-too-late, but it helps bring the plot to a successful conclusion.

Achilla's three arias are similar in style, even though two deal with love and one with anger. Each is relatively fast, accompanied by an "empty" orchestration of unison violins above a bustling bass line, and replete with melismas that pictorialize words but do not move the soul. His first aria of wooing (No. 15, "Tu sei il cor di questo core"—"You are the heart of my heart") is hollow and vain, bassoons doubling first the voice part at the octave then harmonizing the strings in a very distant register; violins drive unsentimentally, both in the introduction and as accompaniment to Achilla's vocal line.[28] "Dal fulgor di questa spada" (No. 30, "By this flashing blade") is a fine example of a rage aria, filled with scales and wide leaps in the melody, and angular, biting intervals in the accompaniment.

Cleopatra (soprano) [kleh-oh-PAH-trah]

Queen of Egypt, ruling jointly with her brother, Tolomeo, whom she plots to displace by enlisting the aid of Cesare. The progress of her personality, from a power-hungry schemer who relies on the political manipulation of men's sexual interests (and thus the complete opposite of Cornelia) to a woman deeply in love and able to face death with dignity and grace makes Handel's heroine one of the most finely drawn of all operatic characters. Her haughtiness is the first attribute presented to us, but as her character is brought into focus through a succession of subtly varied arias, we see her as a young woman capable of guile[29] who is hoisted by her own sexual petard—she falls in love with Cesare and can thus no longer seek to manipulate him.

Defiance, pride, and venomous tongue are the substance of her first aria (No. 6, "Non disperar"—"Despair not," Example GC-5a), a verbal/musical onslaught thrown at Tolomeo: its opening repeated notes in the mordent-decorated[30] violins jab at Tolomeo sarcastically to introduce the idea that Tolomeo is better suited to sexual escapades than to kingship. Her melismas on "amor" ("love") are disjunct and aggressive rather than cooing; clearly, her view of Tolomeo as a lover is not much more respectful than her view of him as dynastic ruler. This spitfire characteristic is but a twist of mind away from rage and a thirst for vengeance, a quality that explodes in the midst of an aria otherwise focused on sadness and resignation (No. 32, "Piangerò la sorte mia—"I shall weep for my fate"; see Example 2.2a).

"Tu la mia stella" (No. 13, "You are my star"; Example GC-5b) is music in a completely different vein, yet it speaks to a similar quality of supreme self-confidence. Its floating rhythm is that of a *siciliano*, decorated with trills

---

28 Winton Dean (*Handel's Operas*, p. 499) says it precisely: Achilla "cannot conceal the cloven hoof."

29 Cf. Richard Strauss's *Salome*, where the European view of the Egyptians as plotters and connivers finds resonance in Salome's distaste for some of the guests at Herodes's banquet: *schweigsame, list'ge Ägypter* ("silent, subtle Egyptians").

30 A mordent is an ornament made up of a quick descent from a note to its lower neighbor and a quick return.

EXAMPLE GC-5: CLEOPATRA IN MUSIC

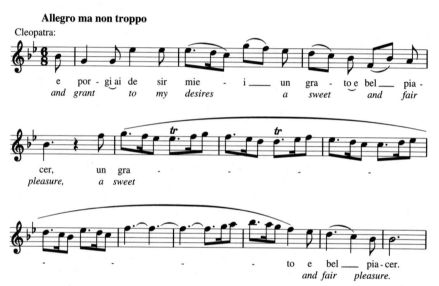

a) Act I, scene v: No. 6, "Non disperar" ("Do not despair")— the taunting violin figure of her sarcasm toward Tolomeo.

b) Act I, scene viii: No. 13, "Tu la mia stella" ("You are my star")—she expects her star to rise.

and quick passing notes that speak directly of a young woman who knows herself and believes in the ultimate triumph of her good fortune.

Cleopatra turns to the subject of sexual allure in "Tutto può donna vezzosa" (No. 10, "A pretty woman can do everything"), "V'adoro, pupille" (No. 17, "I adore you, eyes"), and "Venere bella" (No. 24, "Fair Venus"). The first, with piping oboe, is a jaunty tune serving a text about the unrestricted power of sex ("A pretty girl can do anything"). "V'adoro, pupille" is sung from her place within the stage set of Mount Parnassus, from which lofty spot she spins her sensual web about the entranced Cesare. "Venere bella" is a prayer to Venus, but Cleopatra's treatment of "amor" is more serious than her reference to it in her taunting of Tolomeo, for she is no longer quite so cocksure of herself. By this point, love has become a genuine matter of the heart rather than a tool for manipulating Cesare, so "amor" here flows smoothly and somewhat urgently.

Cleopatra's finest moment is when all thoughts of herself are cast aside and she thinks only of her love for Cesare and his welfare. The conflicting moods of her accompanied recitative (No. 26, "Che sento? O Dio!"—"What do I hear? Oh God!") and the poignant accents of the aria that follows it (No. 27, "Se pietà di me non senti, giusto ciel"; see above, Example GC-1) are the sentiments of a woman whose spirit has become great.

Nireno (alto castrato) *[nee-REH-noh]*

A eunuch completely loyal to Cleopatra. He has no arias but plays an important role in the action, serving as a guide and source of hope for Cornelia and Sesto and leading Cesare to the Parnassus spectacle.

Tolomeo (alto castrato) *[toh-loh-MEH-oh]*

Impetuous, haughty, willful, traitorous, and not terribly bright, Tolomeo is the least attractive figure in the opera. Besides having ordered the murder of Pompeo, Tolomeo buys the loyalty of Achilla without any intention of fulfilling his promise to give the general the gift of Cornelia as a consort, and lusts after a woman (Cornelia) who is old enough to be his mother. His one moment of vocal relaxation and melodiousness, when he contemplates the beauties of his harem and thinks of sexual pleasure with Cornelia, disintegrates into the sparseness of recitativo secco. His arias are fast, angular, and replete with petulance. His rage at Cesare (No. 7, "L'empio, sleale, indegno"—"Infidel, traitor, miscreant") is typical: brusque leaps, a hyperactive bass line, and mechanical sequences of arpeggios reveal an empty mind and an impotent rage (Example GC-6).

EXAMPLE GC-6 ACT I, SCENE VI: NO. 7, "L'EMPIO, SLEALE" ("HEATHEN, TRAITOR")—TOLOMEO, HAVING VOWED TO MURDER CESARE, EXPRESSES HIS ANGER THAT CESARE WOULD PRESUME TO ENTER EGYPT

EXAMPLE GC-6 (*Continued*)

re - gno,   e   di - stur - bar - - -
of   my   kingdom   and   disturb   [my peace of mind]

- - - e di-stur-bar co - sì,
in such a fashion.   etc.

Bibliography

Burrows, Donald. *Handel.* [Master Musicians] New York: Schirmer Books, 1994.

Celletti, Rodolfo. "The Poetics of the Marvelous," in *Opera News* 59, no. 1 (July 1994): 10–14.

———. *A History of Bel Canto,* trans. Frederick Fuller. Oxford: Clarendon Press, 1991.

Dean, Winton. *Handel and the Opera Seria.* Berkeley, CA: University of California Press, 1969.

———. *The New Grove Handel.* New York and London: W. W. Norton, 1983.

———, and John Merrill Knapp. *Handel's Operas 1704–1726,* rev. ed. Oxford: Clarendon Press, 1995.

Freeman, Robert. *Opera Without Drama: Currents of Change in Italian Opera 1675–1725.* Ann Arbor, MI: UMI Research Press, 1981.

Fubini, Enrico. *Music and Culture in Eighteenth-Century Europe: A Source Book,* trans. and ed. Bonnie J. Blackburn. Chicago: University of Chicago Press, 1994.

Keats, Jonathan. *Handel: The Man and His Music.* New York: St. Martin's Press, 1985.

Lang, Paul Henry. *George Frideric Handel.* New York: W. W. Norton, 1966.

Meynell, Hugo. *The Art of Handel's Operas.* Studies in the History and Interpretation of Music, vol. 1. Lewiston, NY: Edwin Mellen Press, 1986.

Raguenet, François, "Parallèle des Italiens et des Français [1702]," in *Source Readings in Music History from Classical Antiquity Through the Romantic Era,* ed. and comp. Oliver Strunk; translation attributed to J[ohn]. E[rnest]. Galliard [1709]. New York: W. W. Norton, 1950, pp. 473–488.

Robbins-Landon, H. C. *Handel and His World.* London: Weidenfel and Nicolson, 1984.

Rogers, Nigel. "Voices," in *Companion to Baroque Music,* comp. and ed. Julie Anne Sadie. New York: Schirmer Books, 1990, pp. 351–365.

Rosselli, John. *Singers of Italian Opera: The History of a Profession*. Cambridge: Cambridge University Press, 1992.

Scott, Michael. *The Record of Singing*. New York: Charles Scribner's Sons, 1977. 2 vols.
Introduction to vol. 1 provides an excellent history of singing.

Smith, Patrick J. *The Tenth Muse: A Historical Study of the Opera Libretto*. New York: Alfred A. Knopf, 1970.

Strohm, Reinhard. "Towards an Understanding of the *Opera Seria*," in *Essays on Handel and Italian Opera*. Cambridge: Cambridge University Press, 1985.

Tosi, Pier Francesco. *Observations on the Florid Song* [1743], trans. John Ernest Galliard. London: William Reeves Bookseller. 1926 .

Winn, James Anderson. *Unsuspected Eloquence: A History of the Relation of Poetry and Music*. New Haven, CT: Yale University Press, 1981.

Chapter 8

IPHIGÉNIE EN TAURIDE

MUSIC: Christoph Willibald von Gluck (1714–1787)
LIBRETTO: Nicolas-François Guillard (1752–1814), probably on an original
  plan by François Louis Lebland du Roullet (1716–1786), after the play by
  Euripides.
PREMIÈRE: Paris, May 18, 1779
TIME AND PLACE OF THE STORY: Tauris, a city-state in Scythia (the modern
  Crimea), perhaps fifteen years after the end of the Trojan War.

*NOTE: In the discussion that follows, references to the characters of the opera will use
their French spellings (thus "Iphigénie," "Oreste," "Pylade," and "Diane"); for the myth,
Euripides, and translations of the libretto, references will use the common English forms
("Iphigenia," "Orestes," "Pylades," and "Diana").*

⁂

Iphigénie en Tauride represents the zenith of the reforms that had been introduced into opera by its composer in *Orfeo ed Euridice*. Direct lines of plot
development, seamlessness of style between declamation and song (all the
recitatives are orchestrally accompanied), reduction of ornament, and a
sense of naturalness in action and characterization marked great changes in
opera and established many approaches to opera as drama of the next two
centuries. Perhaps Gluck's greatest contribution was his use of music for subtle psychological insight as well as pictorialization of text. *Iphigénie en Tauride*
thus represents the completion of the transition from Baroque abstraction
and elaborate metaphor to the probing and very human dramatic goals of
the Enlightenment. The choruses and dance movements are impeccably
wedded to the needs of the plot; the action is compressed into a short period of time, with all of its nuances unmistakably clear from both word and
music. Rhythm, melody, instrumentation, and harmony are wonderfully
varied, yet there is a continuity of mood and style that allows for a natural
flow from lyric episodes to active ones. There are very few self-contained
numbers; indeed, the opera is remarkable for the number of times a songful episode is interrupted by action—and, therefore, by a change in the
music—and for the movement from stark recitative to arioso in accordance
with the demands of plot and emotion.

  Much of the dramatic force comes from ironies: the storm that is in full
torrent at the rise of the curtain of Act I soon subsides as a force of nature

156

but continues its turbulence within the soul of Iphigénie; in Act II, Oreste believes himself to be calmed as he falls asleep, but his dreams are rudely assaulted by the Furies of his conscience; Iphigénie believes that she has dreamt of her mother as a murderess, not knowing that Clytemnestra was indeed the slayer of Agamemnon; Oreste, in his half-sleep in the dungeon, also has a vision of Clytemnestra, but it is Clytemnestra's daughter Iphigénie who actually stands before him.

Simplicity of melody, harmony, mode (few passages are in the minor), rhythm, and texture prevails, yet every thought and turn of action speaks directly through the music. The orchestra is continually expressive of the characters and their moods, even though it is a modest complement of players for the opera houses of the time: pairs of flutes, oboes, clarinets, bassoons, and French horns, plus the usual strings; its group of three trombones is a typical sound element for the supernatural. The only exoticism added to this instrumentation is for the characterization of the Scythians as barbaric through the scoring of their music with piccolo (instead of flute), triangle, cymbals, and a small side drum.[1]

There are but four main characters. The plot is uncomplicated, and the action is a beautifully poised progression from the visions, prophecies, and portents of Acts I and II to the fast-moving and powerful events of Acts III and IV. There is no love story that impedes the basic action or results in distracting billing and cooing, jealousy, and the like. Instead, both the spirit and the straight-line plot of Euripides's drama are maintained. Gluck and Guillard, however, switched the great theatrical moment of recognition from the letter scene to the moment of sacrifice, when Oreste, about to die under the knife, evokes the name of his beloved sister and, thus revealing his identity, precipitates the climax of the opera.

The traditional element of all action being motivated by idealized love and obstructed by greed, jealousy, or ambition is set aside in favor of the grander themes of destiny, conscience, and loyalty. Although Euripides's drama ends in the triumph of its protagonists, its story is nonetheless a capstone of tragic events showing that innocence is often not a shield against victimization nor a perfect defense against guilt. Orestes's anguish is as intense a picture of the ravages of conscience as one can find in theater, but the extent to which he merits being tormented by the Furies is a perplexing question. Of Iphigenia, on the other hand, there is no question that she has come to her present unhappiness through no fault of her own. While her complicity in the ritual sacrifice of any Greek who has come to Thoas's kingdom suggests that she has been a vengeful figure as well as an unfortunate one, her refusal to participate any further is brought forward effectively and early on in the plot. Both play and opera are thus stories of redemption as well as of guilt, and they represent the triumph of strength of noble purpose over passion, revenge, and barbarism.

---

[1] Gluck's score specifies *tamburo*, which can mean either a small drum (without snares) or tambourine. More than likely the side drum was intended: since Gluck specified *tamburino* for his music for *Echo et Narcisse* (1779), it is likely he would have done the same for *Iphigénie* if he had wanted tambourine rather than small drum. Nonetheless, a current recording of *Iphigénie* (Philips 416 148–2) directed by John Eliot Gardiner uses a tambourine to good effect.

The Myth

The characters derive from the legends of the House of Atreus. While assembling the the Greek armies at Aulis for their voyage to Troy, Agamemnon had slain a hart sacred to Diana;[2] as punishment the Greek fleet was becalmed by the goddess. Told by a seer that only the virgin daughter of the offender would serve as a propitiating sacrifice, Agamemnon had ordered his daughter Iphigenia be brought to Aulis for that purpose, although, according to Euripides's *Iphigenia in Aulis*, he told his family that she was to come there to marry Achilles. At the moment he raised his blade to Iphigenia's willing throat, Diana claimed Iphigenia as her own. The girl (with a number of her Greek girlfriends, as Euripides and Gluck have it) was transported to Tauris, there to serve as priestess to Diana and to preside over the ritual sacrifice of any strangers who should come under the power of its fierce king, Thoas.

Between the end of this episode and the start of the events of the opera, the Trojan War has been fought and won by the Greeks, and Agamemnon has returned to his kingdom of Mycenae, there to be slain by his wife, Clytemnestra, and her paramour, Aegisthus. Electra, Agamemnon's younger daughter, has seen to the safety of his son Orestes (who had been a toddler of two or three years of age at the time of the Aulis incident), by spiriting him away to Crisa, the court of his uncle Strophius. Orestes has grown to manhood there, along with his first cousin Pylades, to whom he is bound in deepest friendship and loyalty.

At the demand of the Oracle of Delphos, Orestes returns to Mycenae and wreaks vengeance by slaying his mother, an unnatural act for which he is pursued by the Furies from land to land. An appeal to the oracle reveals a path to salvation—after a year of exile, he is to go to Tauris, seize the sacred image of Diana from its temple, and take it to Athens as a trophy of war for the temple of Pallas Athena.

The opera opens some twenty-five years after the dramatic events on Aulis. Iphigénie is a mature woman of perhaps forty (assuming she was a marriageable fifteen or sixteen when brought to Aulis); Oreste and Pylade are in their mid-twenties.

THE PLOT AND ITS MUSIC

OVERTURE *The music begins with a calm 3/8 time, but there is a sudden shifting of gears when the storm music begins its undulating string scales; as the tempest draws closer, we hear the thumping of timpani and bass drum, rapid alternations of loud and soft accents, and fanfares for winds and brasses. Thunder is stylized by rumbling scales in low strings and percussion, lightning appears via repeated three-note episodes in the French horns, and the shrieking of wind is suggested by sustained high notes in the flute, piccolo, and violins. The curtain is raised as the storm begins to abate, although the cries of Iphigénie and the Priestesses, beginning without any break from the overture, at first show no awareness of this.*

---

[2] Since this opera is about a Greek myth, this goddess should be named Artemis; Guillard uses the Roman/French "Diane," and we're stuck with it.

Act I

Entrance to the Temple of Diana, amidst a sacred grove.

SCENE I

SOLO WITH CHORUS (Iphigénie, Priestesses) *Grands Dieux! soyez-nous secourables* ("Great Gods, help us") The Greek women appeal to the gods to direct their anger toward guilty heads and to release them from their cruel obligations.

Although the stage directions indicate that the tempest is past, the continuing scales and tremolos identify the tempest in Iphigénie's soul.

RECITATIVE (Iphigénie) *Cette nuit j'ai revu le palais de mon père* ("Last night I saw once again my father's palace") The storm ceases, says Iphigénie, but in her heart it is raging still. She tells of her nightmare in which she saw her father's palace engulfed by earthquake, fire, and tempest, Agamemnon stabbed and fleeing from the knife of her mother, and herself unable to prevent using her mother's knife to slay her brother. The Priestesses pray that Heaven will relent.

The narrative is rich in sound pictures: tremolos for the earthquake, fast triplet figures in the strings for fire; descending scales for the collapse of the palace. Her vision comes in gasps— short phrases with detached chords or scale figures. Irregularly spaced woodwind entries identify her hearing a plaintive voice (une voix plaintive et tendre) that turns out to be the tender sound of her dying father; in a later phrase, woodwinds accent her dream of the cry of her brother. An agonized forte dissonance also uses winds to underscore the vision of her mother as a murderess. The choral response, in short phrases appropriate to sobs, is chorale-like and hushed.

RECITATIVE AND ARIA (Iphigénie) *O râce de Pélops,[3] râce toujours fatale. . . . ô toi qui prolongeas mes jours* ("Oh race of Pelops, forever doomed . . . Oh thou [i.e., the goddess, Diana] who hast prolonged my days") Iphigénie grieves over the relentless pursuit of her family by the gods and fates, and laments that she will never see her beloved brother again: *La mort me devient nécessaire*—"Death has become my need."

The ritual quality of her prayer is reflected in the use of a conventional form, ABA with ritornello introduction. Echoes of the ends of the vocal phrases in violins and oboe lend poignancy and sadness. A brief choral response is given a sense of sobbing by weak-beat accents in the strings.

SCENE II

RECITATIVE (Thoas, Iphigénie) AND ARIA (Thoas) *Dieux! le malheur en tous lieux suit mes pas . . . De noirs pressentiments mon âme intimidée* ("Gods! misfortune follows my footsteps everywhere. . . . With black forebodings my soul is frightened") Thoas is terrified by voices that warn him of dire punishment at the hands of foreigners, telling Iphigénie that the gods want blood, not tears.

Thoas's recitative is brusque in the irregularity of its chording and quick dotted rhythms. His fears are set in a pervasive tremolo in the bass and a relentless dotted-rhythm string accompaniment. Thoas's melody is angular and has frequent changes of phrase length. His recalling the

---

[3] Tantalus was a son of Zeus who, in pride and arrogance over his being allowed to sup at the table of the gods, sinned by sharing some of their ambrosia and nectar with his mortal friends. He mocked the gods by cutting up his own son Pelops and serving the pieces of Pelops's body to them for a meal. Iphigénie's allusion, then, is to the cruelty visited on her lineage through the ages.

voice of fate (Tremble, ton supplice s'apprête—*"Tremble, your punishment is being made ready"*) *has a repeated-note quality (cf. the curse motive in* Rigoletto, *Ex.* RI-1a). *His aria has more the quality of recitative than songfulness, his words tumbling from his anxious soul.*

SCENE III

CHORUS and RECITATIVE (Scythians) *Les Dieux apaisent leur courroux* ("The gods abate their anger") Gathering about their King in savage joy, the Scythians exult in the news that two young Greeks have been cast up on their shores and, after a battle, have been captured. One of them, they are told, speaks loudly of his wish for death and of crime and remorse. Thoas orders Iphigénie to repair to the temple and commands his people to rejoice in warlike songs.

Three-part men's voices, with the tenors rather high; bright percussion, shrill woodwinds (esp. piccolo), and a fast, reiterated rhythm suggest barbaric thoughts and movements.

SCENE IV

CHORUS and BALLET (Scythians) *Il nous fallait du sang pour expier nos crimes* ("We had need of blood to expiate our crimes") Joyous anticipation of the forthcoming sacrifice.

The chorus is a reprise of the style above, with unisons and fanfares of militarism, barbarism. Each of four ballet movements has a distinctive percussive timbre; the second of these is especially notable for its venomous swells within what Berlioz described as "sinister stillness."[4]

SCENE V

RECITATIVE (Thoas, Pylade, Oreste) *Malheureux! Quel dessein à vous-mêmes contraire / vous amenait dans mes États?* (Unfortunate men, what scheme contrary to your own interests has led you to my country?") Oreste and Pylade are brought in but refuse to tell Thoas why they have come to his kingdom. Thoas sends the two men to be slain at the altar.

Secco style, but with dramatic tremolo at Thoas's La mort sera le prix (*"Death will be your reward"*). *Brief, expressive strings when Oreste expresses remorse over bringing Pylade to his death.*

CHORUS *Il nous fallait du sang pour expier nos crimes* ("There must be blood to rid us of our crimes") The Schythians again rejoice at the thought of shedding the blood of others.

Choral reprise.

Act II

A room in the Temple reserved for sacrificial victims. An altar is at one side. Oreste and Pylade in chains.

SCENE I

RECITATIVE (Pylades, Oreste) and ARIA (Oreste) *Quel silence effrayant . . . Dieu! qui me poursuivez* ("What terrifying silence . . .Ye gods who pursue me") In spite of the gloom of their cell, Pylades questions Oreste's sighing and suggests that heroes need not be troubled by death. Oreste's response is that he deeply regrets being

---

[4] I am grateful to Richard Mix for calling this comment of Berlioz to my attention. It is found in David Cairns's translation of the Berlioz *Mémoires*, p. 82.

the cause of his friend's dreadful fate. Oreste, blaming the gods for causing him to betray friendship and nature, agonizingly demands that the gods let him die.

The forceful string chords alternating with isolated violin repetitions of a single pitch suggest the starkness of the prison cell. Oreste's distraught state is heard in quick bursts of chords in the recitative, then in full flower in a driven ABA aria, replete with full winds (including French horns and trumpets), timpani, and strings (Ex. IP-3). Scalar passages in the orchestra recall the storm music of the overture.

RECITATIVE and ARIA (Pylade) *Quel langage accablant pour un ami qui t'aime!* . . . *Unis dès la plus tendre enfance* ("Such words for a friend who loves you! . . . United since our most tender childhood") Pylade urges Oreste to cease reviling the gods and join him in welcoming a death that will bind them eternally.

The brevity of Pylade's song—it is an AB form rather than the traditional ABA—is a measure of his simple honesty; the ornaments and flowing nature (grazioso; Ex. IP-5) suggest not only his courtly upbringing and refined nature but also his psychological command of his own emotional state, quite in contrast with the wildness of Oreste's aria.

SCENE II

RECITATIVE (A minister of the temple, Pylade, Oreste) *Étrangers malheureux* ("Unfortunate strangers") Summoning Pylade to the temple, the minister tells them that their appeal to die together is denied.

At first a brittle, quasi-secco style, then hushed repeated chords animating into tremolos. The passage turns to excited dotted rhythms, ending with solemn quiet harmonies appropriate to yet more despair for Oreste.

SCENE III

SCENE and PANTOMIME (Oreste) *Dieux protecteurs de ces affreux rivages . . . Le calme rentre dans mon coeur* ("Ye gods, protectors of these frightful shores . . . peace returns to my heart") Oreste pleads for death's release, then sinks into an exhausted sleep.

Oreste's address to the gods begins with a fanfare motive in full orchestra; stately chords in the low strings are followed at once by ever more agitated figures that reach their most intense point (a spurt of very fast scales) when he begs the gods to strike and crush him ("Tonnez! écrasez-moi!") His melody, "Le calme rentre dans mon coeur," seems restful, but the violin syncopations tell the greater truth (Ex. 3.3a).

SCENE IV

(Oreste, Furies) *Vengeons et la nature and les Dieux en courroux!* ("Let us avenge nature and the angry gods!") In a nightmare, Oreste is besieged by the Furies, who promise eternal punishment for one who has slain his mother.

The appearance of the chorus of Furies is to a return of the fanfares and agitations of the opening of the scene, but now the French horns are replaced by trombones, instruments always associated with the supernatural—the Furies are really present in his mind. Their chorus (in D minor, a key often used by Mozart in association with death and tragedy) is set over a throbbing bass line; imitative entrances suggest that they are on all sides of the sleeping Oreste; the change to a slower, chordal texture emphasizes the extremity of his crime, with a particular accent emphasizing sa mère *("his mother"). Oreste's guilt-ridden cries are short, high gasps.*

SCENE V

SCENE AND RECITATIVE (Oreste, Iphigénie) *Ma mère! Ciel!. . . Je vois toute l'horreur / que ma présence vous inspire* ("My mother! Heavens! . . . I see all the horror that my presence inspires in you") When Iphigénie enters the cell (accompanied by the Priestesses), Oreste awakens; seeing her, he imagines it is his mother's ghost standing before him.

Iphigénie questions Oreste as to his homeland and asks if he knows of Agamemnon. Oreste tells of the awful events at Mycenae without revealing his identity, saying that Oreste is dead and only Electra remains alive. Iphigénie orders him from the room.

The pantomime ends on a dramatically dissonant harmony, as Oreste is startled to awakening by Iphigénie's appearance. Her questions and his evasive answers are given suspense by irregular chords, tremolos, sustained sonorities, and syncopations; the music proceeds from blunt two-note orchestral punctuations to more involved patterns, with snippets of choral response. A long silence follows his news that Electra alone remains in Mycenae.

SCENE VI

RECITATIVE and CHORUS (Iphigénie, Priestesses) *Ô Ciel! de mes tourments la cause et le temoin. . .Patrie infortunée* ("Oh Heaven, cause and witness of my torment . . . Unhappy homeland") An expression of grief and loss.

A simple, two-part lament is made especially moving by the sound of a pair of clarinets; intensity derives from the crossing of the choral parts: each part explores a wider range while the total compass of the sound is tight and narrow.

ARIA WITH CHORUS (Iphigénie, Priestesses) *Ô malheureuse Iphigénie* ("Oh, unhappy Iphigenia") Lamentation.

A flowing song above gentle syncopations and arpeggios, with the timbre of an oboe symbolizing loneliness and grief (Ex. IP-2). Simplicity bespeaks monumental sorrow. The Priestesses, in response to her mêlez vos cris plaintifs, *mingle their cries with hers, extending and altering her lament and preventing it from falling into the mold of a traditional ABA.*

RECITATIVE and CHORUS (Iphigénie, Priestesses) *Honorez avec moi ce héros qui n'est plus! . . . Contemplez ces tristes apprêts* ("With me, honor this hero who is no more . . . Behold these sad offerings") Iphigénie and her compatriots memorialize Oreste.

Clarinets and bassoons give a distinctive flavor of mourning, the falling of tears represented by brief descending scale fragments. At the midpoint of this gentle dirge, Iphigénie thinks of her brother (Ô mon frère) to the same melody but in a different key.

Act III

Iphigénie's living quarters in the temple. Iphigénie is there with her priestess companions.

SCENE I

RECITATIVE and ARIA (Iphigénie) *Je cède à vos desirs . . . D'une image, hélas! trop chérie / j'aime encore à m'entretenir* ("I yield to your wishes. . .Alas, I still love to talk of an image [i.e., of Oreste] that is too dear") Iphigénie sadly confides to her friends that she will save one of the prisoners so that he may carry a letter to her sister, Electra. She admits that she is drawn to one whose *noble fierté* ("noble pride") reminds her of her brother,[5] whom she will see again only *aux sombre bords*—on those "somber shores" beyond the grave.

Iphigénie's recitative of determination to proceed is given at first the regular rhythmic motion of an aria, thus lending it an urgent quality. Her aria, paradoxically, is informed by the assymetry and the irregularity of recitative. The minor mode—relatively rare in the opera—provides an aura of resignation, and frequent appoggiaturas symbolize the sighs and tears of her unhappiness. The restriction of the scoring to strings lends it a quality of intimacy.

SCENE II

RECITATIVE (Iphigénie, Oreste, Pylade) *Voici ces captifs malheureux* ("Here are the unfortunate captives") Seeing the prisoners led in, Iphigénie asks to be left alone with them; the Priestesses leave.

A few orchestral chords under sung declamation.

SCENE III

RECITATIVE (Oreste, Pylade, Iphigénie) *Ô joie inattendue!* ("Oh unhoped for joy!") The men rejoice at seeing each other after their separation. Iphigénie tells them that she too is Greek and would save them if she could, but Thoas's blood lust will not be denied.

TRIO (Iphigénie, Pylade, Oreste) *Je pourrais du tyran tromper la barbarie* ("I could deceive the savagery of the tyrant") She tells them that she can save one of them and asks only that a letter to her friends in Argos be delivered by the survivor. Pylade and Oreste accept eagerly, mutually insisting that the other be saved. To Oreste's despair, Iphigénie chooses Oreste as the one to live and departs to make preparations for his escape.

The music of Iphigénie's first words is artlessly tuneful to the point of being without soul, as if she were unable to bring herself to tell them the reality of what must happen; only the hesitant accompaniment patterns and sustained tones of an oboe suggest her sadness. The responses of Pylade and Oreste are fast and bound together rhythmically. Melody and accompaniment broaden when she tells them that one of them must be a victim; her sympathy for them is in a descending scale in canon with cellos. Quiet chords separated by long rests precede her announcement that Pylade is to die; Oreste's anguish is in vivid, short bursts.

SCENE IV

RECITATIVE and DUET (Oreste/Pylade) *Ô moment trop heureux!. . .Et tu prétends encore que tu m'aimes* ("Oh, a moment too joyous. . .And you pretend that you love me") To Pylade's happiness at being able to die for his friend, Oreste protests that the death of Pylade would be yet another burden of unbearable guilt. Each begs the other to live, each presses his own desire to be sacrificed.

Oreste's explosion recalls the rhythmic fanfares and melodic shape of his Dieux! qui me poursuivez, *but here violins have agitated repeated notes and octave leaps that lend a special desperation. The two protest to each other in overlapping descending scales, starting pitches rising until there is a dramatic pause. More gentle attempts at persuasion ensue, much of it vested in a pleading violin figure, the sound of the oboe, and a pulsating bass line.*

RECITATIVE (Oreste, Pylade) *Quoi! je ne vaincrai pas ta constance funeste?* ("What! Can I not overcome your funereal determination?") Oreste recounts the torments of his guilt. He berates Pylade for denying him the release of death.

---

[5] We must tolerate some fancifulness on the part of Guillard and Gluck here, since the last time Iphigénie saw her brother he was at most three years old. Euripides indicates that, at the time of the Aulis events, Orestes was still a nursing babe.

Oreste's protest is a series of powerful, symmetrical statements accented by groups of three chords that recall the thunder of the overture's storms. Here they are given special weight by the addition of trombones, appropriate to his reminding Pylade that the forces of the gods and the Furies are involved in his torment.

ARIA (Pylade) *Ah! mon ami, j'implore ta pitié!* ("Ah, my friend, I beg for your pity!") Pylade pleads his case—he wishes to die for Oreste.

Pylade's aria is an ABA, with a light, clear string and oboe instrumentation that is in sharp contrast to the heaviness of Oreste's protest, as is the grace and simplicity of the melodiousness his song is given.

SCENE V

RECITATIVE (Oreste, Iphigénie, Pylade, Priestesses) *Malgré tois, je saurai t'arracher au trépas* ("In spite of yourself, I will save you from death") When Iphigénie returns to send Oreste to freedom, he vows to commit suicide rather than let Pylade die on his behalf. Her pleas to no avail, Iphigénie accedes, and Oreste is led away.

The dialogue among the three is standard accompagnato until Oreste resolves to commit suicide, whereupon the music becomes a firmly rhythmed arioso.

SCENE VI

RECITATIVE (Iphigénie, Pylade) *Puisque le ciel à vos jours s'intéresse* ("Since heaven is interested in your life") Iphigénie tells Pylade that the letter she gives him is for Electra but refuses to answer his astonished query as to their relationship.

Quiet chords marked by expressive dissonances.

SCENE VII

ARIA (Pylade) *Divinité des grandes âmes, / Amitié, viens armer mon bras!* ("Friendship, deity of great souls, come strengthen my arm") Pylade vows to save Oreste or die.

Triadic and fanfare figures, drum-like repeated notes in the violas and cellos, and the instrumentation for horns and trumpets provide the symbolisms for this military call to arms. Oboe and vocal line answer each other as a metaphor for Pylade's apostrophe to friendship.

Act IV

Interior of the temple of Diana. A statue of the goddess is at the center, a sacrificial altar to one side.

SCENE I

RECITATIVE and ARIA (Iphigénie) *Non, cet affreux devoir je ne puis le remplir . . . Je t'implore et je tremble, ô Déesse implacable!* ("No, I must not fulfill this horrible duty . . . I beg you and I tremble, Oh goddess unrelenting") Lamenting her terrible duties, Iphigénie is torn between her revulsion at killing the Greek victim and the need to obey the goddess.

Angular and powerful, Iphigénie's prayer approaches the desperation that heretofore had been characteristic of Oreste. The strong accents of bassoons and basses in two-note descending groups point up every phrase (Ex. IP-1).

SCENE II

CHORUS (Priestesses) *Ô Diane, sois-nous propice* ("Oh, Diana, look favorably upon us") A ritual hymn as preparation for the sacrifice.

The first of two hymns. The simple melody of this two-part setting is marked by some poignant dissonances and is accompanied by flutes and clarinets over a steady bass line that evokes the idea of a procession.

RECITATIVE (Iphigénie, Oreste) *La force m'abandonne* ("My strength fails me") Oreste's resolution to die is horrifying to Iphigénie; he is moved by her sympathy for him.

Oreste's Que ces regrets touchants pour mon coeur ont de charmes! *("How these touching regrets touch my heart!" Ex. IP-4) is a flowing arioso over solo flute syncopations, the first isolation of this timbre in the opera and thus a potent symbol for the purity of his feelings.*

HYMN (Priestesses) *Chaste fille de Latone, prête l'oreille à nos chants!* ("Chaste daughter of Latona,[6] lend your ear to our hymn!") Oreste is surrounded ritually by the Priestesses, who lead him to the altar where he is adorned with garlands and purified with libations and perfumes.

A quiet, formal song (ABA); a pair of clarinets contributes to the somber dignity of the Priestesses' prayer.

SCENE (Iphigénie, Priestesses, Oreste) Hesitant, Iphigénie is led to the altar and presented with the sacred blade for the sacrifice. Raising her hand in response to the Priestesses' *Frappez!* ("Strike!"), she is astonished at her victim's final words: *Iphigénie, aimable soeur! C'est ainsi qu'autrefois tu péris en Aulide!* ("Iphigenia, beloved sister, thus did you once perish in Aulis!") Mutual recognition and joy ensue.

The sacrifice begins in recitative, but the orchestra's rhythms intensify as they become faster and more sustained. The progression into full song is seamless, Iphigénie's inner glow of joy set to music that is at once flowing and urgently pulsating.

SCENE III

RECITATIVE (A Greek woman and the preceding) *Tremblez! On sait tout le mystère!* ("Tremble! The whole secret is known") Their happiness is interrupted by news that Thoas has learned of the flight of one of the captives and is rushing in fury to the temple to hasten the sacrifice of the other. Iphigénie charges the Priestesses to assist in saving the life of their [true] king Oreste.

The continuity is unbroken through the frightening news of the coming of Thoas, but all stops when Iphigénie summons the courage of her friends.

SCENE IV

ARIA and SCENE (Thoas; Scythian guards, Iphigénie, Priestesses, Oreste; later, Pylade and Greek sailors) *De tes forfaits la trame est découverte* ("The scheme of your crimes has been discovered") Thoas reviles Iphigénie for deceiving the gods and planning his doom and demands completion of the sacrifice. To her demand that the sacrifice be abandoned because the victim is her brother, Thoas accuses his hesitant guards of cowardice and resolves to slay them both himself.

Thoas's arrival is set to appropriately brusque chords and the military bravado of trumpet rhythms related to the Scythian choruses of Act I. Thoas's threats and the responses of

---

[6] Also known as Leto, Latona was the mother of Apollo and Diana by Jupiter.

Iphigénie, Oreste, and the Priestesses are all sung over this pattern. There is a change marked by tritone harmony when Iphigénie identifies the victim as her brother.

SCENE V

RECITATIVE, CHORUS (Pylade, Greek sailors, and the above) *C'est à toi de mourir!* ("It is you who shall die!") Pylade and the Greek sailors burst upon the scene, Pylade striking Thoas dead with a single blow and, with his colleagues, engaging the Scythians in battle.

When Pylade charges in with his retainers, the music of the overture's storm returns and forms the substance of the battle. The three-part male texture of the Act I Scythians's chorus is retained, but the Greeks are sung by harmonizing tenors, while the Scythians are reduced to a unison bass part.

SCENE VI

RECITATIVE (Diane) *Arrêtez! Écoutez mes décrets éternels* ("Cease! Hear my eternal decree!") The goddess descends suddenly in a cloud and orders a halt to the combat. She accuses the Scythians of profaning her altar and purges Oreste of his guilt, ordering him to Mycenae to reign in peace there and to restore Iphigénie to her homeland.[7] Diane returns to the heavens.

Diane halts the proceedings with a sudden intrusion of accompanied recitative. Her subsequent pronouncements are introduced by descending sweeps of scale figures.

SCENE VII

RECITATIVE, ARIOSO, CHORUS (Pylade, Oreste, et al.) *Ta soeur! Qu'ai-je entendu?* ("Your sister! What have I heard?") Oreste, praising Iphigénie for her compassion and her rescue of him, identifies her as his sister to Pylade and the Greek sailors.

All proclaim a future of peace.

Oreste's arioso is short, simple, and reflective of his new calm spirit. The final chorus is a formal coda by way of its ABA form; its lyrically gracious prediction of peace is pointedly marked by the orchestra's frequent recall of the fanfare rhythm that had moments before heralded Thoas's arrival.

---

[7] Orestes's return to Mycenae results in wedded bliss to Hermione, daughter of Menelaus and Helen (who had become reconciled when Troy fell, because, in spite of her physical attraction to Paris, Helen still loved her husband and was of some aid to the Greeks—and she was still gorgeous). Another telling of the legend has it that Orestes is acquitted of guilt only after a trial at the Court of Areopagus, where Athena/Minerva casts a tie-breaking vote, and could not claim Hermione as bride without first killing Neoptolemus (Achilles's son, also known as Pyrrhus), to whom she was already wed. Pylades marries Electra according to one version of the legends, although Mozart's *Idomeneo* brings her unwed to Crete, where her love for Prince Idamante is a major element in the entanglements of the plot.

Gluck, *Iphigénie en Tauride* (1779), ACT IV, scene v: The terrified Iphigénie (Michal Shamir) and the priestesses observe the final battle between the Greeks and the Scythians. Stadttheater Augsburg, 1995: production by John Dew, sets by Thomas Gruber, costumes by Jose-Manuel Vazquez. Photo Lioba Schöneck, Munich.

The Characters

Iphigénie (soprano) *[ee-fee-zheh-NEE]*

High priestess of Diana but ever more reluctant to participate in the ritual slaughter prescribed by Thoas, who fears that any stranger will cause his death. Iphigénie, aching with longing for her family and racked by a frightful dream of the awful events of her family history, is given stressful recitatives; her appeal to Diane at the start of Act IV (Example IP-1) is marked by a constant alternation of a twisting violin figure and strongly accented two-note descents, swift and unmistakable strokes that show a soul in torment. Her most famous moment, however, her celebrated Act II lament "O malheureuse Iphigénie" ("Oh, unhappy Iphigenia," Example IP-2), is a through-composed melody of great simplicity and unsurpassed dignity. It is given tenderness and poignancy by the commentary of a solo oboe above a steady throb of arpeggios and syncopated violins.

Oreste (baritone) *[aw-REST]*

Iphigénie's younger brother (by about fourteen years). He is perennially on the brink of utter madness, a frame of mind brought out in the first report

EXAMPLE IP-1 ACT IV, SCENE I: IPHIGÉNIE'S APPEAL TO DIANE

EXAMPLE IP-2 ACT II, SCENE VI: IPHIGÉNIE'S LAMENT

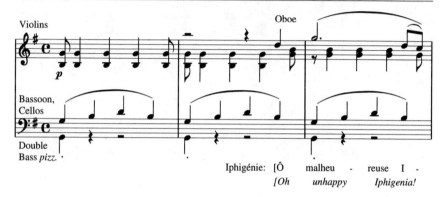

we have of him: a shepherd tells Thoas in Act I that two young Greeks have been driven upon the Scythian shores and one of them had the words "crime" and "remorse" endlessly on his lips. The distress of Oreste's spirit is reflected in his dream in the famous dungeon scene, where syncopations in the strings give the lie to his delusion of calm (see Example 3.3), and unrelenting accents in the following chorus of the Furies attack his sleep without mercy. His mental agony is also reflected in "Dieux qui me poursuivez" ("Ye Gods who pursue me," start of Act II; Example IP-3), where he berates the gods for bringing his life to its present state and begs for death in short phrases accompanied by tremolos, fanfares, and running scales in a fully instrumented aria of remarkable turbulence.

A particularly affecting moment in Oreste's music is the arioso given him in Act IV, when he expresses gratitude to Iphigénie for her sympathy. The pli-

EXAMPLE IP-3 ACT II, SCENE I: ORESTE BERATES THE GODS FOR BRINGING HIM TO HIS PRESENT DESPAIR

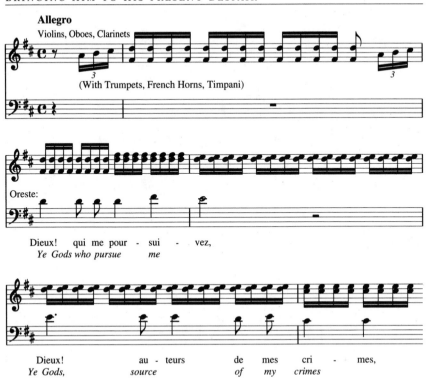

ant beauty of his melody is made poignant there by gentle syncopations and the timbre of a solo flute, the only time in the opera that Gluck isolates this color.

Pylade (tenor) [pee-LAHD]

According to some tellings of the legend, Pylade was disowned by his father for assisting in the murder of Clytemnestra and Aegisthus. There is no evidence of that in the opera, for Pylade sings with consistent grace and rhythmic simplicity even when he speaks energetically. His aria of loyalty, "Unis dès la plus tendre enfance" ("United since our most tender childhood," Act II) is quite different from Oreste's outburst "Dieu! qui me poursuivez," not only in its sense of poise and self-control (as opposed to Oreste's explosive energy) but also in its subtly different use of fast-moving triplets: in Oreste's aria, these are powerful upbeats; in Pylade's, they are decorative grace notes (Example IP-5). Pylade's aria is also quite different because its phrases end on a weak beat of the measure instead of on a strong one,[8] and because its brevity emphasizes a special sincerity and directness of thought.

---

[8] The melodic device by which this is achieved, called an appoggiatura (lit., "leaning note"), provides a dissonant tone on the accented beat and the resolution of the dissonance on the weak beat. This melodic quality, often referred to as a "feminine ending," is a hallmark of the grace and elegance often characteristic of mid- and late eighteenth-century music.

EXAMPLE IP-4 ACT IV, SCENE II: ORESTE RESPONDS TO
IPHIGÉNIE'S TENDER CONCERN FOR HIM

Nonetheless, Pylade has a strong backbone. His Act IV "Divinités des grandes âmes, / Amitiés, viens armer mon bras" ("Friendship, deity of great souls, come strengthen my arm"), when he vows to return to save Oreste, has the militant traits of Oreste's aria—fanfares, scales, trumpets, and drums—but it also has quieter moments that symbolize his resolve and a calm self-reliance.

EXAMPLE IP-4 (*Continued*)

Thoas (bass) *[TOE-ahss]*

Barbarian king who fears any stranger to his land. Like Oreste, Thoas is assaulted by guilt for his past cruelties, but his response is aggressive rather than suicidal. Angular dotted rhythms accompany his first appearance in Act I, when the laments of Iphigénie and the Priestesses cause him to fear his own demise, and his assault on Iphigénie and Oreste in the final scene is stamped with fanfares and bold instrumentation.

Diane (soprano) *[dee-AHN]*

Goddess of the Hunt. Her appearance at the end of the opera is as a typical *dea ex machina*, but, inasmuch as the return of Pylade with his sailors has already saved Iphigénie and Oreste from death, it is a pro forma device that allows for a scenically and aurally solemn finale. Her music is in the secco style, with somewhat more elaborate punctuations from the orchestra.

EXAMPLE IP-5 ACT II, SCENE I: INTRODUCTION TO PYLADE'S
GRACIOUS ARIA WELCOMING THE DEATH THAT WILL BIND HIM
TO ORESTE IN ETERNAL FRIENDSHIP (THE EXAMPLE INDICATES
THAT HIS WORDS FOLLOW THIS INTRODUCTION TO VIRTUALLY
THE SAME MELODY)

Scythian shepherd (bass)

A minister of the temple of Diana (bass)

These are two secondary roles who communicate only in recitative. The former reveals news of the arrival of the Greeks to Thoas; the latter's function
is to escort Pylade to the temple, thus leaving Oreste alone in his cell.

Priestesses (women's chorus)

These companions in suffering are Greek women who accompany Iphigénie
wherever she goes; only once is she alone. They are sympathetic to her and
lament their loss of homeland but are loyal to their duties. Their music is
prevailingly simple, solemn, and hymn-like and never in more than two harmonizing parts, although there are brief passages of independent part-writ-
ing in moments of ritual.

Scythians (men's chorus)

Two high tenor parts and a bass part are the voicing for this wild crew, whose
violent attitude is set out in short choruses that are vivid in rhythm and
tempo. Their special sound is the Janissary instrumentation of piccolo and

percussion (triangle, cymbal, and side drum).[9] The only ballet music in the opera is theirs, although one may presume that the ceremonial comings and goings of the Priestesses are also choreographic.

Furies

The three women of Greek mythology are transformed by Gluck into a chorus of tormenting creatures of conscience. Attacking Oreste by imitative entrances that suggest their coming at him from all sides, their fast, steady rhythms are implacable and throbbing, pausing only for stark, solemn chords when they proclaim no mercy, because "il a tué sa mère"—"he killed his mother." The biting tritone on "mère" is like a savage thrust into Oreste's troubled soul.

Bibliography

Dean, Winton. "Iphigénie en Tauride," in *Essays on Opera*. London: Oxford University Press, 1990 [1961], pp. 94–97.

Einstein, Alfred. *Gluck,* trans. Eric Blom. The Master Musicians. London: Dent, 1936.

Euripides. "Iphigenia in Tauris," in *Alcestis and Other Plays,* trans. Philip Vellacott. Penguin Classics. Harmondsworth, Middlesex: Penguin, 1953.

Grube, G. M. A. *The Drama of Euripides.* New York: Barnes and Noble, 1961 [1941].

Howard, Patricia. *Gluck and the Birth of Modern Opera.* New York: St. Martin's Press, 1963.

See Chapter 8, "Gluck as Dramatist," for focus on this opera.

Newman, Ernest. *Gluck and the Opera: A Study in Musical History.* New York: AMS Press, 1978 [1895].

See pp. 177–189 for a study of Iphigénie en Tauride.

Rushton, Jules. "The Operas of Gluck and Piccini," in *Music and Letters* 53, no. 4 (1972): 411–430.

---

[9] This instrumentation was associated in European minds with the Turkish troops known as the Janissaries; Mozart used it to exotic effect in *Die Entführung aus dem Serail* (especially the overture).

Chapter 9

DON GIOVANNI

Il dissoluto punito, ossia Il Don Giovanni—Dramma giocoso ("The Profligate Punished or The Story of Don Juan—A Humorous Drama"), K. 527[1]

MUSIC: Wolfgang Amadeus Mozart (1756–1791)

LIBRETTO: Lorenzo Da Ponte (1749–1838), based on the Don Juan legend and a libretto by Giovanni Bertati (1735–1815) for *Don Giovanni Tenorio* (Giuseppe Gazzaniga, 1743–1818). It is unclear as to how extensively Da Ponte and Mozart drew on *El burlador de Sevilla y convidado di piedra* (The Deceiver[2] of Seville, or The Stone Guest, 1616) by Tirso de Molina (pseudonym of Gabriel Tellez, 1571–1641).

PREMIERE: Prague (National Theater), October 29, 1787. Two of the opera's best-known arias—Don Ottavio's "Dalla sua pace" and Donna Elvira's "In quali eccessi . . . Mi tradì quell' alma ingrata"—were composed for the Vienna production of 1788, along with a comic duet and scene for Zerlina and Leporello in Act II (with recitatives). The last of these is rarely performed; the first two rarely omitted. The discussions that follow are based on the Prague version, with the two Vienna arias included.

TIME AND PLACE OF THE STORY: A twenty-four-hour period from one midnight to the next in a small Spanish city.

Sui Generis: The Opera as Synthesis

Don Giovanni is the *Hamlet* of opera. Like its Shakespearean counterpart, it is a synthesis[3] of the life around it and speaks for an age caught in an upheaval

---

[1] "K. 527" identifies the number of this opera in the catalogue of Mozart's works published in 1862 by Ludwig von Köchel. *Dramma giocoso* is a generic term synonymous with *opera buffa*; the latter is the way Mozart entered *Don Giovanni* in his own catalogue. In recent times *dramma giocoso* has been applied to *Don Giovanni* as a work sui generis, mixing serious and comic elements. Mozart and his contemporaries did not think in that way.

[2] *Burlador* carries additional connotations of mockery, sneering, and trickery.

[3] The mixing of seemingly unrelated elements was not to everyone's taste. "Musical taste," grumped Antonio Salieri (1750–1825), "is gradually changing to a sort completely contrary to that of my own times; extravagance and confusion of styles have replaced rationality and majestic simplicity." (Quoted in Headington, p. 100.)

for which it was tragically unprepared. By the end of the eighteenth century, the ideals of the Enlightenment—reason, order, and self-restraint—were recognized as wishful thinking.

It is a world apart from *Giulio Cesare*. Ornamentation of melody and extension of phrase are special devices for characterization rather than the lingua franca of the music; its musical texture treats voices and instruments as parts of an interconnected web rather than as separate and complementary elements; its dramatic flow is a steadily mounting sense of climax rather than a series of exit arias; and ensembles are fully fifty percent of its "numbers" rather than occasional events.

Only four arias are soliloquies;[4] in the others, words and music are said directly to someone and are important to the unfolding of the plot. *Giulio Cesare*'s arias freeze action for the sake of emotional response; *Don Giovanni* uses arias and ensembles as dramatic cannons, loading each with the ammunition of response, then discharging the action. *Giulio Cesare* poses magnificently, *Don Giovanni* moves galvanically.

As a composer at the peak of the Classical era, Mozart capitalized on Da Ponte's vivid situations by presenting conflicting emotions, personalities, and motivations simultaneously or within a single passage, adjacent phrases, and so on. Ensembles, accompanied recitatives, and arias not only ring the changes on aspects of mood and feeling but also present a commingling of genres and styles: Ottavio and Anna are characters from the ranks of opera seria; Leporello, Zerlina, and Masetto step into the cast from opera buffa; Elvira is a *mezzo carratere*, a "middle" charater who has aspects of both the farcical and serious. Giovanni is the only character who talks to all of them in their own musical "language" and thus, like the opera, is sui generis.

Different genres of opera are fused in the action, too. The tragic death scene of the Commendatore, for example, is followed by Leporello's bawdy comments in recitativo secco, thus tying high drama to low comedy; a similar fusion comes at the end of the opera, when buffoonery and gluttony (in the Act II supper scene) collapses at the appearance of the Commendatore's statue and the dragging of Giovanni down to the fires of Hell. The Act I finale simultaneously presents three dances—each played by its own orchestra—as metaphors for aristocracy, bourgeoisie, and peasantry; the intermixing of their instrumentations and styles toward chaos and stress offers not only one of the most brilliantly structured and effective curtains in theater but also a musical sermon on the instability of a civilization teetering on disaster.[5]

Ambiguity and "Là ci darem la mano"

Does Anna pursue Giovanni because he failed or because he tried? Does Zerlina love Masetto or settle for him? Is Ottavio a worthless fop or a man of

---

4 Leporello's "Notte e giorno," which opens the opera, Ottavio's Act I "Dalla sua pace" (No. 10b), and Elvira's "Mi tradì quell' alma ingrata" (No. 21c) are sung with no one around to hear. Elvira's "Ah! chi mi dice mai" (No. 3) is sung as a soliloquy but is overheard by Leporello and Giovanni—in opera, private thoughts are public property.

5 See Till, *Mozart and the Enlightenment*, p.203f. Less than two years after the Prague premiere (October 29, 1787), the Bastille fell.

dignity and strength of purpose? Does Anna love Ottavio and delay marrying him because of spiritual exhaustion or does she shrink at the thought of spending her life with him?

The Romantic era's absorption with ambiguity found a mother lode in *Don Giovanni*, and the literature interpreting the opera is enormous. The wonderfully charming Giovanni/Zerlina duet (No. 7, "Là ci darem la mano"— "There we shall give each other our hands") may serve as a paradigm for an endless fascination with the opera's uncertainties and possibilities of meaning. Giovanni has arranged to be alone with this delicious peasant girl; in recitative, he suggests that so lovely a lass should not yield to the rough use of a coarse ploughman ("bifolcaccio") like Masetto but rather should entrust her future to a nobleman like himself. He dismisses her doubts about the usual intentions of the nobility as a vile slander; to prove it, he says, "I want to marry you" ("io vi voglio sposar"). He points to his grand town house, which he refers to as a "casinetto," where they can be alone and where they will be wed.

Is Zerlina taken in by this? Presumably she speaks the same language as he does, so his use of "casinetto" (a little brothel) is not at all confused in her mind with "casetta" (a cottage; "casa" = house). Giovanni's cuteness, then, must be transparent: he is inviting her to have sex, in exchange for which there will be some reward beyond the forthcoming pleasures of the flesh. Having lived on a farm and observed the world of aristocrats and peasants, she knows what's what: "Io sò che raro colle donne voi altri cavalieri siete onesti e sinceri" ("I know how rarely with women you cavaliers are honest and sincere"). On the other hand, maybe she is indeed naive and so overwhelmed by the possiblity of a higher station in life that she quite misses the cynical punning of "casa"/"casino"/"casinetto" and buys into Giovanni's "proposal of marriage." We can't be certain from the words of the recitative, and the music of the duet leaves us in a bit of a quandary.

Consider each person's opening lines. (Giovanni sings first, Zerlina responds, but they are shown simultaneously in Example DG-1a for the sake of comparison.) Giovanni's opening gambit is a serene eight-measure unit that is a paragon of classical symmetry and poise. The grace and simplicity of this elegantly contrived melody (there is but a touch of ornament in m. 7) suggests Giovanni's nobility; by using such a style to address a peasant girl, Giovanni seems to her to be treating her as an equal, without condescension. Zerlina's answer, however, offers a good deal more than a touch of ornament: that her heart trembles a bit is evident from the grace note of m. 12, and mm. 15–18 are not only ornamented but extend the ornamentation two measures beyond Giovanni's original theme. Is Zerlina being flirtatious? Or is she so ill at ease and out of her league socially and musically that she is unable to answer a musical phrase with appropriate symmetry?

When Giovanni urges her to entrust her fate to his care ("Io cangierò tua sorte"), her response is ahead of the beat ("x" in Example DG-1b) instead of on it, and her narrow compass and repetitiousness indicate—what?—coyness? or nervousness? The scene can be staged convincingly both ways, with Zerlina fearfully moving away with quick steps or just standing there playing a delightful game, tilting her head, gazing sidelong at her wooer, and batting her eyelids, while her hand goes pitter-patter in a "be still my aching heart" routine.

Each of the subsequent phrases invites similar disparity of analysis: either Giovanni is interrupting her phrases so that she cannot hear herself (Example DG-1c), or she is delighting in the game and having a merry time taking Giovanni's ornamentation of m. 7 and making it her own by repetition and variation. Are the violins' notes heartbeats? Or orchestral chuckles? The smooth parallel thirds of the *allegro* (Example DG-1d) are either surrender or agreement: take your pick.

EXAMPLE DG-1 ACT I, SCENE III: NO. 7, "LÀ CI DAREM LA MANO" ("THERE WE SHALL GIVE EACH OTHER OUR HANDS")— DON GIOVANNI PROPOSES "MARRIAGE" TO ZERLINA

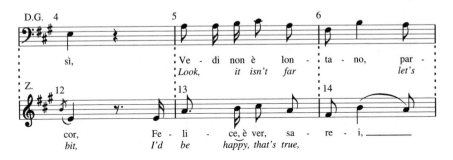

a) Giovanni's offer, Zerlina's response (the melodies are sung in sequence but are shown one above the other for purpose of comparison).

EXAMPLE DG-1 (*Continued*)

Pre - sto non son___ più   for - te, non son___ più___
All   at   once   I   am   no   longer   strong,   I   am   no

for - te, non son___ più   for - te
longer   strong,   I   am no longer strong

b) Zerlina weakening? or flirting?

ma___   può bur - lar   - mi an - cor.   Mi
but   I can still be made   a   fool of.   *I*

Don Giovanni:

Vie - ni, mio bel   di -
Come   my   lovely

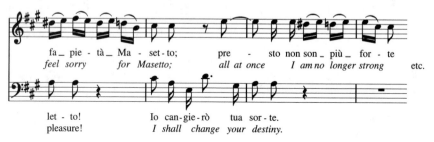

fa_ pie - tà Ma - set - to;   pre - sto non son_ più_ for - te   etc.
feel sorry   for Masetto;   all at once   I am no longer strong

let - to!   Io can - gie - rò   tua sor - te.
pleasure!   *I shall   change   your destiny.*

c) Overlapping of phrase.

Energy and Unity

Violence and cruelty move this opera away from its Classical surroundings
and into the realm of Romantic passion and excitement. Act I begins and
ends with attempted rape—a raw symmetry there—and includes within these
framing elements the killing of the Commendatore. Act II includes the mockery of Elvira, a severe beating of Masetto, a sneering challenge to the spirit of
the dead Commendatore, and the climax of Giovanni being dragged down to
a fiery Hell. All of it, of course, with music to match.

The restlessness and driving energy that are characteristic of this
remarkable score derive not only from the music's rhythmic force but also

EXAMPLE DG-1 (*Continued*)

d) They reach an understanding.

from a musical and dramatic linkage to an extent not found in any of Mozart's predecessors.[6] The opening of the opera, for example, is an extended scene that connects seamlessly Leporello's monologue of complaint, the struggle of Anna and Giovanni, the confrontation between the Commendatore and the Don, and the trio on the death of the Commendatore. The finale of Act I is almost eighteen minutes of connected music drama, and the Act II finale, including the Epilogue, is about twenty-three minutes long. Each segment of these two finales is an intensification and outgrowth of what led up to it, and each finale is a mirror of the other: both offer social structures and convivial situations that collapse, are marked by entertainment and stage music, change dramatic and musical direction at the sound of a woman's scream, have a startling confrontation of someone appearing in a doorway, and turn from a suite-like presentation of pleasant music to tumult and destruction. Their major difference is that the Act I finale represents society plundered, while Act II depicts the final triumph of justice and a restoration of order.[7]

The music is rarely calm. The urgency of melodic or instrumental motion provides a turmoil that is pyschologically disturbing at almost every turn. Only Ottavio's "Dalla sua pace la mia dipende" (No. 10a) and Zerlina's "Vedrai carino" (No. 18) are really serene; his "Il mio tesoro" (No. 21) bus-

---

[6] Don Giovanni is a continuance of this feature as Mozart had developed it in Acts II and IV of *Le nozze di Figaro* (1786).

[7] I have based this description largely on the analysis offered by Allanbrook, p. 277.

tles with fast ornament and rhythmic energy, and Zerlina's "Batti, batti" (No. 12, Example DG-2a) bubbles with a cello obbligato that is as rhythmically propelling as it is delectable. Anna's seemingly placid "Non mi dir" (No. 23), in which she pleads with Ottavio for his understanding of her distress, is a relatively slow tempo (*larghetto*) but throbs with ornament, rhythmic activity, and a frequent exchange of melodic material between voice and instruments (Example DG-2b); the second section of the aria reflects even greater urgency and the sense of torment beyond relief because of its syncopations, abrupt changes of dynamics, gasping broken rhythms (Example DG-2c), extended melismas, and faster tempo (*allegro moderato*).

Large-scale unity is another important feature of this score. The tonality of D is a frame for the entire opera: the overture proceeds from D minor to D major; D minor returns in the final scene with the arrival of the Statue and the destruction of Don Giovanni, and D major returns for the Epilogue and the pointing of the moral.

There is a thematic unity to all this, too, for the supper scene at the end of Act II draws with chilling effect and dramatic horror on the music of the opera's opening moments. The overture's dissonant harmonies recur as the Statue appears in Giovanni's dining hall; Giovanni's astonishment and his order to Leporello to serve the Statue a meal (Example DG-3c) recall not only the overture's throbbing chords and syncopations (Example DG-3a) but also the agonized half-steps in the violins that mark Anna's discovery of her father's body (Example DG-3b); and the Statue's call for repentance (Example DG-3e) is underscored by those same chords and the overture's eerily undulating scales (Example DG-3d).

EXAMPLE DG-2 RESTLESSNESS IN MOMENTS OF APPARENT SERENITY

a) Act I, scene xvi: No. 12 "Batti, batti, o bel Masetto" ("Beat me, beat me, handsome Masetto")—Zerlina cajoles Masetto into forgiveness.

b) Act II, scene xiii: No. 23 "Non mi dir" ("Say not to me")—Anna speaks gently to Ottavio.

EXAMPLE DG-2 (*Continued*)

c) The same: Anna speaks more formally to Ottavio.

Also contributing to the opera's sense of unity is a rhythmic unit (Example DG-4) that informs almost every scene: it is a jabbing snap of scalar sixteenth notes or triplets—rising or falling—with qualities of haste, incisiveness, impetuosity, and straight-line motion that bespeak sword play or—more usually—phallic activity, both of which are closely associated with Don Giovanni.[8] The bold scale figure thus becomes the signature of the opera as a whole and specifically of its central character.

---

[8] Its metaphorical meaning is, of course, derived from the context of the drama and its text, since Mozart used a similar device in *Idomeneo* (1781), an opera seria of a very different dramatic and musical intent.

a) Overture: pulsing chords and syncopations.

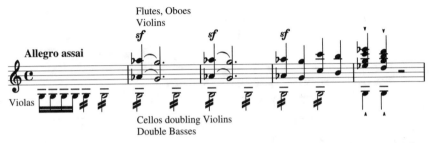

b) Act I, scene iii: No. 2 "Ma qual mai s'offre" ("But what [funereal spectacle] is offered [to my eyes]—Orchestral "cries" at Anna's discovery of her father's body.

Andante

[Note: Violin "cries" are reinforced by Oboes and Bassoons a half-beat later]

c) Act II, scene iv: Finale—Giovanni's consternation at the arrival of the Statue.

EXAMPLE DG-3 (*Continued*)

d) Overture: Rising and falling scales (note dramatic effect of *crescendo* and sudden *piano*).

e) Act II, scene iv: Finale—The Statue calls Giovanni to repent (scales, with chords, as in Example DG-3a).

THE PLOT AND ITS MUSIC

NOTE: Scenes are numbered in accordance with the arrival or departure of characters rather than with changes of location; the latter are identified below as tableaux. All recitatives are secco unless noted otherwise.

OVERTURE *The overture is in two sections, each with the instrumentation of strings, timpani, pairs of woodwinds, trumpets, and French horns. The trombones are significantly silent; they are associated exclusively with the Statue and thus do not appear until it does in Act II, scene xii, and Act II, scene xvi. The music of Section 1 is associated with the supernatural elements of the plot and will be recalled in the supper scene at the end of Act II. The tempo and spirit of Section 2 suggest the comic aspects of the opera; its pattern of development of motives, keys, and recapitulation illustrate the sonata form.*

Section 1 andante: Two dramatic chords set the mode of D minor; then an ominous dotted rhythm accompanies a series of descents in changing woodwind colors, the bass proceeding down by half-steps in an archetypical musical symbol of death. The sense of mystery and portent continues with a syncopated figure in the strings; this is interrupted by sudden flourishes of short scalar figures (Ex. DG-4a) that in turn yield to broken rhythms, suggestive of the sobbing and heart palpitations of Elvira and Anna. Rising and falling chromatic scales ensue, each arch intensified by beginning a half-step higher; each is accompanied by the earlier dotted rhythm and marked by crescendos *and sudden* pianos.

EXAMPLE DG-4 SCALAR MOTIVE FOUND IN VARIOUS CONTEXTS OF
THE OPERA

a) Overture.

b) Act I, scene i: No. 1 *Introduction*—in predawn cold and dark, Leporello paces
back and forth in annoyance and impatience.

c) Act I, scene v: No. 4 "Madamina! Il catalogo è questo" ("Little lady, this is the
catalogue")—from Leporello's catalogue of Giovanni's amours: in brunettes,
Giovanni praises constancy.

d) Act I, scene xiii: No. 10 "Or sai chi l'onore" ("Now you know who [wanted
to ravish] my honor")—Anna swears Ottavio to the cause of revenge.

Mozart, *Don Giovanni* (1787), Act I, scene i: The climax of the duel between the Commendatore (Stephen West) and Don Giovanni (Dwayne Croft). Santa Fe Opera, 1996: production design by Miguel Romero. Courtesy Santa Fe Opera. Photo David Stein.

EXAMPLE DG-4 (*Continued*)

e) Act I, Finale: hearing the scream of Zerlina from a locked room, all rush to the door.

EXAMPLE DG-4 (*Continued*)

f) Act II, Finale: The Statue is heard knocking at the door.

Section 2 **moderato**: *In D major; its spirited principal subject (partially chromatic and syncopated) will recur in the Act II sextet (No. 19), when Ottavio urges Anna to calm her sorrows lest her father's shade "will be pained by your suffering" (pena avrà de' tuoi martir). A second subject is a blunt descending scale with a witty and playful pendant: the scale will accompany Anna's demand that Ottavio avenge her (in No. 2, at Ah! vendicar, se il puoi, giura quel sangue ognor—"Ah! Swear to avenge that blood, if you can"). A sustained chord of unexpected harmony is followed directly by Leporello's No. 1.*

Act I

Tableau 1: *The garden of Donna Anna's palatial home. Midnight. Leporello, cloaked, striding back and forth in boredom and irritation.*

SCENE 1—MIDNIGHT

1 INTRODUCTION (Leporello) *Notte e giorno faticar* ("Night and day I work") Waiting for his master to complete another sexual escapade, Leporello complains about eating and sleeping badly; "I want to be a gentleman (*Voglio far il gentiluomo*) and serve no longer." That Giovanni is inside with a lovely lady while he must stand guard is a prime annoyance to him. Hearing people coming, he withdraws to watch.

Perfect fourths and a stomping scale pattern (Ex. DG-4b) characterize Leporello's back-and-forth pacing. His wish to be a cavalier is given a gallop-like triplet accompaniment of horn calls, and a flourish of woodwinds that is a military swirl gone comic. The flourish returns at Leporello's sarcastic O che caro galantuomo ("Oh that dear gentleman") and points up the grumbling repetitions of Leporello's lowly status as sentinella ("guard duty"). Buffo patter takes over when he hears someone coming, the tuneless repeated notes punctuated by fanfare alternations between winds and strings.

(Anna, Giovanni, Leporello) *Non sperar, se non m'uccidi, / ch'io ti lasci fuggir mai* ("Do not hope, unless you kill me, that I will ever allow you to escape") Don Giovanni exits hastily from within, pursued by Donna Anna. He keeps his cloak over his face while Anna tries to restrain him and see who he is. She vows not to let him escape and calls for help, Giovanni demanding she be silent and fear his wrath (*Taci, e trema al mio furore*), and Leporello (from his hiding place) fearing that Giovanni may make him do something rash (*mi farà precipitar*).

Giovanni offers no melody specifically related to him; his music is only an echo or imitation of Anna's, as if he were disguising himself musically as well as visually. A dotted rhythm and roiling scale patterns characterize the turmoil of their struggle; Leporello's patter adds a buffo element to an otherwise melodramatic duet.

(Commendatore, Leporello, Giovanni) *Lasciala, indegno, / battiti meco!* ("Release her, wretch, fight with me!) The Commendatore appears, bearing his sword and a torch. He demands that the intruder release his daughter. Anna hurries into the house. The Commendatore demands immediate satisfaction; when Giovanni refuses to fight, the outraged father implies he is a coward. Giovanni unwillingly accepts the challenge (*Misero! attendi / si vuoi morir*—"Wretched man! Stay if you want to die").

Tremolos and a scale figure (quoted later at entry of the aristocrats as Maskers in I, xx) announce the entrance of Anna's father. His line is characterized by perfect intervals and simple scale patterns and gains a formal dignity from its short phrasing and triadic melody.

The duel is short and brutal; the Commendatore falls, mortally wounded. Giovanni notes the man's death throes coldly, Leporello with horror and terror.

The duel is compressed into a few measures of vivid rising scales suggestive of sword thrusts (Ex. DG-4c), with tremolos lending tension. The clash of metal against metal is suggested by vividly accented octave leaps in the violins, the fatal blow by a dissonant harmony (a diminished seventh chord). The death scene is in the minor mode over quiet triplets. The final gasps of the Commendatore come in halting phrases of separated notes; Giovanni's comments draw on some of Anna's earlier music; Leporello's dismay is a descending dotted rhythm (picked up momentarily by Giovanni, who still has no music of his own). Chromatic descents in oboe, flute, and bassoon end the scene with ineffable sadness.

SCENE II

RECITATIVE *Leporello, ove sei?* ("Leporello, where are you?") Giovanni calls in a whisper to Leporello, who ironically notes the success of the evening: violate the daughter and murder the father (*sforzar la figlia, ed ammazzar il padre*). To Giovanni's "he asked for it," Leporello asks what Donna Anna had asked for. Giovanni issues a threat of violence for impertinence; both leave quickly.

Anna and Ottavio, with servants bearing torches, appear from the house, Anna urging him to come to her father's aid, he vowing to do so but seeing no one.

SCENE III

2 ACCOMPANIED RECITATIVE . . . DUET (Anna, Ottavio) *Ma qual mai s'offre, O Dei, / spettacolo funesto agli occhi miei! . . . Fuggi, crudele* ("But what tragic sight is offered to my eyes, ye Gods . . . Leave, cruel one") Discovering her father's body, Anna collapses. Ottavio orders the servants to bring smelling salts and calls tenderly to her; then, directing that the corpse be taken away, he tries to calm her.

In rage and grief, Anna demands that death take her also; seeing her fiancé beside her, she swears him to vengeance. He accepts. The two admit to the wavering of their hearts among hundreds of emotions (*Fra cento affetti e cento / vammi ondeggiando il cor*), then leave.

> *The agonized half-steps of Ex. DG-3b over viola tremolos create the horror and agonized cries of Anna's tragic discovery. Her sobs are in short, gasping phrases, with plaintive woodwind echoes. An abrupt change of key and a violin descent at* Padre amato *("beloved father") suggest that she swoons. Ottavio's orders to the servants are given correspondingly quick rhythms. Anna's response to his attempts to offer comfort is a sudden* allegro *in angular and detached phrases; his responses are also in short phrases with a few longer ones, as if he were trying to bridge the emotional gap between them. Fast string scales underly their mutual agitation. The descending scale of the overture's second section announces her call to action, as do dotted-rhythm fanfares. They unite musically in parallel thirds, their phrases sometimes in the broken rhythms of emotional exhaustion, sometimes with repetitions of a tiny rhythmic unit that hint at near hysteria.*

Tableau 2: *A street or plaza on which fronts an inn or hotel; Giovanni's town house can be seen from afar. During scenes iv through vii, dawn breaks and mid-morning is approached.*

SCENE IV—JUST BEFORE DAWN

RECITATIVE (Giovanni, Leporello) *Orsù, spicciati presto. Cosa vuoi?* ("Come on now, quick. What do you want?") Giovanni and Leporello are in the midst of a conversation at the culmination of which Leporello berates Giovanni for leading the life of a rogue (*la vita che menate / è da briccone*). Giovanni warns him of physical punishment. He turns to the matter at hand, the pursuit of a damsel, only to interrupt himself by noting that he senses the smell of a woman. They move aside to see who it might be.

SCENE V

3 TRIO (Elvira, Giovanni, Leporello) *Ah! chi mi dice mai / quel barbaro dov'è* ("Ah! Who will tell me where that cruel man is?") Having just arrived, Elvira, still in her traveling clothes, laments the cruelty that has been visited upon her and avers her eagerness to cut the heart out (*vo' cavare il cor*) of the villain responsible.

Not seeing her face, Giovanni immediately desires to console her (Leporello: *Così ne consolò mille e ottocento*—"As he has consoled eighteen hundred others"). Giovanni steps forward with grand politeness.

Tiny scale fragments and then an explosion of fast scalar descents hint at Elvira's basic state of mind—agitation—and invite a sense of the way she paces about (very different from the blunt intervals of Leporello's first appearance). To Mozart and his audiences her wide intervals, high notes, melismas (on vo' *cavare il cor), and text repetitions (her desire to cut Giovanni's heart out is exclaimed twelve times) suggest the old fashioned (i.e., the music of Handel and his contemporaries) and the comically eccentric (Ex. DG-6a); the literal return of her opening music provides an ABA framework that is similarly archaic in its implications. Syncopations, sudden dynamic changes, and the quick scales found throughout the opera (Ex. DG-4a–f) complete the picture. Giovanni's comments are partly lyrical mockery, partly comic repetitions of a single note; Leporello's music apes his master's.*

RECITATIVE (Elvira, Leporello, Giovanni) *Chi è la?* ("Who's there?") She turns and recognizes Giovanni, whereupon she pours on him a stream of bitter criticism and remonstrance, barely pausing for breath (Leporello: *Pare un libro stampato*— "She's like a printed book"). Giovanni stammers some blather of justification and invites her to turn to his companion for verification. He orders Leporello to tell her everything and, as Elvira redirects her attention, he decamps.

Leporello turns to some doubletalk (*consiossiacosaquandofosseché il quadro non è tondo*—"withthisorthatwhenasitwere a square is not round . . .") to confuse and divert her. She turns to Giovanni to remonstrate and is dismayed at his absence. Feeling some pity for her, Leporello urges her not to trouble herself. He's not worth it, he says, and she's neither the first nor the last. To prove it, he shows her the catalogue he keeps.

4 ARIA (Leporello) *Madamina! il catalogo è questo / delle belle che amò il padron mio* ("My little lady![9] This is a catalogue of the fair ones my master has made love to"). He tallies the record of Giovanni's seductions: Italy 640, Germany 231, France 100, Turkey 91, Spain 1003 (*mille e tre!*). They are of all types and ranks, ages, shapes. Blondes he praises for their gentleness, brunettes for faithfulness, pale ones for sweetness; in winter he prefers plump ones, in summer he likes them lean; large (*maestosa*) or small (*piccina*), young or old—it doesn't matter, although his primary interest is the novice (*la giovin principiante*). "As long as she wears a skirt (*purchè porti la gonnella*) you know what he does (*voi sapete quel che fa*)." Then, as had his master a few moments before, he slips away.

The orchestral accompaniment bubbles with merriment and a rising triad that seems like an elbow in the ribs. The announcement of the numbers is given triumphant woodwind fanfares that create a sense of "Whew! Can you imagine that!" The repetitions and pauses marking the total in Spain are justifiably famous in operatic music. A typical buffo patter is used to regale Elvira with the variety of social classes.

When Leporello turns to physical characteristics, he uses a pseudo-courtly minuet, with flourishes (Ex. DG-4c) that mock the idea of fidelity while at the same time draw on the signature motive of the opera and its theme as a whole. The woman of large dimension is given pompous scales and crescendos, the diminutive one short note values and a wonderfully funny mincing figure in the violins. A sudden turn to the minor mode and a delicate bassoon arpeggio over a descent in the cellos and basses darkens the narrative when Leporello mentions Giovanni's preference for the young and innocent. His leering repeats of "quel che fa" are triads, the next to last of which is traditionally performed as a salacious hum. The Catalogue is given a final dotted-rhythm fanfare, as if trumpeting Giovanni's marvelous achievements.

---

[9] Leporello's diminutive of "Madama" reinforces the idea of Elvira's youth.

SCENE VI

RECITATIVE (Elvira) *In questa forma dunque mi tradì il scellerato!* ("In just this way the wretch betrayed me!") Elvira swears revenge and enters the inn.

SCENE VII—MID-MORNING

5 CHORUS (Zerlina, Masetto, and their friends) *Giovinette, che fate all' amore, / non lasciate che passi l'età* ("Young ladies who think of love, don't let time pass you by") Arriving at the inn to celebrate the wedding of Zerlina and Masetto, the young peasants sing and dance around the bridal couple, Zerlina surrounded by the girls, Masetto by the boys; both happily urge their friends to enjoy love and happiness while they can.

A delightful 6/8 dance in the style of a gigue (a dance type with rural associations). Its rippling triplets and sparkling woodwinds speak of good-heartedness and high spirits. Occasional held notes in lower instruments suggest the drone of bagpipes. The first strophe is for the girls and Zerlina, the second for the men and Masetto; the third for the bridal couple themselves. Parallel thirds in all the verses indicate sweetness and light.

SCENE VIII

RECITATIVE (Giovanni, Leporello; then Zerlina, Masetto) *Manco male, è partita* ("Thank heaven she's gone") Giovanni and Leporello come upon the festivity. Giovanni offers them his protection and directs Leporello to escort everyone to his palazzo (it's just a big house; Giovanni is using some hype here), where they are to be served chocolate, coffee, wine, and ham and given a tour of all the rooms. Putting his arm around Zerlina's waist, he specifies that Masetto is to be made content (*fa' che resti contento il mio Masetto*). Leporello understands and begins to move the peasants toward Giovanni's ample residence.

Masetto, however, will not budge: *La Zerlina / senza me non può star*—"Zerlina cannot remain without me." Giovanni's comment—that Zerlina is in the hands of a cavalier—is echoed by Zerlina, but Masetto is not to be put off until Giovanni pats his sword with a not-so-subtle bit of advice that Masetto might regret his obstinance.

6 ARIA (Masetto) *Ho capito, Signor sì!* (*"I've understood, yes sir!"*) Masetto acknowledges that he has no choice but to bow his head and obey; that Giovanni is indeed a cavalier cannot be doubted. He turns bitterly to Zerlina and denounces her for embarassing him (as, apparently, she has done in the past: *fosti ognor la mia ruina*—"you've always been my ruin"). He leaves angrily, warning her with a coarse pun that the "cavalier" will make a "cavaliera" (wife of a cavalier = a mare) out of her.

Masetto's rhythm and harmonic texture is simpler than Leporello's but made of the same cloth—they're both from the lower strata of society. Repetitive arpeggios in the violins hint at Masetto's one-track mind; the descending line of Ex. DG-8a is a clear pictorialization of his having to bow before the nobility; the lyric violins of Ex. DG-8b are, in context, a snide commentary on the graces of lords and ladies. Repetitions and fast rhythmic patterns speak to Masetto's buffo heritage as well as to his anger and frustration, and the empty octaves accompanying his pun on cavaliere *and* cavaliera *(Ex. DG-8c) have the effect not only of crudity but plain truth—the octave is, after all, second only to the unison as music's most "perfect" interval.*

SCENE IX

RECITATIVE *Alfin siam liberati* ("Finally we're free") Giovanni compliments himself on getting rid of Masetto. Zerlina's hesitancy is brushed off with his assurance that she deserves better than a fool (*scioccone*) and a ploughman (*bifolcaccio*) who is likely to abuse her. He flatters her outrageously, then urges her to go with him to his "little house of joy" (see the discussion of *casinetto*, p. 176), where he promises to marry her.

7 DUETTINO (Giovanni, Zerlina) *Là ci darem la mano, / là mi dirai di sì* ("There we shall give each other our hands, there you will tell me 'yes'"). Zerlina, seeming at first to be uncertain as to whether or not to accompany him, finally agrees to go along. Arm in arm, they head off.

See Exs. DG-1a–d. Giovanni's music begins with simplicity and dignity, its 2/4 rhythm over a gently vamping accompaniment. Zerlina's hesitations (or delay, if one believes that she is as savvy in the flirtation as Giovanni is) are overcome by his singing shorter and shorter phrases and by intruding musically on her responses—in effect, he keeps talking so that she cannot hear her own objections. The songful melody is accompanied by guitar-like string patterns with occasional softening touches of woodwinds and French horn. Giovanni's insistence that she come along (Vieni, vieni) is given the added fillip of the opera's unifying motive (Ex. DG-4a–f). Their coda of togetherness, a lilting 6/8 associated in Mozart's time with rural folk in general and in this opera with Zerlina in particular, has the added spice of string pizzicato.

SCENE X

RECITATIVE (Elvira, Giovanni) *Fermati, scellerato!* ("Stop, you scoundrel!") Out of the inn sails Elvira, halting Giovanni in his tracks with desperate gestures. Giovanni whispers to Elvira that surely she sees he is simply amusing himself; to Zerlina he confides that he must pretend to love this poor unhappy woman who is in love with him, since *per mia disgrazia, uom di buon cuore* ("to my bad luck, I am a man with a kind heart").

8 ARIA (Elvira) *Ah, fuggi il traditor, / non lo lasciar più dir* ("Ah, fly from this betrayer, don't let him say another word") Elvira delivers another torrent of accusation at Giovanni, who, she says, lies and betrays. Insisting that Zerlina must learn from Elvira's torments, she sweeps the country lass from the scene.

Elvira is in her Handelian mode again. Large skips in the introductory violins over a rather clumsy-sounding dotted rhythm make this aria militant in character; the constant variety of phrase length makes it eccentric and a metaphor for a character not quite in control of herself. The angular profile of her melodic line is in keeping with this, as is the grandiose melisma on fallace [il ciglio] *("false [his countenance]"). The aria is the only one in the opera that is accompanied by strings alone, and they are in but two parts, violins against violas and cellos (with doubling basses). This scoring is probably another gesture by Mozart to the sound of the Baroque orchestra's frequent use of an open-textured string sonority for storm-tossed emotions (cf. Handel's* Giulio Cesare: *Cesare's* L'empio, No. 3, *Achilla's* Dal fulgor, No. 30, *and Cleopatra's* Da tempeste, No. 37).

SCENE XI

RECITATIVE (Giovanni, Ottavio, Anna) *Mi par ch'oggi il demonio si diverta* ("I think the devil is having fun today") Giovanni curses the continued round of frustration; seeing the arrival of Anna (dressed in mourning) and Ottavio, he expects things to get worse but is pleased he has not been recognized as the assailant of the previous predawn hours. When Anna proclaims her need for his assistance,[10] he turns on the charm only to be thwarted once again by the swooping Elvira.

---

[10] One wonders why Ottavio has not at this point urged her to go to the "ones to whom we should go"—*a chi si deve*—as he says in the recitativo secco before his second act aria (No. 21, *Il mio tesoro*).

SCENE XII

9 QUARTET (Elvira, Anna, Ottavio, Giovanni) *Non ti fidar, o misera, di quel ribaldo cor* ("Place no trust, unhappy woman, in that perfidious heart") Elvira momentarily gets control of herself and, with dignity, urges Anna to regard Giovanni as a wretch. Seeing that they are moved by her appeal, Giovanni whispers to them that she is a demented girl and they should leave her in his care. Elvira presses her case with ever increasing urgency and anger. While Anna and Ottavio ponder this disturbing encounter and note that Giovanni's reaction is causing them to doubt his goodness, Giovanni draws Elvira aside and browbeats her for making a public spectacle of herself. She exits in dudgeon; he offers some hasty words of politeness and follows her.

Anna and Ottavio sing either in parallel rhythms or in echoes of each other—they are not conversing with Elvira or Giovanni, only listening. Elvira begins with dignified simplicity; a delicate motive in the violins echoes in diminution the rhythm of her avowal that Giovanni will betray Anna as well as her (te vuol tradir ancor). *The Don tries deception via a descending chromatic line in dotted rhythm (Ex. DG-5a). As Elvira becomes more intense, her line becomes more baroque (Ex. DG-6b). The asides of the others are quiet triplets, then dotted rhythms.*

Elvira and Giovanni have at each other with angry spurts of fast note values, while Anna and Ottavio comment aside with short phrases in harmonizing thirds and sixths. The final notes are the orchestra's: the plaintive motive that was heard with Elvira's opening words in this quartet now returns, bearing her from the realm of baroque foolishness into the world of genuine human misfortune.

SCENE XIII

10 ACCOMPANIED RECITATIVE and ARIA (Anna and Ottavio; Anna) *Don Ottavio, son morta! . . . Or sai chi l'onore / rapire a me volse* ("Don Ottavio, I'm dying! . . . Now you know who sought to steal my honor") Having recognized Giovanni's voice as that of her attacker, Anna tells Ottavio the details of the assault: a man had entered her room and grabbed her; she had resisted and cried out, but no one came; with a final burst of energy she had wrested herself from his grasp, redoubled her cries, and boldly followed the miscreant as he sought to flee. Her father's death was the crowning misdeed.

Demanding that Ottavio remember the bloody wound they saw and be the agent of revenge, she departs.

The change from recitativo secco to the quiet rise of double basses is startling. The bass line and the harsh tutti dissonances that follow are both conditioned by the tritone, the archetype interval for murder and betrayal. Anguished orchestral fragments serve as distorted fanfares to introduce Anna's cries. Hushed string chords accompany her parlando account of the attack, freezing both time and breath.

The aria begins like a great march, the motive of Example DG-4d striding under string tremolos. At Rammenta la piaga / del misero seno *("Remember the wound in his poor breast"), the strings turn to descending broken rhythms, as if gasping and sobbing. The aria continues with its mixture of these several elements, Anna's voice proclaiming her demand for revenge in strong dotted rhythms at the top of the staff.*

SCENE XIV

RECITATIVE (Ottavio) *Come mai creder deggio / di sì nero delitto capace un cavaliero!* ("How can I ever believe a nobleman capable of such a dark crime!") Shocked that a gentleman should be guilty of so heinous a deed, Ottavio feels that duty calls him as both betrothed and friend.

10a ARIA (Ottavio) *Dalla sua pace la mia dipende / quel che a lei piace vita mi rende* ("On her peace mine depends, what pleases her gives me life") Ottavio offers a soliloquy of love for Anna and devotion to her happiness.

An ABA aria of lyricism and elegance. The two-note groups in the violins are stylizations of his heartbeats, and his sighs (sospiri) are reflected in a snippet of chromatic slide against string tremolo and abrupt changes from forte *to* piano. *At the end of the reprise of the A section, Ottavio's* quel che le incresce morte mi dà *("whatever grieves her kills me") is given weight by unexpectedly complex harmonies and a more angular vocal line.*

SCENE XV

RECITATIVE (Leporello, Giovanni) *Io deggio, ad ogni patto / per sempre abbandonar questo bel matto* ("I must in any way abandon this maniac forever") Leporello is impatient with his lot, as usual.[11] He narrates his efforts to Giovanni: he has entertained the peasants, kept Masetto amused, and has gotten everyone besotted. Leporello is astonished that Giovanni knows Zerlina has arrived on the grounds and is accompanied by Elvira, who is crying indictments at full voice. Giovanni is delighted at his valet's story of contriving to lock Elvira out of the garden and leaving her alone on the street. What Leporello has begun, he exclaims, he knows how to finish; prizing these country girls all too much, he wishes to amuse them until nightfall.

11 ARIA (Giovanni) *Fin ch'an dal vino / calda la testa, / una gran festa / fa' preparar* ("While their heads are still hot from the wine, prepare a great revelry") His head filled with visions of chaotic hedonism, Giovanni directs Leporello to bring more girls to the party, to have the dances played without any special order, and to let them be danced by whoever wants to without regard to their place in society. By the morrow, he will have ten more to add to his list.

An obsessive motive, a feverish tempo, sliding chromatics, and abrupt dynamic changes are a stunning contrast to the poise of Don Ottavio's testament of love. The aria's insistence that the dances of the fete be without order or regard to who dances them is a metaphor for Giovanni's assault on social order and tradition.

Tableau 3: *The garden of Giovanni's estate, with two gates (locked from the outside) and two alcoves visible. The peasants are scattered about, some sleeping, some sitting on the grassy banks.*

SCENE XVI—MIDDAY OR EARLY AFTERNOON

RECITATIVE (Zerlina, Masetto) *Masetto, senti un po'* ("Masetto, just listen a minute") Masetto berates Zerlina for abandoning him on their wedding day and bringing shame on him by remaining alone with a man. He would beat her if it were not for the fact that it would create an even greater scandal. Proclaiming her innocence, Zerlina invites him to do whatever he wishes with her, *ma poi fa pace* ("but then make peace").

---

[11] In spite of the common practice to stage Scene xv in a room of Giovanni's house, the locale is probably the same as those immediately preceding. Leporello is told in the following aria to bring along any girl he may find in the piazza, so the servant is probably on his way there either to shop for viands or find Giovanni and report to him. If it were in Giovanni's house, the Don would not need to be informed that his lawn is festooned with inebriated peasants.

12 ARIA (Zerlina) *Batti, batti, o bel Masetto, / la tua povera Zerlina: / starò qui come agnellina / le tue botte ad aspettar* ("Handsome Masetto, beat your poor Zerlina; I shall stand here like a little lamb to await your blows") Zerlina, offering herself as a punching bag, winds Masetto around her little finger and promises to pass night and day in pleasures and good cheer (*contenti ed allegria*).

Like her duet with Giovanni, this aria begins in 2/4 and ends with a purling 6/8. A solo cello (Ex. DG-2a) gurgles delightedly all the way through; there are floating counterpoints in gentle woodwinds and soft sighs in the accompanying violins. The first section has the quality of a charming gavotte; Zerlina's begging for peace (pace) *is given a pastoral flavor by the smoothly flowing triplets of melody and accompaniment.*

That Zerlina uses a descending triad borrowed from Giovanni's flattery (Ex. DG-7b) doesn't dilute the exquisite beauty of one of the opera's most popular moments.

SCENE XVII

RECITATIVE *Guarda un po' come seppe / questa strega sedurmi!* ("See how this witch could seduce me!") Masetto becomes mush until he sees Zerlina suddenly frightened when Giovanni's voice is heard from afar; Masetto immediately stiffens with suspicion.

13 FINALE[12] (Masetto, Zerlina) *Presto, presto . . . pria ch' ei venga* ("Quickly, quickly . . . before he comes") Determined to catch Giovanni and Zerlina in untoward behavior, Masetto hides in one of the alcoves in spite of Zerlina's concern and irritation.

Masetto's jealous suspicion is established at once by the hurried repeated chords of the strings and the buffo alternations of wide skips and smooth scales. A twisting string figure over a tapping repeated note in low strings maintains the momentum, as do the quick, simple rhythms of the sotto voce *asides by Masetto and Zerlina.*

SCENE XVIII

(Giovanni, servants) *Su, svegliatevi, da bravi!* ("Come, good people, up and doing!") With four liveried servants, Giovanni enters the garden, urging all inside for the soirée he has had prepared for them. All enter the house, save for Zerlina, Masetto (still in the alcove), and Giovanni.

Giovanni's entry into the garden is proclaimed by wind, brass, and drum fanfares as appropriate to his station. Descending scales in a dotted rhythm add to the pomp of his call to all the peasants to cease drowsing and move into the ballroom.

SCENE XIX

(Zerlina; then Giovanni and Masetto) *Tra quest' arbori celata / si può dar che non mi veda* ("Hidden among these trees, he won't be able to see me") Zerlina's attempt to hide from Giovanni fails; pressing his attentions on her, he leads her into one of the alcoves and is startled to find Masetto there. Giovanni bluffs his way out of the embarassment, using the sound of his orchestra (dance music heard from within) as an excuse to usher them inside.

Violins become sensuously melodic and Zerlina's line more ornamental. The meaning of melodic ornament in Là ci darem *(No. 7) was ambiguous (nervousness? flirtation?); here it is clearly the music of a girl very much ill at ease. Giovanni presses his affection on her in a way reminiscent of that duet. Masetto repeats Giovanni's* la bella tua Zerlina non può . . .

---

[12] The music from here to the end of the act is accompanied orchestrally. The solo passages are best thought of as ariosos.

Mozart, *Don Giovanni*, Act I, scene xxii: Masetto (Theodor Uppman, left) is distracted by Leporello (Fernando Corena) as the worried Zerlina (Roberta Peters) dances with Don Giovanni (Cesare Siepi). Metropolitan Opera, 1957: production by Eugene Berman. Courtesy *Opera News*, Metropolitan Opera Guild. Photo Louis Mélançon.

più star senza di te ("your lovely Zerlina cannot stay here without you") in sarcastic agreement—both men recognize that they are the words Masetto had used earlier, in Scene viii. The music that Giovanni uses as an excuse to get them moving is part of the second of the three dances that will occur simultaneously in the ballroom. The three exit the garden with seeming hilarity and parallel rhythms.

SCENE XX

(Elvira, Anna, Ottavio) *Bisogna aver coraggio* ("We must have courage") Masked, as if for a costume ball, the three wronged aristocrats enter the garden, trying to bolster each other's courage.

As the minuet is heard from the ballroom, Leporello appears at a lighted window and calls to Giovanni that some maskers have arrived. At Giovanni's bidding, Leporello invites them in.[13] When they accept with formal politeness, Leporello closes the window.

A sudden move to the minor mode leads to a passage of mystery and foreboding. Elvira and Ottavio share the same melody to a violin accompaniment of steady sixteenth-notes. This obbligato changes to unsettled chromatic upturns as Anna—desperately afraid—turns to her own melody of higher notes and, at its end, the broken rhythms of sobs and anxiety.

---

[13] He actually invites only the women: "signore maschere," not "mascheri."

When the invitation to enter is accepted (while the minuet is heard from within), the world seems to close in on them. A hesitant, descending rhythm suggests their own uncertainty.

Anna and Ottavio pray for the protection of heaven: *Protegga il giusto cielo*; Elvira prays for heaven to avenge her betrayed heart.

Winds and voices perform the prayer in the manner of the cassation, a genre for wind ensemble that was popular in Mozart's day for outdoor performance. The effect is of total isolation—each voice moves quite independently of the other two and the orchestral sound (no strings) is unlike anything that has been heard in the opera to this moment. Before the party's frenzy, the opera has reached a moment of enormous tension and stasis.

Tableau 4: *A brilliantly lighted hall in Giovanni's residence, with doors leading to adjacent rooms. (These outer rooms are themselves connected, so that one may circumnavigate the ballroom without entering it.) The peasants are milling around; servants pass to and fro with refreshments. A dance has just ended.*

SCENE XXI—MOMENTS LATER

Riposate, vezzose ragazze ("Rest yourselves, you charming girls") Giovanni orders more refreshments to be served. With one of the peasant girls Leporello imitates Giovanni's attentions to Zerlina; the tension between Masetto and Zerlina is palpable to all.

A leaping triad in the strings to accompaniment of full woodwinds and French horns is a catapult to the world of hedonism and splendor. A buoyant 6/8 time and bubbling triplets create an atmosphere of gaiety and light. The music bustles with great energy as people move to and fro, the asides and conversational remarks ripping along restlessly; only Zerlina's outbursts have any sense of melody—all the rest is urgent patter.

SCENE XXII

Venite pur avanti, vezzose mascherette ("Just come forward, charming masked ladies") Anna, Elvira, and Ottavio enter and are greeted with appropriate ceremony. Anna and Ottavio begin to dance the minuet; Giovanni takes up a contredanse with Zerlina; Leporello distracts Masetto by forcing him to dance the *Teitsch*.

The nobility enter to fanfares and flourishes and a sudden key change. The exchange of greetings is through the formality of simple triads and scales (cf. Commendatore and Giovanni at the start of the Duel scene). The ceremony includes exchanges of Viva la libertà *("Long live liberty!"), a phrase that is a token of the new ideals of the Enlightenment to all but Giovanni, who interprets* libertà *as "license."[14] The 3/4 minuet begins, played by a "full" orchestra of strings, oboes, and horns; a second orchestra of violins over a bass line is heard tuning up to open fifths, then playing a sprightly 2/4 contredanse (the* follia *specified in* Fin ch'an dal vino*); as these continue, we hear the third group tuning, then playing a rather twangy German dance (a variant of the* allemande, *or "German dance"; Teitsch = Deutsch = Allemanna/Allemande) for violins above a very simple bass line.*

Giovanni dances Zerlina off to the side, then pushes her ahead of him into an adjoining room. Masetto (*Ah no! Zerlina!*) breaks away and follows. Leporello hastens off to warn Giovanni of Masetto's pursuit. Zerlina's scream brings the dancing to a halt; musicians and peasants exit in confusion. Masetto calls desperately to Zerlina, who is then heard screaming for help (*Scelerato!*—"Villain!") from another side of the stage. Hearing her cries and the sounds of struggle, Ottavio, Anna, and Elvira throw themselves against a locked door just as Zerlina bursts in from another direction.

---

[14] See Till, p. 212.

The piling in of the three dances creates an unbearable tension and seeming complexity. Zerlina's first scream (Gente, aiuto) *brings the pit orchestra in on a* forte *dissonance (a diminished seventh chord) and the pounding scale fragments of Ex. DG-4e. The change of keys is startling; so is the sudden new sweep of rhythmic force as the stage is filled with confusion and the cries of Zerlina and Masetto come from various offstage directions.*

Ecco il birbo ("Here's the rogue") Giovanni suddenly appears with sword in hand, leading Leporello by the arm as if having caught him "in the act," and pretends to have difficulty in drawing his sword to strike the valet. No one is fooled. Ottavio draws a pistol and faces Giovanni.

Matters come to an abrupt halt when Giovanni strides out; the scale fragments now become pompous and proclamatory.

L'empio crede con tal frode / di nasconder l'empietà ("The evil man thinks he can hide his wickedness with such deceit"). In turn, Ottavio, Elvira, and Anna unmask and confront Giovanni. He is at first taken aback but quickly regains his composure. They threaten that a tempest of revenge will loose its lightning bolt upon him. Giovanni brazens it out.[15]

The three nobles denounce Giovanni in a brief canon, its descending scale reminiscent of the second subject of the overture's allegro *section. Tremolos, crescendos, and boiling scales dominate the musical picture of the confrontation.*

*A rising scale from Leporello and Giovanni is in the patter style of opera buffa, but no one laughs here, especially when the others warn him to fear the thundering of heaven (*Odi io tuon della vendetta*): Anna's high F-sharp is a tritone away from the tonic C of Giovanni's scale, and the descending scale of their warning is reinforced by a tutti that sounds like the wrath of heaven itself. Plummeting scales at a faster tempo provide the lightning bolt (*fulmine*) that will fall on his head. Giovanni's defiant retort is curt, triadic, and repetitive; Leporello harmonizes with him at the lower third.*

The tumultuous scene ends with rattling triplets and repetitions and developments of the blistering denunciations.

Act II

Tableau 1: *The inn of Act I, scene iv, but seen from a different angle revealing the window of Elvira's room and an intersection of streets.*

SCENE I—EARLY EVENING

14 DUET (Giovanni, Leporello) *Eh via, buffone, non mi seccar* ("Come on, clown, don't irritate me") Master and valet are in the middle of an argument, with Giovanni trying to persuade Leporello not to quit his service.

The action opens in medias res; *a few brusque chords, then buffo patter by Giovanni who is answered by Leporello in similar musical terms—the two are arguing as equals. The argument is punctuated by a variant of the opera's unifying scale motive and by* forte/piano *alternations, the alternation of* no *and* sì *and the blunt cadences of opera buffa.*

RECITATIVE (Leporello, Giovanni) *Leporello. Signore.* ("Leporello. Sir.") A purse does its work and Leporello agrees to stay, providing Giovanni gives up women.

---

[15] Some may question why Ottavio does not make use of his pistol, a weapon which would clearly grant him control of the proceedings. An answer is proposed by Rushton (p. 61), and I find it persuasive: it would be a lawless act to shoot a man in his own home. The willingness to take a life in Act II is more defensible—it is late at night and Giovanni would be a dangerous intruder in the courtyard of Anna's house.

Lasciar le donne? Pazzo! ("Give up women? You're crazy!") is the response—they are more vital to the Don than bread and air; besides, since he loves all of them and to love only one would to be cruel to the others, his generous nature requires him to continue as he has.

Giovanni turns the conversation to Elvira's maid, who is a beauty with whom he wishes to try his luck. Since an aristocrat's clothing and bearing might put her off, he wishes to change clothes with Leporello; the latter's objections will not be suffered—they exchange cloaks and hats.

SCENE II

15 TRIO (Elvira, Leporello, Giovanni) *Ah! taci, ingiusto core* ("Ah, be still my unjust heart") Elvira appears at her window, wretched and unhappy. Giovanni places himself behind Leporello and calls to her tenderly, asking for forgiveness. Elvira is at first resentful, then affected (*Numi, che strano affetto / mi si risveglia in petto!*—"Heavens, what a strange effect is awakened in my breast!"). She cannot resist Giovanni's blandishments (*Discendi o gioia bella*—"Come down, oh lovely joy") in spite of her efforts to do so (*No, non ti credo, o barbaro!*—"No, I don't believe you, you cruel man!"), then leaves the balcony to join Giovanni at street level. Leporello chokes with laughter over Elvira's foolish credulity but also pities it (*deh, proteggete, o Dei, / la sua credulità*—ah, protect her gullibility, ye Gods").

Elvira's music here is genuinely affecting. As with the Act I quartet (No. 9), she is given a tender violin figure (Ex. DG-6c) that unifies the entire scene; this figure and the gentle meter of 6/8 lend an air of pathos to her music, which tempers the absurdity of her gullibility. Much of the music given to Elvira, Giovanni, and the accompanying violins is inflected by two-note groups (see Ex. DG-5c), the musical "sigh" that is a standard feature of operatic passages dealing with hearts beating for love and/or sadness. Elvira's accusations of perfidy are given the expected angularity and faster rhythms.

The asides of all three characters are in imitation, each using the same music to comment on the action. When Giovanni turns to the tune he will use to serenade Elvira's maid, the key is suddenly changed, and the violins lean on sospiri and background murmurs in a way that is both enriching and comic.

The final thoughts of Giovanni are jokingly angular; Leporello and Elvira both ask the gods to protect her from her credulity in parallel harmonies that are given a touch of seriousness by their beginning syncopation. Elvira's coloratura in the last strains of the trio are in character; so is the blunt cadencing of Leporello, but the middle voice taken by Giovanni is only a harmonic filler and says nothing of himself—as always, his dealing with another person is a charade.

RECITATIVE (Giovanni, Leporello, Elvira) *Spero che cada presto* ("I hope she succumbs quickly") Waiting for Elvira to appear, Giovanni tells Leporello to run to Elvira and press his kisses upon her, then to lead her off. Leporello remonstrates, but the nose of Giovanni's pistol subdues him at once. Giovanni moves into the darker shadows—night has fallen—and watches.

SCENE III

RECITATIVE (Elvira, Leporello, Giovanni) *Eccomi a voi* ("Here I am for you") Elvira, having fallen for the deception, embraces and kisses Leporello, who participates enthusiastically, imitating Giovanni's voice. Impatient at the billing and cooing, Giovanni shouts as if killing someone and frightens them away. Laughing at the success of his ruse, he turns to the window of Elvira's room and prepares to enchant her maid.

16 CANZONETTA[16] (Giovanni) *Deh! vieni alla finestra, o mio tesoro* ("Ah! come to the window, oh my treasure") Accompanying himself with a mandolin, Giovanni offers a serenade to Elvira's maid.

A strophic song with "perpetual motion" scales and triads of a mandolin, the string pizzicatos of the orchestra evoking the strumming of a serenading instrument (Ex. DG-5d).

SCENE IV

RECITATIVE (Giovanni, Masetto) *V'è gente alla finestra* ("There's someone at the window") As Giovanni looks for his target to appear, Masetto and some of his friends enter the square. Armed to the teeth, they are looking for Giovanni. Seeing a person in the shadows, Masetto challenges him; Giovanni tries to imitate Leporello's voice and pretends to be as eager to punish Giovanni as Masetto is.

17 ARIA (Giovanni) *Metà di voi quà vadano / e gli altri vadan là* ("Half of you go there and the others go over there") Giovanni sends Masetto's forces in different directions, urging them to strike (*ferite*) if they see a man and a girl strolling about the square; the man wearing a large hat with white feathers and a sword at his side is their target. (He is, of course, describing the clothing he had exchanged with Leporello.) As the peasants leave, Giovanni keeps Masetto alone with him.

*Syncopations of a single pitch in French horn and violin and tiny supporting rhythmic groups separated by rests create a conspiratorial mood. Giovanni's music broadens into an expansive triad and march-like rhythms when he describes the great cloak "Don Giovanni" will be wearing (*addosso un gran mantello*). Giovanni apes the repetitious patterns of the typical servant of comic opera, especially at* Ferite pur *("Strike well"), when he urges Masetto's friends to beat their quarry thoroughly, and in the middle of the piece, when his impatience gets the better of him (*Andante, fate presto*—"Get going, fast"). The orchestral introduction of this masterpiece of deception threads its way through much of the music, rounding everything off at the end with a hint of plotting and comic conniving.*

SCENE V

RECITATIVE (Giovanni, Masetto) *Zitto . . . Lascia ch'io senta* ("Quiet . . . Let me listen.") Eliciting Masetto's dire ambitions to tear Giovanni into a hundred pieces, Giovanni inquires as to Masetto's weaponry. The not-too-bright peasant hands over his musket and pistol, whereupon Giovanni takes the flat of his sword and administers a hearty drubbing. Giovanni exits, leaving Masetto lying on the ground.

SCENE VI

RECITATIVE (Masetto, Zerlina) *Ahi! ahi! la testa mia!* ("Ow, ow, my head!") Zerlina comes into the square with a lantern, looking for Masetto. Hearing him groaning, she hurries to his side and hears him tell of the thrashing administered by "Leporello." Noting that his bruises are not mortal, she chides Masetto for his jealousy, then helps him to his feet to take him home and heal him.

18 ARIA (Zerlina) *Vedrai, carino, / se sei buonino, / che bel rimedio / ti voglio dar* ("You will see, my sweetheart, if you're a good boy, what a fine remedy I'd like to give you") Offering a love song for their wedding night, she promises a certain balm (*un certo balsamo*) that no druggist can provide but that she carries about with her. She has Masetto touch her heart, where he may feel the beating source of her wonderful remedy. She gently leads him away.

---

[16] See Chapter 3, note 10.

Another triple time piece (3/8) of exquisite charm for Zerlina. It parallels her previous numbers (Là ci darem, *No. 7, and* Batti, batti, *No. 12) in that it flows smoothly and moves to a quicker time in its second part; here the quickening is the result of faster note values provided by the woodwinds and by the repeated notes of cellos and basses. The heart that Masetto is to feel beating* (sentilo battere) *is represented by this cello/bass tapping and by staccati in the woodwinds—the whole thing is delectable.*

Tableau 2: *Courtyard of Anna's house; three doors or gates lead into surrounding streets. The full moon behind the house throws the courtyard into especially dark shadow.*

SCENE VII—NIGHT, AT LEAST AN HOUR LATER

RECITATIVE (Leporello, Elvira) *Di molte faci il lume s'avvicina* ("The light of many torches is nearing") Leporello, seeing the coming of a torchlit procession, guides Elvira into the courtyard to hide. He ignores her query as to why he should fear being seen and tries to find a way out, leaving the now frightened Elvira alone in a dark corner.

19 SEXTET (Elvira, Leporello, Ottavio, Anna, Zerlina, Masetto) *Sola, sola, in buio loco, / palpitar il cor mi sento* ("Alone, alone in this dark spot, / I feel my heart throbbing") Leporello feels his way toward the gate but finds it too late; he quickly scurries into the shadows as Ottavio and Anna, dressed in mourning, enter with their servants bearing lights.

The mood of darkness is set at once by quiet string and wind harmonies, then quick flurries of violins and syncopations. Elvira's fear comes at once in the sudden accent on loco *("place") and the drop of a seventh to which it is set. Broken rhythms suggest Leporello's treading softly in the dark.*

SCENE VIII

Tergi il ciglio, o vita mia! / e da' calma al tuo dolore ("Dry your eyes, my life, and calm your sorrow") Ottavio urges Anna to calm her sorrow so that her father's spirit will not be distressed; she answers that only death can cure her grieving. Unseen by Anna and Ottavio, Elvira and Leporello approach the gate to the street from different directions.

*Trumpets and drums and a key change to D announce the arrival of the torchlit procession. Ottavio's warning of the distress of the ghost of Anna's father—*pena avrà de' tuoi martir *([Your father's spirit] will be troubled by your suffering)—is set to a melody that draws on the opening subject of the overture's allegro. She cannot be consoled: the brief shots of melisma and wide skips, and the half-note sobs (in both voice and orchestra) depict wretchedness that cannot be allayed.*

SCENE IX

Ferma, briccone! Dove ten vai? ("Stop, you wretch, where are you going?") Leporello's effort to escape is thwarted by the arrival of Masetto, now armed with a stick, and Zerlina. He hides his face as Anna, Zerlina, Ottavio, and Masetto call punishment down upon him. They are taken aback to find Elvira there and by her plea for mercy, *È mio marito* ("He is my husband"), but they quickly return to their resolve to do "Giovanni" in on the spot.

Development of these materials plus dramatic punctuations and complex part writing mark the arrival of Zerlina and Masetto and their confrontation with Leporello. Elvira's plangent Pietà! *("Mercy!") is especially poignant, for its descending interval is the tritone—she is about to be deceived again.*

Morrà! . . . Perdon, perdono, signori miei ("He shall die! . . . Pardon, pardon my Lords") As Ottavio prepares to strike him dead,[17] Leporello reveals his identity; falling to his knees, he begs for mercy. *Mille torbidi pensieri / mi s'aggiran per la testa* ("a thousand troubled thoughts spin in my head") is voiced by the accusers: Anna enters the house distraught, Zerlina upbraids Leporello for beating up Masetto, Elvira is outraged at the deceit, and Ottavio expects that some further betrayal is afoot. Zerlina, Elvira, and Ottavio claim the privilege of exacting punishment; Masetto suggests all four of them beat Leporello to death.

> *Leporello begs for mercy to the accompaniment of chromatic descents. The shock of discovery that he is Leporello and not Giovanni brings the five voices together in block harmonies and fanfare rhythms above syncopations synonymous with their confusion and astonishment. They continue thus against the solo voice of Leporello until Anna turns to coloratura despair for a moment; then all six voices form various combinations, their confusion represented by broken rhythms, syncopations, and the intensification of a change to a much faster tempo. Leporello returns to some of the comic characteristics typical of his role in society in the final moments of this amazing and ever-changing ensemble.*

20 ARIA (Leporello) *Ah! per pietà, signori miei!* ("Ah, mercy, my Lords!") Begging for clemency, Leporello admits they are right to be outraged but avers that the crime is not his. He invites them to ask Elvira to confirm that she has been with him for the past hour. He murmurs phrases that cause all to think; during their momentary distraction, he finds his way to the gate and vanishes into the night.

> *That the descending scale of his plea for mercy begins on an off beat suggests genuine fear. The rising arpeggio on* Dò ragione a voi *("I grant you are right"), however, draws suspiciously on the leering end of his Catalogue Aria (No. 4); sure enough, it is the music with which he sidles to the gate and makes his escape when his captors are distracted for a moment. There is a good deal of busy work among a variety of figures in the orchestra during this aria, as if Leporello were quickly developing a scheme of escape in his mind. The rising arpeggio is chief among them and occurs with alternating dynamics that invite images of plotting and conniving—he is his master's shadow here.*

SCENE X

RECITATIVE The four avengers realize too late that Leporello has slipped from their grasp. Ottavio, affirming that Giovanni is undoubtedly the murderer[18] of Anna's father, asks the others to remain in the house with Anna while he makes a formal complaint to the authorities, promising to return in a few moments to avenge all of them.

21 ARIA (Ottavio) *Il mio tesoro intanto / andate a consolar* ("Meanwhile, go and console my treasure") He asks all to comfort Anna while he sets out to avenge her wrongs; he will return only as a herald of destruction and death. All but Elvira leave the scene.[19]

> *A stately aria in ABA form. The outer sections are flowing and lovely, as is appropriate to the Ottavio who is in the mold of the idealized swain of opera seria. The middle section's more*

---

[17] This from a man whom many writers have accused of being a do-nothing fop.

[18] It should be remembered that the Commendatore drew first and challenged Giovanni, who then had to defend himself in a duel. A miscreant, yes; a murderer, no.

[19] For the Vienna production, Mozart inserted a duet here (No. 21a, "Per queste tue manine / candide e tenerelle"—"By these, your hands pure and tender [have mercy on me]") for Zerlina and Leporello, in which she threatens him with a knife and has him bound to a chair. He manages to run off, chair and all.

militant character comes from an increase in fioritura[20] *(in both voice and first violins) and the angularity of perfect interval and triads on such a phrase as* a vendicar io vado *("I am going to gain revenge"). The clarinet sound is especially softening in this aria, but the entire melody bespeaks gentility and grace, even at its most dynamic moments.*

SCENE XI

21a ACCOMPANIED RECITATIVE and ARIA (Elvira) *In quali eccessi, o Numi! in qual misfatti / orribili, tremendi, / è avvolto il sciagurato! . . . Mi tradì quell' alma ingrata / infelice, o Dio! mi fa* ("In what excess, oh Heavens, in what horrible and tremendous crimes is the miscreant involved! . . . I am betrayed by that ungrateful soul, oh God! who has made me unhappy"). Elvira calls down the wrath of God, then admits to herself that, even though abandoned and betrayed, she still feels pity for Giovanni. Her heart speaks of vengeance, but when she sees him in danger, it throbs (*palpitando il cor mi va*).

A twisting low string figure suggests her frustration and confusion; a slash of descending scale illustrates her vision of lightning falling on her betrayer (Ex. DG-6d), but her rage gives way to orchestral sighs (Ex. DG-6e). Her aria (Ex. DG-6f) is a sinfonia concertante movement in rondo form: the main theme continually returns as a kind of self indictment after each melodic excursion, offering pity and understanding. Melismas on key words speak of the Baroque: the hesitant rhythms on palpitando *speak of her throbbing heart, the plunge on* tormento *speaks of her anguish.*

Tableau 3: Full moonlight. A cemetery, with an enclosed mausoleum sheltering a large statue of the Commendatore. Various equestrian statues of other notables may be seen.

SCENE XII—PERHAPS TEN O'CLOCK[21]

RECITATIVE (SECCO and ACCOMPAGNATO) (Giovanni, Leporello, Commendatore) *Ah! ah! ah! ah! questa è buona!* ("Ha, ha, ha, ha, this is good!") Giovanni jumps over a low wall, laughing aloud. His *Or lasciala cercar!* ("Now let her search!") suggests that he has just completed another sexual adventure and has made off in his usual fashion. After commenting on the beautiful light of the moon, he wonders how Leporello has fared; hearing him from the other side of the wall, Giovanni calls Leporello to join him. Taking back his own cloak and hat, Giovanni regales him with a narrative of his affair with a girl who turns out to have been Leporello's inamorata. When she screamed, Giovanni reports, he departed with celerity and has come to this place.

His uproarious laughter at the thought of even greater pleasure had the girl been Leporello's wife is cut off by the sudden sonority of a sepulchral voice warning him that his laughter will end before dawn (*Di rider finirai pria dell' aurora*).

Giovanni speaks alone and to Leporello in secco; the use of trombones and woodwinds (without strings) to accompany the Statue's pronouncements in a chorale-like manner intrudes into Giovanni's ribaldry with mystery and great theatrical effect.[22]

---

[20] Ornamented melody.

[21] Giovanni's *ancor non sono due della notte* ("it's not yet two hours into the night") is often rendered as "it's not yet two o'clock." Given that Leporello has just made his escape from a scene that happened only an hour or so after nightfall and that Giovanni begins this scene by pondering the possibility of finding some girls, the time of 2:00 A.M. is implausible.

[22] Gluck had used the same effect for the pronouncement by an oracle in *Alceste*; Mozart had already used the devise for the Oracle in *Idomeneo*.

Giovanni thrusts his sword here and there to find who would dare make fun of him while hiding among the gravestones. Again the voice calls to him demanding that this bold scoundrel (*ribaldo audace*) leave the dead in peace.

Giovanni, with indifference and disdain, then notices the statue of the Commendatore and orders Leporello to read the inscription underneath it. Leporello, trembling, reads *"Dell' empio, che mi trasse al passo estremo / Qui attendo la vendetta"* ("Here I await revenge on the evil one who brought me to my final moment"). Giovanni orders Leporello to invite the Statue to supper later that evening. The terrified Leporello begs off. As usual, Giovanni threatens violence if his servant does not comply with his wishes. As usual, Leporello yields.

22 DUET (Leporello, Giovanni; then Commendatore's statue) *O statua gentilissima, / benché di marmo siate . . . / Ah! padron mio . . . mirate . . .* ("Oh most gracious statue, though you are of marble . . . Ah! my Lord, look . . .") Leporello tremblingly begins his invitation but falters; when Giovanni threatens him with the sword he continues and is horrified to see the Statue nod its head in assent. He demonstrates to Giovanni what he has seen; astonished, Giovanni turns to look at the Statue and issues the invitation himself. The Statue answers "Yes." Leporello is scarcely able to function; Giovanni finds it strange but determines to see things through. He orders Leporello to accompany him home to prepare the meal.

> *Leporello begins simply and formally—the first and last intervals of his invitational phrases are perfect—but he turns to Giovanni in terror with an interval of a falling seventh and notes aside, in broken rhythms (io sen—to—mi—ge—lar!), that his "blood is freezing." He tries his invitation in a different key, to the same effect. When he tells Giovanni of the Statue's nodding of his head, the falling seventh recurs. Giovanni's impatience is that of a buffo character, but when the Statue responds Sì ("Yes"), Giovanni becomes suddenly more serious and his melody moves to a triadic motion in the minor mode. Leporello continues his falling sevenths. The two express their separate thoughts as the scalar strings busy themselves with restlessness and hushed intensity.*

Tableau 4: *A dimly-lit room in Anna's house.*

Scene XIII—Same hour as the cemetary scene

RECITATIVE (Ottavio, Anna) *Calmatevi, idol mio* ("Calm yourself, my idol") Ottavio assures Anna that her wrongs will soon be avenged and urges her to set her sorrows aside and marry him on the morrow. When she protests the insensitivity of his obviously sincere thoughts, he charges her with cruelty toward him.

23 ACCOMPANIED RECITATIVE and ARIA (Anna) *Crudele? / Ah no, mio ben! . . . Non mi dir, bell' idol mio, / che son io crudel con te* ("Cruel? Ah no, my beloved! . . . Don't say to me, my handsome idol, that I am being cruel to you") Anna confirms her love for Ottavio but, without specifying details, hints that the world might wonder at the haste of their marriage (*ma il mondo, oh Dio!*). The aria is a formal expression of her love and loyalty, asking that he calm his torment (*calma il tuo tormento*) if he does not wish her to die of grief; perhaps, she finishes, someday heaven will again feel pity for her (*forse un giorno il cielo ancora / sentirà pietà di me*).

> *Dotted string fanfares introduce Anna's rejection of Ottavio's suggestion of cruelty. A melting violin melody above a gentle string murmur indicates her love for Ottavio, but the complexity of the textures (especially voice and woodwinds) indicates considerable unrest in her heart. The melody just referred to is the main theme of her aria, introduced now by violins doubled in the woodwinds (Ex. DG-2b). The aria begins tenderly enough, but at the allegro it becomes a formal display piece. The text focuses on herself now, not on her love for Ottavio,*

and the melismas (Ex. DG-2c, for example) rattle on with an almost mindless intensity. It seems now that Anna is on the edge of mental instability; for all the energy of the melodic work, the sentiments seem cold and rigid. Little wonder that she needs to wait a year before she can indeed be a loving consort (see Epilogue).

RECITATIVE (Ottavio) *Ah, si segua il suo passo* ("Ah, I should follow her") After she exits, Ottavio determines that Anna will grieve less if he stays with her and shares her pain. He follows her.

Tableau 5: *The dining hall of Giovanni's house. A table is set for supper; Giovanni's private band of wind instruments sits to one side to provide the obligatory* Tafelmusik *(dinner music).*

SCENE XIV—MIDNIGHT

24 FINALE (Giovanni, Leporello; later Elvira, Statue) *Già la mensa è preparata* ("Now the table is set") Seating himself at the dining table, Giovanni orders the musicians to play and calls Leporello to serve him.

Leporello praises the tune from from Martín's opera *Una cosa rara*[23] as Giovanni begins to eat. Giovanni enjoys seeing Leporello hungry and unable to eat and orders the next course. The musicians begin an aria from Sarti's *Fra i due litiganti il terzo gode*.[24] Giovanni orders wine, noting cooly that Leporello is stuffing himself furtively at every opportunity. As the band begins the *Non più andrai* from the end of the first act of *Le nozze di Figaro* (Leporello: *Questa poi la conosco pur troppo*—"This one I know too well"),[25] Giovanni sees that Leporello's mouth is full, so he orders him to whistle. Leporello begins to bluff his way past the contretemps, and Giovanni exploits his servant's embarassment to the full.

Once again the music goes into a radical change. Full winds and strings erupt with brilliance and rhythmic energy, dotted fanfares introducing a theme that is immediately taken up by Giovanni at a moment of pure hedonism. The opera's scale figures are heard as Leporello announces that the meal is ready.

The onstage winds[26] play dinner music from hit operas, their sonority bright, the melodies tuneful. The quote from Le nozze di Figaro *is a variation of the familiar aria.*

SCENE XV

L'ultima prova / dell'amor mio / ancor vogl'io / fare con te ("I want to make a final proof of my love for you") Elvira bursts in, vowing compassion and love for Giovanni. She kneels desperately before him, but he mocks her by kneeling himself. When she begs him to change his life, he contemptuously returns to the table, inviting her to dine with him. Crying out her distress at his wickedness, she leaves, Leporello commenting on the stone-heartedness of his master.

---

[23] "A rare thing," 1786, by Vicente Martín y Soler (1754–1806), libretto by Da Ponte. The popularity of Martín's opera in Prague had eclipsed that of Mozart's own *Le nozze di Figaro*.

[24] "Between Two Litigants, a Third Rejoices," 1782, by Giuseppe Sarti (1729–1802); libretto by Carlo Goldoni, (1707–1793); the opera was played in Prague in 1783.

[25] *Nozze* had been an enormous hit in Prague. The singers who played Giovanni and Leporello at the premiere had also created the roles of Count Almaviva and Figaro, a double joke that the Prague audiences no doubt enjoyed.

[26] In the palaces of Mozart's Vienna and elsewhere, a small ensemble of this type typically provided entertainment for suppers and the like.

Giovanni offers a credo: *Vivan le femmine! / Viva il buon vino! / Sostegno e gloria d'u-manità!* ("Long live women, long live fine wine, they are the sustenance and glory of humanity!")

Elvira is heard to scream; she reenters the room and runs out another way. Giovanni orders Leporello to investigate. Leporello exits and immediately screams in terror himself.

Ah! . . . signor . . . per carità . . . ("Ah! . . . , my Lord . . . for heaven's sake . . . ") Leporello enters in a state of dire fear and informs Giovanni that the Statue is approaching, imitating the heavy footfalls that sound *Ta ta ta ta ta.* Giovanni rejects all this as nonsense.

Loud knocks at the door are heard. When Leporello refuses Giovanni's order to open it, Giovanni takes a light and his drawn sword and opens the door himself. Leporello hides under the table.

A sudden quickening of tempo and a change to 3/4 meter accompanies Elvira's passionate entrance. Her thoughts are still expressed in a Handelian way in the sense of majesty and grandeur, but there is scarcely any melisma at all. Her plea for Giovanni to reform is made especially earnest by a rumbling figure in the low strings that impels the music relentlessly during Elvira's urgent appeals to Giovanni and his caustic responses to her. He returns to his table to the rhythm and tune of a trivial waltz.

Giovanni's creed of women and wine cuts through the voices and instruments like a militant fanfare; the music of Leporello's comments on Giovanni's hardheartedness share some of Elvira's musical expression of despair.

Elvira's scream is given the same harmony as Zerlina's scream in the Act I finale and the moment of the fatal stabbing of the Commendatore at the beginning of the opera. Tumultuous rhythms, syncopations, and a pounding bass line indicate the emotional pandemonium of those who have seen the Statue approaching. Leporello's report is breathless—his phrases are now half-step patterns interrupted by rests, underscored by string repetitions that seem to depict a heart pounding in sheer terror.

The knocking at the door is thunderous (Ex. DG-4f); Giovanni's orders to Leporello are peremptory perfect intervals; his determination to go to the door himself is a series of self-confident triads accompanied by empty octaves in bassoons and strings.

SCENE XVI

Don Giovanni, a cenar teco / m'invitasti, e son venuto ("Don Giovanni, you have invited me to sup with you, and I have come") The Don is stunned to find the Statue standing in the doorway but orders another place to be set at once, dragging Leporello from under the table to force him to obey.

For the first time in the opera, every orchestral instrument is used together. The dissonant sound, reinforced by a timpani roll, is indeed thunderous and is perhaps the fulfillment of the prediction of Giovanni's opponents at the height of the Act I finale. The pulsing chords and syncopated undulation of the overture's first section (DG-3c) accompany the perfect-interval statement of the Statue. Giovanni's order to Leporello to serve another meal is given the half-step shrieks that heralded Anna's discovery of her father's body. Leporello's terror has the broken sixteenth-note rhythm that was heard when Anna reminded Ottavio (in No. 10, Or sai chi l'onore) of her father's gaping wound.

The Statue's invitation brings back the overture's ghostly scales and their throbbing chords. Giovanni's defiance is short phrased and bold; Leporello's dread finds voice in muttered triplets.

The Statue announces that he needs no earthly food; he has come to invite Giovanni to accept his return invitation. Leporello's *Tempo non ha . . . perdon* ("He hasn't time . . . excuse him") is ignored by Giovanni who accepts. The Statue demands that Giovanni take his hand as a sign of acceptance. Still showing bravado, Giovanni clasps the Statue's hand only to be seized with an icy chill. The Statue demands repentance as Giovanni vainly seeks to tear his hand away.

Giovanni nonetheless remains defiant. When the Statue's repeated demands are rejected, their contact is broken; fire breaks out in the hall, the Commendatore disappears; a chasm opens.

*When Giovanni tries to free himself from the Statue's grasp, the thrusting scales of the duel drive ironically and furiously in the cellos and basses. A stunning tritone marks the Statue's final words—*Ah! tempo più non v'è! *("Ah! You have no more time!").*

Da qual tremore insolito . . . Sento . . . assalir . . . gli spiriti . . . ("By what uncommon trembling . . . do I sense . . . my spirits assailed . . . ") Giovanni quivers with horror as a chorus of dark voices from the underworld summons him to perdition, claiming that what he feels now is not what he deserves—worse awaits him. Leporello watches aghast as Giovanni, writhing in pain and terror, disappears from sight, amid fire and smoke.

*The chords and syncopations of the overture return yet again. Giovanni's melody is barren chanting, accompanied by writhing violin figures (*forte*) alternating with soft minor chords. As an infernal chorus of men's voices pounds its repeated notes, each phrase ending a half-step higher, descending chromatic scales at a fast tempo alternate with* sforzando *(abruptly accented) tremolos and syncopations in a tumultuous picture of the fires of hell and the agony of a damned soul.*

FINAL SCENE/EPILOGUE

Ah! dov'è il perfido? ("Ah! where is the deceitful one?") Accompanied by ministers of justice, Elvira, Anna, Ottavio, Zerlina, and Masetto arrive at the dining hall, seeking to arrest its owner. Leporello narrates the events he has witnessed, to the horror and wonderment of them all.

There is a sudden switch from D minor to D major, with incisive strokes from the strings indicating a total transformation.

Leporello reports to them in solid rhythms and a melodic line that ranges from wide intervals to quick moving half-steps; he has been sobered by what he has seen. The comments of his listeners are generally in block harmonies above sharply accented rising triads, as if the light of day were finally penetrating the night of emotional turmoil and frenzy.

Or che tutti, o mio tesoro / vendicati siam dal cielo ("Now, my treasure, we have been vindicated by heaven in all these matters") Ottavio asks Anna to release him from his languishing and to marry him. She asks for a year of mourning; he assents. Elvira decides to finish her life in a convent. Zerlina and Masetto look forward to getting home and supping together. Leporello determines to head to the inn and find there a better master.

Ottavio tries to return to normality by proposing marriage to Anna in terms of symmetrical phrases and restrained ornament. She answers in kind; even though she will wait a year, the machine-like elaborateness of her Non mi dir *has been set aside. Their common affection and understanding is reached with parallel thirds and a quasi-Baroque melisma (befitting their station) on* amor. *Elvira's decision has a similar quality, but it is in the minor mode— this all-too-loving woman has suffered more than she can bear. Masetto and Zerlina adopt the language of the others but return to the major mode. Leporello picks up a bit of the ornament of the group but quickly becomes his open-intervalled self.*

Resti dunque quel birbon / con Proserpina e Pluton ("Let the wretch then remain with Proserpine and Pluto") Zerlina, Masetto, and Leporello avow that it is proper for the evildoer to remain in the abode ruled by the Queen and King of the Underworld and that all good people should join in the most ancient of songs: *Questo è il fin di chi fa mal, / E de' perfidi la morte / alla vita è sempre ugual* ("This is the end

of those who do evil, and the death of the wicked is appropriate to their lives")
The six survivors address a moral directly to the audience.

Accompanied by the opera's signature motive, Zerlina, Masetto, and Leporello deliver their sentence: Giovanni should burn in Hell. Anna leads off with the moral; it is punctuated by chordal response from the ensemble, then repeated by Zerlina. Scales drive the music on, the sudden piano/forte alternations providing dynamic effects. The final message is orchestral: the opera's scales and a spirited countermelody wrap it all up in music that quivers, bounces, drives, and exults.

The Characters

Leporello (bass) *[leh-pawr-ELL-loh]*

Valet, procurer, catalogue-keeper, Leporello is at first a prototypical comic servant, blunt and earthy. He consoles Elvira by telling her that she is neither the first nor the last of Giovanni's 1,003 Spanish conquests—that is supposed to make her feel good—and takes a lewd delight in his master's sexual plans for the fete that ends Act I. Twice he upbraids Giovanni for his vile behavior, but bribes and a little intimidation quickly bring him back into line. He has some genuine feelings of pity toward Elvira, especially in the balcony scene of Act II, but never acts on them; given the opportunity to emulate his master, as he indicates he would like to do in "Notte e giorno" (No. 1), he takes it. Moral principle is not Leporello's strong point, even though he knows evil when he sees it.

Leporello's music is typically scale steps or simple intervals, the phrases symmetrical and short (see above, Example DG-4b) and shaped by patter in keeping with the stage traditions of operatic comedy. When he fears for his life or comes face-to-face with moral outrage, however, he changes his tune considerably. In the Act II sextet and in all three of the scenes where the Commendatore is present (alive or dead), Leporello's music becomes narrower in compass and more chromatic. If there is any redemption in Leporello's life, it is in these moments.

Donna Anna (soprano) *[DAWN-nah AHN-nah]*

Anna's father is a respected member of the nobility, so she is a person of great social position. Presumably she has been thoroughly schooled in propriety and etiquette, but the events of the opera's opening—the encounter with Giovanni and the subsequent death of her father—unleash passions that were probably kept tightly under psychological lock and key her entire life.

A case can be made for Donna Anna having willingly submitted to Giovanni's advances[27] and an equally convincing one for her having been the victim of an attempted rape. Much of it depends on whether or not you believe her narrative, "Don Ottavio! son morta!" ("Don Ottavio, I'm dying!," No. 10). She tells Ottavio that, confronted with a stranger in her room who

---

[27] See Moberly, 167, et passim.

pressed upon her, she did three things: "vincolarmi, torcermi e piegarmi." The translation of these words is ambiguity itself: "vincolarmi" can mean either "I bound myself" or "I engaged myself" (i.e., made an effort); "torcermi" is clear—"I writhed" or "I struggled"; "piegarmi" can mean either "I submitted" or "I bent myself." If she is thinking of "vincolarmi" and "piegarmi" as restrictive and submissive words, then she is saying she surrendered[28]; if her thoughts are that she struggled and twisted her body, then she fought the good fight and, apparently, succeeded in repelling her attacker, and thus claims complete innocence and success in retaining the purity of her body.

Either she's lying in her teeth or it all happened exactly as she said it did; we don't know and neither does Don Ottavio. Whatever her motivations, she becomes a person possessed. Her Act I "Or sai chi l'onore" (the aria part of No. 10) rumbles with outrage (see Example DG-4d), cries aloud in anguish and a demand for justice (repeated phrases of the vocal line that are echoed in the bass), pants with anxiety (broken rhythm in the violins), and presses its message with relentless rhythmic drive.

Don Giovanni (baritone) [dawn jo-VAHN-nee]

A young, powerful member of the nobility. He has a nice sense of the ridiculous, is quick witted and ingenious, and is equally adept at swordplay, plotting, and—most especially—bedroom tactics. He adopts the music and mode of address appropriate to the person he is dealing with: he can be suave and gracious to Donna Anna, charming to Zerlina, threatening and imperious to Masetto, down-to-earth and common in arguing with Leporello (at the start of Act II), and sentimental and gushy to Elvira (in the Act II balcony-scene trio, No. 15). Whatever he does or sings, his music is energetic and pulsing with life or, as in the case of "Fin ch'an dal vino" (No. 11; see Chapter 4), delirious, repetitive, and obsessive.

Every generation "reads" Giovanni through its own language, and so it is not surprising that Romantics found him as representative of a life force and divine spark, while moderns may find his overthrow of order and indiscriminate taste[29] to be unattractive and revolting. Even a "me-first" civilization has some difficulty with Giovanni's total dedication to self-gratification through sex (wine is second, but not even close), and the casual lack of interest with which he casts women aside once he has conquered them does not sit well with an age intolerant of the physical and emotional abuse of women.

His cruelty assumes different guises. We see it when, encountering Elvira at her hotel, he first deceives her with elaborate flattery then leaves her to be regaled in an insulting manner by his servant. In the great quartet "Non ti fidar" (No. 9), Giovanni turns to character assassination and ridicule: for his insidious suggestion to Anna and Ottavio that Elvira is demented, Giovanni offers a slyly descending chromatic line (Example DG-

---

[28] Moberly, p. 168.

[29] The ecumenism of his catalogue is legendary, his Act I party is "aperto a tutti" ("open to all"), and the dances there are to be played "senza alcun ordine" ("without any order").

5a); then he assumes an attitude of magnanimity through expansive triads[30] bearing his suggestion that she might calm down if left to his care; when neither of these works, he pulls poor Elvira over to the side and whispers viciously in her ear that she ought not to make a spectacle of herself in a rapid parlando that is simply nasty (Example DG-5b).

He puts on the cloak of the confidante in his song to Masetto when, wearing Leporello's cloak and hat, Giovanni whispers a conniving vocal line in broken rhythms, echoed a few beats later by low strings, all to the accompaniment of sustained French horns (a symbol of cuckoldry; see Chapter 3) and hushed violin syncopations. When Masetto is duped into surrendering his weapons, Masetto becomes ripe for the plucking, and Giovanni obliges, administering a vigorous thrashing.

EXAMPLE DG-5 GIOVANNI AS CONNIVING AND CRUEL

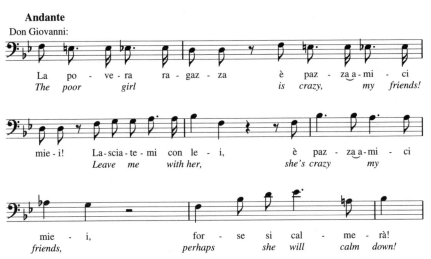

a) Act I, scene xii: No. 9 Quartet, "Non ti fidar"—Giovanni suggests that Elvira is rather dotty and is better left in his tender care.

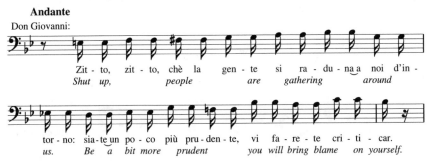

b) In the same ensemble, Giovanni lays aside his grace and snarls angrily at Elvira.

---

[30] A triad is a group of three notes a third apart (thus A-C-E, for example), played either simultaneously as a chord or in sequence as a melody.

His most unkind treatment of a person comes when he persuades Elvira that he is repentant by crooning to her from below her window, knowing that she is a sucker for sentiment and wants desperately to be loved. Not only is his flattery grossly insincere, as evident from the slathering of sospiri (two-note "sighs") in the accompanying violins (Example DG-5c), but it is viciously cynical, since, when Elvira is taken out of the way, he then uses the same melody in a simpler fashion to serenade her serving girl (Example DG-5d). In sum, Giovanni's words of love are tools, not thoughts, and his life history is an ugly swath of broken hearts.

EXAMPLE DG-5 (*Continued*)

c) Act II, scene ii No. 15 Trio, "Ah! taci, ingiusto core" ("Ah, be still my aching heart"[31])—While Leporello makes amatory gestures below Elvira's window at twilight, Giovanni serenades her from the shadows with a melody he will soon use for her servant; the soupy violins are for Elvira's benefit.

d) Act II, scene iii: No. 16 "Deh! vieni alla finestra" ("Ah! come to the window")—A few moments later: Giovanni's serenade to Elvira's servant uses the same melody as in Example DG-5c but with a simple accompaniment on a mandolin.

---

[31] Ingiusto = "unfair," but this translation I found impossible to resist.

Il Commendatore (bass) *[eel koh-mehn-dah-TOHR-reh]*

Anna's father, a knight or member of a chivalric order (not a military leader). As a symbol of rectitude in his first appearance, his music is persistently triadic, turning into the minor mode when he has taken the fatal thrust from Giovanni's sword. His speaking as the Statue in the cemetery is an otherwordly intonation of repeated notes over solemn chord changes in woodwinds and trombones, his few melodic intervals drawing dramatically on the archetypes of open fifths and fourths. A similar quality dominates his appearance in the supper scene (Act II, scene xiv–xvi; Examples DG-3c and e), save for his declining Giovanni's offer of food because he eats no earthly meal ("Non si pasce di cibo mortale / chi si pasce di cibo celeste" ["He who eats celestial food is not nourished by mortal food"]); his music at this point (voice and accompaniment) uses all twelve notes of the octave, an unearthly passage for a phenomenon from another world.

Don Ottavio (tenor) *[dawn aw-TAH-vee-yoh]*

Anna's fiancé. His first aria (No. 10a, "Dalla sua pace") identifies him as a noble lover in the style of the Baroque tradition of sweetness, ornament, and grace. The aria puts the quietus on those who find Ottavio a cynic who is simply out for a financially suitable marriage: characters in theater may lie to others but not to themselves; in opera, to put a finer point on it, their *music* never lies. "Dalla sua pace" is a soliloquy of meltingly tender music; it is telling the truth.

The middle section of his ornate "Il mio tesoro" (No. 21) is a vow to take action, but it is framed and therefore curtailed by the music and text of his concern for his beloved. Moreover, its substance is determined by the secco that precedes the aria: he is going to go to the authorities. The aria, therefore is an exit aria from a bygone convention rather than a springboard for action. In the ensembles, his music is always in the stylistic mode of Anna's music, and the result is that he never emerges in them individually or as a hero worthy of challenging the likes of Don Giovanni.

Although many writers have given Ottavio a going-over as a fop or cold hearted money-grabber, I am comfortable joining the few who have taken up his cause. When Ottavio soliloquizes in "Dalla sua pace" that "qualche le incresce morte mi dà" ("whatever grieves her kills me"), I believe him. He stands, I think, for constancy, dignity, courtesy, respect for law and tradition, and gentleness of spirit in an age that has left those virtues behind. He was an anachronism in Mozart's day; I regret that he is an anachronism in our own.

Donna Elvira (soprano) *[dohn-nah ehl-VEER-rah]*

She is a "povera ragazza" ("a poor girl"), according to Giovanni in the Act I quartet (see above, Example DG-5a), and a "fanciulla" ("lass"), according to Leporello when, in the Act II sextet, he throws off his disguise. In other words, Elvira is young and innocent. We learn from her in the recitative of her first scene that Giovanni had furtively entered her house in Burgos, seduced her with cunning, vows, and flattery ("arte," "giuramento," and "lusinghe") and then declared her to be his wife. Three days later he abandoned her[32] and she has pursued him since.

---

[32] It is perhaps unkind to suggest that there is a kind of distinction in this, for no other Giovanni conquest has been able to keep him around that long.

As a girl of old-fashioned values, she is given old-fashioned music in the form of melodic patterns that seem at times to scramble about like a wing-clipped chicken getting to its roost. In her first appearance, triads mount above the staff, then plunge to the bottom of it; the high notes, broadly phrased angularity, and nose-diving violin scales (Example DG-6a) suggest a woman storming into the fray of wifely turbulence. Mozart stretches her distress into the bizarre in the Quartet (No. 9), when poor Elvira, finding herself once again victimized by the charm of the man she "married," becomes increasingly disoriented melodically as she grows angrier (Example DG-6b).

In Act II, however, she is no longer musically ridiculous but affecting. Her music in the trio "Ah! taci, ingiusto core" (No. 15) lets her speak of genuine heartbreak through the simplicity of her melodic line and the accompanying violins (Example DG-6c); violins then suggest the sighs ("x" in Example DG-6c) that Don Giovanni will soon turn into mockery.

EXAMPLE DG-6 ELVIRA'S MUSIC

a) Act I, scene v: No. 3 "Ah! chi mi dice mai" ("Ah, who can tell me")—Elvira is resolved to track down her errant "husband."

Her most powerful dramatic moment is musically her grandest and most complex. It is the battery of conflicting emotions that shape the accompanied recitative and aria of her Act II soliloquy, "In quali eccessi o numi . . . Mi tradì quell' alma ingrata" (No. 21c; Example DG-6d). In the recitative, word and music mesh with an illustrative quality that is reminiscent of Handel; in the aria, almost every vocal phrase has a response from an instrument (Example DG-6f), the interplay of the parts providing the workings of a tormented and conflicted person.[33]

EXAMPLE DG-6 (*Continued*)

b) Act I, scene xii: No. 9 Quartet, "Non ti fidar" ("Don't give your trust")— Elvira is outraged.

c) Act II, scene ii: No. 15 Start of the trio "Ah! taci, ingiusto core" ("Ah, be still, unjust heart").

---

[33] This interplay is in the style of the *symphonie concertante,* the answer of the Classical era to the Baroque's *concerto grosso.* The aria is a model of the rondo form (a pattern frequently associated with instrumental music) in which a principal theme or episode is alternated with contrasting ones.

EXAMPLE DG-6 (*Continued*)

Allegro assai

Donna Elvira:

Sen-tir già par-mi la fa-ta-le sa-et-ta
It seems I already hear the fatal lightning bolt

Violins

d) Act II, scene xi: No. 21c "In quali eccessi" ("To what excesses")—Word painting à la Handel: Elvira calls down the wrath of heaven.

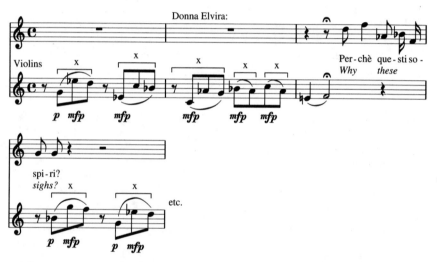

Donna Elvira:

Violins

Per-chè que-sti so-
Why these

spi-ri?
sighs?

etc.

e) The same—more word painting: she asks herself why, being so rightfully angry, she still sighs ("x" = sospiri) with love and pain.

Zerlina (soprano) [tsair-LEE-nah]

A "contadina" (a country girl) whose solo music is entrancingly pastoral, with the flowing triple time of 6/8 governing the little chorus (No. 4, "Giovinette, che fate all' amore") celebrating her wedding to Masetto, and ending both the "Là ci darem" duet and her "Batti, batti" (No. 12); her lovely "Vedrai carino" (No. 18) is in the related 3/8. Both arias are, not surprisingly, labeled *grazioso*. There is a touch of the manipulative in her, too, as suggested by one interpretation of her duet with Giovanni (see Example DG-1a–d). Another hint of this view of her character is derived from her turning the music of Giovanni's flattery of her (Example DG-7a) to good purpose when she is inveigling Masetto to forgive her outrageous behavior (Example DG-7b): the keys are different, but the intended effect of the descending triad is the same.

EXAMPLE DG-6 (*Continued*)

f) Act II, scene xii: No. 21c "Mi tradì quell' alma ingrata" ("I am betrayed by that ungrateful soul")—She still feels pity for Don Giovanni, her anguish voiced by the tumble of a motive through vocal and instrumental parts.

With the Act I finale, Zerlina becomes a different person, frightened and aware of danger at the start of the events in the garden, terrified and abused by Giovanni's vicious attempt at rape by the end of the act; in Act II, Zerlina is again in control of herself, tender to a husband with whom life will have its unhappy and brutal moments and persistent in her efforts to bring a resolution to the tumultuous events of her wedding night.

EXAMPLE DG-7 ZERLINA AS OBJECT OF FLATTERY AND
MANIPULATOR OF IT

a) Act I, scene ix: In recitativo secco, Giovanni speaks honeyed words to Zerlina.

b) Act I, scene xvi: No. 12 "Batti, batti o bel Masetto"—Zerlina, speaking honeyed words, tells Masetto she is ready to submit to whatever he wants to do to her.

Masetto (bass) *[mah-ZET-toh]*

Rustic and unrefined, Masetto is slow to understand and quick to resent and suspect. His one aria, "Ho capito, Signor sì" (No. 6), has the repeated bass notes associated with the droning of peasant bagpipes, the simplicity of unison violins, and the rhythmic monotony of a person who can think only in the simplest terms. The fast repetitions of his phrase endings are right out of the buffo user's guide, but the slower descent of his first long phrase (Example DG-8a) is a bitter reflection of having to bow his head, and the false gentility of the violins (Example DG-8b) sneers at the privileges of the aristocracy.[34] His harping on the *cavalier* who will make a *cavaliera* of Zerlina is a coarse pun on the word for "nobleman" and the neighboring term that can hint not only at the lady of a cavalier but also at "mounting" in its crudely sexual connotation (Example DG-8c). It is reflective of Masetto as a person that this is more an indictment of Zerlina than of Giovanni; it comes after his "bricconaccia, malandrina, fosti ognor la mia ruina" ("Hussy, rascal, you've always been the ruin of me"), so it is more about what Giovanni is doing to Masetto than what is happening to Zerlina. Masetto is not exactly the amorous shepherd of the Enlightenment's Arcadia.

---

[34] It is possible to see the fervor of the Revolution in Masetto's thinking, but if it is there, it is but a momentary digression; *Don Giovanni* is about the assault on the dignity and order of society rather than a critique of the particular abuses of class privilege.

EXAMPLE DG-8 ACT I, SCENE VIII: NO. 6 "HO CAPITO, SIGNOR
SÌ" ("I UNDERSTAND, MY LORD, YES")—MASETTO'S RESENTMENT

a) He must bow his head.

b) Giovanni is a gentleman.

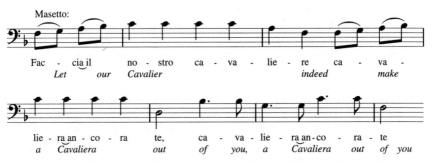

c) Zerlina, says Masetto, will be treated as an object of Giovanni's sexual desires
(and thus will be an embarassment to Masetto).

Chorus of peasant men and women; servants of Giovanni (male voices); demons from Hell (male voices)

Ministers of Justice

Men of the law who accompany Ottavio and Anna to Giovanni's residence at the Epilogue. Although they are silent, their presence indicates that Ottavio has enlisted the aid of the law to bring Giovanni to judgment. Their appearance is often foregone in modern productions.

Bibliography

Allanbrook, Wye Jamison. *Rhythmic Gesture in Mozart:* Le nozze di Figaro *and* Don Giovanni. Chicago: University of Chicago Press, 1983.
   Some very difficult analysis for the nonprofessional but a most perceptive and helpful examination of character and situation as they are illuminated through purely musical means.
Braunbehrens, Volkmar. *Mozart in Vienna, 1771–1791.* New York: Grove Weidenfeld, 1990.
   Pp. 304–309 offer a review of the reception of Mozart's subject matter and his opera.
Dent, Edward J. *Mozart's Operas: A Critical Study.* 2nd ed. London: Oxford University Press, 1947 [1913].
   Although Dent's work has been subject to correction on a number of points and his views of Anna and Ottavio are no longer dominating, this study is still one of the most detailed and helpful.
Einstein, Alfred. *Mozart: His Character, His Work.* London: Oxford University Press, 1945.
   A classic study of the operas as examples of genre and as individual masterpieces.
Heartz, Daniel. *Mozart's Operas,* ed. Thomas Bauman. Berkeley, CA: University of California Press, 1990.
   Four essays on narrow aspects of the opera, with a particularly helpful study of the dance types of the Act I finale.
John, Nicholas, ed. *Don Giovanni: Mozart.* English National Opera Guide 18. New York: Riverrun Press, 1983.
Loft, Abram. "The Comic Servant in Mozart's Operas," in *Musical Quarterly* XXXII, no. 3 (July 1946): 376–389.
Mandel, Oscar, ed. *The Theatre of Don Juan: A Collection of Plays and Views, 1630–1963.* Lincoln, NE: University of Nebraska Press, 1963.
   An invaluable anthology, inlcuding not only the seminal play by Tirso de Molina but also the remarkable treatments of the subject by E. T. A. Hoffmann, Søren Kierkegaard, George Bernard Shaw, and Edmond Rostand. Not included, unfortunately, is Molière's play, Don Juan, ou le festin de Pierre *("Don Juan, or the Stone Guest" [lit., "Don Juan, or the Stone Banquet"], 1665).*
Mann, William. *The Operas of Mozart.* London: Oxford University Press, 1977.

Moberly, R. A. *Three Mozart Operas:* Figaro, Don Giovanni, The Magic Flute. New York: Dodd, Mead & Company, 1968.
   A most willful misreading of many aspects of text and music, but a number of challenging and intriguing insights.

Noske, Frits. *The Signifier and the Signified: Studies in the Operas of Mozart and Verdi.* The Hague: Martinus Nijhoff, 1977.
   Analysis of music and drama; survey of interpretations; examples of archetypical symbols.

Rushton, Julian. *W. A. Mozart:* Don Giovanni [Cambridge Opera Handbooks] Cambridge: Cambridge University Press, 1981.
   Thorny musical analysis, but the discussion of plot and literary/philosophical backgrounds are among the most concise and helpful in a vast literature.

Till, Nicholas. *Mozart and the Enlightenment: Truth, Virtue and Beauty in Mozart's Operas.* New York: W. W. Norton, 1992.

Chapter 10

FIDELIO

MUSIC: Ludwig van Beethoven (1770–1827)

LIBRETTO: Joseph Sonnleithner (1766–1835), with revisions in 1806 by
Stephan von Breuning (1774–1827) and in 1814 by Georg Friedrich
Treitschke (1776–1842), after a libretto by Jean-Nicolas Bouilly
(1763–1842) for Pierre Gaveux's (1760-1825) *Léonore, ou L'amour conjugale* (1798).

PREMIERE: Vienna, November 20, 1805 (with overture known as "Leonore"
No. 2, Op. 72a); rev. Vienna, March 29, 1806 (with "Leonore" Overture
No. 3, also Op. 72a); rev. Vienna May 23, 1814 (with the "Fidelio"
Overture). The "Leonore" Overture No. 1, Op. 138, was composed for a
projected 1806 production in Prague.

TIME AND PLACE OF THE STORY: Time indeterminate but probably late eighteenth or early nineteenth century; a prison near Seville. The action of
the opera takes place within a single day.

Beethoven's only opera, a Singspiel-rescue opera,[1] may be seen as a
metaphor for his life. Like its protagonists, he sought family bliss; like
Florestan, he was a victim of supreme isolation (deafness, of course, being a
special kind of imprisonment for a musician); and, concomitant with the
spirit of struggle found in much of the opera's music, he was a central figure
in the overthrow of conventions of social and musical behavior.

That the opera is one of the world's most revered works, in spite of what
is generally perceived as an uncomfortable mix of domestic comedy (the
opening scene), stark melodrama (the dungeon scene), and dramatic cantata
(the concluding scene), is a result not just of its uplifting music but also of a
grander metaphorical meaning: of all the world's operas, it is possibly the one
most forcefully directed at our aspirations for freedom and human dignity.

---

[1] The Singspiel is a genre of opera using spoken dialogue instead of recitative. The typical
eighteenth-century Singspiel has a strong moralistic bent, with a mix of sentiment and
comedy. In the nineteenth century (*Der Freischütz* and *Fidelio,* for example), serious dramatic tension became an important component as well. The "rescue operas" used stories
of derring-do and the defeat of tyranny, with whatever plot manipulation was required to
produce a happy ending.

It is an opera of struggle against injustice, of loyalty to high-minded principle, and the triumph of good over evil, written during a time of political and stylistic turmoil as European civilization, staggering from the impact of the French Revolution, reeled from eighteenth-century Classicism to nineteenth-century Romanticism. It shows the era's new capacity for a mix of the grisly and villainous with the exalted and the beautiful, and its fascination for real events and real people.[2] Operas of abstraction, stylized metaphor, decorous stage action, and sublimation of violence were long gone.

Beethoven dealt with these aspirations in the full flower of a heroic and distinctively personal musical style that had already found voice in his *Eroica* Symphony (No. 3, Op. 55, 1804) and, in the years of revision and rethinking, in such works as the violin concerto (Op. 61, 1806) and the Symphony No. 5 (Op. 67, 1808).

The *Fidelio* music embraces two distinct elements. One is a propulsive dynamism rooted in the rhythmic forcefulness of three fast pick-up notes and a strongly accented "arrival" note (♪♪♪ | ♩), a motivic concept that is especially well known because of its prominence throughout the fifth symphony and in the first movement of the *Appassionata* Sonata (No. 23, Op. 57, 1804–5). It has a "slingshot" quality that comes from its off-the-beat attack; it is invariably preceded by a short rest on the accented beat and thus springs unavoidably into the listener's awareness, although it may be playful and innocent (see Example FI-1a), breathless and frantic (Example FI-1b), or ecstatic and full of longing (Example FI-1c). It was not unique to Beethoven—it is found in Haydn and Mozart—nor to the fifth symphony,[3] but it symbolizes a drive and theatrical energy that has become especially identified with this composer.

EXAMPLE FI-1 THE PROPULSIVE MOTION (♪♪♪ | ♩) OF *Fidelio*

a) Act I: Introduction to No. 1, Duet, "Jetzt Schätzchen, jetz sind wir allein" ("Now, sweetheart, now we're alone"; Marzelline/Jaquino).

---

[2] Bouilly, who had been an official in Tours during the Reign of Terror, averred that the story of a wife disguised as a boy to enter a prison and rescue her husband actually happened.

[3] The first movements of Haydn's Piano Sonata No. 36 (in c-sharp minor, Hob. XVI:36, from ?1780) and Mozart's String Quintet in c minor, K.406 (1788), offer examples, as do the *Appassionata* Sonata (Op. 57) and the "Egmont" Overture, Op. 84 (1810).

EXAMPLE FI-1 (*Continued*)

b) Act I: No. 10, Finale—Marzelline and Jaquino enter in haste with news of Pizarro's raging return.

c) Act I: No. 10, Finale—The prisoners exult in the warmth and radiance of the sun.

The second type of music found in this opera is precisely the opposite of the first; it is halting and uncertain, suggestive of despair, deep grief, introspection, and uncertainty. Its voice is the dominant tone of the famous *Marcia funèbre* that is the second movement of Symphony No. 3 and is characterized by short phrases, irregular rhythmic groups, frequent rests, and tempos on the slower side.

EXAMPLE FI-2 RHYTHMS IN *Fidelio* ASSOCIATED WITH DESPAIR, GRIEF, INTROSPECTION, UNCERTAINTY

a) Act I: No. 3, Quartet, "Mir ist so wunderbar" ("It's so wonderful to me"; canon theme).

b) Act I: No. 10, Finale—Prisoners return to the darkness of their cells.

EXAMPLE FI-2 *(Continued)*

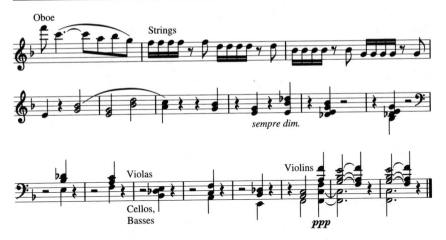

c) Act II: No. 11—End of Florestan's aria.

The extreme difference between these two elements is readily apparent and lends the opera its special qualities of dramatic contrast and intensity, of gloom and of spiritual uplift.

THE PLOT AND ITS MUSIC

Pre-Act I Action

Florestan, having been kidnapped by his personal enemy, Pizarro, has been secretly incarcerated in the deepest part of the State Prison for more than two years. Leonore, disguised as a youth, has been employed as Rocco's assistant for some months. For the past month, Florestan's rations have been steadily reduced; for the last twenty-four hours, he has been given only a little black bread, half a jug of water, no light, and no fresh straw for bedding. An ally of Pizarro has learned that the Minister, having been informed of prisoners being detained by Pizarro without authority, is planning a surprise inspection.

OVERTURE ("FIDELIO") *The overture usually heard at the start of the opera is a symphonic movement based on a virile dotted rhythm heard at its outset. The motives that follow are either derived from it or introduced by it. Although there are quieter materials for the French horns and clarinets, the piece on the whole is vigorous and rhythmically unrelenting, with continuous development of its pithy ideas. The darker elements of the story are nowhere suggested in the overture's music, nor are any of the opera's melodies, but the positive and uplifting qualities of the story suffuse every measure.*

Act I

Courtyard and front of the jailer's lodge of the State Prison. View of the main gate, with a wicket door through which individuals may enter or make deliveries. A smaller lodge for Jaquino is to the side. Marzelline has set up her ironing board in front of her door. (NOTE: in the synopsis below, action taking place via spoken dialogue is indicated as SD.)

1 DUET (Jaquino, Marzelline) *Jetzt, Schätzchen, jetzt sind wir allein* ("Now, sweetheart, now we're alone") Jaquino pleads his suit, Marzelline responding impatiently with insistent "Nos." She understands Jaquino's pleas but is interested only in Fidelio. Jaquino is irritated at the constant interruption of knocking at the porter's gate for delivery of items.

*The pattern of ♪ ♫♫ | ♪ (Ex. FI-1a), lightly scored, provides both drive and a comic element; the marking of **sfp** (suddenly loud, then just as suddenly, soft) suggests Jaquino's fear of pressing too hard, as does the hesitancy of some of his rhythms. Marzelline's Nein, nein, nein, nein, not surprisingly, is a series of repeated notes. The knocking motive is insistent low string repetitions of a single pitch.*

SD Jaquino is summoned to the garden by Rocco. Marzelline notes that her life and hopes have changed ever since Fidelio came.

2 ARIA (Marzelline) *O wär' ich schon mit dir vereint* ("Oh, if only I were wed to you") Marzelline imagines a life of joy and sweet kisses when married to Fidelio.

Interrupted rhythms and the minor mode suggest her dreamy state, but triplets soon lead to the major mode and a bubbling background figure; Marzelline's joy is the source of the quick note values in the tuneful voice part. There are two verses, the refrain of the second using an intensification of rhythmic complexity to suggest her excitement and hopefulness.

SD Leonore (as Fidelio) returns from the village. She carries a heavy burden of provisions and newly repaired chains. Rocco notes that the receipts indicate good business sense and his praise encompasses a hint of reward—marriage to Marzelline. Leonore's embarassment is interpreted by Rocco as shyness.

3 QUARTET (canon) (Marzelline, Leonore, Rocco, Jaquino) *Mir ist so wunderbar, / Es engt das Herz mir ein* ("It's so wonderful to me, it grips my heart") Marzelline believes Fidelio loves her; Leonore frets over the danger she is in (*Wie gross ist die Gefahr, wie schwach der Hoffnung Schein!*—"How great is the danger, how weak the ray of hope!"); Rocco beams with the marriage prospect (*Sie liebt ihn, es ist klar, Ja, Mädchen er wird dein*—"She loves him, that's clear, yes, maiden, he'll be yours"); and Jaquino grumps petulantly (*Mir sträubt sich schon das Haar, der Vater willigt ein*—"My hair bristles, her father favors him").

A hushed introduction by divided violas and cellos over pizzicato basses leads to a mystical canon, each singer beginning with the same hesitant music (Ex. FI-2a) but different words. The accompaniment deepens with each entry, rhythms become more complex, and each voice part moves into its own counterpoint appropriate to the mood of the character.

SD Rocco announces that Fidelio will be his son-in-law in a few days, when Pizarro leaves for Seville for his monthly accounting.

4 ARIA (Rocco) *Hat man nicht auch Gold beineben, / Kann man nicht ganz glücklich sein* ("If a person doesn't have money as well [as love], he can't be completely happy") Rocco offers some advice and his blessing.

A strophic song with refrain, in keeping with the hominess of the advice and its giver. Staccato woodwinds lend a folksy touch, and Rocco's vision of money jingling in his pocket (Doch wenn's in den Taschen fein klingelt und rollt) is expressed in a delightful violin countermelody with woodwind chordings. That gold is a beautiful thing (es ist ein schönes Ding) is driven home by a brief canon between violins and Rocco's part (Ex. FI-3b).

SD Seeing an opportunity, Leonore/Fidelio suggests that Rocco should demonstrate trust in his future son-in-law by allowing him to help with the work in the secret dungeons. Rocco agrees, save for one special place, where an unnamed prisoner, there for more than two years, is soon to die from starvation. Fidelio avers he is strong enough to help.

5 TRIO (Rocco, Leonore, Marzelline) *Gut, Söhnchen, gut, / Hab immer Mut* ("Well said, my son, always have courage") Rocco vows to ask Pizarro for permission to take Fidelio into the dungeon as a helper. Leonore is impatient to join him, while Marzelline, urging Rocco to get the permission, comments lovingly on Fidelio's strength of character.

> *The trio is a response to Fidelio's asserting that "he" is strong, hence rhythmic vigor is immediately asserted in the fast pick-ups of the canonic string introduction and underpinning. Rocco's opening phrase recurs motivically in all the voice parts and in the accompaniment; Marzelline's music is floating and ornamental. Leonore's music is much narrower in compass and less melodic (she has an agenda, here) save for her momentary lapse of disguise, when she avers that love can bear great sorrow (*hohe Leiden tragen*) and when she feels that Hope is bringing her comfort (*Du, Hoffnung, reichst mir Labung dar*).*

6 MARCH (Orchestra) and SD Officers and soldiers parade into the courtyard. Pizarro posts new guards and, looking through the dispatches given him by Rocco, learns of a surprise investigation planned by the Minister. He resolves to take immediate action regarding Florestan.

> *Lively and steadily paced. The prominence of French horns and woodwinds evokes the spirit of a military band. Based on the dotted rhythm heard at the outset, the themes are rhythmically similar to the hesitant or interrupted patterns found throughout the opera, but the context and steady motion in lower voices result in a relentless tread of an unsmiling soldiery.*

7 ARIA w/CHORUS (Pizarro, Soldiers) *Ha! Welch' ein Augenblick! / Die Rache werd' ich kühlen!* ("Ah, what a moment! My rage I shall assuage!") Pizarro exults in anticipation of slaying Florestan and paying him back thereby for past humiliations. The soldiers mutter about Pizarro's evident bloodthirstiness and vow to stick to their rounds with all seriousness.

> *Rapid tempo and varied accompanying figures make for turbulence and violence (Ex. FI-5). The opening violin line devolves into faster descending scales, then tremolos, punctuated by sfp accents on off beats. Sudden fortes and diminuendos suggest a man of wild mood swings. A rolling accompaniment figure underscores Pizarro's resentment of Florestan's having made him the butt of mockery (*Schon war ich nah', im Staube, / dem lauten Spott zum Raube, / dahin gestreckt zu sein—"I was almost, there cast down into the dust, the joke of the mob"*). A high note of gloating (*Nun ist es mir geworden—"Now it has come to me"*) is followed by a chromatic turn at his thoughts of turning the tables through murder (*den Mörder selbst zu morden—"the destroyer himself is to be destroyed"*). Pizarro's high note on* Triumph! *leads the soldiers to mutter low over tremolos and rising chromatics. The aria ends with Pizarro's line restricted to just a few pitches, repeating fiendishly his anticipation of revenge.*

SD Pizarro sends his Captain to the tower with a trumpeter, ordering him to signal at once should a carriage be seen coming from Seville. Unaware that Leonore is overhearing him, he calls Rocco to his side.

8 DUET (Pizarro, Rocco) *Jetzt, Alter, jetzt hat es Eile! / Dir wird ein Glück zu theile, / Du wirst ein reicher Mann* ("Now, old man, we must hurry! This will be good fortune for you, you will be a rich man"). Pizarro offers a purse if Rocco will commit murder, but Rocco demurs. Ordering Rocco to dig a grave for the special prisoner, Pizarro vows to do the deed himself: *Ein Stoss—und er verstummt!*—"One thrust—and he is silenced!"

> *Hesitant rhythms in both vocal line and accompaniment suggest Pizarro's hushed and careful tactical approach. Frequent changes of woodwind color create a sense of an erratic personality (as changes of dynamics did in No. 7). Sudden chord changes punctuate "murder!"*

(Morden!). *Broken phrases reflect Rocco's terror and revulsion, more solid ones his refusal* (Ex. FI-3a); *Pizarro tries to sway him over "soothing" triplets, but they disintegrate into tremolos, bursts of scales, and abruptly loud chords. Quiet strings double Pizarro's description of how he will sidle into the cell to do the deed* (Dann werd' ich selbst, vermummt, / mich in den Kerker schleichen); *a sudden dissonance in the winds highlights his* ein Stoss! *("one thrust"). Orchestral syncopations and fast note values govern the repetitions and the end of the duet.*

9 RECITATIVE and ARIA (Leonore) *Abscheulicher! Wo eilst du hin?. . . Komm, Hoffnung, lass den letzten Stern / Der Müden nicht erbleichen!* ("Vile creature! Where are you rushing off to? . . . Come, hope, let not your last star fade in exhaustion") Leonore vows that, no matter what fury may storm like ocean waves (*Meereswogen*) in Pizarro's blood, for her there is a rainbow of hope. She affirms her determination to rescue her husband, strengthened by the faith of true wedded love (*die Pflicht der treuen Gattenliebe*).

*There is no spoken dialogue. Leonore steps from hiding, her music exploding at once in rapid string figures and a dramatic held chord at her first word. The alternation of violent string and vocal phrases continues until a more gentle motion in Leonore's melody (over held harmony) at her vision of a rainbow (*Farbenbogen*) of hope. A quieter flow sets in as transition to the aria.*

ARIA. A dramatic and moving display piece, very complex melodically and rhythmically. So is the orchestration and variety of accompanying patterns, in accordance with the many emotions that Leonore is experiencing. Melismas of different shape color the repetitions of sie wird's erreichen *("[Love] will attain my goal," Ex. FI-4a) and each line of text has its own music. Her determination (Ich folg' dem innern Triebe—"I follow an inner voice," Ex. FI-4b), is introduced by a strong motive in the French horns and bassoons; rhythms are simple and steady at first (albeit with tremolos), then ever-quickening orchestral and vocal scales lead to the aria's triumphant final bars.*

SD After telling Jaquino his suit is hopeless, Rocco agrees to Fidelio's request to admit the prisoners to the courtyard. Rocco leaves to divert Pizarro's attention, and Leonore and Jaquino open the cell doors.

Finale

10 CHORUS (Prisoners) *O welche Lust, in freier Luft / Den Atem leicht zu heben!* ("Oh what joy to breathe freely in the open air!") The prisoners relish the sun and fresh air, even as they shrink in fear from the constant watching of the soldiers and warn each other to speak softly.

Exquisitely quiet and rising strings lead to faster rising figures in woodwinds (bassoon, then clarinet) over murmuring accompanying patterns. Each pair of vocal entries starts on a dissonance then resolves, as if the restorative influence of sun and air is having its effect. Repetitions of the opening words become faster, higher, stronger, all over gentle figurations, the whole reaching a climax at Nur hier ist Leben *("Only here is life"); sudden low unisons and octaves show that the cell is a tomb (*Der Kerker eine Gruft*), but they disappear as the vision of freedom (*Freiheit*) brings the music to another climax. Held chords accompany the advice to speak softly, the prisoners' whispering of the warning given to polyphony over threatening* **sfp**s *in the woodwinds before their opening music returns. A silence follows.*

RECITATIVE and DUET (Leonore, Rocco) *Nun sprecht, wie ging's . . . Noch heute? O welch ein Glück!* ("Tell me, how did it go? . . . Then it's today? Oh what joy!") Rocco informs Fidelio of Pizarro's permission for the marriage and that Fidelio may help in the dungeon, where, within the hour, the special prisoner is to be slain by Pizarro and buried by them.

Rocco's news comes in suddenly quick patterns. Leonore's joy finds voice in fast rising scales that become even faster as she seeks details. An agitated 6/8 conditions Rocco's task-oriented thoughts; Leonore's deeper feelings are expressed in shorter phrases and faster, more complex rhythms.

ENSEMBLE (Marzelline, Jaquino, Leonore, Rocco; then Pizarro, Soldiers, Prisoners) *Ach Vater, Vater, eilt!* ("Ah Father, Father, hurry!") Marzelline and Jaquino hastily return, describing Pizarro's fury at the kindness shown the prisoners. As Pizarro's angry order for the prisoners to be returned to their cells is carried out, he commands Rocco to hasten to dig the grave in the secret dungeon.

*The panicked arrival of Marzelline and Jaquino is heralded by the opera's drivimg rhythmic pattern (Ex. FI-1b) over **fp** tremolos. Pizarro's furious return is marked by the some of the bristling accompaniment of his earlier aria. Rocco tries to defuse Pizarro's rage by suggesting that letting the prisoners out of their cells is appropriate for honoring the Name Day of the King (some brief fanfares), then Rocco assumes Pizarro's conspiratorial whispers when he turns the Overseer's attention to the special prisoner.*

The prisoners' farewell to the sunlight is sung to separated note patterns. Descending lines in the strings or doubling (and ennobling) French horns accompany a considerable variety of rhythms in the solo parts, appropriate to the different thoughts the characters express. Their return to darkness is described by stuttering descents in both pitch and instrumentation (Ex. FI-2b).

Act II

SCENE I

A subterranean dungeon. A long flight of steps leading up to the courtyard is visible through the grillwork at the back of the cell. An old well is at one side, covered with stone and bits of rubble. Florestan sits dejected, chained to a wall or a pillar.

11 INTRODUCTION (Orchestra)

Soft string unisons alternate with powerful minor chords (woodwinds and French horns); then tritone dissonances, writhing figures low in the strings, softly thudding timpani strokes (tritone pitches of A-natural and E-flat), wild cries in violins and woodwinds. Anguishing syncopations over rolling figurations in the strings lead to Florestan's cry.

RECITATIVE (Florestan) *Gott! welch' Dunkel hier!* (God! what darkness here!) Florestan cries out in anguish at his total isolation and despair but submits to God's will.

A high G on Gott!, then the writhing figure of the Introduction, but in a lower register. Florestan's hatred of the dark silence (O grauenvolle Stille) is given force by the timpani tritones of the Introduction. The wrenching cruelty of this trial of spirit (O schwere Prüfung) is given orchestral syncopation before a more flowing rhythm offers a dignity appropriate to trusting in God's will.

ARIA (Florestan) *In des Lebens Frühlingstagen / Ist das Glück von mir geflohn* ("In the springtime of my life, happiness has fled from me") Although in despair, Florestan does not regret having spoken the truth about Pizarro[4] and having done his duty. He imagines he sees an angel-like Leonore, then collapses in exhaustion.

---

[4] The specifics of this are not revealed.

An ennobling and lyric line (Ex. FI-6a) is broken by shorter rhythms for the pain (alle Schmerzen) he is willing to endure for the sake of duty. A quiet, rising oboe melody (Ex. FI-6b) over murmuring syncopations presents the vision of Leonore to the weakened Florestan, whose gasping phrases suggest both ecstasy and delirium. As he imagines being led to freedom by his "angel, Leonora," his phrases rise; dramatic repetitions of zur Freiheit in's himmlische Reich ("to freedom in a heavenly realm") peak, then the music collapses as a metaphor for Florestan's total exhaustion and fainting, the aria disintegrating into irregularly spaced, ever-slowing patterns and chords (Ex. FI-2c).

12 MELODRAMA[5] (Leonore, Rocco) *Wie kalt ist es in diesem unterirdischen Gewölbe!* ("How cold it is in this underground vault!") They descend into the dungeon area, carrying a pitcher of wine and tools for digging. As Rocco prepares to clear out the well, Leonore tries to get a better view of the prisoner.

Hesitant descending cellos and basses illustrate Rocco and Leonore descending the stairway into the darkness of the dungeon. A solo oboe arpeggio, heard as Florestan stirs in his sleep, suggests that the vision of Leonore is still with him. String and woodwind colors alternate; tempo and melodic shapes adjust to the words of the characters.

DUET (Rocco, Leonore) *Nur hurtig fort, nur frisch gegraben* ("Now quickly to work, to dig the new grave") With the help of Leonore, Rocco lifts stones and rolls them away from the well, urging harder work before Pizarro arrives. To herself, Leonore vows to help the prisoner.

Steady triplets suggest Rocco's working, with contrabassoon and double basses providing a guttural motive suggesting the rolling away of a boulder; Rocco's repeated-note insistence on working is in strong contrast to Leonore's arched, dotted-note assurances of assistance. Her asides become more extended, with an especially affective melisma on the last syllable of her ja, ich will, du Armer, dich befrei'n ("Yes, I will free you, you poor man"). The duet ends with rushing triplets diminishing in loudness to a final return of hesitant rhythm and a hushed ending in stark unisons.

SD During their brief rest for a drink, Florestan awakens. Leonore recognizes him. At Florestan's questioning, Rocco reveals that it is indeed Pizarro who has imprisoned him. When Florestan asks for a drink, Rocco agrees.

13 TRIO (Florestan, Rocco, Leonore) *Euch werde Lohn in bessern Welten, / Der Himmel hat Euch mir geschickt* ("You will have a place in a better world, Heaven has sent you to me") Florestan thanks them for their sympathy; Leonore persuades Rocco to permit her to give the prisoner a piece of bread. Florestan again offers his thanks, with expressions of anguish from Leonore and compassion from Rocco.

Dignified lyricism for Florestan's thanks; trio sections in halting rhythms; Leonore's offering of bread (dies Stückchen Brod) is in the now familiar assertive rhythm associated with much of the opera's action; the rhythm is then applied to Rocco's sympathetic concern, his zu viel wagen ("too much to dare") given a sudden move to the major mode. The final section exchanges two types of materials—lyric and rhythmically broken—among all three voices, suggesting common sympathy and providing for a musically strong and dramatically convincing conclusion.

SD Rocco goes to the door to whistle to Pizarro that the grave is ready. Pizarro enters, orders the "boy" to leave, but Leonore hides in the shadows as Rocco detaches Florestan's chain from the wall. Pizarro draws his dagger.

14 QUARTET (Pizarro/Florestan/Leonore/Rocco) *Er sterbe! Doch er soll erst wissen / Wer ihm sein stolzes Herz zerfleischt* ("He dies! But first he should know whose hand

---

[5] Spoken dialogue with orchestral accompaniment or interludes.

Beethoven, *Fidelio* (1805; rev. 1806, 1814) Act II, scene i: Leonore (Hildegard Behrens) draws a pistol to defend her husband Florestan (Wieslaw Ochman), to the astonishment of the murderous Pizarro (Hermann Becht). Houston Grand Opera, 1984: sets by Neil Peter Jampolis, costumes by Eric Winterling. Photo James Caldwell.

will rip the flesh from his proud heart") Pizarro confronts Florestan triumphantly; Florestan defies him. As Pizarro prepares the fatal thrust of his knife, Leonore leaps between them, protecting Florestan with her body and demanding that Pizarro step back. When Pizarro thrusts her aside, she protects Florestan again, this time challenging Pizarro to first kill his victim's wife (*Töt erst sein Weib!*). When Pizarro steps forward to do them both in, she draws a pistol. At this instant of stunning tableau, the trumpet call from the ramparts announces the approach of the Minister.

There is a moment of reflection, a repeated trumpet call, then the appearance of Jaquino and soldiers with the notice of the Minister's arrival.

The astonished Rocco is relieved at having to serve a tyrant no longer, Pizarro boils with rage and frustration, and Leonore and Florestan express their joy. Pizarro exits hurriedly, followed by Rocco.

A tumult of action and emotions is suggested by a great variety of fast moving configurations. Pizarro's obsession comes via repeated notes and rising patterns; brass fanfares proclaim Florestan's defiance. The musical climax is reached with Leonore's repeated high Gs when she steps before Pizarro; abruptly short phrases mark the others' astonishment, although the rhythmic turmoil never slackens. Perhaps the single most dramatic sequence in opera then occurs: Pizarro moves to stab Florestan, Leonore presents a pistol, and then comes the offstage trumpet fanfare (Ex. 3.5b)—in a suddenly new key—that stops the action cold. The stunned com-

ments of the four are quiet, accompanied by string triplets and rising flute arpeggios. There is a pause for the spoken announcement from Jaquino, then the explosion of full orchestra and vocal quartet. The music boils in fast triplets under a dotted rhythm that binds together the voice parts of Leonore, Florestan, and the relieved Rocco; Pizarro's rhythm maintains his manic repetitions. The presto coda *has two measures of potent silence before concluding orchestral hammerstrokes.*

15 DUET (Leonore/Florestan): *O namenlose Freude! / Mein Mann an meiner Brust / An Leonorens Brust!* ("O nameless joy, my husband in my embrace/Leonore in my embrace!") Ecstatic in their rescue and reunion, the two give thanks to God.

The two exchange the same rising phrase of sheer happiness, strings providing constant impetus of a three-note motive over lyric phrases in various instruments. A sudden adagio *and, a bit later, a turn to the minor, both related to the sorrows they have endured, are but momentary departures from the brilliance and joy of their reunion.*

SCENE II

The courtyard. Soldiers form in ranks to greet the Minister, who enters through the raised main gate, surrounded by villagers. All the prisoners are led in; they kneel before Don Fernando.

Finale

16 ORCHESTRAL INTRODUCTION and CHORUS (Prisoners/People) *Heil sei dem Tag, Heil sei der Stunde / Die lang ersehnt, doch unvermeint* ("Hail to the day and the hour, long sought yet denied") Exuberant joy and excitement.

The broken-note rhythm associated earlier with despair and hesitancy is translated orchestrally into an ever-growing sense of triumphant release.

The choral sound of the people and prisoners is a glorious eruption of jubilation. Fernando's greeting is undergirded with fanfare treatments derived from this same rhythm.

RECITATIVE and ARIOSO (Fernando, Rocco, Pizarro) *Des besten Königs Wink und Wille / führt mich zu euch* ("Our finest King's gracious pleasure leads me to you") Rocco leads Florestan and Leonore to Don Fernando, who demands an explanation from Pizarro. Rocco tells the story of Leonore's disguise and Pizarro's evil intent. Fernando signs for Pizarro to be arrested and instructs Leonore to strike the chains that still bind Florestan.

The music moves freely from one style to another, with an occasional choral punctuation of joy and hailing of the hour. Florestan's astonishment, Rocco's narration, and the arrest of Pizarro are given a new accompaniment rhythm of small melodic compass but steady rhythmic impetus.

ENSEMBLE *O Gott! O welch ein Augenblick . . . Wer ein holdes Weib errungen, / stimm in unsern Jubel ein!* ("O God, what a moment . . . Let him who embraces a loving wife join in our jubilation") All acclaim Leonore a rescuer and savior (*Retterin*), as husband and wife rejoice in each others' embrace.

The recall of the words of Pizarro's moment of exultation in Act I is at once ironic and mystical. Here the text is given a gentle tempo and oboe countermelody over restrained rhythmic background, a quality that continues through the joy expressed by all who observe the striking away of Florestan's chains. The final pages are an ever-intensifying series of rhythms, punctuated by choral responses given dramatic impact by the repeated syncopation on Retterin *(lit., "rescuing woman"). The finale ends with a blisteringly fast choral hymn of praise and thanksgiving.*

Beethoven, *Fidelio,* Act II, scene ii: As Marzelline (Arleen Auger, left), Jaquino (James Atherton), and Rocco (Kurt Moll) look on, Don Fernando (Bernd Weikl) learns of the heroism of Leonore (Hildegard Behrens), who has led her husband Florestan (James King) out of his imprisonment after confronting the now defeated and frustrated Pizarro (Siegmund Nimsgern, far right). Metropolitan Opera, 1970: design by Boris Aronson. Courtesy *Opera News,* Metropolitan Opera Guild. Photo James Heffernan.

The Characters

Marzelline (lyric soprano) (mahr-tseh-LEEN-uh)

The pretty daughter of Rocco, the jailer. Marzelline has fallen in love with Fidelio, her father's new assistant, and is impatient with the attentions of her former beau, Jaquino. Her importance to the plot is momentary, occupying our attention only in the opening scene, where she is given quick, short rhythms and bubbly triplets. Her rejection of Jaquino in the opening duet is highly spirited but her one aria (No. 2, "O wär ich schon mit dir vereint"— "Oh, if only I were wed to you") and her opening melodic line in the Act I canon quartet—in each she ponders her future joy in marrying Fidelio—are both inflected with the hesitant rhythm illustrated in Example FI-2.

Jaquino (lyric tenor) (yah-KEE-noh)

Porter and assistant jailer in the prison run by Pizarro. His expectations to marry Marzelline have been derailed by her attraction to Fidelio. His music in the opera's opening duet is rhythmically insistent but orchestrally insecure, for the light scoring and short phrases suggest his uncertainty even as he presses his suit. His only other solo music is in the canon quartet, where his entry, while melodically the same as the other three characters, has a sense of petulance and discomfort because of the change in the orchestra's accompanying patterns from duplets to more restless triplets.

Rocco (bass) (ROHK-koh)

Chief jailer in Pizarro's prison and Marzelline's father. He looks favorably on the possibility of the marriage of his daughter to Fidelio, whose good sense and hard work speak well of a future son-in-law. Kindhearted, he feels great sympathy for the unknown prisoner whose grave he is charged to dig. As a result, in the generally urgent Act I duet (No. 8, "Jetz, Alter, hat es Eile"— "Now, old man, we must hurry"), his firm rhythm and stolid melodic line (Example FI-3a) show that he has enough courage to refuse the bullying

EXAMPLE FI-3 ROCCO AS COURAGEOUS AND AS REALIST

a) Act I: No. 8, "Jetzt, Alter, hat es Eile"—Rocco refuses to be a murderer.

Pizarro's order to commit murder. Rocco is also a pragmatist; he offers the usual parental advice about happiness and love being directly related to financial security in a bluff and hearty strophic song that ends the domestic-comedy element of the opera with blunt and bustling rhythms and frequent cadences. His philosophy of life is uncomplicated, and so is his tune, although Beethoven invests his orchestral accompaniment with remarkable and subtle details (note the canon in Example FI-3b) that perhaps are meant to imply the richness of life's ordinary experiences.

Leonore (dramatic soprano) (leh-oh-NOH-ruh)

A noblewoman, wife of Florestan. Suspecting that her husband, who has disappeared, has been imprisoned secretly by his personal enemy Pizarro, Leonore has assumed the disguise of an adolescent boy under the name of "Fidelio" and has taken a position as Rocco's assistant in order to gain entry to the prison. She is aware of a special prisoner, access to whom is maintained only by Pizarro and Rocco, and it is her hope to gain the confidence of Rocco in hopes of finding Florestan there and effecting his rescue.

Her first music occurs in the canon quartet, where subtle woodwinds color her innermost and hesitant thoughts. As the opera progresses, however, her rhythms become more driven and her melodic line more affirmative. Her indictment of Pizarro, in the famed recitative "Abscheulicher! wo eilst du hin?" (No. 9, "Vile creature! where are you rushing off to?"), is a vivid and powerful outburst; the aria that follows, "Komm, Hoffnung" ("Come,

EXAMPLE FI-3 (*Continued*)

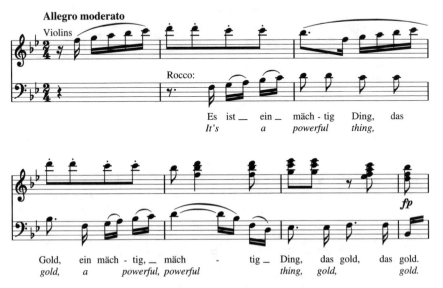

b) Act I: Refrain to No. 4, "Hat man nicht auch Gold beineben" ("If you haven't gold as well"; note canon between violins and voice line).

hope") is more noble and sustained, although its opening longer lines and mellow orchestration yield first to syncopations and rising chromatic scales (Example FI-4a) representative of the great stress she is under. The broadening melisma on "erreichen" ("reign") is an affection in the Baroque vein, suiting the music to the triumphant nature of the word. Steadier rhythms and symmetrical phrases, however, soon underscore her absolute determination to rescue her husband (Example FI-4b). The aria is a tour de force, demanding enormous energy, dramatic talent, and vocal command.

Her sudden stepping forth to challenge Pizarro at the moment he is about to stab Florestan is one of the most celebrated confrontations in opera. As with her aria, the Dungeon Scene requires a soprano of supreme vocal abilities, worthy of one of opera's greatest heroines.

EXAMPLE FI-4 NO. 9, LEONORE'S "KOMM, HOFFNUNG" ("COME, HOPE")

a) Anxiety, stress; then the uplifting melisma on "erreichen" ("reign").

b) Determination.

Pizarro (bass-baritone) *(pee-TSAHR-roh)*

A virulent and vengeful aristocrat, supervisor of the State prisons. His music is constantly turbulent, with scales, tremolos, and fast-moving accompaniment patterns that often lie in the middle and low registers of the orchestra. The swirling and repetitiveness of his phrases indicate his vicious obsession with personal ambition and revenge. Short, blunt interruptions of his music suggest that brutality and unrestrained cruelty easily rip apart any veneer of humanity or high station he may present to others.

EXAMPLE FI-5 ACT I: NO. 7, "HA! WELCH' EIN AUGENBLICK" ("HA! WHAT A MOMENT")—PIZARRO'S TURBULENCE

EXAMPLE FI-5 (*Continued*)

Florestan *(dramatic tenor)* *(FLOH-ress-tahn)*

Leonore's husband. When he first appears, he languishes from long imprisonment and is weak from starvation and deprivation of light. His recitative at the start of Act II is a dramatic cry of a soul exhausted, but his thoughts of his prior happiness are expressed in an aria of surpassing songfulness (Example FI-6a; this melody is also the main lyric theme of the "Leonore" Overture No. 3). His delirium, with a solo oboe floating the melody that represents his vision

EXAMPLE FI-6 NO. 11, FLORESTAN'S ARIA

a) He remembers past happiness.

b) He sees a vision of Leonore.

of Leonore, is voiced in short, rising phrases (Example FI-6b) that clearly represent spiritual exhaustion; his gratitude for the kindness of "Fidelio" is rhythmically steady and melodically flowing; and his defiance of the murderous Pizarro rings heroically, accompanied by rising trumpet flourishes.

Don Fernando (bass) (dawn fair-NAHN-doh)

Minister of State; a nobleman and longtime friend of Florestan. His arrival to inspect the prison has a noble purpose: the King has sent him, he says, to lift the burdens of unjust imprisonment; people must no longer kneel like slaves. This pronouncement is not especially characterized musically, its halting rhythms perhaps suggesting the mystery behind such an unexpectedly libertarian creed. Don Fernando's music is simple and direct, serving primarily as a foil to the more varied and emotional expressions of Florestan and Leonore.

Soldiers (male chorus)

Under strict obedience to Pizarro, they have no lyric moments, just muttered comments. Their orchestral music is a rather coarse march in which woodwinds and low pizzicatos lend a heavy, tread-like timbre suggestive of grim resolve and leaden duties.

Prisoners (male chorus)

Their entrance into the light after months of restriction to their dark cells is one of opera's most spiritual moments. They begin softly, with dissonances between the pairs of voices suggesting fear and tentativeness, but their song becomes louder and more lyrical. Brief bursts of emotion are quickly quelled by short repetitions of the cautionary "sprecht leise, ja leise" ("speak softly, yes softly"), but the music of their momentary happiness returns. In the final scene, they join in full-throated paean to Leonore as their rescuer/savior.

Villagers (mixed chorus)

These men and women appear only in the final scene, where their chorus becomes a kind of cantata of jubilation to end the opera.

Bibliography

Broyles, Michael. *Beethoven: The Emergence and Evolution of Beethoven's Heroic Style.* New York: Excelsior, 1987.

Cairns, David. "Fidelio," in *Responses: Musical Essays and Reviews.* New York: Knopf, 1973.

Conrad, Peter. *A Song of Love and Death: The Meaning of Opera.* New York: Poseidon, 1987.
    See pp. 123–132 for study of Fidelio *as political statement.*

Dean, Winton. "Beethoven and Opera," in *The Beethoven Reader,* eds. Denis Arnold and Nigel Fortune. New York: W. W. Norton, 1971, pp. 331–386. *Detailed study of revisions; discussion of influence of Cherubini and French opera. Reprinted in* Essays on Opera *(New York: Oxford University Press [Clarendon], 1990, pp. 123–163).*

John, Nicholas, ed. *Fidelio.* English National Opera Guide 4. London and New York: Calder Publications/Riverrun Press, 1980.

Knight, Frida. *Beethoven and the Age of Revolution.* New York: International Publishers, 1973.

Lee, M. Owen. "More Than an Opera," in *Opera News* 44, no. 12 (Feb. 2, 1980): 14, 20f. *The themes of freedom, human worth, and spirituality in* Fidelio.

Marek, George. "Where Were You the Night of November 20, 1805?," in *Opera News* 35, no. 10 (Jan. 2, 1971): 24–26. *Atmosphere of first performance, when Vienna had been newly occupied by Napoleon's troops.*

Robinson, Paul. "*Fidelio* and the French Revolution," in *Cambridge Opera Journal* 3, no. 1 (March 1991): 23–48.

Rolland, Romain. *Beethoven the Creator—The Great Creative Epochs. Vol. I: From the Eroica to the Appassionata,* trans. Ernest Newman. Garden City, NY: Garden City Publishing Co., 1937. *Chapter 4 is a perceptive (and romantic) study of the opera.*

Singer, Irving. *Mozart and Beethoven: The Concept of Love in Their Operas.* Baltimore, MD: Johns Hopkins University Press, 1977.

Solomon, Maynard. *Beethoven.* New York: Schirmer Books, 1977. *Freudian study of the opera, pp. 198–200.*

Chapter 11

IL BARBIERE DI SIVIGLIA

MUSIC: Gioacchino Rossini (1792–1868)
LIBRETTO: Cesare Sterbini (1784–1831), after *Le barbier de Séville, ou L'inutile précaution* (1775[1]), by Pierre-Auguste Caron Beaumarchais (1732–1799).
PREMIERE: Rome, February 20, 1816.
TIME AND PLACE OF THE STORY: Seville, in front of and inside the house of Dr. Bartolo, from early morning through just after midnight of a single day.

Rossini's paragon of comedy and tunefulness was a complete fiasco at its first performance in 1816 but very quickly became a benchmark of comedy through music. Beethoven put the basic stamp on it when he told Rossini face-to-face that *Barbiere* "would be played as long as Italian opera exists."[2] Beethoven has proven correct—by the end of 1996, the Metropolitan Opera had performed it more than 300 times, and it's still going strong.

The difficulties of the premiere were more political than musical, because the plot, based on the first of the three plays by Beaumarchais,[3] had already been used for an opera by Paisiello that was enormously successful since its premiere in 1782. It was considered a gross effrontery by the twenty-four-year-old Rossini not only to take up the same subject but to seem to challenge a revered master who was still living.[4] Efforts to divert resentment failed to quench the flames of a partisan first-night audience, but, after the second night, the opera set out on its course of world triumph. That Rossini composed the music in thirteen days is astonishing in itself; more to the

---

[1] Originally written by Beaumarchais as an opéra comique (which he described as a "comedy with songs here and there": (*comédie mêlée d'ariettes*) in 1772 but not accepted for performance. It was re-written as a five-act play in 1773, revised and extended yet again, then finally put into its present—and eminently prosperous—four-act structure for its performance on February 25, 1775.

[2] Weinstock, p. 120. Tactlessly suggesting that serious opera was something for which Italians "don't have enough musical science to deal with," Beethoven urged Rossini to "above all, make a lot of *Barbers*." (p. 122).

[3] The others were *La folle journée, ou Le mariage de Figaro* (1778; set by Mozart in 1786 as *Le nozze di Figaro*) and *La mère coupable* (1792; set by Milhaud in 1965).

[4] Paisiello died on June 5, 1816.

point, his quickness of invention is a metaphor for the opera's verve, brilliant wit, flagrant comedy, and boldness of characterization.

Il barbiere di Siviglia is an opera that exaggerates both incident and character, and its broadly comic pratfalls are everywhere: among them are the shattering of the dawn's quiet by musicians who shout their thanks for being paid for accompanying the Count's serenade; the Count disguised as a drunken soldier slamming around Bartolo's drawing room; the shaving scene, in which no baritone can resist slathering soap over the basso's face; and the grotesque finale to Act I, where all but Figaro and the Count are "freddo ed immobile" ("frozen and immobile").

All the characters are driven by overweening egos. Figaro's "Largo" is both bravura and braggadocio; Almaviva's first serenade splatters ornaments in every direction; Rosina sings directly to the audience about how she can deal with anyone who dares to cross her (and she does so with coloratura that is a sleeves-rolled-up, no-nonsense tour de force; see Example 4.3); and Bartolo's "Un dottor della mia sorte" ("A doctor of my station") is the ultimate musical gesture of overblown self-importance.

The orchestra sparkles with wonderful vivaciousness, the woodwinds especially chattering away at every opportunity, and the opportunity for gross effect via crescendo-cum-repetition (the so-called "Rossini crescendo") is exploited shamelessly. There is a frequent giggling in the orchestra's violins, usually evidenced by a delicate figure while some bizarre situation is taking place or a character is being absurd (see Example BA-2c, for instance). We also should not ignore those moments when the orchestra has *all* the melody, as when Figaro tells the Count where his shop is (Example BA-1).

There are delicious in-jokes for musicians and music lovers. One of them is the spicy key change in the finale of Act I, when, with all on stage

EXAMPLE BA-1 ACT I, SCENE I: NO. 4, "ALL' IDEA DI QUEL METALLO" ("AT THE VERY IDEA OF COIN"). FIGARO GIVES DIRECTIONS TO HIS PLACE OF BUSINESS

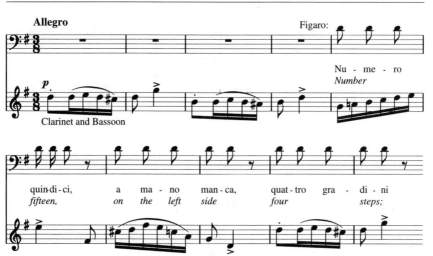

having complained about having their heads "in a frightful forge where the persistent din of ringing anvils grows louder and louder and never ceases" ("in un' orrida fucina, / dove cresce e mai non resta / dell' incudini sonore / l'importuno strepitar") they turn to the basic chords of C major, the simplest of keys, for the text "fa con barbara armonia" ("it makes a barbarous harmony"). Another one occurs a moment later in the same ensemble, where an awkward and flagrantly obvious downward change of key at the unison singing of "dove cresce e mai non resta" ("when [the din of ringing anvils] grows and never stops") is clearly a spoof of heroic opera's cliché of upward key change for heightened drama (a well-known example by Verdi is the "Vendetta" duet, in Act II of *Rigoletto*, composed thirty-five years later). Opera seria is also parodied in the mincing minuet of Bartolo's Act II song about how good music used to be when Cafarelli, the great castrato of opera seria, reigned on the stage.

Other jokes are less subtle but no less pointed: the turn to the minor mode when Basilio is informed that he's as yellow as a corpse ("siete giallo come un morto," in the Act II quintet, No. 13);[5] Rosina's swift melodic plunge that warns us she can be a viper when she doesn't get her way (in "Una voce poco fa," No. 5; see Example 4.3b); the prissy fakery of the formal greetings offered by the Count when he bows and scrapes as the "substitute music teacher" at the start of Act II; and, in the final scene, Figaro's mockery of the billing and cooing cadence endings of the lovers' duet.

The opera draws brilliantly on archetypes of character and plot: the story of the old duffer outwitted by a servant so that the young lovers may be united is an ancient one; so are the devices of letters purloined and/or misinterpreted, constant disguises, and scurrying from under the burden of being caught in a difficult situation by lying and quick-witted invention of excuses.

Vocal brilliance and virtuosity are major features of the score, not only in the elaborate coloratura given to Almaviva and Rosina (and for Figaro, in No. 7, his duet with Rosina in Act I, scene ii), but also in the comic patter of Bartolo and Figaro, whose abilities to articulate at breakneck speed are sorely tested.

The one element of great comedy that is not a part of this work is sentiment and genuine gentleness of feeling. In this respect, then, *Il barbiere di Siviglia* is the supreme example of opera buffa as farce; for a more probing human comedy, one would need to turn to the works of Mozart and to very different masterpieces such as Donizetti's *Don Pasquale* (1843) and the inimitable *Falstaff* (1893) of Verdi.

---

[5] Numbers refer to the identification of set pieces in the Ricordi edition of the score. (Editions vary considerably in this regard.)

The Plot and Its Music

All recitatives are secco unless otherwise identified.

Pre–Act I Action

A year or so before the opera begins, Figaro had been in the employ of Count Almaviva—a rascal serving a playboy. Having left that employment and having been in a number of escapades, Figaro has set up shop in Seville as a barber by day, a guitar-player at night. He rents a house from Doctor Bartolo, whom he serves in a number of capacities.

Six months before the curtain, Almaviva had seen Rosina in Madrid; his pining for her was instantaneous and, when he found out that she had been whisked off to Seville by a man he thinks is her father,[6] he has followed them in hopes of becoming her lover. He has appeared under her balcony each dawn to sing of his love for her.

OVERTURE *The modern audience has no trouble identifying the overture as inseparable from the comic impetus of the opera. Context being what it is, however, it may be unsettling to some that Rossini took it over from a very un-comic* Aureliano in Palmira *(1813), an opera seria dealing with the entanglement between a Roman emperor and a Persian queen. Rossini modified it somewhat for the equally serious* Elisabetta, regina d'Inghilterra *("Elisabeth, Queen of England," 1815).*

Some of the middle section of the overture is manipulated in the storm interlude of Act II; otherwise the overture is isolated from the music of the score as a whole.[7]

Act I

SCENE I

Dawn, outside the Bartolo house, below the balcony. Latticed windows are closed.

1 INTRODUCTION (Fiorello, Count, musicians) *Piano, pianissimo, senza parlar* ("Quiet, very quiet, no talking") Fiorello, having assembled musicians who are to accompany the Count in serenading Rosina, orders that silence must prevail and reports to Almaviva that all is ready.

Soft, detached notes are an archetype for a tiptoeing kind of comic action and sentiment.

1a CAVATINA[8] (Count) *Ecco ridente in cielo / Spunta la bella aurora* ("Behold, smiling in the heaven appears the beautiful dawn") As the sky brightens, he sings of the happiness her love for him would bring.

---

[6] In Beaumarchais, Almaviva thinks Bartolo is her husband, and thus cuckoldry is what he has in mind. The opera deals only with real "amore." Given the Count's sexual appetite and disdain for marriage in the Beaumarchais-Mozart *Le mariage / Le nozze di Figaro*, the Beaumarchais plot twist is more logical but would be an uncomfortably dark current had Rossini and Sterbini incorporated it.

[7] Rossini drew on elements of *Aureliano* for some of the Count's first serenade, Rosina's "Una voce poco fa," and Basilio's "Calumny Aria." See Weinstock, p. 408, n. for p. 40, l. 39. See also Osborne, p. 167ff, for a brief idea of *Aureliano in Palmira*'s plot and music.

[8] The term, most usually descriptive of a short song without extensive repeats, was also applied in nineteenth-century Italian opera to the first solo sung by a principal singer. The cavatina's relatively simple character may be reflected in the brevity of its form rather than the nature of its melody—see Rosina's No. 5, for example.

Accompaniment specifically written for guitars and winds suggests outdoor music and "song." The Count's melody is elaborate (Ex. BA-2a) and formal. A faster second section (O sorte!) is a stylization of intensified rapture.

ENSEMBLE (Count, Fiorello, musicians) *Mille grazie, mio Signore* ("A thousand thanks, my Lord") Disappointed that Rosina has not appeared on her balcony, the Count orders the musicians to be paid. Their gratitude is expressed more and more fervently until there is an uproar of thanks, and the Count and Fiorello must drive them off with curses for their shattering the peace.

The Rossini crescendo is put to effective service, as the mounting expressions of gratitude utterly shatter the mood the Count had hoped to create. Shrieking piccolos help, too.

RECITATIVE (Count, Fiorello) *Gente indiscreta!* ("Unruly mob!") Dismissing Fiorello, the Count resolves to stay in that spot until Rosina appears. Hearing someone coming, he draws aside.

2 CAVATINA (Figaro) *Largo al factotum della città* ("Song of the City's Factotum") On his way to his shop, Figaro sings aloud of his indispensability to Seville and the joy he has in being so important and so good at his work.

The opening flourish (Ex. BA-3a) is clearly the mark of a man who has never known shyness. His song is part narration of how good he is (Ex. BA-3b), part simply exuberant singing on la. The bravura nature of the Largo lies also in its demand for fast articulation and ringing high notes.

RECITATIVE (Figaro, Count) *Ah! Ah! che bella vita!* ("Ha! what a fine life!") The Count and Figaro recognize each other; the Count tells Figaro of his desires, and Figaro explains that he has access to the house.

Rosina appears on the balcony with hopes of dropping a note to her serenader but is interrupted by Bartolo, who demands to know what document she is holding. Explaining that it is the text of an aria from the new opera *Inutile Precauzione* ("Useless Precaution"[9]) she "accidentally" drops it to the street below and importunes Bartolo to get it back for her. When Bartolo leaves, she calls to the Count—whose identity she does not know—to pick it up quickly.

Bartolo comes into the street from the house and, unable to find the "aria," is immediately suspicious of Rosina's suggestion that it must have blown away. He orders her off the balcony and reenters the house.

Figaro reads Rosina's letter aloud: Bartolo is about to leave the house, it says, and she, eager to be told of the serenader's name, position, and intentions, is ready to do anything to break away from Bartolo's close supervision.

Figaro tells Almaviva that Bartolo intends to wed Rosina and gain control of her inheritance. They hide as Bartolo leaves, overhearing him muttering that he is determined to marry Rosina that day.

Almaviva avers that, because he wants to be loved for his own sake and not for his money, he is to be known only as a poor man named "Lindoro." Observing that Rosina is standing behind the latticed window, Figaro urges the Count to explain everything to her in song.

3 CANZONE[10] (Count) *Se il mio nome saper voi bramate* ("If you wish to know my name") The Count sings that his name is "Lindoro" and that he wishes to marry her. Rosina repeats the melody of his refrain with her own amorous words, thus

---

[9] A quite unsubtle metaphor for Bartolo's attempts to keep her under lock and key.

[10] *Canzone* = "song." See Chapter 3, note 10.

urging him to continue. He does in a second verse avowing poverty of purse but possessing eternal love. Her response is interrupted by the slamming shut of the window.

A serenade improvised on the spot, accompanied by guitar and strings pizzicato. The Count's musical uncertainty is suggested by the fact that the music is set often in the passaggio, *the break between chest voice and head voice near the top of the staff, around the pitches from E to G. The ornaments are less flowing than in the earlier serenade, for which the Count had clearly done some rehearsing.*

RECITATIVE (Count, Figaro) *Oh cielo! Nella stanza / convien dir che qualcuno entrato sia* ("Heavens! Someone has entered the room and interrupted her") Upset that Rosina is not free to respond to his wooing, the Count hires Figaro to help him get into the house, promising Figaro generous payment in gold for his service. Figaro accepts gleefully.

4 DUET (Figaro, Count) *All' idea di quel metallo / portentoso, onnipossente* ("The very idea of that heavy, all-powerful metal") Gold, says Figaro, inspires a volcano of ideas. He proposes that the Count disguise himself as a soldier seeking billeting, since a cavalry unit is due in Seville that very day. The Count is immediately responsive, since the colonel of the unit is his cousin. If drunk, Figaro suggests, he will be less likely to arouse suspicion. They join in enthusiastic approval of the plan. Figaro tells the Count of the location of his shop. The Count promises to meet him there, his purse heavy with money; the two joyously anticipate the future. Figaro enters the house as the Count leaves.

*Wide intervals, dotted rhythms, flourishes of scales, and rollicking triplets are symbolic of Figaro's unabashed enthusiasm for himself and for intrigue (Ex. BA-3c). The image of his imagination erupting like a volcano (*un vulcano la mia mente*) finds voice in an upward octave leap and an orchestral tutti chord. Figaro's thinking is given to a sprightly tune in flute and violin; its second phrase is taken up by the Count, who then repeats the "volcano" music in his eagerness to hear what plan Figaro can come up with. Figaro generates the idea of a soldier-disguise to this "thinking" melody as accompaniment to simple declamation as the idea forms in his head. His excitement is infectious, for the Count joins in with the parallel thirds usually associated with love duets and oaths of friendship. The idea of the Count pretending to be drunk (*ubriaco*) occurs in isolated flurries of downward scales, before the two return to the parallel writing of their mutual excitement.*

The detailing of the location of Figaro's shop is precise because of the vocal part's reliance on repeated notes—the sprightly tune is in the clarinet and bassoon (Ex. BA-1). The scene ends with another archetype of comic duetting, lyric roulades for the tenor over fast patter for the baritone, as each anticipates success and its individual rewards. Rossini also exploits his typical, motivically generated crescendo.

SCENE II

A bit later. A room in Bartolo's house. Rosina has a letter in her hand.

5 CAVATINA (Rosina) *Una voce poco fa / Qui nel cor mi risuonò!* ("A distant voice echoes in my heart") Rosina is entranced by Lindoro and vows to win him. She warns anyone who touches her "weak spot" (*il mio debole*) that she will turn from docility to a viper who will play a hundred tricks.

The tutti *introduction is a fanfare: clearly, it introduces a character of self-importance and confidence. Her vow to triumph (*la vincerò*) has rising triplets, her confidence that Lindoro mia sarà ("Lindoro will be mine") is given a melisma all its own. Violins take over the melody as she mutters defiance of her guardian. A flowing melody for flute and clarinet marks her turn to a self-description as a girl of docility and respect (Ex. 4.3a), but that she can be a viper comes through a dramatic plunge of melody below the staff (Ex. 4.3b). The more defiant she becomes, the more florid and diva-like her music.*

RECITATIVE (Figaro, Rosina; then Bartolo, Basilio) *O, buon dì, Signorina* ("Oh, good day, my little lady") Figaro enters to tell Rosina that he has news for her. When Bartolo is heard coming into the room, Figaro hides in an anteroom, where he may overhear any conversation.

Bartolo is irritated with Figaro for the quack nostrums he has given the servants and because he suspects Figaro has been putting wrong ideas into Rosina's head. Bartolo asks if Figaro has been to the house yet. After snippy answers, Rosina flounces out. Determined to know if Figaro is responsible for Rosina's obvious distaste for him, Bartolo questions the sneezy Berta, his housemaid, and sleepy Ambrogio, his servant, but to no avail.

Basilio arrives. To Bartolo's impatient directive to make the wedding arrangements, Basilio responds that Count Almaviva has arrived in Seville and is Rosina's unknown suitor. Basilio suggests that the best strategy is to destroy his reputation. The pedagogue tells his student of slander to *uditemi e tacete* ("listen to me and keep quiet").[11]

6 ARIA (Basilio) *La calunnia è un venticello* ("Slander is a little breeze") Basilio describes how a whispered rumor can grow into a force utterly destructive to a man's honor and name.

The growth of slander from a gentle breeze to a tumultuous roar is, of course, vested in another Rossini crescendo, with bass drum and a tutti *chord marking the* colpo di cannone *("the blast of a cannon"). The preliminary buzzing of rumor is heralded by pianissimo bowing on the bridges of the violins against snippets of viola sounds, the crescendo building by the obsessive repetition of motive, addition of winds, divisions in the strings, and ever intensifying dynamics. Basilio also makes use of the short detached notes of comic plotting (see the No. 1 Introduction) and the numerous scale figures that mark him as musical drillmaster.*

RECITATIVE (Basilio, Bartolo; then Figaro, Rosina) *Ah! che ne dite?* ("Well, what do you say to that?") Bartolo rejects the idea as too time-consuming and ushers Basilio into another room to draw up the wedding contract. As an aside, Basilio confesses his eagerness to get money wherever it is available.

Figaro emerges, having overheard all. Rosina returns and is told by Figaro of Bartolo's plans. Rosina vows defiance, then questions Figaro about the gentleman she saw him with under her window. Figaro describes "Lindoro" as his cousin, a poor man dying of love. He teases Rosina as to the cause of this infatuation, describing the girl as having great beauties and whose name is spelled "R-O-S-I-N-A."

7 DUET (Rosina, Figaro) *Dunque io son—tu non m'inganni?* ("Then I'm the one? You're not deceiving me?") Rosina plays coyly with feigned shyness and surprise, convinced all along that "Lindoro" loves her. Figaro notes her foxiness, then tells her that Lindoro awaits some sign of her affection and that she should write a letter telling him to come to her. He is impressed that, far from needing instruction, she has just such a letter ready for delivery. Rosina urges that Lindoro should come to the house, but prudently; Figaro, promising that Lindoro will come soon, exits with Rosina's letter of invitation.

Rosina plays at being shy, so her first phrases are short and separated by rests (Ex. BA-5a). She cannot resist complete self-confidence, however, so her coloratura quickly takes over, pausing only for a sham coyness when Figaro suggests that she write a letter. Figaro at first matches Rosina's melodic boldness, but the duet ends in typical comic fashion, soprano melismas over a baritone's comic patter.

---

[11] Basilio is apparently a teacher of the old school.

RECITATIVE (Rosina, Bartolo) *Ora mi sento meglio* ("Now I feel better") Bartolo returns, interrupting Rosina's optimism, and demands to know what Figaro was saying to her. He challenges her story of the "aria from 'Useless Precaution'" and accuses her of writing a secret letter, as proven by the stain on her fingers (which she passes off as the remnants of ink she used to cool a burn), a missing sheet of writing paper (which Rosina claims was used to wrap sweetmeats for Marcellina[12]), and the fact that the pen has just recently been sharpened (a natural consequence, says Rosina, of her having to draw the design of a flower on her embroidery work). Bartolo has had enough of her evasiveness and disrespect.

8 ARIA (Bartolo) *A un dottor della mia sorte / Queste scuse, signorina?* ("To a doctor of my status you would make these excuses, little lady?") Bartolo sneers at her lame inventions, claims that she is no match for his intelligence and experience, demands to know about the missing writing paper and, hearing no response to his suggestion that he will forgive her if she confesses all, threatens to lock her in her room. He exits with a flourish.

Pompous fanfares, descending dotted scales, accompanied by sudden woodwind fortes and a flourish of strings, and an obsessively repeated string figure as he recites each of her excuses are all symbolic of his aggrieved ego and self-inflation of his importance. His rage becomes stronger the more he thinks of it, so his phrases get shorter and are puffed up by little fanfares in the tutti. The obsessive string figure accompanies his attempt at wheedling (Via carina, confessate—"come, dear, confess"); when this doesn't work, words and notes gush in a symbol of uncontrollable rage that is a masterpiece of comic puffery (Ex. BA-4).

RECITATIVE (Rosina, Berta) *Brontola quanto vuoi* ("Storm all you want") Rosina vows defiance and sweeps out. Berta comes in, wondering about who has been conversing in the room. Hearing loud knocking, she goes to the door and opens it.

Finale

9 *Ehì, di casa, buona gente* ("Hey, in the house there! Good people!") The Count blusters in, disguised as a drunk soldier. When Bartolo enters to investigate the loud knocking, the Count gets a good deal of mileage out of the twisting of Bartolo's name: *Balordo* = "idiot"; *Bertoldo* = "blockhead"; *Barbaro* = "barbarian." He shows Bartolo a billeting order.

Rosina enters to see the source of all the noise; the Count whispers to her that he is "Lindoro." Bartolo is immediately aware of her reaction to the whisper and, ordering her from the room, looks for and finds the certificate exempting him from having to house military officers. The Count knocks it out of Bartolo's hand. When Bartolo raises his cane in a gesture of outrage, the Count draws his sword and offers to give battle. Pretending to sketch out a battlefield, the Count surreptitiously shows Rosina a letter and whispers to her to cover it with her handkerchief when he drops it. This action ensues: the Count pretends to notice it as something Rosina has dropped and grandly picks it up and gives it to her in spite of Bartolo's demand to see it. Rosina quickly hides the note she has

---

[12] In the play Rosine has prepared the candies for Figaro's sick little daughter. This parentage is glibly forgotten for the rest of the play and its sequel. Marcellina never appears in *Barbiere,* but her presence in the house permits the affair that results in the birth of Figaro and is thus important to the unraveling of the plot in *Mariage/Nozze.*

received from the Count and substitutes for it another paper; to Bartolo's demand to see it, she responds that it is simply a laundry list.

The Count's entrance is announced by fanfares of full orchestra that immediately become a tinny sort of march in the violins and bassoon (Ex. BA-2b). Trills suggest his careening this way and that, as do blurts of rising scales. As Bartolo looks for his exemption, the typical lyricism over patter prevails; Bartolo tries to protest with the dignity of heroic melisma, but he is unable to stay away from the bluster of fast articulation for very long.

As Basilio arrives with some legal materials in hand, Bartolo snatches the paper from Rosina and, to the mingled comments of the observers, expresses his embarassment—it is indeed the laundry list. He tries to make things up to Rosina, who engages in very theatrical weeping (*Ecco qua! sempre un' istoria—*"There it is! Always a story . . . ") over his mistreatment of her.

Figaro and other servants arrive in time to see the Count's pretending to defend Rosina's honor as the servants gather in amazement and excitement at the growing ruckus.

Loud knocking at the door is heard (for the third time in the scene). All are shocked into silence at hearing the militia demand admission. Their officer enters with his men. The testimony of Bartolo (*Questa bestia di soldato, / mio signor, m'ha maltrattato*—"This beast of a soldier, sir, has abused me") is quickly taken up by all observers, with appropriate uproar, whereupon the sergeant announces his arrest of the offender. When the Count draws him aside and shows him a document, the sergeant abruptly withdraws his men and stands to the rear with them, at attention.

The arrival of Basilio is the start of a concerted ensemble, Rosina and the Count distinguished by melodic ornament from the short, dotted phrases of Berta and Bartolo, while Basilio sings his scale of utter befuddlement. Rosina takes full advantage of Bartolo's embarassment to the sound of oboe sobs and a turn to the minor (Example BA-5b).

Figaro enters to triplet fanfares, warning all that the noise is attracting a crowd.

The sudden call of the militia to open the door (La forza, la forza! / Aprite qua!) brings everything to a halt and sudden quiet; the troops enter with the bravado of scales and fast triplets. The explanations pile in canonically at a furious tempo, all punctuated by the deliriously sibilant sì signor, sì signor ("yes sir, yes sir").

9a SEXTET AND STRETTA[13] *Fredda ed immobile / Come una statua* ("Frozen and immobile, like a statue") All but the Count and Figaro are frozen with astonishment. After Bartolo's subsequent protests are rejected by the officer, confusion reigns, with all complaining about the din that beats on their heads like the sound of ringing anvils, reducing all to madness.

The detached notes of comic quiet come again (see No. 1) when the officer suddenly shows deference to the "soldier," in both the introduction and the canonic ensemble, where the idea of immobility finds expression in the seeming break-up of musical continuity. The act ends with yet another Rossini crescendo that starts with quiet unison and obsessive repetition of a motive, the humor given a special wrench by a wonderfully awkward key change and a coda that approaches the speed of light.

Act II

SCENE I

That afternoon. The music room/library of Bartolo's house.

---

[13] Stretta = lit., "tightening" or "squeezing." It is the acceleration of tempo for climactic purposes, usually at the end of a scene.

Rossini, *Il barbiere di Siviglia* (1816), Act I finale: Disguised as a drunken army officer, Almaviva (Francisco Araiza) terrorizes Dr. Bartolo (Sesto Bruscantini, far right), while Figaro (Thomas Allen, center) and Basilio (Paolo Montarsolo, left) do their bits to preserve order, with Rosina (Maria Ewing) observing the whole with astonishment. Houston Grand Opera, 1983: sets and costumes by John Stoddart. Photo James Caldwell.

RECITATIVE (Bartolo) *Ma vedi il mio destino!* ("If I just knew my future!") Bartolo wonders if the soldier had been sent by Almaviva to spy on the house and to explore Rosina's interest. He goes to answer a knocking (!) at the door.

10 DUET (Count, Bartolo) *Pace e gioia sia con voi!* ("Peace and joy be with you!") The Count, disguised as a young priest/music teacher, wearing Basilio-like garb, offers obsequious greetings. Bartolo answers formally and impatiently. In asides, Bartolo finds the man's face familiar and the Count delights in furthering his cause.

> *Deliciously mincing violins and a quasi-intonation by the Count (Example BA-2c) suggest his head-bobbing entrance; Count and Bartolo express their real thoughts in lyric/buffo asides. Their parallel thirds are clearly not in the context of archetypical lovers.*

RECITATIVE (Bartolo, Count; later Rosina) *In somma, mio Signore, / Chi è lei si può sapere?* ("And now, sir, who are you if I may know?") The Count introduces himself as "Don Alonso," a student of Basilio, who is ill and for whom he has come to give Rosina her voice lesson. He tells Bartolo that the Count has taken lodging in the same inn as he and that he, Don Alonso, had found a letter to him from Rosina. Wishing Bartolo's favor, he has brought it directly and, if left alone with Rosina, could persuade her that another girl friend of the Count had given him (i.e., "Alonso") the letter. It would thus be proof that the Count is making sport of her protestation of love.

Bartolo enthusiastically embraces "Alonso" and the plan as a slander worthy of a student of Basilio. Pocketing the letter, he goes to fetch Rosina for the lesson. Alone for a moment, the Count expresses his concern for having used the letter as a ruse to stay in the house but not being able to explain it to Rosina. He resolves to make a clean breast of his intentions at the first opportunity.

Rosina is ushered in by Bartolo to work on her song from "Useless Precaution." Bartolo takes a chair nearby to listen.

11 ARIA (Rosina) *Contro un cor che accende amore / Di verace, invitto ardore* ("Against a heart where love burns with a true, unquenchable fire") Rosina's "lesson" begins as a formal and elaborate tribute to love as unconquerable. When Bartolo nods off, Rosina hurriedly implores "Lindoro" to rescue her from her guardian; he vows to do so. Bartolo reawakens, and the lesson song resumes, although Bartolo is unaware of their continuing to mingle their real thoughts with its elaborate expressions.

A formal, fanfare introduction leads to elaborate melismas for a highly flowery text, interrupted briefly by a change in style for the hurried exchanges between the Count and Rosina.

12 RECITATIVE and ARIETTA (Bartolo) *Bella voce! . . . 'Quando mi sei vicina, / Amabile Rosina'* ("Beautiful voice! . . . 'When you are near me, beloved Rosina'") Almaviva and Bartolo praise Rosina's singing, with Bartolo noting that the music of the present is very boring compared with what "Cafariello"[14] used to sing, whereupon Bartolo demonstrates. Figaro enters at the rear and mimics him.

Preciously thin string writing, with trills, accompanies Bartolo's fatuous attempt to sing in a courtly minuet fashion. He changes the original "Gianina" to "Rosina" and stops to make sure she knows. His flirtation is utterly inane.

RECITATIVE (Figaro, Bartolo, Rosina, Count) *Bravo, signor Barbiere* ("Nice going, Mr. Barber") Figaro diverts Bartolo's irritation at his disrespect by insisting on shaving Bartolo at once. Bartolo reluctantly agrees and leaves to get the necessary towels. Figaro learns from Rosina that the key to the lattice windows of the balcony are on the key ring that Bartolo has taken from his pocket. Bartolo returns, giving the keys to Figaro and telling him to get the towels himself. Figaro exits; almost immediately there is a crash of crockery from his direction.

Although Bartolo hurries off to inspect the damage, there is not time enough for the Count to inform Rosina of his plans, for Bartolo returns almost at once. Figaro returns with him, furtively showing the Count that he has been able to get possession of the balcony-window key. Bartolo takes his seat to be shaved. The "lesson" is about to resume when Basilio arrives.

13 QUINTET (Rosina, Count, Figaro, Bartolo, Basilio) *Don Basilio! Cosa veggo! . . . Buona sera, mio signore* ("Don Basilio! What do I see! . . . Good night, sir") A secretively proffered and very healthy bribe from the Count persuades Don Basilio that he is indeed ill and must "hasten back to bed" (*presto a letto*). With elaborately tendered repetitions of *buona sera, mio signore* from all, Basilio takes his leave.

A good deal of orchestral hurly burly and the archetypical tenor fioritura over bass patter (Count vs. Bartolo) drives the confusion at Basilio's unexpected arrival. Dramatic chords a half step away from the key highlight the suggestion to Basilio that he's as yellow as a corpse (siete giallo come un morto); dotted rhythms drive the command that he go to bed at once; the "good night" is formally presented as a series of statement-and-response phrases, with all having a turn at them.

---

[14] The reference is to the great castrato Caffarelli (1710–1783), for whom Gluck had composed the title role in his *La clemenza di Tito* (1752). The melody of Iphigénie's great "O malheureuse Iphigénie" (in Gluck's *Iphigénie en Tauride*) was first used in this earlier work.

Rossini, *Il barbiere di Siviglia*, Act II, scene 1: While Figaro (Karl-Heinz Peters) shaves Bartolo (Richard Kogel), Rosina (Pari Samar) and Almaviva (Frederic Mayer), in disguise as Basilio's assistant, pretend to pursue a singing lesson. Staatstheater am Gärtnerplatz, Munich, 1968: production by Kurt Pscherer. Courtesy Deutsches Theatermuseum, Munich. Photo Hildegard Steinmetz.

RECITATIVO ACCOMPAGNATO (Figaro, Count, Rosina, Bartolo) *Orsù, Signor Don Bartolo* ("Now then, Mr. Don Bartolo") Bartolo sits down to be shaved; Figaro sets to work, standing between Bartolo and the lovers, who pretend to study the music. The Count whispers his plans for a midnight elopement, but, as he starts to explain about his disguise and having given her letter to Bartolo, Bartolo tiptoes over to them and overhears. His denunciation and demand that Figaro and "Alonso" leave the house are in full voice.

Busy violins accompany the attempt to return to the business of the lesson and the shave.

ENSEMBLE (Rosina, Count, Figaro, Bartolo) *La testa vi gira, / Ma zitto, Dottore, / Vi fate burlar* ("Your head is spinning, but be quiet, Doctor, you're being ridiculous"). In spite of the apparent defiance reflected in the words, all beat a hasty retreat before Bartolo's temper tantrum.

Bartolo's explosion comes with a change of meter and bristling violin arpeggios as accompaniment to his blustering repeated phrases; their attempts to distract him are the repeated notes of desperation—the tune is in the violins, which soon turn to gyrating scale figures as the scene ends chaotically.

RECITATIVE (Bartolo; then Berta) *Ah! disgraziato me!* ("Ah! I'm distracted!") Vowing to guard the door himself, Bartolo sends Ambrogio to summon Basilio, then leaves the room. Berta, contemptuous of Bartolo's trusting no one, complains about the constant tumult in the house.

14 ARIA (Berta) *Il vecchiotto cerca moglie* ("The old fool wants a wife") The elderly maid notes how love drives people crazy. Even she feels its excitement, she says, but she despairs because no one wants her for a wife.

The tiny, doddering footsteps of the old woman are suggested by the staccato notes and shortbreathed phrases of flute and bassoon, with string accompaniment.

SCENE II

The same room as Act I, scene ii. The shutters are barred. Later that afternoon.

RECITATIVE (Basilio, Bartolo; then Rosina) *Dunque voi Don Alonso / Non conoscete affatto?* ("Then you know nothing of this Don Alonso?") Basilio suggests that "Don Alonso" may have been Almaviva himself. In response to Bartolo's order to get the Notary at once so that the wedding contract may be finalized that evening, Basilio says it is impossible, since the Notary is committed to arrange the marriage of Figaro's niece and, besides, it's raining. Bartolo, knowing that Figaro has no niece, realizes something is up and is insistent. He gives the front door key to Basilio, who leaves to do Bartolo's bidding.

Resolving to use the letter "Alonso" had presented as evidence of Almaviva's faithlessness, Bartolo calls Rosina into the room. He shows her her letter to the Count (which presumably the Count has made light of) and advises her that Figaro and "Alonso" plan to hand her over to Count Almaviva as anything but a respected bride.

Enraged, Rosina vows revenge on the false "Lindoro," who is apparently only a pimp for the Count. Agreeing to marry Bartolo at once, she informs him of the elopement plans and that Figaro and Almaviva have a key to the balcony window. He advises her to lock herself in her room while he calls the police to arrest the two "burglars." He exits hurriedly, she sadly.

15 INTERLUDE (orchestral storm) The fury of a tempest marks the passage of time. As the lightning and thunder fade, Figaro and the Count enter by the window.

We are given the usual flute detached notes and/or arpeggios, low string tremolos, and rolling scales and dotted rhythms of orchestral tempest-tossing.

RECITATIVE *Alfine eccoci quà* ("Finally we're here") Rosina enters and upbraids "Lindoro" for planning to deliver her into the hands of his vile Count Almaviva. To the Count's eager question she answers that she did indeed love Lindoro, whereupon he kneels before her, saying he is the one who indeed sighs for her: *Almaviva son io, non son Lindoro* ("I am Almaviva, not Lindoro").

16 TRIO (Rosina, Count, Figaro) *Ah! qual colpo inaspettato!* ("Ah, what an unexpected stroke!") Rosina and Almaviva bill and coo, the Count promising to make her his wife, while Figaro comments aside on the brilliance of his achievement. The lovers ignore Figaro's warnings that time is wasting and they must be off. Suddenly Figaro, looking from the balcony, sees two people at the door. The three warn each other nervously to be quiet and to get going quickly via the ladder from the balcony (*Zitti, zitti, piano, piano, / Non facciamo confusione; / Per la scala del balcone / Presto andiamo via di quà*—Shush, quiet, softly, softly, let's not make a disturbance, let's get away from here by the ladder at the balcony").

Rosina and the Count repeat each other's little blurts of melisma (Ex. BA-5c) and delight in highly melismatic parallel thirds, mocked by Figaro. His quickening rhythms urge departure, but they must finish their formal duetting. His alarm is set to a sudden appearance of tremolos and wide intervals.

Their scurrying to figure a way out is to a whispered tune taken up by each in turn, reaching loud points only quickly to be hushed by their repetitions of piano, piano.

RECITATIVE (Figaro, Count, Rosina, Basilio, Bartolo; then an officer) *Ah! disgraziati noi!* ("Ah! We're undone!") Figaro announces that the ladder has been taken away. Hearing others entering the room, they move off to the side. Basilio enters via the door, leading a Notary with a legal paper in his hand. Figaro recognizes them and seizes the opportunity to turn the tables. He accosts the Notary with the "reminder" that the Notary was to come to Figaro's house to marry Figaro's niece to one Count Almaviva. The Notary, knowing no better, shows him that the appropriate document is ready. Basilio is about to set him straight, but the mutually persuasive powers of an expensive ring and a pistol at his head settle Basilio's hash very readily. The marriage document is quickly signed.

As Almaviva kisses his new bride's hand and Figaro embraces Basilio (grotesquely), Bartolo arrives with an officer and some soldiers and demands the arrest of the intruders. Almaviva announces his true identity.

17 RECITATIVO ACCOMPAGNATO (Bartolo, Count) *Il conte! Ah, che mai sento! . . .* ("The Count! What do I hear . . .) The Count tells the stunned Bartolo that Rosina is now his wife.

One of the few passages of accompanied recitative in the opera, the strings providing theatrical punctuations of pronouncements.

18 ARIA WITH CHORUS (Almaviva) *Cessa di più resistere* ("Cease any further resistance") The Count warns Bartolo that resistance is futile, his power is over, and that innocent love has triumphed.

The Count turns to his generic florid style for his warning to Bartolo to give up before arousing the Count's anger, the recitative yielding to a steadier flow of rhythm as he proclaims the triumph of love. As joy takes over, the music assumes a more sprightly, staccato rhythm, the Count yielding more and more to melismatic type as the finale is reached.

19 RECITATIVE AND FINALE *In somma io ho tutti i torti . . . Di sì felice innesto / Serbiam memoria eterna* (In sum, I've been completely wrong . . . Let us preserve an eternal memory of this happy union") With surprising good nature, Bartolo agrees and bestows his blessing. Led by Figaro, all enter into mutual good spirits and wish joy to the newly wed pair.

Figaro and Rosina sing the verses of a buoyant polonaise, all joining in the spirited refrain that brings the opera to its rollicking close.

The Characters

The characters of Beaumarchais's play are in parentheses.

Fiorello (baritone) *[fee-oh-REL-loh] (no equivalent character in the play)*

Servant to Almaviva. Although he has the important job of hiring the musicians for the Act I serenade and is active in dispersing them when they become overly grateful, Fiorello has no distinguishing musical characteristics.

Count Almaviva (lyric tenor) *[ahl-mah-VEE-vah] (same as in the play)*

Young, dashing, and bold enough to undertake the pursuit of his beloved to the point of assuming ridiculous disguises and carrying a deception as far as it will work. In Act I, scene i, he professes awkwardness in music as far as the guitar is concerned, but he is a good enough keyboardist to accompany Rosina acceptably in the "Lesson Scene" of Act II, scene i. His desire, in the custom of wealthy swains, is to be loved for his own sake, hence he insists on being known as poor "Lindoro."[15]

Almaviva's music is that of the conventional gesture of florid song reminiscent of the opera seria (Example BA-2a); he adopts musical disguises— first a parody of military marches (Example BA-2b) when he barges in as a drunken military horse doctor, and then a tuneless chant (Example BA-2c) when he wears the clergyman's costume as a student of Basilio—but his asides and his music with Rosina are lyrical and graceful.

EXAMPLE BA-2: ALMAVIVA'S DIFFERING STYLES

a) Act I, scene i: No. 1a, "Ecco ridente in cielo"—the florid song of his serenade.

---

[15] This pseudonymous device will find resonance in Verdi's *Rigoletto,* where the Duke introduces himself to Gilda as "Gualtier Maldè—studente sono e povero" ("Walter Maldè—I'm a student and poor").

EXAMPLE BA-2 (*Continued*)

b) Act I, scene ii: No. 9, "Ehì di casa, buona gente!"— his mockery of a military march.

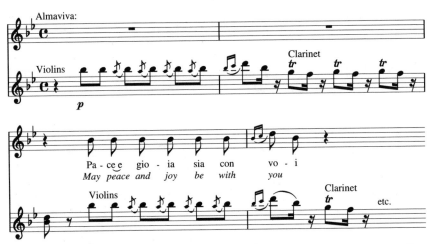

c) Act II, scene i: No. 10, "Pace e gioia sia con voi!"—mincing and coy in a disguise as a ministerial student substituting for Basilio.

Figaro (baritone) *[FEE-gah-roh] (same as in play)*

Figaro is the most engaging entrepreneur in opera and one of the most versatile; lest we have our doubts, he tells us so himself in his famous and bravura "Largo al factotum" ("Song of the Factotum," No. 2). His background is brought out in Beaumarchais's *Le mariage*,[16] where we learn that, after leav-

---

[16] See Figaro's self-histories in the Penguin edition, pp. 41ff and 199ff.

ing an apparently tumultuous period of service as personal attendant to Count Almaviva, he has held a series of jobs and been in all kinds of scrapes in various cities. He was often forced to move on, barely a step ahead of the authorities. He has written poetry, plays, economic tracts, political commentary, and satire (and has done jail time for this activity), and published a journal; his employment in a government bureau as a minister of drugs to horses provided him with some of the background he needed to prescribe a sleeping potion to one of Bartolo's servants and sneezing powder to another. His most recent employment as a barber has gained him entrance to all the best houses in Seville as a shaver of faces, powderer of wigs, puller of teeth, and, most important, bearer of messages.

Little wonder, then, that Figaro's opening music—the "Largo al factotum"—bustles with energy and pride. The opening flourish (Example BA-3a) is as familiar a sound as there is in all opera; and so are the lyric melody given to his expression of delight in his active and involved life (Example BA-3b), and his repetitions of the calling of his name (from every direction: "là," "qua," "su," "giù"—"there," "here," "up," "down").

Figaro loves money, and, when the Count promises to pay him handsomely for his assistance, glorifies its importance as the source of invention with trumpet rhythms and large intervals, to the accompaniment of grandiose scales (Example BA-3c). He tries his hand at florid singing in an aside (Act I,

EXAMPLE BA-3. FIGARO'S MUSIC

a) Act I, scene i: No. 2, The "Largo al factotum"'s introductory flourish.

b) In the "Largo," Figaro delights in his importance.

EXAMPLE BA-3 (*Continued*)

c) Act I, scene i: No. 4, "All' idea di quel metallo." For Figaro, money is powerful and the source of invention.

scene i) that uses a flurry of melismas to suggest that, while Rosina is quite a piece of work, she will have to deal with him. However, his music is usually either a parody of someone else or a fast patter in the opera buffa style.

Bartolo (bass) *[BAHR-toh-loh] (Bartholo)*

A doctor of medicine, well on in years (although not doddering, by any means). He is the guardian of Rosina, whom he plans to marry at once in order to gain control of her inheritance. His bluster is vested in dotted rhythms evocative of fanfares; his temper, obsessiveness, and comic impatience find expression in the repetitious patter style of comic opera, both vocally and in the instrumental accompaniments given him.

Rosina (mezzo-soprano) *[roh-SEE-nah] (Rosine)*

This conniving, delectable wench is one of the great mezzo-soprano[17] roles and one of the first of such stature in opera. References to her are not always flattering: she describes herself in her first appearance as able to act like a viper, Figaro speaks of her as having the slyness of a vixen ("o che volpe sopraffina!," in their duet, No. 7), and Bartolo sarcastically refers to her pre-

---

[17] It is often undertaken by lyric sopranos with great success, but considerable juggling of the parts is required in the ensembles, the soprano exchanging some of her phrases with Berta's or Figaro's.

EXAMPLE BA-4 ACT I, SCENE II. NO. 8, BARTOLO'S "A UN DOT-
TOR DELLA MIA SORTE." DOTTED-RHYTHM POMP AND OBSESSIVE
REPETITIONS, IN THE ARCHETYPE PATTER OF COMIC OPERA

tense of innocence as "making the face of a dead cat" ("faccia pur la gatta
morta," in his No. 8, "A un dottor della mia sorte"), but she is nonetheless so
graced with spirited rhythms and irresistible tunefulness that she comes off
as the paragon of the teenager—able to drive you mad but utterly lovable.
She has just turned fifteen,[18] the age of discretion. Orphaned and left with
a considerable fortune, she had been taken by her guardian, Bartolo, from
her native Madrid to Seville, where Bartolo plans to marry her and has been
keeping her under close watch until she is eligible for marriage.

---

[18] Hispanics celebrate the "Quinceanera," the transition from girlhood to womanhood at
the age of fifteen. See *The New York Times* (Feb. 1, 1996), Section B, p. 1. Mozart's Despina
(*Così fan tutte*) opens Act II with advice that a fifteen-year-old girl must know every means
by which the devil hides his tail, and what's good and what's bad ("Una donna a quindici
anni / Dee saper ogni gran moda, / Dove il diavolo ha la coda / Cosa è bene e mal cos' è . . . ").
Despina and Rosina are among the few operatic teenagers who finish the opera happier
and wiser; among opera's tragic adolescents are Butterfly (fifteen at the start of the opera),
Juliet (fourteen), Gilda (sixteen), and Salome (sixteen).

She takes singing lessons with Basilio—with considerable accomplish-ment for one so young—but needs acting lessons from no one: when Figaro suggests she write a letter to "Lindoro," hesitancy is implied with short phrases and shyness by a musical "blush" in the form of a sudden turn to the minor by the violins (Example BA-5a). Of course she's putting him on: she has already written just such a letter. She turns to theatrical fakery again in the "laundry list" episode near the end of Act I, when, having fooled Bartolo into thinking he has treated her cruelly and unfairly, she feigns deep grief by the same device of a quick turn to the minor; her seeming tunelessness (the musical equivalent of unhappiness that destroys "speech") is accompa-nied by choking sobs in the oboe that are as funny as they are false (Example BA-5b). A tritone on "oppressa" (G in the voice part against C-sharp in the

EXAMPLE BA-5 ROSINA'S MUSIC

a) Act I, scene ii: No. 7, "Dunque io son . . . " Pretending shyness at Figaro's suggestion of writing to the poor man who has serenaded her.

b) Act I, scene ii: No. 9, Finale. Feigned sorrow at having been "falsely" accused of receiving a note from the drunken soldier.

oboe) is a musical in-joke that nails down her counterfeit despair with a ten-inch spike.

That there is no special music to indicate the depth of her love for Almaviva/Lindoro is a function of the farcical nature of the opera and perhaps also due to the fact that Rosina is too young to know what real love is. Both of her expressions of love bubble with ornament and move at a snappy pace, although the revelation that Almaviva and Lindoro are one and the same—and that the latter is not simply pimping for the former—calls from her a kind of short-phrased excitement that suggests genuine wonder and joy (Example BA-5c).

Basilio (bass) *[ba-SEE-lee-oh] (Bazile)*

A man of the cloth who specializes in arranging matrimonials and teaching singing. He will also yield to bribery without compunction. He is also an expert in scandalmongering, a talent that underlies the famed "Calumny Aria" (No. 6), in which Basilio explains how to use slander and innuendo to undermine the Count's wooing. Ever the musician, he gives a battery of performance indications—*piano, sotto voce, crescendo, poco a poco*—to describe how rumor begins as a gentle breeze ("un venticello") and ends up like the roar of a cannon ("come un colpo di cannone"). He presents his ideas with a pervasive orientation to the musical scale (notes marked "x" and "y" in Example BA-6), even though he mentions that the actual timbre of the rumor is wholly non-musical—a subtle hissing ("sibilando") that becomes a buzzing ("ronzando") and eventually, like a raging storm, goes whistling and rumbling ("fischiando," "brontolando").

EXAMPLE BA-5 (*Continued*)

c) Act II, scene ii: No. 16, "Ah! qual colpo!" Astonishment and joy that she has not been deceived in love.

EXAMPLE BA-6 ACT I, SCENE II: NO. 6, "LA CALUNNIA"
("SLANDER"). BASILIO AND THE MUSICAL SCALE

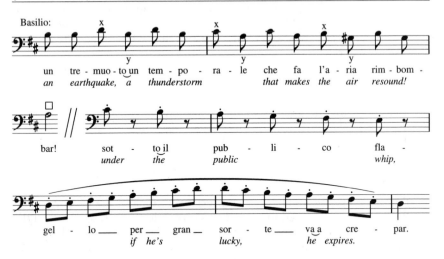

Basilio turns to his scales again in the Act I, scene ii quintet, when Bartolo's search for a love letter as damaging evidence produces only a laundry list and a musical tumult from all involved: all Basilio can do amid the hubbub is rehearse his solfeggio syllables (another musician's in-joke at the hands of Rossini).

Berta (soprano) [BAIR-tah] (La Jeunesse)

Bartolo's elderly housekeeper (the name of "Youth" given her by Beaumarchais is farcical). She has little to do in the plot beyond sneezing and fussing about but provides for the passage of time in Act II with an *aria di sorbetto*—a comic moment given to a secondary character that allows members of the audience to partake of refreshments (sorbetto = sherbet), sanitary facilities, and so forth.

Ambrogio (bass) [ahm-BROH-zhee-oh] (L'Éveille[19])

A virtually narcoleptic servant in the Bartolo household, presumably the least qualified person to be charged with keeping guard over Rosina while Bartolo is out of the house. Ambrogio has no significant solo music.

An officer of the militia (bass)

At the end of Act I, he leads a group of city police to investigate the uproar coming from the Bartolo household and proposes to arrest the "drunken

---

[19] "Wakeful" is a bit of Beaumarchais whimsy.

soldier," not knowing that the uproarious lout is Count Almaviva in disguise. The Count furtively shows him some document, which is never identified, that turns the officer's attitude into respect and humility to the astonishment of all save the Count and Figaro.[20] He has only *recitativo accompagnato* in this scene; when he returns as an arresting officer in the final scene, he has just a moment of *secco*.

A notary

A mime part only; he appears in the final scene to certify the marriage of Rosina to Bartolo but, with the appropriate machinations of the plot, marries her to the Count.

Male chorus

This group plays the ludicrously appreciative bunch of impoverished and rapscallion musicians hired for Almaviva's serenade in Act I, scene i, and the equally inept soldiery at the end of Act I, scene ii. In each case, the choral writing is meant to contribute to a sense of wild disorder and confusion that is exactly the opposite of what the main characters desire.

Bibliography

Beaumarchais, Pierre Augustin Caron de. *The Barber of Seville; The Marriage of Figaro*, trans. John Wood. Penguin Classics. London: Penguin Books, 1964.
   A translation of the two plays. An introductory chapter compares Mozart's Le nozze di Figaro *with* Il barbiere di Siviglia *with respect to the rational thinking of the late eighteenth century and the cynical reactionism of early nineteenth century.*
Gossett, Philip. "Gioacchino Rossini," in *The New Grove Masters of Italian Opera*. New York: W. W. Norton, 1980.
John, Nicholas, ed. *The Barber of Seville / Moses*. English National Opera Guide 36. London and New York: Calder Publications/Riverrun Press, 1985.
   A very free translation of the libretto but helpful articles and a thematic guide.
Kimbell, David. *Italian Opera*. National Traditions of Opera. Cambridge: Cambridge University Press, 1991.
Osborne, Richard. *Rossini*. Boston: Northeastern University Press, 1986.
Robinson, Paul. "Enlightenment and Reaction," in *Opera and Ideas*. New York: Harper and Row, 1985.
   See pp. 363–391 for study of settings by Paisiello and Rossini.
Weinstock, Herbert. *Rossini: A Biography*. New York: Limelight Editions, 1987.

---

[20] The episode is an invention of Sterbini and has no equivalent in the play.

Chapter 12

RIGOLETTO

MUSIC: Giuseppe Verdi (1813–1901)
LIBRETTO: Francesco Maria Piave (1810–1876) after *Le roi s'amuse* ("The King Amuses Himself," 1832), by Victor Hugo (1802–1885).
PREMIERE: Venice, March 11, 1851.
TIME AND PLACE OF THE STORY: Sixteenth century; the duchy of Mantua, in Italy.

Rigoletto was composed at the point in Verdi's life when his genius was in full flower and his reputation had become firmly established as Italy's dominant musical voice. It is one of several works (*Luisa Miller*, 1849, and *La Traviata*, 1853, among them) composed around mid-century that mark Verdi's complete maturation as a composer and reveal his growing predilection for longer musical units[1] in musical and dramatic construction. Numbered items in the score now typically came to include not just a single aria or ensemble but a connected complex of styles and passages of varying musical and textual character.

The melodies of *Rigoletto* range from the simple and tuneful to the pliant and deeply expressive, and delineate persons of striking individuality and reality. Their accompaniments are consistently colored with dramatic force and vividness that result from superbly original combinations of instrumental timbres, independent orchestral lines and motives, and a sophisticated and original manipulation of accompanying rhythmic patterns. The use of thematic recall shows a keen sense of effect and large-scale unity.

Hugo's play *Le roi s'amuse* had been a *cause célèbre*: its story of the amorality of a King of France and a plot to assasinate him by his servant (who was also his court jester and instigator in matters of carnal pleasure) caused Paris authorities to see it as an immediate danger to the order of society and to close it down after one performance. Although it was published and Hugo defended the work in print, the play was absent from the stage for fifty years.

---

[1] In a letter to the husband of soprano Teresa De Giuli, Verdi wrote: "Let me say that I conceived *Rigoletto* almost without arias and finales, only a series of duets without end." (August 9, 1852; *Copialettere*, pp. 497–98). An extended quote from this letter is in Hussey, p. 71; see also Budden's citation, I, 483.

Verdi was captivated by Hugo's story and characters, but his proposal to turn them into an opera ran into a wall of censorship: an opera of threatened regicide and blatant immorality of purpose simply would not do. It took much correspondence, angry confrontation, compromise (including changing of locale and names and omitting one of Hugo's most powerfully licentious scenes), and patient diplomacy on the part of Verdi's collaborators and friends to achieve a rapprochement with the theater and the censors.

The opera was an instant triumph, even though it offered a number of unsettling departures from tradition. The protagonist, Rigoletto, has but one soliloquy. That in itself is unusual; more remarkable is that it is not the expected crowd pleaser but rather an arioso connected to the music that follows in such a way as to stifle any opportunity for applause. Both the appearance and the character of Rigoletto are departures: he suffers the disabilities of being a dwarf with a hunched back and has not one but two very different personae, a loving father in his private world, a man of viciousness and hatred in public life. In fact, none of the men in the plot warrants affection: the tenor is a scoundrel in every respect; the bass is a villain who kills without compunction (albeit with a touch of gallows humor); and among the courtiers there is not a moral principle to be found.

Recitatives are richly melodic and atmospheric, not just connecting tissue between crowd-pleasing arias; the melody of the Rigoletto/Sparafucile duet (see below, Example RI-4) is given to the unique timbre of solo cello/solo double bass instead of voices; and, in the entire opera, there is but one of the *aria-cabaletta*[2] pairings that is a hallmark of Italian nineteenth-century opera. Instead of elaborate ballets and choruses, the only dancing is background for conversation (in Act I, scene i), and all the choral singing is for men's voices only. Opera as a whole is associated with display, but *Rigoletto* offers primarily gloom: the mood of brilliance and sparkle established in the first scene is more than counterbalanced by the dark of night in two of the four scenes, and a prevailing sense of isolation and cruelty informs three of them.

This prevailing mood is reflected in sound as well as sight. The opening notes of the Prelude are the stark Cs of the repeated-note motive of the curse that weighs so heavily on the thinking of the title character (Example RI-1a), and the only other material of the Prelude is the sospiri (Example RI-1b) associated with the grief felt so deeply by both Rigoletto (as in his duets with Gilda in Act I, scene ii) and by Gilda (most notably in No. 16, "Un dì, se ben rammentomi" / "One day that I well remember," the famous quartet of Act III).

Act I, scene ii, and Act III are set in dimly lit, humble surroundings, where the moods of brooding and latent evil are set by chords in low winds and muttering figures in the low strings. Only the opening scene, set in the ducal castle, is brilliant and elaborate; the other castle scene is in an anteroom, where the focus is on dramatic/musical confrontation rather than scenic effect.

---

[2] A *cabaletta* is a brilliant aria in fast tempo, usually paired with a slower preceding one. The aria-cabaletta pair may be the whole or just part of a *scena*, a musical/dramatic unit comprised of a sequence of different styles and musical structures (e.g., recitative/slow aria/recitative with choral interjection/cabaletta/choral stretta).

EXAMPLE RI-1 THE MOTIVES OF THE PRELUDE

a) Curse.

b) Sobbing.

Rigoletto, then, is a very private and dark story. Its moments of brilliance and flair are shortlived, very much like the lightning that snaps through the violent storm of Act III and illuminates the hideous irony of the father having been the agent of the curse that has ended with the murder of his own daughter. Sound and story are the epitome of Romanticism and the Romantic era.

THE PLOT AND ITS MUSIC

Numbers may refer to individual arias and ensembles or to scene complexes involving several musical and/or dramatic units.

Pre-Act I Action

The Duke has enjoyed a sexual liaison with the daughter of the elderly Count Monterone, a nobleman who has plotted against him and been pardoned as a result of the daughter's surrender of her virtue. The Duke's latest interest is a young girl whom he has observed in church every Sunday for three months (thus from the moment of Gilda's arrival in Mantua) and whom he has followed to her secluded small house, where she is visited nightly by a mysterious man.

PRELUDE *The opening trumpet/trombone call is the repeated-note motive of the Curse (Example RI-1a), a dissonant harmony lending it evil portent. Repetitions over a steadily intensifying tremolo lead to a dramatic outburst from which issues a series of descending two-note units (Example RI-1b) associated with Gilda's grief. After hushed returns of the Curse motive, the Prelude ends with a brutal series of two-chord cadences alternating with ominous timpani rolls.*

Act I

Scene I[3]

Ballroom in the Palace of the Duke of Mantua

1 INTRODUCTION *Della mia bella incognita borghese / Toccare il fin dell' avventura io voglio* ("I would soon like to finish my affair with that unknown pretty girl of humble family") A palace revel is underway; passing to and fro, dancing, etc. The Duke comments to Borsa of his new adventure—he has observed a beautiful young girl in church but has not identified himself to her, has followed her to her secluded home (where she is visited nightly by a mysterious man) and plans this evening to bring his desires for her to fruition.

When Borsa's comment on the many beauties present at the revel elicits the Duke's expression of passion for the Countess Ceprano, Borsa warns him of the jealousy of Count Ceprano.[4] The Duke's response is frivolous.

Recitative moves quickly over the playing of a banda, *a small ensemble of wind instruments, performing sprightly dance music. A string "vamp"—the tum-te-tum accompaniment of the Duke's aria—provides the transition from banda to orchestra.*

2 BALLATA[5] (Duke) *Questa o quella per me pari sono* ("This one or that—they're all the same to me") Husbands and lovers, he asserts, are to be ignored in the pursuit of amatory pleasure.

A buoyant 6/8 tune over a stereotyped rhythm characterizes both verses of this lighthearted strophic song.

3 BALLET (Duke, Countess; then Rigoletto) *Partite? Crudele!* ("You're leaving? Cruel one!") A minuet is begun. As the Countess Ceprano crosses the room, the Duke intercepts her and, in an overtly passionate manner, professes undying love and leads her into an adjoining room. Count Ceprano's angry pursuit provokes merriment from all and barbs from Rigoletto. Rigoletto follows to observe and mock the Count still further.

A second stage ensemble, this time of strings, plays a minuet in the manner of the Classical era. As the Duke becomes more ardent, there is intensification of the minuet melody by changing from arpeggio accompaniment to repeated note patterns. Rigoletto's repeated-note jibe is tuneless.

4 ENSEMBLE (Marullo, Courtiers) *Gran nuova! gran nuova!* ("Great news! Great news!") Another dance begins, only to be interrupted by Marullo's laughing account of Rigoletto as cupid; he apparently has a mistress whom he visits nightly.

---

[3] The opera is constructed in three acts, with Act I having two scenes. Some recordings, scores, and productions present each scene as a separate act.

[4] In Hugo's play, De Latour Landry's warning is more pointed—the jealous husband may reveal the King's new amour to "a certain fair lady," who, Hugo tells us, is Diane de Poitiers, daughter of an important nobleman. Although she is not given a name in the opera, the play's allusion makes it clear that the King/Duke's current mistress is the daughter of St. Vallier/Monterone, a relationship occasioned by the girl's sacrifice of herself to stave off the execution of her father.

[5] Ballata = an aria using a dance-like rhythm.

Verdi, *Rigoletto* (1851), Act I, scene i: Monterone (Rodney Stenborg) imposes a father's curse on a horrified Rigoletto (Matteo Manuguerra). Houston Grand Opera, 1983: production Jean-Pierre Ponnelle, costumes by Martin Schlumpf. Photo James Caldwell.

The Duke returns, irritated at Ceprano's close watch over the Countess, and invites advice from Rigoletto (within the hearing of the Count) as to how to be rid of this jealous husband. Rigoletto's suggestions—"Abduct her . . . tonight" (*Rapitela . . . stasera*), imprison or exile the Count, or behead him—enrage Ceprano, who draws his sword.

The banda picks up again as background to Marullo's information.

The Duke laughingly protects Rigoletto (*Ah sempre tu spingi lo scherzo all' estremo*— "You're always pushing jokes too far"), while the courtiers vow revenge for all of Rigoletto's insults. The courtiers agree to meet at Ceprano's house to effect a plan against Rigoletto.

The orchestra joins in as accompaniment to the scherzando dialogue of the Duke and Rigoletto; the courtiers' phrases are short and blunt at first, then rise in a chromatic scale in broken and dotted rhythms toward rancore *("rancor" or "grudge"). Their repetitions of* vendetta *("revenge") serve as counterpoint to the scherzando and syncopation of Rigoletto and the Duke.*

5 CONTINUATION and STRETTA[6] *Ch'io gli parli. Il voglio.* ("Let me speak with him. I desire it.") The festivities resume, only to be interrupted by Monterone. Forcing his way past the guards, Monterone demands that his grievance against the Duke be heard. Rigoletto mockingly imitates him and mounts the ducal throne in a grotesque satire of the Duke's formal hearing of complaints.

The attempts to renew the festivities in a coda in chordal style at a faster tempo are interrupted by a repeated-note fanfare from Monterone, with the chorus calling his name on a diminished-seventh chord. Rigoletto's mockery is accompanied by the halting, lurching pattern in strings suggestive of his limping walk (Ex. 4.1a); he picks up the fanfare style, adds trills of derision.

Monterone upbraids the Duke for his profligacy and for allowing the insult from his Fool. When the Duke orders Monterone arrested, Monterone pronounces a curse on both Duke and jester. He aims imprecation especially at Rigoletto, whom Monterone reviles as a snake.

Monterone's outrage is in orchestrally pounding rising chromatic scales and agitated string patterns. The Curse is pronounced as a fanfare (Example RI-1a); Monterone's indictment of Rigoletto is at first quieter, with short tremolos, then climaxes on a minor chord played by the full orchestra and reinforced by the chorus.

Amid general dismay and repudiation by the court, Monterone is led off to prison, while Rigoletto cowers at the awesome implications of a father's curse.

The chorus of dismay as counterpoint to Rigoletto's Orrore! *begins sotto voce. There is a crescendo to the end of the scene.*

SCENE II

A dead-end street running between the wall of the garden of Ceprano's palace and Rigoletto's modest home. Visible are both the street and the walled-in garden of Rigoletto's house. Later that night.[7]

---

[6] See Chapter 11, note 13.

6 RECITATIVE (Rigoletto) *Quel vecchio maledivami* ("That old man cursed me")
Brooding on the curse, Rigoletto limps homeward.

Hushed dissonances in low woodwinds, then cellos and basses in the limping figure (Ex. 4.1)
are suggestive of Rigoletto's gait. He recalls the repeated-note imposition of the curse; the dis-
sonance on maledivami *("cursed me") is unresolved—the curse is unfulfilled and the*
thought of it will not go away.

DUET (Rigoletto, Sparafucile) *Signor . . . Va, non ho niente* ("Sir" . . . "Go! I've
nothing!") Sparafucile steps from the shadows and softly calls to Rigoletto.
Rigoletto at first thinks Sparafucile is a thief but listens intently to Sparafucile's
offer to get rid of the "rival" for the lady of the house Rigoletto is about to enter.
Sparafucile explains that, with the aid of his sister, a street dancer who entices the
men he is hired to dispatch, he needs but one stab, and the work is done *senza*
strepito ("without a sound"). Should he be needed, he will be at this spot nightly.
Softly intoning his name, Sparafucile leaves.

A sinuous cello melody, with staccato low winds and pizzicato strings (Ex. RI-4), accompa-
nies the dialogue of an unusual duet for two lower men's voices. Sparafucile departs, his
name repeated on a low F.

7 ARIOSO (Rigoletto) *Pari siamo!* ("We are alike!") Rigoletto compares himself to
the assassin, one stabbing with a knife, the other with his tongue. He reviles the
world that has treated him so viciously and is contemptuous of a master who
thinks of his jester as less than human and as a figure existing only to provide
him with entertainment. He vents his hatred of the court and his delight in jeer-
ing at them. When he remembers that there is another side to his nature, the
memory of the curse intervenes. *Mi coglierà sventura?* ("Will it change my fate?")
he wonders. He rejects the idea passionately.

Rigoletto's lurching gait is in the low strings; his indictment of man and nature (O uomi-
ni, o natura) is accompanied by tremolos, then brusque scales of anger; his contempt for the
Duke is accompanied by a hint (Ex. 4.1b) of the banda of the earlier revelry; his hatred is
expressed in more scales, triadic motives, and tremolos (Ex. lc); thoughts of Gilda are given
a solo flute and a more gentle melodic flow (Ex. 4.1d). There is a return of the Curse fan-
fare, then tremolos and scales. A modulation to the major mode occurs as he tries to reject the
idea of the curse and turns to enter his house.

Entering his garden via the gate in the wall, Rigoletto is greeted by Gilda,
who sympathizes with his evident sorrow and worry. She asks him to explain his
troubles and to tell her his name, but he answers only with a demand to know if
she has been out. "Only to church," she responds. She then asks him to tell her
of her mother.

A joyous violin melody (Ex. RI-3a) is illustrative of Gilda's youth and exuberance; its
descending trills will be recalled in the first part of the Act III quartet. Violins continue as
accompaniment to the reunion of father and daughter and Gilda's questioning, but they are
interrupted abruptly when he asks her if she has left the house.

---

[7] In their narration to the Duke in Act II, the courtiers reveal that they assembled outside
Rigoletto's house shortly after sunset (*brev' ora dopo caduto il dì*). This suggests that the
Duke's party was in the afternoon, Rigoletto got home about twilight or just after dark had
fallen, and that the abduction took place fairly early in the evening. Most productions set
the second scene of Act I late at night, however.

DUET (Rigoletto, Gilda): *Deh non parlare al misero / Del suo perduto bene* ("Ah, speak not to an unhappy man of his deep loss") Rigoletto tells of his love for the woman who loved him in spite of his deformity. She died, leaving Gilda as his only consolation. They have no family, no homeland.

> *Longer lyric phrases are given to Rigoletto, with a poignant chromatic emphasis on* moria *("she died"); Gilda's compassion comes in short, faster patterns, suggestive of a mix of sobs and her eagerness to offer solace (Ex. RI-5a). The end of the first section combines arched arpeggios in Rigoletto's music and descending two-note phrases ("sospiri") in Gilda's. Rhythmic motion intensifies for Rigoletto's bitter yet loving assertion that his family, relatives, and homeland* (culto, famiglia, patria) *are vested in her.*

Gilda asks if she may see the city. She reminds him that she was brought to this place three months ago, and she has yet to see the city or speak with anyone other than Giovanna. In a panic over the lust and amorality of courtiers who would make great sport of her innocence and beauty, Rigoletto forbids her to leave the house. He calls loudly for the housekeeper, questioning her with intense nervousness as to the possibility of any strangers loitering about the house and her attentiveness to keeping the house well locked and Gilda well guarded.

> *A violin offers a sospiro effect for Gilda's wheedling; abrupt tremolos accompany Rigoletto's questioning of Gilda, staccato strings his questioning of Giovanna.*

DUET (Rigoletto, Gilda) *Ah! veglia, o donna, questo fiore / Che a te puro confidai* ("Ah, woman, watch over this pure flower whom I entrust to you") Rigoletto implores Giovanna to guard his daughter carefully. Hearing a noise in the street, he breaks off, leaving the gate open while he investigates. The Duke, dressed simply, enters unseen by all save Giovanna, whom he silently bribes with a purse to say nothing. He hides behind some bushes as Rigoletto returns, finishes his charge to Giovanna, and leaves.

> *Broad lyricism characterizes Rigoletto's plea; after a switch to a higher key for Gilda's repeat of the melody, the return of the opening key for Rigoletto's reprise promises a symmetry, but he interrupts his appeal in mid-phrase when, to the accompaniment of agitated strings, he rushes into the street. Returning, he takes up the duet theme a second time, now accompanied by youthful and sympathetic staccati in Gilda's music.*

8 RECITATIVE *Giovanna, ho dei rimorsi* ("Giovanna, I feel remorseful") Gilda tells Giovanna that she feels guilty for not telling her father of the youth who had followed her from church, that she feels his love for her, and that she would not want him to be a lord or a prince (*Signor nè principe*). The words she wants to hear are supplied impetuously by the Duke, who steps from hiding and ardently exclaims *T'amo* ("I love you"). He kneels in the romantic pose she has often envisioned; her momentary fear vanishes.

> *Short repeated rhythms in strings yield to a more flowing rhythm; delicate oboe and clarinet staccati accompany Gilda's lyric vision of her beloved as neither lord nor prince. She is interrupted in mid-phrase by the Duke's quickened music and energetically rising melody. He tries to calm Gilda's fear, but syncopations betray his true thoughts.*

DUET (Duke, Gilda) *È il sol dell' anima, la vita è amore* ("Love is the sun of the soul, life is love") The Duke speaks romantically; she responds wholeheartedly.

> *The melody, over a simple conventional rhythm, is flowing and assured. Gilda's response is derived from his tune (Ex. RI-5b), with more delicate string/flute figural accompaniment. He*

maintains his melody, she accompanies it with staccato patterns. Parallel thirds and sixths at the end are the archetype for lovers.

As Borsa and Ceprano appear in the street, identifying the house as Rigoletto's, the Duke tells Gilda he is Gualtier Maldé,[8] a poor student. Hearing hushed noise in the street (the courtiers assembling to abduct Rigoletto's "mistress" as a present for the Duke), Giovanna is alarmed at the possibility that Rigoletto is returning. Gilda tells her to show the Duke a way out of the house.

The strings move nervously just as the Duke offers his alias: Gualtier Maldè—studente sono e povero.

DUET (Duke, Gilda) *Addio, speranza ed anima* ("Farewell, my hope and my soul") A passionate and hurried farewell between Gilda and and her "Gualtier."

This is the cabaletta of the duet. Its rapid interchange of phrases and the parallel singing at a fast tempo, both over animated rhythmic accompaniment, suggest haste and ardor.

9 RECITATIVE and ARIA (Gilda) *Gualtier Maldè! Nome di lui sì amato . . . Caro nome che il mio cor / Festi primo palpitar* ("Walter Maldè! The name of him so beloved. . .Dear name that is the first to make my heart throb") Gilda sings of this first love in her life; as she mounts the staircase to the balcony outside her bedroom, the courtiers gather in the street, marveling at her beauty.

Flute arpeggios form the introduction as symbol of purity, innocence, and youth. This formal introduction sets out the simple descending scale that is the source of a theme and variations. Gilda's ornaments (Ex. RI-5b) are the metaphor for her fantasy and childlike joy. The violins' tremolo is to return in the first part of the Act III quartet as an ironic recall of this moment of happiness. The scoring is light throughout. At the end, she dreamily reprises the name Gualtier Maldè *and the original theme over delicate tremolos and a hushed, atmospheric bassoon scale. Her final trill is accompanied by quiet chords from the male chorus; the ending is hushed.*

10 RECITATIVE *Riedo! . . . Perchè?* ("I return!. . .Why?") Rigoletto, returning home apprehensively, stumbles into the gathering. They tell him they are there to abduct the Countess Ceprano and allow him to feel the crest on the Ceprano key, allaying his unease. Rigoletto immediately joins them but is duped in the darkness into holding the ladder against his own house. He is given a mask, he thinks, but it is a cloth that covers both eyes and ears, so he hears and sees nothing.

Rigoletto's blundering in the dark is sensed via a staggered rhythm in strings that continues as accompaniment to the dialogue between Rigoletto and Marullo; an agitated pattern in violas intensifies the move toward the actual abduction.

CHORUS (Courtiers) *Zitti, zitti, moviamo a vendetta* ("Hush, we move to vengeance") A few ascend the ladder, climb over the wall and open the gate; others rush into the house, emerging moments later with Gilda. Her scarf, with which she has been gagged, is dislodged in her struggles.

A conspirators' chorus in the typical mode: fast and staccato, with sudden dynamic changes; the bridge to Rigoletto's realization of the deception is a syncopated return of the opening phrase.

---

[8] Hugo's King uses *Gaucher Mahiet*—"left-handed"—for which Piave could not, apparently, find a perfect Italian equivalent.

The street is soon deserted; realizing that the jest has gone on too long, Rigoletto discovers the blindfold. Tearing it off, he recognizes where he is; the light of a lantern left behind reveals Gilda's scarf. Rushing through the house and screaming her name, he comes upon the terrified Giovanna, realizes what has happened, and, choked with fear, acknowledges the fateful work of Monterone's curse.

Frenzied short string phrases are remindful of Rigoletto's lurching gait; the Curse fanfare is sung over tremolos; descending chromatic scales mark Rigoletto's collapse.

Act II

A room in the private apartments of the Duke, adjacent to his bedroom; early the next morning.

11 RECITATIVE *Ella mi fu rapita!* ("She's been taken from me!") The Duke storms in angrily. He had returned to Gilda's house, only to find it open and deserted. He wonders where "that dear little angel" (*quell' angiol caro*) can be, she who for the first time awakened the "flame of faithful affection" (*la fiamma di costanti affetti*), and vows revenge on the person who has taken her from him.

Quick rising scale spurts and detached descents indicate his rapid entrance, his pacing to and fro, and his anger. A see-saw background is appropriate to the flowing melody (Ex. RI-2a) used for his more loving sentiments.

ARIA (Duke) *Parmi veder le lagrime / Scorrenti da qual ciglio* ("I seem to see tears falling from her lashes") He imagines Gilda frightened and alone, calling for her beloved "Gualtier"; but he, who because of her did not envy the angels their heavenly spheres, cannot help her.

The courtiers flood into the room, gleefully announcing the capture of Rigoletto's mistress; the Duke forgets his concern for Gilda and seats himself to hear their story.

The music is lyric, lovely, and tender, with a standard rhythmic um-pa-pa and cadenza.

CHORUS (Courtiers) *Scorrendo uniti remota via* ("We hastened together to a remote street") With obvious relish, the courtiers narrate the events of the abduction.

Detached dotted rhythms and a sprightly tempo exhibit the jocular character of their narration. The trumpet doubling makes for appropriate triteness.

CABALETTA with CHORUS (Duke, Courtiers) *Possente amor mi chiama* ("All-powerful love summons me") When he is told that the girl is there in the palace, the Duke, realizing they are speaking of Gilda, excitedly surrenders to the flush of libido and rushes off to her, leaving the courtiers somewhat puzzled at his reaction.

The Duke explodes into a fast tempo for an aria marked by a bold, angular melody and triplet descents over arpeggiated strings. The blatancy of the woodwind doubling of the vocal line reflects the obviousness of his lust.

12 ARIOSO (Marullo, Rigoletto, Courtiers) *Povero Rigoletto . . . La rà, la rà* ("Poor Rigoletto . . . La ra la ra") Rigoletto enters, trying to appear casual. He delivers a few jibes while looking desperately for signs of his daughter. He inquires after the Duke and is told the Duke is asleep, but a page, entering with a message for the Duke, insists that the Duke must be up and around, since he has just seen him. The courtiers change their story: the Duke is hunting. The page is incredulous, for the Duke would certainly not be hunting without his entourage or his weapons.

The courtiers' impatience is the trigger for Rigoletto's grasp of the truth. He demands the return of the girl they abducted who, to the astonishment of all, he identifies as his child (*Io vo' mia figlia!*—"I want my daughter!"). He starts for the Duke's door, but his way is barred.

*The high violins and thin scoring introduce the jester's innocuous tune and its non-word vocalise (*la rà, la rà*). The mood is made intense by the seeming insouciance of the melody against the sotto voce chording given the chorus. The verbal sparring between jester and courtiers becomes rhythmically steadier and more ominous. The rhythm of Rigoletto's* la rà *is double-timed as accompaniment to the page's comments and the irritated put-offs by courtiers. Tremolos and boiling string figures reveal Rigoletto's realization that Gilda is in the palace.*

ARIA (Rigoletto) *Cortigiani, vil razza dannata* ("Courtiers, you vile, damned breed") Rigoletto pours out his anguish and anger, condemning them for not understanding the treasure they have abused and trying to force his way past them. He is thrown back, then falls weeping to the floor. A plea to Marullo is useless, so he begs them all for mercy and forgiveness.

Rigoletto's violent outburst is expressed in explosive vocal phrases over rampant sextuplets (Ex. RI-3b); there are repeated-note, interrupted triplets as Rigoletto makes for the door and is thrown back. His plea to Marullo is mostly in short, gasping phrases over poignantly descending, sobbing patterns. His final plea is lyric and broad, over solo cello figuration.

13 RECITATIVE *Mio padre! Dio! Mia Gilda!* ("My father!" "Oh God, My Gilda!") Gilda rushes from the Duke's room, her weeping and dishevelment revealing what has happened to her. Rigoletto's demand that all leave is obeyed by the courtiers, who mutter that children and madmen must have their way.

A flurry of rising scale announces Gilda's distraught appearance; Rigoletto asks the courtiers to tell him it was all a joke over disjointed rhythms and broken phrases. When he orders them to leave, it is to the repeated Cs used so often in the opera to recall the Curse.

14 RECITATIVE AND DUET (Rigoletto, Gilda) *Parla, siam soli . . . Tutte le feste al tempio / Mentre pregava Iddio* ("Speak, we are alone . . . Every Sunday in church while praying to God") She tells her father what befell her and how it came about. Rigoletto blames himself and seeks to console her (*Piangi, fanciulla*— "weep, my little girl").

Gilda's sad tale is sung in the minor mode, with the archetypical oboe solo as symbolic of her isolation and grief. As her narration climaxes, the orchestration is gradually enriched. Piangi is in sobbing, two-note groups alternating with lyric phrases over pizzicato arpeggios; Gilda's response is doubled in flute and oboe over tremolos in the violin that are reminiscent of the violin figure of Caro nome. *There is a steady change of figuration as Gilda's music becomes more ornamental, thus maintaining her character vis-a-vis her father's steadier lyricism. Rigoletto's melody of sympathy is rich in character: its broken rhythms speak of his sobs, its repetitious quality hint at a soul that has become obsessive, and the wonderful melody of consolation is warm and deeply moving.*

Monterone, preceded by a herald, is escorted to the dungeons; passing by the doorway, the Count apostrophizes the Duke's portrait, bemoaning that the Duke continues his merry life in spite of the curse. Rigoletto vows that the old man shall be avenged.

Fanfare rhythms over quickly rising scales recall the music of Monterone's appearance in Act I, scene i.

DUET (Rigoletto, Gilda) *Sì, vendetta* ("Yes, revenge") Rigoletto vows revenge. Gilda begs him to forgive and forget, noting in an aside that, even though she has been betrayed, she loves the Duke still. Rigoletto is deaf to her pleas.

An effective bit of theater for all its obviousness, this closing duet features tutti doubling over arpeggios, upward key changes for Gilda's taking up of the melody, and trumpet doubling of the final verse.

Act III

At night; a desolate spot on the banks of the Mincio River. Visible to the audience are the area just outside the door of Sparafucile's wretched hovel, the bank of the river, and both the main room of the tavern and the "guest room" above it. It is a month later, during which time Gilda has been living in the palace as the Duke's mistress.

15 RECITATIVE *E l'ami?* / *Sempre* ("And you love him? . . . Always") While Sparafucile is inside, cleaning his sword, Rigoletto arrives with Gilda, she affirming that she loves the Duke with all her heart. He orders her to put her eye to a crack in the wall of the house and observe.

The Duke, dressed as an army officer, strides in. He demands a room and some wine, then launches into his song on the fickleness of women.

Gloomy low strings invoke the night as does the sparse accompaniment of the hushed conversation between Rigoletto and Gilda.

CANZONE[9] (Duke): *La donna è mobile, / Qual piuma al vento, / Muta d'accento / E di pensiero* ("Women are fickle, like a feather in the wind, changing words and thoughts")

Strophic and tuneful with a strongly accented rhythm background rhythm, this is the archetypical drinking song and seems at one with the spirit of Italian music.

RECITATIVE *È là il vostr' uomo* ("Your man is in there") Maddalena enters the main room of the tavern, flirtatiously eluding the Duke's embraces, while Gilda continues to watch. Sparafucile meets Rigoletto to confirm the assassination of the man inside and delivery of his body later that night.

As unsubtle as the Duke's song is, the recall of it in fragments as background to the whispered arrangements between Rigoletto and Sparafucile is wonderfully atmospheric and rich in dramatic irony.

16 QUARTET (Duke, Maddalena, Gilda, Rigoletto) *Un dì, se ben rammentomi . . . Bella figlia dell' amore* ("One day that I well remember . . . Beautiful daughter of love") Avowing that he has been infatuated since the first time he saw her, the Duke claims that Maddalena has been the only woman he's ever loved and that he is a slave to her charms. Maddalena laughingly enjoys his outrageous flattery, Gilda sobs her disbelief at such betrayal, and Rigoletto, brusquely rejecting her weeping, vows to be Gilda's avenger.

(Part 1: Un dì se ben rammentomi . . .): Short phrases in vocal parts carry on the flirtation while the orchestra states, develops and restates the descending trilled scale of the Rigoletto/Gilda duet in Act I, scene ii, and the violin figure of Caro nome. In other words, the orchestra is vividly recalling moments of Gilda's greatest happiness just as she is at the depths of her misery.

---

[9] See Chapter 3, note 10.

Verdi, *Rigoletto,* the quartet of Act III: As Rigoletto (Hans Choi) and Gilda (Celeste Tavera) listen outside Sparafucile's tavern, the Duke (John Swenson) and Maddalena (Jane Gilbert) engage in outrageous flirtation. San Francisco Opera Center, 1989: sets by Jay Kotcher, costumes coordinated by Walter Mahoney. Photo Larry Merkle.

(Part 2: Bella figlia dell' amore*): The famous, broadly lyric melody of the Duke luxuriates in flattery: the scherzando style for Maddalena, the sobbing two-note groups for Gilda, and the repeated notes and narrow range (= obsession) for Rigoletto are all foils to it. The quartet moves in varied duet patterns: the Duke and Gilda in same rhythm as both talk of love; Gilda syncopated against her father as both talk of their own views of the betrayal, while Maddalena and the Duke sing together in parallel lines.*

17 RECITATIVE *M'odi! Ritorna a casa* ("Listen to me! Return home") With an approaching storm muttering in the distance, Rigoletto bids Gilda to return home, don male clothing, and ride on to Verona, where he will join her the next day. In a brief colloquy with Sparafucile, Rigoletto gives him half the fee due for the murder, the remainder to be paid on delivery of the body at midnight. Rigoletto insists on disposing of the body himself, then leaves.

   As the storm nears, the Duke announces his intention to stay the night, whispering to Maddalena to join him in the room upstairs. The Duke goes there and dozes off.

Rigoletto's instructions to Gilda are unaccompanied. The music for the distant storm uses low strings and perfect intervals, with isolated oboe tones in high register as accompaniment to the dialogues; fast flute arpeggios = lightning, low string tremolos = thunder, chromatic humming by male chorus offstage = wind. The Duke's whispered invitation to Maddalena is unheard by the audience but is suggested by a clarinet snippet of the Bella figlia *tune from the quartet's second section. He falls asleep to snatches of his* brindisi, *some of it sung, some played by clarinet; its final phrase is unfinished.*

18 RECITATIVE *Ah, più non ragiono* ("I reason no longer") Gilda, defying her father's orders, returns to the tavern, only to overhear Maddalena plead for the life of the young officer with whom she has fallen in love. Gilda hears her suggestion to kill the hunchback instead and Sparafucile's response in a crude code of honor: *Che diavol dicesti! / Un ladro son forse? Son forse un bandito? / Qual altro cliente da me fu tradito?* ("What devilment are you speaking? Am I perhaps a thief? A bandit? What other client have I ever betrayed?")

The dialogue leading to the trio and storm is given a mix of storm figures in the orchestra and increasing use of triplet rhythms in both orchestral figures and voice parts.

TRIO (Sparafucile/Maddalena/Gilda) *Se pria ch'abbia il mezzo la notte toccato / Alcuno qui giunga, per esso morrà.* ("If anyone comes here before midnight strikes, he will die instead of him.") As the storm builds, Sparafucile yields to Maddalena's entreaties by finally agreeing to cut the throat of anyone who should come to the tavern before the "delivery" is due; Gilda resolves to be that person. She knocks at the door. The light within is extinguished, she is dragged inside and stabbed.

The argument between Maddalena and Sparafucile takes place during an intensification of humming (= wind), constant tremolos, fast descending scales, and rolling triplets. Gilda's line is in rising chromatics over the less melodious music of Maddalena and Sparafucile. A single church-bell stroke announces the half hour before midnight. There is a sudden hush when Gilda knocks: pretending to be a wayfarer, she calls plaintively on a repeated high pitch that is a perfect fifth above the quiet tremolo in the strings; her murder is consummated in an explosive reprise of the opening of the trio.

INTERLUDE (Orchestra) The tempest rages.

Full tutti treatment of storm figures, timpani rolls, chromatic scales, etc.

19 RECITATIVE (Rigoletto; then Sparafucile) *Della vendetta alfin giunge l'istante!* ("The moment of revenge finally is at hand!") The storm abates; Rigoletto returns and, when midnight is tolled by a distant bell, knocks at the door. Sparafucile delivers the body in a sack; Rigoletto rejects Sparafucile's eagerness to help throw it in the river. The disposal, says Rigoletto, is for himself alone. Sparafucile quickly departs.

The accompaniment to the Rigoletto-Sparafucile dialogue is lean, with flute arpeggios continuing their metaphor of lightning; the stroke of midnight is tolled by six bells, as appropriate for the Italian clock system in the nineteenth century.

Gloating (*Ora mi guarda, o mondo! / Quest' è un buffone, ed un potente è questo! / Ei sta sotto miei piede! È desso! O gioia!*—"Now look at me, world! This man is a clown, and this one a ruler! He lies beneath my feet! It's he himself! Oh joy!"), Rigoletto drags the body toward the river only to hear the Duke caroling his drinking song as he leaves the tavern after his lovemaking with Maddalena.

Arioso is the style for Rigoletto's gloating, but it is suddenly interrupted by the return of La donna è mobile. *The Duke's banal tunefulness has become one of opera's great theatrical strokes.*

20 RECITATIVE (Rigoletto) *Chi è mai? Chi è qui in sua vece?* ("Who is this then? Who is here in his place?") In horror, Rigoletto tears open the sack; a flash of lightning reveals that it is Gilda lying there. His desperate knocking at the inn fruitless, Rigoletto returns to the sack, his anguished call to Gilda eliciting a faint response from her.

Staggered tremolo figures commingled with lightning figures illustrate Rigoletto's disbelief and realization of the awful truth; his appeal to Gilda to speak is voiced in a rich lyric line over syncopations.

DUET (Gilda/Rigoletto): *V'ho ingannato . . . colpevole fui . . . / L'amai troppo . . . ora muoio per lui* ("I deceived you . . . It is my fault . . . I loved him too much . . . now I die for him") Gilda asks Rigoletto for pardon for her deception; when he avers that she has been the victim of his thirst for vengeance and begs her to speak to him, she asks his blessing. As he begs her not to die, she assures him that soon she will be in heaven with her mother, where she will pray for him forever (*Lassù in cielo vicina alla madre / In eterno per voi . . . pregherò*).

> *Gilda's faint voice is undoubled, supported only by a delicate, hesitant background figure that is a very conventional um-pa, yet highly effective. Urgent rhythmic motion and heavily rising chromatic scales underscore Rigoletto's anguish. The innocent child's vision is given delicate flute arpeggiations with high-pitched chords in reduced strings. Rigoletto is reduced to snatches of repeated-note pleas (Example RI-3d).*

Gilda dies in his arms. With a cry of deepest anguish (*È morta! Ah, la maledizione!*—"She's dead! Ah, the curse!"), Rigoletto collapses over the body of his daughter.

> *Plummeting chromatic scales and Rigoletto's recall of the Curse lead to the opera's pounding, final chords.*

The Characters

The characters of Hugo's play are in parentheses

Duke of Mantua *(lyric tenor)* *(MAHN-too-ah)* *(King Francis I; historical figure, 1494–1547)*

Young, wealthy, amoral. That he is married has not prevented him from taking great delight in seductions and rakish escapades, many of them under the tutelage and conniving of his court jester, Rigoletto. As a ruler bound in his public appearances by protocol and custom, he sings most of the time in conventional forms: "Questa o quella" ("This one or that one," No. 2) and "La donna è mobile" ("Women are fickle," No. 15) are strophic; "Parmi veder le lagrime" ("I seem to see tears," No. 11) and "Possente amor mi chiama" ("All-powerful love summons me," the second part of No. 11) are strung together in the traditions of the *scena*, a standard nineteenth-century construction moving from a slow aria through a transition[10] passage (in this case a short chorus) to a fast, virtuosic finale.[11]

Suavity and unctuousness characterize two of his professions of love; each of these is out-and-out flattery and is recognized as such by the women who hear them (Countess Ceprano in Act I, scene i, and Maddalena in the quartet of Act III). He "speaks" in a similar vein to Gilda, but she accepts his flowery hypocrisy without reserve and, as one might expect, suffers egregiously for it. The Duke's lightheartedness and insouciance is in all his music of the first scene and characterizes "La donna è mobile" ("Women are fickle"), the famous brindisi[12] of Act III. Although he is petulant and self-willed

---

[10] Such a transition is called a *tempo di mezzo*, or "middle tempo."

[11] The so-called *cabaletta*, a solo with or without chorus.

to the point of childish excess in the opening recitative of Act II, "Ella mi fu rapita" ("She's been stolen from me," the start of No. 11), he has a moment of real tenderness, in both word and music (Example RI-2a), when he admits to himself that Gilda has awakened real love in his heart. The melody that follows, "Parmi veder le lagrime" ("I seem to see the tears"), is one of Verdi's loveliest and suggests that there is some glow of genuine sentiment in the soul of this callow wretch. But it lasts for only a short time; the moment he learns Gilda is in his bedroom, tenderness yields to a very different urge (Example RI-2b) expressed in an angular, athletic melody over pounding arpeggiation. Six weeks later (Act III) he is on the prowl again, pursuing the luscious Maddalena.

Borsa (tenor) *[BAWR-sah] (De Latour Landry)*

A fawning courtier, Borsa has no characterizing music.

Countess Ceprano (mezzo-soprano) *[cheh-PRAH-noh] (Madame de Cosse)*

She appears only in the first scene, where her music is restricted to recitative-like phrases sung above a sensuous minuet melody. Her beauty is of

EXAMPLE RI-2, ACT II: THE DUKE'S SENTIMENTS TOWARD GILDA

a) Act II: No. 11, after "Ella mi fu rapita!"—He shows genuine concern.

---

[12] *Brindisi* = drinking song.

EXAMPLE RI-2 (*Continued*)

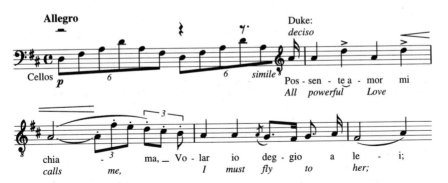

b) "Possente amor"—A moment later, he is alive with the anticipation of sexual delights.

inflammatory attractiveness to the Duke; when Count Ceprano is outraged by the Duke's attentions to her, Rigoletto takes the opportunity to offer venomous mockery of him, thus inciting Ceprano's eagerness to participate in the abduction of Rigoletto's "mistress."

Rigoletto (baritone) *[ree-goh-LEHT-toh]* (Triboulet)

Jester to the Duke of Mantua; a limping dwarf (see Example 4.1) with a hunched back. Rigoletto's life has been virtually nothing but torment, because his deformity has been greeted with scorn, ridicule, and cruel jest by all save one. That one was a lovely woman who not only pitied him but loved him; he still feels most painfully her death in childbirth. By her Rigoletto has a daughter, Gilda, whom he cherishes beyond all else and whose existence he has kept secret from the harsh world in which he moves. Under the protection of the Duke, who enjoys Rigoletto's barbed wit and sarcasm as long as it's aimed at other people, Rigoletto vents his hatred of the courtiers in vicious verbal assaults[13] as well as in his one soliloquy, the "Pari siamo" of Act I, scene ii (No. 7; see Example 4.1c).

---

[13] In Hugo's play, the jester introduces his young master to the fleshpots of the city and abets him in seducing the wives and daughters of the sycophantic nobles of the court. Quoting from H. Morley's *Clément Marot* (the Marullo of the opera), Godefroy (p. 193) cites this description of the original Triboulet by Jean Marot, the poet's father: "Triboulet was a fool, with no strength in his horn, / At thirty as wise as the day he was born; / Little forehead, great eyes, a big nose, figure bent, / Long, flat stomach, hunched back, to bear weight as he went; / He mimicked all people, could sing, dance and preach, / Always pleasant, none ever resented his speech." Considering both the sexual allusion of the first line and the basic personality trait mentioned in the last line, it is clear that Hugo, Verdi, and Piave excercised considerable dramatic license.

Rigoletto lives in a small, secluded house near the Duke's palace, on a deserted street that runs alongside a high wall forming the side or rear of the Ceprano palace. He is musically the most varied of any of the characters in the opera, because he must adapt his behavior to the situation and can only occasionally be himself. His music is rhythmically bold and intrudes spasmodically into the merriment of the first scene, but it drops out quickly after each sally, as if to indicate his scurrying for the Duke's protection immediately after he delivers a barb in someone's direction. His scenes with Gilda, however, are marked by symmetry of phrase and breadth of line; they are surgingly lyrical in Act I, scene ii (Example RI-3a), flowing and gentle (with sobbing two-note accents) in the narrative scene of Act II. When his mind turns to the dangers hovering about them, however, his music turns to quicker tempos and accompaniment by short, staccato figures. In Act II, the accompanying patterns of his cursing of the courtiers (No. 12, Example RI-3b) and the vengeance duet (the end of No. 14) are rhythmically relentless, and his line hammers monomaniacally in the Act III quartet (No. 16, Example RI-3c).

Example RI-3 Aspects of Rigoletto's music

a) Act I, scene ii: No. 7, "Figlia! Mio padre!"—Rigoletto greets his daughter tenderly, accompanied by violin melody associated with her youth and exuberance.

EXAMPLE RI-3 (*Continued*)

b) Act II: No. 12, "Cortigiani, vil razza dannata"—Figure accompanying his indictment of the courtiers.

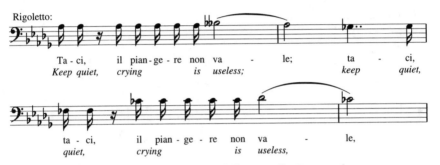

c) Act III: No. 16, Quartet, "Bella figlia dell' amore"—Repeated-note pattern as obsession.

When his beloved daughter lies dying in his arms, he is given a final, searingly lyrical moment before he is reduced to pleading for her to live in gasping, short-breathed descending phrases (Example RI-3d).

Marullo (baritone) *[mah-ROOL-loh] (a conflation of Hugo's De Pienne and Marot)*

The court poet[14] who discovers that Rigoletto nightly visits a beautiful woman and tells the courtiers about it. Marullo does not know she is Rigoletto's daughter. It is to Marullo that Rigoletto especially appeals for sympathy in Act II, because he is not a nobleman and, thus, like Rigoletto, owes his position at court to intelligence, merit, and, presumably, a sense of human worth. Marullo has no individualizing music.

Count Ceprano (bass) *[cheh-PRAH-noh] (De Cosse)*

A courtier forced to endure Rigoletto's mockery when the Duke flirts outrageously with his wife. When the Duke asks Rigoletto how to be rid of the

---

[14]Clément Marot (1496–1544) held several positions at court, but his Lutheran sympathies twice forced him to flee France. He was author of witty poems and a translator of the Psalms, and was among the first French poets to write in sonnet form.

EXAMPLE RI-3 (*Continued*)

d) Act III: No. 20, "V'ho ingannato"—He pleads for Gilda not to die.

annoyingly jealous Count, Rigoletto's suggestion to behead the Count, since "what is one to do with a head like that?" (*Che far di tal testa?*) is probably an allusion to the Count's obesity, of which much is made in the play. He has no distinguishing music, although his explosive reaction ("Marrano!"—"Scoundrel!") to Rigoletto's tasteless comments is the trigger for the first big ensemble of Act I, scene i.

Count Monterone (bass-baritone; originally intended to be sung by a baritone) [mohn-teh-ROH-neh] (St. Vallier)

Father of a girl bedded by the Duke. In the play, St. Vallier had been impli-cated in a plot to overthrow the King; his daughter Diane de Poitier yielded her honor to the King to save her father. (The King issued a last-minute reprieve that, we are told, turned the man's hair gray on the spot.) Thus, when Monterone storms into the palace in the opening scene of the opera to upbraid the Duke on matters of honor, this conspiracy and Diane's sacrifice give meaning to Rigoletto's taunting "Voi congiuraste contro noi" ("You have conspired against us") and "Qual vi piglia or delirio a tutte l'ore / Di vostra figlia a reclamar l'onore," ("What madness takes hold of you to seek at every turn to reclaim your daughter's honor?").

Outraged at the Duke's order to arrest him and the jester's insolence, Monterone curses them both and thus becomes the source of Rigoletto's obsession and the direction of the plot.[15] His fanfare-like Curse motive (RI-1a) is a distinct element in every scene of the opera.

Sparafucile (bass) [spah-rah-foo-CHEE-leh] (Saltabadil)

A sardonic, professional assassin who has observed Rigoletto's nightly visits to a young woman whom Sparafucile, like Marullo, believes to be Rigoletto's mistress. With his alluring sister, Maddalena, he operates from a dilapidated tavern on the outskirts of Mantua, by the banks of the Mincio River. He is first characterized in a sinuous melody (Example RI-4) for solo cello and double bass that glides through his dialogue with Rigoletto at the start of Act I, scene ii; his Act III music is short, sequential, and blunt. When he floats his name into the night air at the end of the Act I, scene ii duet with Rigoletto, he is given a sustained low note that speaks of the shadows from which he strikes; the device returns for his Act III "Buona notte" ("Good night") to Rigoletto, when he delivers the sack and disappears into the dark.

EXAMPLE RI-4 ACT I, SCENE II: NO. 6, "SIGNOR . . . VA, NON HO NIENTE"—THE ACCOMPANIMENT TO THE SPARAFUCILE/RIGOLETTO DIALOGUE

---

[15] Verdi's original title for the opera was *La Maledizione*—"The Curse."

Gilda (lyric soprano) *[JEEL-dah] (Blanche)*

Rigoletto's sixteen-year-old daughter, whose youthful exuberance is immediately represented by the violin melody that accompanies her reunion with Rigoletto in Act I, scene ii (Example RI-3a). We learn in Act I, scene ii, that she has been in Mantua only three months; prior to that her life had probably been spent in the confines of a cloister. Even now she is forbidden to leave the house save to go to church and may not speak with anyone other than Giovanna, the housekeeper. She knows nothing of her father—not even his name—save that he loves her dearly. Her only sense of the world is what she has read in fanciful fictions. Like any teenager, she wants desperately to explore it and find her true love. She has found it, she thinks, in a handsome youth she has seen at church, not knowing it is the Duke disguised as a poor student.

The music of her grief is the second element we hear in the opera: it is the sobbing motive of the Prelude (Example RI-1b) and occurs with dramatic irony as a counterpoint to the mocking laughter of Maddalena in the Act III quartet.

Her counterpoint to Rigoletto's sad telling of their having no family other than each other (Example RI-5a) and the coloratura passages of the Act I, scene ii, "Caro nome" (No. 9, "Dear name"; see Example RI-5b) are representative of her youth, innocence of spirit, and romanticized notions. She is the only character given ornamental music; it is thus representative not only of her girlishness but also her isolation from the real world. She can wheedle and cajole with insistent repetition like any adolescent, but musically she is out of her league with the Duke—in the duet with him she is a follower,[16] her lyricism being a decorative response to his simpler, more assured melody (Example RI-5b).

Gilda is given solo woodwind timbre as accompaniment at key moments, most notably a flute in *Caro nome* as a symbol of purity and innocence, an oboe in her narration of Act II (No. 14, "Tutte le feste al tempio"—"Every Sunday in church"), and flute arpeggios as she sings her dying thoughts of joining her mother in heaven (No. 20, "Lassù in cielo"—"Up there, in heaven").

Giovanna (mezzo-soprano) *[jo-VAHN-nah] (Dame Berarde)*

Housekeeper for Rigoletto and guardian over Gilda when he is absent. She is easily bribed by the Duke to keep silent when he enters the garden, even though she has been charged by Rigoletto with the responsibility of Gilda's protection. She has no distinguishing music.

Page (lyric soprano) *(Vendragon)*

An adolescent boy[17] whose appearance in Act III, with a message that the Duchess wishes to speak with her husband, causes the courtiers' issuance of

---

[16] For an interpretation of this characteristic, see Elizabeth Hudson's "Gilda Seduced: A Tale Untold," in *Cambridge Opera Journal* 4, no. 3 (November 1992): 229–251.

[17] The role of adolescent boys is often assigned to female voices, hence such parts, sung by sopranos and mezzos, are referred to as "trouser roles." Cherubino (*Le nozze di Figaro*), Octavian (*Der Rosenkavalier*), and Nicklausse (*Les contes d'Hoffmann*) are examples.

EXAMPLE RI-5 GILDA'S MUSIC

a) Act I, scene ii: No. 7, "Deh non parlare al misero"—she commiserates with her sorrowing father.

conflicting excuses ("He's gone hunting;" "He's still asleep") and thus Rigoletto's realization that the Duke is in the bedroom with Gilda.

Usher (bass) (Servant)

A herald; he has a brief stint near the end of Act II, when he proclaims the passage of Monterone on the way to the dungeons.[18]

---

[18] It is a curious moment, since Monterone presumably had already been incarcerated since the day before, when he was arrested at the height of the party. Moreover, if he is on the way to the dungeons, how would his route lead him by a room just outside the Duke's bedchamber? Whatever the explanation, it triggers the explosion of the vengeance duet and the climax of the act.

EXAMPLE RI-5 (*Continued*)

e   fin l'ul - ti - mo   mi - o   so - spir,   Ca - ro ___
and even   my   last   sigh,   dear

no -   me, _ tuo _ sa - ra!
name,   will be yours!

b) Act I, scene ii: No. 9, "Caro nome"—coloratura treatment of the aria's melody.

Members of the Court (male chorus)

Fawning, hypocritical, pleasure-seeking members of a good-for-nothing aristocracy. Their resolving on revenge in Act I, scene i, has a mood of building resentment that comes from the rolling lyricism of the music for their repetitions of the word "vendetta"; their choruses of abduction (No. 10, "Zitti, zitti"—"Hush, quiet") and narration of abduction ("Scorrendo uniti"—"We hastened together," in No. 11) are quick and short phrased, the former quiet and conspiratorial, the latter spirited and jocular, with sudden fortes of excitement and crude pleasure. In the last act, the men's voices become a sound device: they vocalize chromatically on an open vowel as the "voice" of the winds of death.

Maddalena (mezzo-soprano) (mah-dah-LEH-nah) [Maguelonne]

Sparafucile's sister. Dressed as a gypsy, she dances in the streets for coins and bats her eyes at Sparafucile's intended victims, thus luring them to his tavern for assassination and robbery. With Rigoletto's cooperation, she has attracted the attention of the Duke; the assignation of Act III is the result. Her music is at first flirtatious with staccatos (suggestive perhaps of the castanets with which she would accompany her dancing) and, in the quartet, amorous lyricism. When she suggests saving the Duke's life, her phrases become irregular and repetitively insistent, with triplets gradually suggesting her growing urgency. In the trio leading up to Gilda's murder, individualized melody disappears from her part: repeated notes or repetition of Sparafucile's music indicates the disappearance of any semblance of affection, good humor, or sensual charm. She becomes as murderous as her brother.

Bibliography

Budden, Julian. *The Operas of Verdi. Vol. I: From* Oberto *to* Rigoletto. New York: Oxford University Press, 1978, pp. 475–510.
   The most thorough and insightful study of the Verdi operas.
Drummond, John D. *Opera in Perspective*. Minneapolis, MN: University of Minnesota Press, 1980.
   See pp. 244–263 for a detailed study of the quartet.
Godefroy, Vincent. *The Dramatic Genius of Verdi: Studies of Selected Operas. Vol. I: "Nabucco" to "La Traviata."* New York: St. Martin's Press, 1975.
Hudson, Elizabeth. "Gilda Seduced: A Tale Untold," in *Cambridge Opera Journal*, 4, no. 3 (November 1992): 229–251.
Hughes, Spike. *Famous Verdi Operas*. Philadelpia, et al.: Chilton Book Co., 1968.
Hugo, Victor. "The King Amuses Himself," in *Three Plays by Victor Hugo*, trans. Frederick L. Slous. New York: Washington Square, 1964.
Hussey, Dynley. *Verdi*. Master Musicians Series. London: J. M. Dent, 1948.
John, Nicholas, ed. *Rigoletto*. English National Opera Guide 15. London and New York: Calder Publications / Riverrun Press, 1982.
Kestner, Joseph. "La Maledizione," in *Opera News* 54, no. 11 (Feb. 17, 1990): 21–25.
Kimball, David R. B. *Verdi in the Age of Romanticism*. Cambridge: Cambridge University Press, 1981.
Lee, M. Owen. "When Verdi's Fathers Sing: *Rigoletto*," in *First Intermissions*. New York: Oxford University Press, 1995, pp.15–24.
Martin, George. "The Curse in *Rigoletto*," in *Aspects of Verdi*. New York: Limelight Editions, 1993, pp. 157–180.
Osborne, Charles. *The Complete Operas of Verdi*. New York: Knopf, 1970.
Sacher, Jack. *A Guide to "Rigoletto."* New York: Metropolitan Opera Guild, 1978.

Chapter 13

DIE WALKÜRE

MUSIC AND LIBRETTO: Richard Wagner (1813–1883).
PREMIERE: Munich (Königliches Hof- und National-Theater), June 26, 1870; its first performance as part of the complete cycle was at Bayreuth on August 14, 1876.
TIME AND PLACE OF THE STORY: primordial times; the forests and mountains along the River Rhine. The action may be presumed to occur within a single day and night in May or over a more extended period in spring.

Die Walküre *("The Valkyrie") is the second of the four operas of* Der Ring des Nibelungen *("The Ring of the Nibelung"). A number of folk sources deal with its characters and events, but Wagner leaned most heavily on* The Nibelung Saga (Das Nibelungenlied, *ca. 1200),* Thidreks Saga af Bern *("Dietrich's Saga," compiled in Norway ca. 1260–70), the* Volsunga Saga *(an anonymous Icelandic prose narrative compiled during the thirteenth century), the* Poetic Edda *(anonymous poems compiled in Iceland ca. 1150–1250; also called the "Verse Edda" or the "Elder Edda"), and the* Prose Edda *(a handbook for poets written ca. 1223 by the Icelandic bard Snorri Sturluson (1178–1241; also known as the "Younger Edda"). The tetralogy's mythic devices and themes also draw on Greek dramatic sources, especially Aeschylus's* Prometheus *and the* Oresteia *for interconnection of separate dramas, linkages of an overarching curse, confrontations of pairs of characters, narrative reviews of past events, and the pursuit of expiation.*

Wagner's Principles of Music and Drama

Wagner believed that opera had developed the wrong musical and dramatic values: instead of music being a means to an end, it had become the end itself, with story and character bent to suit purely musical purposes and thus undermining the drama and its dramatic raison d'être. For Wagner, all the arts—poetry, music, mime, scenic work—should serve the highest goal of drama: the explication of the timeless allegories of legend and the fundamental forces of humanity. "Opera," then, had become too highly specialized and anachronistic a term for him; his vision of a "unified art work" (*Gesamtkunstwerk*) is more properly described as "music drama."

He proposed that psychological action must be a continuous force expressed through "endless melody" unbroken by the closures of musical forms and dramatic units. Present action should be connected with the past and the future by a web of musical ideas or motives associated with the psychological makeup of the characters and related to symbolic events, concepts, and objects. For Wagner, the orchestra was the ideal medium for recalling, coloring, and continually reshaping these musical linkages.

Poet and composer were one in Wagner's thinking. He wrote his own texts because he felt that word and sound were inseparable; their combination of strict meaning and connotation had to be shaped by the same creative force. While it was the job of the actor-singers to declaim the text, it was a basic function of sound—instruments, vowels, harmonies, consonants, melody, etc.—to provide those deeper meanings that could only be felt. Music, he wrote, was the primal force:

> Before starting to write a verse, or even to outline a scene, I must first feel intoxicated by the musical aroma ["aura" is perhaps a better translation of Wagner's *Duft*] of my subject; all the tones, all the characteristic motives are in my head, so that when the verses are finished and the scenes ordered, the opera proper is also finished . . . it falls to the poet and composer of opera to conjure up the holy spirit of poetry which has come down to us from the legends and sagas of past ages. For music offers the means for synthesis which the poet alone, especially in the drama, cannot command.[1]

In explaining how vowel and consonant should be at the service of character and situation, Wagner asserted in his essay *Opera and Drama* (1850–51) that the highest communicative force derived from the interrelationship of specific meaning (*Wortsprache*—"word speech") and expressive/emotional sound (*Tonsprache*—"tone speech"). The fusion of word-meaning and word-sound formed for him a special kind of music for which he found inspiration in the alliterative poetry of the ancient Nordic and Anglo-Saxon *Stabreim* (alliteration).

The opening phrases of Siegmund's Spring Song in Act I offers a prime example of alliteration wedded to poetic, dramatic, and musical intent: embracing Sieglinde, who has been frightened by the sudden blowing open

EXAMPLE WA-1 ACT I, SCENE III: SIEGMUND'S SPRING SONG.

Siegmund:

Win - ter - stür - me wi - chen dem Won - ne - mond,
Winter   storms   have yielded   to   the   month of May,

---

[1] Letter of January 30, 1844, from Wagner to Karl Galliard, in *Letters of Richard Wagner: The Burrell Collection*, ed. John N. Burk (New York: Macmillan, 1950), p. 108.

of the door by a storm's final blast, he consoles her with a lullaby of smooth consonants (the repeated "vee" sounds of "Winterstürme," "wichen," and "Wonnemond," for example [see Example WA-1], and the "els" of "Lichte," "leuchtet," and "Lenz,") that are sung to a gentle triplet figuration over the murmur of hushed strings.

Wotan's indictment of Brünnhilde in the final act of *Die Walküre* provides another famous example of this use of word-as-sound: his images of her as his favorite daughter who carried out his wishes ("Wunschmaid"), bore his shield ("Schildmaid"), and cast her lot with his ("Loskieserin"—"chooser of fates") are set to open vowels and liquid consonants borne by lyric phrases and simple triads; his denunciation of her disobedience is given hard consonants ("gegen" = "against"), gutturals ("mich doch" = "me then"), chromatic twists, and melodic angularity.

Most of all, the Wagnerian approach to drama relies on multidimensional characters who think, feel, and change. As beautiful as the music is, the opera's greatness comes no less from the musical depiction of Wotan's struggle between desire and duty, Brünnhilde's change from a warrior to a

EXAMPLE WA-2 ACT III, SCENE II: WOTAN'S INDICTMENT
OF BRÜNNHILDE

compassionate woman, and Siegmund's blend of courage, ardor, and tenderness. With Handel, we saw mostly steady states of mind glittering in the frozen moments of closed-off arias; with Wagner, we hear the process by which more complex states of mind are achieved.

Wagner developed remarkable techniques of harmonic and melodic inflection that allowed him to override the tendency of tonal music to pause. By drawing freely and extensively on notes not normally found in a key, beginning a new phrase as another was ending, and following dissonance with dissonance or unexpected harmonic resolution, the tonal center of a phrase could be hidden or delayed. Form and harmonic logic underlie all of Wagner's music, but a listener often feels only that the music is continually unfolding and that one is awash in a sea of sound.

The concept of associating a dramatic image with a musical phrase was not new with Wagner; the extent to which his orchestral and vocal fabric made use of recurrent sound images, however, was greater and infinitely more supple than had appeared in any operatic works before his time. These recurrent images are now commonly referred to as *leitmotifs* ("leading motives"), although the term was not coined by Wagner,[2] nor was it used by him. However, it is impossible to deal with Wagner's operas without referring to them, and the only convenient way to do this is by the labels that have been attached to them.

Along with virtually every modern commentator, I must offer a word of caution: the practice of labeling can become misleading and simplistic, because both the "meaning" and the music of a motive may change as plots and characters evolve. Indeed, Wagner's transformation of association and manipulation of rhythm, mode, harmony, timbre, and melody are fundamental to his musical and dramatic thinking.[3]

Consider, for example, some of the music heard in the first scene of *Die Walküre*, when Sieglinde, having found the exhausted Siegmund in her house, offers him a cooling drink while a solo cello plays a long-breathed melody that reflects gentleness and compassion (Example WA-3a).

Near the end of the act, when Sieglinde proclaims to Siegmund "Du bist der Lenz / nach dem ich verlangte / in frostigen Winters Frist" ("You are the spring I have yearned for during the icy cold of winter"), a fragment from her first appearance in the act (marked "a" in Example WA-3a) becomes the main element of her exuberance and unrestrained expression of love (Example WA-3b). In the Prelude to Act II, however, the same fragment is driven by tempo and scoring (high violins and flutes) into a description of Sieglinde's terror as she and Siegmund escape into the night (Example WA-3d).

The fanfare-like *Sword* motive (Example WA-3c) is also prominent in Act I, its trumpet timbre, opening octave descent, and rising triadic blaze making it one of the *Ring*'s most instantly memorable and heroic sounds. When

---

[2] Wagner preferred the terms *Grundthema* ("basic theme") and *Hauptmotif* ("head" or "principal motive").

[3] See William Mann, "Down with Visiting Cards," in Di Gaetani, 303–306. Mann traces the various occurences of the "Renunciation of Love" motive to show the fecklessness of strict labeling.

compressed into a triplet rhythm ("x" in Example WA-3d) in the Act II Prelude, it is transformed into Siegmund's role in the flight from Hunding.

The recall of these same motives may be seen in another light, however. Their excitement, passion, and vibrancy may depict the consummation of the love of Siegmund and Sieglinde rather than their flight. In this view, the Prelude to Act II perhaps reflects an extended passage of time rather than the hour or so immediately after the end of Act I. It is frenzied enough to allow for either interpretation. And it may be all of these things simultaneously.

EXAMPLE WA-3: SOME LEITMOTIFS OF ACT I AND THEIR TRANSFORMATION IN THE PRELUDE TO ACT II

a) Act I, scene i: Sieglinde offers refreshment to Siegmund ("a" is the opening figure of her later song of love to Siegmund, "Du bist der Lenz"; "b" is a figure found first in Siegmund's song to her, "Winterstürme wichen dem Wonnemond.")

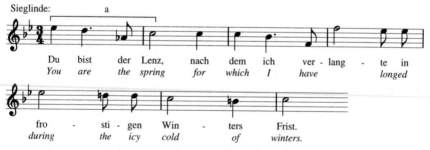

b) Act I, scene iii: Sieglinde declares Siegmund to be the love she has yearned for ("a" extracted from the example above).

c) Act I, scene iii: Sword motive.

EXAMPLE WA-3 (*Continued*)

d) Act II Prelude: Transformation of motives of Sword ("x") and Sieglinde's love ("a").

The orchestra in Wagnerian music drama is a remarkable resource of colors. It is much larger than the orchestras of any of his contemporaries and more varied, able to summon full chords and extensive partwork from any genre of melodic instruments.[4] Wagner's penchant for full exploitation of the orchestra has been one of the factors for making "Wagnerian" into a synonym for grandiosity (not to say bombast), but his achievements in terms of delicacy and intimacy are no less wondrous.

The Ring of the Nibelung: **An Overview**

Because the *Ring* allows for so many layers of meaning and the exploration of ambiguities, no single analysis has been wholly satisfactory.[5] The following is simply a survey of basic events of the four operas as a means of placing *Die Walküre* in its context.

Das Rheingold ("The Rhinegold," first performed in 1869) is the cycle's Prologue focusing on the actions of Alberich, an ugly Nibelung dwarf (*Nebel* = mist, fog), and Wotan, king of the gods. It begins with Alberich's seizure of a hoard of gold capable of being possessed only by one who renounces love. Symbolized by a ring shaped from it, the gold is the source of unlimited power and dominion. Wotan pays for his arrogantly ambitious construction

---

[4] He even required the development of a special valved tuba, played with a French horn mouthpiece, that has come to be known as the "Wagner tuba." It is particularly applied to the motive associated with Hunding.

[5] See Millington, *Wagner*, p. 222ff, for a brief survey of some of the readings.

of the castle, Valhalla, by deceit and by stealing the gold, the ring Alberich made from it, and the helmet that makes its wearer invisible, called the *Tarnhelm*. At the end of *Das Rheingold*, the outraged Alberich imposes a curse of eternal misery and ultimate death on any possessor of the ring (see below, Example WA-4c), and Wotan, realizing that engaging in deeds that violated his own laws has set him on a path of unavoidable destruction, conceives a plan to pass dominion over the universe to a hero free of sin but worthy of the mantle of leadership.

In the years between the end of *Das Rheingold* and the start of *Die Walküre*, Wotan descends to the terrestrial forests and sires Siegmund and Sieglinde by a mortal woman, intending that they will unite as bride and husband, and, by parenting a new race of heroes, fulfill his scheme. During that same timespan, Wotan also fathers by Erda (earth mother and font of natural wisdom) the nine warrior maidens known as the Valkyries. Brünnhilde stands out among them as Wotan's favorite, gifted with the wisdom and prescience of Nature and special representative of his own will and desires.

The plot of *Die Walküre* centers on Wotan's plan gone awry. Wotan is forced to destroy his own children because, even though they have behaved in accordance with his deepest wishes, they have broken divine law: Siegmund and Sieglinde (brother and sister) have consummated an incestuous love; and Brünnhilde has disobeyed his instructions by seeking to help Siegmund instead of slaying him. By the end of the opera, Siegmund has been killed in battle and Brünnhilde lies in magic slumber surrounded by a circle of fire penetrable only by one who has no fear of Wotan's power. Sieglinde survives, however, hidden in the forest to await the birth of the child who will eventually bring the cycle to its heroic conclusion.

Siegfried is the epic of the *Ring* cycle. Siegfried, the child of Siegmund and Sieglinde, is now in the first blush of adulthood. He achieves great deeds (including gaining possession of the ring), brushes aside a now impotent king of the gods, breasts the circle of fire, and claims Brünnhilde as his bride.

Götterdämmerung ("Twilight of the Gods") points the moral. Alberich has not ceased to work to reclaim the ring: he has begotten a son who causes Siegfried to forget his vows to Brünnhilde and to marry another. Believing herself betrayed, Brünnhilde reveals the one weakness by which Siegfried may be murdered, only to learn, too late, that he was never knowingly false to her. As an act of repentence and ultimate fulfillment of natural destiny, she takes the ring from Siegfried's hand and, promising that it shall be returned to its rightful place in the Rhine, rides her horse onto Siegfried's funeral pyre. The Rhine overflows its banks, the nymphs from whom Alberich had stolen the gold reclaim the ring, Valhalla and its denizens are destroyed by fire, and the world is made ready for its inheritors.

The Motives of *Die Walküre*

Here are some of the most prominent leitmotifs of the opera in their most characteristic forms. Note that characters or ideas may be suggested by motivic associations even if they have none of their own: although there is no "Wotan" motive, for example, we sense his central position in the story by motivic reference to things attributed to him—such as his castle (*Valhalla*) and his spear—and we are made aware of his inner thoughts through associations with abstractions such as *Dejection* or *Wrath*. The motives are listed alphabetically by the title most frequently used in commentaries, with the reminder here that the associative meaning of a musical phrase will alter and so will its musical shape. I have provided the equivalent German label if there is one commonly used.

EXAMPLE WA-4 BASIC LEITMOTIFS OR MUSICAL ASSOCIATIONS IN *Die Walküre*.

Annunciation of Death (Todesklang). This leitmotif is the basic thread of the Act II scene between Brünnhilde and Siegmund. It tends to lie in the lower instruments and to appear at a slow tempo, although it moves higher and changes into exuberant triplets when Brünnhilde ecstatically determines to assist Siegmund in spite of Wotan's orders. Its last three notes form the *Fate* motive.

Bliss (Wonne). Invariably associated with sensual excitement, its characteristic upward sixth followed by a half step is always recognizable. It first appears in the happy moments of Act I, when Siegmund and Sieglinde rejoice in their newfound love; in the Act II Prelude, however, it is fast and desperate.

Brünnhilde. Motives connected with her in *Die Walküre* are the *Valkyries*, *Redemption*, and *Volsung Love*, each explained below.

Curse (Fluch). Characterized by the strong ascent of minor thirds and a climaxing major third,[6] it is first heard near the end of *Das Rheingold*, when the outwitted Alberich vows that, until the ring returns to him, unhappiness and death shall come to whoever possesses it. In *Die Walküre*, the Curse motive is a threatening presence whenever it is heard. It is the music of some of Fricka's first moments with Wotan, when she angrily informs him of Hunding's call to her for aid; it is a prominent part of the interlude between Fricka's haughty departure and the arrival of Brünnhilde to start Act II,

---

[6] The rising line of *Curse* is a reversing of the first phrase of *Ring*.

scene ii; and it recurs as a bitter coda to Wotan's admission to Brünnhilde that he has no choice but to destroy Siegmund.

Alberich: (in Das Rheingold)

Wie durch Fluch er mir ge-riet,   ver-flucht sei die-ser Ring!
As through a curse it came to me,   accursed be this ring!

Death (Tod). This archetypical pattern[7] is usually a somber drum tap played with either triplet or duplet rhythm. It also shapes the Hunding motive, inasmuch as Hunding is the agent of Siegmund's death. By extension, then, it makes the Hunding motive a harsh indictment of lovelessness as equivalent to lifelessness. The motive is also heard in fast tempo in connection with the Valkyrie maidens, because they are associated with the deaths of heroes.

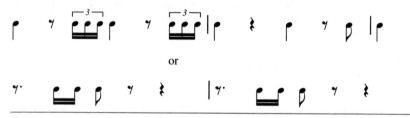

or

Dejection (Unmut) (also Wotan's anger and frustration). Because this opera is largely concerned with the defeat of Wotan's plan to prevent Alberich from regaining the ring, the descending, plodding scale of this motive is one of the most frequently encountered in Act II, where it becomes more and more evident as Fricka's victory becomes inevitable. It is also strongly evident in Act III, where it reflects Wotan's sadness in having to separate himself eternally from his favorite daughter. It forms the second half of *Need of the Gods* and is directly linked to *Spear* by its descending scale, a resonance of the treaties and oaths that have brought Wotan to his despondent state.

Farewell. See *Wotan's Farewell.*

Fate (Schicksal). A consistent element of all four operas, it is also one of the shortest. Its dissonant harmony and generally slow tempo make it a powerfully atmospheric force. It forms the final notes of *Annunciation of Death.*

---

[7] See Chapter 3, pp. 52–54

Fire (*Feuer*) (also Loge, who is the god of fire, intrigue, craft, deceit, and cleverness). This version of the *Fire* motive is the musical depiction of the growing circle of flame summoned by Wotan at the end of the opera; its flickering patterns in high instruments makes it especially pictorial. It is often heard in combination or sequence with a double-dotted rhythm, with trills, and with rapidly descending chromatic scales, all coloring *Die Walküre*'s final tableau.

Flight (*Flucht*). A rhythmic diminution of the *Love* motive (see Example WA-3b).

Frustration. See *Dejection*.

Glorification of Brünnhilde. See *Redemption*.

Hero. See *Siegfried*.

Hunding. This blunt fanfare is invariably scored for low instruments, especially the Wagner tubas. It speaks with a variant of the archetypical rhythms of *Death* and has a coarse vehemence reflective of the brutishness of its subject. We are given a hint of the motive early in Act I in the melody to which Sieglinde tells Siegmund—a complete stranger to her at this point—that both she and the house are Hunding's possessions.[8] Its most threatening and characteristic moment is its announcement of the arrival of Hunding to start the second scene of that act, when it intrudes into the moment of quiet as brother and sister gaze at each other with growing interest.

Last Greeting. See *Wotan's Farewell*.

Loge. See *Fire*.

Love (*Liebe*). The concept is communicated by elements "a" and "b" in Example WA-3a but also by Siegmund's *Spring Song*, *Sieglinde*, and *Wotan's Farewell*.

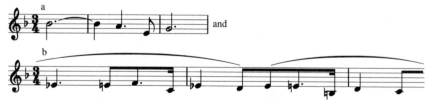

---

[8] Par. 2 in "The Plot and Its Music."

Magic Spell (Zauberschlaf); also *Magic Slumber*. The chromatic downward slide and subtly shifting harmonies, paradigms for the Wagnerian style, depict Brünnhilde's sinking into deep sleep. (See also the smugglers' music of *Carmen*'s Act III, discussed on pp. 352 and 362f.)

etc.

Wotan:
| | In | festen | Schlaf | verschliess' | ich | dich |
| | *In* | *deep* | *sleep* | *I* | *bind* | *you* |

Need of the Gods; Anxiety (Unruhe). Restless dotted rhythms and low instrumentation (especially cellos with bassoons) indicate Wotan's emotional stress; appropriately, its second half is the motive of *Dejection*. The rise-and-fall roils at a good clip whenever it enters the music's fabric (as in Wotan's second scene with Brünnhilde in Act II) and thus represents Wotan's seething desperation.

Dejection

Pursuit (Verfolgung). A short flourish, it forms the first notes of the opera, indicating not only the vehemence of wind and rain but also Siegmund's desperate flight from Hunding's tribesmen. It is also an element of the Valkyries because of its connotation of battle's chase.

Redemption (Erlösung). Learning in Act III that she will bear the world's greatest hero, Sieglinde bursts into this rapturous melody in praise of Brünnhilde. (Wagner himself called it *Glorification of Brünnhilde*.) Its more commonly used label, *Redemption*, derives from its climactic appearance at the end of *Götterdämmerung*.

Sieglinde (deeply moved)

| | O | hehr | - | - | - | stes | Wun | - | der! |
| | *Oh* | *most* | | *sublime* | | | *wonder!* | | |

| | Herr | - | | lich | - | ste | Maid! |
| | *Most* | *glorious* | | | | | *maid!* |

Renunciation of Love (*Entsagung*). Quite the opposite in mood to *Redemption*, *Renunciation* is accompanied by minor harmonies and often by tremolos; it is thus emotionally oppressive and threatening. It is one of the signal musical elements of the *Ring* because, in representing the denial of the greatest of human virtues, it symbolizes one of the principal actions motivating the plot of the entire cycle. Its most dramatic appearance in *Die Walküre* is when Siegmund grasps the haft of the sword to pull it from the tree. By using the motive of *Renunciation of Love*, he symbolically represents the acceptance of Alberich's challenge: the sword is a token of Wotan's love for his daughter and his son; Siegmund will use the sword as a weapon in defense of love; in *Siegfried*, the child of Siegmund and Sieglinde will use it to cut away the armor that covers his bride-to-be, still deep in the spell of the magic slumber placed upon her. Siegmund's quotation of the *Renunciation of Love* thus becomes a wonderful irony, a twisting of hideous negativism into a mighty Affirmation of Love.

 Renunciation also figures naturally in Wotan's farewell to Brünnhilde, when it is given to the mournful sound of the English horn as counterpoint to Wotan's "Denn so kehrt / der Gott sich dir ab, / so küsst er die Gottheit von dir!" ("Thus the God turns away from you, thus he kisses godhood from you!").

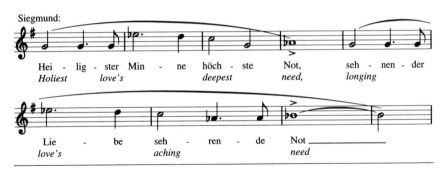

Ring. Descending and rising mostly in minor thirds, the motive is a grim presence in much of Act II. Its construction is interesting, because it is "circular": save for its first note and one passing note, it is the same backward as it is forward, so both its notation and sound represent the image of a ring. Also interesting and allegorically provocative is that it is a minor-mode form of *Valhalla*: both represent ambition, one for evil, the other for noble purpose.[9]

---

[9] Donington offers a challenging (and controversial) study of such relationships and representations.

Siegfried. A dramatically triadic horn call, it begins in the minor and ends blazingly in the major (especially at the end of Act III, with Wotan's "Wer meines Speeres / Spitze fürchtet / durchschreite das Feuer nie!" ("Whoever fears the point of my spear may never pierce the flames!").

Sieglinde (see also *Love*). A gently rising and falling triad, harmonized always in thirds and instrumented quietly in the violins, is Sieglinde's principal characterizing figure and represents her sweetness of spirit in terms of compassion, tenderness, and love.

Siegmund (see also *Volsung, Sword*). Although Siegmund is alluded to by the triumphal sounds of *Sword* and *Volsung Race*, the only motive actually labeled with this hero's name is the somber descending scale associated with *Dejection* and Wotan's *Spear*. It is usually part of a complex of motives involving two archetypes, a brief fanfare suggesting both battle and death, and a series of half-note descents often used as a gesture of sorrow or death.[10]

---

[10] The final interval in the ancient Phrygian mode (a scale pattern found on the piano's white keys descending from e to E) is a half step; melodic patterns that use it are characterized as variants of the "Phrygian cadence" and, in descriptive or dramatic music, are archetypically associated with death. Examples include the orchestral introduction to Donna Anna's "Don Ottavio, son morta" (No. 10a in *Don Giovanni*), the bass line of the *Fate* motive in the *Ring*, and, in a special kind of dying—the ultimate ecstasy of love—the ends of the first two phrases of the "kiss" motive of Verdi's *Otello*. The Phrygian half step is a

Wagner, *Die Walküre*, Act I, scene iii: To the delight of Sieglinde (Gundula Janowitz), Siegmund (Jon Vickers) exultantly draws the sword from the tree. Metropolitan Opera, 1967: production designed by Günther Schneider-Siemssen. Courtesy *Opera News*, Metropolitan Opera Guild. Photo Louis Mélançon.

---

most important element throughout the music of *Peter Grimes* and provides a striking fatalistic character to the Act IV entr'acte of Bizet's *Carmen* (see Example CA-1e, p. 348). The matter is explored extensively in William Kimmel, "The Phrygian Inflection and the Appearances of Death in Music" (1977, typewritten).

Slumber (*Schlummer*). A gently falling figure murmuring throughout the final scene as Brünnhilde sinks into sleep. The image, lulling and sweet, suggests a return to innocence necessary for her rebirth as a mortal woman at the end of *Siegfried*.

Spear (*Speer*) (also *Wotan, Treaty, Honor*). The written notes of the descending scale of this motive suggest the line of the shaft itself. The importance of a spear as an extension of a warrior's right arm and his basic tool of war made a man's spear representative of his honor and was therefore the object on which he took an oath that was inviolable.

In Wagner's reworking of the sagas, Wotan made the spear from a branch of the World Ash Tree. The wound in the tree never healed and the tree's resultant death became symbolic of the destruction of the world.[11] The spear is engraved with Wotan's Runes, written symbols of those mysteries of knowledge, wisdom, and authority especially associated with him, hence it is the fundamental symbol of his integrity and the rule of law. *Spear*, therefore, is inevitably presented with rhythmic vigor and orchestral strength. Wotan is never without his spear, visually or musically; while he does not use it as a weapon, it is inseparable from his soul and his laws and therefore is a symbol of the things he must do as opposed to what he would like to do. The shattering of Wotan's spear in *Siegfried* is one of the pivotal moments of the *Ring*, because it symbolizes the elimination of Wotan as a source of power and influence in the shaping of the universe.

The motive is felt with great emphasis as the pounding of the storm at the very opening of the opera, its driving scale steps harboring images of driving rain and Siegmund's heavy running; it is clear at once that the storm is Wotan's doing and that the arrival of Siegmund at the hut of Hunding and Sieglinde signals that Wotan's plan is afoot.

The scalar feature of *Spear* has a good deal in common with *Dejection/Frustration* because Wotan is sworn to uphold treaties (symbolized by his spear) that are contrary to his deepest desires. He is constrained by his own vows and agreements, so his aims are blunted at every turn. That *Spear* is allied to *Siegmund* by forming its bass line and to *Volsung Love* (a motive associated particularly with Brünnhilde) via its scale pattern and dotted rhythm is another reflection of the lacework of the leitmotifs and thus the subtle indication of character relationships through music.

---

[11] We learn in *Götterdämmerung* that Wotan has had the dead tree felled and its logs piled around Valhalla as fuel for the ultimate funeral pyre.

Spring Song (*Lenzlied*) (also Siegmund, Love). A lyric, smooth flowing triplet passage first heard in Siegmund's Act I "Winterstürme." (See Example WA-1.)

Sword (*Schwert*) (see above, Example WA-3c; also connected with Siegmund, heroism, Wotan's plan, and ultimately Siegfried). One of the most vivid of the cycle's many motives, its octave descent, exploding triad and brassy instrumentation always cut through whatever heavy orchestration may surround it. Siegmund gives the sword its name as he grasps its hilt, preparing to pull it from the tree in Act I: *Notung* (*Not* = "need"; *ung* = "child of").

Treaty. See *Spear*.

Valhalla (*Walhall*) (Wotan; by extension reflective of noble ambition, dignity, and majesty). It is usually in major chords and warmly orchestrated in trombones and French horns, bespeak the dignity, vision, and lofty ambition of Wotan. As a softly developed motive during Sieglinde's narrative of Act I, *Valhalla* implies not only the identity of the stranger (Wotan) who plunged a sword into a tree but also the love and concern that motivated Wotan's appearance and the way he gazed at her. *Valhalla* and *Ring* are virtually mirror images, but the former is most characteristically in the major, the latter inevitably in the minor.

Valkyries (*Walküren*) (thus also Brünnhilde). Vehemence characterizes the nine warrior maidens (Brünnhilde among them) sired by Wotan from Erda. They ride fire-breathing horses, hence the galloping rhythm (Example WA-4c below) and the wild trilling and giddy chromatic slide (Example WA-4d). Their battle cry (Example WA-4e) is recalled in many a cartoon assault on opera, inevitably depicting a breast-plated, horn-helmeted, and fully endowed Valkyrie in full voice. (They ought at least give the girls wings on their helmets; only Hunding's headgear is horned, he being a somewhat oxish character.) The Valkyries are children of nature and uninhibited desire, hence the music especially connected with them is vivid and flamboyant. And loud.

   c) Valkyries' Ride (*Walkürenritt*)

   d) Fiery Steeds; Valkyries' Laughter (no common German label in use)

e) Battle Cry (Walkürenruf)

Ho - jo - to ho!

Volsungs (Wälsungen). When Wotan walked the earth in the years following *Das Rheingold*, he took the name *Wälse* ("Wolf"), and by a mortal member of the Volsung (Ger.: *Wälsung*) Tribe fathered the twins Siegmund and Sieglinde. The following three motives are related to this and thus to Wotan's plans in general and to Siegmund in particular.

f) Volsung Love (Wälsungenliebe) is one of those soaring melodies identified with Wagnerian ecstasy and is reserved for three very special moments in Act III: the hushed interlude at the opening of the third scene when, the exhaustions of Wotan's rage and Brünnhilde's terror having faded, the two silently realize their deep familial love and the implications of the actions that have brought them to their present point; Brünnhilde's affirmation of her having achieved Wotan's will even as she broke his law; and the orchestral coda to Wotan's promise that a hero more free than he will claim her as bride.

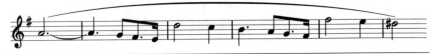

g) Volsung Race (Heldentum der Wälsungen; i.e., "Heroism of the Volsungs") (also *Volsung Victory*). A dotted-rhythm fanfare associated with both the tribe and its courage in battle. Its brass timbres and rhythmic profile speak of strength of purpose and courage while its prevailing minor mode hints of a troubled clan.

h) Volsung Sorrow (Wälsungleid; also *Wälsung-Schicksal).* It is usually scored songfully for instruments in the lower registers of the orchestra, its rising sixth often associated in the music of the nineteenth century with longing and aspiration (also ecstasy: see above, *Bliss*). It is heard during the quiet moment in Act I just before the mood of Sieglinde's and Siegmund's growing awareness of their love is crushed by the arrival of Hunding.

Wotan. See *Spear, Valhalla, Dejection,* and *Wotan's Farewell.*

Wotan's Farewell (Wotans Abschied; also *Wotans Scheidegruss).* This glowing melody comes only in the final pages of the opera, but it is one of its most moving and memorable passages. Accompanied by the purling descents of

Slumber, it is lyric and loving; the final note marks the motive's uplifting turn to the major mode.

Wrath (Frickas Zorn). This jagged music, identified by its violent pattern of a strongly accented short note followed by a longer one (i.e., a reversed dotted rhythm), its dissonance, and its minor harmonies, informs Fricka's outrage. It is also an attribute of Wotan in Act II, first when Brünnhilde suggests she might defy him, and later when, having had to slay Siegmund himself, he vows to punish Brünnhilde for her disobedience. It characterizes Wotan during his first moments in Act III but disappears when his love for Brünnhilde and the inevitability of destiny soften his harsh intent.

THE PLOT AND ITS MUSIC

The paragraph numbers do not refer to arias or other discrete musical forms but are provided for ease of reference to the musical commentary. "Scene" refers to a division of the dramatic action, not a change in the stage set. Motives are identified by the label assigned in Ex. WA-4, with the reminder that a leitmotif may assume many levels of meaning for which the original label might be useless. (Motive labels are in reverse fonts.)

Act I

PRELUDE *The orchestral music represents a driving storm and Siegmund's flight through the forest. Under pervasive string tremolos affected by sudden dynamic changes and quick crescendos,* **Pursuit** *and* **Spear** *hammer away in the low strings. As the scale pattern of* **Spear** *is reversed, the storm's intensity grows; snaps of fanfare rising in sequence from low winds and brass to the higher winds suggest fitful lightning.* **Pursuit** *becomes scattered throughout strings and woodwinds as the storm becomes wilder, the bass tubas shouting out the perfect intervals of the motive associated with* **Donner**, *god of thunder. A slashing, descending dotted rhythm suggests the violence of lightning, with the repetitions of it progressively softer as the violence of the storm recedes.*

The interior of the main room of Hunding's dwelling. In its center is a huge ash tree, its roots spreading widely, its top boughs passing through holes cut specially for them through the roof of the house. The walls of the room built around the trunk of the tree are made of roughly shaped logs, hung here and there with woven rugs and plaited hangings. Entrances may be seen to an inner chamber and a sort of storeroom, with a half-open hanging separating it from the main room. To the rear is the house's main door, with a simple wooden latch. A broad wooden bench is fastened to the wall; also a table, some stools. In the foreground to one side are a fireplace and hearth.

SCENE I

1 Siegmund enters, exhausted and disheveled from running through the storm. Seeing no one, he throws himself down on a bearskin by the fire and lies there, stretched out and motionless. Sieglinde enters from the inner room; astonished to see a stranger there, she quietly steps toward him and bends over him, concerned at his evident exhaustion. Siegmund suddenly raises his head and asks for drink; she quickly gets him a horn of water.

The storm ends in a series of rising scales, interrupted suddenly by Siegmund. *The dissonant harmonies and battle fanfare (French horns and trumpets) of* Siegmund *suggest his exhaustion from combat; occasional recalls of the storm's scales derived from* Spear *remind us that his flight and arrival at this particular place are under the influence of Wotan. A halting rhythm suggests Sieglinde's tentative entrance; her concern is reflected in* Sieglinde *(violins; see Ex. WA-3).*

2 Siegmund drinks thirstily. As he signs his thanks with his head, he gazes at her with growing interest, then expresses his gratitude verbally and inquires as to the identity of this beautiful woman who has served him. Sieglinde tells him that "this house and wife belong to Hunding" (*Dies Haus und dies Weib / sind Hundings Eigen*). When Siegmund suggests that, being weaponless and wounded, he ought not to trouble her husband, she is at once solicitous about his injuries.

The attraction between the two Volsungs is expressed by a cello, its melody drawing on Volsung Love *and* Love *and its solo character hinting at intimacy and thoughts unspoken. The* Sieglinde *motive dominates until her explanation that this is Hunding's house—her simple statement is reminiscent of the rhythm of* Hunding. *A dotted-rhythm treatment of* Spear *punctuates her* Die Wunden weise mir schnell *("Show me your wounds at once"), indicating a sympathy directly related to Wotan's influence and heritage.*

3 Siegmund: *Gering sind sie . . .* ("Slight are they . . . ") He sits up quickly, assuring her his injuries are slight and that, had not his spear and shield been shattered in his recent conflict, he would not have fled. But, he tells her, his faintness has gone and *die Sonne lacht mir nun neu* ("Sunshine now smiles on me anew"). Sieglinde brings him a horn of mead, offering it with friendly eagerness. He asks her to let it touch her lips first; she takes a sip, then he takes a full draught. As he lets the horn sink slowly, his face shows strong feeling and he sighs deeply, lowering his gaze despondently to the floor.

Diminutions of Spear's *dotted-rhythm and snippets of* Pursuit *give way to the loveliness of returns of* Sieglinde *and the fragments of the* Love *theme (found later in their songs of spring).*

4 Siegmund: *Einen Unseligen labtest du* ("You have comforted an ill-fated person") Noting that misfortune follows him, he gets up to leave. She asks why he must flee; he answers that he must not bring evil upon her. Impetuously she calls to him to stay, since he could not bring misfortune to a house where misfortune already dwells. Touched, Siegmund remains where he is, his intent gaze causing Sieglinde to lower her eyes. He returns to the hearth. During a long silence, the two look steadily at each other, with expressions of deep feeling.

Abrupt, irregular phrases in the orchestra accompany his recitative-like declamation.
Volsung Sorrow *(cellos and basses),* Sieglinde, *and* Pursuit *are quietly commingled, syncopations above* Volsung Sorrow *hinting at the stirrings of unnamed emotions in both Siegmund and Sieglinde.*

SCENE II

5 Hunding enters but stops abruptly when he sees the strange man in his house. To his sternly questioning look, Sieglinde tells him of the man's arrival in weakened state and that she had assured him of Hunding's hospitality. Siegmund confirms that she had brought him food and drink, for which surely she would be free of reproach.

Wagner tubas announce Hunding *and its characteristic minor mode; snippets of* Pursuit *establish the connection of Hunding's kinsmen with Siegmund's flight. Sieglinde's earlier tentativeness, established above by separated two-note phrases, is now made tremulous and fearful by triplets. Her explanation is in unaccompanied recitative.*

6 Hunding: *Heilig ist mein Herd: / heilig sei dir mein Haus* ("Sacred is my hearth, sacred must my house be to you") Hunding guarantees hospitality, then orders a meal to be served, noting silently the similarity between his wife and the stranger, both of whom have a brightness of eye like a "glittering snake" (*gleissende Wurm*). Hiding his thoughts, Hunding asks how his guest managed to find his way to this abode. Siegmund answers that he has been driven by the storm and does not know where he is. Hunding identifies himself and asks for identification in return. Observing the apparent interest and sympathy of Sieglinde, Hunding repeats his request.

Hunding's formal hospitality (Ex. WA-7) has lyric breadth, but it is the music of the first half of Ring: *he thinks of power, not love. The* Hunding *motive is developed as he sits for his meal; the violins return with* Sieglinde *as his suspicions grow; the dissonance in low clarinets and bassoons uses the tritone[12] to accompany his thoughts of a glittering snake. His inquiries and Siegmund's answers are recitatives with orchestral punctuations drawn from* Hunding.

7 Siegmund's narrative: *Friedmund darf ich nicht heissen* ("No one may ever call me 'Peaceful'") Siegmund responds that no one should call him by a name signifying contentment or happiness (*Frohwalt*)—instead, his name should be "Woeful" (*Wehwalt*). He relates how, after one of his hunts with his father Wälse, he had returned home to find his mother killed and his twin sister borne off. Thereafter, he and his father had wandered the forest, hunting, living as outlaws, and battling against enemies who came to know him as *Wölfing* ("Wolfcub").

To Sieglinde's question as to where his father is now, he tells of his father's disappearance after one of the many battles, leaving only a wolf skin behind. He had then tried to mingle with warriors and women but was rejected everywhere, his values of good and evil continually at odds with those of other people.

The narrative is introduced by cellos softly intoning Volsung Sorrow. *His tale of hunting is given spirited French horn triplets, but the orchestral depiction of the dreadful sight that greeted him on returning from an expedition is hollow, just as his life was suddenly made empty: a solitary French horn note is sustained under his broken phrases. That the Neidung tribe is related to his host is underscored by* Hunding *and the development of a motive from it (especially death-like in the timpani). The rhythmic movement quickens as he tells of the battles fought by father and son*

---

[12] See Chapter 3, note 3.

The father's identity resonates in the richness of trombones for **Valhalla.** *Siegmund's search for female companionship gains poignance from a clarinet's sweet sounding of the second phrase of* **Love.** *The turmoil of his life of rejection is reflected in dense part work in the strings, and echoes of* **Hunding.**

8 Siegmund: *Ein trauriges Kind / rief mich zum Trutz* ("A sad child called to me for help") After another sympathetic question from Sieglinde, Siegmund continues his story: coming upon a girl being forced into an unwanted marriage and hearing her cries for help, he went to her aid, killing many of her kinsmen. Even though her cries changed to lamentations for her dead relatives, he continued to fight for her. He was then attacked from all sides but was able to shelter her until his weapons were hacked from his hand. Unarmed, he saw the maid killed by her kin, then he fled for his life.

Siegmund's tale of coming to the defense of the girl is dynamic, its melodic triplets and orchestral sorties vividly pictorial. The attack from all sides is narrated to an expansion of the **Hunding** *rhythm, beginning with repeated notes in low strings but quickly adding higher pitch levels;* **Siegmund's** *escape occasions a recall of* **Pursuit** *and the scales of the act's opening storm music. His tale concludes with the pride of* **Volsung Race** *bracketed by recalls of* **Volsung Sorrow.**

9 Hunding: *Ich weiss ein wildes Geschlecht* ("I know of a wild family") Dark with anger, Hunding realizes that his guest is the very man whom he had been summoned by his tribe to fight against; having arrived at the dreadful scene too late, Hunding had returned home only to find the villain in his own house. The vows of hospitality, he avers, will be honored, but on the next day the man's blood will pay for the blood of Hunding's friends. Hunding orders Sieglinde from the room and to prepare his drink for the night.

Hunding's rage is expressed in violent accents and blunt phrases, fragments of his motive continually pointing his threats. Sieglinde anxiously steps between the enemies to a hurried expansion of her motive (**Sieglinde,** *therefore also her compassion), but Hunding's curt order cuts it off.*

10 Sieglinde stands aside thoughtfully, goes to a cupboard, fills a drinking horn, then shakes some spices into it. She looks at Siegmund, who has never stopped looking at her. Seeing that Hunding is watching, she turns toward the bedchamber but pauses on the steps to indicate with her eyes a spot on the trunk of the tree. Hunding starts and drives her from the room with a violent gesture. With one final look, Sieglinde enters the inner chamber; Hunding takes his weapons from the tree and follows her, coldly reminding Siegmund that on the morrow he will need to guard himself well. He closes the door to the bedroom, locking it from within.

An orchestral interlude presents an altered version, in slow tempo, of **Sieglinde,** *first in clarinet then in English horn. These are archetypical instruments of the nineteenth century for depiction of loneliness and psychological isolation; thus, while the original meaning of the motive was compassion, here the instrumentation and rhythmic augmentation add levels of sadness common to both Siegmund and Sieglinde. As she prepares the drugged drink,* **Sieglinde** *(i.e., compassion) occurs in its usual violin timbre. During the interlude, cellos and basses throb softly. When she tries to get Siegmund to see the sword in the tree, a tremolo begins in the violas as accompaniment to the bass trumpet sounding* **Sword.** *The* **Hunding** *motive is, as usual, a coarse rupture of the mood.*

SCENE III

11 In the darkening room, with only a slight glow from the dying fire, Siegmund broods silently; then, in great agitation, he remembers that his father had promised him a great weapon when the hour of his deepest need finally came (*Ein Schwert verhiess mir der Vater*). That hour clearly is now, as he is unarmed in his enemy's house, and his heart is assailed by new emotions occasioned by the beautiful woman who is a slave in her own home. He calls passionately on Wälse, his father, asking desperately for the promised sword. Suddenly the fire collapses; its dazzling reflection from a spot on the trunk of the tree reminds him of the woman's gleaming eyes and the warmth her look occasioned in him, like the sun after the darkness. The fire goes out and the room is completely dark.

Timpani offer the death motive. To powerfully accented tremolos and sudden swells of strings, Siegmund remembers the promised sword by singing its motive altered to the minor mode. By recalls of the Hunding *rhythm, Wagner tubas point up his desperate situation and lend bitter frustration to his lyric thoughts of the woman he has just met. Siegmund's cries to his father are to the descending octave of the start of* Sword. *The trumpet calls of* Sword *beam from a welter of tremolos when the fire's glow reflects from the weapon in the tree; his thoughts of the woman whose bright eyes gave him warmth and light are given harp arpeggios, flowing 6/4 rhythm, and quotations of* Sword. *The darkness becomes oppressive with the return of the* Hunding/Death *motive.*

12 Sieglinde: *Schläfst du, Gast?* ("Guest, are you asleep?") Sieglinde enters quietly. She informs him that Hunding is deep in drugged sleep. There is a weapon awaiting if only he could claim it, she reveals, and then she would be able to proclaim him the noblest of heroes.

Sparse chords, then a rise of flowing triplets mark her whispers and tiptoed entry into the room. As introduction to her tale, a rising fanfare associated with the battle cry of Volsung Victory *mounts with repressed excitement from the woodwinds and French horns.*

13 Sieglinde's narrative: *Der Männer Sippe / sass hier im Sall, / von Hunding zur Hochzeit geladen* ("The men of his kindred sat in this room to witness Hunding's wedding") She relates how, at her forced marriage to Hunding, an old man dressed in gray, with his hat pulled down over one eye, glared at all with a terrifying flash from his other eye; then, with a tender look at her, he thrust a sword deep into the tree. When none of the warriors could remove it, she knew who it was who had come and what the meaning of the sword was. If only she could find here and now the friend[13] (*O fänd' ich ihn heut / und hier, den Freund*) for whom the sword was intended, then all her sorrow and shame would find sweetest revenge (*süsseste Rache*). If only, she concludes, she could find *den heiligen Freund, / umfing' den Helden mein Arm!* ("that divine lover, and encircle that hero in her arms!").

The alliterative poetry of the narrative begins simply; Valhalla *(French horns, bassoons) identifies the man who arrived. That his hat is pulled low is described to notes low in the voice; his tender look is reflected in music not far removed from the sequence of shifting harmonies to be used later in Act III, when Wotan casts Brünnhilde into deep slumber.* Sword *of course figures prominently in Sieglinde's story. Her excitement grows to repeated fragments of* Valhalla; *her cry of earnest desire to find her "friend" is to an outburst of the* Volsung Victory *fanfare in winds and brass, with violins exuberantly providing sparkling scales and rolling arpeggios.*

14 Siegmund: *Dich, selige Frau, / hält nun der Freund* ("Blessed woman, that friend holds you now") Siegmund embraces her, vowing that he is that man and that all he has sought he finds in her. Shame has been hers, woe has been his, he despised and she scorned, but now *freudige Rache / ruft nun den Frohen!* ("joyous revenge calls now on the rejoicers!").

Siegmund embraces her to an expansion of Volsung Race *and roiling string figurations.*

---

[13] In medieval poetry, lovers would use the word "friend" to refer to the beloved. Sieglinde is not thinking just of an ally or rescuer in this urgent passage.

15 A gust of wind blows open the door, allowing the moonlight of the glorious spring night to shine in, revealing each clearly to the other. Sieglinde, frightened, asks who has gone or come.

A blast of trumpets and trombones heralds the sudden swinging wide of the door.

16 Siegmund's Spring Song: *Winterstürme wichen / dem Wonnemond, / in mildem Lichte / leuchtet der Lenz* ("Winter storms have yielded to the month of May, in gentle light smiles the Spring"[14]) Drawing her to him on the bench so that she sits beside him, Siegmund rhapsodizes on the meaning of this moment in their lives: Spring has driven away the harshness of winter and has shattered the doors that have kept them apart. Now Spring embraces its sister, Love, and, having freed her, unites with her.

The song's effect (Ex. WA-1) derives from a floating triplet rhythm accompanied by purling string figurations and gentle syncopations; countermelodies shared by clarinet and oboe add to the magic. As the song progresses, additional woodwind colors are added, drawing on the "battle" figure of the motive of Siegmund's first appearance. The defeat of the rigors of winter and storm by the fragile weapons of Spring are given active dotted rhythms that suggest the battle fought and won. At the high point of the song, flute, oboe, and clarinet give out the second part of Love, with Siegmund's song immediately taking up its first part (at Zu seiner Schwester / schwang er sich her—"to his sister here he flew"). Volsung Victory returns; Die bräutliche Schwester / befreite der Bruder ("The bridal sister is liberated by her brother") is given militant music similar to the earlier allegory of Spring beating back the forces of winter. The song's climax is achieved with lustrous harp arpeggios and soaring vocal line.

17 Sieglinde's Spring Song: *Du bist der Lenz, / nach dem ich verlangte / in frostigen Winters Frist* ("You are the Spring for which I have longed during the icy cold of Winter") Proclaiming that he is the subject of all her fondest hopes, she avers that before this moment all around her had been alien and friendless (*Fremdes nur sah ich von je, / freundlos war mir das Nahe*) but that she knew he was the one intended for her when first she saw him. She embraces him rapturously.

The sweeping introduction swells immediately from the end of Siegmund's song. The primary motive of Du bist der Lenz *(Example WA-3b) is the first segment of the Love motive; she soon takes up its second segment, all to the swirling excitement of violin scales and other patterns. Her memory of alienation and unfamiliarity with all around her halts the rush of the music momentarily but* Doch dich kannt' ich / deutlich und klar *("Yet I knew you clearly and plainly") returns to the* Love *motive ("b"), surging music, and rich orchestration.*

18 Siegmund: *O süsseste Wonne* ("Oh sweetest rapture") The two sit in a blissful embrace, sharing thoughts of tenderness and love. She looks intently at him, brushing the hair back from his brow, sure that she has seen his face before, in the stream where she has seen her own reflection. She remembers his voice from her childhood, and his "gleaming glance" (*Auges Glut*) reminds her of the gaze of the man who came to her wedding.

Their rapture is voiced in the motives of Bliss *and* Love*. The stirring of her memory is echoed in fragments of* Valhalla *and* Volsung Race.

19 Sieglinde: *Wehwalt heisst du fürwahr?* ("Are you really called 'Woeful'?") Some urgent and quick questioning ensues: "Is your name *Wehwalt* and would you like

---

[14] Wagner's choice of words is particularly affective: "Wonnemond" is literally the "moon [month] of ecstasy" and "Lenz" characterizes the warmth and bloom of that period of time rather than simply the calendrical season of "Frühling" ("spring"). The etymology of old Norse and Teutonic words for the seasons and their relations to Wagner's expressive use is discussed by Cord, *Teutonic Mythology*, III, Part 2, pp. 386ff.

to be called *Friedmund* ('Peaceful')? Was Wälse your father? Full recognition is achieved, and she returns his rightful name to him: *Siegmund! So nenn' ich dich!*

Her questioning is quiet at first; when she turns to the subject of Wälse, the battle figure of Siegmund *stirs up the tempo and the music's intensity. A brief touch of* Valhalla *is overwhelmed by boiling triplets of excitement in voice and orchestra. Her "Siegmund" is like a great trumpet call.*

20 Siegmund: *Siegmund heiss' ich / und Siegmund bin ich* ("Siegmund I am named and Siegmund I am") Exultantly calling aloud his name, he rushes to the tree and grasps the hilt of sword. Affirming it as the weapon promised at the time of his greatest need (*Heiligster Minne höchste Not* ("Holiest love's deepest need") and acclaiming it as *Notung* ("Child of Need"), Siegmund draws the sword from the tree. He shows it to the astonished and enraptured Sieglinde, vowing to lead her away from this house and calling her to follow him to the bright land of Spring. He embraces her as if to draw her away with him.

Rattling triplets in winds and brass, the dotted rhythm of Volsung Race, *and* Sword *provide a thrilling counterpoint to Siegmund's acceptance of his name and his preparation to pull the weapon from the tree. His acclamation of the* Sword (Heiligste Minne . . .) *is to* Renunciation *and thus illuminates his part and the Sword's symbolism in the progress toward a world ruled by love rather than by greed or ambition. The richness of implication is heightened by dramatic dynamic changes and chromatically rising tremolos that accompany it. Siegmund repeatedly intones* Notung *on the octave interval of* Sword; *the moment of drawing the sword is acclaimed by its triumphant trumpet call, with lush tremolos and arpeggios swirling around it. He urges Sieglinde to go off with him to echoes of* Spring Song *and* Love.

21 Sieglinde: *Bist du Siegmund, / den ich hier sehe?* ("Are you Siegmund, you whom I see here?") She steps back in highest excitement and identifies herself as Sieglinde, the sister and the bride he has won with the sword. To a full-throated *Braut und Schwester / bist du dem Bruder / so blühe denn, Wälsungenblut!* ("Bride and sister are you to your brother, thus let the blood of the Volsungs blossom!), he embraces her with passionate fervor. The curtain falls quickly.

Sieglinde identifies herself ecstatically to the violins' repeated and ever rising Bliss. *The two rush into the night to a thunderous coda featuring wild figuration,* Sword, *and a diminution in the high violins of her* Du bist der Lenz.

Act II

PRELUDE *The stormy fusion of* Sword *and* Love *depict the flight of Siegmund and Sieglinde and also the passionate consummation of their love. The frenzy abates momentarily until the motive of* Bliss, *starting with a smaller interval then gradually expanding to its definitive form, brings matters to a head again. There is a dramatic transition from this stormy music via a heavily accented descent of dotted rhythms, with the* Death *motive thudding in the trombones and tubas, to the rising of the* Valkyries *in the trombones and bass trumpet.*

A wild, craggy pass in the mountains. A high peak dominates the scene, with a gorge seen leading down from it toward the rear and the forepart of the stage sloping up toward it.

SCENE I

22 Wotan: *Nun zäume dein Ross, / reisige Maid* ("Now bridle your horse, warrior maid") Wotan, in full battle array, orders Brünnhilde to ride to Siegmund's aid and help him to victory. Hunding, unworthy of Valhalla, is to be left dead on the field of combat. Shouting the Valkyrie *Battle Cry*, Brünnhilde leaps from rock to rock toward the peak,[15] stopping suddenly when she sees Fricka furiously driving her chariot toward them. Half-humorously commenting that she prefers *Männer Schlacht* ("the battle of men") to domestic strife, Brünnhilde departs hurriedly.

Wotan's battle lust (Ex. WA-9a) is a mix of quick descending trumpet-like triads and fast descending scales derived from Spear. The Valkyrie Battle Cry is related to Love ("a") in its contour—Valkyries are, after all, agents of Wotan's desire, hence his love children—but the bold intervals, angular melody, dotted rhythm, tempo, and dynamic level—it's always loud—make it a militant yell. Rolling triplets, Pursuit, and a parody of Bliss illustrate Fricka's obsessed driving. Brünnhilde takes her leave to the music of the Battle Cry, snippets of Valkyrie Ride, and the chromatic descent associated with the Valkyries' fiery demeanor and steeds.

23 Wotan: *Der alte Sturm, / die alte Müh'* ("The old storm, the ancient strife") As Fricka strides imperiously toward him, Wotan, muttering that once again he must face domestic conflict, readies himself for Fricka's blasts. They come at once: Fricka having heard Hunding's call and sworn to fulfill her role as the guardian of marriage, demands punishment for those who have wronged a husband and insulted her. Wotan's falsely innocent "What so wrong have the pair committed, these lovers joined by Spring?" (*Was so Schlimmes / schuf das Paar, / das liebend einte der Lenz?*) is quickly brushed aside and so is his suggestion that marriage without love is a meaningless vow. Fricka demolishes Wotan's evasion with her caustic "When has it ever come to pass that brother and sister would be lovers?" (*Wann ward es erlebt, / dass leiblich Geschwister sich liebten?*)

Fricka's mood is that of Wrath, the woodwinds in shrill cry above the higher strings. Hunding's presence is quickly felt via his motive; Fricka's use of Curse for Ich vernahm Hunding's Not, / um Rache rief er mich an reminds us of Alberich's curse from Das Rheingold (no possessor of the Ring will enjoy happiness) and thus foretells the gloom in Wotan's future. Wotan's cynicism uses Love (Ex. WA-3b). Fricka's first retort is to Hunding's sense of hospitality (Ex. WA-7); her Wann war es erlebt. . . ("When has it ever come to pass. . .") is to a manipulation of Curse, with vivid pointing by whipping segments of scales derived from the bass line of Hunding.

24 Wotan: *Heut—hast du's erlebt!* ("Today—you have lived to see it!") Wotan answers that it has happened now, that things without precedent can occur, and that, since she is the patroness of lovers, she should bestow her blessing on Siegmund and Sieglinde's love.

Wotan responds with studied restraint and sweetness, accompanied by the cellos' recall of the love music of the two Spring Songs (see Ex. WA-9b).

25 Fricka explodes: *So ist es denn aus / mit den ewigen Göttern?* ("Is this the end of the eternal gods?") She vehemently reminds Wotan that he has forgotten his obligations and has cast aside his treaties and laws so that these twins, born as "the fruit of your immoral infidelity" (*deiner Untreue zuchtlose Frucht*) may enjoy their incestuous pleasure.

A tremolando scale jets from the strings and erupts into the wind/string dissonances of Wrath.

26 Fricka's lament: *O, was klag ich / um Ehe und Eid, / da zuerst du selbst sie versehrt* ("Oh, why do I sorrow over marriage and vows when you yourself were the first to betray them?") Grieving and resentful, Fricka launches into an indictment of

---

15 ↓

Wotan's sexual excursions and betrayals of her. Until now, she complains, she has at least been respected and even those "wretched girls . . . the Valkyrie herd" (*schlimmen Mädchen . . . der Walküren Schar*) have obeyed her. But now Wotan has stooped to the abyss of dishonor by siring whelps from a she-wolf[16]—he might as well fill Fricka's cup and trample even further the wife he has betrayed.

Wrath mingles with Fricka's arioso phrase that twists the first motive of Love in a way that is both agonizing and parodistic (Ex. WA-10a). Triplet figurations in the violins and violas writhe throughout her lament. The interval climaxing her jetzt dem Wurfe der Wölfin / wirfst du zu Füssen dein Weib! *("now at the feet of a she-wolf's litter you would throw your wife!") is a tritone, the archetype interval of betrayal. Her accusation ends, not surprisingly, with another fully orchestrated explosion of* Wrath.

27 Wotan: *Nichts lerntest du* ("You have learned nothing") Wotan tries to calm things down by pointing out that Fricka has never been able to understand larger meanings and future implications of events in spite of his efforts to teach her. All she understands is custom and tradition. He tries to explain his plan: a free hero must be found to accomplish deeds needed by the gods but denied to them.

Wotan's attempt to rationalize his actions begins patiently: he sings in recitative with virtually no accompaniment. As he turns to the serious matters before him (Ex. WA-9c), Sword *(bass trumpet),* Treaty *(i.e.,* Spear; *cellos and basses), and* Ring *(clarinets and bassoons) make their presence felt softly.*

28 Fricka: *Mit tiefem Sinne / willst du mich täuschen* ("With deep thoughts you want to confuse me") Fricka suspects deceit. This Volsung, she avers, is no free hero, only Wotan's agent. Wotan's defense—that Siegmund had to grow up by himself, without help from him—is at once deflated: if he is truly independent, says Fricka, let him be independent now and have the sword taken back.

Fricka and Wotan exchange tuneless thrust and riposte, with spurts of Wrath, Treaty *, and, when Fricka demands* Nimm ihm das Schwert / das du ihm geschenkt *("Take from him the sword that you gave him"),* Sword. *The crucial moment comes with this statement, for the sword is the symbol of Wotan's direct intervention: Siegmund is not free and therefore cannot serve the ultimate need of the gods.*

29 Fricka: *Du schufst ihm die Not* ("You created the need for him") Wotan from this point on recognizes his defeat and becomes ever more morose. Fricka drives her point home relentlessly: the creation of the Sword and the winning of it were all Wotan's doing. Wrathful gestures from Wotan are to no avail; seeing her logic winning, Fricka presses on, and insists that a mere mortal must be a slave to her and may not be allowed to humiliate her.

It is at this point that Dejection/Frustration *is first heard (bassoon and bass clarinet over a deep and hushed tremolo). The vehement fanfare of* Wrath *and the stirring of unrest through syncopations and dissonances inform much that follows, but the* Dejection *motive is pervasive.*

30 Wotan: *Was verlangst du?* ("What do you want?") Fricka's answer to Wotan's asking for the terms of surrender is a firm *Lass von dem Wälsung!* ("Abandon the Volsung!"). In deep gloom, Wotan agrees. She insists that the Valkyrie must be commanded to let Siegmund die and the magic of the Sword must be broken. Brünnhilde's call is heard; as Wotan dejectedly notes that Brünnhilde has been summoned to go to Siegmund's aid, the Valkyrie appears but stops suddenly and, tethering her horse in a nearby cave, observes the seriousness of the situa-

---

16 The play on words is on Wotan's having walked the earth with the name *Wälse* ("wolf").

tion. Fricka presses on: Brünnhilde must shelter Fricka's honor—will Wotan give his oath on it? In terrible dejection, Wotan submits: *Nimm den Eid!* ("Take my oath!"). Fricka takes imperious leave, passing Brünnhilde with nose high in the air: the warlord, she tells Brünnhilde, will give his orders.

Wotan's Was verlangst du? *is low in pitch, halting in rhythm; a violent dissonance marks the end of his question and her triumphant* Lass von dem Wälsung! *Dejection sounds, then his broken-rhythm* Er geh' seines Weg's *("He goes along his own path"; Ex. WA-8d). Irregularly spaced chords help hammer down her case. The coming of Brünnhilde is announced via the several* Valkyrie *motives and the usual accompanying trill.*

Fricka's aria-like envoi is in the major mode, with a rhythmically steady orchestral background. An ironic use of Spear *precedes her demand for his oath. As low strings offer a rhythmically staggering* Dejection, *Wotan gives his oath a hollow perfect interval, each syllable separated from the others by rests.*

SCENE II

31 Brünnhilde: *Schlimm, fürcht ich, / schloss der Streit* ("Badly, I fear, has the quarrel ended") Seeing Wotan brooding, Brünnhilde goes to him slowly and asks the cause of his mood. Wotan's answer is an outburst of shame (*Schmach*), divine distress (*Götternot*), eternal remorse (*endloser Grimm*), and everlasting grief (*ewiger Gram*). Frightened, Brünnhilde throws down her spear, shield, and helmet and kneels at his feet, laying her head and hands on his lap. Wotan looks long and lovingly in her face, stroking her hair gently. She asks what has filled him with such dismay and to confide in her, since she is at one with his will. When he talks to her, he admits, he is only talking to himself.

Brünnhilde quietly draws near as Dejection *plods its way in low winds and cellos. The motive erupts in inversion, its violent rise framing the bass trumpet's recall of the curse and Wotan's* O heilige Schmach! *("Oh solemn shame!"). His outburst is studded with* Wrath *and the savagely ironic quote of the first unit of the* Love *motive (WA-3b) for* Endlose Grimm *("endless rage") and* ewiger Gram *("eternal remorse"). When he calms down, the bass clarinet dolefully presents more of the* Love *theme. His gentle response, acknowledging her oneness with himself, turns to the soothing major mode and held chords in the warm sonority of French horns.*

32 Wotan's narrative: *Als junger Liebe / Lust mir verblich, / verlangte nach Macht mein Mut* ("When the joy of youthful love faded, my spirit longed for power") Wotan relates the story of his enlisting the craft of Loge, of engaging in wrongful treaties to win the world, of Alberich's theft of the gold and shaping from it the ring, and of Wotan's theft of the ring to pay for Valhalla.

He begins in somber recitative above sparse orchestration: only basses at first, then but a handful of cellos and basses with touches of low brass for Dejection *(see also Ex. 9.4a) and bassoons for* Ring. *Trombones, then tubas intone* Valhalla, *while a bass trumpet mutters the triplet version of the* Death *archetype.*

33 *Die alles weiss, / was einstens war, / Erda, die weihlich weiseste / Wala* ("She who knows all that ever was, Erda, the sacred all-wise Wala"[17]) He tells of seeking out Erda, goddess of the earth, and compelling her to give him wisdom. To divert her prophecy of doom, he forced her to conceive the nine Valkyries who were to assemble an army to be made up of mortals who, as a result of Wotan's treacherous treaties and shameful agreements, were bound to serve him blindly. The Valkyries were to stir them to strife and to gather them in Valhalla.

---

[17] *Wala* allows for no exact translation beyond a generic reference to the ancient Norse imagery of the all-knowing female figure. See Cord, *Teutonic Mythology,* III, pp. 497ff.

Erda's rising motive is given to clarinets. An obsessive repetition of Dejection *and a return to the minor illuminate his visiting her to force knowledge from her; Erda's giving birth to Brünnhilde* (der Welt weisestes Weib / gebar mir, Brünnhilde, dich—*"the world's wisest woman bore to me, Brünnhilde, you") is given the gentle accent of* Love *("a"); Valkyrie rhythms, and the major mode point up the birth of the other sisters and the enslavement of mortals, as low winds intone the duplet version of* Death *(Ex. 4.4c).*

34 *Ein Andres ist's: / achte es wohl, / was mich die Wala gewarnt!* (There is something else: listen carefully to what the Wala warned me about!") Wotan narrates Erda's foretelling of Alberich's plans to regain the ring and of the doom of the gods should Alberich succeed. The ring, he continues, is now possessed by the dragon Fafner, one of the giants who had built Valhalla and had been paid with the gold, ring, and magic helmet stolen from Alberich. Wotan must regain the ring from Fafner but cannot because of his promise to Fafner not to harm him.

A slower tempo, the minor mode, the brooding of Ring, *and the ornamented first note of* Dejection/Frustration *color Wotan's turn of his tale to Alberich;* Treaty *underlies his inability to wrest the* Ring *(motive, of course) from Fafner.*

35 *Nur Einer könnte, / was ich nicht darf* ("There is only one who could do what I could not do") He then tells Brünnhilde of the need for a hero who owes nothing to the gods, is free of their entanglements, and who can act fearlessly and wholly independently. "How am I to find him?" he cries (*wie fände ich ihn?*). In terrible despair, Wotan sees no answer, no hope, "For he must fashion his freedom himself, I can only make slaves!" (*denn selbst muss der Freie sich schaffen; / Knechte erknet ich mir nur!*).

In answer to her question, he informs her that Siegmund is not free: even though Wotan had brought him up to be a rebel, Siegmund's sword is god-given. Fricka knows this and Wotan has had to admit his defeat.

Wotan's plan is narrated to faster tempo and a more complex array of motives: syncopations associated with Alberich lend turmoil, first to the symphonic fusion of Dejection *and* Sword, *then the relentless dotted rhythms of* Need of the Gods. *Increasing rhythmic and dynamic urgency characterize the progress to another outburst: the one who must make himself free is identified by the strings giving forth* Volsung Victory, *but* Dejection *quickly smothers it and the trumpet's attempt to proclaim* Sword *is cut off after two notes.*

36 Brünnhilde: *So nimmst du von Siegmund den Sieg?* ("Then you must take victory away from Siegmund?") When Brünnhilde asks if Siegmund must indeed perish, Wotan acknowledges that, having grasped Alberich's ring, he is subject to the curse of eternal misfortune: he must forsake and murder his beloved son.

Tremolos and abrupt accents underscore Wotan's wretchedness and dire frustration, as does the quick succession of Ring, Curse, Sword, *and turbulent strings.*

37 Wotan: *Fahre denn hin / herrische Pracht* ("Away then with noble pomp") Wotan yields to terrible despair and now wishes only for all to be over (*das Ende, / das Ende!*). He turns his thoughts to Erda's prophecy that, "'when the dark foe of Love begets a son'" (*Wenn der Liebe finstrer Feind / zürnend zeugt einen Sohn*) the doom of the gods is nigh, noting that he has indeed learned of a woman pregnant with Alberich's son.

The orchestral and vocal fury continues, reaching its peak on Wotan's high F and then a sudden rhythmic and melodic collapse. His repeat of das Ende *is followed by a variant of Erda's ascending motive.[18] His telling of her prediction (Ex. 4.4e) is given bite by the*

---

[18] This variant is presented in *Das Rheingold* as a suggestion of premonition and acquisition of the knowledge that leads the psyche away from natural instincts.

snarling syncopated thirds (low winds, with bitingly short surges in low strings) associated with the grinding, lightless life of the Nibelung dwarfs.

38 Wotan: *So nimm meinen Segen* ("So take my blessing") Rising in bitter anger, Wotan invites Alberich to claim his victory and orders Brünnhilde to carry out Fricka's will. Brünnhilde's urgent plea to relent is rejected.

Wotan's blessing of Alberich and his son distorts Valhalla *into a violent fanfare of triplets (*Death*). Brünnhilde's plea uses the* Du bist der Lenz *figure (at* Du liebst Siegmund— *"you love Siegmund"), accompanying it with* Dejection *and troubled but lyrical string triplets. Wotan's rejection converts these triplets to powerful fanfares.*

39 Brünnhilde: *Den du zu lieben / stets mich gelehrt* ("You have constantly taught me to love him") Brünnhilde claims she will defy her father and refuses to kill Siegmund. Wotan berates her furiously, warning that he will crush her if she disobeys and that she must fear his awesome anger. Ordering her again to carry out his will, he storms away, disappearing quickly. Brünnhilde sadly resigns herself to do as bid.

Brünnhilde's threat of defiance (Ex. WA-9a) is to the rhythmic confusion of duplets against triplets and complex part work in the instruments, all suggestive of her being torn and uncertain; her music here is thus similar to her plea. Livid tremolos, turbulent rhythms, Spear, *and fragments of* Wrath *define Wotan's anger and dire warning. The orchestral vehemence signifying Wotan's departure is based on* Need of the Gods *with the intense accompaniment of rushing scale ascents and downward arpeggios; the rhythms of* Wrath *are violent. The concluding* Dejection *begins roughly but quickly diminishes for Brünnhilde's brief recitative. Her resolve to do Wotan's bidding is set out by the* Death *motive in the timpani and by* Valkyrie Ride *in trombones and bass trumpet.*

SCENE III

40 Seeing the approach of Sieglinde and Siegmund, Brünnhilde conceals herself in the cave. Siegmund attempts to restrain and calm the frenzied Sieglinde, who has been rushing ahead of him in her terror. He draws her gently to him; she embraces him ardently then suddenly starts up once more in panic.

The approach of Siegmund and Sieglinde reprises the Act II Prelude's anxious treatments of Love *and* Bliss, *as does her hysteria and his attempts to calm her.*

41 Sieglinde: *Hinweg! hinweg! / Flieh die Entweihte!* ("Away! Shun the defiled one!") Sieglinde reviles her body as unworthy of Siegmund: she has been dishonored (*entehrt*), violated (*geschändet*); her body now is dead (*schwand dieser Leib*) and she, who had found such delight in his arms, has disgraced their love by having been owned as wife and lying loveless in Hunding's arms. Siegmund vows to avenge her wrongs.

Sieglinde's self-condemnation is to interrupted phrases and short, dissonant chords (Ex. WA-6). Love *("a") moves gently among various timbres; agitated strings describe her disgust at having to submit to Hunding's desires. Siegmund's response is emphasized by* Volsung Victory *and* Sword.

42 Sieglinde: *Horch! die Hörner! / Hörst du den Ruf?* ("Hark! the horns, do you hear their call?") Sieglinde hears Hunding's horn call and his summoning kinsman to his aid. Gazing madly before her as she hears the howling of his dogs, she begs Siegmund not to disdain her. She throws herself sobbing on his breast only to start up again in terror as the imagery of the dogs tearing at Siegmund's flesh horrifies her. She screams her vision of the Sword splintered, the ash tree destroyed. With cries of *Bruder, mein Bruder! / Siegmund! Ha!*, she faints.

Timpani sound the rhythm of Hunding; *cellos in fast tempo take up the scales of the opera's opening storm music, then the French horns' grace notes and dissonant chords indicate her vision of Hunding's hounds. Ominous scales in dotted rhythms suggest her hysteria even as they evoke the imagery of* Need of the Gods; *the splintering of the sword is vividly conveyed by a diminution of its motive.*

43 Siegmund: *Schwester! Geliebte!* ("Sister! Beloved!") Siegmund listens to her breathing; realizing she still lives, he settles into a sitting posture, letting her slide downward so that her head rests in his lap. There is a long silence, during which Siegmund bends over Sieglinde tenderly and presses a kiss on her brow.

The love music of the opening scene of the opera is recalled in turn by English horn, clarinet, and cellos.

SCENE IV (*TODESVERKÜNDIGUNG*—"ANNUNCIATION OF DEATH")

44 Leading her horse by the bridle, Brünnhilde issues from the cave slowly and solemnly, bearing her spear and shield in one hand, the other resting on her horse's neck. She pauses and observes Siegmund for a time, then draws closer, regarding him gravely.

Brünnhilde's approach is marked by Fate *(Wagner tubas),* Death *(timpani), and* Annunciation of Death *(trumpet).*

45 Brünnhilde: *Siegmund! / Sieh auf mich! / Ich bin's / der bald du folgst* ("Siegmund! Look upon me! I am the one whom soon you follow") She calls to him quietly to follow her. When he asks who she is, she tells him that those doomed to death are the only ones who see her, for her gaze is fatal and those whom she chooses have no choice but to die. Siegmund asks where he will be led; she tells him of Valhalla, where he will be welcomed. In response to his further questions, she informs him that his father Wälse waits there to greet him and that wish maidens hold sway there (*Wunschmädchen / walten dort hehr*); Wotan's daughter will bear his cup.

French horns and bassoons provide a Valhalla *fragment as a hymn-like introduction to her summons.* Valhalla, Fate, *and* Annunciation *form the fabric of the ensuing dialogue in both voice and orchestra, all of it quiet and somber. The timpani strokes of* Death *are also contributory, as are the touches of* Valkyrie Ride *when she describes the joys of life in Valhalla. The workings of Siegmund's questioning mind find their sound in syncopations given first to woodwinds, then to violas and cellos, and introduce a rhythmic restlessness that subtly alters the mood and flow of the scene.*

46 Siegmund: *Hehr bist du: / und heilig gewahr ich / das Wotanskind* ("Radiant you are: and I recognize Wotan's holy child") Siegmund formally acknowledges Brünnhilde as Wotan's daughter, but his next question is crucial: will Sieglinde accompany him to Valhalla? When Brünnhilde responds that Sieglinde will be left behind and that he will see her no more, Siegmund kisses Sieglinde gently and, turning calmly to Brünnhilde, suggests she greet Valhalla, and all its inhabitants for him, for he will not follow her there.

Siegmund's broad melodic line extends Annunciation; *the underlying syncopations in violas and cellos make it both dignified and urgent. His rejection of Valhalla occasions repeated fragments of the castle's motive; his turning away from the destiny of heroes is noted by his melodic use of* Fate *for his concluding* zu ihnen folg' ich dir nicht! *("to them I follow you not!")*

47 Brünnhilde: *Du sah'st der Walküre / sehrenden Blick* ("You have seen the Valkyrie's baleful glance") She tells him he has no choice, but Siegmund is not intimidated nor is his resolve shaken. When she tells him that death by

Hunding's hand is near, Siegmund's scorn is evident—he will kill *him*. Siegmund calls attention to his sword; when Brünnhilde informs him with loud emphasis that the god who gave him the sword has removed the magic from it, he sharply orders her not to disturb his sleeping sister.

A twisting idea in muted strings, connected with Siegmund's imminent death, is encountered here for the first time as accompaniment to Brünnhilde's response (to the music of Annunciation) *and to Siegmund's growing agitation and bitterness; it will become a prominent element in* Siegfried's Funeral Music *in* Götterdämmerung *(the concluding opera of the cycle).*

48 Siegmund: *Weh! Weh! / Süssestes Weib!* ("Woe! Woe! Sweetest wife!") Siegmund bends over Sieglinde, acknowledging with heavy heart that the one she trusted must leave her alone. Angrily, he calls shame on the one who had given him the sword only to withdraw its power and vows once again not to go to Valhalla even if it means he must descend to Hel.[19]

Muted violas and cellos underlie Siegmund's sad concern for his beloved with gentle triplets that develop the first phrase of Siegmund's Love *(Ex. WA-5). His anger builds musically from this, the triplets rising in pitch and loudness and becoming militant fanfares. Their rhythmic strength is broken as the vocal line angrily twists both* Sword *and* Annunciation. *His final words of willingness to go to* Hel *is followed by cellos and bassoons in a blistering upward scale (a reverse motion of* Spear) *and an immediate quote of the first phrase of* Love, *thus condensing at once the elements of the cycle's conflict between love and ambition for power.*

49 Brünnhilde: *So wenig achtest du / ewige Wonne* ("So cheaply do you value eternal bliss?") Brünnhilde is astonished that he would surrender an eternity in Valhalla for *das arme Weib / das müd' und harmvoll / matt von dem Schosse dir hängt* ("that poor woman who, weak and timorous, droops feebly in your arms") and questions his resolve. When he affirms it, she promises to care for Sieglinde, but Siegmund will not entrust her to anyone: if he must die, he will kill her in her sleep. Brünnhilde's information that she will bear a son does not deter him. Seeing him draw his sword to carry out his intent, Brünnhilde casts off her duty and, in a passionate outburst of sympathy, vows that both of them shall live and that she will side with him in the battle against Hunding.

After the timpani tap the motive of Death *and the strings play* Fate *softly, rhythmic motion quickens in accordance with Brünnhilde's growing compassion and excitement. His affirmation is a diminution of* Annunciation. *Her sympathy intensifies its rhythmic drive still further in the vocal line; the orchestral treatments of it also contribute to the emotional ferment. Rhythmically altered fragments of* Sword *and* Annunciation *mark his move to spare Sieglinde a life of loneliness, but they are overcome by Brünnhilde's joyous, short phrases and, in the orchestra, the transformation of* Annunciation's *gloom, first through exuberant triplets, then vibrant dotted rhythms.*

50 Storm clouds gather and veil the cliffs and crags from view as Brünnhilde rushes off, Siegmund staring after her in exultation. He once more bends over Sieglinde.

The storm's gathering again draws on the diminution of Love *("a") found in the Prelude to Act II.*

SCENE V

51 Siegmund: *Zauberfest / bezähmt ein Schlaf / der Holden Schmerz und Harm* ("Like a magic spell sleep subdues my beloved's tears and pain") Noting that sleep

---

[19] *Sic.* "Hel" is the underworld reserved for the souls of women, children, and those men not selected to reside in Valhalla.

shields her from the horrors of the moment, he lays her gently down. Hearing Hunding's horn-call, he stands determinedly, draws his sword, and heads toward the pass, a flash of lightning breaking from the clouds as he does so.

The second phrase of Love is murmured by muted cellos. Sieglinde's sleep gives rise to the first hint of Slumber (violas), then to cellos recalling Siegmund's Winterstürme (Ex. WA-1). An Alphorn[20] plays the Hunding rhythm from offstage. This rhythm and Sword (in dotted-rhythm diminution) compress the coming fight into a few bars. The jagged rhythm of the music of the lightning is recalled from the opera's opening storm as Siegmund heads off to do battle.

52 Sieglinde: *Kehrte der Vater nur heim!* ("If only Father would come home!") Sieglinde stirs in her dreams, reliving the tragedy of the murder of her mother, the burning of their home, and her abduction. Crying wildly for Siegmund, she awakens and is newly terrified by the breaking of the storm about her. Hunding's call to "Wehwalt" and Siegmund's answering challenge sound from afar. Lightning reveals them locked in battle. Sieglinde rushes toward them screaming to them to stop but she is arrested by an even more brilliant bolt of lightning that staggers and halts her. In the blaze of light, she sees Brünnhilde, hovering above Siegmund and protecting him with her shield. Just as Siegmund aims a deadly blow, a glowing red light breaks through the clouds: Wotan is revealed standing above Hunding and holding his spear in front of Siegmund.

Sieglinde's dream is troubled by the echoes of Hunding as a vicious undercurrent to a development of her Du bist der Lenz (from Act I). A sudden upward chromatic scale mirrors her starting up from sleep. The music recalls the lightning flashes of the Act I storm; Hunding's calls are to the half-note descent found in many operas as a symbol of grief and sorrow. The orchestral action stirs with increasing convulsion: dynamics are ever louder, tempo quickens; tremolos, sudden accents, perfect-intervalled calls from the combatants, manipulations of the motives of Sword, Pursuit, and Valkyrie Ride, and a tumbling array of triplets combine in a musical picture of mortal struggle.

53 Wotan: *Züruck vor dem Speer!* ("Stand back from my spear!") Brünnhilde shrinks back in terror. Siegmund's sword breaks upon contact with Wotan's spear, whereupon Hunding impales Siegmund, who falls lifeless. In the ensuing darkness, Brünnhilde spirits the collapsing Sieglinde away. The clouds part again, revealing Hunding standing above Siegmund's body, and Wotan sadly standing on a rock behind him.

Sword is snapped off by the thundering motive of Wotan's Spear in the heavy brasses and low strings; at the end of Spear, a violent dissonance and its resolution mark the death blow to Siegmund and, at the same time, the agonizing shriek of Woe. Three times this chord sequence is repeated, each time diminishing until there is no breath left in Siegmund's body, just as there is nothing left to the orchestration but a hushed drumroll. Volsung Victory, in the French horns and bassoons, becomes an ironic funeral fanfare. The clouds part to the motive of Fate.

54 Wotan: *Geh' hin, Knecht! / Knie vor Fricka!* ("Go from here, cur! Kneel before Fricka!") With a contemptuous wave, Wotan slays Hunding, snarling to him to kneel before Fricka to inform her that Wotan's spear has worked her revenge. Then, in an outburst of wild fury, Wotan swears punishment for the disobedient Brünnhilde and disappears amid the fury of the tempest.

The contemptuous killing of Hunding is stamped by the Death archetype; a soft reminder in horns and bass trombone recalls the pompous music of Hunding's Act I hospitality (Ex. WA-7). Wotan's hoarse Geh! ("Go!") is slammed home by a plummeting scale and finalized by

---

[20] A wooden trumpet with a very long bore (either S-shaped or slightly turned up at the end), thus very low in pitch and capable of carrying a great distance. It is primarily a signaling instrument among Alpine shepherds, although not unknown elsewhere in Europe.

the thuds of timpani and pizzicato basses. Dejection *begins softly but ends in a crescendo that is a metaphor for Wotan's turn of mind from sadness to fury. The act's final musical tempest uses rising and falling scales (that hark back to both* Spear *and* Need of the Gods*) and fuses the music of lightning with the rhythms of* Wrath. *A bitter wrenching of the* Valhalla *motive leads to the titanically harsh and abrupt final measures.*

Act III

The summit of a rocky mountain; a pinewood and crags to either side, with an open vista to the rear. To one side, a cave entrance. Clouds scud by as if driven by a storm.

Scene I

55 The Valkyries reunite joyously, bringing on the backs of their flying horses the bodies of the heroes they have gathered from various battles, calling to each other as they arrive, and laughing at their several adventures. They wonder where Brünnhilde is, since they dare not arrive at Valhalla without her. Siegrune sees her coming in furious haste. All watch Brünnhilde's approach with astonishment, noting the exhaustion of her horse and that the person on the horse with her is not a dead warrior but a woman. They rush toward the wood where Brünnhilde has landed, then return, Brünnhilde supporting and leading Sieglinde.

The Valkyries' several motives are presented amid a tumult of figures, the heavy brasses of Valkyries' Ride *dominating and cutting through one of music's most familiar orchestral commotions. The dotted-rhythm scale of* Need of the Gods *lends an added dimension to their astonishment over the frenzied approach of Brünnhilde.*

56 Brünnhilde: *Schützt mich, und helft / in höchster Not!* ("Protect me and help me in my deepest need!") Breathlessly, Brünnhilde asks for protection, for Wotan is pursuing her. When Wotan is seen hurtling toward them in a thunderstorm, Brünnhilde again begs them to help, telling them of the events leading to this moment. As Wotan nears, she once more asks for assistance, but the others fear to defy their master.

The short phrases of Brünnhilde's appeal for help evokes her panic and breathlessness; the frantic questions of her sisters pour out in a jumble of independent parts. Need of the Gods *becomes the music of Wotan's wild ride. Brünnhilde's panting narrative is a melange of triplet and duplet rhythms, as if the words were tumbling out of her. The chromatic descents associated with the Valkyries' fire-breathing horses become the frightening sounds of Wotan's furious approach.*

57 Sieglinde: *Nicht sehre dich Sorge um mich* ("Do not trouble yourself worrying about me") When Brünnhilde puts her arm around her, Sieglinde rejects her and asks for death. Brünnhilde tells her of the child now in her womb, eliciting elation from Sieglinde and a plea for life and shelter. Realizing that Wotan is very close now, Brünnhilde resolves to face him alone and draw his revenge on herself, thus allowing Sieglinde to escape.

Sieglinde's music is slow and dark, her voice rising from below the staff to its top as she proclaims her resentment at having been denied the privilege of dying with Siegmund. Brünnhilde's message turns the orchestral music to a boil; Sieglinde's thought of the life within her is given rhythmic vitality and notes well above the staff, evidence of a mood both joyous and desperate. The words of Brünnhilde's resolve are set to a triadic melody in the minor mode; a moment later the melody appears in the major, as the music of Siegfried/Hero *becomes emblematic of Brünnhilde's heroism and sacrifice.*

58 Siegrune: *Nach Osten weithin / dehnt sich ein Wald* ("To the East far from here a forest stretches") Siegrune and Schwertleite remind Brünnhilde that in a gloomy forest to the East is the lair of Fafner, the dragon who broods over the ring and the horde of gold. Realizing that Wotan fears to go there, Brünnhilde charges Sieglinde to head in that direction. All sorrows and deprivations will be hers, but she will bear the noblest hero of all. Brünnhilde gives her the pieces of the sword, predicting that her son will forge them together once more. "His name take from me—'Siegfried'—he who shall rejoice in battle" (*den Namen nehm er von mir: / 'Siegfried'—erfreu' sich des Siegs!*).

An eerie bassoon countermelody lends an air of mystery to Siegrune's information about the dragon's lair to the East; Ring *informs Schwerleite's addition that Fafner guards the Rhinegold, and an undulating motive in low winds and French horns describes the lumbering dragon's movements. Brünnhilde's hail and farewell to Sieglinde turns to the* Siegfried *motive in its full glory.*

59 Sieglinde: *O hehrstest Wunder* ("Oh most sublime wonder") In a burst of elation, Sieglinde marvels at these words and proclaims Brünnhilde "most noble maiden" (*herrlichste Maid*). Praying that someday her son will be able to thank Brünnhilde himself, she rushes off into the forest.

Sieglinde's rapture is to the ecstatic setting of Redemption *(Wagner's "Glorification of Brünnhilde"), the music soaring in a broadly lyric vocal line doubled by violins and flutes. The* Siegfried *motive follows on its heels in Sieglinde's* Für ihn, den wir liebten, / rett' ich das Liebste *("For him whom we loved I shall save the beloved child").*

60 Wotan: *Steh'! Brünnhild'!* ("Stay, Brünnhilde!") Wotan's voice is heard demanding that Brünnhilde remain to face him. Turning their attention to his imminent arrival, the Valkyries draw Brünnhilde into their midst as if to hide her.

The pounding scales of the Act I storm and vicious dissonances in the brass bespeak Wotan's fury; his offstage voice is given a muffled, distant sound by the use of a speaking trumpet. The disjointed writing for the Valkyries is the image of their shared terror.

SCENE II

61 Wotan: *Wo ist Brünnhild'? / Wo die Verbrecherin?* ("Where is Brünnhilde? Where is the lawbreaker?") Wotan strides into view in a fearsome rage, calling to Brünnhilde to appear and reviling the cowering Valkyries for trying to shield her. Their pleas on her behalf are unavailing; his summary of her perfidy is lashing, his bitterness intensified by the fact that she was closest to his heart.

Wotan enters to the music of Wrath, *with vivid dissonances and heavy orchestration. Powerful low strings frame each of his statements with the music of* Dejection.

62 Brünnhilde: *Hier bin ich, Vater* ("Here I am, Father") Brünnhilde steps into view and moves close to her father, announcing her readiness to hear her sentence. Wotan greets her unkindly—she has brought doom upon herself. Again he summarizes the nature of her betrayal and concludes that she will no longer be a Valkyrie. Her sentence is abandonment of all the deeds and joys of being with him and serving him. Never again will he offer her his kiss—she is banished from his sight. Here on this rock she will lie in undefended slumber, prey to the first man to come upon her and awaken her.

Hesitant patterns in low woodwinds and the darkly ornamented first note of Dejection *represent the mood of Brünnhilde's emergence. Wotan's reminder of what she had meant to him is lyrical, diatonic, and set to flowing vowels and consonants; what she has become reverses sound and style (see Ex. WA-3).*

His sentence is imposed above bursts of wildly ascending chromatic scales. His listing of the deeds she will no longer perform begins with Annunciation of Death *(he is dooming her to mortality) and continues with variants of that motive above syncopations that grow in intensity. His final word of expulsion is to an eruption of mounting scales and a powerful beginning of* Spear; *the decrease in* Spear's *loudness makes his banishment of her even more intense and painful.*

63 The Valkyries: *Halt ein, O Vater! / Halt ein den Fluch!* ("Stop, Father! Hold back your curse!") The Valkyries are horrified; they beg him to relent only to have him turn on them once again, repeating the terms of his punishment and emphasizing that Brünnhilde's beauty will fade, that she will be reduced to menial work, and that "she will sit by the fireside and spin, the target and fun of all mockers" (*am Herde sitzt sie und spinnt, / aller Spottenden Ziel und Spiel!*). Brünnhilde sinks to the ground with a cry, as Wotan threatens them with his dire wrath should they dare even to console her. With open fury and contempt, he orders them off before they suffer the same fate. With loud cries of anguish, the Valkyries separate and run desperately into the woods. Lightning reveals them close-grouped, their bridles hanging loosely as they ride off wildly.

The ensemble of Valkyries is a richly textured variant of Annunciation of Death, *their musically independent lines seeming to come from all sides.* Spear *informs Wotan's detailing of Brünnhilde's punishment. Violently decorated chords suggest the debasement that is to be her future. The motives of the fleeing Valkyries (minus their battle cry) are given a disjointed treatment by full orchestra.*

SCENE III

The storm subsides and the clouds dissipate. The weather becomes increasingly calm; twilight falls, then night.

64 Brünnhilde: *War es so schmählich / was ich verbrach* . . . ("Was what I did so shameful . . .") Beginning timidly but gaining confidence as she speaks, Brünnhilde asks if what she has done was so shameful that he should abandon her so. They debate calmly but gravely the subtleties of his command and his desire, she noting that as agent of his will she had no choice, he insisting that his spoken order was what she had to obey.

Brünnhilde asserts an unassailable truth: Wotan loved the Volsung. She recounts her confrontation with Siegmund and how his bravery and love moved her. She was overcome by a new emotion and became willing to share victory or death with Siegmund because of it. It was her only thought and she had no choice. The love that Wotan had inspired in her heart (*Der diese Liebe / mir ins Herz gehaucht*) means that Wotan was not betrayed even though his command was defied.

The wildness diminishes. Volsung Love *appears softly in the bass clarinet, then oboe. Brünnhilde begins her defense to a subtle reworking of* Spear *(Ex. WA-9b), breaking its straight line and turning it into a lyrical and pliant song. That it is unaccompanied after the maelstrom of the first two scenes makes this gentle but assertive melody especially poignant and deeply felt. The motives of* Valkyrie Ride, Fate, *and* Valhalla *provide meaningful counterpoints to the dialogue.* Volsung Love *returns as the setting for her* Nicht weise bin ich, / doch wusst' ich das eine, / dass den Wälsung du liebtest ("Unwise I am, yet I know one thing, that you loved the Volsung") *and (with subtle woodwind shadings) for her assertion that the same love was in her heart.*

65 Wotan: *So tatest du, / was so gern zu tun ich begehrt* ("So you did what I wanted so much to do") Wotan understands and pours out his grief to her. Nonetheless, she has determined her own path, and it must be parted from his forever. Her

Wagner, *Die Walküre*, Act III, scene iii: A traditional staging of the closing scene of the opera, as Wotan (Roger Roloff) summons Loge, god of fire, to surround the sleeping Brünnhilde (Ute Vinzing) with impenetrable flame. Seattle Opera, 1975: sets and costumes by John T. Naccarato. Photo (1984) © Chris Bennion.

response is that any disgrace to her will be disgrace to him, since they are of one mind and spirit. Therefore, she continues, let her become the consort of a great hero, not a coward. He resists and when she reminds him of the Volsung race he has created and of the sword now held by Sieglinde, his anger rises again. Brünnhilde is to be bound in long, deep sleep, claimed by the man who awakens her. Once again she pleads that this man be fearless and free or else let her be slain on the spot. With excited inspiration, she asks for a circle of fire to dissuade any craven man from taking her.

> *Wotan's response is clearly difficult for him, for his reminder that she had turned against him is voiced in repetitions of* Spear *that have no authority about them: his oath of banishment is as troubling as all the other promises he has made. The scalar direction of this motive reverses as Brünnhilde begins to focus on the idea of diverting the shame he has imposed.* Volsung Victory *softly issues from the French horns and bassoons, followed shortly by* Siegfried. *Turbulence accompanies the renewal of his anger when she tells him that Sieglinde is with child. The* Death *figure is an ominous preface to* Magic Spell. *The* Siegfried *theme rises again when she asks that a hero be the one to claim her; there are the motives of* Spear *and* Valkyrie Ride, *but the motives of* Slumber *and* Fire *become more and more prominent.*

66 Wotan's Farewell: *Leb' wohl, du kühnes / herrliches Kind!* ("Farewell, you dauntless, most noble child!") Overcome with deep feeling, Wotan raises his daughter from her knees and bids her farewell. He agrees that she shall be guarded by a bridal fire (*ein bräutliches Feuer*) and that "one alone will win you as bride, one freer than I, the god!" (*Denn einer nur freie die Braut, / der freier als ich, der Gott!*)

Wagner, *Die Walküre*, Act III, scene iii: A contemporary design for the Magic Fire scene, with Roger Roloff as Wotan and Linda Kelm as Brünnhilde. Seattle Opera, 1985: sets and costumes by Robert Israel. Photo © Chris Bennion.

Wotan's Leb' wohl . . . *rises thrillingly from the swelling music of Brünnhilde's appeal. The orchestral array of figures and fire motives swirls luxuriantly, but Wotan's lyricism is the dominant element, speaking of love and richness of heart. His ordaining that only a fearless hero will claim her is imposingly reinforced by the* Sword's *opening octave and the portentous trombone pronouncement of the* Hero/Siegfried *motive.*

67 Brünnhilde sinks on his breast in exaltation, Wotan embracing her. She throws her head back and gazes at him with solemn rapture. He sings of her radiant eyes (*Der Augen leuchtendes Paar*) that he had so often kissed, eyes that had given him cheer and gladden him even now. He lovingly kisses the godhood from them; she sinks, unconscious, in his arms. He supports her to a mossy bank, where he lays her to rest. He closes the visor of her helmet, covers her with her shield, then turns away, pausing to look at her once more with sorrow and love.

With the orchestral richness of full woodwinds supported by all the other instruments, Volsung Love *is given out expansively.* Slumber *becomes an omnipresent murmur as background to Wotan's sentiments, his melody of* Farewell *being especially touching and enriching.* Fate *and* Renunciation *add their special meanings to the scene, as does* Magic Spell *(woodwinds, with harp arpeggios). As Wotan gazes at the sleeping form of his beloved daughter, the* Farewell *motive again works its wonders.*

68 *Loge, hör' !* ("Loge, hear me!") With decisiveness and solemnity, Wotan strides to the middle of the scene. He points with his spear to a rock and summons Loge to surround the rocks with flame. He stretches out his spear as if casting a spell and with his final words, keeps his promise to Brünnhilde: *Wer meines Speeres / Spitze fürchtet, / durchschreite das Feuer nie* ("He who fears the point of my spear shall never pierce the flames"). With one more look at the sleeping Brünnhilde, he departs slowly, disappearing amid the fire.

Brusque figures in the low strings indicate his stride to the center of the scene; brasses pronounce Spear *once again. Tremolando strings, dotted rhythms in woodwinds and French horns, and the rush of a chromatic scale lead to the bursting of fire as evoked by piccolo and a steady intensification of string arpeggios.*

Wotan's final words are to the music of Siegfried, *the motive echoed immediately in the sonority of full brasses. The orchestral panorama that concludes the opera is a glorious dilation on* Wotan's Farewell, Fire, Fate, *and* Slumber.

The Characters

Siegmund (tenor) [ZEEK-moont]

Child of Wotan; twin brother of Sieglinde. We learn from his Act I dialogue with Sieglinde that his life has been troubled and lonely. In his later narration to Hunding and Sieglinde, he gives his name as *Wehwalt* ("Woeful") and tells of the murder of his mother, the abduction of his sister, and the destruction of his home; of years of wandering and living as an outlaw with his father Wälse, ever battling against their Neidung enemies; of the disappearance of his father; and of his own isolation and unending struggle against the enemies of man and nature.

The *Siegmund* motive suggests this torment, but he is no less characterized by the boldness of *Volsung Race*, the éclat of *Sword*, and the gentleness of his *Spring Song*.

Siegmund's greatest and most complex moment psychologically is his rejection of Brünnhilde's summons to Valhalla, thus becoming truly free of Wotan's control.[21] To fragments of *Valhalla*, Siegmund sings with quiet dignity that Brünnhilde should convey his greetings to the castle and its residence, for he will not follow her there if it means leaving Sieglinde.

That the power of the sword is to be denied him is a frightful disillusion: to the accompaniment of violas and cellos playing a triplet variation of her Spring Song (Example WA-5, which draws on *Love*), he sings unhappily and lovingly of the fate of his wife; then, after military fanfares underscore his anger and frustration, he calls shame on Wotan's head by bitterly twisting *Sword* into the minor mode and caustically combining *Sword* and *Annunciation of Death*. Only when Brünnhilde is overwhelmed with compassion and excitement at his grandeur of spirit does Siegmund turn once again to loving concern for Sieglinde and, finally, to heroism: knowing he is doomed, he goes off to do battle with Hunding.

Sieglinde (soprano) [ZEEK-lin-duh]

Daughter of Wotan; Siegmund's twin sister. Abducted in childhood by Hunding's Neidung tribe, she was forced into a loveless, brutal marriage.

---

[21] It is a passage of bitter irony, for even as Siegmund is now fulfilling Wotan's great vision of a hero free of the gods, Wotan must destroy him in accordance with the implications of laws Wotan has himself created.

EXAMPLE WA-5 ACT II, SCENE IV: SIEGMUND'S LOVE—AS HE
BENDS TENDERLY IN AN OUTBURST OF GRIEF OVER THE UNCON-
SCIOUS SIEGLINDE, VIOLAS AND CELLOS ACCOMPANY HIS CONCERN
WITH A TRIPLET VARIATION ("a") OF SIEGLINDE'S SONG OF
SPRINGTIME AND LOVE, *Du bist der Lenz* (WA-3B)

Having suffered much, she has achingly longed for the "spring" to follow the
"winter" of her life with Hunding. From Siegmund's narrative and from seeing herself in him, she recognizes him as her brother, restores to him his
rightful name—*Siegmund* ("Conquering Protector")—and impels the final
passions of Act I.

Sieglinde's music in Act I is prevailingly soft-mannered, the soothing
thirds of her motive warm and fully expressive of a woman who has retained
compassion and concern for others in spite of the harshness of her life. As one
might expect of a person abused by hostile people for much of her life, she is
hesitant and tentative early in the act when she sings in short phrases and
quick note values; the swinging open of the door near the end of the act frightens her as if she were a doe. As her inmost feelings and her recognition of
Siegmund as the fulfillment of her dreams well up in her heart, however, her
melodic line blossoms to the point that her "Du bist der Lenz" floods forth as
an instantaneous response to Siegmund's "Spring Song" ("Winterstürme").
Sieglinde becomes one of opera's truly impassioned heroines.

Act II finds her in a state of physical exhaustion from the flight through
the forests and emotional torment from the memory of years of disgusting
treatment by her brutish husband. She is convinced that her body is now a
corpse and can never be a reservoir of love. Her anguish bursts out breathlessly in irregular gasps of words, wide intervals, and frantic chromatic
upward shifts (Example WA-6). Even when her melody broadens into a
grander expression of anxiety, it retains this sense of hysteria. Uncontrolled

EXAMPLE WA-6 ACT II, SCENE III: SIEGLINDE'S TERROR
AND SHAME

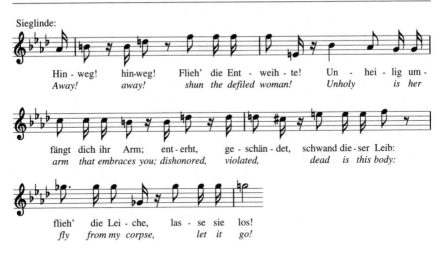

terror and the same kind of music (with appropriately harsh dissonances)
dominate her imagining Siegmund being torn apart by Hunding's dogs and
precipitate her collapse.

The last we see of Sieglinde, however, is as a heroine in the Wagnerian
vein: the expansive melody with which she embraces the wonder of her
child's future and extols the nobility of Brünnhilde is one of the great
moments in opera and presents the motive that will eventually epitomize
Redemption as the ultimate musical message of the *Ring* as a whole.

Hunding (bass) *[HOON-ding]*

The crudeness of his motive tells us all we need to know of his inner self,
revealing one of opera's least attractive personalities. His assertion of his
respect for the traditions of hospitality seems conventional enough
(Example WA-7), but it is set to the first notes of the *Ring* and thus connects
him to the cycle's primary symbol of lust for power minus the balms of compassion and love.

EXAMPLE WA-7 HUNDING'S HOSPITALITY

Wotan (bass-baritone) *[VOH-tahn]*

In *Die Walküre*, Wotan grows from an ambitious conniver and bullish warrior to a person of consummate wisdom, compassion, and understanding. In pre-*Ring* history he had yielded an eye[22] for the privilege of drinking from the Spring of Wisdom at the base of the World Ash Tree; now, in *Die Walküre*, the partial loss of his external vision has finally resulted in genuine insight and introspection (see Chapter 4 and the discussion illustrated by Example 4.4).[23]

Wotan is the protagonist and the linchpin of *Die Walküre*. All of Act I is the result of his doing: the storm that drives Siegmund through the track-less forest to Sieglinde's arms is musically based on the motive of Wotan's spear; the weapon (*Sword*) Siegmund calls for in his hour of greatest need and that had been promised him in his boyhood is identified motivically as the "great idea" that had seized Wotan at the end of *Das Rheingold*; and the connection of the weapon to Sieglinde's sorrows and hopes is firmly cement-ed in her narrative of Act I, scene iii, where *Sword* and *Valhalla* mingle as her story develops.

All of Act II may be seen as Wotan's extensive self-examination, with Fricka representing his conscience, Brünnhilde his desires, and Siegmund and Sieglinde his actions and their implications. His narrative, then, is far more than a saga's relation of a tale oft told; it is the troubled working of his memory and his recognition of truth. The act begins promisingly for him but, when his plan is blunted by the irrefutable logic of Fricka, it ends terri-bly: he must order his "wish maiden" to destroy his son; she disobeys; and he must kill Siegmund himself. Act III is no less tragic for Wotan, for he must banish Brünnhilde from his presence and turn her into a mere mortal. Yet these deeply troubled scenes also represent true grandeur: Act II is a time of true self-understanding and acknowledgement of the responsibility for his actions; Act III is the time when he sets aside rage and the injury to his pride of place in favor of love and acceptance of a future in which world dominion will pass from him.

Wotan is only a presence (albeit strong) in Act I. He first appears in Act II, when his opening music is militant with dotted rhythms, simple har-monies set out in blunt chords in low brass and strings, and short phrases. Five times *Spear* rumbles in vivid triplets, as if Wotan himself were joyfully leading his forces into battle (Example WA-8a).

---

[22] In the second scene of *Das Rheingold*, Wotan tells Fricka that he yielded an eye to her family as a pledge of his wooing. There is nothing in myth that equates to this and it is flat-ly contradictory to the First Norn's narration of the eye-for-wisdom story in the Prologue of *Götterdämmerung*. Cooke (p. 151) sees no contradiction: that Wotan yielded an eye to drink from the spring allowed him to shape a spear from the World Ash Tree; this in turn caused him to think in terms of loveless power, hence his entitlement to a wife like Fricka, whose addiction to law and convention is paralleled by the Spear's representation of treaty and oath. It could be, I suppose, that Wagner simply forgot to clean up the inconsistency: the poem for *Das Rheingold* was undertaken some three years after that of *Götterdämmerung*, and the whole cycle went through years of work and revision. Suggestion that Wagner nod-ded in this respect is anathema to some, so I float the theory that perhaps, *pace* Cooke, Wotan was flattering Fricka with an attractive falsehood.

[23] Cooke (p. 261) proposes that the loss of an eye "symbolizes . . . lovelessness of the author-itarian state-ruler" and that Wotan yielded that half of his understanding/insight "which is the instinct for mutual love and fellowship."

EXAMPLE WA-8 THE PROGRESS OF WOTAN'S MUSIC IN ACT II

a) Act II, scene i: As warlord, he summons Brünnhilde to battle on Siegmund's behalf.

The scene with Fricka begins with Wotan in a confident frame of mind, expecting dignity, his overriding authority, and the divine nature of love to persuade his outraged wife that love is more important than law. He assumes a simple melodic line accompanied by soothing cellos cooing the second half of the motive of *Love* (Example WA-8b), but it does not work. He turns therefore to music of dark foreboding, trying to explain to Fricka his plan that depends on a hero free of the encumbrances of past treaties and misdeeds (Example WA-8c), drawing on the motives of *Spear* (as "Treaty") and *Ring*, but Fricka can smell a rat and traps him: Siegmund is not free, he is Wotan's pawn.

This is a turning point in the opera and in Wotan's maturation, because he realizes his plan is futile and assumes there is no hope. Thus his music turns to the gloom of frustration and *Dejection*. His last words to Fricka are muffled and halting in rhythm; bound by laws and deeds of his own making, he must now yield to them and to her completely (Example WA-8d). Despair dominates his vision of Alberich's triumph (Example WA-8e, a distortion of *Valhalla*), and the turmoil of *Wrath* becomes his music at the end of Act II and the start of Act III.

At the close of the opera, however, the turbulence of rage and despair fade, and Wotan becomes majestic and loving. His music predicting the hero who knows no fear (*Siegfried*) is imposing and grand, and his farewell is ennobling and endearing. Wotan bestows the greatest gifts of parenthood: the independence, talents, and wisdom with which a child may face the future free of a parent's errors and emotional baggage.

EXAMPLE WA-8 (Continued)

b) Act II, scene i: He tries to persuade Fricka to bless the union of Siegmund and Sieglinde ("b" = fragment of *Love* from Example WA-3a).

Brünnhilde (soprano) [BRUEN-hil-duh]

She is a warrior maiden when she appears at the start of Act II, so her first music is based on that of the Valkyries and their famous battle cry. Her questions for details during Wotan's narrative are recitative-like and are accompanied by the motives of the characters or qualities he refers to rather than music of her own.

Wotan's orders to her to carry out Fricka's will and slay Siegmund start a move to an entirely different musical personality, however. For the first time, her music (Example WA-9a) becomes turbid and complex, as if she were unable to determine where Wotan's will really lies: syncopations, overlapping triplets, chromatic changes, and harmonic uncertainty roil the

c) Act II, scene i: He turns to the serious business of the gods needing a hero free of divine control.

d) Act II, scene i—He surrenders: Siegmund must move on his own path without the sheltering of Wotan's power.

EXAMPLE WA-8 (*Continued*)

e) Act II, scene ii: In greatest frustration, he calls to Alberich's son to take the prize of world power.

EXAMPLE WA-8 (*Continued*)

nich - ti - gen Glanz: zer -
empty   *pomp:*   *feed*

più p

na - ge ihn gie - rig dein Neid!
your   envy   greedily   from it!

Strings
p   cresc.

e) (*Continued*)

strings as she threatens to defy her father's command. Brünnhilde's commitment to saving Siegmund and Sieglinde marks her full appearance as her own person. The music is not yet fully hers, because it is based on manipulations of *Annunciation of Death*, but clearly she is reworking that material in accordance with psychological independence and her own motivations, just as Siegmund had a short time before.

In Act III she works the same change and takes matters into her own hands more completely. Standing alone before Wotan and ready for his punishment, she takes the melody of his authority (*Spear*) and, by moving segments of it up an octave, turns it into an eloquent expression of herself: womanly, nobly motivated, and, in spirit, still inseparable from Wotan's most precious desires (Example WA-9b). With her broadly lyric statement of *Volsung Love*, Brünnhilde, once a warrior maiden, is transfigured and becomes the great heroine of the cycle's final two operas.

EXAMPLE WA-9 BRÜNNHILDE'S EMERGENT INDEPENDENCE
OF SPIRIT

Brünnhilde:

Den   du zu   lie - ben stets   mich ge - lehrt,   der in
The   one whom you   have   always   taught   me to love,   the one whose

heh - rer   Tu - gend dem Herz - en dir
noble   virtues   are dear   to your

a) Act II, scene ii: She threatens to defy Wotan's order.

Fricka (mezzo-soprano) [FRIK-ah]

The imperious goddess of marriage and the hearth. Her marriage to Wotan
has been barren, and she has long been aggrieved over her husband's sexual profligacy.[24] Adamant that the treaties of social behavior will be honored,
she represents Wotan's conscience and logic and holds him to account for his
past actions.

---

[24] Wagner rearranged the myth considerably; the Fricka of legend was not only the goddess of the hearth but also of physical love, and was thus sexually promiscuous. See Cord,
Teutonic Mythology, II, pp. 35–39.

EXAMPLE WA-9 (*Continued*)

teu - er,   ge - gen   ihn   zwingt   mich
heart   *against   him   I   will   never be*

nim - mer dein   zwie - späl - tig Wort!
turned by your two - timing   word!

a) (*Continued*)

Brünnhilde:

War   es   so schmä - lich   was   ich   ver - brach, dass mein Ver -
Was   it   so shameful,   what   I   did,   that my misdeed

bre -   chen so schmä - lich du be - strafst?
so shamefully   you   punish?

b) Act III, scene iii: She stands before Wotan as a person of self-will and dignity.

Her arrival in Act II is signalled by triplets so often associated with galloping or dynamic action; in this case, they represent the rolling wheels of her chariot, drawn by a pair of rams with which she is associated mythologically. The snapping, rising scale of *Pursuit* punctuates her approach; clearly she is arriving hurriedly and in an unpleasant frame of mind.

Fricka's resentment is represented by the turbulence of *Wrath* and by peremptory, demanding phrases. Her attack on Wotan's casual handling of his own laws and his illogic is grand in scope; the rhythm of her peroration is relentless, its dynamic level is strong, and, at the frequent peaks of her chastisement of Wotan's perfidies, the orchestra is fully instrumented.

Fricka is not all virago, however one may feel about Wotan's children and Fricka's attitude toward them. While Wagner's/Wotan's sympathies are unmistakable, she has some very moving arioso (Example WA-10a) that mingles her indignation with a genuine sense of unhappiness over love denied (a manipulation of the first phrase of *Love*). Finally, having won her case, she is given a passage (Example WA-10b) of simple dignity, broadly melodic in the major mode and accompanied by the steady pulsing of fundamental harmonies. Even though the bass line descends chromatically as a darkening subtext, Fricka's insistence that Brünnhilde be instructed to use her shield in defense of the honor of the gods shows a side of her that is often given short shrift: in spite of the lovelessness of her life, she is a goddess of great dignity.

The Valkyries

The nine daughters of Wotan and Erda; they ride fire-breathing horses and stir mortal men to strife. They defend great heroes in battle, then bring the

EXAMPLE WA-10 ACT II, SCENE I: FRICKA'S SADNESS AND DIGNITY

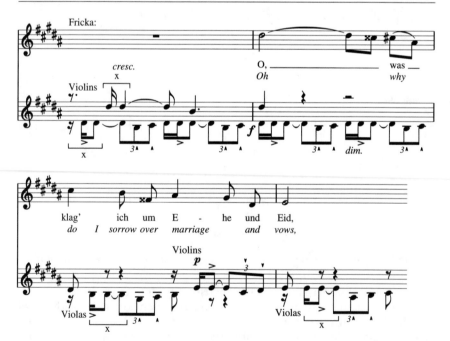

a) Albeit with flashes of anger (x = *Wrath*), she laments Wotan's infidelity.

EXAMPLE WA-10 (*Continued*)

b) Having shown Wotan that Siegmund must be punished and that he cannot be at the same time free and a tool of Wotan's strategy, she demands that Brünnhilde fight for the dignity and integrity of herself and the gods.

souls of those slain in combat to Valhalla to form Wotan's army. In Valhalla, they serve the heroes as "wish maidens," giving them food and drink and bringing to fruition their loftiest desires.[25]

Their music represents the only ensemble writing of the opera; other than Brünnhilde, none has individualizing music. The part work of their ensemble is often intensely complex, first as a mirror of the chaos of the battlefield that they represent and later as a metaphor for their terror and confusion in the face of Wotan's anger and Brünnhilde's disobedience. The basic materials of their warrior characteristics are the three motives of

---

[25] In other words, they are not merely sexual slaves.

Examples WA-4c, d, and e, although their pleading with Wotan to spare Brünnhilde is a contrapuntal working of *Annunciation of Death*.

The Valkyries' voice classifications are somewhat loosely specified in Wagner's score as "sopranos and altos"; they are usually identified in recordings and programs by the voice type of the artist performing the role. The list below is in order of their appearance on a page of the score from top voice to lowest voice, the identification of voice type reflecting general casting practices. Other than Brünnhilde, the Valkyries are:

Helmwige (soprano) [HELM-vee-guh]

Gerhilde (soprano) [GAIR-hil-duh]

Ortlinde (soprano) [AWRT-lin-duh]

Waltraute (mezzo-soprano) [VAHL-trow-tuh; "ow" as in "how"]

Siegrune (mezzo-soprano) [ZEE-groo-nuh]

Rossweise (mezzo-soprano or contralto) [RAWSS-vy-suh]

Grimgerde (mezzo-soprano or contralto) [GRIM-gair-duh]

Schwertleite (mezzo-soprano or contralto) [SHVAIRT-ly-tuh]

Bibliography

Bailey, Robert. "The Structure of the Ring and Its Evolution," in *Nineteenth-Century Music* I, no. 1 (July 1977): 48–61.

Cooke, Deryck. *I Saw the World End: A Study of Wagner's "Ring."* London and New York: Oxford University Press, 1979.
Examination of Das Rheingold *and* Die Walküre *in terms of sources, allegory, characterization, and music. The author's untimely death prevented completion of one of the best books on the* Ring.

Cord, William O. *The Teutonic Mythology of Richard Wagner's "The Ring of the Nibelung."* Studies in the History and Interpretation of Music. Lewiston, ME: Edwin Mellen Press, 1991. 4 volumes.
Studies of the characters, concepts, and etymologies of terms as found in the original legends and as adapted by Wagner.

———. *An Introduction to Richard Wagner's "Der Ring des Nibelungen,"* 2nd ed. rev., enl. Athens, OH: Ohio University Press, 1995.
Mythological backgrounds, index of characters, study of poetry and drama, description of Wagner's theater in Bayreuth, details of the plots, and much more.

Dahlhaus, Carl. *Richard Wagner's Music Dramas*, trans. Mary Whittall. Cambridge: Cambridge University Press, 1979 [1971].

Di Gaetani, John L., ed. *Penetrating Wagner's* Ring. New York: Da Capo Press (Associated University Presses), 1978.

Donington, Robert. *Wagner's "Ring" and Its Symbols: The Music and the Myth*, 3rd ed. New York: St. Martin's Press, 1974.
Controversial but insightful examination of how motives are interrelated musically and thus reveal Jungian psychological meanings.

Gregor-Dellin, Martin. *Richard Wagner: His Life, His Work, His Century*, trans. J. Maxwell Brownjohn. San Diego, CA: Harcourt Brace Jovanovich, 1983.

Hamilton, David. "How Wagner Forged His Ring," in *Opera News* 39, no. 15 (February 15, March 1, 15, 29, 1975): 21–26.
See pp. 23ff for a clear explanation of the musico-dramatic workings of the Brünnhilde-Siegmund scene.

———. "Crux of the Ring," in *Opera News* 41, no. 5 (February 19, 1977): 9–12.
Overview of Act II.

John, Nicholas, ed.. *The Valkyrie*. English National Opera Guide 21. New York: Riverrrun Press, 1983.
Articles and a libretto. The table of motives is free of any labels, keyed into the libretto only by number. Their associations, however, are explained in Barry Millington's brief but extremely helpful study of the music.

Lee, M. Owen. *Wagner's Ring: Turning the Sky Around—Commentaries on* The Ring of the Nibelung. New York: Summit Books, 1990.
Nontechnical interpretations of the drama and its music.

McDonald, William E. "What does Wotan Know? Autobiography and Moral Vision in Wagner's *Ring*," in *Nineteenth-Century Music* 16, no. 1 (Summer 1991): 36–51.
A close reading of Wotan's Act II narrative.

Millington, Barry, ed. *The Wagner Compendium: A Guide to Wagner's Life and Music*. New York: Schirmer Books, 1992.

———. *Wagner*. Princeton, NJ: Princeton University Press, 1984.
The best short "life and works" in English.

Newman, Ernest. *The Wagner Operas*. New York: Alfred A. Knopf, 1949.
Although subject to criticism here and there, this is still one of the best and most detailed studies of the plot and characters, and the relation of leitmotifs to them.

———. *Wagner as Man and Artist*, 2nd ed. New York: Vintage Books, 1960 [1924].

Potter, John. "Brünnhilde's Choice," in *Opera News* 47, no. 14 (March 26, 1983): 9–11.

Sandow, Gregory. "Uninterrupted Flow," in *Opera News* 47, no. 14 (March 26, 1983): 12f.

Chapter 14

CARMEN

MUSIC: Georges Bizet (1838–1875)

LIBRETTO: Henri Meilhac (1831–1897) and Ludovic Halévy (1834–1908),[1] after a short story (1845) by Prosper Mérimée (1803–1870), who derived its events from an episode in real life narrated to him by the Countess de Montijo.[2]

PREMIERE: March 3, 1875, in Paris at the Opéra-Comique,[3] with spoken dialogue; October 23, 1875, in Vienna (in German), with recitatives composed by Ernest Guiraud (1837–1892).

TIME AND PLACE OF THE STORY: Spain, in and near Seville, in 1830.[4]

NOTE: There is no single version of Carmen's words and music that is definitive. For the Opéra-Comique, Carmen's arias, ensembles, and choruses were part of a chain that included spoken scenes, some orchestrally accompanied spoken dialogue (melodrama), and some recitative. For Vienna, some spoken dialogue was retained for more intimate moments, but most of it was replaced by Guiraud's recitatives (Bizet having died in June, three months after the Paris premiere). The Guiraud version,

---

[1] Halévy, well known in his own right as a librettist (for this work and collaborations with Meilhac on librettos for Offenbach), was the nephew of Fromental Halévy (1799–1862), a celebrated opera composer (whose works include *La Juive,* 1835) and father-in-law of Bizet.

[2] Her daughter, Eugénie, became Empress of France when she married Napoleon III in 1853.

[3] In this hyphenated and capitalized form, the term refers to a company or the theater in which the company operated. The theaters have had several names: in addition to Opéra-Comique, the same building has been called Salle Favart, Comédie Italienne, and Théâtre-Italien; the company has also been housed in the Salle Feydeau, Salle Ventadour, Théâtre des Nouveautés, and a second Salle Favart, where it is currently in residence. When written as "opéra comique," the term refers to a French genre of opera that uses spoken dialogue.

[4] The G. Schirmer score and the *New Harvard Dictionary of Music* (p. 140) both place the opera in 1820, but a Mérimée footnote (p. 89, n. 11 to p. 46), noting that as a gentleman (*hidalgo*) Don José was entitled to the garotte rather than simple hanging, indicates that the nobility "enjoyed" this privilege in 1830, clearly the time of José's execution for the murder of Carmen.

published by Choudens in 1877 and later by C. F. Peters under the editorship of Kurt Soldan, became the basic Carmen score for almost a century before opera houses began to restore the original comique form.

Bizet went through several weeks of frenzied revision without living long enough to prepare a definitive score; the remnants of these efforts include fragments of correction or insertion, some of them discarded in favor of later versions, some of them sketches for changes never incorporated, some of them final versions. Having discovered these and a lode of the original orchestral parts and conductor's manuscript score, Fritz Oeser published an edition[5] that sought to reestablish Bizet's intentions. Unfortunately, he included many segments that Bizet had rejected, banishing final and therefore authentic versions to appendices or commentary, and, with particularly egregious enthusiasm, added some of his own stage directions that quite distort Bizet's intentions and mangle the connection between text and music.[6] Although only the original piano score of 1875 can be considered definitive, the majority of performances and recordings tend to present Bizet's music through the separate or combined filters of Oeser or Guiraud.

Each recording and performance, therefore, tends to be a different document. Some major differences: the spoken dialogue includes José's mention of killing a man, but not the recitative; the recitative has José saying that he loves Micaëla, but the spoken dialogue does not; Carmen's greeeting of José in Act II is rather stilted and formal in the recitative, but full of life, wit, and exuberance in the spoken dialogue; the knife fight with Escamillo was cut by Guiraud from eight pages of score to three, eliminating Escamillo sparing José's life; in the Guiraud version, Micaëla finds the smugglers' resting place in the wild mountains by herself, but the comique version gives her a villager as a guide whose terror establishes the danger of the moment and serves as a device to set forth her courage. There are many, many more such differences.

Carmen as Heroine: "Reading" the Opera

There is no opera that has entered the awareness of the public quite like *Carmen*. Simply in terms of a love of its music, it holds an unrivalled position. Its irresistible melodies and vibrant rhythms have sparkled and enticed in thousands of performances in the world's opera houses, over thirty films, countless radio and television commercials, student recitals, public-school songbooks, singers' auditions, and opera workshop scenes. Almost two dozen recordings, not to mention a clutch of highlight albums and suites of instrumental arrangements of the opera's hit tunes, continue to be viable commercially.

Serving as opera's most popular entertainment is quite enough, of course, but *Carmen* has filled another function as well, becoming in its own time the focus of argument over the goals of theater, the nature of love, and

---

[5] Kassel: Alkor Editions, 1964.

[6] A sharply critical discussion of the Oeser edition is provided by Winton Dean in "The True *Carmen?*," in *The Musical Times* 106 (November 1965): 846–55. A shorter critique is found in his 1975 revision of *Bizet*, p. 294f.

the relation of man to woman. Nietzsche (1844–1900), for example, rejecting the sentimentality and idealization of love that he saw in such treatments
as the Senta/Dutchman love of Wagner's *Der fliegende Holländer*, described
Carmen as ". . . love translated back into *nature!* Not the love of a 'higher virgin'! No Senta-sentimentality! But love as *fatum*, as fatality, cynical, innocent,
cruel—and precisely in this a piece of nature. That love which is war in its
means, and at bottom the deadly hatred of the sexes!"[7]

The view of Carmen as the archetype of woman as destructive *femme fatale*,
luring men from the paths of righteousness to denial of honor and social
order, carbuncled the earliest reviews of the opera, of which this excerpt from
Paris's *La Patrie* is a particularly virulent but not atypical example:

> [Carmen is] . . . mad over her body, giving herself to the first soldier
> who comes along, out of caprice, bravado, by chance, blindly. Then,
> after having lost him his honor, treated him with scorn, she deserts him
> to run after a handsomer fellow whom, in turn, she will leave when she
> likes. . . . [She is] savage; half gypsy, half Andalusian; sensual, mocking,
> shameless; believing neither in God nor in the Devil . . . she is the ver-
> itable prostitute of the gutter and the crossroads.[8]

Recent studies have used *Carmen* as a *locus classicus* of different agendas
and subtexts relating to gender and sexuality, with scarcely any aspect of
the novella or the opera escaping analysis. Even the mountain setting of
Mérimée's tale has served symbolically, as witness Peter Robinson's suggestion that the narrow gorge in which the narrator first meets Don José "can
only be described as an uncannily feminine landscape . . . a small stream
trickling through high, narrow foothills," a "body [that the narrator] has
penetrated."[9]

The literature of opera-as-gender study has consistently turned to the
identification of Carmen as a victim. She is seen as an "Other" who must be
destroyed by men because her independence, vitality, and sexual power constitute gross impropriety to a white male establishment and a threat to masculine dominance. Catherine Clément finds Carmen "the most feminist, the
most stubborn of [opera's] dead women . . . the image . . . of a woman who
refuses masculine yokes and who must pay for it with her life";[10] Susan
McClary asserts that ". . . because [Carmen] apparently has the power to
deliver or withhold gratification of the desires she instills, she is immediately marked as a potential victimizer."[11]

---

[7] 1888. See Friedrich Nietzsche, "The Case of Wagner," Section 2, in *Basic Writings of
Nietzsche*, trans. and ed. Walter Kaufmann (New York: Modern Library, 1992), p. 614f.

[8] Achille de Lauzières, in *La Patrie*, March 8, 1875, quoted in Curtiss, p. 399.

[9] Peter Robinson, "Mérimée's *Carmen*," in McClary, p. 4f.

[10] Clément, p. 48.

[11] *Feminine Endings: Music, Gender, and Sexuality*, p. 57.

Whether one buys into this sort of interpretation or not, there is no question that the filter of history continues its work; it is no longer possible for the thinking operagoer to experience this opera as a pretty stage entertainment with nice tunes. It has become a linchpin for the sexual politics of our time.

Realism and Romanticism

In 1866, Émile Zola (1840–1902) asserted that the days of a "complicated and improbable story" were gone and that the sole object of fiction was "to register human facts [and] to lay bare the mechanism of body and soul [with] the first man one comes across as hero."[12] Mérimée, Gustave Flaubert, and Guy de Maupassant were on the cutting edge of this anti-Romanticism, which sought to illuminate its subjects with the harsh light of clinical observation, to let the events and locales speak for themselves, and to use language that was relatively unadorned and free of moralizing.

Half of *Carmen* is set in places that are seamy or ugly: outside a cigar factory for Act I, a smuggler's den of iniquity for Act II. The characters show none of the traits of the larger-than-life protagonists of grand opera: there are no princesses or military heroes here, nor are there events that call from its protagonists deeds of derring-do, noble sacrifice, or expression of lofty ideals.[13]

Tenderness of expression is the exception rather than the rule, and the only love-duet provided in the music is a snippet between Carmen and Escamillo in Act IV. The other duets are not at all the traditional expression of man-woman mutual affection: the Act I duet between José and Micaëla is about his mother; José's comments during the "Seguidilla" (No. 10) and in various moments of Act II are those of a man being seduced into betraying his duty; the ensemble between him and Escamillo is prelude to a fight to the death; and the scenes between José and Carmen in Acts III and IV are contentious, to say the least. Neither of the protagonists is impelled by what Western society, in our time or Bizet's, would identify as "true love": Carmen's interest in José is sparked only by the fact that he pays no attention to her; his passion for her is driven by infatuation motivated by her sexual allure and, from the end of Act II until the opera's final moments, by jealousy and posessiveness.

Yet *Carmen* is a most romantic score. Its two main characters are explosively emotional and given to moods that vary in character but never slacken in intensity. Its orchestration is as colorful and scintillating as that of any opera in the repertory, and its melodies are unsurpassed in lyricism and

---

[12] Zola's speech is quoted in Mosco Carner's *Puccini: A Critical Biography* (New York: Knopf, 1959), p. 239.

[13] Whatever there may be of these romanticisms is found in the secondary figures: Micaëla, José's presumed fiancée from his native village of Elizondo, in the Basque country, is the only one who presents faith in God as a bulwark for her venture into dangerous land; and Escamillo, the glamorous and victorious matador, for all his fatuous posturing as an athletic hero (in Act II), holds back from killing José when the Act III knife fight gives him the opportunity to do so.

appropriateness for its characters. Although its musical atmosphere is manu-factured and Spanish audiences find *Carmen* to be anything but Spanish,[14] its gestures of melody, instrumentation, and rhythm have become the paradigm of Spanishness and exotic local color for opera audiences everywhere; in bull-fight arenas of southern France, it is the source of *corrida*[15] procession music.

The reason for this near-universal acceptance of Bizet's atmospheric devices is his skillful manipulation of Spanish stylistic elements, most of which he apparently derived from a single anthology of Spanish songs, *Échos d'Espagne,* borrowed by him from the library of the Paris Conservatoire de Musique. Among them is a song that Bizet actually adapted as the second phrase of the Act IV entr'acte, but more important is a consistency of style elements that he applied to striking effect: a frequency of triple time; the use of reiterated, hypnotic rhythms; the prevalence of the minor mode; the strumming of guitars (evoked by the use of pizzicato strings); and the inflec-tions of vocal and instrumental melodies by characteristic intervals, arabesques of ornament, and harmonies.

Among the exquisite touches in the score are the frequent niceties of harmony, instrumentation, and counterpoint. The flute is particularly

EXAMPLE CA-1 SPANISH ELEMENTS IN BIZET'S MUSIC FOR *Carmen*

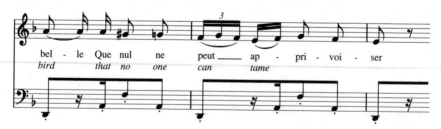

a) Act I, No. 5: "Habanera," with its typical background rhythm.

---

[14] Carmen's "Habanera" is modeled after a Cuban song by Sebastián Yradier (1809–1865), a Spanish composer who lived for a time in Cuba; Escamillo's Song of the Toreador is a French boulevard song *par excellence,* Micaëla's Act III aria of faith in God is right out of the pages of nineteenth-century French opera, and, in spite of the jangle of a tambourine, the gypsy dance of Act II uses the appurtenances of the mainstream European orchestra.

[15] A *corrida* is a bullfight.

EXAMPLE CA-1 (*Continued*)

b) Act I, No. 10: Andalusian dance rhythm, fast 3/8 meter, and melodic ornament in Carmen's "Seguidilla."

c) Act II, No. 12: Hypnotic rhythm and melodic ornament in the "Chanson bohème" ("Gypsy Song").

d) Act IV, Entr'acte, first phrase: Evocation of flamenco guitar strumming.

EXAMPLE CA-1 (*Continued*)

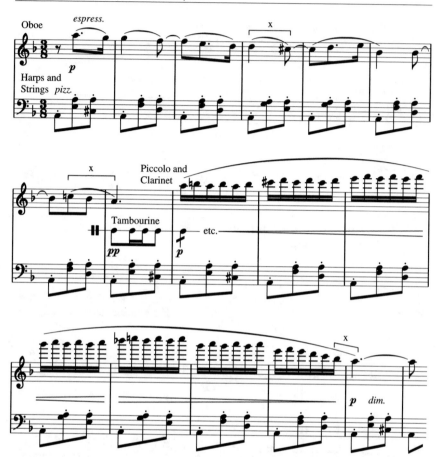

e) Act IV, Entr'acte, second phrase (adapted by Bizet from a Spanish folk song): Characteristic half-step phrase ending ("x"),[16] melodic flourish, guitar-like accompaniment, fast triple time.[17]

atmospheric throughout the score, but its associations with moral virtue and innocence as found in *Lucia di Lammermoor* or *Rigoletto* are at some remove. In *Carmen,* the sound of the flute is more directed at the rural or the scenically untamed as emblematic of the free gypsy life or the purity of nature: it introduces the "Seguidilla"—Carmen's promise of special entertainment at Lillas Pastia's tavern—and the "Chanson bohème" that is actually danced in that gypsy hangout; it is a consistent tone color in the quintet (No. 15, in Act II), when the mix of comedy and plotting among the gypsies goes on apace;

---

[16] See the discussion of the Phrygian cadence in Chapter 13 *(Die Walküre)*, note 10.

[17] This melody is from a *cante jondo* (lit., "deep" or "profound song"), a kind of flamenco music with text of tragic import or protest against injustice and an accompaniment of a fast-moving guitar pattern. See Nettl, p. 115.

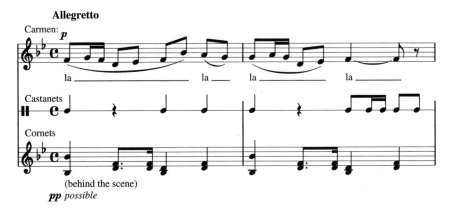

a) Act II, in No. 17: Cornets sound Retreat to Barracks as offstage counterpoint to Carmen's castanet-accompanied dance.

b) Act III, No. 19: Chromatic harmonies of smugglers' cautious descent down the mountain pass.

EXAMPLE CA-2 (*Continued*)

c) Act III, No. 20: Card Scene, with sprightly violins suggesting carefree attitudes of Frasquita and Mercédès, while cellos and double basses underscore Carmen's brooding over the cards' prediction of death.

it is the definitive timbre of the entr'acte before Act III's mountain scene; and it is a vital feature of the festive music outside the arena in Act IV. The swirling of the piccolo (lit., a "small" flute) to the children's chorus (No. 3, in Act I) plays simultaneously on the innocence of children and their toy-soldiering mockery of the soldier's march.

EXAMPLE CA-2 (*Continued*)

c) (*Continued*)

Convention and Controversy

Carmen is an opéra comique in several respects: plot development through spoken dialogue; tunefulness; picturesque settings; humor (in flirtation between the soldiers and Micaëla in Act I and the banter between the smugglers and the helpless Zuniga in Act II); and a heroine good and true (Micaëla) with sweetness of music to match.

From the outset, however, it was clear to Bizet's contemporaries that the Opéra-Comique, a theater of family entertainment and a frequent venue for the first social gathering of families to be joined by matrimony, was being turned inside out: the motivation of the action is often tawdry; the audience sees the death of the female lead and the degradation of the male lead; and the treatment of love that ranges from the cynical to the contemptuous implies the sterility of traditional sentiment and the power of the carnal. Among the most striking departures from tradition was the presentation of a "heroine" who does not suffer and refuses to surrender to the demands of society or those around her.

Bizet had not only to contend with those who expected "niceness" from the stage of the Opéra-Comique but also with anyone who sensed a touch of Wagner in his sound. Although Wagner was revered in some Parisian quarters, he and his music were profoundly despised in others, and the anti-Wagner crowd were ready to let fly at any manipulation of a recurrent motive or tonality-muddling chromaticism (such as the wonderful side-slipping harmonies accompanying No. 19, the chorus sung as the smugglers descend a mountainous slope; Example CA-2b. See also the *Magic Spell* motive of *Die Walküre*, p. 300).

The Fate Motive

The ominous melody (Example CA-3) of the last of the Prelude's three segments was a special target for the contra-Wagnerians. It occurs only in instruments, never in the voice, and appears in a variety of guises, always associated with Carmen's inexorable destiny and with her darker side as gypsy, seductress, and untamed spirit in a world that cannot tolerate untrammeled female independence. Critics heard with disparagement the chromatic twist

EXAMPLE CA-3 THE FATE MOTIVE.

a) Prelude to Act I, concluding section.

b) Act I: In No. 4, in diminution as introduction to Carmen's arrival in the square.

of its augmented second (marked "x" in the example) without giving credit
to its special importance: it is a startling change from the character of the rest
of the Prelude, and thus representative of the way tragedy can slash into life's
normalcy, and it is a sound indigenous to both Spanish folk music and some
Gypsy music,[18] and therefore fundamental to the atmosphere of the opera as
a whole. When we hear the motive for the first time, after the zesty sparkle of
the Prelude's festive music associated with fiestas and the excitement of the
corrida, it is announced portentously by tremolos and is punctuated by double bass thuds; when it heralds Carmen's flouncing into public view for her
Habanera in Act I, it is playful and bewitching (CA-3b). It snaps through
many of the vital scenes of the opera, but its most telling appearances are in
Act I, when Carmen first appears; in Act II, when it forms the substance for
the English horn introduction to José's Flower Song; in Act III when the
cards foretell Carmen's death; and in the final moments of Act IV when, after
the last reprise of Escamillo's song, it returns over the tremolos of the Prelude
to mark Carmen's murder and José's total abjection—his fate has become
inextricably linked to hers.

EXAMPLE CA-3 (*Continued*)

c) Act IV, José's final despair.

---

[18] It is associated with Hungarian gypsies in particular. The scale c / d / *e-flat/f-sharp* / g /
a-flat / b / c is usually described as the "gypsy scale"; the intervals emphasized here are augmented seconds. See, for example, *The New Harvard Dictionary of Music*, ed. Don Michael
Randel. Cambridge, Mass.: Belknap Press/Harvard University Press, 1986, p. 360.

THE PLOT AND ITS MUSIC

NOTE: "SD/R" refers to spoken dialogue in the opéra comique version. It is compressed into recitative in the Guiraud grand opera revision. "Recitative" refers to music composed by Bizet.

1 PRELUDE *Essentially a distillation of the action of Act IV, the music begins with festive fanfares associated with the procession and excitement of the act's bull fight ambience. A lyric statement of the refrain of Escamillo's Toreador Song is followed by a martial treatment of it and then a return to the brilliant materials of the* corrida. *The joyous mood is abruptly shattered by tremolos, then statements and expansions of the Fate motive. (Ex. CA-3a)*

Act I

A square in Seville; to one side is a guardhouse, to another the entrance to a tobacco factory; seen also is a bridge leading out of the square. At curtain, a group of Dragoons of the Regiment of Alcala are lounging about, waiting for the changing of the guard. Citizens, merchants, etc., wander to and fro.

2 SCENE and CHORUS (Morales, Dragoons; then Micaëla) *Sur la place, chacun passe, chacun vient, chacun va* ("In the square, everyone passes by, everyone comes, everyone goes") The troops idly observe the quiet and boring life of the city. Micaëla arrives to give José a message from his mother. Morales tells her that José is to come on duty soon and flirtatiously invites her to await José's arrival with him in the guardhouse. She laughingly refuses his offer and leaves. The troops resume their comments on the comings and goings around the square.

Flowing scale fragments in woodwinds and strings, with occasional, accented syncopated chords in the violins, suggest the bustle of the square. The music of the chorus is easygoing; their sense of detachment is pointed in the first-note accents of their short-phrased Drôles de gens que ces gens-là *("Funny people, these folks"). Light triplets in the violins intimate Micaëla's tentative entrance and uncertainty as to how to find José. The questions and hints of Morales and the soldiers are in lighthearted recitative; his information that José will soon arrive is to a buoyant, joking march tune.*

3 MARCH and CHORUS OF STREET CHILDREN *Avec la garde montante, / Nous arrivons, nous voilà!* ("With the mounting of the guard we arrive, here we are!") The military band is heard from afar. As the soldiers on duty form up for the ceremony and passers-by gather to watch, the relief unit parades over the bridge, led by Zuniga and Don José. Urchins run in from all sides, forming their own parade.

A cornet fanfare on stage announces the ceremony of the changing of the guard. The children's toy soldiery is proclaimed by scoring for piccolo and flute duet above cornet fanfares and pizzicato strings; the bugle is imitated via "ta ra ta ta ta ta ra." The orchestration remains effervescent, although instrumentation increases as the soldiers arrive, with piccolo and flute swirling above the march theme.

SD/R[19] (Morales, José) During the posting of the new sentries, Morales tells José of the visit of the girl from his home province. The retiring troops are called to order.

---

[19] This scene was a melodrama in the earliest versions of the opera, but it is spoken dialogue in the 1875 Choudens score.

MARCH (Street children) The old guard leaves while the children march off and the onlookers resume their business. The new guardsmen assume their duties, stack their lances, etc.

A reprise of the above.

SD/R (Zuniga, José) Zuniga tells José that he's only been with the regiment for two days and has never been to Seville before; he inquires about the large building across the square. José informs him that it is the tobacco factory, where many young girls are employed; in hot weather, he adds, they work in various stages of undress, although he professes disinterest. He tells Zuniga, who had overheard Morales relating the visit of the girl with braids and a blue skirt, of how that costume reminds him of home and how he was forced to leave home and join the army. The factory bell rings, announcing a break in the workday.

4 INTRODUCTION and CHORUS (Young men of the city and factory girls) *La cloche a sonné . . . Dans l'air nous suivons des yeux / La fumée / Qui vers les cieux monte* ("The bell has sounded . . . Our eyes watch the smoke climbing to the sky") José speaks of his resolve to make a chain for the priming pin for his rifle and moves off to the side, ignoring the people in the square. Soldiers issue from the guard-house, and the young men of the area saunter into the square to do some ogling. The factory girls appear, singly or in small groups. Smoking cigarettes, they liken the words of their lovers and the flattery of the onlookers to the smoke that rises in the air and vanishes.

> *Quickly rising upper string figures over timpani strokes and a cello/bass tremolo indicate the excitement of the men. The girls' languorous relaxation and the rising smoke of their ciga-rettes are vested in graceful string arpeggios, the gentle triplet sway of the 6/8 melody, and soaring woodwind scales and arpeggios. The vanishing of the smoke and the moment of peace of the scene comes through the divided final harmony of the women's chorus under a string tremolo that slowly fades.*

RECITATIVE (Soldiers, Men) *Mais nous ne voyons pas la Carmencita!* ("But we don't see la Carmencita!") The men eagerly ask the girls where Carmen is. Carmen saunters in, to their excitement; they crowd about her, asking her when she will bestow her favors on them. "When?" she asks. She cannot say: perhaps never, perhaps tomorrow, but certainly not today.

> *An abruptly heavy tremolando arpeggio is a prelude to the men's urge to see Carmen. The Fate motive in diminution (Ex. CA-3b) announces her sudden appearance. The men's sexu-al arousal is implied by their phrases of narrow melodic compass and hurried rhythms. Carmen's flippant response is to further snips of her motive in piccolo and flute; the finality of c'est certain ("That's for sure") is pointed by a loud pizzicato.*

5 HABANERA (Carmen) *L'amour est un oiseau rebelle / Que nul ne peut apprivoiser* ("Love is a free-living bird that no one can tame") Love is like a gypsy's life, she sings, unpredictable, perverse, untamable. "If you don't love me, I love you, and if I love you, watch out." *(Si tu ne m'aime pas, je t'aime; / Si je t'aime, prends garde à toi!).* During the aria, José pays no attention.

> *A seductive, steady-state rhythm (Ex. CA-1a) underlies the verse (a descending chromatic scale with brief triplet flourishes) of her strophic song. A sudden forte points her advice to men to watch out for themselves (Prends garde à toi!). As a refrain, she croons the word l'amour, the mode slipping sensuously into the major when the chorus takes up her melody. Two orchestral notes in unison give a closing fillip to one of opera's most remarkable and insightful moments.*

6 SCENE (Men) *Carmen! sur tes pas / Nous nous pressons tous!* ("Carmen! we follow your every step") The men gather around her as she heads back to the factory. Seeing that José is ignoring her, she saunters toward him.

The men's hurried phrases occur as before, to further appearances of the Fate motive in diminution.

6A MELODRAMA and **RECITATIVE** Carmen asks José what he is doing. Only then does he look at her. Told that he is fixing a chain for his priming pin, she laughingly suggests that it is the pin of her soul, throws at him the acacia flower she has been wearing and runs into the factory. All laugh; at the sound of the bell, the girls return to their work. José expresses annoyance at her boldness but, unobserved by anyone, picks up the flower, inhales its strong aroma and notes that if witches were real, this woman would certainly be one. Seeing Micaëla enter the square, he hurriedly hides the flower in his jacket and turns to greet her. She tells him she has been sent to him by his mother.

Carmen's approach to José is marked by darker appearances of the Fate motive and tremolos (similar to the Prelude's final episode). Brusquely dissonant brasses mark her toss of the flower; an animated reprise of part of the Habanera by the factory girls accompanies her run into the factory and expresses their merriment at Carmen's effrontery. A broadly lyric melody—perhaps the pivot-point of the opera—illuminates José's sudden surge of deep feeling as he picks up the blossom. His description of Carmen as a witch is to yet another diminution of the Fate motive, first in high strings, then more ominously but still quickly in the cellos. As he takes in the flower's aroma, woodwinds taunt us with the memory of the Habanera's second phrase. His surprise at seeing Micaëla is symbolized by disjointed orchestral fragments.

7 DUET (José, Micaëla) *Parle-moi de ma mère!* ("Tell me about my mother!") His mother, she says, has sent her with a letter, some money, and a kiss. The letter, she tells him, speaks of missing her long-absent son and forgiving him. Micaëla chastely delivers the kiss, too. The two sing of José's happy memories (*Ma mère, je la vois*—"My mother, I see her") and his longing to return home.

José mutters his relief that his mother has diverted him from an obviously dangerous path (*Qui sait de quel démon j'allais être la proie!*—"Who knows of what demon I was about to become the prey!") Sloughing off Micaëla's puzzlement, he gives her words of love and repentance to his mother and—through Micaëla—returns his mother's kiss.

When Micaëla begins, the music turns to a calm and steady pulse in the strings. Each of her phrases is tenderly lyric, as is the rising scale heard first in strings, then in horns, the latter consistently adding dignity to her character. She begins shyly, oboe and piccolo suggesting purity (she was, she says, given her instructions as she and José's mother left a service in the chapel), but her music becomes richly flowing (Ex CA-4a), with harp arpeggios and warm scoring. The kiss is "delivered" at the end of a rising chromatic line (the opposite of Carmen's descending chromaticism) and a brief but rich string episode that leads to a second, equally lovely melody (Ma [Sa] mère, je la [Il la re-]vois—"My mother, I see her [His mother, he sees her again") sung by the two in a sweet canon. The ardent orchestration and rhythmic murmuring are momentarily set offstride by the return of a quick recall of the Fate motive and some anxious recitative before the two songful themes return in a free mix to conclude the duet. The duet is ineffably lovely; its mood is not encountered again in the opera.

SD/R José reads that his mother wants him to behave well and, when he has completed his military service, to return home and marry Micaëla. Micaëla leaves, promising to return soon to get José's reply. Alone for a moment, José promises himself to follow his mother's wishes. He begins a dismissive comment about the gypsy and her bewitching flowers when chaos erupts from the factory.

8 CHORUS *Au secours!* ("Help!") Screaming for the guards, factory girls pour into the square, calling for the soldiers to break up a vicious fight between

Carmen and another girl. Zuniga orders José to take two men and investigate; while José is doing so, factions besiege Zuniga as to who was at fault. As the crowd is pushed back, Carmen appears at the factory door, led by José and followed by the soldiers.

Tremolos and scales boil out of the strings; chromatic slides follow them as accompaniment to wild trills. The conflicting narrations of women's voices are in bursts of repeated notes, the whole turmoil accented by blunt chords in winds and brass.

SD José reports that, in a wild battle, Carmen had knifed an "X"—a St. Andrew's cross—on the cheek of her opponent but has submitted to his arresting her as meekly as a lamb.

9 SONG and MELODRAMA (Zuniga, Carmen) *Tra la la la . . . Coupe-moi, brûle-moi* ("Tra la la la . . . Hit me, burn me") Carmen answers Zuniga's spoken questions with a saucy song, alternating snippy "tra la las" with vows to say nothing, because, although she loves someone (and will until she dies) she keeps such matters as secrets in her heart. Some women break through the cordon with more accusations; Carmen is prevented by José from striking one of them. As the soldiers clear the square entirely, Zuniga orders José to bind Carmen's wrists, promising Carmen a prison term. He leaves José to guard her while he goes into the guardhouse to write out the warrant, after which José is to conduct her to jail.

Carmen's appearance in the square is heralded by a return of the grandly romantic melody heard earlier when José had picked up the flower. Here it is given additional lushness by a countermelody high in the cello range. Zuniga and José speak during the scene; Carmen sings. Carmen's sauciness is set to a an actual folksong,[20] here given a sensuous depth by low string harmonies and countermelodies for solo flute and solo violin, both in their low registers.

A wild flurry of tremolando *arpeggios is a momentary interruption for the eruption of violence, before Carmen returns to her insinuating song. The tune continues in staccato fashion on solo violin, then solo cello, yielding to a hushed return of the Fate motive in low flute and clarinet as Zuniga withdraws.*

SD/R Alone with José, Carmen asks where he is to take her. He loosens the rope when she complains that it is bruising her wrists. When she suggests that he should help her escape because he loves her, José forbids her to speak.[21] She agrees not to talk.

10 SEGUIDILLA and DUET (Carmen; Carmen and José) *Près des remparts de Séville, / Chez mon ami Lillas Pastia* ("Near the Seville ramparts, at my friend Lillas Pastia's place") Looking at José purposefully, she sings of the tavern where she will dance and drink Manzanilla, hopefully with a new lover, since being alone is so dull and her heart is free for the taking (*Elle est à prendre . . .*).

José, who has come close to her as she sings, again forbids her to talk, but she responds that she is free to sing and think of the Dragoon—only a corporal—who loves her and with whom she has decided to be content.

---

[20] Its text was a satire on hair styles, hinted at by Carmen's "cut . . . burn."

[21] Dialogue usually omitted draws from a Mérimée passage in which Carmen, recognizing that José is a Basque from Navarre, claims to be a nice girl from that area who was kidnapped by gypsies and is simply trying to work her way back home. Out of loyalty to one from his own country, José should help her, she suggests. José challenges her veracity, whereupon she unconcernedly admits she is indeed a gypsy, but that it was a nice thing for her to take the trouble to lie to him. A fascinating woman.

Completely hooked, José unties her wrists, whispering his demand that she keep her promise to love him and to meet him at Pastia's. She reaffirms the happy prospects she has laid out for him.

The seduction of José is in three parts: Carmen's song, a brief duet, then a return of the song. The song's graceful melody, with occasional ornamental embellishments, is set over a hypnotic, guitar-like accompaniment of harp and strings (Ex. CA-1b), spiced with brief woodwind colorings. As she poses the question Qui veut mon âme? *("Who wants my heart?"), she enters into a brief canon with low flute, implying a dialogue with an unnamed lover. In the duet, José is restricted to patches of repeated notes, becoming songful only when he presses her to keep her promise (*Ta promesse, tu la tiendras . . . si je t'aime, Carmen, tu m'aimeras?—*"Your promise, would you hold to it . . . If I love you, Carmen, would you love me?") She practically hypnotizes him by sighing repeated-note patterns over a chromatic descent (Ex. CA-5a). When he unties her hands, the recapitulation of the Seguidilla nails him for good, her concluding "tra la la la la" providing an exuberant and triumphant finis.*

11 FINALE Zuniga returns with the arrest order and directs José to escort Carmen to prison. *Sotto voce,* Carmen instructs José to march behind her and to fall heavily when she gives him a push; she will take care of the rest. Softly singing her song of gypsy love, Carmen is led toward the bridge as people return to the square. On the bridge, she turns and shoves José, who acts his part. Amid confusion and disorder, and to the general enjoyment of the crowd, Carmen laughs and makes her escape as the cigarette girls surround Zuniga with great merriment.

To the strings' hushed four-part fugue based on the music of the tumultuous argument of the factory girls after the stabbing incident, Zuniga issues his orders loudly; Carmen whispers hers. She walks ahead of José in her hip-twitching way to the tune of the Habanera. She pauses significantly on the phrase Prends garde à toi, *then moves along as flute and clarinet twist the tune subtly and suggestively in both melody and harmony; there is a pianissimo timpani roll, then a boisterous eruption of the fight music as she runs off.*

ENTR'ACTE Bassoons, accompanied by a ruffling snare drum, present the tune that José will be heard singing as he comes from barracks to the tavern. A good-humored dialogue that alternates high woodwinds with strings presents a light, dotted-rhythm motive before the clarinet takes up a repeat of José's melody. The entr'acte ends quietly with a final reprise of the melody sifting down in fragments through the various woodwind timbres.

Act II

A month later, at Lillas Pastia's tavern. Gypsies are dancing, while others play guitar and tambourine. Carmen, Frasquita, and Mercédès are at a supper table with Zuniga and other officers. Zuniga is talking to Carmen softly, but she ignores him, watching the dancing.

12 CHANSON BOHÈME [Gypsy Song] (Carmen, Frasquita, Mercédès) *Les tringles des sistres tintaient / Avec un éclat métallique* ("The sistrum[22] bars jangled with metallic sparkle") Carmen leaves Zuniga and begins to sing and dance, soon joined by Mercédès and Frasquita. The text of their song is the substance of the

---

[22] The sistrum is an ancient Egyptian percussion instrument (with a rounded frame and a handle, crossed with loose, jangling bars (called *tringles* or *baguettes*) used in the worship of Isis. Given the Egyptian provenance of the Gypsies, the reference to this instrument in their song is appropriate, although most performances use tambourines instead.

music—gypsies dancing to Basque[23] guitars and tambourines, their red and orange dresses swirling as their dance gains speed and spins wildly.

Above pizzicato harp, violas, and cellos, harmonizing flutes begin a delicately ornamented dance in triple time (Ex. CA-1c). Sudden fortes and decorations in other woodwinds provide exciting accents before a momentary quieting down. When Carmen begins the first of the three verses of the song, horns join the flutes in a descending chromatic countermelody. Tambourines are soon added, then a rhythmic intensification via off-beat woodwind chords. As the song progresses, accompanying figures become more complex, tempo becomes more animated, and the dance moves swiftly to a wild, whirling climax.

SD/R Asked to observe closing time, the officers invite the girls to the theater for the hour before roll call. The girls decline. Zuniga, asking Carmen if she is angry with him for sending her to prison, tells Carmen that the soldier who let her escape has been demoted and this day been released from a month's incarceration.

13 CHORUS and MELODRAMA *Vivat! Vivat le toréro!* ("Hurrah! Hurrah for the matador!") A passing torchlight procession is heard; Frasquita recognizes the parade's honoree as Escamillo, a celebrated matador from Granada. Zuniga invites him in for a toast, all raising their glasses to Escamillo and the art of bullfighting.

The offstage chorus is a brief fanfare that, like the Chanson bohème, *is intensified with repetitions, addition of instruments, and a dramatic crescendo.*

14 COUPLETS [Toreador Song] (Escamillo, et al.) *Votre toast je peux vous le rendre* ("I can return your toast") Escamillo offers his own toast to the drama of the arena, likening himself to the soldiers who also live to fight. He finishes each stanza with the image of dark eyes watching the victor and love as his reward. At the pinnacle of the final verse, he shares the idea of love with Frasquita, Mercédès, and, in a special way, Carmen.

Accompaniment by brass and woodwind fanfares is appropriate to Escamillo's noting that both soldiers and toreadors live to fight. Triplet figures spurt upward and orchestration becomes more complex as his verse proceeds; the tuneful refrain is simple. When Escamillo describes the love awaiting the victor, Carmen's echoing of l'amour *uses an interval that goes beyond the octave (Ex. CA-6c) and thus puts her in a world of her own.*

SD/R Escamillo asks Carmen her name. His supposition that they might be lovers gets her rejoinder that if he were seriously to think such a thing, he'd be out of his mind. Zuniga promises to come back in an hour, in spite of Carmen's advice not to do so.

CHORUS Singing the Toreador Song, all leave save Carmen, Frasquita, Mercédès, and Lillas Pastia.

SD/R Pastia informs them that Dancaïre and Remendado have arrived with "Egyptian business" on their minds. The two smugglers enter as Pastia shutters the windows and locks the doors. Dancaïre tells the girls that plans are afoot to smuggle some English goods into the Gibraltar area.

15 QUINTET (Dancaïre, Frasquita, Mercédès, Remendado, Carmen) *Nous avons en tête une affaire* ("We have an idea for some business") Dancaïre asserts that the participation of the girls is necessary, for, when it comes to deception, trickery, and thievery *(Quand il s'agit de tromperie, de duperie, de volerie)*, women are indispensable. Carmen, however declines to join them, for she is hopelessly in love.

---

[23] The reference to José's native dialect is not especially pointed.

The ensemble is a breathtaking, fleet-footed masterpiece of everchanging yet always gossamer color, both vocal and instrumental; voices and instruments share the motives, developed in the manner of a symphonic movement in sonata form. Flecks of woodwind and string timbres are occasionally softened by quiet horns, but the mood is never chastened until the unexpected intensity of Carmen's announcement that she is in love (Je suis amoureuse!). Her announcement is in a suddenly slower tempo, with accompaniment reduced to divided violas and cellos. The quickness of the opening returns as accompaniment to a lyric statement by Carmen that they can go if they want, but she will remain. The music of Quand il s'agit returns, slightly altered, when the five agree that nothing can beat women when it comes to conniving.

SD/R To their incredulous questions and pleas for pragmatism (love is no reason not to be useful), Carmen admits she is awaiting the soldier who went to jail for her. They doubt he will come.

16 CANZONETTA[24] (José) *Halte-là! / Qui va la? / Dragon d'Alcala!* ("Halt! Who goes there? A Dragoon of Alcala") José is heard singing as he nears the tavern. Apparently just a soldier's tune, its words have special meaning for Carmen, for when she learned he had been incarcerated, she had sent to him a bread loaf of a special type made in the nearby town of Alcala and had hidden in it a gold coin and a file. José's honor would not allow him to take advantage of her gift, but now he is coming to her, knowing of her concern for him.

An unaccompanied, fanfare-like tune in two strophes, characterized by dotted rhythms and open fifths (Ex. CA-5b). It starts in the minor and ends in the major, as did Carmen's Habanera. Perhaps, then, this innocent-seeming song, with its hidden textual message that only Carmen understands, is also meaningful to her in its musical language.

SD/R Dancaïre urges Carmen to persuade José to join them.

CANZONETTA (José) *Halte-là* etc. José sings a second strophe.

SD/R (Carmen, José) Telling Carmen that he has been free only two hours, José confesses that he adores Carmen; he admits to jealousy when Carmen informs him that his superior officer enjoyed her singing and dancing and is in love with her. Now, however, she will dance for him alone.

NOTE: The music and texts of the following scene, including Carmen's dancing, José's Flower Song, and the Là-bas, là-bas dans la montagne *are printed in the scores as parts of a single "number." I have broken them into segments for ease of description.*

17 DUET (Carmen, José) *Je vais danser en votre honneur* ("I will dance in your honor") She sings quietly as she dances, accompanying herself on castanets.[25] The Retreat to Barracks, played by a military band[26] parading through the area, is heard. José takes Carmen's arm, pointing out the fanfare that orders his return, but she is unconcerned. Declaring that it will serve as additional accompaniment, she resumes, but José forces her to stop.

---

[24] See Chapter 3, note 10.

[25] In the novella, Carmen has misplaced her castanets, so she breaks a plate and clacks the fragments of it.

[26] Bizet requires cornets, not bugles or trumpets, in spite of the indications in the Oeser and Soldan scores.

Castanets and pizzicato strings accompany Carmen's wordless, swaying melody in a simple but richly atmospheric fashion. The enrichment by fanfare music of the two cornets (Ex. CA-2a) is wondrously subtle and effective. José's music is also somewhat in the manner of fanfare, for it is reflective of the soldier's mind, not the lover's.

Carmen is outraged that she could be so stupid as to fall in love with someone who prefers the army to her. She crudely makes fun of the bugle calls and, throwing his headgear at him, orders him to leave.

A single note low in the clarinet punctuates Carmen's astonishment. A rush of violin scale opens the floodgates of her anger, her first phrase plummeting from the top of the staff to below it (cf. Ex. CA-6b). With the woodwinds, she mocks military tattoos, dismissing him from her presence to a boiling tremolo and further instrumental parodies of bugle fanfares.

He tries to explain, but she will have none of it until he violently demands she listen to him.

José's first remonstrance is urgent yet dignified, clarinet arpeggios lending rhythmic regularity to an arching melody in which he proclaims that no woman has ever troubled his soul so much. Carmen's derision returns unabated. José's demand that she listen to him is angular in melody, powerful in high-note climax, and rhythmically turbulent in its accompanying figures.

ARIA[27] (José) *La fleur que tu m'avais jetée, / Dans ma prison m'était restée, / Flétrie et sèche* ("The flower that you threw at me, stayed with me in my cell, dried and withered") José reveals that all during his imprisonment the acacia blossom kept its scent and kept her image before him. Although he cursed her, vowed to hate her, and asked Fate why she had been placed in his path, he became consumed with but one desire, to see her again, for he loves her *de tout mon être*—"with all my being."

José's aria is an elegy, a lament to the loss of traditional expressions of love and to the complete subjugation to Carmen's spell. His through-composed melody is appropriate for a man who acts impetuously and departs readily from the traditional configurations of behavior (or musical form). The English horn mournfully introduces it with the Fate motive, extremely soft and accompanied by tremolos. His narration is melodically elegant and poetic, with subdued string syncopations hinting at his troubled spirit. As his song unfolds, it becomes more stressful, rising in a sequence of short phrases (Ex. CA-5c) to an ever-changing background until it reaches a climactic B-flat at the end of Et j'étais une chose à toi! *("I was utterly yours" [lit., "I was a thing to you"]). His final avowal of love elicits harmonies from another key, much as Carmen's* l'amour *had gone out of key at the end of the Toreador Song. Both thus speak of love as a phenomenon that transcends mundane experience.*

RECITATIVE *Non! tu ne m'aimes pas* ("No, you don't love me") Carmen says to José that if he really loved her he would go off with her.

To muttered dotted figures in the orchestra (related to the death archetypes discussed in Chapter 3), Carmen responds at first with the intonation of a single pitch, her whispered "No, you don't love me" perfectly calculated to ensnare José still further.

DUET (Carmen, José) *Là-bas, là-bas dans la montagne. / Là-bas, là-bas tu me suivras* ("Over there, over there in the mountains, Over there you would follow me") Carmen paints a romantic picture of the free life of the gypsy, riding in the open country with the only law being one's own desires.

---

[27] This is not identified as a separate number in the score but is part of an extended scene.

The flow of labial consonants and the narrow compass of the melody seem to enmesh José, whose participation is restricted to sighs in 2/4 while she floats her image of life, love, and liberty in an alluring 6/8. Her enticement ends with a flute's murmur of her melody, but the resolution of the accompanying evocative woodwind chords is broken off by José's fanfare-accompanied resolve to be true to his duty.

RECITATIVE José is hesitant; then, to her contempt, he refuses to desert the army and turns to leave. A knock at the door stops him in his tracks.

18 FINALE (Zuniga, José, Carmen, the gypsies) *Holà! Carmen! Holà! Holà!* Zuniga knocks again, then forces open the door. Seeing José, he chides Carmen for rejecting an officer in favor of a soldier. When he orders José to decamp, José angrily refuses; when Zuniga strikes him, José draws his sword. Carmen leaps between them, calling to her companions for help.

Zuniga's sight of José leads him to a joking, lightly accompanied ditty for his teasing of Carmen; his peremptory order to José is curt and angular. José's response of jealous rage is accompanied by a violent tutti; *tumbling triplets accentuate Carmen's effort to separate the men and the running in of the gypsies.*

Zuniga is disarmed. Under the persuasion of a pistol at his head, he accepts with good grace the "invitation" to come along with them for a time (*Bel officier, l'amour / Vous joue en ce moment un assez villain tour*—"My handsome officer, love has just played a rather dirty trick on you"). Zuniga promises José a reckoning.

A scherzando style takes over for the poking of fun at the discomfited but gracious Zuniga, who accepts the music of the gypsies just as he accepts their invitation; trills in the strings, however, make his warning to José quite menacing.

To Carmen's *Es-tu des nôtres maintenant?* ("Are you one of us, now?") José sorrowfully admits to having no choice. All enthusiastically urge him to look forward to the liberty of their life in the country.

A powerful appeal to liberty is given a new series of mounting melodic fragments before the music of Carmen's enticement returns climactically and quasi-militarily to sweep José into a world that every instinct tells him to reject.

ENTR'ACTE *A serenely flowing flute melody over harp arpeggios suggests the quiet picturesqueness of the scene to be revealed when the curtain rises. Repetitions of the theme are given to clarinet, then bassoon with English horn; fragments of it under a string countermelody end the beautifully atmospheric piece quietly.*

Act III

Months later. Night. A cleft in the mountain wilderness not far from the valley where José's mother and Micaëla live.

19 SEXTET and CHORUS (Smugglers) *Écoute, compagnon, écoute! / La fortune est là-bas, là-bas* ("Listen, friend, listen, fortune is over there") The gypsies, many of them carrying bales of illicit goods, carefully make their way down the mountainside, anticipating success in spite of the dangers they face.

The careful progress of the gypsy band is set out in delicate dotted rhythms and muted dynamics, above a plodding, rising scale in low strings, suggestive of their labored ascent to the lip of the mountain pass. To a sudden forte *and a quick* diminuendo, *as if someone might overhear them, they warn each other of the danger of a false step* (Prends garde de faire un faux pas; *Ex. CA-2b) to an intensely chromatic series of falling parallel harmonies, suggestive of the steep descent they must traverse to their resting place.*

SD/R They pause to rest so that Dancaïre and Remendado can scout ahead. Relations between José and Carmen having become seriously strained, José tries to make peace, but her cold response is that she loves him less now than before. Seeing him gaze down at the valley, she asks what he is thinking about. His answer is that he is thinking of his mother who, he knows, still believes him to be honest. Carmen is scornful and suggests that José would do well to rejoin his mother, since it is clear he is not cut out for gypsy life. The implied threat of José's demand that she not speak again of their separating is clear to her.

20 TRIO [CARD SCENE] (Frasquita, Mercédès, Carmen) *Mêlons! Coupons!* ("Let's shuffle! Cut!") Frasquita and Mercédès begin to tell their own fortunes with tarot cards. Mercédès finds a romantic young lover who will carry her off into the mountains, Frasquita a rich old husband who dies and leaves his fortune to her. Happily, they reshuffle and try again.

Carmen, who has been watching them, takes up her own cards. The import of the sequence of diamonds and spades is unavoidable: death.

The cards are shuffled to the scurrying of scale fragments in the strings; sparkles of wood-wind and string sounds mark the turnover of the cards, and a buoyant lyric melody informs the pleasure and superficiality of Frasquita and Mercédès.

The light tremolo that accompanies some of their card playing is transformed into a brooding moment for strings and octaves in the low brass as Carmen takes up the cards. The Fate motive in fast tempo snaps in the flute before a sudden chromatic scale descent as she reveals the death-predicting diamonds and spades (Carreau! Pique!). Minor chords plod ominously in the strings, as Carmen acknowledges the inevitability of Fate (Ex. CA-6a), her repetitions of La mort! ("Death") in marked contrast to the babbling of her companions (Ex. CA-2b). Cellos and basses land heavily on the Fate motive, the trio ending abruptly and harshly.

SD/R Dancaïre and Remendado return, announcing that there are only three guards. The girls assure them that there is nothing to worry about. Dancaïre instructs José to control his jealousy and to keep watch while they set about the matters at hand.

21 ENSEMBLE (Carmen, Frasquita, Mercédès and gypsies) *Quant au douanier, c'est notre affaire!* ("As for the customs official, that's our business!") As all head for the path, the girls promise the men that they can be trusted to use their wiles to proper effect. All but José set out for the border.

A self-confident march is undertaken by Frasquita, Mercédès, and Carmen, with the other women of the gypsy band soon joining in. A perky dotted rhythm is given to the topmost voices over an energetic countermelody for Carmen and, later, the lower voices of the women's chorus.

SD/R Micaëla and a villager come on the now apparently deserted scene. She assures him that she is not afraid; she is willing to be left alone in an area known to be used by the smugglers because she wants to speak to one of them. The guide leaves, nervously and hurriedly.[28]

---

[28] This passage is often omitted, Micaëla beginning her aria after a brief, tremulous recitative.

22 ARIA (Micaëla) *Je dis que rien ne m'épouvante* ("I say that nothing frightens me") Micaëla tries to build up her own courage by affirming her faith in God. She is terrified but determined to confront the woman who has brought crime and dishonor to the man she loves.

The aria (Ex. CA-4b), an ABA form, is given pastoral atmosphere and personal dignity by the rich writing for French horns; a cello underpinning recalls the harp arpeggios of her Act I appearance but moves faster and covers a wider range so as to suggest her unease. The middle section of the aria is given over to Micaëla's determination to confront the woman who has lured José away from duty and honor, her determination made all the more worthy by the syncopations that indicate the fear and desperation that assail her. The conclusion of the aria is a literal return of the opening section.

SD/R She sees José aiming his rifle in another direction. When he fires, she fearfully darts into hiding. Escamillo appears, pondering a bullet hole in his hat. José steps forth and angrily demands that he identify himself.

23 DUET (Escamillo, José) *Je suis Escamillo* ("I'm Escamillo") Escamillo complies, averring that he has come to the mountains because he's in love with a gypsy girl. When he informs José that it is Carmen in whom he is interested and that he knows she is now tired of her former dragoon lover, José warns him that to take a gypsy girl from her lover involves a cost—payment in *coups de navaja* (blows from a brutally sharp type of clasp knife).

Escamillo, realizing that he stands before the man to whom he has just referred, accepts the challenge. The battle is engaged.

Escamillo slips and is about to be killed by José.[29]

The duet begins in a jocular fashion, Escamillo wryly noting his narrow escape to a sprightly triplet figuration in the woodwinds. Love being the reason for his venturing into the wild begets quieter strings; his announcement that he is seeking Carmen produces for José's outburst an abrupt orchestral crescendo and a flurry of orchestral figures. Escamillo settles into an insouciant tune for his tale of Carmen's readiness to take another lover, with punctuating explosion from José's music (as one might expect). The two share the same militant rhythms and brass chords as they ready themselves for the fight. The battle is a blistering array of rising string scales and answering woodwind motives around heavy brass accents; it ends abruptly.

24 FINALE Carmen and Dancaïre arrive just in time to save him. Thanking Carmen for saving his life and inviting José to resume their rivalry anytime he wishes, Escamillo invites all to the bullfights at Seville. His pointed remark that anyone who loves him will be there elicits a threatening gesture from José. Escamillo takes his leave calmly and somewhat disdainfully.

As the gypsies prepare to resume their expedition, Micaëla is discovered hiding nearby. Her brief tale of José's mother's grief and longing for her son induces a sarcastic suggestion from Carmen that gypsy work is not for José and that he ought to go. That, of course, produces a furious reaction from José, who, viciously jealous over the likelihood that she is eager to join a new lover, cries, "You are mine, you she-devil, and I will force you to submit to the destiny that binds your fate to mine (*Ah, je te tiens, fille damnée, / Et je te forcerai bien / À subir la destinée / Qui rive ton sort au mien*). He rejects the warning of the ensemble that his actions are likely to result in heavy cost, but, when Micaëla adds to her narrative that his mother is dying and would not wish to pass on without forgiving him, his determination vanishes.

---

[29] The original form of the opera has a more extended combat in which Escamillo is clearly in control of things at first, but declines to strike.

Dramatic recitative is shaped by the turn of fortunes, Escamillo returning to the easy grace of his arrival music for his invitation to all to attend the bullfights and his warning to José; he departs to divided strings harmonizing a solo cello insinuatingly playing the refrain of the Act II Couplets.

As they take up their bundles, the gypsies reprise the music of their cautions to each other from the start of the act; the discovering of Micaëla interrupts them. Micaëla's appeal to José is to the music of her Act I delivery of the message from José's mother (Ex. CA-4a). Carmen's disdain is accompanied by tremolos; so is José's response, culminating in his defiant vow to stay and force her to submit to his will (Ex. CA-5d), a melodic line that is made threatening and powerful by its climactic arches, strong accents, and heavy trombone harmonies. His repeat of this music a half step higher lends it desperation as well.

He agrees to leave but warns Carmen that they will meet again. As he and Micaëla begin their descent, Escamillo is heard singing his Toreador Song. José pauses to stare at Carmen who is listening intensely; he then turns and leaves with Micaëla. The gypsies take up their bales and set out once again.

José's response to Micaëla's brief but effective rising scale announcing the imminent death of his mother is again desperate, his warning to Carmen pointed by blunt horns and strings. The Fate motive and its attendant tremolos loom once again, the distant singing of the Toreador Song refrain being another of the multitude of master strokes in the opera. Ominous timpani strokes lend a macabre quality to a final appearance of the gypsies' Écoute! compagnon, écoute music; a potent triplet tutti ends the act.

ENTR'ACTE *A vigorous, strum-like fanfare (Ex. CA-1d) precedes a spirited oboe melody that is in turn followed by an ornament in the Spanish style (Ex. CA-1e). A sense of ornamental flourish pervades the piece; even the hushed ending is arrived at through quick scale ascents and trills before the final guitar-like pizzicatos.*

Act IV

A square before the walls of the Seville arena on the day of the bullfight. An entrance to the arena is closed off by a long canvas curtain. Crowds press their way forward.

25 CHORUS *A deux cuartos, / des éventails pour s'éventer* ("For two cuartos, fans to cool yourself . . .") Vendors of fans, oranges, and other items hawk their wares.

Festive triplets, repeated notes for trumpets and French horns, and sparkling woodwind scales characterize the brilliance and spirited movement of the crowds. The calls of the vendors are fragments that add to the general vivacity of the scene.

26 MARCH and CHORUS *Les voici, voici la quadrille, / la quadrille des Toréros* ("Here they are, the cuadrilla, the team of matadors") The parade of corrida participants and celebrities arrives, each acclaimed except the ugly-faced sheriff— *l'alguazil*—who is heartily booed with *À bas! À bas!* The greatest cheers are for Escamillo who arrives last, Carmen on his arm.

Cornet fanfares (akin to the March of the street children of Act I) announce the arrival of the important personages; their rhythms sparkle though much of the procession, which becomes musically more expansive and coloristic with the return of the opening music of the opera's Prelude. At the climactic entrance of Escamillo and Carmen, Escamillo's signature tune is sung by the acclaiming crowd to greet him.

Escamillo advises Carmen that if she loves him *(Si tu m'aimes)*, she will be proud of him before long. She responds that she hopes to die if she has ever loved anyone as she loves him.

> *The exchange of sentiments between Escamillo and Carmen (Ex. CA-7) is a relaxed, lyric interlude; Carmen responds with his music—for both of them it is easygoing and sincere for the moment, and that's all either of them would want.*

As the mayor *(alcalde)* arrives and leads the rest of the procession into the arena, Frasquita and Mercédès whisper to Carmen to leave the area, for they have seen José lurking nearby. Carmen dismisses their fears—she is not one to tremble before him, so she will wait and speak to him. Mercédès and Frasquita warn her to be careful, then follow the rest of the crowd to watch the fights.

> *The parade resumes, but now it has become background action, its music restricted to harmonizing flutes and the counterpoint of bassoons as an ironic commentary to the warnings of Frasquita and Mercédès.*

27 DUET and CHORUS (Carmen, José) *C'est toi! C'est moi!* ("It's you!" "Yes, it's me.") José begins calmly: he is not there to threaten but to implore her to forget the past and to find a new life with him under other skies.[30] Carmen quietly avers that all is over between them *(Entre nous, tout est fini!)*

> *The fanfares of the arena quickly move into the background via restriction to woodwind timbres; a descending chromatic fragment in the strings brings the final confrontation into the foreground. José's first utterances have dignity and rhythmic flow; Carmen's answers are short and blunt. José appeals to her with a broad and moving theme (Carmen, il est temps encore—"Carmen, there is still time"), but the string syncopations and increasingly complex accompanying figures belie his attempt at dignity, just as they had in the Flower Song. Her angry rejection is to quick spurts of trembling scale fragments.*

José begs Carmen to let him save her, but she answers that even though she knows her hour has come, she will not give in to him. The two "talk at" each other, neither hearing what the other is trying to say.

> *The only real duet passage is simultaneously sung with different words and different melodies, his a repeat of the broad melody he has just sung, hers short phrased and increasingly varied in its note durations as her patience wears thin. The section ends with a death motive throbbing in the timpani.*

When Carmen says flatly that she no longer loves him *(Non, je ne t'aime plus)*, José's desperate response is that he loves her and will do anything she wants if only she will stay with him. Carmen cries that she never surrenders; she was born free and will die free *(Libre elle est née et libre elle mourra!)*.

> *Low clarinet, then horns point to José's shocked realization that she no longer loves him; a measure of orchestral silence followed by poignant brass and winds is an effective exclamation point to it. At her hollow reinforcement of that truth (No, je ne t'aimais plus), José bursts into begging (CA-5e) and pleading, his melody reaching and plunging, doubled by strings at pitch and the octave.*

The shouts of excitement from the bullring impel Carmen to head for the entrance, but José bars the way, vowing that she will not pass but will follow him. As hurrahs are again heard, Carmen tries again to enter the arena; when José asks furiously if she loves Escamillo, she proclaims firmly that she does and will repeat that she does even in the face of death *(Je l'aime, et devant la mort même / Je répéterai que je l'aime)*.

---

[30] In the novella, José proposes that they go to America.

Bizet, *Carmen* (1875), Act IV: The tragic climax of the final confrontation between Don José (Anton de Ritter) and his beloved Carmen (Pari Samar). Staatstheater am Gärtnerplatz, Munich, 1971: production by Kurt Pscherer. Courtesy Deutsches Theatermuseum, Munich. Photo Hildegard Steinmetz.

The choral fragments from the arena are drawn from the processional music of the Prelude and the opening of Act IV; between these episodes we have the musical struggle of Carmen and José, their phrases now short and violently disjunct, the orchestral music writhing with vivid tremolos and eruptions.

José draws his knife and demands twice more that she go with him. Furious and impatient, she takes the ring he had given her and throws it away (*Tiens!* "There!").

Her contempt grows apace, her melody now stretching angrily across the breadth of the staff (Ex. CA-6b), culminating in a shout as she hurls the ring into the street.

While the crowds inside the arena exult with Escamillo's song of victory, José fatally stabs Carmen. As people enter the square from the stadium, singing the song of the victorious Escamillo, José kneels by her body. To their shock, he tells them they may arrest him, for he has slain his beloved Carmen.

She is stabbed to death as the Toreador Song refrain is heard for the last time; as it reaches its climactic note, the Fate motive lances into the musical picture, a plangent and agonizing commentary on the gypsy girl who gave her life rather than surrender love and liberty, and the despairing soldier who has destroyed every reason for living.

The Characters

Morales (baritone) *[morr-AHL-less]*

A *brigadier*[31] who appears only in the first scene in a brief flirtation with Micaëla as she comes with a message for José. Morales's easygoing, melodious, and symmetrical phrases are valuable for establishing a mood of calm and ordinariness.

Micaëla (soprano) *[mee-cah-yeh-LAH]*

A character not found in the novella, she is an orphan raised from childhood by José's mother. Now seventeen, wearing a blue skirt and her hair in the two braids customary to Navarre, she comes to José in both Act I and Act III with messages from his mother. She and José share his mother's expectation that they will marry.

Micaëla's music symbolizes the traditional values she brings to the action. The harmonies accompanying her are simple and steady, and she sings in the regular phrases of conventional song. Her one aria, the Act III "Je dis que rien ne m'épouvante" (No. 22, "I say that nothing will frighten me"), is the only soliloquy of the opera; it is a prayer in the most conventional of forms, the ABA.[32] This aria features the opera's only prominent music for French horn, a warm sound that lends her dignity and strength of purpose found in no other character of the opera. Commentators often find Micaëla a cardboard figure who is simply a foil for the sensuality of Carmen, but this aria and the courage-cum-terror it represents provide an alternate view.

Characteristic of her Act I music and "Je dis" is the gentle rise and fall of arpeggio (lit., "harp-like"), an archetypical pattern[33] that represents the angelic and pure aspects of her personality and thus of the middle-class values so dear to the patrons of the Opéra-Comique; the use of harp in her Act I music (Example CA-4a) is especially pointed, whereas the fast arpeggiation by the cellos in the Act III aria (Example CA-4b) is much more active and perhaps meant to be suggestive of the anxiety explicit in her words.

---

[31] A lower-ranked, noncommissioned officer, equivalent to the modern corporal, or perhaps "buck sergeant."

[32] Cf. Don Ottavio's two arias in *Don Giovanni*.

[33] Used by Verdi in *Rigoletto* for Gilda's dying words, "Lassù in cielo vicina alla madre . . ." ("Up there in heaven next to my mother . . .").

EXAMPLE CA-4 MICAËLA AS REPRESENTATIVE OF TRADITIONAL VALUES

a) Act I, No. 7: She brings a message from José's mother.

Don José (tenor) [dawnh zhaw-ZEH]

A brigadier. One of the most varied and developed characters in opera, his spiritual disintegration is as much the substance of this opera as is Carmen's tragic life. The novella tells us that José, having sorely beaten another man who resented being defeated in a game of *pelota*,[34] fled his town and, having met up with some dragoons, enlisted in their company. He is of noble rank, hence the title "Don,"[35] and is apparently a gifted and intelligent person, having risen quickly in the noncommissioned ranks. He is torn between loyalty to his mother and family traditions and the consuming impulses of infatuation and jealousy; the latter are his downfall.

His first music shares the phrases and qualities of Micaëla's, thus reflecting their common interests and backgrounds. Once Carmen begins to weave her spell, however, he is reduced to short intonations that contrast most effectively with her chromatic insinuations and the underlying dance rhythms of the Seguidilla (Example CA-5a). His soldier's song (No. 16, *Halte-là! / Qui va là? / Dragon d'Alcala?*—"Halt there! Who goes there? Dragoon of Alcala?), as he finds his way to Lillas Pastia's tavern in Act II, has the happy-

---

[34] A source of the modern jai alai, pelota's various forms involved hitting a ball against hard surfaces either with the hand or bats. José and his opponent fought with *maquillas*, iron-tipped staves used by Basques and quite devasting on impact with skin and bone.

[35] His full name is Don José Lizzarrabengoa.

EXAMPLE CA-4 (*Continued*)

b) Act III, No. 22: She affirms her faith in God even though she is terrified.

go-lucky dotted rhythms of military music (Example CA-5b) and the perfect intervals so often associated in opera with purity, innocence, and nature, although its move from minor to major suggests an ambivalence not unrelated to the modal shifts of Carmen's songs.

His music with Micaëla is flowing and lovely. His most moving lyricism, however, lies in his emotional response to Carmen's Act II expression of contempt for his readiness to return to barracks and his duties as a soldier: the gorgeous melody of "La fleur que tu m'avais jetée" (No. 17, "The flower that you threw at me") follows no standard pattern; that it is through-composed separates his music from that of other characters and is appropriate for a person who acts impetuously rather than in obedience to convention. Its upwardly pressing melodic motion and climactic phrasing are expressive of desperation and pleading (Example CA-5c) and thus reflective of a person governed by emotion, not common sense or the dictates of idealized heroism.

a) Act I, No. 10: In the Seguidilla, José seems hypnotized by Carmen's enticements.

EXAMPLE CA-5 (*CONTINUED*)

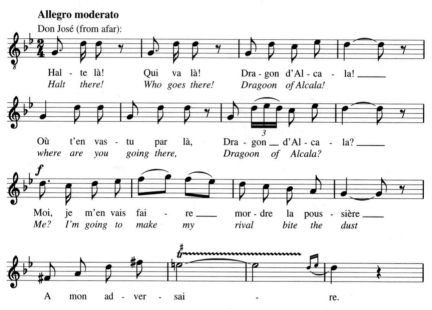

Allegro moderato

Don José (from afar):

Hal - te là!   Qui va là!   Dra - gon d'Al - ca - la! ___
Halt   there!   Who goes there!   Dragoon of Alcala!

Où   t'en vas - tu   par   là,   Dra - gon ___ d'Al - ca - la? ___
where are   you   going there,   Dragoon of   Alcala?

Moi,   je m'en vais fai - re ___   mor - dre la pous - sière ___
Me?   I'm going to make   my   rival   bite the   dust

A   mon ad - ver - sai - re.

b) Act II, No. 16: José nears Lillas Pastia's tavern after being freed from jail.

Andantino

Don José:

cresc. molto

Et   je   ne sen - tais   en moi - mê - me,   Je ne sen -
and I   felt   in   myself,   I   felt

stringendo _ _ _ _ _

tais ___ qu'un seul dé - sir,   un seul dé - sir,   un seul es -
but   one desire,   only one desire,   only one hope:

_ _ _ _ _ Tempo I

f   rit.

poir: Te re - voir, ô Car - men, ___ oui, te re - voir! ___
to   see you again,   Carmen,   yes,   to   see you again!

c) Act II, No. 17: In the Flower Song, José admits to being completely lost in his love for Carmen.

In Acts III and IV, José's music is often spasmodic and angular (Example CA-5d).[36] Even in the Act IV duet with Carmen, the only songfulness given to him is for his begging, first when he implores Carmen to let him save her (Example CA-5e)[37] and then when he puts forward the impossible suggestion that, even if she does not love him, they could be happy together because he loves her. When this is rejected, José's composure vanishes, and so does any semblance of melodic flow.

Zuniga (bass) *[tsoo NEE gah]*

A young lieutenant of Dragoons, and José's immediate superior. Zuniga has an eye for the ladies: in Act I he is interested that the tobacco factory is staffed by partly undressed and good-looking young girls; and he enjoys the "Chanson bohème" dancing and singing in Act II. His primary functions are narrative and as a precipitator of irreversible action: it is Zuniga who tells Carmen of José's imprisonment for dereliction of duty and ultimate release at the start of Act II; as a would-be suitor of Carmen, he arouses José's uncontrollable jealousy, thus inciting José to draw his sword, leaving him with the dismal choice of submitting to court-martial or deserting. Either way, the confrontation with Zuniga is José's step into an abyss.

EXAMPLE CA-5 (*CONTINUED*)

d) Act III, No. 24: José vows that Carmen will be his forever, come what may.

---

[36] It is in these scenes that Bizet composed recitatives for him; elsewhere, the recitatives are by Guiraud.

[37] That, of course, is the last thing in the world she would ever want.

EXAMPLE CA-5 (*CONTINUED*)

e) Act IV, No. 27: José begs Carmen to let him save her.

Zuniga's nice sense of irony and humor is evidenced in lighthearted trills in the strings and the bassoon counterpoint that accompany his smiling acceptance of being tied up so that the smugglers can take their leave.

Carmen (mezzo-soprano) [KAHR-men]

Earthy, intense, fatalistic, fun-loving, sensuous, clever, courageous, amorous, amoral, cruel, fickle, self-willed, outrageous, libidinous, alluring, exciting, dynamic, and free and determined to be as she pleases—these are characteristics that performers, readers, listeners, scholars, and just about anyone else who has ever come across Bizet's astonishing creation have found in Carmen's words and music. Bizet's gypsy is a fascinating, unique, and ultimately mysterious creature, never to be mastered completely.

Writers have a great deal of difficulty with the principles by which she is guided, applying qualities of evil and immorality to a person who has no principles at all and for whom concepts of good and evil are irrelevant. I rather like Maria Callas's proposal that "Carmen's only morality is never to pretend what she does not really feel. She's not calculating but she is without pity."[38]

---

[38] Interview with Jacques Bourgeois, 1964, in album notes to *Bizet: "Carmen,"* EMI compact disk set CDS 7473138, p. 9.

When she is enjoying her world, Carmen's soul is inseparable from song and dance: her Act I arias are identified in the score by dance type *(Habanera* and *Seguidilla)*, not by the words of the first line of text; her comments to Zuniga, when she is arrested in Act I, are in the guise of an impertinent street song; her confidence of success in the Act III smuggling venture (shared musically with Frasquita and Mercédès) is similarly saucy and vibrant; the "gyspy song" (see above, Example CA-1c) is a real foot-stomper (also with Frasquita and Mercédès); and her Act II scene with José is a sensuous dance accompanied by her own singing and castanet playing (Example CA-2a).

However, her music also includes the brooding, unremitting rhythm of her acceptance of destiny (in No. 20, the Act III Card Scene, Example CA-6a). In the Act IV confrontation with José, her phrases run the gamut from above the staff to below it in such a way that at least part of her melodic line must sound harsh (Example CA-6b). This roughness of sound also characterizes her contempt for weakness, as in her snarling in wonderment (in Act II) that she could be so stupid as to fall for someone who would rather return to barracks than spend the night with her, and, in the final scene of Act IV, her throwing away the ring José had given her.

Also important in Carmen's music is the prevalence of the minor mode, made especially noticeable when the involvement of others—none of whom are anything like her—is represented by a shift to the major.[39] This is underscored by the orchestra in the *Habanera*, for example, when she croons "l'amour" as the chorus takes up her melody. It is a feature of other promi-

EXAMPLE CA-6 CARMEN'S MUSIC.

a) Act III, No. 20, the Card Scene: Carmen acknowledges that destiny cannot be avoided.

---

[39] Furman, p. 174, points out that "carmen" is Andalusian for "a villa or country house, a residence between town and country, between civilization and nature," thus suggesting a spirit that hovers between different worlds. Add to this notion that "carmen" is also Latin for "song" or "poem," and we have a name for the opera's protagonist that is wonderfully appropriate.

EXAMPLE CA-6 (*CONTINUED*)

b) Act IV, No. 27, the final duet with Don José: She vows never to yield to him.

c) Act II, No. 14: At the end of Escamillo's song, the three gypsy girls echo "l'amour."

nent passages: the *Seguidilla,* when Carmen refers to the boredom of being alone ("Oui, mais toute seule on s'ennuie"); the "Chanson bohème"; and the Card Scene, where Carmen's minor mode is in stark contrast to the flighty major-mode fortune telling of her friends.

It is interesting that in her brief duet with Escamillo in Act IV, she responds to him with *his* music, not her own—for the moment Carmen indeed belongs to someone and, as it turns out, is willing to die rather than deny it.

At the end of the Toreador Song, her response to the idea that love awaits the victorious bullfighter is in strong contrast with the unthinking sentimentality of Escamillo, Frasquita, and Mercédès: when Carmen sings "l'amour," she pulls the music out of key with a striking interval of a descending augmented octave (Example CA-6c).[40] For Carmen, love is serious business.

Frasquita (soprano) [frahss-KEE-tah], *and*
Mercédès (soprano) [mair-SEH-dess]

Carmen's gypsy companions. They are consistently lighthearted and frivolous and share tuneful, bouncy, major-mode music in almost every situation. Their gaiety and melodic ornament in the Card Scene are important foils to Carmen's fatalism and are fundamental to the scherzando flavor of the Act II quintet.

---

[40] See also the use of the rising ninth in the music of *Peter Grimes.* If Carmen's D-flat were written as C-sharp, the "spelling" would be a minor ninth.

Lillas Pastia (spoken part)   [LEE-lahss PAHSS-tee-ah]

Owner of the disreputable inn where the gypsy smugglers gather; the place has other attractions, apparently, because Zuniga and his fellow officers come there, too.

Andrés (spoken part)   [AHN-dress]

A lieutenant of Dragoons. The part is often omitted, because it serves no vital function in the plot.

Escamillo (baritone)   [ess-kah-MEE-yoh)

A famous matador[41] from Granada who has come to Seville to fight bulls. His character is often described as thinly drawn, but I think it is well dimensioned by both music and dialogue. The "Toreador Song" is so blatantly tuneful and crowd-rousing—especially with the extensive use of brass for fanfares and accompanying chords—that it is a perfect mirroring of Escamillo as athletic hero.[42] Bizet is reported to have said of it that "They wanted ordure, and they've got it,"[43] but this self-deprecation should not be taken too seriously—it is clear that he was referring to its obviousness but was not negating the validity of it for the character or the situation.

Like Carmen's solo pieces, Escamillo's one aria is identified by type, not text: it is headed *Couplets* ("stanzas").[44] Like her, he takes life as it comes and deals with people as they are, without any false pretense or sentimental idealization. Given that the crowd breaks into the refrain of the Toreador Song at his Act IV moment of triumph, it seems that this part of his Act II aria sung in Lillas Pastia's tavern is Escamillo's "music" and is well known to his fans. It is not operatic "speech"; thus, like Carmen, Escamillo's most characteristic moments are expressed through song *qua* song.

In Act III, Escamillo cuts a jaunty figure. According to some oft-omitted spoken dialogue, he is ostensibly in the hill country to find bulls suitable for the arena; one may assume, however, that a more pressing reason is that he has heard of Carmen's becoming bored with her ex-dragoon and so is ready to offer himself. His dialogue with José is bluff and good-hearted, even when he knows that José is now his rival. That the two share the same rhythm as they gird themselves for their fierce duel shows that he is as determined as José; unlike José, however, Escamillo is not a killer of men: he merely defends himself and purposely avoids the opportunity he has in the first phase of the fight to stab his opponent. His departure from the mountains,

---

[41] "Toréador" is apparently a coinage by Bizet. "Torero" is a generic term for anyone involved in fighting bulls, including not only matadors but also banderilleros and picadors. Clearly the text of the opera is aimed at the top of the ranks. (I am grateful to Sandra Darling for pointing this out.)

[42] The score indicates it is to be sung *avec fatuité.* Of course.

[43] The identity of "they" is never made clear; presumably Bizet was thinking of the Comique's impresario, Camille Du Locle (1832–1903), Meilhac, and Halévy, or perhaps he had in mind the Opéra-Comique audiences in general.

[44] This two-stanza form is a common feature in nineteenth-century operas where characters introduce themselves to listeners on both sides of the proscenium.

marked by his carolling his matador's song as he moves off into the distance, is pointedly a musical elbow-dig at José and a reminder to Carmen of the panache she has never seen in José.

Escamillo's final music is his Act IV comment (Example CA-7) to Carmen before he enters the arena. Significantly, its text speaks of what Carmen will do if she loves him, not of his love for her. There is a certain tenderness in the music, expressed through its melodiousness, soft dynamic, relaxed tempo, simplicities of harmony and rhythm, and gentle orchestration of interwoven cellos and violas, but it is not deeply moving musically and bears a certain detachment textually; it is thus as appropriate to the moment and to his character as is the macho imagery of his music in Act II.

Le Dancaïre [luh dahn-kah-EER], also listed as El Dancairo (tenor) [el dahn-ka-EER-roh]; and Le Remendado (tenor) [luh reh-mehn-DAH-do]; also listed as El Remendado

Smugglers who urge Carmen to join them on an expedition. Dancaïre is the leader of the band; Remendado, who serves as a comically over-talkative figure in the spoken dialogue, has little purpose other than to provide a voice in the Act II quintet.

Miscellaneous parts

There are snippets of song for a woman vendor of oranges and a gypsy seller of opera glasses in Act IV. There is also some spoken dialogue for a sol-

EXAMPLE CA-7 ACT IV, NO. 26: ESCAMILLO TELLS CARMEN
THAT SOON SHE WILL BE PROUD OF HIM IF SHE LOVES HIM.

dier who gets the rope to tie Carmen's hands in Act I, and a villager who guides Micaëla to the smugglers' resting place in Act III.

Bibliography

Clément, Catherine. *Opera, or The Undoing of Women,* trans. Betsy Wing. Minneapolis: University of Minnesota Press, 1988.

Curtiss, Mina. *Bizet and His World.* New York: Knopf, 1958.

Dahlhaus, Carl. *Realism in Nineteenth-Century Music,* trans. Mary Whittall. Cambridge: Cambridge University Press, 1985.

Dean, Winton. *Bizet.* Rev. 3rd ed. The Master Musicians. London: J. M. Dent, 1975.

———. "The True *Carmen?*" in *Essays on Opera.* Oxford: Clarendon Press, 1990 [1965], pp. 281–300.
    Critique of the Oeser edition.

Furman, Nelly. "The Languages of Love in *Carmen,*" in *Reading Opera,* ed. Arthur Groos and Roger Parker. Princeton, NJ: Princeton University Press, 1988, pp. 168–183.

John, Nicholas, ed. *"Carmen"—Bizet.* English National Opera Guide 13. New York: Riverrun Press, 1982.

Kestner, Joséph. "The Cruelest Story," in *Opera News* 53, no. 6 (December 10, 1988): 13–16, 68.
    Study of themes of Mérimée's writings as found in Carmen *and* Colomba.

Martin, George, "Sounds of the Orchestra (cont.): II. The Scoring for *Carmen,*" in *The Opera Companion.* London: John Murray, Ltd, 1984, pp. 82–86.

McClary, Susan, ed. *Georges Bizet: "Carmen."* Cambridge Opera Handbooks. Cambridge: Cambridge University Press, 1992.

———. *Feminine Endings: Music, Gender, and Sexuality.* Minneapolis: University of Minnesota, 1991.

Mérimée, Prosper. *Carmen,* trans. Walter F. C. Ade. Woodbury, NY: Barron's Educational Series, 1977.

Nettl, Bruno. *Folk and Traditional Music of the Western Continents.* Prentice-Hall History of Music Series. Englewood Cliffs, NJ: Prentice-Hall, 1965.

Sacher, Jack. *A Teacher's Guide to "Carmen."* New York: Metropolitan Opera Guild, 1968.

Scherer, Barrymore Laurence. "Storyteller," in *Opera News* 51, no. 13 (March 14, 1987): 32+.
    Brief study of Mérimée's life and work.

Tiersot, Julien. "Bizet and Spanish Music," trans. Theodore Baker, in *The Musical Quarterly* XIII, no. 4 (October 1927): 566–581.

Wright, Leslie. "A New Source for *Carmen,*" in *Nineteenth-Century Music* II, no. 1 (July 1978): 61–71.
    Textual and musical revisions as affected by various factors, among them censorship regulations and the emotional climate in the theater during the final weeks of preparation for the opera's premiere.

Chapter 15

SALOME

MUSIC: Richard Strauss (1864–1949)

LIBRETTO: Strauss's adaptation of a translation by Hedwig Lachmann of *Salome,* a play (1891; written originally in French) by Oscar Wilde (1854–1900).

PREMIERE: Dresden Court Opera (Hofoper), December 9, 1905.

TIME AND PLACE OF THE STORY: 30 C.E., during the reign of Tetrarch Herod Antipas of Judaea and the early ministry of Christ. The action of the one-act opera takes place on the terrace of the fortress of Machaerus, in the Roman province of Peraea, about nine miles from the eastern shore of the Dead Sea, fifty miles southeast of Jersualem.

Salome and the Dawn of Modernism

Toward the end of the nineteenth century, a number of striking changes affected Western art, music, and literature. Among them were a turn toward an unflinching presentation of the darker side of the human condition and the unrestrained release of attendant emotions. The ultimate flowering of this was Expressionism, a style of dramatic angst that stripped away all pretense and facade to bare the suffering and decadence of the soul. This went far beyond the movement toward realism represented by *Carmen;* as Zola noted in reviewing a group of songs, "the whole disgusting sore of our social inferno shouted and spat out its sickness in revolting words, full of blood and fire."[1]

A fascination for near-Eastern orientalism in particular and non-Western artistic resources in general was also a feature of the century's final quarter. Treatments abounded of women as exotic, dangerous, immoral, and destructive,[2] especially but not exclusively at the hands of French artists, composers, and writers. The particular story of Salome and/or her mother

---

[1] Quoted in Willett, p. 16.

[2] Modern commentaries often use the term "The Other" when referring to women whom artists have nihilistically or pejoratively placed beyond societal conventions. Among the frequently staged operas relevant to such attention are *Carmen* (1875), Saint-Saëns's *Samson et Dalila* (1877), Delibes's *Lakmé* (1883), and Massenet's *Thaïs* (1894).

was the focus of a short story by Flaubert (*Hérodias*, 1877), poetry by Mallarmé (*Hérodiade*, 1869) an opera by Massenet (*Hérodiade*, 1881), and celebrated paintings by Gustave Moreau (*Salome Dancing Before Herod* and *The Apparition*, both exhibited in 1876).

In music and painting, the traditions of centuries were dissolving: Wagner's chromaticism and seemingly rootless harmonies had undercut the foundations of the tonal system with the music of *Tristan und Isolde* (1865, see Example 3.17, p. 57); Debussy had weakened it still further with the use of five-tone and whole-tone scales and a gradual abandonment of harmony and timbre as unifying forces.[3]

Many of the defining attributes of the modern world and thus many of its symbols appeared in the last five years of the nineteenth century and the first five years of the twentieth. Among them were the openly sensual acting on the stage by Sarah Bernhardt; anarchy as a political movement; "fauvism"[4] as a label for the painting of Matisse and others; the development of the airplane (the Wrights' first flights in 1903) and the automobile; Planck's Quantum Theory (1900); the Curies's discovery of plutonium and radium in 1898; and Freud's *Study of Hysteria* (1895) and *Interpretation of Dreams* (1900).

Instability is a common thread here: inherited certainties in science were no longer consistently valid; populations and individuals could move with ever greater swiftness from one cultural center to another; the theater was no longer a pulpit honoring commonly understood virtues; painting and sculpture seemed more and more removed from traditional principles of beauty; and time-honored concepts of behavior, philosophy, taste, and restraint were stretched beyond recognition, if they were observed at all.

Into this world came Strauss's *Salome*, its instability of moral principle given voice through the instability of its music. Glissandos, slithering half-step progressions of melodies or chords, melodic fragmentation, frequent alteration of rhythmic groups and change of metric pulse, and the permutations of timbre via the thirty-eight different instruments (requiring over a hundred players) give this opera its special sense of musical and psychological ferment.[5]

Music: Imagery and Obsession

Strauss drew uninhibitedly on Wagner's chromaticism, orchestral opulence, broad-phrased melodic lyricism, and intricately meshed symphonic leitmotifs. As with Wagner, the associations and musical shapes of the motives change with the psychological aspects of the story. The motive first present-

---

[3] Like the Impressionists in painting, Debussy manipulated "color"—in his case, harmony, rhythm, and instrumentation—to produce a mosaic of fragments that gave the perceiver a feeling that form and "meaning" were imprecise and pointedly vague, even though every element was calculated and detailed.

[4] Freely translated as "wild beasts." *Fauves* are deer; wild beasts more properly are *grands fauves*.

[5] Described by Strauss's father as "similar to having ants in your pants." "Cockchafers" (scarab beetles; *Maikäfer*) is what he said, but the literal translation doesn't quite, well, fly.

Richard Strauss, *Salome* (1905): Narraboth (Mark Baker) pleads with Salome (Inga Nielsen) to have nothing to do with Jokanaan (Richard Cowan).
Santa Fe Opera, 1995: production by Tom Hennes. Courtesy Santa Fe Opera.
Photo Hans Fahrmeyer.

ed in connection with Narraboth's obsession for Salome, for example ("x" in Example SA-2a), flowers into the motive of Salome's demand for the head of Jokanaan (Example SA-2b). The thread of obsession remains, but the object of its application and the details of its music have shifted.

Salome's incessant change of tempo, dynamic, timbre, key center, and motivic manipulation has a febrility unlike any opera in the repertory. Consider Narraboth's despair, for example: he has violated his orders to prevent anyone from speaking to Jokanaan, finds the Princess of the kingdom on a precipice of a disastrous scandal for which he is responsible, and, worst of all, knows that his desperate love for her is utterly doomed. Little wonder, then, that Strauss composes flurries of scales, syncopations, varied meters, fluctuating dynamics, a panoply of orchestration, a shiver of high tremolos, and melodic fragments and harmonies spattered everywhere with sharps and flats. Above them all, Narraboth's vocal line of accented notes climbs the staff in a manner appropriate to a character just eight quick measures away from stabbing himself to death.

As a body that can only reflect light, the moon serves as the pervasive symbol for the inner thoughts and perturbations of the main characters, and its illumination of the castle terrace or its being darkened by the passing of clouds is intimately connected with the action. The libretto continually glows with references to it or to images derived from it: to Narraboth, the moon is like a princess who has little doves for her feet, and Salome is like the reflection of a white rose in a mirror of silver; Jokanaan predicts a Judgment Day when the moon shall seem to be made of blood; to Herodes, the moon is like

EXAMPLE SA-1 NARRABOTH BEGS SALOME TO HAVE NOTHING TO
DO WITH JOKANAAN.

EXAMPLE SA-1 (*Continued*)

a deranged woman looking for lovers everywhere or a drunken woman reeling through the clouds; to Salome the moon hovers like a silvery[6] flower, and
Jokanaan looks pale and wan as if carved from ivory. For the crassly materi-
alistic Herodias, however, "The moon is like the moon, that's all."

Wilde's original text and the Lachmann translation of it are liberally
sprinkled with other colorful images, too, and Strauss lavished his gift of
musical pictorialism on them: when Salome describes Jokanaan's hair as
standing like the cedars of Lebanon giving shade to lions and robbers, trombones roar appropriately; rising and falling chromatic scales describe the icy
wind that only Herodes feels; a wildly descending glissando in the double
basses expresses the "howling" of arguing rabbis; woodwinds and horns
evoke raucous clamor when Herodias sneers at her husband's nomadic
ancestors as camel drivers; the brittle sound of the celesta's metal bars
accompanies Salome's moment of utter stillness as she stares at the cistern in
the final moment of her dance and, in a very different context, Herodes's

---

[6] And, of course, Jokanaan's head is delivered on a silver platter.

mincing offer of fruits to her and his slavering urging of her to "take just a tiny bite of them" ("Beiss nur ein wenig ab"); and, in the opera's final sounds, there is the hideous crunching by strings, percussion, and heavy brass of the archetypical motive of Death as the soldiers crush Salome with their shields. A list of such momentary effects would be a catalogue of almost every measure.

The main thread of the drama is obsession. The quarrelsome Jews are wholly taken up with the minutiae of their religion; the Page idolizes Narraboth; both Narraboth and Herodes are obsessed with Salome; Salome's mother, Herodias, thinks only of assuring her place of privilege and carnal pleasure; Salome becomes obsessed with Jokanaan; and Jokanaan is consumed with the coming of Messiah.

Of the many motives of the opera (there are thirty or so), three are especially associated with obsessive behavior and thought and are thus among the most prominent elements of the score. Although there is a family resemblance among them (especially the use of the interval of a third), each has a distinctive melodic and rhythmic profile that is noticeable even when buried under a welter of other motives or manipulated into other shapes.

The first of these, Narraboth's obsession for Salome ("x" in Example SA-2a), opens the opera as a pendant to an upward chromatic rush played by the clarinet. It jabs through the orchestral texture time after time, becoming associated with the obsession of Herodes for Salome when the soldiers, gazing at the offstage banquet, observe that Herodes is "looking darkly" ("Der Tetrarch sieht finster drein"). They cannot tell what he is looking at, but the return of this motive and its original clarinet sonority at the moment of the soldiers' comment is unmistakable evidence that Herodes is staring at Salome, just as Narraboth had. It eventually appears in the ghastly sequence of Salome's demands for the head of Jokanaan as her reward (Example SA-2b), when, in altered form, it has become *her* motive of obsession.

EXAMPLE SA-2 MOTIVES OF OBSESSION

a) The opening notes of the opera: Narraboth's fixation ("x") on Salome.

b) After the Dance of the Seven Veils, Salome, with seeming innocence, asks for her reward.

The second of these three motives, with its characteristic shape of three repeated notes followed by a jump of a minor third, is heard barely three minutes into the opera when the Page urges Narraboth not to look at Salome (Example SA-2c). Among its many appearances are Jokanaan's first utterance (Example SA-2d) and the climax of the confrontation between Salome and Jokanaan (Example SA-2e). Fused with variants of the twisting "obsession figure" of Example SA-2a, it becomes the music of Salome's ultimate demand for her reward; then, a few bars later, in shortened time values, it is a viciously ironic symbol of Herodes's inability to avoid granting her any wish: it becomes the music of his surrender.

The motive of Salome herself (Example SA-2g), the third of these obsession figures, is inseparable from her fixation on Jokanaan. It seems to float

EXAMPLE SA-2 (*Continued*)

c) The Page warns Narraboth about his staring at Salome.

d) Jokanaan predicts the impact of the coming of Messiah.

e) Salome is obsessed with kissing Jokanaan's mouth.

EXAMPLE SA-2 *(Continued)*

f) Salome demands the head of Jokanaan.

g) Salome and her obsession with Jokanaan.

on the evening air when the clarinet plays it as she sees Jokanaan for the first time and comments on how terrible ("schrecklich") he appears (see bracketed notes "b" in Example SA–2g and SA–5d). It is never far from the music for the rest of the opera. It is more than a symbol of Salome's obsession with Jokanaan, however; it is also a suggestion of her own willowy, graceful body and the sensuality of a sixteen-year-old.

The Historical Background

The treatments of the story by Flaubert, Wilde, Mallarmé, and Strauss conflate several historical characters and events from the years between the birth of Christ and the start of his ministry. All of them deal with the descendants of Herod the Great, who, having learned of the birth of the ruler of a new Kingdom of God and fearing a threat to his own reign, had instigated the

"Slaughter of the Innocents" (Matthew 2:16).[7] Herod the Great had numerous wives and offspring. One of his sons[8] was given the name Herod as a birthright; he is identified as Herod Phillipus in the Gospels of Matthew and Mark. Another son, by a different wife,[9] was named Antipas; as Tetrarch of Gallilee and Peraea, he assumed the name "Herod Antipas" to symbolize the legitimacy of his title. This Herod Antipas is the "Herodes" of Strauss's opera.

Herod the Great's granddaughter Herodias married her uncle, Herod Phillipus, by whom she gave birth to Salome. When Herod Antipas visited his half brother in Rome, Herodias promptly entered into a sexual liaison with him.

Wilde and Strauss depend on an invented narrative for events immediately preceding their dramas: according to this fiction, Phillipus visited his half brother in Peraea, where he was thrown into a cistern-as-dungeon for twelve years and finally strangled. That Herodias became the wife of her half brother-in-law/half-uncle[10] and that Salome was thus Antipas's stepdaughter is factual, as is the quick departure of Antipas's first wife for the safety of her own family without any formal divorce having been undertaken by her husband.[11]

In the year 30 C.E., then, Herod Antipas lives incestuously and adulterously with Herodias, whose dissolute sexual proclivities are well known in her own land and abroad. Princess Salome is an adolescent, well into the stage of life where she is aware of human sexuality. The bearded prophet known as John the Baptist has been preparing his people for the coming of Messiah, urging them to purge themselves of their sins and continually pointing to the life of Herodias as a lesson in moral outrage and violation of Jewish law. John has been arrested by Herod as a troublemaker in a Judea already politically unsettled and economically miserable. Moreover, John's acid indictments of the wife of the Tetrarch of Judaea is not only an irritant but a threat to the legitimacy of Herod's marriage. Although John/Jokanaan is incarcerated in the same cistern that had held Salome's father, Herod/Herodes has resisted the urge to kill him since, according to Matthew, Herod "feared the multitude, because they counted him as a prophet."[12]

---

[7] Dating is confusing under the best of circumstances. Sources usually place the lifespan of Herod the Great as 73 B.C.E.–4 B.C.E., which would remove him from the scene before the birth of Christ and thus render implausible the "Slaughter of the Innocents." But then, Christ was probably born sometime before the putative year of zero; or after. See Keller, p. 333f.

[8] By a Jewish wife with the resonant name of Cleopatra.

[9] The entanglements of people, events, and places have of course been subject to merging and confusion as a result of the distance of history, ambiguity of sources, and—not least of all—artistic license.

[10] Anna Russell's inimitable narration of the plot of Wagner's *Ring* comes to mind. Describing the love connection between Siegfried (Wotan's grandson) and Brünnhilde (Wotan's daughter), Russell reminded us that "She's his aunt, by the way." See *Anna Russell Sings! Again?* Columbia Masterworks LP ML 4733.

[11] There was, apparently, some military retribution exacted by her family. Their defeat of Herodian forces contributed to the unrest besieging Herod's kingdom.

[12] The fullest account of the history of John the Baptist is in Mark 1:4–9 and 6:14–29; shorter accounts are in Matthew 3:13, 4:12, and 14:1–12, and Luke 3:1–20. Salome is not mentioned at all by name, entering Mark's narrative only as a daughter obeying Herodias. Her name is given by the Jewish historian Flavius Josephus (37? C.E.–ca. 100); her personality has been shaped by the passage of time and the imagination of creative artists.

THE PLOT AND ITS MUSIC

NOTE: The opera is in one act. The paragraph numbers do not refer to arias or other discrete musical forms but are provided for ease of reference to the musical commentary. "Scene" is used in Strauss's score to delineate dramatic episodes, not a change in time or place.

The action takes place at night on the moonlit terrace of Herodes's palace. Toward the rear is an ancient covered cistern. A noisy banquet honoring the Tetrarch's birthday is underway in a palace hall that opens onto the terrace. Herodes, Herodias, Salome, and their guests are within. Keeping guard on the terrace are some soldiers under the command of Narraboth. Also on the terrace are some Cappadocians and Herodias's young page.

There is no Prelude, the curtain rising abruptly with the upward sweep of the clarinet and the tremolo-accompanied motive of Narraboth's fixation on Salome (Ex. SA-2a).

SCENE I

1 Narraboth cannot take his eyes off Salome, whom he watches from afar. The Page comments gloomily on the moon, which he likens to a woman rising from the tomb, while Narraboth compares Salome to a little princess who has white doves for feet *(deren Füsse weisse Tauben sind)* and who seems to dance whenever she moves.

The music of Ex. SA-2 leads at once to Narraboth's rhapsody to Salome's beauty, his vocal line arching eagerly above the high quivering of violins. The Page's music moves more sombrely below the staff, its low notes appropriate to his dark metaphor. A light, spirited figure in oboes and flutes paints the picture of Salome's dove-like feet.

2 The soldiers comment sarcastically on the uproar of theological argument among the Jews attending the banquet. The Page warns Narraboth of the danger of looking at people the way Narraboth is staring at Salome. The soldiers note that Herodes is looking darkly at someone but cannot tell at whom.

Brittle rhythms are given to biting woodwinds, the "howl" of their uproar finding voice in plummeting glissandos of the double basses. The Page's warnings (Ex. SA-2c) are set to a motive of obsession characterized especially by its opening repeated-note pattern. The soldier's comment on the Tetrarch's dark look is accompanied by Ex. SA-2a, the music of Narraboth's gazing at Salome; if it is not clear to the soldiers, it is clear to the listener that, like Narraboth, Herodes is staring at Salome.

3 Narraboth comments on the paleness of Salome, who seems "as pale as the shadow of a white rose in a mirror of silver" *(wie der Schatten einer weissen Rose in einem silbernen Spiegel)*. The Page gives voice once more to his fear that something terrible may happen.

Flurries of rising woodwind scales above string tremolos accompany Narraboth's continued rapture; the music of the Page's repeated caution (Ex. SA-2c) is intensified by a brief canon with bassoon.

4 From the cistern comes the sonorous voice of Jokanaan, predicting that when the Messiah comes the desolate shall be made glad, the blind shall see, and the ears of the deaf shall be opened.

A hushed timpani roll and strokes of the tam-tam[13] punctuate the solemn harmonies of Jokanaan's first statement. He predicts the state of the world at the coming of Messiah to the music of Ex. SA-2d.

---

[13] A tam-tam is a large, suspended gong.

5 One of the soldiers tells the others that this prisoner is a holy man and a gentle person who thanks him when he is brought something to eat. He has come from the desert where many followed him. The soldier is unable to explain the meanings of his sayings and adds that the Tetrarch has forbidden anyone to see the man.

The grace and holiness of Jokanaan is communicated by the First Soldier in the simple and sonorous music of Ex. SA-3. The impatience of the Second Soldier and the blunt questioning of a Cappadocian are given short, percussive rhythms (cellos and basses) that yield quickly to the more convincing lyricism expressive of Jokanaan as an inherently good person.

SCENE II

6 Narraboth sees that Salome is rising in agitation and that she is leaving the banquet. She comes onto the terrace hurriedly and excitedly, complaining that the Tetrarch looks at her constantly with "his mole's eyes under quivering eyelids" *(seinen Maulwurfsaugen unter den zuckenden Lidern)*.

A nervous variant of Ex. SA-2a accompanies Narraboth's observation. Salome hurries onto the terrace to the rapidly flowing violin music of Ex. SA-5a, with oboe and celesta lending it special colors. The "mole-like" eyes that repel her are suggested by the oily sound of the bass clarinet and cellos.

7 She breathes deeply of the fresh air, a relief from the atmosphere of the banquet, where the Jews from Jerusalem "tear themselves to pieces" arguing "over their foolish ceremonies" *(die einander über ihre närrischen Gebräuche in Stücke reissen)*, and the Egyptians sit silently and subtly *(Schweigsame list'ge Ägypter)*. She especially despises the brutal, coarse Romans and their "uncouth speech" *(plumpen Sprache)*. The moon appears like "a silver flower" *(eine silberne Blume)*, cool and chaste, with "a virgin's beauty" *(die Schönheit einer Jungfrau)*.

A floating waltz melody (Ex. SA-5b), given to strings and celesta, yields to the quiet but flurried scales of Ex. SA-5a. Salome's contempt for the theologians is expressed to the accompaniment of vividly angular spurts of woodwinds and pizzicato violins. Horns, contrabassoon, and double basses brood in their lowest registers for the unpleasant Egyptians; harsh strokes of the bow in the entire string section delineate the Romans' brutality.

The Page warns of trouble in his own 4/4 rhythm over a stressful 3/4 rhythm in celesta, harps, solo violin, and string tremolos, but the intensity of the music lessens as Salome turns her attention to the moon (high tremolos, with Ex. SA-5a); the images of silver flowers and virginal beauty are in delicate woodwind shadings.

8 Salome is startled by the sudden intrusion into her reverie of the voice of Jokanaan, booming from the cistern with a prediction that "the Son of Man is nigh" *(des Menschen Sohn ist nahe)*. Told it is the voice of the prophet, she quickly realizes that it is the voice of the man of whom the Tetrarch is afraid and who says "terrible things" *(schreckliche Dinge)* about her mother.

Narraboth's attempts to divert her are useless; she rejects a message from the Tetrarch requesting her to return and questions further about the prisoner.

The sudden sound of Jokanaan's voice is punctuated by the brasses on a chord that is abruptly struck then quickly softened. In a more mellow vein, the brasses offer a soft touch of Ex. SA-3, a motive originally heard in connection with Jokanaan's goodness but now transferred to Christ, the subject of his prediction.

Salome's realization that Jokanaan is referring to her mother is clear from the the violas' giving out the music of "y" of Ex. SA-7.

Narraboth's efforts to divert her are lyric, with delicate piccolo and harp sounds on the offbeats, but the tremolos in middle strings and a brooding bass line suggest his unease. His request that she accede to the message from Herodes is more urgent: his phrases are shorter, more angular. Her questions recall fragments of Exs. SA-5a (the music of her arrival on the terrace) and b, as if her curiosity is that of a young girl facing a potentially exciting event.

9 When she hears Jokanaan predict the punishment of sinners, she asks to see him. The soldiers demur, unable to disobey the orders of Herodes. She gazes into the cistern, noting "how terrible it must be to live in such a dark hole. . . . It is like a tomb" (*Es muss schrecklich sein, in so einer schwarzen Höhle zu leben. . . . Es ist wie eine Gruft*). She demands that the prisoner be brought before her; again, the soldiers refuse.

Salome approaches the cistern as clarinets and strings offer a hurried descending scale; the sense of the blackness of Jokanaan's cell is the effect of heavy brass and a low string tremolo. A brusquely rising chromatic scale in the violins, over thrusting syncopations in the other strings, heralds her order to produce the prisoner, but the soldiers' polite refusal is made final by the harsh chords with which the scale is chopped off.

10 To the Page's dismay, she turns coyly to Narraboth, promising that she will drop "a little green flower" (*ein kleines grünes Blümchen*) for him when she passes in her litter on the morrow. When he hesitates, she promises to look at him through the muslim veils of her litter and to smile at him. *Ich weiss, du wirst das tun!* she says—"I know you will do this." To the simple, love-struck Captain, a smile is enough: her cajoling reduces him to putty. He acquiesces and issues the order for the prophet to be brought forth.

Salome cajoles Narraboth with flowing tunefulness that recalls the triple time of her waltz; the harps accompany her with chords that seem delicate and simple, but the detached notes of the melody that comes from them are an augmentation of the motive of Narraboth's obsession (Ex. SA-2a)—Salome knows her quarry very well. Trills give point to her suggesting that the Tetrarch fears the prisoner.

Narraboth's lyricism is gone, taken over by repetitions of single pitches and a generally static line. Salome's final snare—the promise of a smile—is to a lilting tune over floating arpeggios.

11 The soldiers descend into the cistern; Salome breathlessly awaits their return. As Jokanaan appears, she steps back slowly, looking at him.

The orchestra describes Salome's growing excitement by a steadily rising pitch level, intense string figurations, high woodwind tremolos, and a steady development of the triplet of Ex. SA-5a. Jokanaan steps into view as Ex. SA-3 appears in sonorous French horns; Ex. SA-4 follows at once in the more austere combination of tuba and contrabassoon. At the peak of a vivid rising chromatic scale in the violas, Ex. SA-5c appears grandly in the violins—the woman in Salome has suddenly flowered. The remainder of this interlude is given to expansion and development of these motives.

SCENE III

12 Jokanaan's first words are a demand to meet the man "whose cup of sins is now full" (*dessen Sündenbecher jetzt voll ist*). Although Jokanaan's meaning is not clear to Salome, she immediately recognizes the significance of Jokanaan's reference to the woman who gave herself up to the lust of her eyes (*die sich hingab der Lust ihrer Augen*)—it is unmistakable to her that he means Herodias.

Jokanaan calls Herodes to justice as French horns intone fragments of Ex. SA-3. His eagerness to confront the unnamed sinful woman is voiced solemnly over the playing of Ex. SA-7 by the French horns, while chromatic descents in piccolo and flutes slither above it all.

13 Salome is both horrified and entranced at the sight of the man whose eyes are like "black caverns where dragons dwell" (*schwarzen Höhlen, wo die Drachen* *hausen)* or "black lakes troubled by a fantastic moon" *(schwarze Seen, aus denen irres Mondlicht flackert).*

The sinuous contour of Ex. SA-2g appears in the clarinet. Salome's phrases seem distracted and irregular as spurts of half-step scale fragments rush quietly through various registers of the orchestra, as if the dragons she imagines or the currents of dark lakes are circling about, unseen but ominously present.

14 In spite of Narraboth's remonstrance, she steps closer to gaze at Jokanaan and is caught by the paleness of his skin, which she compares to "an ivory image" *(ein Bildnis aus Elfenbein).* He demands to know who she is and, resentful of her staring at him with "golden eyes under gilded eyelids" *(Goldaugen unter den gleissenden Lidern),* that she be gone from him.

The open fourths of Ex. SA-4 capture her awe and her unhealthy absorption in Jokanaan's gaunt appearance. Her melody broadens as her fascination controls her, reaching a rapturous pause on a pianissimo *high pitch as she imagines that "he is as chaste as the moon" (ist er keusch wie der Mond). Jokanaan's vocal line is solidly rhythmed, but a roiling line in the cellos and basses represent his anger and resentment. Even though he does not know the identity of the bejeweled and heavily made-up girl standing before him, the presence of a variant of Ex. SA-7 (fragment "b") in bassoons and cellos connects her to Herodias.*

15 When Salome identifies herself as the daughter of Herodias, Jokanaan erupts with condemnation, but Salome, ever more enraptured, finds his voice to be "like music in her ears" *(wie Musik in meinen Ohren).*

Salome identifies herself proudly to a triadic, fanfare-like melody. A solo violin punctuating it with the motive of Narraboth's and Herodes's fixation (Ex. SA-2e) gives the motive the additional identity of Salome herself and connotes the obsession that is now overtaking her. Her reference to the sound of his voice as sweet music is given an expansively lyrical vocal line.

16 Jokanaan urges her to don sackcloth and ashes and go to the desert to meet the Son of Man. When she asks if this person is as beautiful as Jokanaan himself, he warns her that he hears the "beating of the wings of the Angel of Death in the palace" *(die Flügel des Todesengels im Palaste rauschen).*

Among the motives boiling under Jokanaan's reviling of Herodias's daughter are the chromatic fillip of the Herodias figure (Ex. SA-7 "b") and the opening notes of the Jokanaan/Christ theme (Ex. SA-3). His urging her to seek the Son of Man is given majesty by simplicity of melody and harmony. Her naive questioning is to Ex. SA-2g in the sound of the flute; his vision of the Angel of Death is pictorialized vividly by a fluttering figure in clarinets.

17 Salome becomes ecstatic over Jokanaan's body, which to her is like the lilies of an unscythed field, as white as the snows of the mountains of Judaea, even whiter than "the breast of the moon on the sea" *(die Brüste des Mondes auf dem Meere).* She longs, she says, to touch his body *(Lass mich ihn berühren, deinen Leib).*

Calling his name, Salome turns to a beautiful, long-phrased cantabile *in the major mode; as she proclaims her love for his body, violins and clarinets (above a whispered trembling in the harp) give emphasis to the music of Ex. SA-2g. She proclaims the whiteness of his body to the motive of her sensual excitement (Ex. SA-5c). Her eagerness to touch him moves into the minor, with cellos and bassoons making a point of the Herodias motive (Ex. SA-7 "b").[14]*

18 His vigorous rejection causes her to revile his body, which now seems to her to be like "the body of a leper" *(der Leib eines Aussätzigen),* a plaster wall "where vipers have crawled" *(wo Nattern gekrochen sind)* and scorpions have made their nest. It is, she avers, like "a whitened tomb" *(ein übertünchtes Grab).*

---

[14] Mann (p. 54) nicely compares this concluding passage to "the rotten center of a toothsome apple."

Sharply accented music reveals her revulsion. The motive of Jokanaan's gauntness (Ex. SA-4) is played brusquely by bassoons and French horns in short note values; angular motives and chromatic scales jab their way upward. Pizzicatos add to the bite of Aussätzigen *("lepers"); Ex. SA-2g insistently whines in the clarinets and piccolo, then in the violas (the use of the wood of the bow on the strings results in a specially thin sound). Images of vipers and other loathsome things writhe in twisted figures above dissonant harmonies.*

19 It is his hair, she says, of which she is truly enamored. It is like "clusters of grapes" *(Weintrauben),* like the cedars of Lebanon shading lions and robbers, like black nights "when the moon hides her face" *(wenn der Mond sich verbirgt),* and like "the forest's silence" *(des Waldes Schweigen).*

The vocal line broadens again, the violins providing the exuberance first of Ex. SA-6a (the music of her hurrying into the fresh air), then of Ex. SA-5b (the waltz melody of her delight in breathing the fresh air at her leaving the banquet). A blurt of trombone crescendo provides the roars of lions; her melody slows and lowers in pitch as the blackness of Jokanaan's hair reminds her of the dark nights when the face of the moon is hidden. Her rapture explodes on a high A when she avers that nothing in the world is as black as his hair.

20 Her "Let me touch your hair" *(Lass mich es berühren, dein Haar)* produces another outburst from Jokanaan that in turn stimulates a revulsion of his hair, which is like "a crown of thorns" *(eine Dornenkrone)* on his head or "a knot of black serpents writhing around his neck" *(ein Schlangenknoten gewickelt um deinen Hals).*

As Salome coos her desire to touch his hair, Ex. SA-2g sighs quietly in the violins and Ex. SA-7 "b" rises sinuously (it is the motive of Herodias) in the cellos. Jokanaan's reaction is melodically vehement and powered further by trombones hammering the repeated-note introduction of Ex. SA-2d. That she should not profane the Temple of the Lord is strongly reinforced by Ex. SA-3, first in the French horns, then in the strings. Salome's abruptly negative turn of mind is as before.

21 She loves not his hair, but his mouth, she declares. It is like "a band of scarlet" *(ein Scharlachband)* on a tower of ivory, more red than "the red blasts of trumpets that herald the coming of Kings" *(die roten Fanfaren der Trompeten, die das Nah'n von Kön'gen künden)* or the "feet of the men who tread wine in the winepress" *(Füsse der Männer, die den Wein stampfen in der Kelter).* His mouth is "like a branch of coral that fishermen find in the twilight of the sea" *(wie ein Korallenzweig in der Dämm'rung des Meers). Lass mich ihn küssen, deinen Mund—*"Let me kiss your mouth."

The luscious cantilena of Salome's glorification of Jokanaan's mouth is given constant irony by variants of the motive of obsession (Ex. SA-2c, introduced by the Page in the first scene), sometimes forcefully and in broad note values, sometimes subtly and quickly. Text illustrations abound: trumpets echo the motive of Ex. SA-2c when she speaks of the red blare of Kings' fanfares, staccato bassoons and pizzicato cellos and basses alternate with French horns to depict the soft tromping of feet in the winepress, trills and runs in the woodwinds describe the doves whose feet are not as red as Jokanaan's mouth, and celesta and glockenspiel "color" the redness of the coral of the dark seas. Jokanaan's blunt Niemals! *("Never!") excites Salome's obsession even more, her eagerness to kiss his mouth soaring at the top of the staff to the music of Ex. SA-2e (derived from Ex. SA-2c); each repetition is a half step higher. This paean to Jokanaan's mouth is the opera's first climactic moment; there will be a grisly and ironic recall of much of it in the final scene.*

22 Narraboth becomes utterly distraught as Salome repeats her craving to kiss Jokanaan's mouth; he stabs himself and dies at once, his body rolling down the terrace steps and ending sprawled between Salome and Jokanaan. Neither notices him at all.

Narraboth's death is to fortissimo *recalls of the opera's opening motive (Ex. SA-2a). Any musical awareness of his tragic end is quickly obliterated by a quick thrust of Herodias's motive (Ex. SA-7 "b") and Salome's final cry of Ex. SA-2e, now reaching a high B-flat before concluding ecstatically in the major mode.*

23 Jokanaan reviles Salome as a "daughter of adultery" *(Tochter der Unzucht)* and calls her to repent on her knees before the One who can save her; even as they speak, avers Jokanaan, He is in a boat on the Sea of Galilee talking with His disciples.

Jokanaan delivers his mini-sermon in a lyrical line that draws on the flowing triad of Ex. SA-3 and is accompanied by warm orchestral colors. Ex. SA-2e appears often in forceful orchestrations, as if Salome hears nothing but her own demands for sexual gratification. The gentle waves of the Sea of Galilee find expression in a quiet ostinato of string triplets; Christ's quiet voice speaking to his disciples is suggested by a floating, lovely melody played by solo violin. His final urging of repentance is to the sonorousness of string tremolos, rich chords in French horns, and powerful accents in trumpets and trombones.

24 She does not relent. With a final *Du bist verflucht* ("Thou art accursed"), Jokanaan returns to his dungeon.

Ex. SA-2e is sung by Salome yet again. Jokanaan's curse builds suddenly from hushed intensity to an explosion, the orchestra accenting it with the now not-so-sinuous Ex. SA-2g. Motives from the above passages thrash about in the various voices of the orchestra as the two call loudly to each other but hear only themselves. Jokanaan returns to his cell to a great pounding of Ex. SA-4 in the timpani, bassoons, and low brasses. The orchestral interlude that follows is dominated by the concept of Salome's obsession (represented by Ex. SA-2g in a hysterical canon), but other figures associated with her (Ex. SA-2e) and Jokanaan (Ex. SA-3) are also potently present.

25 Salome remains, staring at the cistern. It is a pivotal moment in the drama, for it is here that the plan for revenge takes shape in her mind.

The music sinks to a hush. Salome is silent, but her thoughts of revenge are given voice in the instruments: string tremolos persist and create unbearable tension; they are suddenly cut into by harsh crescendos and violent accents; the contrabassoon mutters Ex. SA-2, then turns to rushes of chromatic scales and abrupt triadic spurts (Ex SA-5f); the sopranino clarinet suddenly squeals a caricature of the motive of Jokanaan's asceticism (Ex. SA-4) before the brasses proclaim Ex. SA-2d.

SCENE IV

26 Herodes, Herodias, their guests, and attendants bustle onto the terrace, Herodes looking angrily and desperately for Salome. Ignoring his wife's admonishment that he must cease his constant staring at Salome, Herodes comments that the moon has "a strange look" *(ein seltsames Bild)*, like "a mad woman seeking everywhere for lovers" *(ein wahnwitziges Weib, das überall nach Buhlen sucht)*, reeling through the clouds like a drunken woman. Herodias rejects any fanciful interpretation of the moon: *Nein, der Mond ist wie der Mond, das ist alles* ("No, the moon is like the moon, that's all").

The jagged descents of the quarreling Jews knife into the music as the banquet attendees move out of the hall. Herodes's vulgar mind and behavior is expressed in descending whole-tone eruptions in the strings. When he sees Salome, his glee is to mercurial viola chromatics. As he comments on the moon, the orchestra provides a vivid picture of a man consumed with neuroses, alternating the viola figure with fast-moving whole-tone scale descents (Ex. SA-6) that provide no melodic continuity but constant—and pointless—busyness. Herodias throws cold water on his thoughts whenever she can, commenting on his visions of the moon in the major mode to harmonies so simple (in this context) as to sound bald and crass.

27 Herodes slips in the blood of the dead Narraboth, whose body is still sprawled in the middle of the terrace. Only momentarily puzzled by the death of the handsome Captain, who, he noticed, had looked languorously at Salome, Herodes offhandedly orders the body carried away.

Violins distort the viola's chromatic music (played when Herodes first appeared; see par. 26) as Herodes puzzles over the blood and body of Narraboth. An oboe's glimmer of the opera's first motive (Ex. SA-2a) and the cellos' touch of Salome's Ex. SA-5a establish musically Herodes's connection of the body of Narraboth with the fact that Narraboth was seen to look at Salome with languorous eyes (schmachtenden Augen); *for the listener, the connection is sarcastic—Herodes does not see the connection between himself and his infatuated Captain of the Guard. The music of Herodes's orders to clean things up is abrupt and unfeeling— only three notes are needed for him to snap a blunt* Fort mit ihm *("Off with him"), as if the body were a dead leaf to be swept off the terrace.*

28 Herodes suddenly feels, then hears, a chill wind that seems to him like "the beating of vast wings" *(Das Rauschen von mächt'gen Flügeln).* Herodias feels and hears nothing; he is ill, she suggests, and they should go back inside. She again protests his looking at Salome, who, says the Tetrarch, has never been so pale.

The cold wind is symbolized by rushing chromatic scales that rise and fall in muted violins. These scales return with unsettling ebb and flow of loud and soft, as he thinks he hears the wind again, while horns and timpani alternate hurried two-note groups to suggest the beating of wings (they may also represent the pounding of his heart.) The music for Herodes's fervid imagination is wholly different from that of Jokanaan's vision (see above, par. 16): Jokanaan recognized the wings of the Angel of Death; Herodes, thinking only of a great bird, is fearful but uncomprehending.

29 Herodes importunes Salome to join him in drink; she answers flippantly that she is not thirsty *(Ich bin nicht durstig, Tetrarch).* Herodes throws an irritated remark at Herodias about her daughter's impertinence, then cozily offers Salome some fruit in which "I would so joyously see the bite mark of your tiny teeth" *(Den Abdruck deiner kleinen, weissen Zähne in einer Frucht seh' ich so gern). Ich bin nicht hungrig,* is the response—"I'm not hungry." Herodes's annoyance elicits Herodias's sneer that his ancestors were camel drivers and his father a robber.

As the orchestra hints at the motive of Salome's youthfulness (Ex. SA-5a), Herodes invites her to sip wine with him; his tune is a heavy-footed waltz. Tiny pricks of woodwinds make grotesque his flirtatious "then would I drain the cup" (dann will ich den Becher leeren). Salome's response is accompanied by the heckelphone's[15] *staccato augmentation of Ex. SA-2a. Herodes and Herodias snarl at each other tunelessly. Herodes turns to a more sweeping melody to invite Salome to taste rare fruits, the violins offering a banal, mincing little tune to suggest Herodes's envisioning her delicate biting. Salome's answer again elicits an unpleasant colloquy between Herodes and Herodias; the trade of his ancestors is given vulgar point by the squealing*[16] *of clarinets-as-camels. The vulgar argument between Mr. and Mrs. Tetrarch is mercifully brief.*

30 Herodes invites Salome to sit next to him on her mother's throne. Again a rejection from Salome: *Ich bin nicht müde, Tetrarch* ("I'm not tired, Tetrarch").

Herodes's third enticement is to a variant of Salome's youthful waltz (Ex. SA-5b). At Salome's "I'm not tired," a contrabassoon recalls Ex. SA-2a as a reminder of both the opera's first music of obsessiveness and Salome's idea of revenge (Ex. SA-5f).

31 The voice of Jokanaan once more issues from the cistern. Herodias accuses Herodes of being afraid of the prophet, else surely he would have surrendered the prisoner to the Jews for execution. When Herodes protests that Jokanaan is

---

[15] The heckelphone is a baritone oboe (used rarely).

[16] Reference books describe the camel's sound as "bubbling bellows." To my ears, camels squawk. Whether or no, Strauss's clarinets squeal.

a holy man who has seen God, the Jews enter into yet another of their theological arguments.

Jokanaan's words and music are strongly reminiscent of the moment when Salome first heard his voice. Herodias's calm is obviously unsettled; her accusation that Herodes is afraid of Jokanaan bites with a plummeting whole-tone scale in the bass clarinet. The rabbinical debate becomes intensely convoluted and multi-voiced: rhythmic elements of their fractious music pop in and out of a hubbub, the only extended ensemble of the opera.

32 Hearing Jokanaan predict the coming of "the Savior of the World" *(der Erlöser der Welt)*, Herodes asks the Nazarenes about the Prophet's meaning. Their faith that Messiah indeed now walks the earth is unsettling to Herodes, who wants no new king or kingdom to rival his precarious reign. (Nor can he tolerate the thought that the powers of Messiah to bring the dead to life might cause his murdered brother to walk the earth again.)

Jokanaan's music continues and flattens the religious squabble; replayings of Ex. SA-3 are quietly intoned like a mantra in mellow French horns, then bassoons. When the Nazarenes sing of the meaning of Jokanaan's prediction, the combination of their soft and steady A-flat major key against the A minor of the Jews is a brief moment of bitonality[17] that sets the different religious forces worlds apart from each other. When the First Nazarene's tale of Christ's raising the dead ends graciously and melodiously in A-flat major, Herodes's upward spurt in A minor—Wie, er erweckt die Toten? ("What, he raises up the dead?")—is bitingly satiric and an echo of the harmonic contrast between the Nazarenes and the theologians.

33 Jokanaan's denouncing voice continues to resound from the cistern, predicting that a multitude of men will stone the daughter of Babylon and that her body will be "pierced with soldiers' swords" *(Schwerten durchbohren)* and "crushed with their shields" *(Schilden zermalmen)*. Herodias becomes more and more agitated.

The responses to Jokanaan's predictions are to a jumble of motives, some literal recalls, some variants. The mood of the passage is combined outrage, frustration, hysteria, and fear.

34 As Jokanaan's prediction of the coming of a new King resounds from the cistern, Herodes asks Salome to dance. Salome's refusal is greeted triumphantly by Herodias, but Salome is toying with Herodes's panic, lust, and neuroticism, knowing that she has him right where she wants him. He promises Salome anything she wants if she will dance for him. She rises to ask if he really means what he says; her persistent asking results in his swearing several times over to keep his word, ultimately swearing by life, crown, and gods *(Bei meinem Leben, bei meiner Krone, bei meinen Göttern)*.[18]

Herodes's invitation to dance is musically a sudden switch, deriving in part from the eccentricity of his mind and his own absorptions, and in part from a frantic desire to get away from the sound of Jokanaan's voice. A triplet (associated with the first notes of Ex. SA-5a) scurries in the orchestra as Salome and Herodes spar with each other and Jokanaan's voice continues to resound. Things suddenly become quiet when Salome asks, over a hushed trill high in the clarinet, Du schwörst es, Tetrarch? ("Do you swear it, Tetrarch?"). After a rising flurry of whole-tone fragments when he vows to keep his word, the trill returns as Salome drives his oath into the memory of the observers.

35 Herodes is in the midst of mental collapse: again he feels the chill of an imagined icy wind and hears once more the beating of wings, fancying that "a monstrous black bird" *(ein ungeheurer, schwarzer Vogel)* hovers over the terrace.

---

[17] "Bitonality" refers to the simultaneous use of two keys at the same time. A prominent example of this is found in the duet at the end of the Prologue of Britten's *Peter Grimes;* see Examples 3.11a and b.

[18] A remarkable assertion by the ruler of a monotheistic nation.

Strauss, *Salome:* Salome (Birgit Nilsson) begins her Dance of the Seven Veils for Herodes, as the page (Marcia Baldwin) crouches at the feet of Herodias (Irene Dalis). Metropolitan Opera, 1965: production designed by Rudolf Heinrich. Courtesy *Opera News,* Metropolitan Opera Guild. Photo Louis Mélançon.

Suddenly the air feels hot to him, and he demands snow to eat and that his cloak be loosened. Desperately, he throws his floral crown to the ground, for the "roses on it feel like fire" *(Diese Rosen sind wie Feuer).*

Chromatic scales swirl again. A waltz, distorted and syncopated, marks his throwing down his floral crown.

36 Over the continuing sonority of Jokanaan's voice and Herodias's insistence that Salome not dance, Salome agrees to Herodes's request. Slaves bring perfumes and seven veils, and remove her sandals. Yet again the voice of Jokanaan is heard, enraging Herodias, who demands that all return to the Palace. Herodes will not leave until Salome has danced. Salome ends all argument with *Ich bin bereit, Tetrarch* ("I'm ready, Tetrarch").

Roiling string arpeggios announce the general excitement. Jokanaan's motives are absent, his voice becoming part of a rush to the sudden chords that mark Salome's readiness to perform.

37 The musicians begin a wildly thrumming introduction, but Salome stills them; she then begins her Dance of the Seven Veils in a gently rocking way. As it progresses it becomes more and more impassioned. She wearies for a moment near the end, regains her strength and continues with increasing wildness. She pauses by the cistern as if in a trance; then, in a sudden rush, throws herself at Herodes's feet.

The Dance falls into five sections:

1. A barbaric Introduction, with percussive sounds and accents from all instruments; trumpets and trombones give a snippet of the music Salome will use to demand the head of Jokanaan before the flurry of wild music diminishes in response to Salome's gesture.

2. A slow, swaying dance in 3/4 time, with oriental flourishes in solo oboe and flute over a hypnotic accompanying pattern, extensive permutations of fragments associated with Salome and those obsessed with her (especially Exs. SA-2e, SA-2g, and SA-5a), increasing enrichment of timbre (especially in percussion), and brief flurries of passion.

3. A lyrical waltz (Ex. SA-5g), announced by the French horns and strings, voluptuous in melody and timbre. An expansion of Exs. SA-2g and SA-5c becomes more and more lush. After exotic castanets and chromatic ebbs and flows, the music manipulates Salome's waltz tune (Ex. SA-5b).

4. A presto, loud and wild, with a recall of the Introduction, the whole-tone fragments of Herodes's music, and the revenge figure (Ex. SA-5f) in harps, piccolo, and clarinets. After a stressful recall of Ex. SA-5c, it ends with a hushed trill as Salome pauses.

5. A furious Coda, based on the music of Ex. SA-5c (the motive associated with Salome's sexual excitement and fully aroused lust).

38 Herodes gleefully invites her to name her reward. She would like, she answers, to have brought to her "on a silver charger" *(in einer Silberschüssel)*—there she pauses, while Herod chortles unsuspectingly and gushingly over the idea of a material award that would fit so charmingly on a silver platter—the head of Jokanaan.

The whole orchestra becomes busy with the mood of Herodes's neurotic joy, his gratitude coming in lyrical lines above rippling arpeggios. A wonderfully ironic touch is the stinging trumpet sound of the rhythm of a death archetype ♫ ♪, heard when Herodes asks Salome to name anything she desires. The idea of a silver charger is entrusted to the crystal-clear arabesques of flute, harp, and celesta. The accompaniment to Salome's identification of her reward echoes the clarinet trills of her moment of pause in her Dance, their chromatic rise and fall creating an ironic and vicious expectancy. Flute and piccolo provide added meaning with the motive of Salome's sensuousness and obsession (Ex. SA-2g); the music of Salome's request is Ex. SA-2b.

39 Herodias is delighted; Herodes nervously suggests that Salome is speaking for her mother, but Salome insists it is her own will she is putting forward. She holds him to his promise.

Herodes's music is jumbled, of course. Salome's insistence that the choice of prize is her own is shaped by the pounding repeated notes of several motives of obsession (Exs. SA-2c, d, e, and f). The sound of the revenge figure (Ex. SA-5f) in the bassoons and contrabassoon is a spike driven home with terrible thrust. Her insistence that the Tetrarch honor his oath is to persistent clarinet trills.

40 Herodes offers half his kingdom, but Salome's insistence is vivid and uncompromising; her mother supports her case with obvious pleasure.

Herodes offers half his kingdom over an orchestral sound filled with bubbling triplets, his own line reaching anxiously to the top of the staff. Salome's response is a powerful repetition of a single pitch until she pronounces the name of her victim to the dotted rhythm of the opera's first motive (Ex. SA-2a). Herodias exults with harshly accented chords in strings, horns, and bassoons, the orchestral fabric turning to brass-driven treatments of Ex. SA-7 "b" and the opening fragment of SA-2c and its derivatives.

41 Desperately, Herodes asks if perhaps he has loved her too much, urges her to believe that the head of a dead man is vile to look at, and offers her the largest emerald in the world. Salome is unrelenting.

Strauss, *Salome,* Salome (Inga Nielsen) demands her reward from Herodes
(Ragnar Ulfung). The Rabbis express dismay over Herodes's promise to give
her the sacred veil of the Temple if she will relent and ask for something other
than the head of Jokanaan. Santa Fe Opera, 1995: production by Tom
Hennes. Courtesy Santa Fe Opera. Photo Hans Fahrmeyer.

*Herodes's agitation comes in wide skips and abrupt changes of direction. Salome's music of
insistence is in the same cast as before, but now low in register and more ominous. His desperation is again expressed in orchestral triplets.*

42 In a frightened outburst, half forgetting what he wants to say, Herodes then
offers his white peacocks. Salome insists on her prize.

*Herodes turns to a wheedling, waltz-like melodic line to offer his white peacocks. Salome's
renewed demand is the music of Ex. SA-2f.*

43 Herodes begs her to remember that Jokanaan is a holy man; if she will not
think of that, she should think of what might happen to Herodes himself. Her
words of rejection are the same. With unknowing irony, he frenziedly urges
Salome to be calm, then turns to an extended and desperate enumeration of his
treasury of jewels, some with magic powers, that he will give her if she will yield.
To the horror of the rabbis, he even offers her the sacred veil of the temple.

*His agitated music returns as he desperately seeks release from his vow. The picture he paints
of his jewels is mirrored in high chinks of color: glockenspiel, celesta, and upper woodwinds.
The disjunct nature of his music takes on a melodic flow, but it is clearly the mouthing of a
man quite out of control. His shocking offer of the Temple's holy veil is on a high A.*

44 Salome is implacable; he surrenders. Herodias draws the Ring of Death from
Herodes's finger and gives it to the First Soldier, who takes it to the Executioner
(see note 19). As the Executioner descends into the cistern, Herodes blabbers
pointlessly about needing wine and that surely evil will befall someone.

Herodes's final offer has no effect. Salome's insistent music moves higher and sweeps away all resistance; the opening words of his surrender are sung to a diminution of her Ex. SA-2b, the music of her first request for the head of Jokanaan. Violent syncopations, seething recalls of Ex. SA-2g, harsh dissonances, and tumbling triplets mark Herodias's removal of the ring. Herodes mumbles to hurried and disjunct phrases accompanied by descending whole-tone patterns. Quiet distortions of Jokanaan's Ex. SA-3 in strings and muted French horns are foreboding and reveal the Tetrarch's troubled mind.

45 Salome waits anxiously by the edge of the cistern. She hears no sound and wonders aloud why there is only silence. "If anyone tried to kill me, I would cry out, I would struggle"—*Wenn einer mich zu töten käme, ich würde schreien, ich würde mich wehren.* She is on the verge of insanity.

The sound of a note very high in a solo double bass marks Salome's anxious expectancy. Created by drawing the bow sharply across a high part of a string pinched between thumb and forefinger, this eerie timbre is for a pitch that is octaves away from the accompanying dark roll of the bass drum; the combination of these sounds is, in Strauss's words, not "cries of pain uttered by the victim, but sighs of anguish from the heart of an impatiently expectant Salome."

Her frantic puzzlement over hearing nothing comes softly and low in pitch at first, but, as frenzy takes over, her notes quickly spring to the top of the staff, above a clamor of French horns and the revenge motive (Ex. SA-5f) as punctuation to her eagerness for Naaman, the Executioner, to strike. The "pinched" double bass effect returns, this time with violin tremolo. A horrible tremolo in basses and cellos is the moment of the sword stroke, but Salome thinks the executioner has dropped his sword and has forsaken his duty.

46 She calls to the Page to get soldiers to carry out the Tetrarch's command when suddenly the huge black arm of the Executioner appears from the cistern, bearing Jokanaan's head on a silver platter.

Salome's music becomes demented again, as woodwinds shriek with the tension of the moment. She reaches a peak of frenzy when the musical storm stops suddenly; the numbing pianissimo *roll of the bass drum is the only music for the grisly sight of the prophet's head.*

47 Taking the charger into her own hands, Salome sings an extended love song to the head of the prophet. She triumphantly calls on the head to open its eyes, asks why its tongue no longer speaks to her, and exults in the fact that, in spite of Jokanaan's imprecations, she lives and can do with his head what she wants.

Her cry of triumph is introduced by a wild fanfare that draws on the music of Ex. SA-2a and the revenge figure of Ex. SA-5c. Salome's extended solo is in the grand manner, marked by long phrases and exultant high notes, yielding at times to equally broad melodies in the violins. Underneath much of this, however, are brutal percussive effects in the lower registers of all sections, and above and around these broad phrases are surging chromatic scales in the clarinets that recall the icy wind of Herodes's guilty imagination. As she imagines biting his red lips, the music of Herodes's offering of rare fruit (see above, par. 29) returns in an altered way; as she calls to Jokanaan's eyes, she draws on the music of her first encounter with him, when she had found his eyes as black and as deep as dark caverns or lakes at night (par. 13).

She extols the beauty of a body that was "a column of ivory set on silvery feet" *(eine Elfenbeinsäule auf silbernen Füssen);* she revels in the blackness of his hair and the redness of his mouth. She confesses to unrequited passion for him even though he is dead and laments that he never even looked at her when he was alive. "I know well," she says, "that you would have loved me" *(Ich weiss es wohl, du hättest mich geliebt).*

She extols the whiteness of his body to the quiet recall of Ex. SA-2g; that nothing on earth was so white is sung to the string-supported richness of Ex. SA-5c. Her lament that he never looked at her recalls the accompaniment of her facing the living Jokanaan and turning her attention to his mouth. SA-5c returns again as the underpinning of her vow that the fires of her desire (dieses brünstige Begehren löschen) *can never be quenched; when she imagines that, had he looked at her, he would have loved her* (du hättest mich geliebt), *Jokanaan's motive (Ex. SA-3) returns, now in diminution and rhythmic reworking by violins. As she thinks of the "mystery of death"* (das Geheimnis des Todes), *her music sinks below the staff, as if in total exhaustion.*

48 Herodes's shock and revulsion at Salome's monstrous behavior is not matched by Herodias. He frantically orders all the lights extinguished and unknowingly echoes the Page's prediction from the opening of the opera that *Es wird Schreckliches gescheh'n* ("Something terrible will happen").

Herodes's revulsion is muttered over the strange sound of timpani recalling Salome's Ex. SA-2g. Herodias's approval is sung while trumpets sting again (see par. 38) with the rhythm of a death archetype. Herodes is reduced to recitation on rapid single pitches, his emotional terror mirrored in the tremolos that have characterized the emotional and moral instability of the opera from its beginning.

49 The moon and stars are suddenly hidden by clouds, and all is dark. From the darkness Salome's voice is heard, confessing to having kissed Jokanaan's mouth *(Ah! Ich habe deinen Mund geküsst, Jokanaan)* and that it had a bitter taste. *Ich habe deinen Mund geküsst, Jokanaan,* she repeats.

After Herodes, on repeated notes, snarls his fear that something terrible will happen, violins issue an evil-sounding half-step tremolo. In a low voice, Salome is heard from the darkness as the violins, flute, and clarinet turn to a trill (heard consistently in this opera as an omen of the unspeakable), piccolo and oboe offer Salome's Ex. SA-2g, and a brooding dissonance in lower strings and brass swells and fades, is silent, then swells and fades again. The dissonance returns under the trill as reinforcement of Salome's wry thought that love has a bitter taste. Her final words are triumphant and explosive, a gorgeous arch of melody ending in a major chord, given the pendant of her motive of sexual excitement (Ex. SA-5c).

50 A moonbeam penetrates the blackness, revealing Salome and her ghastly prize.

A sudden and violent dissonance in full orchestra represents the revelation of the total horror for all to see, the clarinets wailing the Salome motive of Ex. SA-2g one last time.

51 At Herodes's shouted order (*Man töte dieses Weib!*—"Let that woman be killed!"), the soldiers crush her with their shields.

Herodes's shout is on an agonized high note. A hideous rush of chromatics explodes in the supreme violence of heavy brass, low strings, and percussion in a crushing Death archetype ♫|♪ᵧ↯ ↯ ᵧ ♫|♪, *ending the opera with unbridled viciousness and finality.*

The Characters

Narraboth (tenor) *[NAHR-ah-boat]*

A young Syrian captain in Herodes's army. His passion for Salome is communicated with the music of the opera's first notes (Example SA-2a) and is consistently portrayed by floating lyricism. He readily falls prey to Salome's enticements, surrendering to her promise of a smile if he will order Jokanaan to be brought from the cistern for her to see. Salome's infatuation for Jokanaan is too much for Narraboth; he falls on his sword in a useless suicide and disappears from the opera when Herodes, momentarily irritated by stepping into his blood, orders his corpse to be dragged away.

Page to Herodias (contralto)

An adolescent boy (a "trouser role") who idolizes Narraboth and dreads the implications of Narraboth's infatuation for Salome. From the outset, the Page's thoughts are of death (the moon "is like a woman rising from the tomb"—"wie eine Frau, die aufsteigt aus dem Grab") and that "terrible things can happen" ("Schreckliches kann geschehn"). His music moves in somber rhythms pitched low on the staff at first, but as Narraboth's rapturous thoughts become increasingly assertive, the Page's become more active, wide-ranging, and angular. From the moment of Salome's arrival on the terrace, the Page falls silent, remaining only as an observer of the opera's "schreckliche" events.

Two soldiers (basses)

Acid comments among the military's lowest ranks are among opera's time-honored features, opening the action in Monteverdi's *L'incoronazione di Poppaea* (1643) and providing a moment of comic relief toward the end of Berlioz's *Les Troyens à Carthage* (1856–58). In *Salome,* the Soldiers sing in short, diatonic phrases, their words describing the offstage fete where Herod looks lustfully at Salome and the rabbis argue eternally. When one tells the other about the prisoner whose voice comes to them from the cistern, their conversation[19] allows for the important presentation of a primary motive (Example SA-3) associated with Jokanaan and, through him, the Messiah. Its warmth of scoring and simple dignity is strikingly different from the musical ambience of the opera as a whole.

When Salome demands they bring Jokanaan out of his cell, they must of course be polite in refusing, so their responses to her are somewhat longer and more gracious in phrase than are their comments to each other, but the simplicity of their music remains an emblem of their humble station.

EXAMPLE SA-3 MOTIVE OF JOKANAAN AS A HOLY MAN AND OF THE CHRIST WHOSE COMING HE PROCLAIMS

First Soldier:
(doubled by French Horns)

Er   ist   ein   heil' - ger   Mann.
He   *is*   *a*   *holy*   *man.*

---

[19] Omitted from Wilde's drama is an extension of this conversation in which one of the soldiers tells of the murder in that cistern of Herodias's first husband. The order to execute him was ceremonial: the Tetrarch removed from his own finger the Ring of Death and ordered it to be conveyed to the Executioner, for whom the ring served as a written command. In the opera, Herodes is virtually paralyzed after surrendering to Salome's demand, so Herodias removes the ring from the fainting Herodes's finger. She gives it to the First Soldier who in turn bears it to Naaman, the Executioner, thus mirroring the ritual authorization of the murder of Salome's father.

A Cappadocian (bass)

A visitor (from what is now East-Central Turkey) or perhaps another soldier on duty on the terrace. His function in the plot is to ask questions about the man whose voice emanates from the cistern and thus to elicit from the soldiers the information that all are forbidden to see him.

Five Jews (four tenors, one bass)

Five rabbis in attendance at Herodes's court who continually debate fine points of religion. The Soldiers describe them as wild, howling beasts, Salome finds their ceremonies foolish, and Herodias is irritated by their constant bickering. They provide the only ensemble of the opera when, after the banquet, they argue about whether Elijah did or did not see God, and contribute thereby to the general ambience of excess and discord in Herodes's court. Their theological bickering is depicted in an orchestral "argument" among jagged woodwind descents and contrabassoon triplets.

Jokanaan (bass-baritone) [yo-KAH-nah-ahn]

A young man—about thirty years of age—wholly convinced that the world is about to change with the coming of One greater than he. He sings consistently in diatonic, firmly rhythmed melodies sharply contrasted with the frenetic music of the Herodian court. He has his fierce side, too: he can chastise with the best of the biblical figures, roaring fanfare indictments of Herodias (see below, Example SA-7) above the seemingly omnipresent tremolos of the score and repetitions of his own motive as a holy man (Example SA-3).

Three motives are associated with him. One is his own expression of his unshakable religious convictions (Example SA-2d) and a second, set out first by the soldiers when they talk about him, is his nobility of spirit (Example SA-3).

The third (Example SA-4), reflecting his asceticism, gaunt appearance, and strength of purpose, is a sequence of descending open fourths that draws on the archetype of the perfect interval as suggestive of purity, truth, and grandeur. This motive, consistently given a rhythmic stride and orchestral power, resounds for the first time in trombones and cellos as Jokanaan mounts the steps from the cistern to the terrace.

EXAMPLE SA-4 JOKANAAN AS AN ASCETIC, GAUNT IN
APPEARANCE AND STRONG IN PURPOSE

Salome (soprano) [ZAHL-o-meh]

The sixteen-year-old daughter of Herodias, stepdaughter of Herodes.

We are aware of her at the instant of the opera's opening through Narraboth's opening words, "Wie schön ist die Prinzessin Salome heute Nacht" ("How beautiful Princess Salome is tonight"). A shriek from the clarinet after Narraboth's "Niemals habe ich sie so blass gesehn" ("Never have I seen her so pale") suggests she is ready to explode unless she can escape the filthy leering of Herodes and the oppressive atmosphere of the royal banquet's arguing Jews, silent Egyptians, and brutal Romans. She is at the point in life where all teenagers find parental guidance a bore and an irritant; her parents are, of course, the worst possible role models and she is, I assume, fully aware of their carnal proclivities.

Salome is no hootchy-kootchy hip-swinger that carnival sideshows and some operatic attempts would have her appear. She is, of course, a princess and therefore rigorously supervised and guarded. And chaste. "Anyone who has been in the Orient," wrote the composer, "and has observed the decorum of its women will appreciate that Salome should be played as a chaste virgin, an oriental princess, with but the simplest, most dignified gestures, if her shipwreck on encountering the miracle of a brave new world is to arouse compassion and not horror and disgust."[20]

Although she must be aware of the sexual undertones of the court's activities, it is clear from the opera's final moments that she knows of love only from what she has heard or been told, not from experience, for she says after she has kissed the severed head, "Sie sagen das die Liebe bitter schmecke"—"They say [not "I know"] that love tastes bitter." The libidinous insanity that ultimately consumes her is undoubtedly the result of her living in a court where the satisfying of the pleasures of the flesh is instantly gratified. Given the environment of her upbringing and the fact that she is accustomed to instant obedience and deference to her wishes, Salome is fully poised to take her place in the court's debauchery.

The opera, then, is a terrible progress in Salome's life from the seeming innocence and girlishness of her first appearance to the depravity of unchecked sexual desire. When she excitedly leaves the banquet as if suffocating, violins, oboe, and celesta gush a lyric melody at once exuberant and feverish (Example SA-5a); a few seconds later her music is a lilting waltz (Example SA-5b) that is girlishness personified. Her adolescence becomes less attractive when the triple time of waltz music is used to suggest her wheedling of Narraboth to bring Jokanaan out of his dungeon. When she first sees Jokanaan and hears him denounce her mother and predict a terrible and wonderful future, her fascination takes hold, asserted in a sinuous motive of obsession (Example SA-2g).

A motive associated with the stirring of her sensuality (Example SA-5c), heard first when she awaits Jokanaan's exit from the cistern, becomes an expression of passion and desire as she gazes on his gaunt, ivory-like body.

---

[20] Mann, p. 50f.

When she praises his beauty, her music is long-phrased, glowing with melodic warmth, and climactically arched toward a final harmony that is fulfilling and wondrously sensuous (Example SA-5d). Her response to rejection, however, is perverse: what she has just praised is now disgusting to her, so her vocal line is eruptively disjointed; the orchestral motives (especially that of her obsession) bite and dig about as illuminations of the vile pictures she paints with her words (Example SA-5e).

Her mind turns to brutality and revenge after Jokanaan goes back to his cell to the music of an orchestral passage remarkable for its tension and dramatic insight: under an intensely quiet violin tremolo that shivers in the silent air, the contrabassoon blurts several chromatic scales, then, from its depths, snaps out an ugly series of rising thirds (Example SA-5f) that returns shriekingly during the *presto* of the Dance of the Seven Veils and

EXAMPLE SA-5 MOTIVES OF SALOME

a) Salome rushes from the banquet hall onto the terrace.

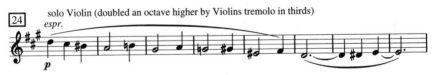

b) Salome's adolescence and chasteness expressed in a waltz.

c) The stirrings of sensuality and passion as she awaits the appearance of Jokanaan from the cistern.

EXAMPLE SA-5 *(Continued)*

d) She praises Jokanaan's body.

with brutal obviousness during Salome's frantic wait for the executioner to return from the cell.

Her dance begins chastely enough: when the musicians offer a wild introduction, she stops them with an imperious gesture, then proceeds with studied simplicity. It soon becomes a flood of the opera's motives, however. Its high point is dominated and shaped by waltz rhythms (Example SA-5g), symbolic of the lavishness of late-nineteenth-century Vienna and thus of a grossly inflated sensuality.

The claiming of her reward is set to music that is cold and calculating. Her first request is a skittish and almost whimsical recall of the opera's open- ing motive (Example SA-2b) as she seems to flirt girlishly with a Herodes

EXAMPLE SA-5 (*CONTINUED*)

e) She reviles Jokanaan's body.

EXAMPLE SA-5 *(Continued)*

Contrabassoon

p

f) The idea of revenge occurs to her as she stands by the cistern, having been rejected by Jokanaan and watched his return to the cistern.

Ziemlich langsam
(fairly slow)
Violins, Violas

p espr.

g) The waltz melody of the Dance of the Seven Veils.

who is out of his mind with the ecstasy of what he has seen and what he imagines. When Herodes, shocked by her demand, accuses her of being the voice of her mother, Salome's music uses the heavily accented rhythm of an obsession motive that is now turned to vicious expression of self-will: it is *her* desire, not her mother's, to have the prophet's head on a silver charger.

Salome's final music is womanly in its melodic grandeur, lush orchestration, dramatic high notes, and full-throated emotionalism. It is a scene all by itself, terribly demanding, terribly orgiastic, terribly beautiful, and quintessentially romantic.

A Slave *(tenor or soprano; unspecified in the score)*

In five measures of quasi-recitative, scarcely accompanied, the slave brings Salome Herodes's request to return to the banquet. The request is rejected peremptorily.

Herodes *(tenor)* *[heh-ROH-des]*

A man in his mid-fifties, terrified of the supernatural, dissipated with self-indulgences of every kind, devoid of any moral principle, and close to mental collapse. Sometimes he forgets what he is about to say, and he usually turns abruptly from one emotion to another. His attempts at flirtation with Salome are waltzes, albeit clumsy ones, and there is also lyricism (some of it in a banal major mode) when he tries to change her mind.

Herodes's most characteristic music, however, is restless and tonally vague. The harmonically ambiguous whole-tone scale, used when he first appears and remarks on the strangeness of the moon ("x" in Example SA-6), is typical; another is his use of tiny germs of rhythmic and chromatic movement that scurry through the orchestra like cockroaches suddenly exposed to the light.

EXAMPLE SA-6 THE NEUROTICISM OF HERODES EXPRESSED IN THE WHOLE-TONE SCALE ("X") AS HE SEES STRANGE IMAGES IN THE MOON

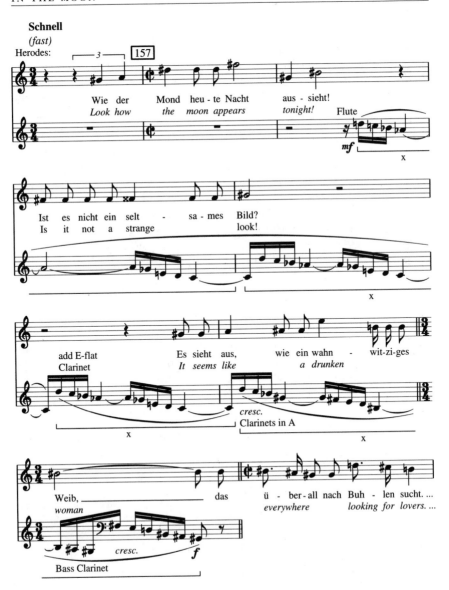

Herodias[21] [hair-ROH-dee-ahss]

A woman of about thirty, imperious, volatile, and calculating; she is as dissolute as her husband, for whom she has nothing but contempt. The use of blunt major harmonies for her sneering rejection of Herodes's neurotic view of the moon is caustically witty: Herodias knows the political realities of life and has no compunctions about doing anything that will further her interests.

Like Herodes, she is often characterized by quick rhythms and spurts of restlessly moving motives, but she is also represented by a sardonic figure ("b" in Example SA-8) that twists the simple triad pattern associated with Jokanaan's goodness ("a" in Example SA-8) into a venomous representation of her corrupt soul. The juxtaposition of the two motives provides a subtle but effective dramatic point: Herodias is the target of Jokanaan's unrelenting condemnation of iniquity. The difference between the two musical figures is subtle, but unmistakable: there is a sudden and biting chromatic slide upward at the end of the Herodias motive ("y" in the following example; it is heard as a motive in itself) and an occasional manipulation of its opening interval through the tritone (the augmented fourth, the archetype of cruelty, moral decay, and falsity; marked "x" in Example SA-7).

Two Nazarenes (tenor, bass)

In lyric and gracious lines that contrast boldly with the squabbling of the rabbis, their music is always in the major mode, even when their key occurs simultaneously with a different key[22] given to one or more of the prattling theologians. They tell Herodes of the miracles being worked by the man (from their hometown, Nazareth) of whom Jokanaan has been speaking. The opera's only comic moment occurs in this episode, when, hearing that Messiah raises people from the dead, Herodes forbids him to do so, for it would be terrible ("schreckliches" again) if the dead were to return.

Naaman (silent part) [na-ah-MAHN]

The Executioner. He is given Herodes's Ring of Death as token of the command to behead Jokanaan. The appearance of his muscular arm bearing the head aloft is one of the great theatrical strokes in opera.

---

[21] In Wagner's *Parsifal*, we learn that Herodias was the first incarnation of Kundry and that it was Herodias who scoffed at Christ on his way to Golgotha. See Lucy Beckett, *Richard Wagner: "Parsifal,"* Cambridge Opera Handbooks (Cambridge: Cambridge University Press, 1981), p. 147.

[22] See note 17 for another example of bitonality.

EXAMPLE SA-7 JOKANAAN ("a," HERE IN THE MINOR MODE)
INDICTS HERODIAS ("b," TRITONE MARKED BY "x,"
CHROMATIC SLIDE BY "y").

Bibliography

Abbate, Carolyn. "Opera, Or the Envoicing of Women," in *Musicology and Difference: Gender and Sexuality in Music Scholarship,* ed. Ruth A. Solie. Berkeley, CA: University of California Press, 1993.

Focusing on Gluck's Orfeo ed Euridice *and* Salome, *Abbate proposes that operatic music allows the true voice of women to speak even when the plot line suggests restriction, repression, and destruction by men. For a balanced critique of Abbate's analysis, see p. 113f. in the review of Solie's anthology by Edmund J. Goehring,* Opera Quarterly 12, no. 2 (Winter 1995–96): 107–115.

Bird, Alan. *The Plays of Oscar Wilde.* Barnes and Noble Critical Studies. New York: Harper and Row, 1977.

Del Mar, Norman. *Richard Strauss: A Critical Commentary on His Life and Works.* Ithaca, NY: Cornell University Press, 1986 [1978]. 3 volumes.
   The most thorough study in English. The analysis of Salome *is in Volume I, 239–286.*

Dijkstra, Bram. *Idols of Perversity: Fantasies of Feminine Evil in Fin-de-Siècle Culture.* New York: Oxford University Press, 1986.

Gilman, Sander. "Strauss and the Pervert," in *Reading Opera,* ed. Arthur Groos and Roger Parker. Princeton: Princeton University Press, 1988.

Grant, Michael. *Herod the Great.* New York: American Heritage Press, 1971.
   An excellent history of the Herodian dynasty, more popular in style than Hoehner's (see below); photos, maps (see esp. Judaea under "Herod's sons," p. 258), Chronology (p. 259ff.), and Genealogy of Herod's children (p. 263).

———. *The Jews in the Roman World.* New York: Charles Scribner's Sons, 1973.
   A broader historical survey than the above. See pp. 103ff for overview of John the Baptist, Salome, etc.

Hoehner, Harold W. *Herod Antipas.* Cambridge: Cambridge University Press, 1972.
   A scholarly, highly detailed study of sources, people, places, events. A Genealogy is provided on p. 349, a Chronology on p. 350.

John, Nicholas, ed. English National Opera. *Salome/Elektra.* English National Opera Guide No. 37. New York: Riverrun Press, 1988.
   Librettos of the two operas, short essays on their literary backgrounds and music, and identification of important motives.

Kennedy, Michael. *Richard Strauss.* Master Musicians. London: Dent, 1976.

Kestner, Joseph. "Born of Obsession," in *Opera News* 53, no. 12 (March 4, 1989): 24–26.

Kramer, Lawrence. "Culture and Musical Hermeneutics: The Salome Complex," in *Cambridge Opera Journal* 2, no. 3 (November 1990): 269–294.
   An examination of attitudes toward the Salome story and treatments of it in the late nineteenth century.

Lingg, Ann M. "Meet Herodias," in *Opera News* 29, no. 18 (March 13, 1965): 16.
   Brief historical background of the figures of the opera.

Mann, William. *Richard Strauss: A Critical Study of the Operas.* New York: Oxford University Press, 1966.

Markow, Robert. "Fatal Scherzo," in *Opera News* 55, no. 6 (December 8, 1990): 20–24.
   Overview of the role of the orchestra in Salome.

Osborne, Charles. *The Complete Operas of Richard Strauss.* North Pomfret VT: Trafalgar Square Publishing, 1988.
   Somewhat less detailed than Mann or Del Mar, but easier reading.

Praz, Mario. *The Romantic Agony,* 2nd ed., trans. Angus Davidson. London: Oxford University Press, 1970.
   Study of various treatments of the theme of the femme fatale, *with references to Wilde, Moreau, and others.*

Puffett, Derrick, ed. *Richard Strauss, "Salome".* Cambridge Opera Handbooks. Cambridge: Cambridge University Press, 1989.

Schmidgall, Gary. *Literature As Opera*. NewYork: Oxford University Press, 1977. *Excellent study of the interactions between Wilde's play and Strauss's music. See pp. 247–286.*

Wilde, Oscar, and Aubrey Beardsley. *Salome,* trans. Alfred Douglas. New York: Dover Publications, 1976 [1894].

Willett, John. *Expressionism*. World University Library. New York: McGraw-Hill Book Co., 1970.

Chapter 16

PORGY AND BESS®[1]

MUSIC AND LIBRETTO: George Gershwin (1898–1937), DuBose (1885–1940) and Dorothy Heyward, and Ira Gershwin (1896–1983), after a play (*Porgy*, 1927, by DuBose and Dorothy Heyward) taken from DuBose Heyward's 1925 novel, *Porgy*.

PREMIERE: Boston, September 30, 1935. [Some sources refer to this as the "tryout" for the New York production of October 10, 1935.]

TIME AND PLACE OF THE STORY: A bayside area of Charleston, South Carolina, and Kittiwah, an offshore barrier island, in August-September in the 1920s. The bulk of the action is set in Catfish Row, a connected series of buildings on three sides of a courtyard in what used to be an elegant part of the city but is now a group of ramshackle tenements inhabited by blacks of meager income. They have a strong sense of their community, which is quite separated from the rest of the world.

Idiom and Motive

One of America's greatest operas has taken a long time to gain full acceptance in its own country, although it enjoyed instant and lasting success in Europe[2] and Russia. That a Caucasian would evoke a distinct and highly localized ethnicity—the Gullah[3] dialect of South Carolina—has curled the lips of many black musicians and writers; that a writer of popular songs,

---

[1] The title of this opera is copyrighted and protected by trademark. In addition, the work is considered to be of joint authorship, hence reference to "the Gershwins" rather than simply to the composer.

[2] In World War II, the Danish underground interrupted broadcasts of German propaganda with a recording of "It Ain't Necessarily So."

[3] "Gullah" is a name given to the residents (and their speech habits) of the Sea Islands and tidewater areas of South Carolina and Georgia. Geographic, social, and economic isolation has resulted in a distinct anthropological unit, characterized by a mix of archaic West African and Elizabethan English roots. Gullah religious themes are Christian and their melodies derive from white hymns and folk songs, but performance practices are distinctly African. For a discussion of the Gullah community, see Joyner, Chapter 7.

revues, and musical comedies would seek to write a serious opera has invited the sneers of journalists and critics, both black and white. Imamu Amiri
Baraka, for example, has described its music as "kind of pleasant, but in reality, hideous and dishonest dilution,"[4] and Lawrence Gilman, a prominent
newspaper critic at the time of the premiere, castigated "the song hits" as
"cardinal weaknesses" and "blemishes upon its musical integrity."[5]

The negatives have faded, however, for it has come to be generally recognized that, in keeping with the best traditions of Western opera, *Porgy and
Bess*® speaks with a unified and cogent dramatic voice in music that is incisive, memorable, and highly persuasive. Its heritages and influences are
diverse: Tin Pan Alley strophic song ("I got plenty o' nuttin'") shares the
score with folklike music composed in the black idiom ("It take a long pull
to get there"); timbres move smoothly among the sounds of jazz and the
modern symphony orchestra; and harmonies derive equally from the patterns of blues progressions and the American neo-Romantic movement.
There are beautiful, long-phrased melodies that shape self-sufficient song
forms; and there are supple motives that recur frequently in the musical fabric so as to bind one dramatic moment to another.

The essential nature of plot and music were set out by George Gershwin
himself in an October 20, 1935, piece for the *New York Times:*

> *Porgy and Bess* is a folk tale [whose] people naturally would sing folk
> music. . . . because *Porgy and Bess* deals with Negro life in America it
> brings to the operatic form elements that have never before appeared
> in opera, and I have adapted my method to utilize the drama, the
> humor, the superstition, the religious fervor, the dancing and the irre-
> pressible high spirits of the race.

> . . . opera should be entertaining. . . . Therefore, when I chose *Porgy and
> Bess* . . . for a subject, I made sure that it would enable me to write light
> as well as serious music and that it would enable me to include humor
> as well as tragedy. . . . This humor is natural humor—not "gags" super-
> imposed upon the story but humor flowing from the story itself. . . . The
> recitative I have tried to make as close to the Negro inflection in speech
> as possible, and I believe my song-writing apprenticeship has served
> invaluably in this respect, because the song writers of America have the
> best conception of how to set words to music so that the music gives
> added expression to the words. I have used sustained symphonic music
> to unify entire scenes . . .

> . . . thus *Porgy and Bess* becomes a folk opera—opera for the theater, with
> drama, humor, song and dance.

Gershwin spent five weeks living and working among the Gullah of Folly
and James Islands, both off the coast of Charleston, South Carolina, and vis-

---

[4] Imamu Amiri Baraka, "Porgy and Bess," in *Jazz Review* 2, no. 10 (November 1959), p. 50f.

[5] Quoted in David Ewen, *A Journey to Greatness: The Life and Music of George Gershwin* (New York: Henry Holt, 1956), p. 268f.

ited various black communities on the mainland. With great delight and fascination, he absorbed musical and speech habits that were rooted in African sources and improvisational performance practices. Gershwin's insistence on a valid representation of the Gullah people is evident not only in the musical aspects of *Porgy and Bess*® but also in the requirement that only blacks play blacks, a stipulation that will continue to affect national and international performance rights until the copyright expires early in the next century.[6]

The musical personality of *Porgy and Bess*® is derived from the blues and jazz, interrelated genres of performance that rely extensively on improvisation and ornament and that are solidly rooted in the musical Africanisms that Gershwin knew from his barrier islands stay and also from his numerous visits to New York's Harlem theaters and nightclubs. At their core is inflection of pitch, especially the micro-flattening of the third, the seventh, and, sometimes, the fifth of the scale, and the departure from a solid beat by subtle and wonderfully inventive syncopation. Important also in the opera is the use of the perfect intervals of the open fifth and fourth, for they lend a sense to the people of Catfish Row as residents of a kind of Eden, a pure if primeval world free of the grimness and superficiality of urban America. And one should not forget the influence of the qualities of Jewish music that were fundamental to Gershwin's childhood and with which the Gullah sound has strong affinities.[7]

The motive associated with Porgy (Example PB-1), heard when he arrives on the scene early in Act I, is the embodiment of all of these: its first element is a rhythmic figure falling from B to E, an open fifth; its next element uses an ornament (written always in small notation and necessarily performed with a freedom that cannot be notated)[8] and a syncopated falling minor third (G to E). It is heard throughout the opera and conditions much of its music, including the cynicism of Sportin' Life's "It ain't necessarily so" (see below, Example PB-3b), which is a twisted version of it, and the jazz piano playing of the opera's opening, where the two elements of the Porgy motive are reversed.

This connection of one melodic idea from another is an important feature of the music and the drama: Porgy's loneliness, for example, is linked

EXAMPLE PB-1 PORGY MOTIVE

© WB MUSIC CORP. (ADM.)

---

[6] *Porgy and Bess*® was not the first opera to have an all-black cast; Virgil Thomson's *Four Saints in Three Acts* (1934; libretto by Gertrude Stein) was originally cast this way.

[7] See Schwartz, pp. 322ff., for a study of the Jewish elements in George Gershwin's style.

[8] This sort of ornament is called an *acciaccatura* (lit., "crushed note"). Derived from the keyboard literature of the Baroque era, it is the simultaneous sounding of a melodic note and an adjacent note, without the resulting dissonance being resolved. In vocal music, the acciaccatura is a lower inflection of the main melodic pitch. It is this latter fashion that informs much of the musical personality of *Porgy and Bess*®.

to the solace offered him by life with Bess by the recurrence of the Act I music of the lot of a crippled beggar ("Night time, day time, he got to trabble") in the great Act II duet with Bess, when Bess assures him "I ain't goin'! You hear me sayin' . . . ." Another instance is the connection between Porgy's invocation to the dice (in the first scene's crap game) with the song of his happiness: the falling minor third of " 'leven little stars come home" shapes the music of his tribute to having "plenty o' nuttin' " when he sings "got no car, got no mule."

The minor third (marked in the segments of Example PB-2) is itself a source of thematic unity, lending many of the melodies a kinship without diminishing their individuality or aptness to a character or situation. The same is true of syncopation, especially the short-long rhythmic units that result from the natural accents of the English language (in all its dialects).

EXAMPLE PB-2 MELODIC EXAMPLES SHOWING MINOR THIRDS (MARKED "M3") AND SYNCOPATED OR SHORT-LONG RHYTHMS ("X")

a) Act I, scene i: Porgy's comments on his lonely life.

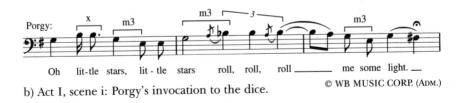

b) Act I, scene i: Porgy's invocation to the dice.

c) Act II, scene i: Porgy's song of contentment in spite of being poor.

d) Act II, scene ii: Bess resists Crown.

EXAMPLE PB-2 (*Continued*)

e) Act III, scene ii: Greetings among the residents of Catfish Row.

The recurrent motives are striking, individual, and rich in character. The falling tritone, for example (see Chapter 3), the archetype of deviousness and cynicism, is particularly associated with the oily Sportin' Life. It is one of the most familiar sounds of the opera, because it is the first melodic element of his "It ain't necessarily so" (see Example PB-3b), and therefore darts frequently in and out of the various confrontations that involve him.

A trio of figures lends a harshness central to the drama: the two scenes given over to fights to the death (Act I, scene i, and Act III, scene i) are vividly punctuated with the hammering syncopations of Crown's motive (Example PB-4a; note the acerbic effect of a archetypical rhythm of death accompanying it) and a jagged motive that is always connected with harsh reality (Example PB-4b); also prominent in the darker aspect of the opera is the appropriately slithery figure representative of cocaine, the "happy dust" that is Bess's undoing Example PB-4c).

EXAMPLE PB-3 THE TRITONE OF CYNICISM

a) Act II, scene i: Accompaniment to Maria's confrontation of Sportin' Life.

b) Act II, scene ii: Start of Sportin' Life's cynical appraisal of inherited truth.

EXAMPLE PB-4 OTHER MOTIVES

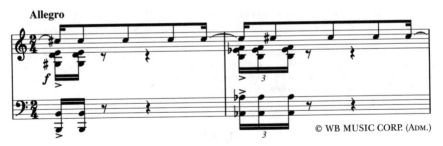

© WB MUSIC CORP. (ADM.)

a) Act I, scene i: Crown (accompanied by variant of death-rhythm archetype).

© WB MUSIC CORP. (ADM.)

b) Act I, scene i: Reality, harshness of life; also Sportin' Life.

© WB MUSIC CORP. (ADM.)

c) Act III, scene ii: Cocaine (the motive appears in varied shapes in each of the three acts).

THE PLOT AND ITS MUSIC

NOTE: There are no score designations such as "song," "episode," or "ensemble," nor are the various passages numbered. I have provided these for ease of reference.

INTRODUCTION *The orchestral prelude is short and snappy. After a quick rising scale and a trill, the xylophone starts a rapid, high ostinato figure, marked by continually changing accents. The figure becomes accompaniment to a syncopated set of chords taken over by Jasbo Brown's upright piano when the curtain rises.*

Act I

SCENE I

Saturday night in the courtyard of Catfish Row. Late summer.

1 ENSEMBLE and SONG (Clara) *Summertime* Couples dance in the court as Jasbo Brown plays blues piano in his room. Clara sings a lullaby to her baby.

A floating melody is accompanied by a lulling ostinato (instruments at first, then humming women) and quiet scale figures. The extensive use of falling minor thirds and fifths (as at "[liv-]in' is easy") connect the song with Ex. PB-1 and the spirit of Catfish Row.

2 ENSEMBLE A crap game begins. Robbins, drinking heavily, insists on joining it, despite Serena's plea not to gamble.

Ex. PB-4b plus a variant of the syncopated pattern of Jasbo's piano music underlie the start of the scene. Sportin' Life mocks the lullaby by using its dotted rhythm; there is a return of the xylophone ostinato of the overture, then a reprise of Clara's song over the jagged rhythms associated with the crap game.

3 SONG (Jake) *A woman is a sometime thing* Hearing Clara take up her lullaby again, Jake takes the baby and sings to it a humorous critique of the frailties of women (as seen by men). When Jake proudly notes that his baby is finally asleep, the child awakes with a loud wail.

Jake's dotted rhythm and the similarity of sound of "sometime" parodies Summertime. The baby's wail produces laughter as a rising chromatic scale accompanied by a descending chromatic scale in triplets.

4 EPISODE Porgy arrives in his goat cart and is ready to join the game. When someone suggests they wait for Crown's arrival before continuing, Porgy's inquiry about Bess elicits some teasing of his apparent interest in her.

Porgy's arrival is marked by the first appearance of Ex. PB-1. The suggestion to wait for Crown is given the Crown motive in dissonant triplets in low woodwinds.

5 SONG (Porgy) *They pass by singin'* Porgy suggests that women have no concern for him, averring that the life of a cripple is lonely.

Porgy's song is characterized by minor thirds and a "crushed" note on "cryin'." "When Gawd make cripple" (Ex. PB-2a) is pentatonic and gently rhythmed, thus very different from the sharp angularity and biting rhythms of much of the opera. "Night time, day time, you got to trabble . . ." will occur at the end of the act and in the duet with Bess in Act II, scene i.

6 EPISODE Crown and Bess enter the court. He demands liquor from Sportin' Life, drinks fully of it, then joins the craps circle after handing the bottle to Bess.

The Gershwins, *Porgy and Bess*®, Act I, scene i: The dice game. Sportin' Life
(Larry Marshall) prepares to roll, while Porgy (Terry Cook), Jake (Elex Lee
Vann), and Robbins (Richard Taylor, with whiskey bottle) await the result.
San Francisco Opera, 1995: sets by Ken Foy, costumes by Judy Dearing.
Photo Larry Merkle.

Bess takes a swig, then pointedly offers it to Robbins, knowing that the women
are watching angrily. As the game progresses, Crown, too drunk to read the dice
clearly, becomes angry at losing and at others' picking up the dice too quickly.
His purchase of cocaine from Sportin' Life exacerbates his loss of self-control.

*The orchestral accompaniment is dominated by the Crown motive (Ex. PB-4a) and fast
accompanying figures, often wavering between the major and the minor third. Porgy teases
Robbins by reprising Jake's song. As the game intensifies, so does Ex. PB-4b, a motive associated with the harshness of life, and the febrile repetitions of Ex. PB-4c ("cocaine").*

7 ARIOSO (Porgy) *Oh little stars* Porgy croons to the dice and wins. The dice then
pass to Robbins.

*Porgy's incantation starts in chant style over a held major chord, then turns to the music of
Ex. PB-2b. Porgy's melodic minor thirds are accompanied by undulating major chords—he
expects to win.*

8 ENSEMBLE *Nine to make, come nine* Robbins's sweeping up the dice too fast is
the last straw for Crown. Crown attacks and, in the ensuing fight, stabs Robbins
fatally with a cotton hook. Bess warns Crown to get away quickly before the
police come. At mention of "police," the crowd disappears. Bess, Crown, and
Sportin' Life remain, as does Serena, weeping over the body of her husband.

*Individual voice parts overlap more and more, and orchestral motives become shorter. Phrases
associated with life's harshness (Ex. PB-4b) and Crown (treble of Ex. PB-4a) pile in, often
with furious chromatic scale fragments in voices and/or instruments. The fight is an orches-*

tral fugue based on these figures. The death blow to Robbins is accompanied by a rushing chromatic rise, harmonized dissonantly.

9 FINAL EPISODE Crown, warning Bess that any man she takes up with before he returns is temporary, leaves to go into hiding. Sportin' Life accedes to Bess's request for some cocaine to relieve her "shakin' so I can hardly stan'," inviting her to head off to New York with him. Bess rejects him, then runs to door after door to find shelter. All save one are either already locked or are slammed in her face. About to take Maria's scornful advice to leave, Bess hears police whistles and, in desperation, enters Porgy's dwelling, the only haven open to her.

The crowd scatters, and Bess and Crown have their hurried dialogue in fast recitative over the frantic pounding of the motive associated with the world's harshness and cruel reality (Ex. PB-4b). Bess's frantic search for shelter is acted to a return of the fugue of the fight scene. Her turn to Porgy's room is reflected in a sudden calming of the music, with recalls of the melody of Porgy's song of loneliness.

SCENE II

The next night. Serena's room. Robbins's body is on the bed, a saucer on his chest.

10 ENSEMBLE *Where is Brudder Robbins?* As mourners file in, they lay coins in the saucer so that Robbins may have a decent burial. Bess's contribution is rejected until Bess assures Serena that the money is Porgy's, not Crown's.

The contributions are not yet enough, so all urge greater giving ("Overflow, fill up de saucer till it overflow.")

The music is patterned after a call-and-response spiritual. The "Gone, gone" refrain is a harmonization of a descending whole-tone scale, its death symbolism reinforced by plodding quarter notes and the half-step move of the scale's last two notes.[9] "Overflow" is more spirited, thus more encouraging of generosity. It is built on the model of the "shout," with one or more leaders supported by echo responses from the group until the main melody becomes a large choral movement. Pleas of "Lawd send down yo' blessing" are set to a long-note chromatic fall; optimism that the "Lawd will fill de saucer" is set to scales that quickly rise.

11 EPISODE A detective (a white man) arrives, accompanied by two policemen. He warns Serena that Robbins must be buried within the next twenty-four hours. He accuses Peter of the murder as a way of frightening him into giving information. When Peter identifies Crown as the murderer and is arrested as a material witness, the police leave.

The police do not sing, only speak; responses to their questions are sometimes spoken, sometimes sung in short bursts of recitative, with irregular orchestral patterns. There is a reprise of the "Gone, gone" text, but now set as simultaneous scales, the basses descending, the sopranos rising.

12 LAMENT (Serena) *My man's gone now* The mourning resumes.

A rhythmic, swaying spiritual, over a regularly recurring syncopated accompaniment. Serena's moans are short melismas on "Ah"; those of her friends are a wail on a dissonant, upward glissando.

13 EPISODE The Undertaker agrees to give Robbins a burial even though the money is not sufficient.

Recitative; rhythmic motion is quiet until the Undertaker agrees to go ahead with the burial. There is a quick flurry of violins, then a reprise of "Gone, gone."

---

[9] The Phrygian cadence; see Chapter 13, note 10.

14 ENSEMBLE (Bess and Chorus) *Oh we're leavin' for the Promise' Lan'* Bess leads all in a song of religious jubilation.

Bess leads a march-like spiritual of fervent joy. There are two verses in the call-response format, then a coda in which the main tune is set out in slower note values, while accompanying voices provide an uplifting countermelody and quickened tempo.

Act II

Scene i

A month later. 9 A.M.

15 SONG (Jake and fishermen) *It take a long pull to get there* The men repair fishing nets.

Jake's song is a strophic song with refrain; the effort of rowing is expressed in strong grunts on an accented beat.

16 EPISODE Jake's intention to make a particularly long trip out to Blackfish Banks worries Clara, who warns him that September storms are due.

Recitative and spoken dialogue are accompanied by several repeats of a lighthearted and lyric orchestral syncopation, as Jake tries to ease Clara's fears.

17 SONG (Porgy) *Oh, I got plenty o' nuttin* At his window, Porgy sings of his happiness and that the things that are important—the stars, his girl, Heaven, and his song—are all free.

Porgy has a buoyant, vamping[10] rhythmic background to one of opera's most singable, simple melodies and one of its happiest moments. It is in a standard song form (AABA') in three verses with choral comments and also chorus as a humming timbre. The melody of "I got no car" (Ex. PB-2c) recalls his invocation to the dice. In a way, the piece is a tribute to music, for its final phrase gives the climactic note not to his "gal" or his "Lawd," but to his song.

18 SPEECH-SONG (Maria) *Friend wid you lowlife, hell, no!* Confronting Sportin' Life, Maria blows the cocaine powder from his hand. At his sly offer of friendship, she threatens him with a knife and reviles everything he stands for.

Sportin' Life saunters over to Maria to a string/woodwind rush of Ex. PB-3a. Her rhymed tirade is over a jocular vamping accompaniment, with wood blocks as hollow orchestral laughter and little bursts of orchestral colors as punctuations.

19 EPISODE Frazier, a black lawyer, points out (to the interest and amusement of onlookers) that it takes an expert to divorce people who aren't married. He dupes Porgy into buying a divorce for Bess from Crown.

Archdale enters the court to tell all that, because Peter's folks "used to belong" to the Archdales, he has put up the bond for Peter. Archdale's mixed annoyance and amusement at Frazier's selling of a divorce is interrupted when all cower from the shadow of a buzzard. Porgy explains that, once a buzzard folds his wings above a person's house, that person's happiness is "done dead."

Frazier's recitatives and spoken phrases are given the scherzando elements of staccato patterns and a witty 6/8 lilt. Sudden chords, flourishes of clarinet, and choral comments mock his pre-

---

[10] A vamp is a simple figure repeated by accompanying instruments until a vocalist begins.

tentiousness. Porgy's payment is accompanied by his motive. Archdale is a speaking part; responses to him are at first very short, with orchestral music limited to brief flurries of scale patterns and held chords. Agitation over the buzzard's hovering is symbolized by short rushes of rising and falling chromatics.

20 SONG (Porgy) *Buzzard keep on flyin' over* Porgy defies the superstition, expressing his new state of life by averring that "Porgy, who you used to feed on, don' live here no mo'" and laughing at the bird and its omen.

Flurries of flute sextuplets create the image of flight; phrases of narrow compass and repeated short-long two-note patterns suggest both obsessiveness with the superstition and defiance of it. Porgy's self-confidence and joy ("Step out, brudder") is hymn-like. The conclusion of the song draws on the music of its opening, with added emphasis from choral reinforcement.

21 EPISODE Overhearing Bess's rejection of Sportin' Life's renewal of his offer of happy dust and a life in New York, Porgy grabs Sportin' Life's wrist, almost breaking it, and warns the dope peddler to stay away.

Sportin' Life's enticement is again punctuated by Ex. PB-3a (eventually to become the opening of It ain't necessarily so) and also the Cocaine motive (Ex. PB-4c). When Porgy orders him off, Ex. PB-3a (descending tritones, heard here in the bass clarinet, then in low strings) musically turns the tables on him.

22 DUET (Porgy, Bess) *Bess, you is my woman now* The two sing of the passing of unhappiness and their pledge of faith to each other, as "De real happiness is jes' begun."

The duet is shaped by long, lyric phrases, inflected with blue notes and subtle but continual changes in the accompaniment patterns. Each major phrase begins on the downbeat, separating the duet from most of the opera's music, making syncopation incidental rather than fundamental, and thus giving both characters a special sincerity and depth of feeling. Bess's "I ain't goin'" recalls the melodic shape of Porgy's Act I song (Ex. PB-2a) and is at once soothing, because she vows to relieve his loneliness, and ironic, because she eventually does leave him. "Mornin' time an' ev'nin' time" are on open fifths, an interval symbolic of basic truth. The final return of the main melody is in Bess's voice, with Porgy lending assurance and strength by singing a counterpoint to it; brief half-step descents are like sighs as they sing each other's name, the duet ending with the unisons and parallel sixths of the universal musical language of love.

23 ENSEMBLE *Oh, I can't sit down!* The parade to the steamer boat to Kittiwah Island forms, all dressed in the regalia of the "Repent Ye Saith the Lord" Lodge for the annual picnic. As a band marches by, Maria urges Bess to come along; Bess's reluctance to leave Porgy is calmed by Porgy, who urges her to go.

Flourishes (trumpet and xylophone) and string fanfares herald an infectious choral march, its off-beat rhythm derived from the Jasbo Brown blues of the first scene of Act I. Bess's reluctance to leave uses a recall of the duet's principal melody; his answer recalls the duet's "Mornin' time . . ."; their farewell is accompanied by the principal theme of the duet played tenderly by French horn. The scene ends with a reprise of Porgy's "I got plenty o nuttin'" and one more recall of the duet.

SCENE II

That evening, by a palmetto grove on Kittiwah Island. Moonlight.

24 INTRODUCTION and ENSEMBLE *I ain' got no shame* As the picnic reaches its end, all are dancing and singing in an uninhibited way.

African drums pound in cross-rhythms as introduction, then accompaniment to the unisons and blunt rhythms of the people.

The Gershwins, *Porgy and Bess*®, Act II, scene ii: On Kittiwah Island, Sportin' Life (Krister St. Hill) regales the picknickers with his views of biblical truths. Houston Grand Opera, 1976: sets by Douglas W. Schmidt, costumes by Nancy Potts. Photo (1987) James Caldwell.

25 SONG (Sportin' Life) *It ain't necessarily so* Sportin' Life mocks the inherited tales told in the Bible.

> *The song (Ex. PB-3b) is marked by tritones, vamping in the low strings, a 3-against-2 contrast between voice and accompaniment, and a penetrating doubling of the melody by muted trumpet. All these traits lend twists of mockery and cynicism. The nose-thumbing is given vehemence by scat singing. The momentary outbursts by the folk, who are quite carried away by Sportin' Life's insinuating denial of all inherited truth, are given a sudden change of tempo and meter.*

26 EPISODE Serena scolds the revelers. At the sound of the boat's whistle, all gather their belongings and leave the picnic area. As Bess follows them, Crown steps before her from the thicket. Telling her that he has been hiding there, he brusquely rejects her avowals of being part of a new life. Swearing that he will come for her and incredulous that she would prefer a cripple to him, he laughs at Bess's sensitivity to Porgy's need for her.

> *Serena's outburst is in the grand manner, ringing the changes between held high notes and repeated, fast low ones. The sudden appearance of Crown is heralded by an unexpected chromatic rush; his words are given an ominous cast by a halting rhythm in low brass and quiet dynamics, then a throbbing syncopation in the double basses that soon merges into the rhythm of his motive (PB-4a) and variants of a rhythmic archetype for death (see Ex. 3.15). Bess's attempt to explain Porgy's need for her is a recitative over held chords.*

27 DUET (Bess, Crown) *What you want wid Bess?* Bess begs Crown to let her go, suggesting that there are younger and prettier girls eager to be his. Crown is contemptuous of her plea. She is unable to resist his kiss. He hurls her into the edge of the thicket; she rises and backs into the woods, Crown following.

The Gershwins, *Porgy and Bess*®, Act II, scene ii: Crown (Stacey Robinson) attacks Bess (Roberta Laws). San Francisco Opera, 1995: sets by Ken Foy, costumes by Judy Dearing. Photo Larry Merkle.

Her plea is dominated by the music of Ex. PB-5. Her "five years I been yo' woman" ironically recalls Jake's "A woman is a sometime thing"; her "you could whistle an' there I was" recalls Porgy's motive (Ex. PB-1). As Bess gets more desperate, the broad range of her opening melody is replaced by a wail in the form of a rising and falling scale constrained to the distance of a minor third as she sings "I am his woman" and "He would die without me." As Bess's resistance weakens, the music is colored by lurid chromatic scales and Bess's begging (the descending minor thirds of Ex. PB-2d). The violent end of the scene is dominated by the Crown motive; a final anguished and bitter playing of Bess's opening phrase by harmonizing trumpets is accompanied by pounding dissonances.

SCENE III

The court, before dawn, nine days later.

28 EPISODE Jake and his crew complete preparations for fishing and depart. Bess has been in a delirium for a week, having returned to Catfish Row after two days on the island. As Peter returns from jail, she is heard feverishly reliving the agony of Crown's abusiveness. Serena disdains Peter's suggestion of hospitalization for Bess, assuring the distressed Porgy that Bess will be well by five o'clock.

Flowing triplets and musical calm are an introduction to a return of Jake's "It take a long pull." That they tack on the last words of the finale to the Funeral Scene ("[I'll anchor] in de Promise' Lan'") is both ironic and prophetic. Bess's delirium is given expression in wideranging vocal phrases sung over tremolos.

29 PRAYER (Serena, Porgy, Peter) *Oh, Doctor Jesus* Serena invokes the aid of Jesus.

A chant is intoned over held chords, with brief outbursts from Peter and Porgy. Serena's calm at the end of the scene is accompanied by flowing perfect intervals—she has no doubt that her prayer will work.

30 EPISODE Vendors enter the court, hawking strawberries, honey (Peter), and crabs. As the nearby Church of St. Michael strikes five o'clock, Bess appears in Porgy's doorway, now recovered as Serena had predicted. Porgy insists she should stay with him as long as she wants, no matter what her relation to Crown.

Each street call is based on a basic rhythmic and melodic pattern, with perfect fourths and fifths prominent either as intervals or as defining limits of the range of the call. Bess's return to health is marked by cellos and bassoon recalling the theme of "Bess, you is my woman now."

31 DUET (Bess and Porgy) *I wants to stay here, but I ain't worthy* To Bess's confession of inability to resist Crown, Porgy affirms his love for Bess and assures her that she may rely on him.

A melody of arpeggios over simple, unsyncopated accompaniment lends a quality of tenderness and sincerity until her anticipation of Crown's rough physicality, when her music becomes scalar over syncopated dissonances in the clarinets. Porgy's reassurance has a solid rhythmic underpinning that suggests a march to battle, the duet ending with Bess returning to her melody over Porgy's energetic countermelody. As they hold their final notes, the Porgy motive is heard in affirmation by the violins.

32 EPISODE Clara's fear of the forthcoming storm is realized by the sudden clanging of the hurricane bell and the dramatic upsurge of wind.

The surges of wind use the archetypes of storm: waves of fast chromatic scales, punctuations by flute snippets, pounding figures in the low brass, dissonant fanfares, and heavy percussion.

SCENE IV

Serena's room, dawn of the next day. The room is crowded with people, huddling in fear as the storm rages.

33 ENSEMBLE *Oh Doctor Jesus . . . Oh, de Lawd shake de Heavens . . . Oh, dere's somebody knockin' at de do'* All pray for heaven's mercy and relief from the storm. Clara tries to soothe her baby. As the prayers continue, Porgy and Bess consider the possibility that Crown will be drowned when the sea engulfs Kittiwah.

A choral hum accompanies six independent melodies in solo voices, each melodically and rhythmically independent of the others. The orchestra is a hushed doubling of the hum, its open fifths (cf. the storm in Rigoletto*) suggesting the vastness and mystery of nature. "Oh de Lawd shake de heavens" is a spiritual based on dotted rhythms suggesting fanfares acclaiming the power of God. The storm music of the previous scene is recalled as an interlude before Clara takes up her lullaby of Act I, scene i, in an attempt to keep herself and her baby calm. The spiritual resumes as accompaniment to the recitative-like dialogue between Bess and Porgy.*

34 EPISODE There is furious knocking at the door. In superstitious dread, men try to hold it closed, but Crown forces his way in. Sneering at the fear of all and at the disability of Porgy, Crown grabs Bess, then throws Porgy to the floor. Bess tears herself loose and assists Porgy. Crown claims to be "havin' it out" with God in a mutually respectful combat ("Gawd an' me is frien'").

The violence of the storm music returns, with percussive fanfares derived from a Death-rhythm archetype. The people turn to a new spiritual for "Oh, dere's somebody knockin',", with brief musical hints of the storm's fury. Crown's sneering is accompanied by storm figures that are soft but nonetheless menacing. The dialogue between Bess and Crown is accompanied by the "Bess you is my woman" music until Crown's physical brutality is expressed in harsh 2-against-3 rhythms and furious scale patterns.

35 SONG (Crown) *A red-headed woman makes a choo-choo jump its track* Crown laughingly starts a boisterous song about his own irresistibility while the people beg God to ignore his heresy.

Brutally accented rhythms define Crown's unpretty, sardonic song, even when its second verse is sung over the people's appeal to God to reject his blasphemy.

36 EPISODE Clara, staring through the window, sees Jake's boat capsized in the bay. Handing her baby to Bess, she rushes out. Crown is the only one to respond to Bess's request for someone to go to Clara's aid. Vowing to return to reclaim Bess and challenging God once more, he charges into the ever intensifying hurricane. In terror, the people return to their prayers.

The music for this frenzied action is dominated by the storm motives and the opening motive of the fugue of the Act I, scene i fight. The final prayers are a return of the music of the scene's opening, accompanied by high woodwind tremolos.

Act III

SCENE I

The courtyard. The next night, after the storm.

INTRODUCTION (Orchestra) *Quiet, falling intervals are a stylization of the lament of the people's prayer; they continue in the* ENSEMBLE.

37 ENSEMBLE The people lament the loss of Clara, Jake, and Crown in the storm.

A quiet orchestral introduction leads to falling intervals as a musical stylization of the people's lamenting prayer (cf. the sospiri *of Gilda's sobbing in* Rigoletto).

38 EPISODE Sportin' Life mockingly hints that Crown is still alive and that Bess has two men, not just one. Bess is heard singing Clara's lullaby to the baby. As night darkens, all enter their homes.

The colloquy between Maria and Sportin' Life is dominated by the easy, lilting swing of the dope peddler's music and hints of the opening figure of his It ain't necessarily so. *Bess takes up* Summertime, *since she has now assumed the rearing of Clara's baby.*

Crown stealthily enters the court and picks his way carefully to Porgy's door. As he crawls under Porgy's window, the shutter opens; an arm is extended, the hand grasping a long knife that is plunged into Crown's back, then withdrawn and hurled into the center of the court. Crown staggers to an upright position, whereupon Porgy leans from the window and clasps both hands around Crown's throat, strangling him. Porgy hurls Crown's body away from the house, laughing in triumph.

The melody that had been a precursor of violent death in Act I, scene i, and in the hurricane of Act II, scene iv, is so once again: Crown's furtive approach is reflected in the orchestra's mix of his own motive with that of Ex. PB-4b. As in the fight scene of Act I, scene i, the orchestra tells all by intensifying and developing these two motives; a climactically rising chromatic flourish is followed by an archetypical Death motive. The scene ends with strings majestically playing Porgy's motive as accent to his triumphant laughter.

SCENE II

Catfish Row, the next afternoon.

39 EPISODE The Detective and the Coroner arrive to investigate the murder of Crown. Serena claims to have seen nothing, her avowal of three days of sickness verified by her friends. Porgy's unwillingness to identify the body is ignored by the Detective, who tells Porgy that the police will come for him. Porgy panics when Sportin' Life says that Crown's wounds will bleed if his murderer gazes on his body. When the police haul Porgy off to the morgue, Sportin' Life cynically tells Bess that Porgy is likely to be away for a year or two. He renews his offer of the life of New York yet another time; Bess, in spite of her words of rejection, suddenly takes the cocaine he extends to her and claps it to her mouth.

The introduction is vigorous, strings turning quickly to a twisted version of Bess's plea to Crown (Ex. PB-5). The music becomes more lilting until the arrival of the police, when it returns to the spasmodic alternation of spoken dialogue with instrumental bits and sung recitative. Sportin' Life's song of mockery intrudes more and more into the scene (see Ex. PB-3c), ultimately becoming an ironic counterpoint to the Crown motive as Porgy struggles against the police who come to take him to the morgue. His song is then commingled with the Cocaine motive (Ex. PB-4c) as he tempts Bess.

40 SONG (Sportin' Life) *There's a boat dat's leavin' soon for New York* He paints an alluring picture of strutting through Harlem, with Bess in silks and satins and all unhappiness forgotten.

A writhing melody in the bass clarinet under a series of vamping off beat chords introduces a strophic song. Instrumentation is brassy and sassy, the melody inflected with blue notes on key words ("come wid me"). The piece is at once conniving, enticing, and entertaining.

41 EPISODE Bess furiously rejects him. Sportin' Life hands her a second paper of happy dust, which she knocks to the ground. She storms into the house, but Sportin' Life tosses yet another packet of cocaine at the doorstep and saunters off, smiling.

Bess's rejection is over the tritone motive of It ain't necessarily so, *suggesting that her resistance is on a weak foundation indeed. The motive is important in the music of the rest of the scene.*

SCENE III

Pre-scene action. Bess, believing Porgy will not return for years, has gone off with Sportin' Life. While in jail for refusing to look at Crown's body, Porgy has been victorious at craps. Now released from jail, he has purchased a number of gifts for his friends and a beautiful hat and dress for Bess.

A week later, early morning.

PRELUDE The orchestra begins pastorally, with gently descending woodwind scales over purling triplets. As the courtyard fills with people undertaking the day's affairs, the music turns to jaunty dotted rhythms (notably in low brass) and bouncy scales; the triplets begin to frolic. The normalcy of Catfish Row's innocence, good humor and untroubled life is suggested first by an easygoing passage for alternating clarinet and flute, then by an *allegro* marked by xylophone dissonances and vivacious music for violin. The more relaxed mood returns before the prelude ends with sparkling rhythms and timbres.

42 ENSEMBLE The people greet each other. Children frolic about. Porgy's arrival, courtesy of the police wagon, is a matter of consternation, since all know of Bess's departure. As he tells of his winning at dice and distributes his gifts, his friends begin to desert the court. Porgy suspects nothing until he sees Serena with the baby Clara had entrusted to Bess. His joy changes suddenly to desperate questioning as to Bess's whereabouts.

The introductory music is cheerful and flowing, violins recalling the opening of the previous scene. As the morning draws on and the people enter the court, rhythms become faster, orchestration brassier and melody more spirited. The greetings among the passersby (Ex. PB-2e) draw on the minor third of the blues, the children's song on those thirds and also on open fifths (Ex. 3.12b). This genre scene turns to strong rhythmic work by timpani and African drums before it concludes with the folk taking up the second phrase of the children's song. Porgy's entrance is to the xylophone ostinato of the opening of the opera; the choral greeting to him is derived from the Porgy motive, which is then heard in its original form. Porgy's questioning his friends about the strangeness of their attitude occurs to the accompaniment of the theme of the first love duet (Bess, you is my woman now), *with his motive (Ex. PB-1) also used prominently as he presses for the truth.*

43 TRIO (Porgy, Serena, Maria) *Oh, Bess, oh where's my Bess* While Porgy despairs, Maria blames Sportin' Life and cocaine for Bess's departure; Serena, averring that she had been right about Bess all along, assures Porgy that he is better off without her.

A broadly lyric line over warm orchestral doubling is characteristic of Porgy's line; Maria's indictment of Sportin' Life is couched in repeated note patterns and varied phrase shapes; Serena's self-righteousness comes out in her frequent reliance on an accented descending scale.

44 EPISODE Porgy at first thinks Bess is dead, but, on learning that she has gone to New York, vows to go to her and asks for someone to bring his goat and cart.

His realization that Bess is not dead and that therefore there is hope is set to a rising chromatic scale; a growing rhythmic excitement underscores his resolution to go to her.

45 FINALE (Porgy and Chorus): *Oh Lawd, I'm on my way* His friends lift him into his cart, and Porgy, full of hope and determination, sets off to find New York and his beloved Bess.

The opera's opening ostinato (see Introduction to Act I, scene i) introduces the uplifting sentiments of the final spiritual; its simple rhythms and short, symmetrical phrases lead easily to a theatrical, showtime climax.

The Characters

Jasbo Brown (pianist)

In his room at curtain rise in Act I, scene i, Jasbo is playing a slow blues on the piano, immediately establishing the mood of Saturday night in Catfish Row, not only because of its syncopated chord pattern but also because it is the music to which "half a dozen couples can be seen dancing in a slow, almost hypnotic rhythm." It is Jasbo's only appearance.

The people of Catfish Row (mixed-voice chorus)

The people are the central element of the plot; it is against their life and mores that the main action is set, and they are prominent in every scene. We hear them in the archetypical open fifths of the Children's Song of Act III, scene iii; the ritual patterns of the street vendors' cries of Act II, scene iii; the astonishing rhythmic freedom and complexity of the Hurricane Scene of Act II, scene iv (where we hear six completely independent prayers simultaneously[11]); the scat singing of both Act I, scene i, and the start of the Kittiwah Island episode of Act II, scene ii; and the call-and-response spiritual, with its funereal whole-tone descent of "Gone, gone, gone, gone" in Act I, scene ii. Their African roots are in the worksong grunts of Jake's fishing song (Act II, scene i) and the African drumming and wild dance music of the Kittiwah scene.

Ebullience of spirit is also a characteristic of Catfish Row, and it comes out in the timpani and trumpet fanfares and buoyant, tuneful syncopation of the parade *(Oh, I can't sit down)* of Act II, scene i, and the mix of spiritual and show tune that shapes the finale of the opera, *I'm on my way.*

---

[11] This polyphony was modeled after the "shout," an improvised religious communal singing as heard by the composer at a worship service in Hendersonville, S.C., inland from Charleston. An account of a similar experience was offered in 1867 by one William Francis Allen, who noted that ". . . the intonations and delicate variations of even one singer cannot be reproduced on paper. And I despair of conveying any notion of the effect of a number singing together. . . . There is no singing in *parts* [Allen's emphasis], as we understand it, and yet no two appear to be singing the same thing . . . [They] seem to follow their own whims, beginning when they please and leaving off when they please . . . or hitting some other note that chords, so as to produce the effect of a marvelous complication and variety, and yet with the most perfect time, and rarely with any discord. . . . [L]ike birds, they . . . strike sounds that cannot be precisely represented . . ., and abound in slides from one note to another . . ." Quoted in Kingman, p. 39; see also Hamm, pp. 136ff.

While a number of individual roles are set out from the people by solo lines, only the lawyer Frazier (baritone) has a music that identifies him: the scherzando rhythms (especially a jaunty 6/8) and light orchestration accompanying his one scene is genre writing and interpolated comedy in the manner of the musical. Among the other individual roles are:

Mingo (tenor)

Annie (mezzo-soprano)

Lily (mezzo-soprano)

Jim (baritone); a fisherman

Undertaker (baritone)

Nelson (tenor); a fisherman

Scipio (a twelve-year-old boy, child of Robbins and Serena)

Strawberry Woman (mezzo-soprano)

Crab Man (tenor)

The white folk

These are speaking parts only, because they represent the outside world; each of their appearances is an intrusion into the closed society of Catfish Row. They include a Detective, a Policeman, the Coroner, and Mr. Archdale, a friendly and compassionate lawyer.

Clara (lyric soprano)

A young mother of a babe-in-arms, married to Jake. Clara has the opera's opening solo passage, the famous Summertime, and thus establishes the mood of Catfish Row as a world in itself, with its languorous pace and sense of purity and simplicity of values. Clara's other music is less an indication of her personality than her response to a situation: the wild chromatic scales heard when she sees her husband's overturned boat are the music of the hurricane rather than her own.

Sportin' Life (tenor)

In a way, Sportin' Life is the Don Giovanni of the story, for he has an ingratiating way about him and an ironic sense of humor (in the mockery of "It ain't necessarily so") that is entertaining and delightfully spirited. He is nonetheless an insidious villain, associated musically with the infamous tritone, deviously lilting syncopations, or small chromatic twists that speak of a soul without even a hint of morality. "There's a boat dat's leavin' soon for New York" is a masterpiece of musical enticement: the opening writhing bass clarinet melody synthesizes descending chromaticism, blue notes, supple manipulation of offbeat patterns, and an ominous tone color, all belying the apparent grace and insouciance of his very singable melody.

Jake (baritone)

A fisherman whose basic outlook is to support and enrich his family except on Saturday night, when he insists on his right to lose a bit at craps. His Act I, scene i lullaby to his wailing infant is a peppy, dotted-rhythm song, with regular rhymes and phrases, and its humorous take on women as abusers and controllers of men recalls the comic moment found in the typical Broadway musical. On the other hand, his work song ("It take a long pull to get there," Act II, scene ii) is a strophic song with refrain. Modeled after African work songs and based on the pentatonic scale (a pattern based on the division of the octave into five notes instead of the usual eight or twelve), it lends a strong Gullah ambience that shapes the musical personality of the opera.

Serena (soprano)

The wife of Robbins, Serena is the religious leader of the community, leading the prayers for Bess's recovery from illness and delirium after Bess is assaulted by Crown on Kittiwah Island. She is, however, quick to condemn Bess for her surrender to the lure of cocaine. Serena sings mystically (as in her free rhythmed incantation for the health of Bess) and more dramatically than anyone in the cast but Bess herself. Her music lies high on the staff, especially in the funeral and hurricane scenes, and is frequently supported by warm string instrumentation.

Robbins (tenor)

Serena's husband, a cotton worker. He also is committed to the Saturday night crap game and he likes his liquor. He sweeps up the dice before the besotted/doped up Crown can read them and sparks Crown to his murderous attack. Robbins's music has a rhythmic sway between 3/4 and 4/4 at first, and his one songlike passage is accompanied by a spirited vamp, but he soon loses any musical individuality and becomes part of the situational music that intensifies from Crown's entrance to the fight scene.

Peter (tenor)

An eighty-two-year-old seller of honey who lives with the much younger Lily (it is unclear as to whether he is related to her or not, although she identifies him in Act I, scene i as her "ol' man"). Peter's role is important in emphasizing the nature of life in Catfish Row: the pentatonic nature of his ritualized vendor's call (Act I, scene i, and Act II, scene iii) speaks of the area's Gullah character, and the disrespectful way the police arrest him as a material witness reflects the low status and isolation of the Catfish Row community vis-a-vis white Charleston.

Maria (contralto) *[muh-RYE-uh]*

The doyenne of Catfish Row; she runs a restaurant of sorts, from which place of modest business she sees all and reigns, as it were. Maria is less judgmental than Serena, blaming Bess's downfall on Sportin' Life and narcotics rather than on Bess herself. Maria's most defining moment is her rejection of Sportin' Life's sneering "le's you an' me be frien'" in Act II, scene i, when she speaks rhythmically in rhyme over a muffled drum and a perky, vamping accompaniment that is at once sarcastic, humorous, and very strong. The rest of Maria's music is confined to recitative and ensemble work.

Porgy (bass-baritone)

As described in the play, Porgy is "no longer young, and not yet old." His dignified acceptance of his status as a beggar and cripple (see Example PB-2a) and his positive, good-sense attitude toward life have endeared him to everyone. He is a consummate—and inveterate—craps player, winning regularly through means unspecified, although one assumes he never cheats. He is devoutly religious but is ready to believe what he is told, as witness his immediate fear when Sportin' Life tells him in Act III, scene ii that "when the man that killed Crown go in that room an' look at him, Crown' wound begin to bleed." On the other hand, he can summon enough courage to cast off the superstition of the buzzard, whose alighting, according to the legend of the Gullah, foretells the loss of happiness to anyone nearby.

Porgy's motive (Example PB-1) is the most prominent of the opera, but it describes him more as a denizen of Catfish Row than as a person. The solid tunefulness of "I got plenty o' nuttin'" is greater in its depth of characterization: its symmetrical phrasing, simple harmonies, solid melodiousness, and steady rhythmic underpinning reflect a person confident of himself and willing to take life's small pleasures as blessings, with a good sense of what's important.

The incapacity of Porgy's legs is more than matched by fullness of chest and strength of arm, derived from his life of moving about with crutches or by dragging himself here and there. This physical strength, which is vital in the conquering of Crown, is a mirror of his even more important strength of spirit, represented musically in the celebrated duet of Act II, scene i, "Bess, you is my woman now." The duet's long phrases and firm rhythms sing of a heart full of tenderness, compassion, dignity, and ampleness of spirit. His love that forgives all makes Porgy one of opera's most attractive characters.

Crown (baritone)

A stevedore, described by Porgy in the play as "a nigger . . . dat Gawd start to make a bull, den change He min'." Crown is a self-interested brute with no sense of good and evil and with appetites for booze, cocaine, and sex that are animalistic and brook no delay. The singlemindedness of his purpose in any endeavor is clear in the pounding repetitions of his one motive (see Example PB-4a). This trait is also seen in the relentless scale patterns of his duet with Bess on Kittiwah Island, where her nervously syncopated music is at first crudely dominated by the scales, then rudely mocked by his making her syncopation his own.

Crown's muscular forcefulness is matched by his bravado when, in the hurricane scene, he challenges even God in a brazen song about his sexual invincibility. His exiting to help Clara, however, is a redemptive act of considerable interest, albeit brief and soon forgotten. Crown's final appearance, to reclaim Bess in Act III, scene i, is orchestrally sinister and vicious; he never says or sings a word, but the development of the motives of Examples PB-4a and b describes the crude violence of his spirit.

Bess (soprano)

Drug addict and Crown's woman at first, then a person seeking redemption and a place in society as Porgy's beloved. At first despised by the women of the community as, in Maria's words, "a liquor guzzlin' slut," Bess gains acceptance slowly. She becomes a full member of society when Clara entrusts her with the future care of her baby.

Bess is a tragic figure who is unable to resist the force that compels her—the sexual attractiveness and strength of Crown—even when she knows that her happiness lies elsewhere. Her weakness is reflected in the fact that she has little music of her own: her parts in the duets with Porgy derive from themes introduced by him; and the indication of her as someone accepted by the community is through her reprise of "Summertime," a song associated with Clara.

In the scene with Crown on Kittiwah Island, Bess protests with the nervousness of repeated notes over fast syncopations, and her pleading with Crown ("What you want wid Bess?") is descending, angular, and accompanied by a mix of vamped and triplet rhythms that tell of weakness and instability (Example PB-5).

She has one other moment of music that is clearly hers, the overtly dramatic rejection of Sportin' Life, in Act III, scene ii, but this music is made of short, wide-ranging phrases that tell of desperation rather than resolve.

EXAMPLE PB-5 ACT II, SCENE III: BESS PLEADS WITH CROWN

Bibliography

Armitage, Merle, ed. *George Gershwin*. New York: Longman's Green, 1938.

Block, Geoffrey Holden. "Gershwin's Buzzard and Other Mythological Creatures," in *Opera Quarterly* 7, no. 2 (Summer 1990): 74–82.

Crawford, Richard. "George Gershwin," in *The New Grove Twentieth-Century American Masters*. New York: W. W. Norton, 1988.

Ewen, David. *A Journey to Greatness: The Life and Music of George Gershwin*. New York: Henry Holt, 1956. Rev. and enl. as *George Gershwin: His Journey to Greatness*, 1970.

Gershwin, George. "Rhapsody in Catfish Row," in *The New York Times* (October 20, 1935), section 10, p. 1f.
Reprinted in whole in Armitage; in part in Ewen and Jablonski.

Gilbert, Steven. *The Music of Gershwin*. New Haven: Yale University Press, 1995.

Hamm, Charles. *Music in the New World*. New York. W. W. Norton, 1983.

Heyward, DuBose, and Dorothy Heyward. "Porgy," in *Famous American Plays of the 1920s and 1930s*. Garden City, NY: Fireside Theatre, 1988.

Heyward, DuBose. *Porgy*. New York: Doubleday and Co. [Norman S. Berg], 1925.

Jablonski, Edward. *Gershwin: A Biography*. Boston: Northeastern Press, 1990 [1987].

Joyner, Charles. *Down By the Riverside: A South Carolina Slave Community*. Blacks in the New World. Urbana, IL and Chicago: University of Illinois Press, 1984.
See Chapter 7 for "Gullah: A Creole Language."

Kingman, Daniel. *American Music: A Panorama*. New York: Schirmer Books, 1979.

Mellers, Wilfrid. *Music In a New Found Land: Themes and Developments in the History of American Music*. New York: Knopf, 1965.

Rorem, Ned. "Living With Gershwin," in *Opera News* 49, no. 13 (March 16, 1985): 11–14, 16, 18f.

Rosenberg, Deena. *Fascinating Rhythm: The Collaboration of George and Ira Gershwin*. New York: Dutton, 1991.

Schwartz, Charles. *Gershwin: His Life and Music*. Indianapolis and New York: Bobbs-Merrill, 1973.

Southern, Eileen. *The Music of Black Americans: A History*. 2nd ed. New York: W. W. Norton, 1983.

Starr, Lawrence. "Toward A Reevaluation of Gershwin's *Porgy and Bess*," in *American Music* 2, no. 2 (Summer 1984): 25–37.

Chapter 17

PETER GRIMES

MUSIC: Benjamin Britten (1913–1976)

LIBRETTO: Montagu Slater, derived from the poem *The Borough—A Poem in 24 Letters* (1810) by George Crabbe (1754–1832), after a scenario by Benjamin Britten and Peter Pears.

PREMIERE: London, June 7, 1945, Sadler's Wells.

TIME AND PLACE OF THE STORY: Aldeburgh,[1] a fishing village on the coast of the North Sea, in Suffolk, England, about 1830. The action takes place over a period of perhaps a week.

Peter Grimes is one of a handful of twentieth-century operas that are not only generally acknowledged as modern masterpieces but have been embraced unreservedly by the opera-going public. Although there was some early hostility to the composer and the work during the preparation for its premiere, the expressive power of this opera was, generally, immediately felt and acclaimed. Admiration for it is ever expanding. The imageries of the sea at peace, in turmoil, and as symbolic of the actions on land are among the wonders of tone painting, the inexorable march of the story line is fascinating and deeply moving, and the characters are limned with decisive strokes.

The Opera As Symbol

This opera is a multiple metaphor, for its protagonist may be seen to represent Britten himself, while the work as a whole speaks to the relation of the outsider to society and the tragedy inherent in the denial of love and compassion. Britten was a pacifist and a homosexual in a time that had no tolerance for either:[2] the blossoming of his career in the 1930s and 1940s was in a Western civilization in which only the traditional heterosexual relation-

---

[1] Britten's world-famous Aldeburgh Music Festival is not far from his birthplace of Lowestoft, Suffolk.

[2] Alex Ross, in "In 'Grimes,' Low Tragedy Makes for Great Opera," in *The New York Times*, (*Arts and Leisure* section, December 11, 1994, p. 33) proposes that the opera has "an atmosphere of self-loathing. . . . Britten equates his [own] unfulfilled desires with murder and sends Grimes to an awful demise."

ships were countenanced—homosexuality was a criminal offense in England—and to be against war when England was in the midst of the most dire threat to its existence was to invite isolation and hatred. Britten's private life, like that of his protagonist, was thus on the fringe of his society, and his views toward the world conflict and his nation's struggle for survival were distinctly unpopular. Resentment among the singers of the Sadler's Wells company preparing the premiere was rife, openly and bitterly in terms of his pacifism, unspoken but nonetheless potent because of his sexual orientation.

Like the composer, Grimes has a poetic imagination and depth of spirit, but, save for a minority of sympathetic persons, those qualities are unrecognized by those around him, who see only rough behavior and unwillingness to "get along" as signs of someone different from them and hostile to them. To the world of the Borough and to the England of 1945, Grimes/Britten was an anti-hero.

Societal indifference, rigidity of custom, self-satisfaction, hypocrisy, and the human propensities for indifference, hatred, and viciousness are the antagonists here. They are present in one way or another in every scene and are represented in the two pervasive elements of the score, the choral music of the people of the Borough and the presence of the sea as metaphors for social forces that are unconquerable, insensate, ultimately mysterious, and infinite in mood.

The Opera as a Point of View

The philosophical positions underlying this tragedy are set out powerfully in two passages given to the sympathetic Balstrode.

The first of these concepts is the right of a person to be apart, to answer to his own calling. It is set out in the tavern scene (Act I, scene ii) as a song among the people of the Borough who have come together for shelter and community but fall to bickering, drunkenness, and violence. Balstrode reminds his fellow citizens ". . . we live and let live, and look, we keep our hands to ourselves" in a passage that starts as a mini-sermon but immediately becomes a folk tune with a simple oom-pah accompaniment, becoming at once a communal statement supported by all the others. The moment is both metaphorical and ironic: the text speaks of letting people alone, while the musical unison binds all of them into a single social unit; words and song symbolize the delicate balances between individuals and society; and it is sung with fervor by people who mouth the sentiments without applying them for a moment to themselves.

The second thesis of the opera is correlative to the first, because it acknowledges that people must care about each other, even as they acknowledge a person's right to be different. It is in Act III, scene i (Example PG-1), that Ellen and Balstrode realize the enormity of Peter's distress and ultimate tragedy. The apprentice's sweater has been found washed up by the tide and the message of its discovery is clear: the boy has lost his life in the sea and Peter is somehow involved in his death. Ellen at first feels wholly powerless, her despair set to an unvaried pitch (accompanied only by the hollow sound of a doubling trombone) that implies an inescapable hopelessness through

EXAMPLE PG-1 ACT III, SCENE I: BALSTRODE POINTS THE
MORAL; HE AND ELLEN AFFIRM THEIR COMMITMENT TO HELP
PETER ("X" MARKS THE QUOTATION OF PETER'S CRY FROM
ACT II, SCENE I, "AND GOD HAVE MERCY UPON ME")

its repetitiveness, but Balstrode breaks its bonds with a rising, heavily accented and rhythmically animated, affirmative power. His music moves from her sparsely accompanied pitch, climbs through crushing dissonances, and leads to their mutual renewal of commitment to Peter's welfare in the major mode. It is one of the opera's few uplifting moments.

The Threads of the Music

Peter Grimes stands firm in the tradition of Romantic grand opera. The atmosphere is vitally important as an illumination of the dramatic forces at work, the story writhes with human torment, and the scenes of conflict and outburst are as violent and explosive as they are inexorable. The opera's elements are also derived from grand opera, because it relies extensively on recitatives, arias, choral songs, grand set pieces, and such standard devices of its nineteenth-century model as Tempest and Mad Scene.

These units, while strikingly individual, are tightly unified, because Britten has threaded them together with recurrent motives that at times are literal returns and at other times are recalled as subtle transformations. The former are easily recognized when their recalls are fundaments of the dramatic moment, as in Peter's Mad Scene (Act III, scene ii). The transformations are less obvious but always potent; I have already pointed to one of them in Examples 3.2a and b, where a simple dance tune, heard as background to Mrs. Sedley's poisonous suggestions in Act III, scene i, is reworked into a raving mob's wordless howl.

A more frequently exploited motive is one heard first with harsh irony in front of the church, in Act II, scene i, when Peter rejects Ellen's remonstrances over his excessive work and harsh treatment of John, the apprentice. In an uncontrollable explosion of frustration and obsession, Peter strikes her, then cries out in agonized bitterness, "So be it, and God have mercy upon me" (Example PG-2a).

Throughout the scene there has been an ironic interplay between the mouthings of the congregation within the church and the action outside; this climactic moment is given its point by the "Amen" droned within, as Peter's shouted anguish traverses an octave down from a high B-flat. The bitterness and irony of text and music are driven immediately and ineradicably into our memory, for we hear this music at once as a canon[3] in the brass instruments as an orchestral punctuation of the moment's violence. It is taken up moments later as the sardonic music for the crowd's "Grimes is at his exercise"[4] (Example PG-2b) and "Now the church parade begins," and becomes the substance for the growing hostility of a lynch mob in the making.

Its basic intervals—a descending third and a descending fifth (marked respectively "a" and "b" in Example PG-2)—are the substance of the ground

---

[3] A note-for-note imitation of one musical line by another, the first continuing independently against the second.

[4] The words were taken directly from Crabbe.

EXAMPLE PG-2 THE IRONIES OF PETER'S CRY FOR GOD'S MERCY.

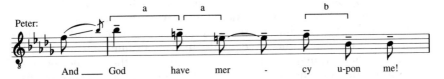

a) Act II, scene i: On Sunday morning, as people are in church, the climax of
the quarrel with Ellen.

b) Act II, scene i: The people of the Borough comment sarcastically on
Grimes's abuse of Ellen as typical of his behavior.

c) Act III, scene ii: In the Mad Scene, Peter inverts his plea.

bass of the passacaglia that constitutes Interlude IV (see below, Example PG-
4e) and thus provide the pizzicato strings there with an ironic, thudding,
relentless reminder of a man who has found no surcease from misery, and
no mercy, even from God.

The motive is transformed in combination with its original version near
the opera's final moments as the punctuation of Balstrode's and Ellen's
pointing of the opera's moral (see "x" in Example PG-1, above): the music
of their unflinching support of their friend, no matter what his horror,
becomes the metaphor for the path of God's mercy.

We hear it yet one more time at the most wrenching moment of Peter's
suffering, when, cowering from the ravages of total dementia and the obsessive voices of his pursuers floating through the fog, he keeps the motive's
music but inverts the message: "To hell with all your mercy." It is the ultimate sorrow: the loss of hope of any kind for any ray of love or understanding.

There are many other melodic reminiscences, notable among them the
acidly rhythmic motive of Peter's obsession with material wealth, the interval
of an ascending ninth with which several of his utterances begin, his frequent repetition of his dream of a "harbour that shelters peace," and Ellen's
scalar descents and brief moments of melodic ornament. They will be quoted in the discussions that deal with Peter and Ellen as they are characterized through their music.

An important device for unifying music and drama is Britten's use of key and pitch relationship. The move between a note or key and a half step (or minor second) below it[5] is often associated in Western music with death or suffering and is the relationship between the two keys of most of the Peter-Ellen duet at the end of the Prologue (he in F minor after starting in a different key; she in E major). The minor second is also the distance between the first two notes of the keening of the high violins at the start of the first Sea Interlude (see below, Example PG-4a), and between the notes of each of the first seven word groups of the Mad Scene (Example PG-6).

Key relationship is also at work on a broader scale, ranging across the the opera as a whole. We see (and hear) the people of the Borough at their daily work in the first scene of Act I and again in the final scene of the opera: in both cases, they sing similar music and they sing it in the same key, the key of A. In Act II, scene i, however, their opening hymn ("Now the daylight fills the sky") is recited on E-flat, a pitch that is in a potent dissonance—the tritone/augmented fourth—with the pitch and key of A. The connection between keys is extremely subtle for even the sophisticated listener, who will probably not remember the harmonies of Act I while listening to Act II, but nonetheless the dramatic point is caustic: the music of the people's Christian worship has nothing whatever in common with the music related to what they do or think in their real world.

EXAMPLE PG-3 ACT III, SCENE II: THE DESCENDING MINOR SECOND AT THE START OF THE MAD SCENE

---

[5] See the discussion of the Phrygian cadence, Chapter 13, note 10.

The Pervasiveness of the Sea

The sea atmosphere invests the entire score, orchestrally and vocally, deriving in part from Britten's own identity with the locale of the plot and in part from the words of Crabbe, whose poem, while often somewhat in the nature of a rigidly rhymed sociological report, is wonderfully vivid in this respect:

> From parted clouds the moon her radiance throws
> On the wild waves, and all the danger shows;
> But shows them beaming in her shining vest,
> Terrific splendor! gloom in glory dressed!

In describing Peter's oneness with the sea and marsh in spite of the dullness and hopelessness of his life, Crabbe characterizes how Peter would

> . . . sadly listen to the tuneless cry
> Of fishing gull or clanging golden-eye;
> What time the seabirds to the marsh would come
> And the loud bittern, from the bull-rush home,
> Gave from the salt-ditch side the bellowing boom.

The sea is most apparent in the six "Sea Interludes."[6] Three of these, Interludes I, III, and V, are preludes to acts, each setting the mood of the following action and threading its way motivically through that action. The other interludes are transitions between scenes. They are no less atmospheric, but they are pointed more to Peter's state of mind than to staged events.

Interlude I (Example PG-4a) introduces Act I, scene i, and also provides the closing music of the opera, thus, Prologue aside, framing the whole. It shows the expanse of the water and the natural world of birds and breeze that exists above it, vital but unsentient, active but uninvolved: calls of gulls squeal in high violins; waves of arpeggios (clarinet, harp, and viola) swoop up and down like birds careening over the water; and low, sustained chords in the brass move slowly in unrelated harmony to symbolize the depths and expanse of the ocean, supremely mysterious and dangerous for all its neutrality.[7]

Drawn from the music of Balstrode's warning in Act I, scene i (Example PG-4b), Interlude II (Example PG-4c) portrays the tempestuous sea as viciously as any in opera; its pounding, percussive bass and raging scales are powerfully individual even as they make us aware of musical-tempest archetypes. Interlude III, on the other hand, presents an entirely different mood: it uses detached, high woodwind pitches to evoke the water's shimmer and

---

[6] Four of these have become concert pieces as a suite independent of the opera in the following order: I ("Dawn"), III ("Sunday Morning"), V ("Moonlight"), and II ("Storm"). The Passacaglia that is Interlude IV is sometimes included as a fifth movement.

[7] White (p. 130) interprets the three elements of Interlude I as "(a) the wind that 'is holding back the tide,' as it blows through the rigging of the boats on the beach and over the chimney-pots of the Borough, (b) the lapping of the water, and (c) the scrunch of the shingle beneath the tide."

the sparkle of white caps on a brilliantly sunny morning (Example PG-4d; moments later the same music will accompany Ellen's song of encouragement to the apprentice).

The sea as symbol of human torment is the substance of Interlude IV. It is a passacaglia[8] built on the strange, syncopated descents of a theme in the violas (Example PG-4e) over a brooding ostinato rich in the suggestions of Peter's tormented mind in particular and the darker side of humanity in

EXAMPLE PG-4 THE SEA INTERLUDES

a) Interlude I, "Dawn": Calls of gulls, swoops of bird and breeze, the still depths of the waters.

---

[8] A set of variations on a continually repeated theme that is heard most often in the bass.

EXAMPLE PG-4 (*Continued*)

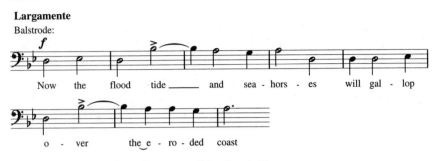

b) Act I, scene ii: Balstrode warns of the flood tide.

c) Interlude II: Storm motive derived from Balstrode's warning.

d) Interlude III: "Sunday Morning"—the glint of sunshine on the sea.

general. The sea at night as portrayed in Interlude V is unruffled and serene, but crescendos and diminuendos underlying its quiet syncopations suggest the swells that imply unknown and dangerous depths. Interlude VI is an instrumental transition to the Mad Scene and is directly parallel to it: both offer reminiscences of a number of motives in a somewhat fragmentary way, and both are haunted by distant sounds evocative of fog, the murk of night, and unseen peril.

EXAMPLE PG-4 (*Continued*)

e) Interlude IV: Passacaglia theme and ground bass.

The imagery of the sea informs many other passages of the opera: its metallic glint is the first thing we hear in the Prologue, where angular, biting woodwind notes set out a motive (Example PG-5a) that will be transformed into the gossiping of the onlookers at the inquest; Swallow's irritated and caustic verdict; the play of sun and wave in Interlude III (see above, Example PG-4d); and Peter's bitter and demented recall in the Mad Scene of Act III, scene ii.

The sense of the vastness and the undulations of the sea can be felt in the vocal music as well as in the instruments, as illustrated by the opening chorus of Act I, scene i (Example PG-6a; this music is also the substance of the concluding choral moments of the opera) and the anguished cry of Peter in the Mad Scene (Example PG-6b).

Peter Grimes is now more than half a century old, yet its resonances of the sufferings and longings of the isolated human soul, be he dreamer or non-hero, are as tragic and poignant as when they were first heard. The voices of Peter and Ellen's duet still call to us, reminding us that "a voice out of the pain is like a hand that one can feel and know." The whole world longs for some-one—anyone—to say with them the duet's closing words, "Here is a friend."

EXAMPLE PG-5 THE HARSH GLINT OF THE SEA AS VERDICT AND GOSSIP IN THE FIRST NOTES OF THE PROLOGUE

EXAMPLE PG-6 THE UNDULATIONS OF THE SEA IN VOCAL LINES

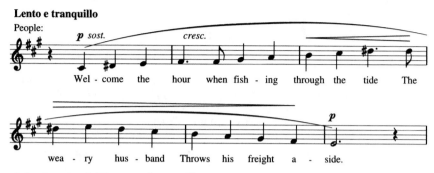

a) Act I, scene i: The people mending nets.

b) Act III, scene ii: Peter's Mad Scene.

THE PLOT AND ITS MUSIC

NOTE: The music moves unbroken from unit to unit, and there are no score designations such as "aria" or "scene with chorus." I have provided them and the numbering of paragraphs as points of reference.

PRE-CURTAIN ACTION As was a common custom, Peter had given a sum to a workhouse to "purchase" an orphan boy to serve as his apprentice. Subsequently, having made a huge haul of fish, Peter had attempted to sail directly to London to market his catch there, but he had to jettison his load when he was blown off course. The boy became ill, the drinking supply ran out, and the boy died of thirst. An investigation has begun.

Prologue

A crowded room inside the Moot Hall, arranged for a coroner's inquest. Swallow is sitting at a raised table.

1 As first witness in the investigation of the death of his apprentice, Peter is sworn in. He tells of having been blown off course by the wind and, after three days at sea, of the death of the boy. Swallow's questions indicate that there had been an uproar when Peter had returned, that he had verbally abused Mrs. Sedley, and that Ellen had helped him carry the boy home.

The questions are quick, with jagged rhythms and intervals, usually with accompaniment of staccato woodwinds (see Ex. PG-5). Peter's responses are in slower time values, accompanied by quiet strings.

The women of the crowd mutter that Ellen should open her eyes to the truth.

The choral muttering is canonic, often over reiterative, fast background patterns.

Noting that Peter had rescued the boy from drowning on an earlier occasion, Swallow pompously warns Peter not to obtain the services of another youth but to hire an adult "big enough to stand up for himself." He issues the verdict that the boy died of "accidental circumstances." The audience mutters angrily that the guilt should be fixed more precisely.

Swallow's verdict is in the style of Ex. PG-5. The crowd continues its sotto voce comments in canon.

Peter desperately asks for the truth to be examined at a trial, for "the case will go on in people's minds," but the inquest is adjourned. At Hobson's call to clear the court, all but Peter and Ellen leave.

Peter's desperation is in short phrases, faster rhythms.

2 RECITATIVE/DUET (Peter, Ellen) *The truth, the pity* Peter's bitterness over the viciousness of gossip is assuaged by Ellen's reassurance that his name will be cleared. The two go off together.

Unaccompanied throughout. Peter and Ellen start in different keys (See Ex. 3.11). Her lines are flowing and gentle, his jagged and irregular, covering a wide range. They end in a unison that begins with the rising minor ninth consistently associated with Peter's special world.

3 INTERLUDE I (Orchestra) Depiction of the sea at dawn.

See Ex. PG-4a Violins and flutes use high notes, with grace notes a minor second above, to suggest the squalling of gulls; clarinets, harps, and violas provide rising and falling arpeggios that call up images of swooping sea birds; rich major chords in low brass and timpani imply the mysterious depths and the eternity of the sea.

Act I

SCENE I

Oceanfront of the Borough, on a cold, grey morning. Visible are mooring spots for fishing boats and, in the background, facades of Ned Keene's Apothecary Shop, the Moot Hall, The Boar Tavern, and the church. Fishing boats are moored at their anchorages.

4 CHORUS *Oh, hang at open doors the net, the cork* The Borough's normal life is underway: children scamper and people are busy mending nets or completing other tasks of their daily lives. Banter and various conversational exchanges. Some comment about the possibility of a storm, Balstrode noting that if the wind that holds back the tide should shift, the storm would be terrible and destructive.

While the orchestra continues motives from Sea Interlude I, the rise and fall of steady-rhythmed phrases suggest the ocean's ebb and flow (Ex. PG-6a). Boles's haughty condemnation of Auntie's tavern has brief melismas and a very narrow melodic span until the notes of "your hot desires" move jaggedly and widely, suggesting his own hidden lusts.

Peter calls for help in docking his boat; no one but Balstrode and Keene move to help him. Keene informs Grimes that a boy from the workhouse is available, but Keene's call to Hobson to set out in his cart to fetch the lad is met with a refusal.

The efforts of Keene and Balstrode have short rests between phrases, suggesting their gasping for breath as they turn the capstan.

5 SONG (Hobson) *I have to go from pub to pub, picking up parcels* Hobson's excuse is that the cart is full, and he has too much to do.

The slow, dotted rhythms of his grousing are comically reinforced by the double basses, as if to mock his exaggeration of his heavy work.

6 ARIA AND CHORUS (Ellen) *The carter goes from pub to pub* Overhearing Hobson's refusal, Ellen offers to go along but the people object to her being "Grimes's messenger."

Ellen parodies Hobson's melody by using it for her first words. The objections of the people are over the now ironic playing of Hobson's melody by the double basses.

7 ARIOSO (Ellen) *Let her among you without fault cast the first stone* Ellen politely upbraids all for their coldness by quoting Jesus's words at the stoning of the Magdalene. She sets out with Hobson for the long journey to the workhouse.

She continues to turn Hobson's music on its ear, inverting the scalar direction of his "My journey back is late at night" for her "Let her among you without sin" (Ex. PG-10a). Her "Mr. Hobson, I'm ready" offers quiet determination to simple recitative, accompanied by steady chords in the brass.

Responding to Mrs. Sedley's request for replenishment of her laudanum, Ned tells her to come to The Boar that night, when Carter Hobson will return with a supply.

Mrs. Sedley's addiction is suggested by short, gasping phrases.

8 ENSEMBLE (Balstrode, people) *Look, the storm come! . . . Now the flood tide* Balstrode notes with alarm that the wind has turned and that the flood tide will soon be upon them. Fearing the storm's potential for devouring the land, all hasten home or into The Boar.

A dissonant hushed tremolo hints at the awesome power of the storm that is to come. Balstrode's warning is in a broad, arching melody accompanied by panicky bursts of rising scale patterns from the people, creating a musical effect of great power that drives the angry spurts and roilings of violent waters and winds. Balstrode's theme (Ex. PG-4b) becomes the subject of an elaborate fugue.

Left alone with Grimes, Balstrode suggests that, since the town hates him and distrusts him so, he should find employment as a seaman somewhere else.

9 ARIA (Peter) *We strained into the wind, heavily laden* Peter tells of "that evil day" when a storm threatened the survival of him and his first apprentice, who, "among the fishing nets," died "a childish death."

Peter's narrative is a set of six, hypnotically similar phrases, each beginning with his intervallic signature, the rising minor ninth (Ex. PG-7b), each accompanied by fragments of quickly rising woodwind scales. An occasional harp glissando evokes wind and wave.

10 DUET (Peter, Balstrode) *They listen to money. . . . Man, go and ask her* Peter asserts that the only way "to answer the Borough" is through money. Balstrode urges him to marry Ellen at once and suggests that the tragedy of his life is about to begin all over again unless he conducts himself differently. The two begin to argue angrily, their mood matched by the rising gale. Balstrode stomps into the tavern.

Peter's obsessiveness is set in the short repeated phrases of Ex. PG-8a; when he even applies it to his determination to marry Ellen, it becomes clear that love and tenderness are not in his thoughts at this moment, only respectability.

11 ARIA (Peter) *What harbour shelters peace?* Alone, Peter wonders if he can ever find a life free of tribulation.

Peter's narrative uses the music of his narration to Balstrode, but here it is mostly in the major mode. Several phrases begin with the rising ninth (major, in each case) and is accompanied by quick woodwind rising scales regularly associated with movements in sea and sky. His music contrasts arching phrases and long-breathed note values with jagged spurts of lower pitches. The former are associated with his vision of shelter and freedom from quarrel; the latter, associated with the "tidal waves, . . . storms, . . . terrors and tragedies," comprise an inversion of the woodwind figure used in the Prologue to accompany the gossiping and muttering of the people.

12 INTERLUDE II (Orchestra) Storm.

The battering of the storm is a metaphor for the uncontrollable forces that assault Peter's peace of mind and will eventually destroy him. Low brass and percussion, with angry syncopations, pound away. The harsh opening motive (Ex. PG-4c), the main material of a rondo form, derives from Balstrode's Act I, scene i warning. The three contrasting episodes are (1) largamente ("broadly"): expansion of the motive played in the low brass in Interlude I; (2) molto animato ("very animated"): disjunct rhythms and triplet figures; and (3) largamente: a diminuendo ("quieting") leads to expressive reminiscences of the music of Peter's "What harbour shelters peace" and, shortly after the intrusion of more musical violence, of "with her there'll be no quarrels."

SCENE II

That night, inside The Boar's common room. The storm is at full fury; people struggle to close the door against the wind after every person's entrance.

13 RECITATIVE Mrs. Sedley's presence—she is waiting for the delivery of her laudanum—elicits sarcasm from Auntie and Balstrode. More and more people arrive for shelter and community. Fearful commentaries about the wildness of the storm are followed by news of washouts and landslides, especially at the cliff near Grimes's hut.

At curtain rise, the violent music disintegrates into a brooding low trill. The dialogue is sung without musical measure over the trill or dissonant tremolos that tell of the ravages of nature outside the tavern. Each time someone enters the tavern, the storm music erupts, its appearances following the sequence of the episodes of the Interlude.

14 SONG (Balstrode, People) *We live and let live* As the drinking continues, Boles drunkenly paws one of the Nieces; when Balstrode restrains him, Boles takes a swing, and a fight is about to erupt. Balstrode calms everyone down with a reminder that people need to "keep our hands to ourselves." All join in that sentiment.

A rather awkward melody of short phrases and no real lyricism, thus suggesting the unease that all feel. The people join in briefly, sotto voce.

Grimes suddenly appears in the doorway, looking wild. Mrs. Sedley faints at the sight of him; all mutter "talk of the devil and there he is" and shrink from him as he moves into their midst. There is a moment of quiet.

Grimes's sudden appearance is to a shrieking recall of the music of "What harbour shelters peace"; the people "speak" in canon in hushed tones.

15 ARIA (Peter) *Now the Great Bear and the Pleiades* Peter muses to himself about the meaning of the universe and of life.

See Ex. 5.3. Four segments are in the form of four strophes that outline an AABA form. The enormity of sky and space arching over the sea is implied by the contrast between Grimes's repeated high notes and the canon started by low strings. The turmoil and uncertainties of life are set out in the complex, fast rhythms and polyphony of the third section; the cyclic nature of existence is suggested in the final section by a reverse canon from high to low strings and the return of the aria's opening materials.

The onlookers comment *sotto voce* that Peter is either mad or drunk and should be thrown out.

The onlookers comment quietly in tiny segments set in a highly complex polyphony.

16 ROUND (All) *Old Joe has gone fishing* At Balstrode's suggestion, a song is struck up, but Peter's participation is rhythmically, textually, and melodically disjointed; the people set the music aright with some difficulty.

A most complex 7/4 rhythm for a canon with three subjects: "Old Joe . . .," "Pull them in in han'fuls . . .," and "Bring them in sweetly, gut them completely." Little wonder that Peter gets it mixed up by singing the first in augmentation, altering the words, changing the notes, and eventually composing his own music ("O haul away!"), which is far more expansive and arching than anything that the people have sung previously.

17 Ellen, Hobson, and John arrive, all three of them soaked to the skin and, as Ellen announces, "chilled to the bone." Auntie urges Peter to let the boy warm up, but Peter insists on leaving at once. Ellen kindly tells the boy that Peter will take him home, but, as Peter and John step out into the howling tempest, the people caustically roar, "Home! do you call that home!"

The final moments of the scene are heralded by an explosive return of the storm's tremolo and continuous repetitions under the dialogue of the eruptive motives of Sea Interlude II.

Act II

SCENE I

18 INTERLUDE III (Orchestra) The sea in bright sun.

French horns in warm thirds underlie bright, detached woodwind patterns (Ex. PG-4d) that frame this ABA piece; high-pitched minor seconds recall Interlude I. In the center section, rushing chromatic descents and other fast figures suggest wind and the splash of waves on the shore, while a warm, expressive theme in the viola and cello (Ex. PG-4e) suggests the smoothness of the ocean surface.

Village scene as in Act I, scene i, some weeks later. Church bells ring on a bright and sunny Sunday morning. Villagers are arriving for church services; Ellen and John enter against the flow of citizens heading for the church.

19 ARIA (Ellen) *Glitter of waves and glitter of sunlight* Ellen notes the beauty of the day as something to make the heart rejoice and invites the boy to talk to her as she does some knitting for him. He plays silently beside her.

Ellen sings to the accompaniment of elements heard in Interlude III. The first church bell's B-flat is a semitone from Ellen's A-major; the second bell, on E-flat, is a tritone away. The playful quality and key of her suggestion that they not go to church derives from the opening of Interlude III, implying that there is little sympathy between her and the people. Ex. PG-4e is in canon, in the strings.

20 HYMN with ARIOSO (Congregation, Ellen, Rector Adams) *Now that the day-light fills the sky . . . Nothing to tell me?* As the opening hymn is heard from within the church, Ellen tries to draw the boy out a bit and tells him that, in spite of what he may have heard about Peter's first apprentice, she prays that John's arrival will mark a new start.

> *Virtually tuneless, the hymn seems a matter of habit rather than conviction. The hymn's "Shield from anger's din [and] earth's absorbing vanities" contrasts with Ellen's tale of reaching out to help with children's problems. As she speaks of the "story of the prentice [sic] Peter had before," the hymn's text ironically notes that "shades of night return once more."*

21 RESPONSES and GLORIA with RECITATIVE (Rector, Congregation, Ellen) *Wherefore I pray you and beseech you . . . There's a tear in your coat . . . Glory be to the Father* As the Rector and congregation intone the litany's words of people as errant who "have done those things which we ought not to have done," Ellen, observed by Mrs. Sedley, notices a tear in John's coat and finds a bruise on his neck. Her sad observation, "A bruise . . . well it's begun!" is ironically punctuated from within by the intonation from the *Gloria:* "As it was in the beginning, is now and ever shall be."

> *As the church music continues to be intoned tunelessly, Ellen's discovery is to a series of agitated rising phrases; her reassurance is to a gently bending series of rising and falling scale figures. Her "After the storm will come a sleep" (Ex. PG-11a) is to prove all too true. Her caressing words are followed by the bitter recall of the music of her discovery of the bruise in an oboe's staccato patterns.*

Ellen tries to assure the boy that his present unhappy days will soon be resolved by peaceful ones.

22 DUET and BENEDICITE (Peter, Ellen, Congregation) *Come boy! . . . O all ye works of the Lord* Peter arrives unexpectedly and orders the boy to join him in heading out to sea again. As the congregation intones the canticle that praises God for the plenitude of the earth, Peter announces excitedly that he has seen a shoal and they must set out for fishing.

> *The litany's repeated units of melody underscore Peter's own obsession. His "I've seen a shoal" uses the music of his "They listen to money" (Ex. PG-8a).*

Ellen's protests are rudely rejected, Peter once again insisting that only money will buy them respect. (His statement of reliance on money is a bitter gloss on the Creed heard from the congregation.) As their discussion intensifies, Peter rudely demands that Ellen remove her hand from his arm. As Auntie observes the dispute from The Boar, Ellen asks Peter if they were mistaken in their plans "to solve [Peter's] life by lonely toil." Boles[9] and Keene enter the area from the street nearby and also observe the argument.

> *Peter continues the musical style of Ex. PG-8a; Ellen's descending scale fragments are consistently marked diminuendo, as she tries to calm his excitement with "Hush, Peter!," but to no avail. Peter's plea, "Believe in me," on an F-sharp, is a semitone away from the congregations' F-natural for the intoning of the Creed. He becomes more agitated, rejecting her proffer of a gentle touch to the music of Ex. PG-7a.*

---

[9] The libretto does not explain why Boles is not in the church with the others. Perhaps his Methodist congregation met elsewhere, earlier that morning.

Britten, *Peter Grimes* (1945), Act II, scene i: Peter (Peter Pears) strikes Ellen (Joan Cross), when, having accused him of ill treating his apprentice (Leonard Thompson), Ellen laments, "We were mistaken to have dreamed . . . Peter! We've failed, we've failed!" Sadler's Wells Opera, 1945 (premiere production): scenery and costumes by Kenneth Green. Courtesy *Opera News,* Metropolitan Opera Guild. Photo British Information Services.

When Ellen disappointedly whispers that all their plans and hopes have failed, Peter, with an agonized cry, strikes her, calling aloud in a powerfully ironic counterpoint to the *Amen* from the church, "So be it, And God have mercy upon me!" Ellen leaves, weeping; Peter pushes the boy ahead of him roughly, in the other direction.

The blow comes as a visual climax to the orchestra's biting echo of Peter's "Wrong to try, wrong to plan." His cry "And God have mercy upon me!" (Ex. PG-2a) ensues almost immediately, first in the vocal line, then in jagged canonic treatment by the brass.

23 TRIO (Auntie, Keene, Boles) *Fool! to let it come to this* Those who have overheard the scene between Ellen and Peter comment angrily ("Grimes is at his exercise") on what they have seen and heard, then caustically on the religiosity of the people who begin to exit the church ("Now the church parade begins").

The prevailing music is the continual recitation of Ex. PG-2b, with new texts commenting sarcastically on the habitual behaviors of both Peter and the people in church. "Grimes is at his exercise" becomes the dominant motive of the scene.

24 ENSEMBLE (Auntie, Keene, Mrs. Sedley, Balstrode, Boles, People) *Doctor! Leave him out of it! What is it? . . . Grimes is at his exercise!* Balstrode tries to soften the stirring up of the people by the eager-to-moralize Mrs. Sedley and Boles, but they intensify their talking among themselves, gathering about Boles in growing agitation.

Balstrode's remonstrance draws on the people's song opening Act I, scene i, suggesting that Peter is a skilled fisherman like them. Ex. PG-2b becomes a mantra between the snaps of angry questions and comments of the people.

Ellen returns to pick up her workbasket, left behind when Peter struck her. The crowd demands that she speak out.

The crowd's demands on Ellen recall the reciting tones of the church service, but here potently rhythmic and accompanied by offbeat heavy accents of the full orchestra.

25 ARIA with CHORUS (Ellen, People) *We planned that their lives should have a new start* As she tells them of her hopes and plans for a new start, the crowd's anger grows. She and Balstrode attempt to dissuade them from rage (Ellen: "O hard, hard hearts!"), but they peremptorily condemn her softness of heart that "tried to be kind [but helped] Murder." At the Rector's suggestion, all determine to go to Peter's hut to find out the worst.

Ellen's repetitions of small ornaments and of plodding descents suggest her deep sadness; her music is mocked by quotations of it from some and by attacks from others through angular, heavily accented, faster patterns. The people interrupt or jab at her musically even as she tries to explain (Ex. PG-10b)—no one listens or cares. The rage of the crowd expands into a concertato, with an ensemble of ten solo lines using these two ideas alternating with choral episodes punctuated by a hammering rhythm.

26 ENSEMBLE (People) *Now is gossip put on trial* Hobson gets his drum, a procession is formed, and all the men set off, the women following.

Diminution of time values and orchestral complexity intensify the pace. The sudden hollowness of Hobson's drum begins a pagan-like march, with thudding oom-pahs from low strings; brasses provide portentous swells, low strings offer deep trills.

27 QUARTET (Ellen, Auntie, Nieces) *From the gutter, why should we trouble* The four women remain behind dejectedly, wondering whether they should "be ashamed because [they] comfort men from ugliness" and not knowing whether to "smile . . . weep or wait quietly" until the foolishness of human behavior abates.

Interludes of dissonant descents from a pair of flutes alternate with passages where the steady lyricism of the women's voices is accompanied by harmonized arpeggios in the low strings. The mood is a mix of weariness and discontent, but the mission all feel of extending solace to others is expressed in the ending of each phrase on a softening major chord.

28 INTERLUDE IV (Orchestra)—PASSACAGLIA—The tormented soul of Peter.

(Ex. PG-4e) The ground bass is the music of Ex. PG-2 in slow pizzicato strings. The theme, set out by a solo viola, is given nine variations, the last a fugue that suggests a grotesque revisiting of Interlude I, just as the whole Interlude is a visiting of the turmoil in Peter's mind.

SCENE II

Later that morning. Interior of Peter's hut, made from an upturned boat. A door leads to the path to the Borough; another door exits to the cliff behind the hut, with a way down to the sea.

29 RECITATIVE (Peter) *Go there! Here's your sea boots!* Peter rudely thrusts John into the hut, demanding that he hurry into his work clothes and threatening to tear his Sunday clothes from his body.

A plummeting melisma suggests the violent push that sends John stumbling into the room. Orchestral fragments from Interlude IV alternate with Peter's erupting orders.

30 RECITATIVE and ARIA (Peter) *They listen to money . . . In dreams I've built myself some kindlier home* He talks hurriedly to himself about his ambitions to get a great catch, make money, and marry Ellen; when he sees the boy sitting and crying, Peter tears the boy's coat off, throws Ellen's knitted jersey at him, and shoves him to the ground. Then, in a complete change of mood, Peter speaks of his dreams of happiness with Ellen and tries in his own rough way to soothe John.

Peter, unaware of the sounds of the villagers approaching his hut and with madness coming upon him, remembers the last moments of his first apprentice.

Peter's rambling mixes recitative with propulsive orchestral rhythms, his music drawing on Ex. PG-8a. His dream of a "kindlier home," however, moves into the major mode, with softer instrumentation (especially flutes and clarinets) and rising sixths and small ornamentations (see Ex. PG-11c) characteristic of much of Ellen's music. It is possibly the loveliest moment in the entire score. His memories of the death of his first apprentice are to a more disjointed accompaniment and a reduction of the lyricism of the vocal line; the distant sound of Hobson's drum turns the music into an intensifying and dreadful dirge, with a continual narrowing of the melodiousness of Peter's part, to the point of his nonrhythmic intoning on a single pitch.

31 ARIOSO and CHORUS (Peter; then Men of the Borough) *You've been talking! . . . Or are shouted in the wind.* Suddenly, Peter is aware of the procession. He accuses the boy of talking about him to Ellen ("You and that bitch were gossiping!") and shouts at him to get moving, to go down the cliff, and catch the gear Peter throws to him. John climbs through the door onto the cliff edge, holding tightly to anything he can.

Playing col legno (with the wood of the bow), the strings pick up the rhythm of Hobson's drum. Peter's phrases are disjointed, rapid short bursts. His accusations ("You sit there watching . . . And you're the cause of everything . . . Your eyes are like his . . . With an idiot's drooling gaze . . .") are inversions of "And God have mercy upon me" (Ex. PG-2a).

Just as the procession arrives at the hut and Peter hears loud knocking at the door, John loses his grip and falls off the cliff with a scream. Peter runs to the door and climbs down quickly.

The death of John and arrival of the procession are heralded by violent orchestration: a screamingly dissonant tremolo, cymbal crash, muted brass, and an enormous crescendo.

Moments later, the citizens enter through the other door, somewhat tentatively. Some look out the door to the cliff, noting the steep precipice that is there. Rector Adams and Swallow note that the hut is neat and clean and that there is no evidence of anything wrong. All leave save Balstrode, who, in looking about the place, finds John's Sunday clothes in a heap. He goes to the door that leads to the cliff and hurriedly leaves by it to climb down toward the place where Peter would usually tie up his boat.

The entry of the citizens and their dialogue is to the otherworldly sound of a repeated arching figure played by a celesta; all other instruments are silent. Swallow's embarassment and pompous posturing is mocked by a staccato counterpoint in a bassoon. When all leave but Balstrode, the sound of the celesta returns as accompaniment to a solo viola's sad inversion of the Passacaglia theme. The last sounds suggest the drama's emptiness of spirit—they are the notes of the ground bass of the Passacaglia, the music of Peter's cry for God's mercy, diminishing to quasi niente—"almost nothing."

Act III

32 INTERLUDE V (Orchestra)—The sea at night

Subtle dynamic swells, syncopations, the use of perfect intervals, and dramatic pauses suggest the expanse of a quiet sea; brief flourishes of harp and flute are evocative of the reflections of moonlight.

SCENE I

Scene as in Act I, scene i, three nights later. Moonlight. A dance is taking place in the Moot Hall. Busy passage of men between the Moot Hall and The Boar.

As dance music is heard from within, there is uninhibited flirtation among the Nieces, Swallow, and Keene.

A "barn dance" in 12/8 is set out by a "local" band of violin, two clarinets, and double bass; the main orchestra accompanies with glimmers of Interlude V. Swallow's lust is suggested by his bizarrely wide intervals; the Nieces flirt in more controlled staccati, occasionally in canon.

33 ARIOSO (Mrs. Sedley, Keene) *Mr. Keene! Mr Keene! Can you spare a moment?* Mrs. Sedley accosts Keene with the fact that neither Peter nor the boy have been seen and that the boy has disappeared. For two days, she says, she has pieced bits of information together and is convinced that Peter has murdered his apprentice. Keene, with irritation, breaks away from her and goes into the tavern.

As a slow waltz (i.e., alla Ländler[10]) begins, Mrs. Sedley calls in an urgent, repeated-note fashion, her narrative melodramatically dark with her almost spoken (senza voce—"without voice") low Gs. The music of Keene's rebuff is a fragment of the dance (Ex. 3.2a). Mrs. Sedley's chromatic rise and fall (Ex. 3.4) moans in the low strings.

34 ENSEMBLE (Rector, Men) *Come along, Doctor!* The Rector and some town burgesses leave the dance and bid goodnight.

To an animated hornpipe,[11] the men bid their farewells in a conventionally harmonized and pretty tune, the Rector chattering in a jaunty manner.

---

[10] See Chapter 3, note 5.

[11] The hornpipe is a vigorous dance characterized by short, blunt phrases and stamping rhythms.

35 ARIOSO (Mrs. Sedley) *Crime which my hobby is* . . . When they leave, Mrs. Sedley remains in front of the Moot Hall, brooding in the shadow of the boats.

Ex. 3.4 returns, the dance music reduced to a distant tremolo.

36 RECITATIVE (Ellen, Balstrode) *Is the boat in?* Mrs. Sedley overhears Ellen and Balstrode walking up from the beach, Balstrode noting that Peter's boat has landed, but Peter is nowhere to be seen. Ellen shows him the watersoaked jersey that she had found at the water's edge. It is the one she had embroidered for John.

The whispered conversation of Ellen and Balstrode is on a repeated pitch accompanied by the piercing doubling of that note by an English horn, timpani strokes, and fragments of the ground bass of the Passacaglia (Interlude IV).

37 ARIA (Ellen) *Embroidery in childhood* Ellen admits that, although she had hoped to bring some softness into John's and Peter's lives, it is clear that she and Balstrode must face a difficult truth.

A supple 5/8 meter is used for this tender, richly ornamental (Ex. PG-11b), ineffably sad aria. The steady flow of a descending scale pattern at each occurrence of "Now my embroidery affords the clue" (Ex. PG-10c) lends the music its spirit of exhausted resignation.

38 RECITATIVE and ARIOSO (Balstrode, Ellen) *We'll find him* . . . *We shall be there with him* The two agree that, despite the tragedy that has unfolded, they must never turn their backs on their friend.

They return to the repeated F-sharps, Ellen's despair now doubled by solo trombone with no other accompaniment. Their resolve not to fail Peter is given strength by intensifying rhythmic drive and deepening instrumentation (see Ex. PG-1).

39 ENSEMBLE (Mrs. Sedley, Auntie, Swallow, et al.) *Mister Swallow! Mister Swallow!* When Ellen and Balstrode have left, Mrs. Sedley breathlessly calls at the door of The Boar. Auntie tries to give her short shrift but Swallow comes to the door and, when informed that Grimes has apparently returned, charges Hobson to gather a posse and search for him.

Hurried, short phrases, obsessively repeated, suggest Mrs. Sedley's determination and intent. Ex. 3.4 returns, doubled by a solo cello and trumpet, as the dance band begins a spirited galop[12] over hushed string tremolos.

40 CHORUS *Who holds himself apart, lets his pride rise, Him who despises us we'll destroy!* The folk of the Borough gather around, becoming rapidly more and more caught up in the excitement of the moment and their passion for bringing to heel someone different from them.

An expanding, grand concertato, layering two musical elements (repeated major seconds and a rising figure, both obsessive) into an elaborately polyphonic climax. It ends with wild laughter on a waltz fragment (Ex. 3.2b).

Calling aloud the name of their quarry, they set out, hunting in different directions.

The mob's calling into the night of "Peter Grimes" capitalizes on the name's anapestic rhythm (⌣ ⌣ —), a rhythmic archetype associated with death. The fortissimo orchestra boils with figures in two keys at once (F minor, E major), a semitone apart (reminding us of the bitonality of the Prologue's duet and other passages in the opera).

---

[12] A galop is a fast dance in 2/4 time; couples form a line and move about with quick steps.

41 INTERLUDE VI (Orchestra)—Night, fog

Three muted horns are a steady presence under recalls of disjointed fragments: flute for Ex.
PG-8a, 3 violins (and, later, double bass) for PG-7c, clarinet for his argument with Ellen.
The music fades away with descending minor seconds.

SCENE II

The same, some hours later.

42 MAD SCENE (Peter) *Steady! There you are! Nearly home!* A foghorn and the calls
of the hunters can be heard from afar. Peter enters, exhausted and demented.
He babbles and cries out fragmented recalls of all that has transpired.

The mob is heard calling "Peter Grimes" from afar. Peter begins with a memory of the expe-
dition that resulted in the death of his first apprentice (the minor seconds of Ex. PG-3).
Frequent quotations from all the scenes of the opera occur in disconnected keys; among them
(in order of Peter's singing) Exs. PG-5, 5.3, PG-7a, PG-2c, PG-6b, PG-3, and PG-7c.
They move in and out of his mind while the calls of his name come from all sides. A foghorn
is suggested by a slightly off-pitch tuba, but the pitch is unrelated to either Peter or the mob.

SPOKEN DIALOGUE Ellen and Balstrode come upon him. Balstrode tells him
to sail out until he loses sight of the Moot Hall, then to sink his boat. Balstrode
helps the silent Peter push out the boat; he returns to Ellen and, taking her by
the arm, leads her away.

Peter is unaware of the arrival of Ellen and Balstrode; his last thoughts are of her (Ex. PG-9).
The last sound of the foghorn is a half-step descent. There is silence, then the last words of
Ellen and Balstrode, spoken, without music.

43 CHORUS with RECITATIVE (People; Swallow, a fisherman, Auntie) *To those*
who pass, the Borough sounds betray / The cold beginning of another day . . . In ceaseless
motion comes and goes the tide As dawn begins, people return from the hunt or
come out of their houses, setting about their usual tasks.

The music of Interlude I (Ex. PG-4a) returns as a transition to the coming of dawn and as
underpinning to the people's taking up their music of Act I, scene i (Ex. PG-6a). Words and
music are thus a metaphor for the continuance of attitudes and life, the strong, unbroken
rhythm and descending line for "Then back to sea with strong majestic sweep it rolls" sug-
gesting the great swell of the eternal ocean and the wash of its tides.

Swallow notes that a fishing boat has been reported to be sinking at sea. A
look through a telescope reveals nothing.
The people resume the business of their daily affairs.

The Characters

The Borough

The people of the Borough are gossipers and whisperers, quick to mock the
foolishness of someone else, quick to resent difference, and swayed easily this
way and that by a rumor or demagogic leadership. Their thoughts are usually expressed in short but intensely contrapuntal spurts, as in the inquest of
the Prologue and their post-worship service coming together in Act II, scene
i. They are squabblers, too, as in the tavern scene of Act I, scene ii, and the
elaborate finale of the Sunday morning scene (Act II, scene i) when fourteen
vocal parts are embroiled in intense argument.

Their indifference and their resistance to change and diversity are vested in the steady-state harmonies and even, flowing rhythms of the choral work given to them when they are at their seaside work (Act I, scene i, and Act III, scene ii) and, no less pointedly, in their relentless, one-note parroting of the litany of humility as they sing in church (Act II, scene i).

When they wrench a fragment of the Ländler dance tune of Act III, scene i, into hysterical laughter, as they set out to bring Peter to "justice" (see Examples 3.2a and b), they become a mindless mob that evokes witchhunts from Savonarola to Kristallnacht. At the end of the opera, callous about news of a boat sinking at sea and wholly forgetful of their previous night's bloodlust, they return to the music of the net-mending of Act I, scene i. They frame the opera: they are the first voices of Act I, scene i, and they return to their music of that scene as the last voices of Act III, scene ii. Like the sea, they exist.

Jim Hobson (bass)

A carter who is also the Town Crier. Hobson's first music is in the Prologue, where he is given a peremptory repeated-note fanfare summoning Grimes to appear before the inquest. In Act I, scene i, his song uses a wearisome dotted-note rhythm to create a lumpen complaint about all the work he has to do when he is asked to fetch Peter's new apprentice. This rhythmic quality applies also to Hobson's most grim function in the opera, the beating of the drum that leads the hunt for Grimes in Act II, scene i.

Swallow (bass)

The town lawyer and mayor; in the Prologue, he is also the Coroner. His music is persistently arid, vested either in repeated-note nonmelodiousness or in a brittle angularity.

Peter Grimes (tenor)

Slater and Britten departed significantly from Crabbe's portrait of the opera's main character by placing him at the center of the Borough's concerns and by deepening his humanity. Crabbe's Grimes is a drunkard, a thief, and a lazy lout; his desire for an apprentice is motivated largely by a thirst for someone to abuse. The opera's Grimes is a man of contradictions and ambiguities, of bitter resentments and aching longing, of hating the Borough and wanting to be part of it, of poetic visions and inarticulateness, of impetuously insensitive cruelty, and of remorse and tenderness. For Crabbe, Peter was "untouched by pity, unstung by remorse and uncorrected by shame." For Britten and Slater, Peter can speak (in Act II, scene ii) of "some kindlier home, warm in my heart" and of Ellen as his wife, "wrapped round in kindness like September haze."

Moreover, that the opera's Peter "can see the shoals to which the rest are blind" (Act II, scene i) represents the insight of an imaginative dreamer and wonderer, far beyond the ken or experience of the Borough's inhabitants. That his residence is not a house but a hut constructed around an overturned boat, and that he lives well away from the town rather than near its center, are obvious metaphors for his spiritual and intellectual isolation.

His being different has its voice in the ascending ninth, an interval that exceeds the range of an octave and thus seems to transcend the "normal" world of melodic thinking and to float him musically into a world of his own.[13] The interval characterizes a burst of anger and frustration, as when, in Act II, scene i, he rejects Ellen's touch (Example PG-7a), but most often it leads to a softer, translucent lyricism that represents a side of his behavior wholly unobserved or imagined by the people. In Act I, scene i, for example, it initiates his remorseful narrative to Balstrode of the death of his first apprentice (Example PG-7b); it is also the springboard for one of Peter's most poignant expressions, his soliloquy at the end of Act I, scene i, when he dreams of the peace that marriage to Ellen would bring (Example PG-7c).

EXAMPLE PG-7 PETER AND THE RISING NINTH

a) Act II, scene i: He rejects Ellen's placement of her hand on his arm.

b) Act I, scene i: He relates to Balstrode the death of William Spode, his first apprentice.

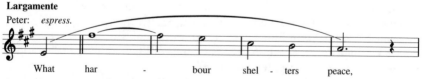

c) Act I, scene i: He dreams of a life free of turmoil.

---

[13] It is most often a minor ninth, the distance between first-line "e" and top line "f" on the treble staff. A similar effect was used by Bizet in the descending pitches of Carmen's response to Escamillo; see Example CA-6c.

Peter's isolation is portrayed in his music in other ways, too. The very first impression we receive of him is at the start of the inquest in the Prologue, when, in response to Swallow's loud and peremptory "Do you wish to give evidence," sung over crackling woodwind staccati, Peter takes the oath softly and in slower note values, with the major mode accompaniment of quiet strings. He often sings in a key different from those around him: the duet with Ellen after the inquest, for example, begins with him in the key of A-flat minor, while she answers in E major; a sudden jolt of a tritone marks the change in Act I, scene i, from the A major of the people's daily work to E-flat, when he steps on shore to tie up his boat; and the insanity of the Mad Scene moves aimlessly through one key after another, none of them connecting with the tonality of the distant calls of "Peter Grimes" from the people as they hunt for him through the fog.

The most remarkable of Peter's appearances as different and visionary is his wonderment about the universe and the fortunes of men. "Now the Great Bear and the Pleiades" (see Example 5.3), Peter's quiet musing amid the crowd in the tavern, is an enthralling moment of melodic lyricism, exquisitely refined instrumentation, and subtlety of musical form. It is a most affecting moment, a time of the expansion of the human spirit in an ambience where storms rage outside in nature and within the petty minds of those around him.

EXAMPLE PG-8 PETER'S OBSESSION WITH MATERIAL WEALTH
AS A MEANS OF GAINING RESPECT

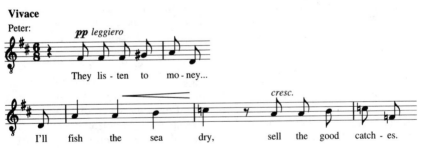

a) Act I, scene i: He is convinced that the Borough is impressed only with wealth.

b) Act I, scene i: Marriage to Ellen as a way to join the conventions of the Borough.

EXAMPLE PG-9 ACT III, SCENE II: PETER'S LAST THOUGHTS

The less attractive side of Peter is revealed through music that is quick-rhythmed, short-phrased, and repetitive, particularly when he sees money as the only way out of his troubles.

In spite of the crudeness and harshness of Peter, however, we remember him primarily in terms of his vision of the "harbour that shelters peace" (Example PG-7c), for the last thought we have from him, at the end of his insane rambling in Act III, scene ii, is his textual and melodic allusion to that moment.

Mrs. Nabob Sedley (mezzo-soprano)

The town gossip and scandal mongerer. Mrs. Sedley considers herself morally above everyone else: the tavern, she harrumphs in Act I, scene ii, "is no place for me," and her contempt for Auntie, the manager of The Boar, is expressed by a series of spurts of notes for her reiterations of "You baggage, you baggage!" (with eight repeats of "baggage" for good riddance).

In spite of a pompous sense of herself, Mrs. Sedley is addicted to laudanum, eavesdropping, and, with great relish, planting ideas of evil at work. Her poisonous urge is set in brief chromatic, snaky phrases that are given a twist of the parodic by an accompaniment of extremely low, often grotesque timbres, such as the combination of double bass and contrabassoon for her "Murder my hobby is, sweetens my thinking"[14] (see Example 3.4). She gets the mob passion flowing when, having overheard Balstrode and Ellen conferring about the significance of finding the apprentice's embroidered sweater (knitted for him by Ellen), she hints at the need for vigilante pursuit.

Ellen Orford (soprano)

Widowed teacher of the the Borough's schoolchildren, she and Peter plan to marry. Ellen represents all the gentleness that Peter's troubled soul so desperately needs, and her steadfastness and graciousness of spirit come through melodies that are solid in rhythm, diatonic, and songful.

---

[14] And later: "Murder most foul it is, eerie I find it, my skin's a prickly heat, blood cold behind it."

Particularly noticeable in her music is a descending lyric line: it characterizes her effort to soften the crowd's attitude (Example PG-10a), her urging Peter to be more tender and considerate toward his apprentice (see above, Example PG-7a), her noting how difficult it is for those who try to better the lives and spirits of others (Example PG-10b), and her sad realization of the significance of finding on the beach the sweater she had embroidered for Peter's apprentice (Example PG-10c).

The last two examples begin with a rising sixth, an interval (in either its major or minor shape) that is often associated with softness, gentleness, and tenderness,[15] and is therefore especially appropriate to her music.

EXAMPLE PG-10 ELLEN'S USE OF DESCENDING SCALAR PATTERNS

a) Act I, scene i: To the people, who support Hobson's unwillingness to provide transport for Peter's new apprentice.

b) Act II, scene i: To the people on Sunday morning, defending her support of Peter.

c) Act III, scene i: She recognizes the significance of discovering the boy's sodden sweater, washed up by the sea.

---

[15] Some examples are Sieglinde's "O süsseste Wonne!" ("Oh sweetest wonder!") in Act I of *Die Walküre;* the song of Berlioz's lonely sailor, Hylas, in Act III of *Les Troyens à Carthage;* Pamina's call just before the trial by fire and water in Act II of Mozart's *Die Zauberflöte* ("Tamino mein!"—"My Tamino"); and in the Act I duet of Verdi's *Otello,* Desdemona's first words to her loving husband, "Mio superbo guerrier!" ("My splendid warrior!").

In the grim world of the Borough, Ellen is the only person with a sense of loveliness. It appears when she comforts John, promising him that happiness will eventually come to him (Example PG-11a), and, most particularly, in the elaborate aria she sings about the embroidered sweater, which symbolizes to her her wish to "bring some silk" into the lives of others (Example PG-11b). Naturally, it also conditions how Peter thinks of her (Example PG-11c).

Ellen is not without a sense of humor and irony: when Hobson, reluctant to fetch the apprentice for Peter, grumps his plodding "I have to go

EXAMPLE PG-11 ORNAMENTAL ELEMENT IN MUSIC SUNG
BY ELLEN OR ASSOCIATED WITH HER

a) Act II, scene i: Ellen comforts John that a happier time will come in his life.

b) Act III, scene i: Having found the embroidered sweater washed up by the sea, Ellen thinks back to what beauty had once meant in her life.

EXAMPLE PG-11 (*Continued*)

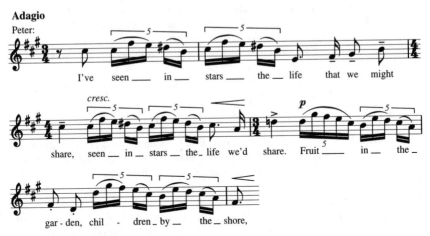

c) Act III, scene ii: Peter thinks of her love and graciousness.

from pub to pub" (Act I, scene i), Ellen remonstrates—not all that gently—by quoting his melody right back at him, mocking his rising scale of "My journey back is late at night" with "the boy needs comfort late at night."

Ellen's last appearance once more brings her warmth and compassion into the foreground. Recognizing the final measure of Peter's life, she joins with Balstrode in "we shall be there with him," her voice firming up in simple, repeated phrases of solid harmony and rhythm (see Example PG-1) as a reworking of the music of Peter's "And God have mercy upon me."

Auntie (*contralto*)

Landlady of The Boar Tavern. Auntie—her "real" name is never identified—is a realist of good humor and common sense. A jocular, angular *marcato* usually identifies her music, but her sensitivity to Ellen's despair over the borough madness and the difficulties associated with Peter are vested in an ascending scale that parallels Ellen's at the gentle interval of a sixth.

Bob Boles (*tenor*)

A fisherman and Methodist preacher whose pious mouthings are a metaphor for the hypocrisy of the Borough as a whole. He preaches whenever he can, it seems, but his seriousness scarcely masks his self-righteousness and religious quackery. In Act I, scene i, when he spouts of Peter that "this lost soul of a fisherman must be shunned by respectable society!," he becomes representative of a repulsive hypocrisy. Boles's pronouncements are given to short ornamental turns of melody and repeated-note phrases that are a parody of chant and liturgical intonation, often ending with an angry or pompous burst of melisma or angular melody.

Horace Adams (tenor)

Rector of the church. His intonations, in Act II, scene i, are taken from the litany traditions of the Anglican Church. He is a good public relations man, we suppose, because his "goodnights" to the townsfolk in Act II, scene i, form the most traditionally tuneful moment in the score, to the point of being a ditty. He is not of a very independent mind, sad to say: he joins the now-we'll-get-him procession of Act I, scene ii, with the rest of them.

The Nieces (sopranos)

The town's sluts; they live in The Boar, flirt outrageously a good deal of the time, and serve more as an atmospheric element than as furtherers of the plot. They invariably sing as a pair, sometimes in unison, sometimes in harmony, and sometimes in imitation. They are given some genuinely moving music as part of the women's quartet with Ellen and Auntie: as the procession marches up the hill toward Peter's hut at the end of Act II, scene ii, their syncopations provide a rhythmic distress that lends unhappiness to the harmonizing scales of Ellen and Auntie. The girls usually appear as flighty nitwits, but here they contribute significantly to one of the opera's many affecting moments.

Ned Keene (baritone)

The Borough's Apothecary, part quack[16] and part man of common sense who knows himself and the foolishness of people. He cynically provides Mrs. Sedley with her laudanum, noting to himself in Act II, scene i, that "thanks to flinty hearts, even quacks can make a profit," but he does not hesitate to tell off Mrs. Sedley for her nosiness. Keene is neither hero nor villain, but his music has a jaunty, brisk flavor that bespeaks a good heart and an openness of mind.

Balstrode (baritone)

A retired sea captain; his music reflects his bluff and good-natured attitude toward those around him by generally defining him in short, blunt, diatonic phrases. He is the first to help Peter beach his boat in the opening scene of Act I and the first to plant in our minds that the tragedy of Peter's life is not necessarily his fault. Balstrode is very much a person of the Borough in that he believes in leaving people alone (his song in the tavern, Act I, scene ii: "We live and let live and look, we keep our hands to ourselves"), but, when a person is in need and is his friend, he is commited to supporting him. To Balstrode falls the basic moral of the opera, set to music that is true to his character yet broader in line and more lyrically expressive than his usual utterances (Example PG-1).

---

[16] Crabbe wrote of [Abel] Keene that he "could neither reason, write, nor spell."

Dr. Crabbe

A silent part with no function in the story; his presence is Montagu Slater's gesture to the source of the plot of the opera, perhaps there in the town as an observer.

John

Peter's apprentice. A silent but important part, because it is the suspected treatment of him that transforms the minds of the people of the Borough to a mob mentality.

Bibliography

Brett, Philip, comp. *Benjamin Britten: "Peter Grimes."* Cambridge Opera Handbooks. Cambridge: Cambridge University Press, 1983.

Carpenter, Humphrey. *Benjamin Britten: A Biography.* New York: Charles Scribner's Sons, 1992.

Crabbe, George. *The Poetical Works of George Crabbe,* ed. A. J. Carlyle and R. M. Carlyle. London: Oxford University Press, 1914.

Crozier, Eric, and Nancy Evans. "After Long Pursuit: Memoirs," in *Opera Quarterly* 10, no. 3 (1994): 5–18.
   This first of a four-part set of articles reminiscing about Britten and his works includes the early shaping of Peter Grimes.

———. "After Long Pursuit: Eric's Story Continues: Fifty Years of *Peter Grimes,*" in *Opera Quarterly* 10, no. 4 (1994): 7–20.
   The second article of the Crozier-Evans reminiscences. Pp. 15–18 detail some of the hostilities within the Sadler's Wells company during preparations for the first performance of the opera.

Elliott, Graham. "The Operas of Benjamin Britten: A Spiritual View," in *Opera Quarterly* 4, no. 3 (Autumn 1986): 28–44.

Evans, Peter. *The Music of Benjamin Britten.* Minneapolis: University of Minnesota Press, 1979.

Garbutt, J. W. "Music and Motive in 'Peter Grimes,'" in *Music and Letters* 44 (October 1963): 334–42.

Howard, Patricia. *The Operas of Benjamin Britten: An Introduction.* New York: F. A. Praeger, 1969.

John, Nicholas, ed. *Peter Grimes; Gloriana—Britten.* English National Opera Guide 24. New York: Riverrun Press, 1983.

Kennedy, Michael. *Britten.* The Master Musicians. London: J. M. Dent, 1981.
   Best short biography; pp. 168–176 is an appreciation of Peter Grimes.

McDonald, Katherine. "At Home With the Sea," in *Opera News* 31, no. 16 (February 11, 1967): 24f.

Mitchell, Donald, and Hans Keller. *Benjamin Britten: A Commentary on His Works from a Group of Specialists.* Westport, CT: Greenwood Press, 1972 [1952].
   Essays on the music (Arthur Oldham), plot (Hans Keller), and musical characterization and mood (Erwin Stein).

New, Peter. *George Crabbe's Poetry*. New York: St. Martin's Press, 1976.
   See pp. 93–100 for an extended study of Crabbe's picture of Peter.
Sadler's Wells Opera. *Benjamin Britten:* Peter Grimes, ed. Eric Crozier. Sadler's Wells Opera Book 3. John Lane: The Bodley Head, 1945.
Schmidgall, Gary. "Out of the Borough," in *Opera News* 41, no. 6 (December 10, 1977): 11–15.
   Study of Crabbe's text and the adaptation by Britten and Slater.
Simon, John. "The Defiant One," in *Opera News* 59 (December 24, 1994): 8–11.
White, Eric Walter. *Benjamin Britten: His Life and Operas*. 2nd ed. Berkeley, CA: University of California Press, 1983.

A Glossary of Operatic Terms

An explanation of the pronunciation guide prefaces Part III (see p. 116).

Cross-referenced terms are printed in small capital letters. The list below includes a few terms not exclusive to the description of operatic music. It. = Italian, Fr. = French, Ger. = German, Lat. = Latin, Sp. = Spanish.

AB, AAB, ABA, ABACA, etc.   outlines of musical forms, each letter representing a distinct and recognizable melody or section and its repeats.

accidental   (1) a note not normally found in the key; (2) a flat, sharp, or natural sign placed before such a note.

accompagnato   see RECITATIVE.

affection   in BAROQUE music: (1) the prevailing mood or musical character of an instrumental or vocal passage; (2) the musical pictorialization of a specific word or phrase. See also DOCTRINE OF AFFECTIONS.

allemande [ahl-luh-MAHND; Fr., Ger.]   as written in the Act I finale of *Don Giovanni*, a duple-time, fast dance of German origin; the name, however, has also been applied to dances of other characters.

argument; argomento [ahr-goh-MAIN-toh; It.]   a summary of pre-Act I events printed in a LIBRETTO.

alto   see CONTRALTO.

aria [AH-ree-ah; It.]   song; the focus of NUMBER OPERA and the vehicle for expression of a character's sentiments or reactions to the plot of an opera. An aria is usually quite separate from the music and action that precedes and follows it and is most often in a patterned form such as ABA, a RONDO, etc., although it may be THROUGH-COMPOSED and connected musically to its surroundings. See ARIETTA, BALLATA, BRINDISI, CABALETTA, CANZONE, CANZONETTA, CAVATINA, COUPLET, DA CAPO ARIA, EXIT ARIA, MOTTO ARIA, SCENA. See also ARIOSO, BEL CANTO, CADENZA. Cf. RECITATIVE.

arietta [ah-ree-EH-tah; It., "little song"]; **ariette** [ah ree ET; Fr.]   a relatively simple, lighthearted, and tuneful ARIA. See also CANZONETTA.

arioso [ah-ree-OH-zoh; It., "song-like"]   (1) an orchestrally accompanied passage that draws on the THROUGH-COMPOSED and declamatory style of the RECITATIVE while retaining the melodious expressiveness of the ARIA; (2) a short aria.

arpeggio [ahr-PEH-gee-oh; It., "harp-like"]   the notes of a chord played in sequence rather than simultaneously.

atonality   absence of key or tonality.

augmentation   the lengthening of time values.

ballad opera   a type of COMIC OPERA (often satiric) developed in the eighteenth century in England and popular for a time in both Ireland and the British colonies in America. Its plot, dealing with ordinary people in commonplace situations, is developed through spoken dialogue; songs and ARIAS (either newly composed or adapted from other musical-textual sources) are interspersed (e.g., *The Beggar's Opera*, text by John Gay, music arranged/ compiled/composed by Johann Pepusch). See also PASTICCIO.

ballata [bahl-LAH-tah; It.]   an ARIA set to a dance-like or dance-derived rhythm.

banda [BAHN-dah; It.]   a small band or orchestra playing as part of the action.

baritone   the male voice classification between TENOR and BASS in terms of RANGE, TESSITURA, and TIMBRE. As with other voice types, baritones may be described as dramatic (Verdi's Rigoletto, Bizet's Escamillo, Gluck's Oreste, the Gershwins' Crown) and lyric (Mozart's Don Giovanni, Rossini's Figaro). See also VOICES, BASS-BARITONE.

baroque   (1) the period from the birth of opera at the end of the sixteenth century through the middle of the eighteenth century (Monteverdi, Purcell, Alessandro Scarlatti, Lully, and Handel). See also AFFECTION, BASSO CONTINUO, BEL CANTO, CASTRATO, DA CAPO ARIA, DOCTRINE OF AFFECTIONS, OPERA SERIA, RITORNELLO; (2) any style that is elaborately decorative; (3) in a pejorative sense, the overly-complicated or ornate.

bass; basse; Bass; basso [BASE; BAHSS, Fr. and Ger.; BAHSS-soh, It.]   the lowest male voice RANGE. Basses are also classified by TIMBRE and special skills of the performer, identified most typically for English-speaking audiences by Italian terminology, such as: *basso buffo*—virtuosity in diction, ability to negotiate wide leaps, breadth of range (Bartolo, *Il barbiere di Siviglia;* Leporello, *Don Giovanni*); *basso cantante* (kahn TAHN teh), also known as BASS-BARITONE—ability to sing lyrically, and with warmth of tone, especially in the higher notes of the range (Wotan, in *Die Walküre*, Mozart's Figaro); *basso profondo* (proh FAWN doh; also, if less accurately, *profundo*)—capacity for dark sonority and deep pitches (Sparafucile, *Rigoletto;* Don Basilio, *Il barbiere di Siviglia;* and Musorgsky's Boris Gudonov). The several national schools of singing offer their own terminologies. See also TIMBRE, VOICES.

bass-baritone   a powerful FACH, which is more brilliant than the *basso cantante* yet darker than the baritone (e.g., Wotan in *Die Walküre*, although identified in the score as a bass; Pizarro in *Fidelio*, identified in the score as baritone).

basso continuo [BAHSS-so kawn-TEEN-oo-oh; It.]   an accompanying pair of players, one a low sustaining instrument (such as a violoncello) giving strength of line and rhythm to the bass notes of the harmony, the other improvising chordal patterns (typically on the harpsichord) above the written bass notes with the aid of a musical shorthand called "figured bass." In BAROQUE opera, all RECITATIVO SECCO was accompanied only by the continuo players, and virtually all orchestrated pieces were reinforced by them.

bel canto [bell KAHN-toh; It., "beautiful singing"]   a term coined in the mid-nineteenth century to refer to the eighteenth- and early nineteenth-century traditions of singing that stressed skill in ornamentation; unforced, beautiful tone; evenness of sound across all REGISTERS; perfection of LEGATO and PORTAMENTO; and refinement of style and taste.

belt   a style of singing used in modern MUSICALS and MUSICAL COMEDY that involves carrying the qualities of the CHEST VOICE into higher notes.

bitonality   see TONALITY.

bravura [brah-VOO-rah; It.]   display, BRIO, virtuosity, panache.

break   a noticeable change in TIMBRE when a singer moves ineffectively from one REGISTER to another.

breeches part   see TROUSER ROLE.

brindisi [BREEN-dee-zee; It.]   an ARIA presented as a drinking song (e.g., Libiamo ne' lieti calici"—"Let's drink from the happy chalice," in Verdi's *La Traviata*, Act I).

brio [BREE-oh; It.]   spirit, zest.

buffa [BOOF-fah; It.]   comic.

cabaletta [kah-bah-LEHT-tah; It.]   in nineteenth-century Italian opera, the concluding ARIA or duet of a SCENA; usually fast and virtuosic.

cadenza [kah-DEHN-tsah; It.]   an unaccompanied virtuoso passage interpolated by a singer at the end of an ARIA or an aria section; also a frequent feature of the instrumental concerto.

Camerata dei Bardi [kah-mair-AH-tah deh-ee BAHR-dee; It., "club," "society," "academy"]   a group of intelligentsia in late-sixteenth-century Florence whose meetings were under the sponsorship of Giovanni de' Bardi. Their discussions of the interrelationships of music, poetry, and drama led to the creation of the declamatory style now known as RECITATIVE and thus the development of opera.

cantabile [kahn-TAH-bee-leh; It.]   (1) lyric, songful, and flowing; (2) in nineteenth-century Italian opera, the opening, slow ARIA of a SCENA.

cantilena [kahn tee LEH nah; It.]   the lyric aspect of a melody or of a singer's delivery.

canzone; canzonetta [kahn-ZOH-neh; kahn-tso-NEHT-tah; It.]   an ARIA occurring within the action as a song. The former applies to more extended, elaborate moments (e.g., Almaviva's florid "Se il mio nome saper" in Act I of *Il barbiere di Siviglia*), the latter to shorter, simpler songs (Don Giovanni's Act II "Deh vieni alla finestra").

castrato [kahs-TRAH-toh; It.]   the male singer turned at puberty into a soprano or alto as a result of an operation on the testicles. Also known as *evirato* or *musico*. Major female and male roles were commonly assigned to the castrati in the seventeenth and eighteenth centuries; the practice died out after that, although some parts were created for them in the early nineteenth century. The last castrato died in 1922. Handel's Giulio Cesare, Gluck's Orfeo, and Mozart's Idamante (*Idomeneo*)   and Sesto (*La clemenza di Tito*) are important castrato roles. See also PRIMO MUSICO.

cavatina [kah-vah-TEE-nah; It., "carved out"]   (1) a short ARIA, without the return of the opening section (e.g., the Countess's "Porgi, amor" in *Le nozze di Figaro*, Act II)—cf. DA CAPO ARIA; (2) in eighteenth- and nineteenth-century opera, an important character's first aria (e.g., Almaviva's "Ecco ridente in cielo" in *Il barbiere di Siviglia*, Act I); (3) a short aria using words originally meant for RECITATIVE.

chaconne   see PASSACAGLIA.

chest voice   the lowest, heaviest, and strongest REGISTER of the singing voice.

chromaticism [kro-MAT-ih-sizm]   (1) the use of pitches not normally found in the scale or key of a passage; (2) the use of a succession of half steps.

clarin; clarino [klah-REEN, klah-REE-noh; It.]   the upper range of the BAROQUE trumpet, brilliant and pealing in TIMBRE.

classical   (1) the historical period from the mid-eighteenth century through the 1820s, beginning with the emergence of OPERA BUFFA as an independent genre (e.g., Pergolesi's *La serva padrona* ; see INTERMEZZO) and some of the reform operas of Gluck, and reaching its apex with Mozart; (2) a style associated not only with simplicity, serenity, translucent instrumentation, bold wit, and a seemingly natural sentimentality and human warmth, but also the synthesis of these with their opposites, as often found in the mature operas of Mozart.

coloratura [koh-lawr-ah-TOO-rah; It., derived from Ger. *Koloratur*]   (1) vocal display, including FIORITURA, high notes, articulation of MELISMAS, and agile skips; (2) a singer who specializes in roles requiring it (e.g., Rosina in *Il barbiere di Siviglia*, Olympia in Offenbach's *Les contes d'Hoffmann*, Donizetti's Lucia di Lammermoor).

comic opera   see BALLAD OPERA, INTERMEZZO, OPERA BUFFA, OPÉRA COMIQUE, SINGSPIEL, TONADILLA, ZARZUELA.

commedia dell'arte [kawm-MEH-dee-ya dell-AHR-teh; It., "a comedy of types"]   spoken theater with interspersed songs and small vocal ensembles, the dialogue improvised by actors playing stock roles (the SOUBRETTE, the clever servant, the old man wishing to marry the soubrette, etc.) in accordance with standard plots or story elements. Simple songs, comic pratfalls and routines (the so-called *lazzi* [LAHT tsee]) were performed by the *zanni* [TSAH nee], the clowns. The plot devices, rapid development of action, ensemble acting, simple music, down-to-earth characters and situations, and vigorous spirit of the commedia troupes exerted a powerful influence on the character and emergence of OPERA BUFFA.

comprimario [kawm-pree-MAH-ree-oh; It., "with the lead"]   a role of secondary importance.

concertante [It., kawn-chair-TAHN-teh; Fr., kohn-sair-TAHNT; "concertizing"]   the participation of two or more instruments as important and contributing soloists in an ARIA or an instrumental segment (e.g., Elvira's "Mi tradì quell' alma ingrata" in *Don Giovanni*).

concertato [kawn-chair-TAH-toh; It., "concerted"]   an elaborate passage involving soloists and chorus, usually at the climax of an act or scene.

consonance   a concept of pleasing harmony; the opposite of DISSONANCE. The identification of what is dissonant or consonant is a matter of historical and musical-dramatic context rather than an absolute set of sounds that can be classified one way or the other.

continuo   see BASSO CONTINUO.

contralto   the lowest female voice, associated with richness and darkness of TIMBRE as well as power and low pitches (e.g., Cornelia in *Giulio Cesare*, Auntie in *Peter Grimes*, Erda in Wagner's *Das Rheingold*, Maria in *Porgy and Bess®*).

contredanse [KAWNH-truh-dahnss; Fr.]   any of several simple, spirited dances in duple meter associated with the good nature of simple folk.

counter-tenor;   also **contra-tenor** a tenor who often relies exclusively on FALSETTO but in other cases on an extended range upwards. In modern performance practice, roles once assigned to a CASTRATO are often taken by a counter-tenor (e.g., Gluck's Orfeo). Oberon (Britten's *A Midsummer Night's Dream*, 1960) is an important modern role for this voice classification. See Giles, *The History and Technique of the Counter-Tenor*.

couplet [koo-PLEH; Fr.]   a witty or convivial STROPHIC song used by a character to introduce him/herself (e.g., Escamillo's "Toreador Song" in *Carmen*, Act II).

da capo aria [dah KAH-poh; It., "from the top"]   an ABA aria form fundamental to OPERA SERIA.

deus ex machina [DEH-uhs eks MAH-kee-nuh]   (Lat., "a god from a machine") (1) the visually exciting arrival of a supernatural figure by mechanical stage contrivance; (2) the resolution of a plot by an unexplained or clearly illogical plot twist, the arrival of last minute rescuers, and the like.

diminution   (1) the shortening of time values; (2) ornamentations added to a melody.

dissonance   any simultaneously sounding combination of pitches that produces a tension or a need for harmonic resolution; the opposite of CONSONANCE.

diva [DEE-vah; It., "goddess"]   a popular or celebrated female singer. See also PRIMA DONNA.

divertissement [di-vair-teess-MAHN; Fr.]   (1) in French BAROQUE opera, a scene or activity of display, dance, etc., which may or may not be related to the development of the plot; (2) an entertainment presented as part of festivities required by a plot.

doctrine of affections   an aesthetic concept of the BAROQUE era (but given the name only by later historians) in which a single emotion (AFFECTION) was to be presented at a time and was to dominate an entire movement, section of a movement, or ARIA.

dotted rhythm   a sequence of alternating long and short notes, the durations of which result from the addition of a dot to a written note symbol indicating that its duration is to be lengthened by half, and the shortening of the note preceding or (more usually) following the lengthened note; a sequence of these two-note units results in a jagged, tripping, or fanfare rhythmic pattern (e.g., see HABANERA).

dramatic   a term used to describe voices that communicate emotional urgency through power and sonic "weight," as well as beauty of sound. Cf. LYRIC, SPINTO.

dramma giocoso [DRAHM-mah joh-KOH-zoh; It., "humorous drama"]   in the mid-eighteenth century, a term synonymous with OPERA BUFFA as descriptive of a comic opera, but later associated with works that mixed comic elements and characters with serious ones (e.g., *Don Giovanni*).

drame lyrique [DRAHM lee-REEK; Fr.]   a genre of French opera of the late Romantic era. While drawing on the expressive richness of GRAND OPERA, its more natural subject matter, scenery, and cast of characters derive from the OPÉRA COMIQUE.

dramma per musica [DRAHM-mah pair MOO-zee-kah; It., "a play for music"; later, "a play through music"]   in the seventeenth and eighteenth centuries, a phrase used by a LIBRETTIST to indicate that his play was intended to be set to music; eventually the term came to refer primarily to the drama as told *by* the music.

duple   rhythmic pulse in groups of two beats (or multiples of two).

dynamics   varieties and levels of loudness and the way a composer moves either abruptly or smoothly from one level to another. Abrupt changes from loud to soft (or vice-versa) are referred to as *terraced dynamics; graded dynamics* involves the use of *crescendo* and *diminuendo* and/or such distinctions as *mp* (*mezzo-piano,* moderately soft), *pp* (*pianissimo,* very soft), *mf* (*mezzo-forte,* moderately loud), and *ff* (*fortissimo,* very loud).

ensemble   (1) a musical passage or NUMBER involving two or more solo singers whose parts are to a significant extent performed simultaneously; (2) any group of performers, large or small; (3) excellence of rhythm, intonation, etc., within such a group.

ensemble finale [fee-NAH-eh; It.]   the musical-dramatic coming together of characters at the end of a scene, especially in comic opera. See also VAUDEVILLE FINALE.

entr'acte [ahn-TRAHKT; Fr., "between the acts"]   an instrumental composition played between acts or as a prelude to any act other than the first one (e.g., Acts II, III, and IV of Bizet's *Carmen*). See also INTERMEZZO (definition 1).

exit aria   in BAROQUE opera, an elaborate ARIA followed at once by the departure of the character who sang it.

fach [FAHCH; Ger., "specialty"]   type of role appropriate to a singer's voice and career.

falsetto   (It., "little falsity") the thin, high sound of a male singer's exclusive reliance on HEAD VOICE without connection to lower resonances while using only part of the length of the vocal cords, thus the basic technique for COUNTER-TENORS. Discussion of it is inconsistent and often unclear, some sources identifying it as the higher of two male REGISTERS, others as an artificial (and, for many, undesirable) vocal technique. While a number of writers suggest that, prior to the 1830s, all tenor notes near or above the top of the staff were sung in falsetto, it seems more likely that tenors used a light head voice for those pitches. Whatever the truth may have been, the operatic use of falsetto became passé when the urgency and overt passion of romantic characters and orchestrations demanded the more vigorous and stentorian sound of the chest-supported head voice for the higher notes.

fanfare   a ceremonial melodic flourish, especially (but not exclusively) in brass instruments.

figured bass   see BASSO CONTINUO.

finale [fee-NAH-leh; It.]   a climactic conclusion to an act or scene.

fioritura [fee-oh-ree-TOO-rah; It., "flourish"]   an ornamental passage or figure, either written by a composer or interpolated by a singer; an aspect of COLORATURA.

French overture   an orchestral introduction to an opera, oratorio, or ballet; its first section is slow, majestic, chordal, and marked by a dotted rhythm, the second by a fast tempo and FUGAL style. If there is a third section, it is either lively and dance-like or a reprise of the opening. Standardized by Lully in the mid-seventeenth century, the genre is a consistent feature of Handel's operas and oratorios.

fugato   see FUGUE.

fugue [FYOOG]   a procedure in which a theme (called the "subject") is first set out by a single part or voice and is then imitated by subsequent parts; each entry is accompanied by the continuation of parts that have already stated the subject. Once all the parts have entered (in a section called an "exposition"), the fugue will have "episodes" devoted to free manipulation of segments of the subject. (E.g., the FINALE to Verdi's *Falstaff,* when all involved participate in a rollicking fugue to the text "Tutto nell' mondo è burla"—"All the world's a joke" [thus it is a CONCERTATO]). A passage involving this procedure within a larger context is called a *fugato* [foo-GAH-toh].

gavotte [gah-VAWT; Fr.]   a simple, gracious, courtly dance in duple time.

Gesamtkunstwerk [guh-SAHMT-koonst-vairk; Ger., "collected art work"]   a term for Wagner's MUSIC DRAMAS, which the composer described as fusing the elements of mime (acting), visual arts (scenic construction and design), poetry, and music.

grand opera   a genre of opera involving elaborate visual effects, rich scenery, large casts, virtuoso singing, grand choral confrontations, luxuriant orchestration, and sung recitative (that there was no spoken dialogue is an important distinction; cf. OPÉRA COMIQUE), the whole at the service of a story placing impassioned lovers into historical settings and events conspiring against their happiness. This term is especially associated with opera in Paris (e.g., Rossini's *Guillaume Tell*, Giacomo Meyerbeer's *Les Huguenots* [libretto by Eugène Scribe], Saint-Saëns's *Samson et Dalila*), but it is applicable also to works by Donizetti (*Lucia di Lammermoor*) and Verdi (*La forza del destino*, *Aida*, and *Otello*), and influenced the musical and dramaturgical devices employed by Wagner (*Götterdämmerung*) and a number of twentieth-century composers (Prokofiev in *War and Peace*). See also DRAME LYRIQUE.

ground; ground bass   a repeated figure or melodic unit played in the lowest accompanying instruments. (e.g., Orfeo's appeal to Caronte, in Monteverdi's *L'Orfeo, Favola in musica*, and Dido's lament, "When I Am Laid In Earth" [Purcell's *Dido and Aeneas*]). See also OSTINATO, PASSACAGLIA

habanera [hah-bah-NAIR-ah; Sp.]   a nineteenth-century Cuban song and dance form, marked by a characteristic accompanying rhythm (♪ ♫ ♫), duple meter, a swaying melody, and a hypnotically slow tempo (e.g., the first aria of Bizet's *Carmen*).

head voice   a singer's natural upper REGISTER; lighter and brighter than the CHEST VOICE.

Heldentenor [HELT-en-ten-awr; Ger., "heroic tenor"]   a dramatic tenor FACH of special power and brilliance associated especially with the MUSIC DRAMAS of Wagner (Siegmund, Tristan) and such virile parts as Peter Grimes.

hornpipe   a vigorous dance using short phrases that usually end with a well-accented stamping rhythm.

interval   (1) the distance between two pitches, measured in scale steps (thus from A to C is described as a third—see also MODE; (2) in British opera houses, the intermission between acts.

intermedio [een-tair-MEH-dee-oh]   in the late Renaissance in Italy, a musical-dramatic-scenic interlude performed between the acts of a play and thus an important forerunner of opera. Some intermedio plots were independent of the play, others were allegorically connected to it.

intermezzo [een-tair-MEDZ-zoh; It.]   (1) an orchestral composition played within a scene or between scenes to indicate the passage of time or summarizing events through purely musical means; (2) in the seventeenth and eighteenth centuries, a short comic scene performed between the acts of an OPERA SERIA; the scenes between the several acts were in some cases themselves a consistent plot (e.g., Pergolesi's *La serva padrona*). As the mirror image of the OPERA SERIA, the intermezzo reversed everything: scenes of ordinary life and people; simple melodies; a variety of song forms (see DA

CAPO ARIA); naturally expressed sentiments rather than elaborately metaphorical ones; quick physicality rather than poses; and a special interest in the bass voice. See also BAROQUE, CLASSICAL, OPERA BUFFA.

introduzione [een-troh-doo-tsee-OH-neh; It.] the opening musical moments (chorus, RECITATIVE, etc.) of a nineteenth-century Italian opera, culminating in the opera's first ARIA. See also CAVATINA.

Italian overture an orchestral introduction to an opera, oratorio, or ballet, cultivated in Italy in the late seventeenth and much of the eighteenth century, its most consistent three-movement pattern (fast-slow-fast) standardized in the 1680s by Alessandro Scarlatti.

janissary music; also **janizary** [JAN-iss-sar-ee] the use of cymbals, triangles, drums, and piccolo to suggest the sound of Turkish army bands. The sound was used by Gluck in *Iphigénie en Tauride,* Mozart in *Die Entführung aus dem Serail,* and Beethoven in the last movement of his Symphony No. 9.

Ländler [LENT-lur; Ger.] a graceful, lighthearted dance in triple time.

lazzi see COMMEDIA DELL' ARTE.

legato [leh-GAH-toh; It., "connected"] a flowing, smooth, and unbroken vocal delivery. See also PORTAMENTO, BEL CANTO.

leggero; also **leggiero** [ledge-JEH-roh; It., "nimble," "light"] see SOPRANO.

leitmotiv, also **leitmotif** [LIGHT-moh-teef; Ger., "leading motive"] a melodic or rhythmic fragment associated with a person, object, or concept, especially in the MUSIC DRAMAS of Wagner and his successors. The leitmotiv is more than a recalled tune: its dramatic and musical effectiveness derives from musical development and manipulation, so that the related dramatic element is continually given new meanings or symbolisms.

libretto [lee-BREHT-toh; It., "little book"] the list of characters, ARGOMENTO, dialogue, and scenic instructions of an opera.

lieto fine [lee-EH-to FEE-neh; It.] happy ending; the customary conclusion for OPERA SERIA.

lyric (1) songful, tuneful; (2) descriptive of VOICES marked by clarity and sweetness of tone and flexibility in articulation. See SOPRANO, MEZZO-SOPRANO, TENOR. Cf. DRAMATIC, LEGGERO, SPINTO.

major see MODE.

masque a spectacular entertainment involving song, dance, dramatic scenes (oriented to mythological subjects), and elaborate scenery, especially popular in England in the sixteenth and seventeenth centuries; a forerunner of opera.

melisma [mell-IZ-mah] several notes set to a single syllable of text; an important feature of COLORATURA and FIORITURA.

melodrama spoken dialogue accompanied by orchestral music (e.g., dungeon scene of Beethoven's *Fidelio*). Cf. MELODRAMMA.

melodramma [MEH-loh-drahm-mah; It.]   a play created for the purpose of being set to operatic music. Cf. MELODRAMA.

messa di voce [MESS-ah dee VOH-cheh; It., "placement of the voice"]   the dynamic crescendo and diminuendo of a single pitch, regarded as an important element of BEL CANTO technique.

mezza voce [MEDZ-zah VOH-cheh; It., "half-voice"]   sung very softly. Cf. SOTTO VOCE, MESSA DI VOCE, MIDDLE VOICE.

mezzo-soprano [MEDZ-oh soh-PRAH-noh; It., "middle soprano"]   the female voice lying between the high SOPRANO and the low CONTRALTO in terms of RANGE and TIMBRE, the mezzo being richer and more comfortable in the lower pitches than the former, higher and brighter than the latter. This voice type is especially associated with TROUSER ROLES and operatic "heavies," the FACH often summarized as appropriate for witches, bitches, and boys. Among the subclassifications are lyric/coloratura (Rosina in *Il barbiere di Siviglia*), dramatic (Fricka in *Die Walküre* [but see VOICES], Herodias in *Salome*, and Amneris in Verdi's *Aida*), and lyric (Dalila in Saint-Saëns's *Samson et Dalila*, Maddalena in *Rigoletto*). Many mezzo roles are pitched high enough to be taken by SOPRANOS; among them are Cherubino *(Le nozze di Figaro)*, Carmen, and Kundry (Wagner's *Parsifal*).

middle voice   the singing REGISTER between the CHEST VOICE and HEAD VOICE, involving elements of both of them.

minor   see MODE.

minuet   a graceful, courtly dance in TRIPLE TIME, identified musically by symmetry of phrase, smoothness of melody, and a firmness of rhythm that results in part from the beginning and ending of each phrase on a strong beat of the measure (e.g., the first dance of the Act I finale of *Don Giovanni*).

mise-en-scène [meez ahn SEN; Fr.]   (1) the stage picture or design; (2) the arrangement of actors, props, etc., within a stage setting; (3) environment or mood established by a stage picture.

mode   (1) a scale pattern from which the pitches of melodies and harmonies are derived; (2) a quality of melody, harmony, and TONALITY described in relation to the scale pattern governing the pitches that are used. The most common modes employed in the familiar operatic repertory are the major (represented by the INTERVAL of two whole steps between the first note of the scale and the third note, such as from A to C-sharp), the minor (represented by the interval of one-and-a-half steps between a scale's first and third notes, such as from A to C-natural), and the chromatic (extensive use of half steps). Other important modes are the PENTATONIC and the WHOLE TONE; (3) a pattern of rhythmic stresses important in the relation of music and poetry in the Middle Ages.

motive; also **motif** [mo-TEEF]   a recognizable rhythmic or melodic fragment. See also LEITMOTIF.

motto aria   a type of solo song, especially used in BAROQUE OPERA SERIA, in which a melody or melodic fragment (the "motto") is sung unaccompanied, then played by the orchestra before the melodic flow of the aria is undertaken in earnest. See also RITORNELLO.

music drama a term consistently preferred for Wagner's operas (and other works, especially by Richard Strauss and Alban Berg) because of its elaborate philosophical ambitions and intended mutual importance of orchestral and vocal music, poetry, and scenic elements; see also GESAMTKUNSTWERK, LEITMOTIV.

musical an American-British dramatic genre using spoken dialogue as well as song and extensive choreography (often for solo songs as well as for choral passages). The musical has emerged as distinct from the MUSICAL COMEDY because of the musical's association with more insightful and continuous music and dramatic seriousness of purpose. *Porgy and Bess*®, originally thought of as a musical, is now widely recognized as an opera, and one can make a case for identifying Bernstein's musical *West Side Story* as an American opera derived from the musical.

musical comedy an American-British entertainment using song and dance (for virtually every musical moment), spoken dialogue, happy ending (see also LIETO FINE), unabashed sentiment, a plot line of love thwarted and then requited, obligatory comic diversions, and a popular style of singing.

musico [MOO-zee-koh; It.] a CASTRATO; see also PRIMO MUSICO.

number; number opera a section of an operatic score that stands by itself and is identified as such in a title and/or table of contents, where each unit is listed as part of a numerical sequence; an opera in which the score is divided in separable and self-sufficient sections, such as ARIAS and choruses.

octave (1) the INTERVAL between a pitch and its next repetition at a higher or lower level, the higher pitch vibrating at twice the frequency of the lower; (2) a sequence of eight pitch names, the last a higher or lower repetition of the first, each a step or a half step distant from its nearest neighbor. The division of the octave may also be in whole steps (thus only six pitches plus the repetition), or half steps (twelve pitches plus the repetition).

ombra scene [OHM-brah; It., "shadow"] action with supernatural personages.

opera a dramatic, staged vehicle in which music is the primary purveyor of text, character, and plot. See the genres immediately following; see also BALLAD OPERA, GRAND OPERA, INTERMEZZO, SINGSPIEL, ZARZUELA. Cf. MUSICAL, MUSICAL COMEDY.

opéra bouffe [oh-peh-rah BOOF; Fr.] farcical comic opera, using spoken dialogue.

opera buffa [OH-peh-rah BOOF-fah; It.] comic opera, derived from the plots and characters of the COMMEDIA DELL' ARTE and the musical characteristics of the INTERMEZZO (especially the BASS or BARITONE voice as clever servant-protagonist and the use of ensemble), and using RECITATIVO SECCO (and occasionally RECITATIVO ACCOMPAGNATO) for all dialogue (e.g., Rossini's *Il barbiere di Siviglia*). Cf. SINGSPIEL, OPÉRA COMIQUE, BALLAD OPERA, MUSICAL COMEDY, ZARZUELA.

opéra comique [oh-peh-rah koh-MEEK; Fr.]   originally comic opera using spoken dialogue; in the nineteenth century, an opera with any kind of plot in which the dialogue was spoken. Characters, scenery, and plots are typically drawn from the more common aspects of life (e.g., Bizet's *Carmen*). Cf. GRAND OPERA; see also DRAME LYRIQUE.

Opéra-Comique   a Parisian theater and/or its performing company devoted to the presentation of OPÉRA COMIQUE.

opera semiseria [OH-pair-ah sem-ee-SEH-ree-ah; It.]   a nineteenth-century Italian hybrid mixing overtly serious elements with sentimental and/or comic ones (e.g., Bellini's *La sonnambula*—"The Sleepwalking Woman," 1831).

opera seria [oh-pair-ah SEH-ree-ah; It., "serious opera"]   the archetypical genre of the BAROQUE era (and important also in the CLASSICAL era), the genre is characterized by plots and characters drawn primarily from classical mythology, history, or literature; the domination of the DA CAPO ARIA and its florid musical expression (see COLORATURA); the vocal principles of BEL CANTO; and the aesthetic principles of the DOCTRINE OF AFFECTIONS. See also BASSO CONTINUO, CASTRATO, EXIT ARIA, MOTTO ARIA, RECITATIVO SECCO. Cf. INTERMEZZO, OPERA BUFFA.

operetta [It., "little opera"]   lighthearted drama, important in its own right and a progenitor of the MUSICAL COMEDY. Traits: spoken dialogue; picturesqueness of setting; romanticized and sentimentalized love interest; comedy; dance; solo and ensemble music of varying degrees of complexity and form (e.g., Johann Strauss's *Die Fledermaus*—"The Bat," 1874). See also MUSICAL COMEDY; cf. GRAND OPERA.

ostinato [ohss-stee-NAH-toh; It., "obstinate"]   a steadily repeated melodic figure, especially in the bass line or an accompanying part.

overture   any orchestral introduction to a staged drama. An overture is generally considered to be longer and musically more complex than a PRELUDE, but composers have not used the term with refined consistency. (Wagner's "prelude" to *Die Meistersinger von Nürnberg,* for example, is one of the grandest and most expansive works in the literature.) See also FRENCH OVERTURE, ITALIAN OVERTURE.

parlando [pahr-LAHN-doh; It., "speaking"]   evoking the flow of natural speech.

passacaglia [pahss-ah-KAHL-yah; It.] also **chaconne** [shah-KAWN]   a structure presenting continually changing music or variations above a GROUND BASS or a repeated figure heard most often in the lower instruments (e.g., fourth Sea Interlude of Britten's *Peter Grimes*).

pasticcio [pahss-TEECH-ee-oh] (It., "mess," "muddle"; also a cake or pie involving a variety of ingredients)   a play with incidental NUMBERS in which the music is cobbled from a variety of sources and composers.

patter song   a comic solo characterized by syllabic settings of a profusion of words, the whole to be delivered in as rapid a fashion as possible. This genre of ARIA is a frequent feature of the music of the BASSO BUFFO and is a hallmark of the OPERETTAS of Gilbert and Sullivan.

pentatonic   a MODE in which the OCTAVE is divided into five (not necessarily evenly spaced) scale steps (e.g., the black keys of the piano keyboard). Pentatonic and WHOLE-TONE scale patterns are especially evocative of Oriental and Pacific cultures.

Phrygian cadence [FRIDGE-ee-an]   the final descending notes of a medieval MODE (found on the piano by playing the white keys within an OCTAVE defined by E), identified by the interval of a half step between the first and second notes of its rising form (and consequently the last two steps in its descending form). The descent of a half step down to the final note is often a musical symbol for death.

polytonality   see TONALITY.

portamento [pawr-tah-MEHN-toh; It., "carrying"]   (1) the steady support of the voice by a healthy reservoir of breath; (2) a smooth vocal transition from one pitch to another that results in a seamless LEGATO. Both concepts are important aspects of BEL CANTO.

prelude [PREL-lood; Fr.]   an orchestral introduction to an act or scene, generally thought of as short and establishing one or two moods; but see OVERTURE. See also ENTR'ACTE.

prima donna [PREE-mah DOHN-nah; It., "first lady"]   (1) a principal female singer (almost always a soprano) of a company or dramatis personae; (2) any female star singer; (3) a person of unbearable ego and temperament, the term derived from the pride of place often exhibited and insisted upon by a company's star soprano. See also DIVA.

primo musico [PREE-moh MOO-zee-koh; It.]   (1) the leading CASTRATO of an opera company or cast of an opera; (2) in the early nineteenth century, a female singer performing a TROUSER ROLE. See also MUSICO.

primo uomo [PREE-moh WOH-moh; It.]   the leading male singer of a company or cast; in the seventeenth and eighteenth centuries, the term was synonymous with PRIMO MUSICO (definition 1); in the nineteenth century, it referred to the leading tenor, who was not infrequently a male version of the PRIMA DONNA (definition 3).

range   (1) the highest and lowest notes called for in a NUMBER or a role; (2) the highest and lowest notes of practical use in a singer's voice; (3) a broadly if imprecisely used term offering a distinction among the six basic types of singing voice—SOPRANO, MEZZO-SOPRANO, CONTRALTO, TENOR, BARITONE, and BASS.

recitative [ress-ih-tah-TEEV; also retch-ih-tah-TEEV]; **recitativo** [retch ee tah TEEV oh; It.]   sung declamation used for dialogue and the unfolding of a plot and therefore in a polar relationship with ARIA and ENSEMBLE. Only one voice sings at a time, the accompaniment is prevailingly chordal, and tempos and rhythms are designed to fit the natural accents and inflections of the words. Each note is given but one syllable, the THROUGH-COMPOSED melody arranged so as to provide for the greatest clarity of text. The rapid style of recitative that is accompanied only by a keyboard instrument or BASSO CONTINUO is called SECCO [SEK koh; It., "dry"]; orchestrally accompanied recitative, more songful and more varied in tempo than the secco, is known as ACCOMPAGNATO [ah-kawm-pah-NYAH-toh; It., "accompanied"] or STROMENTATO [stroh-mehn-TAH-toh; It., "instrumented"].

register   (1) a division of the sound and concept-sensation of placement of the singing voice. Authorities are not consistent in their analysis of these, most dividing both male and female voices into CHEST VOICE, MIDDLE VOICE, and HEAD VOICE, while some reserve these nomenclatures for women and divide the male sound into heavy and light "mechanisms" with a middle register mixing the two. Others consider the male voice in terms of CHEST, MIDDLE, and FALSETTO, some have divided the voice into seven registers, and some claim there are no such divisions. All writers on the voice, however, stress the importance of a seamless movement from one register to another and insist that the most viable singing for sopranos, tenors, and basses comes in the middle and upper parts of the voice, where head and chest are appropriately blended in accordance with the demands of pitch level and emotional-musical communication. See R. Miller, *English, German, and Italian Techniques of Singing,* Chapters X and XI, for a discussion of these different points of view. See CHEST VOICE, HEAD VOICE, MIDDLE VOICE, FALSETTO, BREAK. See also BEL CANTO; (2) a portion of the range of pitches available on an instrument, often identifiable by TIMBRE as well as pitch level.

reform opera   a work by Gluck representing the mid-eighteenth-century values of simplicity (plot, characters, music), naturalness of emotional expression, and consistency of style (*Orfeo ed Euridice, Alceste, Paride ed Elena, Iphigénie en Aulide, Iphigénie en Tauride,* and *Écho et Narcisse*).

rescue opera   a genre of opera especially popular in the decades following the French Revolution, when tales of sacrifice for love and/or noble ideals, unmitigated villainy and heroism, unjust imprisonment, natural catastrophe, and last-minute salvation (see also DEUS EX MACHINA) resulted in plots and librettos calling for extremes of passion and action (e.g., Beethoven's *Fidelio*).

ritornello [ree-tawr-NEL-loh; It., "a little return"]   (1) a melody that returns in whole or in part within a single NUMBER (cf. LEITMOTIV); (2) the principal melody of a DA CAPO ARIA.

romance [ro-MAHNSS; Fr.], **romanza** [roh-MAHN-tsah; It.], **romanze** [ro-MAHN-zuh; Ger.]   a relatively simple ARIA (often in STROPHIC form), its text dealing with love or sentimental soliloquizing.

romantic   (1) (when capitalized) the era embracing the diversity of the nineteenth century and, in some periodizations, continuations of nineteenth-century aesthetics during the first half of the twentieth century (under the rubrics of Expressionism and neo-Romanticism); (2) overtly emotional, richly expressive, warmly or picturesquely colored.

rondo   a form alternating a principal melody with contrasting episodes.

scena [SHEH-nah; It., "scene"]   (1) the stage; (2) the scene or location of a segment of the action; (3) in nineteenth-century Italian opera, a sequence of differing styles (such as ARIA, RECITATIVE, CABALETTA-with-chorus) given over to a particular dramatic segment of a plot.

scherzando [skair-TSAHN-doh; It., "joking"]   lighthearted, jocular.

secco   see RECITATIVE.

siciliano   a simple, graceful, relatively slow dance type in 6/8 or 12/8, often used in BAROQUE opera for passages of melancholy or tenderness, or for scenes of a pastoral nature.

sinfonia [seen-foh-NEE-ah; It., "symphony"]   in the BAROQUE era, an independent composition for orchestra, including interludes, OVERTURES, etc.

Singspiel [ZEENG-shpeel; Ger., "sung-play," "sing-play," "song-play"]   a type of German opera using spoken dialogue (rather than RECITATIVE), ARIAS, choruses, etc. Originally comic and sentimental in nature (e.g., Mozart's *Die Entführung aus dem Serail*), the term came to include more serious fare (e.g., *Fidelio*, which begins with a scene of homeyness and comedy, and Weber's *Der Freischütz*—"The Free Marksman"). Cf. OPÉRA COMIQUE, OPERA BUFFA.

singing   see RANGE, REGISTER, TESSITURA, VOICES, BEL CANTO.

sonata form   a musical structure in which a theme(s) is set out in an exposition, subjected to fragmentation, manipulation, and change of key in a development, then freely recalled in a recapitulation. The form is often preceded by a slow introduction and concluded with a climactic passage called a "coda." Although associated especially with instrumental music, Mozart and others made extensive use of it in ARIA forms as well.

soprano   the highest classification of the singing voice. Sopranos may also be classified by the TIMBRE and dramatic "weight" of their sound, hence the distinctions among the "dramatic" soprano (associated with power and weight: Anna in *Don Giovanni*, Leonore in *Fidelio*), the SPINTO (urgency and incisiveness: Puccini's Butterfly and Manon), the LYRIC (clarity of tone and flexibility, as with Marzelline in *Fidelio* and Micaëla in *Carmen;* but often called to sing with dramatic stress: Cleopatra in *Giulio Cesare;* Iphigénie; Gilda in *Rigoletto;* Bess), and the LEGGERO (nimbleness and lightness; also called "lyric coloratura": Norina, in Donizetti's *Don Pasquale*). A special terminology, "heroic," is applied to such dramatic soprano roles as Brünnhilde and Salome, where the enormity of orchestration demands special strength and projection. Descriptive terms in other languages reflect national schools of singing. See also TIMBRE, VOICES.

sotto voce [SAWT-toh VOH-che; It., "under the voice"]   muttered, extremely soft.

soubrette [soo-BRET; Fr.]   a soprano role or FACH calling for flirtatiousness, cleverness, and lyric singing.

spinto [SPEEN-toh; It., "pushed"]   a FACH or voice type characterized by energy and dramatic cogency; the term is applied to SOPRANO and TENOR voices. Cf. LYRIC, LEGGERO, DRAMATIC.

Sprechgesang; also sprechstimme [SPRECH-guh-zang; SPRECH-shtim-muh; Ger., "speech-song," "speaking voice"]   a twentieth-century technique of declamation for which pitches are indicated on the staff but are to be delivered in a manner closer to natural speech than RECITATIVE (e.g., Marie's Bible-reading scene in Berg's *Wozzeck*, Act III, scene i).

Stabreim [SHTAHP-rime; Ger.]   the type of ancient Teutonic alliterative poetry used by Wagner for his *Der Ring des Nibelungen*.

stretta [STREHT-tah; It., "squeeze," "pressure"]   acceleration of tempo at the end of a NUMBER, scene, or act for the purpose of climactic effect.

stromentato   see RECITATIVE.

strophe [STRO-fee]   a verse, either textual or musical. The Duke's BALLATA in *Rigoletto*, Act I, is in two strophes. So is his "La donna è mobile," in Act III.

syncopation   (1) the accenting of a note that normally would be unaccented in the metric-rhythmic scheme of a measure; (2) the shifting of accent from the expected strong beat to a weak beat.

tableau [TAB-lo]   (1) a scene or division of an act; (2) a posed moment when all action is halted for the purpose of presenting an effective stage picture.

tempo [TEM-poh; It.]   speed.

tempo d'attacco [TEM-poh dah TAHK-koh; It., "attack speed"]   in nineteenth-century Italian opera, the fast opening section of a multisection ENSEMBLE.

tempo di mezzo [TEM-poh dee MEDZ-oh; It.]   in nineteenth-century Italian opera, a freely composed, transitional section of a SCENA.

tenor   the standard designation for the highest male voice (but see also CASTRATO, COUNTER-TENOR). As with SOPRANOS, tenors may be classifed as DRAMATIC (Florestan in *Fidelio*), SPINTO (Rodolfo in Puccini's *La bohème*, Wagner's Lohengrin), and LYRIC (the Duke in *Rigoletto*, Pylade in *Iphigénie en Tauride*); the *tenore di grazia* (Almaviva in *Il barbiere di Siviglia;* Sportin' Life in *Porgy and Bess*®) equating to the *soprano leggero*, although more associated with sweetness of sound than his singing sister. Within the dramatic FACH, singers speak of the *tenore di forza* or *tenore robusto* to describe roles (Wagner's Siegfried, Herodes in *Salome*, Verdi's Radames, in *Aïda*) requiring powerful voices that are particularly ringing and brilliant and slightly higher in TESSITURA than the HELDENTENOR (Siegmund, Peter Grimes). There are a number of other classifications of the tenor voice that are derived from national schools of singing. See also HELDENTENOR, TIMBRE, VOICES.

tessitura [tess-ee-TOO-rah; It., "texture"]   the general placement on the staff of a melody or role (rather than the highest or lowest note called for; cf. RANGE).

through-composed   a term descriptive of music that proceeds freely, without following any standard pattern of repeats or formal units (e.g., Don José's "Flower Song" in *Carmen*, Act II).

timbre [TANHM-bruh; Fr.] the quality or color of an instrumental or vocal sound.

tonadilla [toe-na-DEEL-yah; Sp.] a satirical or political one-act comic opera in popular style and, in the tradition of other genres of COMIC OPERA, focusing on the people and situations of daily life; important in Spain in the eighteenth century as a kind of INTERMEZZO (definition 2).

tonality key; the tendency of a composition or passage to end on a specific pitch. The use of two or more keys at once is called "polytonality" or "bitonality." Cf. ATONALITY.

Tonsprache [TONE-sprach-chuh; Ger., "musical speech"] Wagner's concept of the word-music relationship in which the sound of a word suggested its connotive associations.

travesti [Fr., "disguised"] (1) a TROUSER ROLE; (2) a part requiring a singer to wear the costume of the opposite sex (e.g., the witch in Humperdinck's *Hänsel und Gretel*).

tremolo [TREM-oh-loh; It., "trembling"] the rapid repetition of a single pitch on a stringed instrument or the rapid alternation of two or more pitches (such as the notes of a CHORD or pitches an OCTAVE apart).

trill a melodic ornament involving the alternation of two adjacent notes in the same key, the note of the melody in relatively rapid exchange with the note above it.

triple a rhythmic pulsation in three (or multiples of three).

tritone the INTERVAL of an augmented fourth/diminished fifth, i.e, any two notes separated by three whole steps (such as A to D-sharp/E-flat or F to B-natural/C-flat). In traditonal harmony, the tritone is regarded as the most DISSONANT of intervals and is thus an archetypical symbol for betrayal, misfortune, and the like.

trouser role a male role sung by a female; while the practice is most often thought of as a way of distinguishing the parts of adolescent boys (e.g., the Page in *Salome;* Octavian in R. Strauss's *Der Rosenkavalier*) from the sound of adult characters, a number of important heroic roles were created for women's voices in the continuance of the CASTRATO tradition and the concept of heroes as lovers and men of grace (e.g., Bellini's Romeo, a MEZZO-SOPRANO in *I Capuleti e i Montecchi;* the CONTRALTO title role of Rossini's *Tancredi*). See also TRAVESTI.

tutti [TOOT-tee; It., "all"] the simultaneous playing of all the instruments and/or singers.

vaudeville finale [VOHD-veel fee-NAHL; Fr., although the latter word is often pronounced in the Italian way, fee-NAHL-leh] a STROPHIC finale with refrain, each stanza taken by a solo singer, the others (chorus and/or soloists) joining in with a choral response at the end of each verse.

vamp a repeated rhythmic pattern used as an introduction to a song or ARIA, usually one that is convivial or comic in nature (e.g., Sportin' Life's "It ain't necessarily so" in *Porgy and Bess*®).

verismo [vair-EESS-moh; It., "truth"]   a late-nineteenth-century Italian approach to opera that applied seriousness and tragedy to the events and characters of ordinary life, the plot and music presenting moments of extreme passion and violent action (e.g., Leoncavallo's *Pagliacci*, Mascagni's *Cavalleria rusticana*)

vibrato [vee-BRAH-toh; It.]   a variation of a pitch to include microtones above and below so as to lend richness of TIMBRE to a sound; an excessively wide or slow vibrato is called a "wobble"; one that is too fast or tight is called a "flutter"; a voice without vibrato is usually described (pejoratively) as "straight," "flutey," or "white."

voices   The categories of the voices are fundamentally six, arranged from high to low—SOPRANO, MEZZO-SOPRANO, CONTRALTO, TENOR, BARITONE, and BASS. Each, however, has subcategories named in accordance with TIMBRE, and the qualities associated with a particular type of voice are by no means exclusive to it. The assignment of roles is often a matter of the availability and skills of individual singers, changes in audience taste, and dramatic necessity. The role of Fricka in *Die Walküre*, for example, is identified in the score as soprano but is usually taken by a strong mezzo-soprano to avoid aural distraction from the music of Brünnhilde. The role of Carmen is often associated with the supposedly sultry qualities of the mezzo-soprano but is frequently taken by a lyric soprano. And Don Giovanni, composed with a baritone in mind, is more often than not taken by a basso cantante. The nature of singing itself is a matter of imprecise understanding and vocabulary, since the "instrument" is an inherent part of the psyche as well as hidden within the body and therefore cannot be comfortably subjected to scientific analysis. See R. Miller's *English, French, German, and Italian Techniques of Singing*, Chapters XIII–XVI, for a discussion of vocal categories vis-à-vis national schools and historical perceptions.

Vorspiel [FORE-shpeel; Ger.]   the German word for PRELUDE.

Wagner tuba   a tenor or bass brass instrument, pitched between the French horns and the trombones, developed at Wagner's suggestion for use in the operas of the *Ring* (especially for the LEITMOTIV associated with Hunding).

whole tone   the division of the OCTAVE into whole steps (such as C, D, E, F-sharp, G-sharp, A-sharp, C) and the use of CHORDS using the notes of this scale.

zanni   see COMMEDIA DELL' ARTE.

zarzuela [tsahr-TSWEH-lah; Sp.]   Spanish comic opera, usually in a satiric vein and in one act, alternating improvised spoken dialogue with singing and dancing.

Works Consulted, Recommended

The sources cited below are in addition to those noted in the chapters dealing with individual operas. When the content of a source is more generally applicable, I have listed it here as well. The Bibliography is restricted to books and articles in English.

In the Key to the Bibliography, I have marked with asterisks some "first choices" for the operagoer. Sources listed under a particular heading may, of course, be also relevant to another. Not all sources consulted are included in the Key.

Key to the Bibliography

Aesthetics

Dean, Drummond, Kerman, *Kivey, *Strunk, Sutcliffe, Weiss/Taruskin, Weisstein
See also *Appreciation, Drama, Libretto, Symbolism*

Appreciation

Lee, *Knapp, Lindenberger, Littlejohn, Pauly (*Music and the Theater*)

Drama

Dahlhaus, R. Freeman, Kerman, P. Robinson, Stein, Wagner
See also *Appreciation, Libretto*

History of Opera; Performance Practice

General: Donington (*Opera*), Grout, *Headington, Kimbell (*Italian Opera*), *S. Sadie, MacClintock, *Oxford History
Baroque: Donington ("Rise . . ."), R. Freeman, Fubini, Palisca, M. Robinson, Roselli, J. Sadie
Classical: Barzun, Fubini, Pauly, Rosen
Romantic: Barzun, Bloom, Dent, Donakowski, Fulcher, Maguire, Pendle, Tomlinson

Twentieth Century: Barzun, Botstein, Martin, Mellers, Mordden, Nichols, Sutcliffe
See also *Singing*

Libretto, Literary Backgrounds

Conrad, Dean, Schmidgall, P. Smith, Weiss, Winn

Musical, Musical Comedy

Boardman, Gänzl, C. Smith

Plots, Studies of Individual Operas

Curtis, Dean, *Jacobs/Sadie, *Kobbé, Lee, Locke, P. Robinson, *Viking

Reference

New Grove (*Dictionary of Opera* is multivolume and the most complete), New Harvard, *Oxford, *Viking

Singing

Bergeron, Burney, *Celletti, Ellison, Giles, Heriot, Keyser, Maguire, Mason, *R. Miller, Newton, *Pleasants, Reid, Rogers, *Roselli, *Scott, Steane, Tosi

Symbolism

Adorno, *Campbell, Chailley, *Cone, Conrad, Fenlon/Miller, Ferguson, Fulcher, Groos, *Kivey, Langer, Lindenberger, Maguire, Merriam, Nattiez, *Noske

Bibliography

Adorno, Theodor W. "Music, Language, and Composition," in *The Musical Quarterly* 77, no. 3 (Fall 1993): 401–414.

Barsham, Eve, "The Orpheus Myth in Operatic History," in *C. W. von Gluck: Orfeo*, ed. Patricia Howard. Cambridge Opera Handbooks. London and New York: Cambridge University Press, 1981, pp. 1–9.

Barzun, Jacques. *Classic, Romantic and Modern.* 2nd ed. New York: Little, Brown and Co., 1961.

Bergeron, Katherine. "The Castrato as History," in *Cambridge Opera Journal* 8, no. 2 (July 1996): 167–184.

Bloom, Peter, ed. *Music in Paris in the 1830s.* Stuyvesant, NY: Pendragon Press, 1987.

Boardman, Gerald. *American Musical Theatre: A Chronicle.* 2nd ed. New York: Oxford University Press, 1992.

Botstein, Leon. "The Opera Revival," in *The Musical Quarterly* 78, no. 1 (Spring 1994): 1–9.

Burney, Charles. *Music, Men, and Manners in France and Italy, 1770*, ed. H. Edmund Poole. London: Eulenburg, 1974.

Campbell, Joseph, assisted by M. J. Abadie. *The Mythic Image.* Princeton: Princeton University Press, 1974.

———. *Transformations of Myth Through Time.* New York: Perennial Library, 1990.

Celletti, Rodolfo. *A History of Bel Canto,* trans. Frederick Fuller. Oxford: Clarendon Press, 1991.

———. "The Poetics of the Marvelous," in *Opera News* 59, no. 1 (July 1994): 10–14.

Chailley, Jacques. *The Magic Flute Unveiled: Esoteric Symbolism in Mozart's Masonic Opera; An Interpretation of the Libretto and the Music.* Rochester, VT: Inner Traditions International, 1992 [1971].

Cone, Edward T. "The World of Opera and Its Inhabitants," in *Music: A View from Delft,* ed. Robert P. Morgan. Chicago: University of Chicago, 1989, pp. 125–138.

Conrad, Peter. *A Song of Love and Death: The Meaning of Opera.* New York: Poseidon Press, 1987.

Curtis, Alan. "'La Poppea Impasticciata' or Who Wrote the Music to 'L'incoronazione' (1643)," in *Journal of the American Musicological Society* XLII (Spring 1989): 23–54.

Dahlhaus, Carl. *Realism in Nineteenth-Century Music,* trans. Mary Whittall. Cambridge: Cambridge University Press, 1985.

Dean, Winton. *Essays on Opera.* Oxford: Clarendon Press, 1990.

Dent, Edward J. *The Rise of the Romantic Opera,* ed. Winton Dean. The Messenger Lectures at Cornell University, 1937–38. Cambridge: Cambridge University Press, 1976.

Donakowski, Conrad L. *A Muse for the Masses: Ritual and Music in an Age of Democratic Revolution 1770–1870.* Chicago: University of Chicago Press, 1972.

Donington, Robert. *The Opera.* Harbrace History of Musical Forms. New York, et al. Harcourt Brace Jovanovich, 1978.

———. *The Rise of Opera.* London, New York: Faber and Faber, 1981.

———. *Wagner's 'Ring' and Its Symbols: The Music and the Myth.* London: Faber and Faber, 1963.

Drummond, John D. *Opera in Perspective.* Minneapolis: University of Minnesota Press, 1980.

Einstein, Alfred. *Gluck,* trans. Eric Blom. The Master Musicians. New York: E. P. Dutton, 1936.

Ellison, Cori. "Cafés and Catechisms," in *Opera News* 58, no. 12 (March 5, 1994): 23–25, 53.

———. "Breaking the Sound Barrier: How Women Finally Made Their Way to the Opera Stage," in *Opera News* 57, no. 1 (July 1992): 14.

Fenlon, Iain, and Peter Miller. "Public Vice, Private Virtue," in *The Operas of Monteverdi.* English National Opera Guide 45, ed. Nicholas John. London: Calder; New York: Riverrun Press, 1992, pp. 129–137.
Study of musical symbolism in Monteverdi's L'incoronazione di Poppea.

Ferguson, Donald N. *Music As Metaphor: The Elements of Expression.* Westport, CT: Greenwood Press, 1973 [1960].

Freeman, John. "Viewpoint," in *Opera News* 53, no. 10 (February 4, 1989): 4.

Freeman, Robert. *Opera Without Drama: Currents of Change in Italian Opera 1675–1725.* Ann Arbor, MI: UMI Research Press, 1981.

Fubini, Enrico. *Music and Culture in Eighteenth-Century Europe: A Source Book,* trans. and ed. Bonnie J. Blackburn. Chicago: University of Chicago Press, 1994.

Fulcher, Jane. *The Nation's Image: French Grand Opera as Politics and Politicized Art.* Cambridge: Cambridge University Press, 1987.

Gänzl, Kurt. *The Encyclopedia of the Musical Theatre.* New York: Schirmer Books, 1994. 2 volumes.

Giles, Peter. *The History and Technique of the Counter-tenor.* Aldershot, England: Scolar Press, 1994.
A superb study of voice production, with related information on voice types, registers, history of singing, etc.

Groos, Arthur, and Roger Parker. *Reading Opera.* Princeton: Princeton University Press, 1988.

Grout, Donald Jay, with Hermine Weigel Williams. *A Short History of Opera.* 3rd ed. New York: Columbia University Press, 1988.

Headington, Christopher, Ray Westerbrook, and Terry Barfoot. *Opera: A History.* New York: St. Martin's Press, 1987.

Heriot, Angus. *The Castrati in Opera.* New York: Da Capo Press, 1974 [1956].

Hitchcock, H. Wiley. *Music in the United States: A Historical Introduction,* 3rd ed. Prentice-Hall History of Music Series. Englewood Cliffs, NJ: Prentice-Hall, 1988.

Howard, Patricia. *Gluck and the Birth of Modern Opera.* New York: St. Martin's Press, 1963.

Hughes, [John]. *Lives of the English Poets.* Oxford English Classics, Dr. Johnson's Works, vol. 7. New York: AMS Press, 1970 [1825].

Jacobs, Arthur, and Stanley Sadie. *The Limelight Book of Opera.* Rev., enl. edition of *Great Operas in Synopsis.* New York: Limelight Editions, 1992.
Synopses of eighty-seven operas. Also an excellent bibliography oriented to composers and works about them.

Jellinek, George. *History Through the Opera Glass: From the Rise of Caesar Through the Fall of Napoleon.* White Plains, NY: Pro/Am Music Resources, 1994.

Jennings, Gary. "Opera's First Step Was a Stumble," in *Opera News* 31, no. 16 (February 11, 1967): 6f.

Kennicott, Philip. "Poised in Time," in *Opera News* 57, no. 11 (February 13, 1993): 16–18.

Kerman, Joseph. *Opera As Drama.* New, rev. ed. Berkeley, CA: University of California Press, 1988.

Keyser, Dorothy. "Cross-Sexual Casting in Baroque Opera," in *Opera Quarterly* 5, no. 4 (Winter 1987–88): 46–57.

Kimbell, David R. B. *Italian Opera.* National Traditions of Opera. Cambridge: Cambridge University Press, 1991.

Kingman, Daniel. *American Music: A Panaroma.* New York: Schirmer Books, 1979.

Kivey, Peter. *Osmin's Rage: Philosophical Reflections on Opera, Drama, and Text.* Princeton: Princeton University Press, 1988.

———. *Sound and Semblance: Reflections on Musical Representation.* Princeton: Princeton University Press, 1984.

———. *The Fine Art of Repetition: Essays in the Philosophy of Music.* Cambridge: Cambridge University Press, 1993.
See especially pp. 137–159, "Opera Talk: A Philosophical Phantasie," and pp. 160–177, "How Did Mozart Do It?"

Knapp, J. Merrill. *The Magic of Opera.* New York: Da Capo Press, 1984 [1972].

Kobbé, Gustav. *The Definitive Kobbé's Opera Book.* Ed., rev., and updated by the Earl of Harewood. New York: G. P. Putnam's Sons, 1987.

Lang, Paul Henry. "The Birth of Comedy," in *Opera News* 27, no. 15 (February 16, 1963): 8–11.

Langer, Suzanne K. *Feeling and Form: A Theory of Art Developed from "Philosophy in a New Key."* New York: Charles Scribner's Sons, 1953.

Lee, M. Owen. *First Intermissions: Twenty-One Great Operas Explored, Explained, and Brought to Life from the Met.* New York: Oxford University Press, 1995.

Levenson, Thomas. *Measure for Measure—A Musical History of Science.* New York: Simon and Schuster, 1994.

Lindenberger, Herbert. *Opera—The Extravagant Art.* Ithaca, NY: Cornell University Press, 1984.
See especially Chapters 2 and 3, "Opera as Representations," and thoughts on the roles of words and music.

Littlejohn, David. *The Ultimate Art—Essays Around and About Opera.* Berkeley, CA: University of California, 1992.

Locke, Ralph. "Constructing the Oriental 'Other': Saint-Saëns's *Samson et Dalila,*" in *Cambridge Opera Journal* 3, no. 3 (November 1991): 261–302.

———. "Reflections on Orientalism in Opera and Musical Theater," in *Opera Quarterly* 10, no. 1 (August 1993): 48–64.

MacClintock, Carol. *Readings in the History of Music in Performance.* Bloomington, IN: Indiana University Press, 1979.

Maguire, Simon. *Vincenzo Bellini and the Aesthetics of Early Nineteenth-Century Opera.* New York: Garland Publishing Co., 1989.
Includes survey of bel canto tradition.

Mann, William. *Richard Strauss: A Critical Study of the Operas.* New York: Oxford University Press, 1966 [1964].

Martin, Frank. *Aspects of Verdi.* New York: Limelight Editions, 1993.

———. *The Opera Companion to Twentieth Century Opera.* New York: Dodd, Mead, 1979.

Mason, David. "Voice," in *New Oxford Companion to Music,* ed. Denis Arnold. Oxford: Oxford University Press, 1983, vol. 2, 1939–1946.

Mellers, Wilfrid. *Francis Poulenc.* Oxford Studies of Composers. New York: Oxford University Press, 1993.

Merriam, Alan P. *The Anthropology of Music.* Chicago: Northwestern University Press, 1964.

Miller, Richard. *English, French, German and Italian Techniques of Singing: A Study in National Tonal Preferences and How They Relate to Functional Efficiency.* Metuchen, NJ: Scarecrow Press, 1977.

Millington, Barry. *Wagner,* rev. ed. Princeton: Princeton University Press, 1992.

Mordden, Ethan. *Opera in the Twentieth Century: Sacred, Profane, Godot.* New York: Oxford University Press, 1978.

Morford, Mark P. O., and Robert J. Lenardon. *Classical Mythology,* 5th ed. White Plains, NY: Longman Publishers, 1995.

Nattiez, Jean-Jacques. *Music and Discourse: Toward a Semiology of Music,* trans. Carolyn Abbate. Princeton: Princeton University Press, 1990.

———. *Wagner Androgyne: A Study in Interpretation,* trans. Stuart Spencer. Princeton: Princeton University Press, 1993.

New Grove Book of Operas, ed. Stanley Sadie. New York: St. Martin's Press, 1992, 1996.
Plots and a glossary. A most useful reference.

New Grove Dictionary of Music and Musicians, ed. Stanley Sadie. London: Macmillan Publishers Ltd. 20 volumes.

New Grove Dictionary of Opera, ed. Stanley Sadie. New York: Grove's Dictionaries of Music, 1992. 4 volumes.

The New Harvard Dictionary of Music, ed. Don Michael Randel. Cambridge, MA: Belknap Press of Harvard University Press, 1986.

Newman, Ernest. *Wagner as Man and Artist.* New York: Vintage Books, 1960.

Newton, George. *Sonority in Singing: A Historical Essay.* New York: Vantage Press, 1984.

Nichols, Roger. "Francis Poulenc," in *The New Grove Twentieth-Century French Masters.* New York: W. W. Norton, 1986.

Noske, Frits. *The Signifier and the Signified—Studies in the Operas of Mozart and Verdi.* The Hague, Netherlands: Martinus Nijhoff, 1977.
 Appendix I deals with "Semiotic Devices in Musical Drama." See also pp. 171–214 for a discussion of "The Musical Figures of Death."

The Oxford Dictionary of Opera, ed. John Warrack and Ewan West. Oxford: Oxford University Press, 1992.

The Oxford History of Opera, ed. Roger Parker. Oxford and New York: Oxford University Press, 1996.

Palisca, Claude V. *Baroque Music.* 2nd ed. Prentice-Hall History of Music Series. Englewood Cliffs, NJ: Prentice-Hall, 1981.

Pauly, Reinhard G. *Music in the Classical Period.* 3rd. ed. Prentice-Hall History of Music Series. Englewood Cliffs, NJ: Prentice-Hall, 1988.

———. *Music and the Theater: An Introduction to Opera.* Englewood Cliffs, NJ: Prentice-Hall, 1970.

Pendle, Karin. *Eugène Scribe and French Opera of the Nineteenth Century.* Studies in Musicology, No. 6. Ann Arbor, MI: UMI Research Press, 1979.

Pinker, Steven. "The Game of the Name," in *The New York Times* Op. Ed. (April 5, 1994): A, 5.

Pleasants, Henry. "How High Was G?," in *Opera News* 35, no. 17 (February 20, 1971): 25f.

———. *The Great Singers: From the Dawn of Opera to Our Own Time.* New York: Simon and Schuster, 1966.

Reich, Willi. *The Life and Works of Alban Berg,* trans. Cornelius Cardew. London: Thames and Hudson, 1965 [1963].

Reid, Cornelius. *The Bel Canto Principle and Practices.* New York: Coleman-Ross, 1950.

Robinson, Michael. *Naples and Neapolitan Opera.* Oxford: Oxford University Press, 1972.

Robinson, Paul. *Opera and Ideas From Mozart to Strauss.* New York: Harper and Row, 1985.

Rosen, Charles. *The Classical Style: Haydn, Mozart, Beethoven.* New York: Viking, 1971.

Rogers, Nigel. "Voices," in *Companion to Baroque Music,* comp. and ed. by Julie Anne Sadie. New York: Schirmer Books, 1990, pp. 351–365.

Rosselli, John. "From Princely Service to the Open Market: Singers of Italian Opera and Their Patrons, 1600–1850," in *Cambridge Opera Journal* 1, no. 1 (March 1989): 1–32.

———. *Music and Musicians in Nineteenth-Century Italy.* Portland, OR: Amadeus Press, 1991.

———. *Singers of Italian Opera—The History of a Profession.* Cambridge: Cambridge University Press, 1992.

————. *The Opera Industry in Italy from Cimarosa to Verdi: The Role of the Impresario.* Cambridge: Cambridge University Press, 1984.

Rothstein, Edward. "Gluck's Doomed Lovers of 1774," in *The New York Times* (January 14, 1995): A, 13.

Rysanek, Leonie, "Total Woman," in *Opera News* 49, no. 15 (April 13, 1985): 30f. *Characterization of* Parsifal's *Kundry.*

Sadie, Julie Anne, ed. and comp. *Companion to Baroque Music.* New York: Schirmer Books, 1990.

Sadie, Stanley, ed. *History of Opera.* Norton/Grove Handbooks in Music. New York, London: W. W. Norton, 1990.
Includes a helpful glossary.

Schmidgall, Gary. *Literature as Opera.* New York and Oxford: Oxford University Press, 1977.

————. *Shakespeare and Opera.* New York and Oxford: Oxford University Press, 1990.

Scott, Michael. *The Record of Singing.* New York: Charles Scribner's Sons, 1977. 2 volumes.
The introduction to Volume 1 provides an excellent history of singing.

Smith, Cecil, and Glenn Litton. *Musical Comedy in America.* New York: Theatre Arts Books, 1981.

Smith, Patrick J. *The Tenth Muse—A Historical Study of the Opera Libretto.* New York: Alfred A. Knopf, 1970.

Steane, J. B. *Voices—Singers and Critics.* Portland, OR: Amadeus Press, 1992.
Examination of aural characteristics of voice types and the roles suited to them.

Stein, Jack. *Richard Wagner and the Synthesis of the Arts.* Westport, CT: Greenwood Press, 1973 [1960].

Strunk, Oliver, ed. and comp. *Source Readings in Music History from Classical Antiquity Through the Romantic Era.* New York: W. W. Norton, 1950.

Sutcliffe, Tom. *Believing in Opera.* Princeton: Princeton University Press, 1996.
Problems and solutions of staging, audience reception, compositional directions in modern opera.

Swain, Joseph. *The Broadway Musical: A Critical and Musical Survey,* New York: Oxford University Press, 1990.

Tomlinson, Gary. "Italian Romanticism and Italian Opera: An Essay in Their Affinities," in *Nineteenth-Century Music* 10, no. 1 (Summer 1986): 43–60.

Tosi, Pier Francesco. *Observations on the Florid Song,* trans. John Ernest Galliard. London: William Reeves Bookseller, ltd. 1926 [1743].
Also available as Opinions of Singers Ancient and Modern, or Observations on Florid Singing, *trans. and ed. Edward Foreman. Minneapolis, MN: Pro Musica Press, 1986.*

Troy, Charles E. *The Comic Intermezzo: A Study in the History of Eighteenth-Century Opera.* Studies in Musicology No. 9. Ann Arbor, MI: UMI Research Press, 1979.

Vickers, Hugh. *Even Greater Operatic Disasters.* New York: St. Martin's Press, 1984.

————. *Great Operatic Disasters.* New York: St. Martin's Press, 1985 [1980].

Viking Opera Guide, ed. Amanda Holden, with Nicholas Kenyon and Stephen Walsh. London, New York: Viking, 1993.
Synopses of familiar and unfamiliar operas, definitions of terms, studies of composers, etc.

Wagner, Richard. *Wagner on Music and Drama—A Compendium of Richard Wagner's Prose Works*, sel. and arr. Albert Goldman and Evert Sprinchorn, trans. W. A. Ellis. New York: Da Capo Press, 1981 [1964].

Warrack, John. *Carl Maria von Weber.* 2nd ed. Cambridge: Cambridge University Press, 1976.

Weiner, Marc. *Richard Wagner and the Anti-Semitic Imagination.* Lincoln, NE: University of Nebraska Press, 1995.

Weiss, Piero. "'Sacred Bronzes': Paralipomena to an Essay by Dallapiccola," in *Nineteenth-Century Music* 9, no. 1 (Summer 1985): 42–49.
  Study of word choice in the nineteenth-century Italian opera libretto.

——— and Richard Taruskin, comps. *Music in the Western World: A History in Documents.* New York: Schirmer Books, 1984.

Weisstein, Ulrich, ed. *The Essence of Opera.* New York: Norton, 1969 [1964].
  Anthology of letters and other documents (translated into English) pertaining to opera and its aesthetics.

Winn, James Anderson. *Unsuspected Eloquence—A History of the Relation of Poetry and Music.* New Haven, CT: Yale University Press, 1981.

Index

Page numbers of extended or focused treatments of a topic are in bold face. Page numbers of illustrations (*Ill.*) of productions are italicized. Dates of individual works correspond in most cases to the world premiere, which usually followed close on the time of composition. Where there is a significant time gap, date of composition is given, marked with an asterisk (*). Operas, plays, etc., are indexed under the composers' or authors' names, which are provided for each title entry. "Def." = definition; "descr." = description. See also Glossary entries.

A

ABA, AABA form, 36, 36n. 15 (def.), 368, 368n. 32, 423. *See also* Aria da capo
Abstraction. *See* Opera, abstraction in
Absurdity, **94–104**, 243
  comic aspects, 94–102
  serious aspects, 102–104
Acciacatura, 416n. 8 (def.)
Accidentals, 32n (def.)
Acting. *See* Opera, acting in
Addison, Joseph (1672–1719), 26n (quoted)
Aeschylus (525–456 B.C.E.)
  Prometheus, 290
Aesthetics, 3–6, 7, 9, 10, 10n. 23, 14, 16n, 18, 20, **104–114**. *See also* Opera, text and music in; Opera, history of
  Wagner, 290–295
Affection, 119 (def.)
Age of Reason, 133n. 21
Aida (Verdi, 1871)
Alceste (Gluck, 1767)
Alceste (mythological figure), 13n. 5
Alcides. *See* Hercules
Allen, William Frances, 431n (quoted)
Almaviva, ossia L'inutile precauzione. See Rossini, *Il barbiere di Siviglia*
Alphorn, 321n (descr.)

Anapest, 54, 457. *See also* Archetypes, death rhythm
Appoggiatura, 169n (def.)
Apparition, The (painting, Moreau, 1876)
"Appassionata" sonata for piano, op. 57 (Beethoven, 1804–1805)
Arabella (R. Strauss, 1933)
Archetypes, **33–57**, 90, 244. *See also* Symbolism
  chromaticism, **56–57**
  death rhythm, 41, 49, **52–56** (Exs. 3.15 a–c), 71, 92, 298, 302, 385, 398, 401, 418, 425, 427, 457
  form and genre, **35–41**, 37n
  intervals, perfect, **45–51**, 427
  march, 36–37, 37n
  melody, **41–46**
  ostinato, 37n
  parallel voicing, **41–45** (Exs. 3.8a–c, 3.9), 57, 87, 177, 251, 424
  Phrygian cadence 302n (def.), 348 (Ex. CA-1e), 348n. 16, 410, 410n, 442, 458
  scale, 41, 54, 56–57, 75 (Ex. 4.5d), 78, 90
  song and singing, **33–35**
  tempest, **38–41**. *See also* Symbolism
  tritone **45–47**. *See also* Symbolism, intervals

Aria, 6, 18, 20, 102n, 118–119, 175,
175n. 4, 266, 266n, 293. *See also*
Opera, time in; Opera seria, action
and music in
aria-cabaletta, 266, 266n (def.), 279n. 11
aria da capo, 102n (def.), 119. *See
also* Opera seria
metaphor/simile aria, 135n. 23 (def.)
Ariadne auf Naxos (R. Strauss, 1912)
Ariodante (Handel, 1735)
Arioso, 40, 40n (def.), 119, 169, 196n
Artwork of the Future, The (essay,
Wagner, 1849)
Atonality, 104. *See also* Bitonality;
Tonality
Atonement, 73–74, **87–93**. *See also*
Conscience; Redemption
Auden W[ystan] H[ugh] (1907–1973),
4 (quoted)
Aureliano in Palmira (Rossini, 1813)

B

Bach, Johann Sebastian (1685–1750),
80
*Back to Methuselah: A Metabiological
Pentateuch* (play, Shaw, 1922)
Ballad opera, 99n (def.), 100
Ballata, 268n. 5 (def.)
Ballet. *See* Dance music
Ballo in maschera, Un (Verdi, 1859)
Baraka, Imamu Amiri, 415 (quoted)
Barber, Samuel (1910–1981), 22
Barbier de Séville, Le (play,
Beaumarchais, 1775)
Barbiere di Siviglia, Il (Rossini, 1816)
Baroque era (1600–1750), 5, 8, 14, 16,
16n, **18–21**, 19n. 15, 21n, 31n. 7,
38, 40, 98, 102n, **120–121**, 175,
213–214, 416n. 8. *See also* Age of
Reason; Basso continuo; Bel
canto; Castrato; Handel (*Giulio
Cesare*); Monteverdi; Mozart (*Don
Giovanni*, baroque elements in);
Opera, women singers in; Opera
seria; Orchestra and orchestra-
tion; Ornamentation; Singing;
Symbolism, pictorialization
Basso continuo, 18, 18n. 13 (def.),
118
Beaumarchais, Pierre Augustin Caron
de (1732–1799), 4 (quoted)
*Le barbier de Séville, ou L'inutile pré-
caution* (The Barber of Seville, or
The Useless Precaution, play,

1775), 242, 242nn. 1, 3; 245n. 6,
249n, 257n., 256–259 *passim*,
263n, 264n
*La folle journée, ou Le mariage de
Figaro* (The Crazy Day, or The
Marriage of Figaro, play, 1778),
242n. 3, 245n. 6, 249n
La mère coupable (The Guilty Mother,
play, 1792), 242n. 3
Beethoven, Ludwig van (1770–1827),
21, 222, 242, 242n. 2, 21
Bibliography, 240–241
Fidelio (1805, rev. 1806, 1814), 6n. 8,
9nn. 11, 17; 56, 77, 37, **222–241**,
223n. 2; *Ill. 231, 233*
  CHARACTERS: **Don Fernando**, 240;
  Florestan, 225 (Ex. FI-2c),
  238–240 (Exs. FI-6a, b); **Jaquino**,
  233–234; **Leonore**, **235–236** (Exs.
  FI-4a, b); **Marzelline**, 233;
  Pizarro, 77, 92, **237–238** (Ex. FI-
  5), **Prisoners**, 224 (Exs. FI-1c; FI-
  2b), 240; **Rocco**, 78, **234–235**
  (Exs. FI-3a, b); **Soldiers**, 240
  domestic comedy, 222, 235
  metaphorical meaning, 222, 235
  musical idiom, 223–225
  music and plot, **225–233**
  overtures, 222, 225
  prelude to Act II, 229
  revolutionary fervor, 223
  other works: Concerto in D for violin, op. 61 (1806), 223; *Egmont*
  overture (1810), 223n. 3; *Die
  Ruinen von Athen*, op. 113 (1811),
  100n; Sonata No. 23 in f minor
  for piano, op. 57 ("Appassionata,"
  1804–1805), 223, 223n. 3;
  Symphony No. 3 in E-flat, op. 55
  ("Eroica," 1804), 223, 224;
  Symphony No. 5, in c minor, op.
  57 (1808), 223; Symphony No. 9,
  in d minor, op. 125 (1824), 98n,
  100n
Beggar's Opera, The (Gay and Pepusch,
1728), 98–100
Bel canto, **121–123**. *See also* Baroque
era; Opera seria; Ornamentation;
Singing
Bellini, Vincenzo (1801–1835), 21
Berg, Alban (1885–1935), 22
Wozzeck (1925), 5, 61, 93, 104
Berlioz, Hector (1803–1869), 160
(quoted)

Les Troyens (1856–58*), 12, 28, 29
  (Ex. 3.3b), 34, 36–37, 37n, 42
  (Ex. 3.8b), 52 (Ex. 3.15a), 57,
  77n. 7, 463n
Bernstein, Leonard (1918–1990)
  Candide (1956), 7
  West Side Story (1957), 26–27 (Ex.
  3.1)
Bertati, Giovanni (1735–1815), 174
Billy Budd (Britten, 1951)
Bitonality, 47–48 (Exs. 3.11a, b), 396n.
  17 (def.), 410, 442, 461. *See also*
  Tonality
Bizet, Georges (1838–1875), 22, 376f
  (quoted)
  bibliography, 378–379
  Carmen (1875), 6n. 8, 33n. 10, 34n.
  11, 36, 56, 87, 303n, **342–379**,
  380, 380n. 2, 342n. 4, 460n; *Ill.
  35, 367*
    CHARACTERS: **Carmen**, 34, 36, 344,
      346 (Ex. CA-1a), 346n. 14, 347
      (Ex. CA-1b), **349–353** (Exs. CA-
      2a, c; CA-3b), 357n. 21, 371 (Ex.
      CA-5a), **374–376** (Exs. CA-6a–c);
      Dancaïro/Remendado, 377; **Don
      José**, 34, 113, 342n. 4, 353 (Ex.
      CA-3c), 361, **369–373** (Exs. CA-
      5a–d), 369nn. 34, 35; **Escamillo**,
      345n. 13, 346n. 14, 375, **377–378**
      (Exs. CA-6c; CA-7), 376nn. 41,
      42; **Frasquita/Mercédès**, 376 (Ex.
      CA-6c); **Lillas Pastia**, 377;
      Micaëla, 36, 345n. 13, 346n. 14,
      368–370 (Exs. CA-4a, b); **Morales**,
      368, 368n; **Smugglers** 349 (Ex.
      CA-2b), 352; **Zuniga**, 373–374
    dance music, 36n. 14, 346–349, 374
    departure from convention, 344,
      345, 345n. 13, **351–352**
    entr'actes: II, 358; III, 350; IV,
      347–348 (Exs. CA-1d, e), 348n.
      17, 362, 365
    fate motive, **352–353** (Exs.
      CA-3a–c)
    feminist viewpoint, 344
    gypsy atmosphere, 352n. 18, 359n.
      23. *See also* Bizet, *Carmen*,
      Spanish elements
    literary background, 342n. 4, 357n.
      21, 360n. 25, 366n
    metaphorical meanings, 343–344,
      348, 350
    musical idiom, 345, **346–351**, 353,

346n. 14, 359, 359n, 360n. 26
    music and plot, **354–368**
    prelude, 352–353 (Ex. CA-3a), 354
    reality, 345
    Spanish elements, 346–349 (Exs.
      CA-1a–e), 348n. 17, 353
    versions, 342–343, 343nn. 5, 6
Blues, 47, 415–417, 432
Bohème, La (Puccini, 1896), 7, 61, 87
Boito, Arrigo (1842–1918)
  Mefistofele (1868), 75–77
Boris Godunov (Musorgsky, 1868–69;
  rev. 1871; rev. 1874)
Borough - A Poem in 24 Letters, The
  (poem, Crabbe, 1810). *See*
  Britten, *Peter Grimes*
Botstein, Leon, 4 (quoted)
Bouilly, Jean-Nicolas (1763–1842),
  222, 223n. 2
Bravura, 94, 100, 244, 246. *See also*
  Coloratura
Breuning, Stephan von (1774–1827),
  222
Brindisi, 280n (def.)
Britten, Benjamin (1913–1976), 22,
  437–438, 437nn. 1, 2
  bibliography, 467–468
  Peter Grimes (1945), 5, 9nn. 15, 21;
  10, **24–25**, **27–28**, 38, 41, 54, 79,
  84–86, 93, **437–468**; *Ill. 25, 453*
    CHARACTERS: **Auntie**, 465;
      Balstrode, **438–440** (Ex. PG-1),
      441, 445 (Ex. PG-4b), **466**; **Bob
      Boles**, 465; **The Borough**, **24–25**,
      27–28 (Ex. 3.2b), 79, 93, 438,
      440, 441 (Ex. PG-2b), 447 (Ex.
      PG-6a), **458–459**; **Dr. Crabbe**,
      467; **Ellen**, 41, **47–48** (Exs.
      3.11a–c), 44l, **438–439** (Ex. PG-
      1), **462–465** (Exs. PG-10a–c; PG-
      11a–c); **Horace Adams**, 466; **Jim
      Hobson**, 459, 464–465; **John**,
      467; **Peter Grimes**, **47–48** (Exs.
      3.11a–c), **84–86** (Exs. 5.3a–e),
      440–441 (Exs. PG-2a, c), 447 (Ex.
      PG-6b), **459–462** (Exs. PG-7a–c;
      PG-8a, b; PG-9); **Ned Keene**,
      27–28 (Ex. 3.2a), 466, 466n; **The
      Nieces**, 466; **Mrs. Sedley**, 27–28,
      32–33 (Ex. 3.4a), 56, 440, **462**,
      462n; **Swallow**, 459
    literary background, 443, 459, 466n
    as metaphor, 437–438, 441. *See also*
    Sea Interludes

Britten, Benjamin (*continued*)
  musical idiom, 47–49 (Exs. 3.11a, b),
    303n, 375n, **440–446**, 442n, 457,
    461
  music and plot, **447–458**
  philosophical positions, 24–25, 438,
    440, 446
  sea imagery, 437, 438, **443–447**, 459
  Sea Interludes, 440–441, **443–446**,
    443nn. 6, 7; I, 443–444 (Ex. PG-
    4a), 443n. 6, 448; II, 443, 443n.
    6, 445 (Ex. PG-4c), 450; III,
    443–445 (Ex. PG-4d), 443n. 6,
    451; IV (Passacaglia), 444–446
    (Exs. PG-4e), 455, 456; V, 443n.
    6, 445, 456; VI, 458
  unity, **27–28**, **440–443**, 445–446, 458
  Other works: *Billy Budd* (1951), 77,
    78; *Death in Venice* (1973), 33
Broschi, Carlo. *See* Farinelli
Busenello, Gian Francesco
    (1598–1659), 5 (quoted)
Bussani, Francesco (fl. 1673–1680), 118

C

Cabaletta. *See* Aria-cabaletta
Cadenza, 124n. 16
Caesar, Julius (historical figure,
    104–44 B.C.E.), 125, 129
Caffarelli (né Gaetano Maiorano,
    1710–1783), 123, 252n
Callas, Maria, quoted, 374
Calzabigi, Ranieri di' (1714–1795), 18
Candide (Bernstein, 1956)
Canon, 440 (def.)
Cante jondo, 348n. 17 (def.)
Canzone, canzonetta, 33n (def.)
Capriccio (R. Strauss, 1942)
Carmen (Bizet, 1875)
Carmen (novella, Mérimée, 1845)
Carousel (Rodgers/Hammerstein, 1945)
Castrato, 19, 19nn. 14, 15; 121, 123.
    See also Baroque era; Bel canto;
    Opera seria; Singing; Symbolism,
    voice as; Voice types, use of
Cavalleria rusticana (Mascagni, 1890)
Cavalli, Pier Francesco (1602–1676),
    5n. 7
Cavatina, 245n. 8 (def.)
Celesta, 87, 87n. 9 (descr.)
Choral music, 47–48, 76, 100–101, 266n
  Il barbiere di Siviglia, 264
  Boris Godunov, 47–48, 50 (Ex. 3.12c)
  Carmen, 349, 352

Dialogues des Carmélites, 81, 83–84
Fidelio, 224 (Exs. FI-1c; FI-2b), 240
Iphigénie en Tauride, 156
Die Meistersinger von Nürnberg, 96
in opera seria, 124n. 15, 130n. 19
Orfeo ed Euridice, 14–16 (Ex. 2.1b)
Peter Grimes, 24, 28, 438, 446,
    458–459
Porgy and Bess®, 47, 50 (Ex. 3.12b),
    422, 423, 431
Rigoletto, 266, 277, 278, 288
Chromaticism, 32 (Ex. 3.4), 32n (def.),
    34, 54 (Exs. 16a, b), 56–57 (Ex.
    3.17), 74, 75 (Ex. 4.5d), 78, 94,
    342, 349, 381
Clarin trumpet 19, 19n. 15 (descr.). *See
    also* Overtone series
Classical era (1750–1820), 14, 16, 18,
    21, 36, 38, 78n, **156–157**, 169n,
    174–175, 178, 222n. *See also* Gluck
    (Iphigénie en Tauride); Mozart *(Don
    Giovanni)*; Beethoven *(Fidelio)*
Clément, Catherine, 344 (quoted)
Clemenza di Tito, La (Gluck, 1752)
Cleopatra (historical figure, 69–30
    B.C.E.), 125, 127
Coloratura, 41, 41n. 21 (def.), 100,
    252. *See also* Bel canto; Bravura;
    Ornament; Singing
Comedy, 26, 49, **94–102**. *See also*
    Comic opera
  Il barbiere di Siviglia, 67, 94, 243–244
  Carmen, 348, 351
  Falstaff, 31–32
  Fidelio, 222, 235
  Madama Butterfly, 49, 51
  Die Meistersinger von Nürnberg, 95
  Le nozze di Figaro, 32
  Porgy and Bess®, 415, 433, 434
  Der Rosenkavalier, 32, 84
  Salome, 410
Comic opera, 20, 21, 31–32, 100–101,
    174n. 1. *See also* Gilbert and
    Sullivan *(The Mikado)*, Rossini *(Il
    barbiere di Siviglia)*, Mozart *(Così fan
    tutte, Don Giovanni, Die Entführung
    aus dem Serail, Le nozze di Figaro)*
  as farce, 244
Commedia dell' arte, 111, 111n. 13
    (def.). *See also* Lazzi; Zanni
Communication to My Friends, A (essay,
    Wagner, 1851)
Concerto for violin, in D, op. 61
    (Beethoven, 1806)

Conscience, 28, **71–79**. *See also* Atonement; Opera, good and evil in
Aida, 74–76 (Ex. 4.6)
  Boris Godunov, 68–70 (Exs. 4.4a–d)
  Iphigénie en Tauride, 28 (Ex. 3.3a), 74
  Die Walküre 68–70 (Exs. 4.4a–e)
Contes d'Hoffmann, Les (Offenbach, 1880; completed in 1881, Guiraud)
Context, 26, **27–33**, 45, 47, 49n, 245, 251
  leitmotiv in, 293
  metaphorical meaning in, 182n
Cornelia (historical figure), 128
Così fan tutte (Mozart, 1790)
Couplets, 377n. 44 (def.)
Coward, Noel (1899–1973), 4 (quoted)
Crabbe, George (1754–1832), 437, 440n. 4; 459, 467
  The Borough—A Poem in 24 Letters (poem, 1810), 437, 443, 466n
Crespi, Antonio, 19n. 15
Crossover role, 6, 7, 7n

D

Da capo aria. *See* Aria da capo
Dance music, 26, 33, 56, 80–81, 173
  Carmen, 36n. 14, 346–349, 374
  Don Giovanni, 78, 175, 198–199, 210n. 29
  Iphigénie en Tauride, 156
  Orfeo ed Euridice, 15 (Ex. 2.1a), 16
  Peter Grimes, 27–28 (Ex. 3.2a, b), 79, 440, 456, 456n. 11, 459
  Rigoletto, 64–65 (Ex. 4.1b), 266, 268
  Salome, 397, 404–406 (Ex. SA-5b), 408 (Ex. SA-5g)
Da Ponte, Lorenzo (1749–1838), 174, 175, 206n. 23
Dean, Winton, 14 (quoted)
Death, 41, 54, 88. *See also* Archetypes: death rhythm, Phrygian cadence, scale
Death in Venice (Britten, 1973)
De Brosses, Charles (1709–1777), 123 (quoted)
Debussy, Claude (1862–1918), 22, 381n. 3
  Pelléas et Mélisande (1902), 34, 41
De Giuli [-Borsi], Theresa, 265n
Delibes, Léo (1836–1891)
  Lakmé (1883), 34, 380n. 2
Deus ex machina, 88n, 171
Dialogues des Carmélites (Poulenc, 1957)
Dido and Aeneas (Purcell, 1689)

Didone (Cavalli, 1641)
Don Giovanni (Mozart, 1787)
Donizetti, Gaetano (1797–1848), 22
  Don Pasquale (1843), 34, 244
  L'elisir d'amore (The Elixir of Love, 1832), 61
  Lucia di Lammermoor (1835), 38, 41, 93, 348
Don Pasquale (Donizetti, 1843)
Down in the Valley (Weill, 1948)
Dramma giocoso, 174n. 1 (def.)
Drummond, John, 14 (quoted)
Dvořák, Antonín (1841–1904), 22
  Rusalka (1901), 9nn. 19, 20; 33, 46 (Exs. 3.10a, b), 55 (Ex. 3.16b), 90–92 (Exs. 5.7a–c)

E

Echo et Narcisse (Gluck, 1779)
Eddas, 290
Egmont Overture (Beethoven, 1810)
Elegy Written in a Country Churchyard (poem, Gray, 1751)
Elisabetta, regina d'Inghilterra (Rossini, 1815)
Elisir d'amore, L' (Donizetti, 1832)
England, audience taste in, 21, 26n
Enlightenment, 16, 175, 198. *See also* Classical era
Entführung aus dem Serail, Die (Mozart, 1781)
Entr'acte. *See* Bizet, *Carmen*
"Eroica" Symphony (Beethoven, 1804)
Euripides (ca. 480–406? B.C.E.) 156
  Iphigenia in Aulis, 158
  Iphigenia in Tauris, 157
Evil. *See* Opera, good and evil in; *see also* Conscience
Expressionism, 380

F

Falstaff (Verdi, 1893)
Fanciulla del West, La (Puccini, 1910)
Fanfares, 36, 36n. 16, 49, 94
Farce, 244
Farinelli (né Carlo Broschi, 1705–1782) 19n. 15, 123
Faust (Gounod, 1859)
Faust Symphony, A (Liszt, 1857)
Fauvism, 381, 381n. 4
Fidelio (Beethoven, 1805, rev. 1806, 1814)
Fioritura, 204n. 20 (def.). *See also* Coloratura

Flaubert, Gustave (1821–1880), 381, 387
    Hérodias (1877), 381
Flavius Josephus. *See* Josephus, Flavius
Fliegende Holländer, Der (Wagner, 1843)
Floyd, Carlisle (b. 1926), 22
Folk music, 47–49, 51 (Exs. 3.14a–c), 414–415, 431n, 438. *See also*
    Blues; Bizet, *Carmen* (Gypsy atmosphere, Spanish elements)
    gullah, 11, 11n, 30, 433, 433n
Folle journée, La, ou Le mariage de Figaro (play, Beaumarchais, 1778)
Form and genre, **35–41**, 265n, 266, 266n, 293. *See also* Strophic form
Forza del destino, La (Verdi, 1862; rev. 1869)
Four Saints in Three Acts (Thomson, 1934)
Fra I due litiganti il terzo gode (Sarti, 1782)
France, 16n, 19n. 14
Freeman, John, 5n. 5 (quoted)
Freischütz, Der (Weber, 1821)
French overture, 129n. 17
French Revolution, 81, 223
Freud, Siegmund (1856–1939), 381
Furman, Nelly, 375n. 39 (quoted)

G

Galop, 457n (def.)
Gardner, Ed, 4 (quoted)
Gaveaux, Pierre (1760–1825)
    Léonore, ou L'amour conjugal (1798), 222
Gay, (John, 1685–1732), and Pepusch (Johann, 1667–1752)
    The Beggar's Opera (1728), 98–100
Gazzaniga, Giuseppe (1743–1818), 174
Gender issues, 20, 411, 380–381
Genre, **36–41**
Germany, nationalism in, 11, 31
Gershwin, George (1898–1937), 415 (quoted), 415–416
    bibliography, 436
    Porgy and Bess® (1935), 9nn. 13, 16, 20; 11, 11n, 24, 30 (Ex. 3.3d, e), 33, 77, 93, **414–436**, 416n. 6; *Ill. 421, 425, 426*
        CHARACTERS: **Bess**, 417 (Ex. PB-2d), 434, **435** (Ex. PB-5); **Children**, 47, **50** (Ex. 3.12b); **Clara**, 41, 432; **Crown**, 77, 93, 93n, **418–419** (Ex. PB-4a), **434–435**;

Jasbo Brown, 431; **Maria**, 433–434; **People of Catfish Row**, 431–432; **Peter**, 433; **Porgy**, 34, **416–417** (Exs. PB-1; PB-2a–c), **434**; **Robbins**, 433; **Serena**, 433; **Sportin' Life**, 24, 416, **418–419** (Exs. PB-3b; PB-4c), **432**; White folk, 432
        comedy, 415, 433, 434
        gullah music, 11, 11n, **414–416**, 414n. 3, 431n, 433
        harshness, 418–419 (Exs. PB-3a, b; PB-4a–c)
        musical idiom, **415–418**, 416n. 8, 431
        music and plot, **420–431**
        preludes, 420, 428, 430
        spirituals, 422, 423, 431
        syncopation, 30 (Exs. 3.3d, e), 416, 417, 424, 431, 434
        unity in, **415–419**
Gershwin, Ira (1896–1983), 414
Gesamtkunstwerk, 290. *See also* Wagner, aesthetics
Gilbert (William Schwenk, 1836–1911) and Sullivan (Arthur, 1842–1900), 49
    H.M.S. Pinafore (1878), 100–101
    The Mikado (1885), 49, 51 (Exs. 3.14a, c), 100
    The Pirates of Penzance (1879), 100
Gilman, Lawrence, 415 (quoted)
Gioconda, La (Ponchielli, 1876)
Giulio Cesare (Handel, 1724)
Gluck, Christoph Willibald von (1714–1787), 9n. 12, 16n. 11, 18, 21, 28, 33, 252n
    bibliography, 173
    Iphigénie en Tauride (Iphigenia in Tauris, 1779; rev. Vienna, 1781), 9n. 12, 28, 38, 74, 100, **156–173**, 252n; *Ill. 167*
        CHARACTERS: **Diane**, 158n, 171; **Furies**, 75, 173; **Iphigénie**, 157, 158, **167–168** (Exs. IP-1; IP-2); **Oreste**, 28 (Ex. 3.3a), 74, 157, 158, **167–170** (Exs. IP-3; IP-4); **Priestesses**, 172; **Pylade**, 158, **169–172** (Ex. IP-5), **Thoas**, 171; **Scythians**, 100n, 172
        choral music, 75, 156, 172–173
        dance music, 156, 173
        musical idiom, **156–157**, 157n
        music and plot, 157, **158–166**

mythological background, 158, 158n, 159n, 163n, 165n, 166n
overture, 158
scene construction, 156,
Orfeo ed Euridice (1762; rev. Paris, 1774), **12–20**, *Ill. 14*
compared to Handel's *Giulio Cesare*, 13–18
metaphorical meanings, 14, 16
mythological backgrounds, 12–15
Orfeo, 14–16 (Ex. 2.1b)
Paris revision, 14, 19n. 14
as reform opera, 14, 16, 18
voice types in, 20
and reform of opera, 14, 16, 18, 156–157
other works: *La clemenza di Tito* (The Mercy of Titus, 1752), 252n; *Echo et Narcisse* (1779), 157n, *Alceste* (1767; rev. Paris, 1776), 18, 204n. 22
Good and evil. *See* Opera, good and evil in; *see also* Conscience
Götterdämmerung (Wagner, 1876)
Gounod, Charles (1818–1893), 22
Faust (1859, rev. 1860, 1869), 10, 34, 35, 36, 41, 45, 73, 75, 80n. 2
Grand opera, 21, 440
Grande-duchesse de Gérolstein, La (Offenbach, 1867)
Gray, Thomas (1716–1771)
Elegy Written in a Country Churchyard (poem, 1751), 12
Gregor, Joseph (1888–1960), 109n
Ground bass, 35n (def.), 54 (Ex. 3.16a), 105 (Ex. 6.5a), 107 (Ex. 6.5d)
Guillard, Nicolas-François (1752–1814), 156
Guiraud, Ernest (1837–1892), 34n. 11, 342, 373n. 36
Gullah. *See* Folk music; *see also* Gershwin, *Porgy and Bess*®
Guys and Dolls (Loesser, 1950)
Gypsy music. *See* Bizet, *Carmen*, gypsy atmosphere
Gypsy scale, 352n. 18 (def.)

H

Halévy, Fromental (1799–1862, uncle of Ludovic), 342n. 1
Halévy, Ludovic (1834–1908, nephew of Fromental), 342
Handel, George Frideric (1685–1759), 6, 21, 24, 191, 193, 293

bibliography, 154–155
Giulio Cesare (Julius Caesar, 1724), 9nn. 14, 18; 30, 38, 40, 56, 102, **118–155**; *Ill. 130, 131*
CHARACTERS: **Achilla**, 123; **Cesare**, **16–17** (Ex. 2.2b), 31, **102–104** (Exs. 6.4a, b), 113, 120, 120n. 3, 123, **124–127** (Exs. GC-2a–c), **145–147** (Exs. GC-3a, b); **Cleopatra**, 16 (Ex. 2.2a), 18, 38, 40 (Ex. 3.7), 122 (Ex. GC-1), **151–153** (Exs. GC-5a, b); **Cornelia**, 56, 141n. 26, **148–150** (Exs. GC-4a–c); **Curio**, 148; **Nireno**, 153; **Sesto**, 56, 148, 150 (Ex. GC-4c); **Tolomeo**, 77, **119–120, 153–154** (Ex. GC-6)
compared to Gluck's *Orfeo ed Euridice*, 13–18
compared to Mozart's *Don Giovanni*, 175
and conventions of opera seria, **123–125**
forms and genres of Baroque music, 102–104, **118–120**, 124, 137n. 24
historical background, 125, 127–129
musical idiom, **16–18, 19–20, 121, 123–125**
music and plot, **129–145**
overture, 129, 129n. 17
Parnassus scene, 16, 17–18 (Ex. 2.2b), **120–121**, 124
voice types in, 19, 20, 121, 123n. 10
other works: *Ariodante* (1735), 77; *Jephtha* (1752), 129n. 17; *Judas Maccabaeus* (1747), 129n. 17; *Rodelinda* (1725), 77
Hartmann, Rudolf (1900–1988), 109n
Harmony, 16, **41–49**, 121, 169n, 293, 459. *See also* Archetype, parallel voicing; Chromaticism; Tritone
Haydn, Franz Josef (1732–1809), 100, 233n. 3
Haym, Nicola (1678–1729), 118, 127, 128
Heckelphone, 395n. 15 (descr.)
Henry VIII (play, Shakespeare, 1612)
Henze, Hans Werner (b. 1926), 22
Der junge Lord (The Young Lord, 1965), 96
Hercules (mythological figure), 13n. 5, 129

Hérodiade (Massenet, 1881; poem, Mallarmé, 1869)

Herodias (historical figure), 388, 388n. 12

Herod the Great (73–4 B.C.E.), 387–388, 388n. 7

Heyward, Dorothy, 414

Heyward, DuBose (1885–1940), 414

History. *See* Opera, history of; Medieval era; Baroque era; Classical era; Romantic era; Twentieth century

H.M.S. Pinafore (Gilbert and Sullivan, 1878)

Hoffmannsthal, Hugo von, 87 (quoted), 109n

Hornpipe, 456n. 11 (def.)

Hugo, Victor (1802–1885), 265
   Le roi s'amuse (The King Amuses Himself, play, 1832), 265, 273n, 279–281 *passim*, 283–288 *passim*, 281n

I

Idomeneo (Mozart, 1781)

Impressionism, 381n. 3

Incoronazione di Poppea, L' (Monteverdi et al., 1643)

Instrumentation. *See* Orchestra and Orchestration

Intervals. *See* Symbolism, intervals; *see also* Harmony; Overtone series

Introspection, **62–71**. *See also* Conscience
   in *Il barbiere di Siviglia*, **66–68** (Exs. 4.3a, b)
   in *Boris Godunov*, 68, **74–75** (Exs. 4.5a–d)
   in *Otello*, **63–66** (Exs. 4.2a–c)
   in *Pagliacci*, 70–71
   in *Rigoletto*, **63–64** (Exs. 4.1a–d)
   in *Die Walküre*, **68–73** (Exs. 4.4a–e)

Iphigenia in Aulis (Euripides)

Iphigenia in Tauris (Euripides)

Iphigénie en Tauride (Gluck, 1779; rev. Vienna, 1781)

Irony, 27, 156, 327n, 438, 464

Italy, 16n, 19n. 14, **118–124**, 266. *See also* Madrigal, Italian

J

Janáček, Leoš (1854–1928), 22

Janissary music, 100n, 172–173, 173n

Japan, folk music of, 48–49, 51 (Exs. 3.14a–c)

Jazz, 419. *See also* Blues

Johnson, Samuel (1709–1784), 3 (quoted), 3n (quoted)

John the Baptist (historical figure), 388

Josephus, Flavius (37? C. E.–ca. 100) 388n. 12

Junge Lord, Der (Henze, 1965)

K

Kampf und Sieg (cantata, Weber, 1815)

Kaye, Danny (1913–1987), 3, 4, 113

Key. *See* Tonality

Krauss, Clemens (1893–1954), 109n

L

Lachmann, Hedwig, 380, 384

Lady in the Dark (Weill, 1941)

Lakmé (Delibes, 1883)

Ländler, 28, 28n (def.), 456, 459

Langer, Suzanne, 23 (quoted)

Lauzières, Achille de, 344 (quoted)

Lazzi, 111n. 13 (def.). *See* Commedia dell' arte

Leier und Schwert (song cycle, Weber, 1814)

Leitmotiv, 23, **293**, 293nn. 2, 3. *See also* Thematic recall
   in *Salome*, **381–382**, **385–387**, **404–406**
   in *Die Walküre*, **296–307**

Leoncavallo, Ruggiero (1857–1919)
   Pagliacci (Clowns, 1892), 46 (Ex. 3.10c), 70–71, **111–114** (Exs 6.7a–c)

Leoninus (ca. 1163–1201), 24

Léonore, ou L'amour conjugale (Gaveaux, 1798)

Libretto *See* Opera, plots in; Opera, text and music in; Poetry

Lieto fine,88, 88n (def.). *See also* Deus ex machina

Liszt, Franz (1811–1886)
   A Faust Symphony (1857), 77

Little Night Music, A (Sondheim, 1973)

Lloyd Webber, Andrew (b. 1948)
   The Phantom of the Opera (1986), 7n

Loesser, Frank (1910–1969)
   The Most Happy Fella (1956), 7

Look-In, 3

Love, Lovers, **41–45** (Exs. 3.8a–c; 3.9), **56–57**, 87, 424
   Boris Godunov, 44 (Ex. 3.9), 45
   Carmen, 345, 352
   Iphigénie en Tauride, 157
   opera seria, 19, 123

Der Rosenkavalier, 84–85, 87
Tannhäuser, 110n. 10
Die Walküre, 299
Die Zauberflöte, 73n
Lucia di Lammermoor (Donizetti, 1835)
Luisa Miller (Verdi, 1849)
Lully, Jean-Baptiste (1632–1687), 21, 129n. 17

M

Macbeth (Verdi, 1847; rev. Paris, 1865)
Madama Butterfly (Puccini, 1904)
Madrigal, Italian, 9, 10
Mallarmé, Stéphane (1842–1898), 387
  Hérodiade (poem, 1869), 381
Mann, William, 392n. 14 (quoted)
March, 36–37, 37n, 424, 440
Marot, Clément (historical figure, son of Jean, 1496–1544), 281n, 283n
Marot, Jean (father of Clément), 281n (quoted)
Mascagni, Pietro (1863–1945)
  Cavalleria rusticana (Rustic Chivalry, 1890), 28, 29 (Ex. 3.3c), 87
Massenet, Jules (1842–1912)
  Hérodiade (1881), 381
  Thaïs (1894), 380n. 2
Maupassant, Guy de (1850–1893), 345
Mazzochi, Domenico (1592–1665), 10n. 23 (quoted)
Medieval era (800–1450), 24, 24n. 3, 81, 110n. 10, 311n
Mefistofele (Boito, 1868)
Meilhac, Henri (1831–1897), 342
Meistersinger von Nürnberg, Die (Wagner, 1868)
Melodrama, 230n (def.), 342
Melody, 21, 26, 175, 265, 291, 381–382, 415. *See also* Chromaticism; Leitmotiv; Ornamentation; Thematic recall
  as symbol, 14, 16, 23, 26, 34, **41–56**, 108, 108n
Menotti, Gian Carlo (b. 1911), 22
Merchant of Venice, The (play, Shakespeare, 1596)
Mère coupable, La (play, Beaumarchais, 1792)
Mérimée, Prosper (1803–1870), 342, 345
  Carmen (novella, 1845), 344, 357n. 21, 360n. 25, 366n. 30, 369nn. 34, 35
Metaphor. *See* Symbolism

Metaphor aria, 135n. 23 (def.)
Meyerbeer, Giacomo (1791–1864), 22
Mikado, The (Gilbert and Sullivan, 1885)
Modern opera. *See* Twentieth century
Molina, Tirso de (1571–1641), 174
Monteverdi, Claudio (1567–1643), 20, 108
  L'incoronazione di Poppea (The Coronation of Poppaea, 1643, with Sacrati et al.), 19, 42n, 57n, 77, 88, 93
  CHARACTERS: **Nerone**, 42 (Ex. 3.8a), **96–98** (Exs. 6.2a–c); **Poppea**, 42 (Ex. 3.8a)
  L'Orfeo, favola in musica (Orpheus, A Legend in Music, 1607), 8, 10n. 23, 12, 34, 35–36, 35n, 61, 88
  CHARACTERS: **Euridice**, 45 (Ex. 3.10a); **Orfeo**, **105–108** (Exs. 6.5a–d)
  metaphorical meanings in, 34, 105, 108
  prelude (Toccata), 36–37 (Ex. 3.5a)
Moreau, Gustave (1826–1898), 381
  The Apparition (painting, 1876)
  Salome Dancing Before Herod (painting, 1876)
Moreschi, Alessandro (1858–1922), 19n. 14, 123
Most Happy Fella, The (Loesser, 1956)
Mozart, Wolfgang Amadeus (1756–1791), 6, 6n, 21, 33, 56
  bibliography, 220–221
  Don Giovanni (1787), 9nn. 17, 20; 33n. 10, 56, 78n, 93, **174–221**, 203n. 19, 368n. 32; *Ill. 79, 187, 197*
  ambiguity in, **175–178**, **209–210**
  characters: **Donna Anna**, 56, 175, **181–183** (Exs. DG-2b,c; DG-3b), 186 (Ex. DG-4d), **209–210**; **Il Commendatore**, 185 (Ex. DG-3e), 213; **Donna Elvira**, 175, 191n, **213–216** (Exs. DG-6a–e); **Don Giovanni**, 34, 35, 36, 41, **77–78**, 93, 175, **176–178** (Exs. DG-1a–c), 184, 188 (Ex. DG-4f), 203n. 18, **210–212** (Exs. DG-5a–d), 218 (Ex. DG-7a); **Leporello**, 78, 175, 186 (Exs. DG-4b, c), 188 (Ex. DG-4f), **209**; **Masetto**, 175, **218–219**, (Exs. DG-8a–c), 218n; **Don Ottavio**, 36, 175, 199n, 203n. 17, **213**, 213n; **Zerlina**, **175–178** (Exs. DG-1a–c), 180 (Ex. DG-2a), 187 (Ex. DG-4e), **216–218** (Exs. DG-7a, b)

Mozart, Wolfgang Amadeus (*continued*)
   dance music in, 78, 175, 195,
     198–199, 210n. 29
   ensemble in, 175, 176–178
   finales of, 179
   "La ci darem" analyzed, 175–178
   metaphorical meanings in, 175, 179,
     182, 182n, 218n
   musical idiom, **174–175**, **178–182**,
     215–216
   music and plot, **182–209**
   orchestra, 56, 183 (Ex. DG-3b), 196n
   overture, 180, 183 (Ex. DG-3a),
     185–188 (Exs. DG-3d; DG-4a)
   time sequence, 174, 189, 190, 192,
     195, 198, 199, 202, 204, 204n. 21,
     205, 206
   uniqueness, 174–175
   unity, **178–182**, **185–188**, 212
   Die Entführung aus dem Serail (The
     Abduction from the Seraglio,
     1782), 6n. 8, 9n. 14, 33, 173n
     Osmin, 34, **100–101** (Exs. 6.3a, b)
   Le nozze di Figaro (The Marriage of
     Figaro, 1786), 26, 32, 34, 34n. 12,
     37–39 (Exs. 3.6a, b), 38n. 18, 75,
     93, 179n, 206, 206n. 25, 245n. 6,
     249n, 286n. 17
   and synthesis, 21, **174–175,** 178,
     213–214
   other works: *Così fan tutte* (Thus Do
     All Women, 1790), 49, *Ill. 52*, 54
     (Ex. 3.15c); *Idomeneo* (1781), 38,
     166n, 204n. 22; String Quintet in
     c minor, K. 406 (1788), 223n. 3;
     Rondo alla turca, K. 331 (1781–83),
     100n; *Die Zauberflöte* (The Magic
     Flute, 1791), 6n. 8, 41, 57n, 71,
     73n, 463n
Musical, musical comedy, 6–8, 11
Musorgsky, Modeste (1839–1883), 22
   Boris Godunov (1868–69; rev. 1871;
     rev. 1874), 9nn. 16, 19; 37 (Ex.
     3.5c), 44 (Ex. 3.9), 45, **47–48**, 50
     (Ex. 3.12c), 68, **73–75** (Exs. 4.5a–d)
Mythological backgrounds, 12, 13,
   13nn. 5, 6; 20, 129n. 18, 158,
   159n, 163n, 165n, 166n, 290,
   316n, 320n, 330nn. 22, 23

N

Nabucco [*Nabucodonosor*] (Verdi, 1842)
Nationalism, 11, 31, **47–49**
Nibelungenlied, Das, 290

Nietzsche, Friedrich (1844–1900), 344
   (quoted)
Nos (Shostakovich, 1930)
Notation, pitch and, 8n. 10
Nozze di Figaro, Le (Mozart, 1786)

O

Obsession, 100,
   in *Salome*, **385–387**
Offenbach, Jacques (1819–1880), 22,
   342n. 1
   Les contes d'Hoffmann (The Tales of
     Hoffmann, 1881), 34, 34n. 11, 41,
     63, 77, 286n. 17
   La grande-duchesse de Gérolstein (The
     Grand-Duchess of Gerolstein,
     1867), 101–102
Oklahoma! (Rodgers and Hammerstein,
   1943)
Opera. *See also* Choral music; Dance
   music; Orchestra and orchestration; Singing
   abstraction, 8–9, 16, 19, 23, 26, 38,
     119, 125; *see also* Opera seria;
     Symbolism
   acting, 7
   adolescents, 286n. 17, 402; *see also*
     Trouser role
   audience perception, 3, 8, 11–12,
     14, 18, 20, **22–27**, 31, 119, 210,
     343, 351, 415, 437n. 2, 438
   centrality of music, **5–8**
   characters as singers, 33–34
   devil in, 75–77; *see also* Opera, good
     and evil in
   elements, **5–8**
   as entertainment, 4–5, 415
   evaluation of, 10
   gender issues, in *Carmen*, 344,
     352–353; in *Salome*, 380–381, 411;
     in *Peter Grimes*, 437–438; *see also*
     Opera, women singers in
   good and evil, 34, **75–79**, 432, 462;
     see also Conscience
   history, 5, 8, 9, 10, **20–22**, 43, 56,
     88, 99–100, 123n. 9; *see also* indi-
     vidual eras, introductions to indi-
     vidual operas
   human condition, 4, 8, 9, 14, 34–35,
     45n, 56, **61–114**, 266, 380, 446;
     see also Absurdity; Atonement;
     Aesthetics; Conscience;
     Introspection; Love; Redemption;
     Spirituality; Wonderment

intellectual discussion in, 9, 76, 114
musical and, **6–8**
non-singing characters, 33
ordinary people, 22, **75–76**, 78, 98
parody of, 44 (Ex. 3.9), 45, 49, *Ill.
    52*, 54 (Ex. 3.15c), 100–102
    (Exs. 6.3a, b), 251; *see also*
    Singing, parody of
pejorative comments on, 3–4, 3n
plots, 5, 20, 21, 38, 41, 62, 88n, 157
poverty in, 61
reality in, **4**, 22, 75–76, 98, 111, 113,
    223, 344, 380, 418–419; *see also*
    Opera, truth in
religion, religiosity in, **24–25**, 80,
    80nn. 1, 2; 90, 368, 368n. 33,
    440, 442, 459, 465, 466
spoken dialogue, 6, 6n; *see also*
    Ballad opera; Opéra comique;
    Singspiel
text and music, 3, 4, **9–10**, 23–24,
    26, 10n. 23, 57n, 104–105,
    118–121, 291–292
time in, 5, 5n. 6, 9, 84, 84n
translation, 26n
truth in, **4**, 5n.5, **35**, **111–114** (Exs.
    6.7a–e), 213; *see also* Opera, reali-
    ty in
voice, *see* Crossover role; Musical,
    musical comedy; Opera seria;
    Singing; Travesti; Trouser role;
    Voice types, use of
women singers, 19, 121, 123,
    123n.10
Opera and Drama (essay, Wagner,
    1850–1851)
Opera buffa, 100, 174n. 1, 175. *See
    also* Comedy; Comic opera
Opéra comique, 6n. 8 (def.), 100,
    342n. 3. *See also* Comedy; Comic
    opera
Opéra-Comique, 342n. 3, 351–352
Opera seria, 19, 20, 21n. 17, 38,
    118–120, 182n, 175. *See also*
    Baroque era; Bel canto, Castrato;
    Handel, *Giulio Cesare*;
    Ornamentation; Singing
    abstraction, 119, 125
    action and music, 5, 118
    audience sociology, 119n. 2
    chorus, 124n. 15, 130n. 19
    lovers and heroes, 123
    parody of, 98–100
    scene division, 117

voice types in, 123, 123n. 9
Operetta, 7, 100
Orchestra and orchestration, **7–8**, 13,
    18, 19n. 15, 20–21, **30–32**, 34,
    38–41, 48, 56, 63, 87. *See also*
    Arioso; Symbolism, orchestra as;
    Symbolism, pictorialization
    Il barbiere di Siviglia, 243
    Carmen, 346, **348–350**, 346n. 14,
        359
    Don Giovanni, 175, 179–180, 182,
        183–186, 212, 214–216, 217
    Fidelio, 223–224, 238–239
    Giulio Cesare, **18**, **120–121**
    Iphigénie en Tauride, **157**
    Orfeo ed Euridice, **18**
    Peter Grimes, **443–446**
    Porgy and Bess®, 415
    Rigoletto, **265–267**
    Salome, 381–382, **384–385**, 405
    Die Walküre, **291**, 293, **295**, 295n. 4
Oresteia, 158, 166n, 290
Orfeo ed Euridice (Gluck, 1762; rev.
    Paris, 1774)
Orfeo, favola in musica, L' (Monteverdi,
    1607)
Orient, folk idiom of, 48–49
Ornamentation, 4, 4n. 4, 14, 16, 16n.
    11, 19, 20, 119, 121–122, 175,
    244, 347, 416n. 8, 441. *See also*
    Baroque era; Bel canto; Singing;
    Symbolism, melody as
Orpheus and Euridice. *See* Mythology;
    see also Gluck, *Orfeo ed Euridice*;
    Monteverdi, *L'Orfeo, favola in
    musica*
Otello (Verdi, 1887)
Othello (play, Shakespeare, 1604)
Overtone series, 25n, 36, 36n. 16. *See
    also* clarin trumpet
Overtures and Preludes, 129
    Il barbiere di Siviglia, 245
    Carmen, 352–353 (Ex. CA-3a), 354;
        see also Entr'actes
    Don Giovanni, 180, 185–188 (Exs.
        DG3d; DG-4a)
    Die Entführung aus dem Serail, 173n
    Fidelio, 222, 225, 229
    French overture, 129n. 17
    Giulio Cesare, 129, 129n. 17
    Iphigénie en Tauride, 38, 158
    L'Orfeo, favola in musica, 37
    Peter Grimes, *see* Sea Interludes
    Porgy and Bess®, 420, 428, 430

Overtures and Preludes (*continued*)
  Rigoletto, 266–267 (Exs. RI-1a, b)
  Die Walküre, 293–295 (Ex. WA-3d),
    307, 313

P

Pagliacci (Leoncavallo, 1892)
Paisiello, Giovanni (1740–1816), 242,
    242n. 4
Parody. *See* Opera, parody of; Singing,
    parody of
Parsifal (Wagner, 1882)
Passacaglia, 444n (def.). *See also* Britten,
    Peter Grimes, Sea Interlude IV
Pears, Peter (1910–1986), 437
Pelléas et Mélisande (Debussy, 1902)
Pentatonic scale, 49n, (def.), 433
Pepusch, Johann (1667–1752) *See* Gay
    and Pepusch
Pergolesi, Giovanni Battista
    (1710–1736)
  La serva padrona (The Maid-Mistress,
    1733), 21
Peter Grimes (Britten, 1945)
Phantom of the Opera, The (Lloyd
    Webber, 1986)
Phrygian cadence. *See* Archetypes
Piave, Francesco Maria (1810–1876),
    265, 273n
Pictorialization. *See* Symbolism
Pinker, Stephen, quoted, 24n. 2
Pirates of Penzance, The (Gilbert and
    Sullivan, 1879)
Pirithous the Lapith (mythological fig-
    ure), 13n. 5
Pitch, 8n. 10, 19n. 15
Plots, 5, 20, 21, 38, 41, 62, 88n, 157.
    See also individual operas;
    Symbolism, entire opera as
Poetry, 5, 23, 26, 96, 119, 121,
    290–292 (Ex. WA-2), 311n, 312n.
    See also Opera, text and music in
Pompey, Gnaeus (historical figure,
    106–48 B.C.E.), 125, 128
Ponchielli, Amilcare (1834–1886)
  La Gioconda (The Joyful Girl, 1876),
    34
Porgy and Bess® (George and Ira
    Gershwin, 1935)
Porgy (novel, DuBose Heyward, 1925)
Porgy (play, Dorothy and DuBose
    Heyward, 1927)
Poulenc, Francis (1899–1963), 22,
    80–81

Dialogues des Carmélites (Dialogues of
    the Carmelites, 1957), 29, 37n,
    81–84 (Exs. 5.1; 5.2)
Prelude. *See* Overtures and Preludes
Procter-Gregg, Humphrey, 144n. 27
    (quoted)
Prokofiev, Sergei (1891–1953), 22
Prometheus (play, Aeschylus), 290
Pronunciation guide, 116
Ptolemy XIII (historical figure, 63–47
    B.C.E.), 127
Puccini, Giacomo (1858–1924), 22
  La bohème (Bohemian Life, 1896), 7,
    61, 87
  La fanciulla del West (The Girl of the
    [Golden] West, 1910), 49n
  Madama Butterfly (1904), 26, 48–49,
    51 (Ex. 3.14b)
  Tosca (1900), 34, 77
  Turandot (1924), 48, 78
Purcell, Henry (1659–1695), 21n. 17
  Dido and Aeneas (1689), 21n. 17,
    35n, 54 (Ex. 3.16a)

Q

Quartet, strings, in c minor, K. 406
    (Mozart, 1788)

R

Raguenet, François (1660–1772?), 123
    (quoted)
Rake's Progress, The (Stravinsky, 1951)
Realism, 22. *See also* Opera, reality in;
    Opera, truth in
Recitative, 6, 18, 18n. 12 (def.), 102,
    118–119, 119n. 1
Redemption, 73, 78, **87–93**
  Der fliegende Holländer, 88–89
    (Exs. 5.5a–c)
  Otello, 90–91
  Parsifal, 90–91 (Exs. 5.6a, b), 90n
  Porgy and Bess®, 93
  Der Ring des Nibelungen, 90, 300
  Rusalka, 91–92 (Ex. 5.7c)
  Tannhäuser, 89
Reign of Terror, 81, 223n
Rescue opera, 222n (def.)
Rheingold, Das (Wagner, 1869)
Rhythm, 20, 26, **28–30** (Exs. 3.3a–c),
    38, **41–56**, 73 (Ex. 4.4e), 75, 90,
    169. *See also* Archetypes, death
    rhythm
  Don Giovanni, **178–182**
  Fidelio, **223–225**

Porgy and Bess®, **30** (Ex. 3.3d, e), 416, 417, 424, 431, 434

Rigoletto (Verdi, 1851)

Ring des Nibelungen, Der (Wagner, 1876). *See also* Wagner's *Das Rheingold, Die Walküre, Siegfried, Götterdämmerung*

Robinson, Paul, 12n. 2 (quoted)

Robinson, Peter, 344 (quoted)

Rodelinda (Handel, 1725)

Rodgers (Richard, 1902–1979) and Hammerstein (Oscar II, 1895–1960)
  Carousel (1945), 7
  Oklahoma! (1943), 7
  The Sound of Music (1960), 7
  South Pacific (1949), 7

Roi s'amuse, Le (play, Hugo, 1832)

Romantic era (1800–1900 [1920? 1950?], **21–22**, 38, 88, 222, 222n, **266**, **380–381**. *See also* Beethoven (*Fidelio*); Bizet (*Carmen*); Britten (*Peter Grimes*); Romanticism; Rossini (*Il barbiere di Siviglia*); Verdi (*Rigoletto*); Strauss (*Salome*); Wagner (*Die Walkure*)

Romanticism, 14, 408, 415. *See also* Romantic era; Wagner, *Die Walküre*, musical idiom
  Carmen, 351–352, 345–346, 348, 350
  Don Giovanni, 175–178, 210
  Fidelio, 223
  Peter Grimes, 440
  Salome 380–381, 398, 408

Rondo alla turca (Mozart, piano sonata movement, 1781–1783)

Rosenkavalier, Der (R. Strauss, 1911)

Ross, Alex, 437n. 2 (quoted)

Rossini, Gioacchino (1792–1868), 6, 21
  bibliography, 264
  Il barbiere di Siviglia (The Barber of Seville, 1816), 9n. 14, 26, 33n. 10, 38, **242–264**; *Ill. 251, 253*
    CHARACTERS: **Almaviva**, 34, 244, **256–257** (Exs. BA-2a–c); **Ambrogio**, 263; **Berta**, 263; **Bartolo**, 94, **259–260** (Ex. BA-4); **Basilio**, **262–263** (Ex. BA-6); **Figaro**, 244, **257–259** (Exs. BA-3a–c); **Fiorello**, 256; **Officer of Militia**, 263–264; **Rosina**, **66–68** (Exs. 4.3a, b), 244, **259–262** (Exs. BA-5a–c)
    comedy in, 94, **243–244**

musical idiom, 94, **243–244**, 246, 248, 250
  music and plot, **245–255**
  overture, 245
  other works: *Aureliano in Palmira* (1813), 245, 245n. 7; *Elisabetta, regina d'Inghilterra* (Elizabeth, Queen of England, 1815), 245

Rothstein, Edward, 14 (quoted)

Roullet, Louis Lebland du (1716–1786), 156

Ruinen von Athen, Die, op. 113 (overture and incidental music, Beethoven, 1811)

Rusalka (Dvořák, 1901)

Russell, Anna, 388n. 10 (quoted)

Russia, folk music of, in *Boris Godunov*, 47–48

S

Sacrati, Francesco (1605–1660), 42, 42n

Sacred/secular meaning in music, 80–81. *See also* Opera, religion in

Saint-Evrémond, Charles de (1614–1703), 4 (quoted)

Saint-Saëns, Camille (1835–1921)
  Samson et Dalila (1877), 61, 380n. 2

Salieri, Antonio (1750–1825), 174n. 3 (quoted)

Salome (historical figure, ?-?), 388, 388n. 12

Salome (play, Wilde, 1891)

Salome (R. Strauss, 1905)

Salome Dancing Before Herod (painting, Moreau, 1876)

Samson et Dalila (Saint-Saëns, 1877)

Sarti, Giuseppe (1729–1802)
  Fra I due litiganti il terzo gode (Between Two Litigants A Third Rejoices, 1782), 206, 206n. 24

Sartorio, Antonio (1630–1680), 118

Satire. *See* Opera, parody of; Singing, parody of

Scale. *See* Archetypes, scales as; *see also* Chromaticism

Scarlatti, Alessandro (1660–1725), 21

Scena, 266n (def.)

Scenery, symbolic use of, 57

Sea Interludes. *See* Britten, *Peter Grimes*

Senesino (né Francesco Bernardi, ca. 1680–1759), 123

Serva padrona, La (Pergolesi, 1733), 21

Sextus (historical figure, 75 B.C.E.–?), 128

Shakespeare, William (1554–1616), 125
 Henry VIII (1612), 14n. 10
 The Merchant of Venice (1596), 57
 Othello (1604), 39, 63n. 3

Shaw, George Bernard (1856–1950), 125
 Back to Methuselah: A Metabiological Pentateuch (play, 1922), 4, 5n. 5

Shostakovich (Dmitri (1906–1975), 22
 Nos (The Nose, 1930), 96

Siciliano, 135n. 22 (def.)

Siegfried (Wagner, 1876)

Simile aria, 135n. 23 (def.)

Sinfonia,137n. 24 (def.)

Singing, 6, 7, 16n, 18, 26, 244, 252, 255. *See also* Bel canto; Castrato; Coloratura; Crossover role; Opera seria; Romantic era
 in Baroque era, **16–20, 121–122**, 123, 123n. 9
 in Classical era, **14–16, 18**
 as metaphor, 18; *see also* Symbolism, singing as
 in musical, musical comedy, **6–7**
 parody of, **94–96** (Exs. 6.1a, b), **98–99** (Ex. 6.2c), **100–102** (Exs. 6.3a, b)
 and pitch level, 8n. 10
 in Romantic era, 21

Singspiel, 6n. 8 (def.), 99n, 100, 222n

Sistrum 358n. 22 (descr.)

Slater, Montagu, 437, 467

Soler, Vicente Martin y (1754–1806)
 Una cosa rara (A Rare Thing, 1786), 206, 206n

Sondheim, Steven (b. 1930)
 A Little Night Music (1973), 7

Song, 16, 33n, **33–35, 105–108**, 268n. 5, 280n. *See also* Canzone, canzonetta; Symbolism, song as

Sonnleithner, Joseph (1766–1835), 222

Sospiro, 56 (def.), 215, 216 (Ex. DG-6e), 266, 267 (Ex. RI-1b), 429

Sound of Music, The (Rodgers and Hammerstein, 1960)

South Pacific (Rodgers and Hammerstein, 1949)

Spirituality, 61, **80–84**, 110n. 10. *See also* Wonderment

Star Spangled Banner, The, 26

Sterbini, Cesare (1784–1831), 242, 245n. 6, 264n

Strauss, Franz (1822–1905, father of Richard), 381n. 5 (quoted)

Strauss, Richard (1864–1949, son of Franz), 22, 109n
 bibliography, 411–413
 Der Rosenkavalier (The Knight of the Rose, 1911), 5n. 6, 9n. 15, 32, 43 (Ex. 3.8c), 84–85, 84n, 87–88 (Ex. 5.4), 286n. 17
 Salome (1905), 54, 130n. 20, **380–413**; *Ill. 382, 397, 399*
  CHARACTERS: **Cappadocian**, 403; **Five Jews**, 403, 410; **Herodes**, 382, **384–385**, 388, 402n, **408–409** (Ex. SA-6); **Herodias**, **384–385**, 388, **410–411** (Ex. SA-7), 411n. 21; **Jokanaan**, 382, 385–386 (Ex. SA-2d), 388, 402 (SA-3), **403** (Ex. SA-4), **410–411** (Ex. SA-7); **Naaman**, 410; **Narraboth**, 78, **382–384** (Ex. SA-1), 385 (Ex. SA-2a), 401; **Page**, 385–386 (Ex. SA-2c), 402; **Salome**, 92, 384, **385–387** (Exs. SA-2b, e), **404–408** (Exs. SA-5a–g); **Slave**, 408; **Two Nazarenes**, 410; **Two Soldiers**, 402
  Dance of the Seven Veils, **397–398**, 406, 408 (Ex. SA-5g)
  exoticism, 380–381
  historical background, 387–388, 388nn. 7, 9, 11, 12
  imagery, **382–385**, 409
  leitmotives, **385–387** (Exs. SA-2a–g), 402 (Ex. SA-4), **404–411** (Exs. SA-5a–g; SA-6; SA-7)
  literary background, 384, 381, 402n
  musical idiom, **381–382**, 381n. 5, **384–387**, 398, 401
  music and plot, **389–401**, 402n
  obsession, **385–387**, 408
  other works: *Arabella* (1933), 8, 32–33 (Ex. 3.4b), 56; *Ariadne auf Naxos* (Ariadne on Naxos, 1912), 41, 108–109 (Ex. 6.6); *Capriccio* (1942), 109–110

Stravinsky, Igor (1882–1971)
 The Rake's Progress (1951), 75

Stretta, 250n (def.), 266n

Strophic form, 35–36, 105–108 (Exs. 6.5a–d), 235
 in *Porgy and Bess*®, 415, 423, 425, 428, 429, 433
 in *Carmen*, 36, 374

Sturluson, Snorri (1178–1241), 290
Swarowsky, Hans (1899–1975), 109n
Symbolism, 8, 12, **23–57**, 62, 294. *See
    also* individual operas; Leitmotiv;
    Orchestra and Orchestration;
    Sospiro; Thematic recall
  archetypes, **33–57**
  dance music, 26–28, 33, 37–38,
    64–65, 78, 175, 195, 198, 398,
    404, 406
  entire opera, 57, 57n, 62, 218n,
    222, 437–438, 437n. 2, 446
  form and genre, **35–41**, 105–108,
    110–111, 444
  harmony, 32, **41–56**, 124, 459; *see
    also* Symbolism, intervals;
    Symbolism, parallel voicing
  intervals, **47–51**, 375, 375n. 40,
    416–417, 427, 431, 440–441, 460
    (Exs. PG7a–c), 460n, 462 (Ex. PG-
    9); *see also* Symbolism, harmony;
    Symbolism, melody
  march, 36–37
  melody, 26, 32, **41–56**, 464; *see also*
    Symbolism, singing; Symbolism,
    song
  national idiom, 26–27
  in opera seria, **119–121**
  orchestra and orchestration, 18,
    31–32, 63, **120–121**, 124,
    238–239, 261, 288, **348–351**,
    384–385, **443–446**
  ornamentation, 108, **14–18**, 98, 98n,
    108, 464, 465; *see also* Bel canto
  parallel voicing, **41–45**
  pictorialization, 13, 16, **38–41**,
    120–121, 158, 215–216, 244, 288,
    348–351, **384–385**, 437, **443–446**,
    443n. 7, 464
  pitch, 19n. 15
  recitativo secco, 120
  rhythm, **26–27**, 32, **41–56** (Ex. 3.1),
    169, **223–225**, 459; *see also*
    Archetypes, death rhythm
  singing, 18, 41, 98, 98n; *see also* Bel
    canto; Ornamentation; symbol-
    ism, voice as
  song, 16, **33–35**, **105–108**, 423
  tempest, **38–41**, 47, 156–158, 254,
    267, 278, 307, 425, 440, 443,
    450, 461
  tonality, **24–25**, 120, 145
  voice as, **19–20**
Symphony No. 3 in E-flat, op. 55

("Eroica"; Beethoven, 1804)
Symphony No. 5 in c minor, op. 67
    (Beethoven, 1808)
Symphony No. 9 in d minor, op. 125
    (Beethoven, 1824)
Syncopation. *See* Rhythm

T

Tamburo, 157n (descr.)
Tam-tam, 389n. 13 (descr.)
Tannhäuser (ca.1205-ca.1270), 110n.
    10
*Tannhäuser und der Sängerkrieg auf
    Wartburg* (Wagner, 1845; rev.
    Paris, 1861)
Tchaikovsky, Pyotr Ilich (1840–1893),
    22
Tempest. *See* Symbolism
Tempo di mezzo, 279n. 10 (def.)
Text. *See* Opera, text and music in; *see
    also* Poetry
Thaïs (Massenet, 1894)
Thematic recall. *See also* Leitmotiv
  Il barbiere di Siviglia, 245
  Carmen, 352–353
  Don Giovanni, 180–182, 185–188,
    212
  Peter Grimes, 440–442, 443, 446, 458;
    see also recall of tonality, 27–28
  Porgy and Bess®, 415–419
  Rigoletto, 63, 265–266, 285
  Rusalka, 92
  Salome, 385–387, 402, 404–411
  Die Walküre, 293–295, 296–307
Theorbo, 120n. 4 (descr.)
Theseus (mythological figure) 13n. 5
Thiedreks Saga of Bern, 290
Thomson, Virgil (1896–1989)
  Four Saints in Three Acts (1934),
    416n. 6
Through-composition, 102, 113, 119,
    291, 361
Timbre, 30n (def.). *See also* Orchestra
    and orchestration
Tonality, **24–26**, 45, 56, 56n (def.),
    120, 145, 180, 293, 352, 381, 442,
    461. *See also* Atonality; Bitonality;
    Symbolism
Tonsprache, 291 (def.)
Tosca (Puccini, 1900)
Tosi, Piero Francesco (ca. 1653–1732),
    121 (quoted)
Travesti role, 123n. 9 (def.). *See also*
    Trouser role

Traviata, La (Verdi, 1853)

Treitschke, Georg Friedrich
(1776–1842), 222

Tristan und Isolde (Wagner, 1865)

Tritone, 24, 24n. 3 (def.), **45–46** (Exs.
3.10a–c), 173, 261, 309, 315, 410,
418, 425, 442, 461

Trouser role, 286n. 17 (def.), 402. *See
also* Travesti role

Trovatore, Il (Verdi, 1853)

Troyens, Les (Berlioz, 1856–68*)

Turandot (Puccini, 1924)

Twentieth century, 20, **22**, 57, 96,
380–381. *See also* Britten, *Peter
Grimes*; Gershwin, *Porgy and Bess®*;
Strauss, *Salome*

U

Una cosa rara (Soler, 1786)

V

Vamp, 423n. 10 (def.)

Verdi, Giuseppe (1813–1901), 265n
(quoted)
  Bibliography, 288–289
  Otello (1887), 9n. 17, **38–41**, 98n,
    302n, 463n
    CHARACTERS: **Iago**, 34, 63, **65–67**
      (Exs. 4.2a–c), 73, 77, 104; **Otello**,
      90–91, 91n
  Rigoletto (1851), 6, 9nn. 12, 13; 22,
    33n. 10, 38, 38n. 19, 100, 244,
    265–289, 368n. 33; *Ill. 269, 277*
    CHARACTERS: **Borsa**, 280; **Count
      Ceprano**, 283–284; **Countess
      Ceprano**, 281; **Courtiers**, 266,
      271, 288; **Duke of Mantua**, 34,
      63–64 (Ex. 4.1b), **279–280**
      (Exs. RI-2a, b); **Gilda**, 41, 56, **267**
      (Ex. RI-1b), 286n. 16, **286–288**
      (Exs. RI-5a, b); **Giovanna**, 286;
      Maddalena, 288; **Marullo**, 283,
      283n; **Monterone**, 268n. 4,
      284–285; **Page**, 286, 286n. 17;
      Rigoletto, **63–65** (Exs. 4.1a–d),
      63n. 2, 71, 113, 266, **281–283**
      (Exs. RI-3a–c), 281n, 287 (Ex. RI-
      5a); **Sparafucile**, **285** (Ex. RI-4);
      Usher, 287
    curse motive, 160, **266–267** (Ex. RI-
      1a), 285
    departures from convention,
      266–267
    literary background, 265–266
    mood, **266–267**
    musical idiom, **265–266**, 268, 285
    music and plot, **267–279**
    prelude, 266–267
    scene construction, 265, 265n,
      268n. 5
    thematic recall, 63, 265–266, 285
    time sequence, 272n
  other works: *Aida* (1871), 48, 51
    (Ex. 3.13), 61, **74–76** (Ex. 4.6); *Un
    ballo in maschera* (A Masked Ball,
    1859), 73; *Falstaff* (1893), **31–32**,
    244; *La forza del destino* (The
    Force of Destiny, 1862; rev. 1869),
    45, 87; *Luisa Miller* (1849), 265;
    Macbeth (1847; rev. Paris, 1865),
    87; *Nabucco* (also *Nabucodonosor*,
    1842), 61; *Simon Boccanegra* (1857;
    rev. 1881), 77; *La Traviata* (The
    Lost Woman, 1853), 265; *Il
    Trovatore* (The Troubadour, 1853),
    34, 53 (Ex. 3.15b), 61, 93

Verismo, 22

Viola da gamba, 120n. 4 (descr.)

Vivaldi, Antonio (1678–1741), 80–81

Voice. *See* Crossover role; Opera,
  women singers in; Singing;
  Symbolism, voice as; Travesti role;
  Trouser role; Voice types, use of

Voice types, use of, 19–20, 120n. 3,
  121, 123, 123n. 9, 259n

Volsunga Saga, 290

W

Wagner, Richard (1815–1883), 6, 22,
  23, 291 (quoted), 295n. 4, 352,
  381
  aesthetics, **290–295**
  anti-Semitism of, 61n. 1, 96n
  bibliography, 340–341
  departures from convention, 290
  essays 110n. 9
    The Artwork of the Future (1849), 110
    A Communication to My Friends
      (1851), 110
    Opera and Drama (1850–51), 110,
      291
  Der fliegende Holländer (The Flying
    Dutchman, 1843), 38, 47, 50 (Ex.
    3.12a), 88–89 (Exs. 5.5a–c), 344
  and leitmotiv, 69–71 (Exs. 4.4a–c),
    88–89, **293–295** (Exs. WA-3a–d),
    293n. 3, 296–302; *see also Die
    Walküre*, leitmotives

Die Meistersinger von Nürnberg (The
   Mastersingers of Nuremberg,
   1868), 11–12, 34, 62, 111n. 12
   Beckmesser, 95–96 (Exs. 6.1a, b),
   111, 111n. 12
   metaphorical meanings in 110–111
Parsifal (1882), 90, 90n, 91 (Exs.
   5.6a, b), 410n. 21
Poetry/music relationship, **290–292**
   (Exs. WA-1, WA-2), 312n
prose writings of, *see* Wagner,
   essays
Der Ring des Nibelungen (The Ring of
   the Nibelung, 1876), 57n, 61n. 1,
   77, 77n. 6, 90. *See also* Wagner,
   Die Walküre; Wagner, other works:
   *Das Rheingold, Siegfried,
   Götterdämmerung*
   literary background, 290
   metaphorical meanings, 295, 295n.
      5
   mythological background, 290, 304,
      316n, 320n, 330nn. 22, 23; 388n.
      10
   plot overview, **295–296**
Die Walküre (The Valkyrie, 1870),
   9n. 15, 10, 18, 21, 38, 71 (Ex.
   4.4c), **290–341**, 463n; *Ill. 72, 303,
   325, 326*
   CHARACTERS: **Brünnhilde,** 68,
      292–293, 297, 300, **304–306,** 330,
      332, **335–336** (Exs. WA-9a, b);
      Fricka, 307, **336–338** (Ex. WA-
      10); **Hunding,** 295n. 5, **299, 329**
      (Ex. WA-7); **Sieglinde, 293–294**
      (Exs. WA-3a, b), **299, 327–329**
      (Ex. WA-6); **Siegmund,** 291,
      299–302, 305, 327–328 (Ex. WA-
      5); **Valkyries, 305–306, 338–340;**
      Wotan, 68–73 (Exs. 4.4a–e), 292
      (Ex. WA-2), **295–296, 298–301,
      304,** 304n, **305–307, 330–335**
      (Exs. WA-8a–e), 330n. 22
   leitmotives, **69–71** (Ex. 4.4a–c),
      296–307 (Ex. WA-4)
   metaphorical meanings, **68–73,** 294,
      301n
   musical idiom, **291–295**
   music and plot, **302–327,** 68n,
      296
   mythological backgrounds, *see*
      Wagner, *Der Ring des Nibelungen*

preludes: Act I, 307; Act II,
   293–295 (Exs. WA-3a–d), 313
time sequence, 290, 294
other works: *Götterdämmerung*
   (Twilight of the Gods, 1876), 77n.
   6, 78, 90, 93, 296, 304n, 330n.
   22; *Das Rheingold* (The Rhinegold,
   1869), 61, 61n. 1, 77n. 6, 276,
   298, 317, 330n. 22; *Siegfried*
   (1876), 296; *Tannhäuser under der
   Sängerkrieg auf Wartburg*
   (Tannhäuser and the Singers'
   Contest on the Wartburg, 1845;
   rev. Paris, 1861), 34, 62, 62n, 89,
   110n. 10; *Tristan und Isolde* (1865),
   56–57 (Ex. 3.17), 381
Wagner tuba, 295n. 4 (descr.)
Walküre, Die (Wagner, 1870)
Walther von der Vogelweide (ca. 1170-
   ca. 1230), 110n. 10
Weber, Carl Maria von (1786–1826),
   21, 31, 31n. 8
   Der Freischütz (The Free Marksman,
      1821; *also* The Charmed Bullet),
      30–31, 33, 38, 75, 222n
   other works: *Kampf und Sieg*
      (Struggle and Victory, cantata,
      1815), 31n. 8; *Leier und Schwert*
      (Lyre and Sword, song cycle,
      1814), 31n. 8
Weill, Kurt (1900–1950)
   Down in the Valley (1948), 6n. 8
   Lady in the Dark (1941), 7
West Side Story (Bernstein, 1957)
White, Eric Walter, 443n. 7 (quoted)
Whole-tone scale, 409
Wilde, Oscar (1854–1900), 380
   Salome (play, 1891), 380, 384, 387
Wolfram von Eschenbach (fl.
   1170–1220), 110n. 10
Wonderment, **84–87** (Exs. 5.3a–e), 88
   (Ex. 5.4), 461
Wortsprache, 291 (def.)
Wozzeck (Berg, 1925)

Z

Zanni, 111n. 13 (def.). *See also*
   Commedia dell' arte
Zauberflöte, Die (Mozart, 1791)
Zola, Émile (1840–1902), 345 (quot-
   ed), 380 (quoted)
Zweig, Stefan (1881–1942), 109n 66